MICROECONOMICS

MICROECONOMICS

TENTH

Richard G. Lipsey

Simon Fraser University

CANADIAN

Christopher T. S. Ragan

McGill University

EDITION

Addison
Wesley
Longman

Toronto

Canadian Cataloguing in Publication Data

Lipsey, Richard G., 1928-
        Microeconomics

10th Canadian ed.
ISBN 0-201-66469-0

1. Micoeconomics. I. Ragan, Christopher. II. Title.

HB172.L56 2001   338.5   C00-930276-X

0-201-66469-0

Vice President, Editorial Director: Michael Young
Acquisitions Editor: Dave Ward
Marketing Manager: James Buchanan
Developmental Editor: Maurice Esses
Production Editor: Mary Ann McCutcheon
Copy Editor: Edie Franks
Production Coordinator: Deborah Starks
Page Layout: Carol Magee
Permissions and Photo Research: Susan Wallace-Cox
Art Director: Mary Opper
Interior Design: Anthony Leung
Cover Design: Artville LLC
Cover Image: Artville LLC

2 3 4 5   05 04 03 02 01

Printed and bound in the United States

BRIEF CONTENTS

v

CONTENTS

LIST OF BOXES

Applying Economic Concepts

Extensions in Theory

Lessons from History

TO THE INSTRUCTOR

Economics is a living discipline, changing and evolving in response to developments in the world economy and in response to the research of many thousands of economists throughout the world. Through ten editions, *Microeconomics* has evolved with the discipline. Our purpose in this edition, as in the previous nine, is to provide students with an introduction to the major issues facing the world's economies, to the methods that economists use to study those issues, and to the policy problems that those issues create. Our treatment is everywhere guided by three important principles:

1. Economics is *scientific,* in the sense that it progresses through the systematic confrontation of theory by evidence. Neither theory nor data alone can tell us much about the world, but combined they tell us a great deal.

2. Economics is *useful* and it should be seen by students to be so. An understanding of economic theory combined with knowledge about the economy produces many important insights about economic policy. Although we stress these insights, we are also careful to point out cases where too little is known to support strong statements about public policy. Appreciating what is not known is as important as learning what is known.

3. We strive always to be *honest* with our readers. Although we know that economics is not always easy, we do not approve of glossing over difficult bits of analysis without letting readers see what is happening and what has been assumed. We take whatever space is needed to explain why economists draw their conclusions, rather than just asserting the conclusions. We also take pains to avoid simplifying matters so much that students would have to unlearn what they have been taught if they continue their study beyond the introductory course. In short, we have tried to follow Albert Einstein's advice:

Everything should be made as simple as possible, but not simpler.

Current Economic Issues

In writing the tenth edition of *Microeconomics*, we have tried to reflect the major economic issues that we face as we begin the twenty-first century.

Globalization

Enormous changes have occurred throughout the world over the last few decades. Flows of trade and investment between countries have risen so dramatically that it is now common to speak of the "globalization" of the world economy. Today it is no longer possible to study any economy without taking into account developments in the rest of the world.

What is true for most countries is also true for Canada. Economic relations between Canada and the rest of the world have a significant impact on most of the major "domestic" issues in the news.

For example, some observers believe that the difficulties faced by Canadian farmers in recent years is caused partly by subsidies that U.S. and European governments provide to their farmers. Students should know how subsidies to foreign farmers affect farmers in Canada. They should also be able to discuss the overall costs and benefits to Canada from agricultural income-support policies, whether they are subsidies or supply-management schemes. We address these issues in some detail in Chapter 5.

In recent years, many Canadians have begun worrying about a possible "brain drain" to the United States. The fear is that Canada's "best and brightest" are leaving in increasing numbers, in pursuit of greater employment prospects, lower income taxes, and higher living standards available south of the border. How mobile is labour across international borders? Does such labour mobility imply that Canada's policies cannot diverge significantly from those in other countries? We explore these issues at various points throughout the book, especially in Chapters 13, 14, and 18.

Another example of the importance of globalization for domestic policy is related to the Asian economic crisis that began in the summer of 1997 and lasted into 1999. The Asian crisis represented both a negative demand shock and a positive supply shock for Canada. The importance of the open economy appears throughout the macroeconomics half of the book—we place a greater emphasis on the importance of exchange rates than we have in past editions.

The forces of globalization are with us to stay. In this tenth edition of *Microeconomics*, we have done our best to ensure that students are made aware of the world outside Canada and of how events elsewhere in the world affect the Canadian economy.

Transition and Development

Over the past decade, the century-long ideological conflict between capitalism and communism has virtually ended. The most powerful communist economy in the world, the Soviet Union, has disappeared, both as a nation and as a planned economy. Mixed capitalism, the system of economic organization that has long prevailed in much of the industrialized world, now prevails in virtually all of it. Many of the developing economies are also moving in this direction. The reasons for the failure of the planned economies of Eastern Europe and the Soviet Union are discussed in Chapter 1 as a contrast to the reasons for the relative success of mixed capitalism.

Developing countries face many of the same problems being experienced by the transition economies of Eastern Europe and the former Soviet Union. Countries in the developing world have been trying—some for many years—to make the difficult transformation from agricultural-based economies to industrialized ones. In many cases, they lack the same institutions that the centrally planned economies had failed to develop. Thus the "development" challenges faced by these economies are very similar to the "transition" challenges faced by the formerly centrally planned economies.

The Role of Government

The political winds appear to have shifted in Canada, the United States, and many other countries over the past two decades. Political parties that once advocated a greater role for government in the economy now argue the benefits of proscribed government. But has the fundamental role of government really changed? In order to understand the role of government in the economy, students must understand the benefits of free markets as well as the situations that cause markets to fail. They must also understand that governments often intervene in the economy for reasons related more to equity than to efficiency.

In this tenth edition of *Economics*, we continue to incorporate the discussion of government policy as often as possible. Here are but a few of the many examples that we explore:
- the effects of payroll taxes (in Chapter 4)
- the effects of minimum wages (in Chapter 5)
- the disincentive effects of income taxes (in Chapters 6 and 18)
- economic regulation and competition policy (in Chapter 12)
- pay equity policy (in Chapter 13)
- environmental policies (in Chapter 17)
- trade policies (in Chapter 35)

The Book

Globalization, growth and development, and the role of government are pressing issues of the day. Much of our study of economic principles and the Canadian economy has been shaped by these issues. In addition to specific coverage of growth and internationally oriented topics, growth and globalization appear naturally throughout the book in the treatment of many topics once thought to be entirely "domestic."

Most chapters of *Microeconomics* contain some discussion of economic policy. We have two main goals in mind when we present these discussions:

1. We aim to give students practice in using economic theory, because applying theory is both a wonderfully effective teaching method and a reliable test of students' grasp of theory.

2. We want to introduce students to the major policy issues of the day and to let them discover that few policy debates are as "black and white" as they often appear in the press.

Both goals reflect our view that students should see economics as useful in helping us to understand and deal with the world around us.

Structure and Coverage

Beginning Part 1, Chapter 1 presents the market as an instrument of coordination. We introduce the issues of scarcity and choice and then briefly discuss alternative economic systems. The problems of converting command economies to market economies will be with us for some time, and comparisons with command economies help to establish what a market economy is *by showing what it is not*. Chapter 2 makes the important distinction between positive and normative inquiries and goes on to an introductory discussion of the construction and testing of economic theories. We also discuss graphing in detail.

Part 2 deals with demand and supply. After introducing price determination and elasticity in Chapters 3 and 4, we apply these tools in Chapter 5. The case studies are designed to provide practice in applying the tools rather than a full coverage of each case.

Part 3 presents the foundations of demand and supply. The theory of consumer behaviour is developed via marginal utility theory in Chapter 6, which also provides an introduction to consumer surplus and an intuitive discussion of income and substitution effects. The Appendix to Chapter 6 covers indifference curves, budget lines, and the derivation of demand curves using indifference theory. Chapter 7 introduces the firm as an institution and develops short-run costs. Chapter 8 covers long-run costs and the principle of substitution, and goes on to consider shifts in cost curves due to technological change. The latter topic is seldom, if ever, covered in the micro part of elementary textbooks, yet applied work on firms' responses to changing economic signals shows it to be extremely important.

The first two chapters of Part 4, Chapters 9 and 10, present the standard theories of perfect competition and monopoly with some discussion of international cartels. Chapter 11 deals with monopolistic competition and oligopoly, which are the market structures most commonly found in Canadian industries. Strategic behaviour plays a central part in the analysis of this chapter. The first half of Chapter 12 deals with the efficiency of competition and the inefficiency of monopoly. The last half of the chapter deals with regulation and competition policy.

Part 5 begins in Chapter 13 by discussing the general principles of factor pricing and how factor prices are influenced by factor mobility. Chapter 14 then examines the operation of labour markets, addressing issues such as wage differentials, discrimination, labour unions, and the "good jobs/bad jobs" debate. Chapter 15 discusses capital and nonrenewable resources.

The first chapter of Part 6 (Chapter 16) provides a general discussion of market success and market failure, introduces social choice theory, and outlines the arguments for and against government intervention in a market economy. Chapter 17 deals with environmental regulation. In addition to providing current applications of microeconomic theory to policymaking, it contains a boxed discussion of the U.S. experience with tradable emissions permits for sulfur dioxide. Chapter 18 analyzes taxes, public expenditure, and the main elements of Canadian social policy. These three chapters expand on the basics of microeconomic analysis by providing current illustrations of the relevance of economic theory to contemporary policy situations.

Substantive Changes to This Edition

We have done a major revision and update of the entire text with guidance from an extensive series of reviews and feedback from both users and nonusers of the previous editions of this book. As always, we have strived very hard to improve the teachability and read-ability of the book. We have shortened the overall length by two chapters (from 38 to 36) and by roughly 10 percent in terms of the number of words. There are two entirely new chapters, and several chapters have been completely rewritten. In the following subsections, we summarize the major changes that we have made for this edition. Later, in a separate section, we will describe the important new features that we have added in order to better accommodate the needs of both instructors and students.

Here is a brief description of the major changes in *Microeconomics*.

Part 1 What Is Economics?

- Chapter 1 has been completely rewritten, incorporating some material from the previous Chapter 3 (which has been removed). The chapter now begins with a discussion about how market economies are self-organizing entities that coordinate the decisions of decentralized agents. This is not an analytical section, but rather an easy introductory discussion. The chapter then goes on to discuss resources, scarcity, opportunity cost, the economy's decision makers, specialization, the division of labour, money, and globalization.
- Chapter 2 is a new chapter that examines how economists think. We begin by discussing normative and positive advice. We then go on to describe theories and models. The section on graphing appears in the main text (rather than the appendix) and shows how economists think about data and how they test their theories. The result is a discussion of graphing that is livelier than in the previous edition.

Part 2 An Introduction to Demand and Supply

- Chapter 3, on demand and supply, has been streamlined but its basic structure is unchanged. In the section on price determination we have added an initial discussion on the concept of a market in which we provide a rough definition of competitive markets. We have added a brief discussion of the 1998 Quebec ice storm in a box. We have also added a new box discussing technical progress and falling computer chip prices.
- Chapter 4 on elasticity has been restructured. We have put the section on supply elasticity as the second section. After discussing supply elasticity, we then go straight into an examination of tax inci-

dence as an important example of why elasticity matters. We have added a new box on the incidence of payroll taxes.

- Chapter 5 begins with an entirely new section on market linkages. We introduce the distinction between partial and general equilibrium, and we go on to consider several ways that seemingly unrelated markets are nonetheless connected. We then discuss administered prices, a section that we have streamlined from the previous edition. We have added a new box on minimum wages. The section on agricultural policies has been updated, and we have added a brief discussion about opposition to the Wheat Board. The section on international trade has been moved to the trade chapter (34).

Part 3 Consumers and Producers

- Chapter 6, on consumer theory, is largely unchanged from the previous edition. We have eliminated the section on free and scarce goods, but have added a small discussion of how information from consumer surveys can easily be misinterpreted because of the failure to distinguish total from marginal value. In the section on income and substitution effects, we have added a box applying the idea to the disincentive effects of income taxation.
- Chapter 7, the first on the theory of the firm, has been extensively rewritten. We begin by discussing the organization and financing of firms, which leads to a new box on debt instruments. We address Coase's ideas regarding why firms exist, and the role of transactions costs. We then go on to discuss production, costs, and profits, explicitly introducing a production function. In the section on short-run production relationships, we have used new numbers in the table and have plotted these values for the diagrams. This should improve the message for the student. We also plot the associated cost data when we discuss the short-run cost curves. Finally, we have a new appendix that explores the issue of whether firms really do maximize profits, and how the market for corporate control places limits on the behaviour of non-profit-maximizing firms. This appendix includes a discussion of the principal-agent problem as applied to the firm's owners and managers.
- Chapter 8 deals with firms in the long run and very long run. It is largely unchanged from the previous edition. The focus on the long run is the cost-minimizing choice of factor mix. The focus on the very long run is how the firm responds to technological change. The chapter's appendix contains a detailed treatment of isoquants, isocosts, and cost minimization.

Part 4 Markets, Pricing, and Efficiency

- Chapter 9 on competitive markets is substantially unchanged from the previous edition, though we have tried to streamline and clarify wherever possible. The box on the seaside inn has been brought forward to the middle of the chapter where it fits naturally as an example of a firm that continues to operate even though it is not covering its total costs. The section of the appeal of perfect competition has been removed.
- Chapter 10 examines monopoly. The figure on elasticity and revenue has been deleted. We have added a new discussion on the comparison of monopoly and competition, introducing the reader to the idea of allocative efficiency (which we explain in detail in Chapter 12). In our discussion of entry barriers we have added a new box showing how legislation has created local monopoly power for Irish pubs. We have added a discussion and figure to explain how firms price discriminate among markets; this adds to a current example dealing with Levi jeans.
- Chapter 11, on imperfect competition, has been shortened. There is less emphasis on the concentration ratio. We have added new examples of co-operation (diamonds and coffee cartels) and have also updated the OPEC box to include some of the recent political frictions that have contributed to OPEC's inability to restrict output.
- Chapter 12, which deals with efficiency, has been updated. The discussion of productive and allocative efficiency has been clarified, and we have added a diagram to emphasize the importance of equating marginal cost across firms. We have streamlined the discussion of regulation, in part by deleting the box on hydro authorities. The section on competition policy has been updated. We discuss the challenge of weighing a merger's efficiency gains against the reduction in competition. The importance of entry barriers is illustrated in an example regarding the 1998 proposed bank mergers. There is a new box on the U.S. antitrust case against Microsoft and some discussion of the Air Canada merger with Canadian Airlines.

Part 5 Factor Markets

- In Chapter 13, we have shortened the opening discussion of income distribution. We have a new figure on earnings distribution, and have both pre-tax and after-tax Lorenz curves. The box on backward-bending labour supply has been removed. We have added a new box on labour mobility—using current data on Canadian-U.S. migration patterns that has recently been the focus of the "brain drain" debate. We have removed the discussions of regional income equalization and of Canadian interprovincial labour mobility. We now give examples of rent to help the student better understand this important concept.

- Chapter 14 deals with labour markets. It has been shortened considerably from the previous edition. We get more quickly through the section on competitive wage differentials, in which we have incorporated a shortened discussion of discrimination. We have a new figure for education and earnings. We have added a new figure for union membership, and have added discussion of some of the things that we *don't* know about unions, especially their effect on productivity. The "good jobs—bad jobs" debate remains, but we have added a figure showing the long-term changes in employment.
- Chapter 15 deals with capital and nonrenewable resources and is largely unchanged from the previous edition. We have improved the discussions of present value and of the firm's demand for capital. The box on interest rates and inflation has been shortened.

Part 6 Government in the Market Economy

- Chapter 16 examines market failures and government intervention. It has been significantly modified from the previous edition. The opening section on market coordination has been removed, since

much of this appears in Chapter 1. We have added a new diagram in the discussion of externalities, as well as a discussion of transactions costs in the discussion of the Coase theorem. We have added an extensive discussion about excludability and rivalry, which then leads to the discussion of public goods. This includes a brief discussion of congestion on roads and road pricing. We have added two new boxes on common property resources. Finally, we have emphasized that the government has other motives for intervention (such as altering the income distribution) that are not based on market failures.

- Chapter 17 is devoted to environmental policy. The discussion in the previous edition on health and safety regulation has been removed. We have added a diagram to remind students about the basic economics of externalities. We then go through direct controls, emissions taxes and tradable emissions permits. The old box on resistance to market-based schemes now appears as an expanded final section entitled "the politics of pollution control".
- Chapter 18 covers taxation and public expenditure. It has been significantly shortened and rewritten from the previous edition. The first section on taxes has been shortened considerably, but we have spent more time discussing progressivity. In the second section we have added a figure to help explain direct and excess burdens. We have also shortened the section on expenditures. There is a brief review of Canadian social policy and the recent reforms, including the challenges facing the Canada Pension Plan and the concerns surrounding reforms that may lead to a two-tiered health-care system.

TO THE STUDENT

A good course in economics will give you insight into how an economy functions and into some currently debated policy issues. Like all rewarding subjects, economics will not be mastered without effort. A book on economics must be worked at. It cannot be read like a novel.

You must develop your own technique for studying, but the following suggestions may prove helpful. Begin by carefully considering the Learning Objectives at the beginning of a chapter. Read the chapter itself relatively quickly in order to get the general run of the argument. At this first reading, you may want to skip the boxes and any footnotes. Then, after reading the Chapter Summary and the Key Concepts (both at the end of each chapter), reread the chapter more slowly, making sure that you understand each step of the argument.

With respect to the figures and tables, be sure you understand how the conclusions that are stated in boldface at the beginning of each caption have been reached. You must not skip the captions. They provide the core of economic reasoning. You should be prepared to spend time on difficult sections; occasionally, you may spend an hour on only a few pages. Paper and pencil are indispensable equipment in your reading. It is best to follow a difficult argument by building your own diagram while the argument unfolds rather than by relying on the finished diagram as it appears in the book.

The end-of-chapter Study Exercises require you to practise using some of the concepts that you learned in the chapter. These will be excellent preparation for your exams. The Discussion Questions require you to apply what you have studied. We advise you to outline answers to some of the questions. In short, you should seek to understand economics, not to memorize it.

The bracketed boldface numbers in the text itself refer to a series of mathematical notes that are found starting on page M-1 at the end of the book. For those of you who like mathematics or prefer mathematical argument to verbal or geometric exposition, these may prove useful. Others may disregard them.

A time line, which runs from the mid 1600s to the mid 1900s, follows the mathematical notes. Along this time line we have placed brief descriptions of the life and works of some great economists, most of whom you will encounter in the textbook. So that you have a better appreciation of *when* these economists did their work, the time line also lists some major world events. We hope this will improve your sense of history and your sense of who these great economists are.

In this edition of the book, we have incorporated many elements to help you review material and prepare for examinations. Pay special attention to the learning objectives, the important concepts highlighted in red, the key terms that are boldfaced and restated in the margins, the captions that accompany the features and tables, the lists of key concepts, and the chapter summaries. A brief description of all the features in this book is given in the separate section that follows.

We strongly suggest you make use of the excellent *Study Guide* written expressly for this text. It will test and reinforce your understanding of the concepts and analytical techniques stressed in each chapter of the text and will help prepare you for your examinations. The ability to solve problems and to communicate and interpret your results are important goals in an introductory course in economics. The *Study Guide* can play an important role in your acquisition of these skills.

We hope you will find the book rewarding and stimulating. Students who used earlier editions made some of the most helpful suggestions for revision, and we hope that you will carry on the tradition. If you are moved to write to us (and we hope that you will be!), please do. You can send any comments or questions regarding the text (or any of the supplementary material, such as the *Study Guide*) to:

Christopher Ragan
Department of Economics
McGill University
855 Sherbrooke St. West
Montreal, Quebec
H3A 2T7

Or, if you prefer to communicate through e-mail, send your comments to:

ragan@leacock.lan.mcgill.ca

We have made a careful effort with this edition to incorporate features that will facilitate the teaching and learning of economics.

- **A new single-column design** has been created for the book, making it more accessible to today's reader.
- A new set of **Learning Objectives** at the beginning of each chapter clarify the skills and knowledge to be learned in each chapter. These same learning objectives are used in the chapter summaries, as well as in the *Test Item File* and the *Study Guide*.

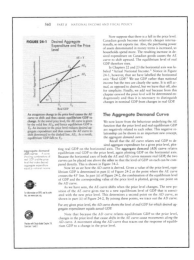

- **Major ideas** are highlighted in red in the text.
- **Key terms** are boldfaced where they are defined in the body of the text and they are restated with their definitions in the margins. In the Index at the back of the book, each key term and the page reference to its definition are boldfaced.
- **Weblinks** to useful Internet addresses are given in the margins. Each weblink presents a URL address, along with a brief description of the material available there. Some links are to government home pages where much data can be obtained. Other links are to organizations such as OPEC, the UN, and the WTO. We have also included links to selected articles from *World Economic Affairs* that we have posted on the Companion Web Site for this textbook.
- **Study Guide** references in the margin direct students to appropriate questions in the *Study Guide* that reinforce the topic being discussed in the text.

- **Applying Economic Concepts** boxes demonstrate economics in action, providing examples of how theoretical material relates to issues of current interest.

- **Lessons from History** boxes contain discussions of a particular policy debate or empirical finding that takes place in a historical context.

- **Extensions in Theory** boxes provide a deeper treatment of a theoretical topic that is discussed in the text.

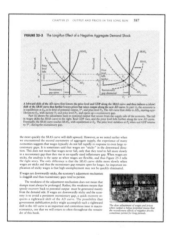

- **A caption for each Figure and Table** summarizes the underlying economic reasoning. Each caption begins with a boldfaced statement of the relevant economic conclusion.
- **A new colour scheme for Figures** has been established to make the use of colour in the graphs consistent. Curves of a particular type are now always presented in the same colour. For example, all demand curves are blue, whereas all supply curves are red.
- **Photographs with short captions** are now interspersed throughout the chapters to illustrate some of the arguments.

- **Chapter Summaries** are organized using the same main heading as found in the body of the chapter. And the relevant learning objectives (LO) numbers are given in red next to each heading in the chapter summary

- **Key Concepts** are listed near the end of each chapter.
- A new set of **Study Exercises** has been created for each chapter. These quantitative exercises require the student to analyze problems by means of computations or graphs.
- A set of **Discussion Questions** is also provided for each chapter. These questions require the student to synthesize and generalize. They are designed especially for discussion in class.

- A set of **Mathematical Notes** is presented in a separate section near the end of the book. Because mathematical notation and derivations are not necessary to understand the principles of economics but are more helpful in advanced work, this seems to be a sensible arrangement. References in the text to these mathematical notes are given by means of boldfaced numbers in square brackets.
- A **Time Line of Great Economists**, running from the mid seventeenth century to the mid twentieth century, is presented near the end of the book. Along this time line we have placed brief descriptions of the life and works of some great economists, most of whom the reader will encounter in the textbook. Along this time line we have also listed some major world events in order to give readers an appreciation for when these economists did their work.

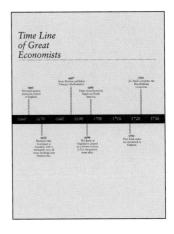

SUPPLEMENTS

The following supplements have been carefully prepared to accompany the new edition:

- A **Study Guide**, written by E. Kenneth Grant and William J. Furlong, is designed for use either in the classroom or by students on their own. The *Study Guide* offers additional study support and reinforcement for each text chapter. It reuses the same learning objectives that appear in the textbook. For each chapter, it provides a prose Overview, a Chapter Review consisting of multiple-choice questions, Exercises, Extension Exercises, and a Practice Multiple-Choice Test.
- An **Instructor's Manual**, written by Christopher Ragan, provides for each text chapter an overview (with teaching suggestions), solutions to the Study Exercises, and suggested answers to the Discussion Questions.
- A **Test Item File**, written by Greg Flanagan and Mike Fellows, contains more than 3300 multiple-choice questions. For each question, the authors have identified the relevant learning objective from the textbook, and they have classified each question by difficulty type (i.e., definitions, using definitions, key concepts, and applying one or more concepts).
- A **Computerized Version of the Test Item File** will enable instructors to edit existing questions, create new questions, generate tests, and administer tests on line over a variety of networks. It also includes a powerful grading system that combines a powerful database with analytical capabilities so that instructors can generate a full set of statistics.
- **Transparency Masters** of all the Figures and Tables in the textbook are available to instructors.
- **Electronic Transparencies** of all the Figures and Tables in the textbook are also available to instructors.
- A special **Companion Web Site** has been created for this book at **www.pearsoned.ca/lipsey**. It includes, among other elements, self-test questions for students, CBC Video Cases, hotlinks to the home pages of governments and other organizations that provide much current data, and the posting of articles from *World Economic Affairs* that are cited in the text.

ACKNOWLEDGEMENTS

It would be impossible to acknowledge here by name all the teachers, colleagues, and students who contributed to the development and improvement of this book over its previous nine editions. Hundreds of users have written to us with specific suggestions, and much of the credit for the improvement of the book over the years belongs to them. We can no longer list them individually but we thank them all sincerely.

For the development of this tenth edition, we are grateful to the many people who offered informal suggestions. We would also like to thank the following instructors who provided us with formal reviews of the textbook:

- Panos C. Afxentiou (University of Calgary)
- Jeremiah Allen (University of Lethbridge)
- F. Michael Bradfield (Dalhousie University)
- Rosilyn G. Coulson (Douglas College)
- Melvin L. Cross (Dalhousie University)
- Martin Dooley (McMaster University)
- Paul Geddes (Columbia College)
- Jack Guthrie (Camosun College)
- Cheryl Jenkins (John Abbott College)
- Eric Kam (York University)
- Susan Kamp (University of Alberta)
- Nargess Kayhani (Mount Saint Vincent University)
- Robert R. Kerton (University of Waterloo)
- Ralph Kolinski (University of Windsor)
- Irwin Lipnowski (The University of Manitoba)
- Rocky M. Mirza (Langara College)
- Robin Neill (University of Prince Edward Island)
- Victor C. Olshevski (The University of Winnipeg)
- Dan Otchere (Concordia University)
- Ian Parker (Scarborough College, University of Toronto)
- Arne Paus-Jenssen (University of Saskatchewan)
- Laurie Craig Phipps (Camosun College)
- Don Reddick (Kwantlen College)
- Charlene Richter (British Columbia Institute of Technology)
- Gary E. Riser (Memorial University)
- James Sentance (University of Prince Edward Island)
- Larry Smith (University of Waterloo)
- Bertram A. Somers (John Abbott College)

In addition, we would like to thank the following instructors for providing formal reviews for some of the supplements that accompany this tenth edition;

- Peter R. Burrell (University of Windsor)
- David M. Cape (Ryerson Polytechnic University)
- Michael F. Charette (University of Windsor)
- Greg L. Flanagan (Saint Mary's University)
- Paul A. R. Hobson (Acadia University)
- Cheryl Jenkins (John Abbott College)
- Eva Lau (University of Waterloo)
- Charlene Richter (British Columbia Institute of Technology)
- Larry Smith (University of Waterloo)
- Donna J. Tibbett (University of Lethbridge)

We would like to acknowledge the work of David Gray (University of Ottawa), who performed a technical review of the textbook.

We would also like to express our thanks to the many people at Pearson Education Canada who spent long hours editing and producing this text.

Our special thanks go to Ingrid Kristjanson, who did a tremendous amount of editing and also carefully reviewed all changes made to this edition. Her comments led to many improvements. For her diligence and hard work we are especially grateful.

Photo Credits

Chapter 1 Canapress/Associated Press/Lionel Cironneau – 2, 6; Tony Stone Images/Daniel Bosler – 1, 9; PhotoDisc, Inc. – 15

Chapter 2 Tony Stone Images/Steven Peters – 28; Dick Hemingway – 1, 24, 31

Chapter 3 Tony Stone Images/Chris McCooey – 50; Saskatchewan Travel – 47, 48, 57; Canapress/Jacques Boissinot – 65

Chapter 4 Imperial Oil Limited – 47, 70, 77; Dick Hemingway – 87

Chapter 5 PhotoDisc, Inc. – 47, 98, 113; Saskatchewan Wheat Pool/Frank Fohr – 120; Ontario Ministry of Agriculture and Food – 102

Chapter 6 Tony Stone Images/Frank Siteman – 127, 128, 135

Chapter 7 Courtesy MacMillan Bloedel Limited – 160; PhotoEdit/Vic Bider – 127, 157, 170

Chapter 8 PhotoDisc, Inc. – 127, 184, 185; Corbis-Bettmann – 192

Chapter 9 Alberta Government Services – 211; Tony Stone Images – 205, 206, 223; Barrett & McKay Photographers – 218

Chapter 10 Dick Hemingway – 205, 230, 237; PhotoDisc, Inc. – 239

Chapter 11 Dick Hemingway – 256; Canadian Press Archives/AP Photo/Miller Brewing Co. – 205, 253, 270

Chapter 12 CRTC – 289; Canapress/Associated Press/Shuji Kajiyama – 205, 279, 297

Chapter 13 The Stock Market/Blaine Harrington III – 313; Canapress/John Lehmann – 303, 304, 324

Chapter 14 Abitibi-Price Inc. – 303, 330, 341; Foote Collection Manitoba Archives/N2762 – 344; Boeing Commercial Airplane Group – 346

Chapter 15 Canapress/Mike Ridewood – 354; Imperial Oil Limited – 303, 352, 362

Chapter 16 Canapress/Nick Procaylo – 371, 372, 382; Dick Hemingway – 387; CP Archive Photo/Roy Antal – 395

Chapter 17 British Columbia Forest Service/Barbara Davies Photo – 408; The Slide Farm/Al Harvey – 412; CP Archive Photo/Red Deer Advocate/Randy Fiedler – 371, 405, 417

Chapter 18 Tony Stone Images/Christopher Bissell – 425; CP Archive Photo/Paul Chiasson – 371, 423, 437; Dick Hemingway – 439

Chapter 34 PhotoDisc, Inc. – 827; British Columbia Forest Service/R.J. Challenger Photo – 821, 822, 831

Chapter 35 Superstock, Inc./Ping Amranand – 821, 841, 842; Agriculture Quebec – 856

Your Internet companion to the most exciting, state-of-the-art educational tools on the Web!

The Pearson Education Canada Companion Website is easy to navigate and is organized to correspond to the chapters in this textbook. The Companion Website is comprised of four distinct, functional features:

1) Customized Online Resources

2) Online Study Guide

3) Reference Material

4) Communication

Explore the four areas in this Companion Website. Students and distance learners will discover resources for indepth study, research, and communication, empowering them in their quest for greater knowledge and maximizing their potential for success in the course.

A NEW WAY TO DELIVER EDUCATIONAL CONTENT

1) Customized Online Resources

Our Companion Websites provide instructors and students with a range of options to access, view, and exchange content.

- **Syllabus Builder** provides *instructors* with the option to create online classes and construct an online syllabus linked to specific modules in the Companion Website.

- **Mailing lists** enable *instructors* and *students* to receive customized promotional literature.

- **Preferences** enable *students* to customize the sending of results to various recipients, and also to customize how the material is sent, e.g., as html, text, or as an attachment.

- **Help** includes an evaluation of the user's system and a tune-up area that makes updating browsers and plug-ins easier. This new feature will enhance the user's experience with Companion Websites.

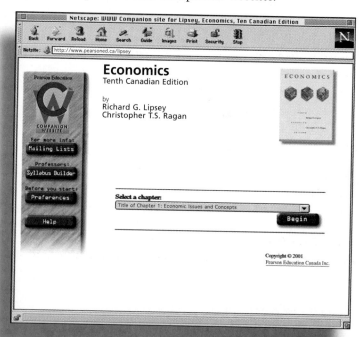

www.pearsoned.ca/lipsey

Pearson Education

COMPANION
WEBSITE

2) Online Study Guide

An Interactive Study Guide forms the core of the student learning experience in the Companion Website. Multiple Choice modules, organized by text chapter, provide students with the ability to send answers to our grader and receive instant feedback on their progress through our Results Reporter. Students can check suggested answers after submitting their problems.

3) Reference Material

Reference material broadens text coverage with up-to-date resources for learning. We have posted more than 35 journal articles from *World Economic Affairs*. Each article is cited by a special icon in the margin of the textbook. Special **CBC Video Case Studies** provide instructors and students with interesting video segments and stimulating cases for discussion. **Web Destinations** provides direct links to websites relevant to the subject matter in each chapter. **Net News (Internet Newsgroups)** are a fundamental source of information about a discipline, containing a wealth of brief, opinionated postings. **Net Search** simplifies key term search using Internet search engines.

4) Communication

Companion Websites contain the communication tools necessary to deliver courses in a **Distance Learning** environment. **Message Board** allows users to post messages and check back periodically for responses. **Live Chat** allows users to discuss course topics in real time, and enables professors to host online classes.

Communication facilities of Companion Websites provide a key element for distributed learning environments. There are two types of communication facilities currently in use in Companion Websites:

- **Message Board** – this module takes advantage of browser technology, providing the users of each Companion Website with a national newsgroup to post and reply to relevant course topics.

- **Live Chat** – enables instructor-led group activities in real time. Using our chat client, instructors can display Website content while students participate in the discussion.

Chapter 1
Multiple Choice
World Economic Affairs
CBC Video Cases
Destinations
Net News
Net Search

Update
Message Board
Help
Preferences
Feedback
Undock

Companion Websites are currently available for numerous Pearson Education Canada books, including

- Case, Fair, Strain, and Veall, *Principles of Microeconomics and Macroeconomics*, First Canadian Edition
- Miller and Clegg, *Economics Today*, First Canadian Edition
- Brown, Chambers, and Currie, *Personal Finance for Canadians*, Sixth Edition

Note: CW content will vary slightly from site to site depending on discipline requirements.

The Companion Website can be found at:

www.pearsoned.ca/lipsey

PEARSON EDUCATION CANADA

26 Prince Andrew Place
Don Mills, Ontario M3C 2T8

To order:
Call: 1-800-567-3800
Fax: 1-800-263-7733

For samples:
Call: 1-800-850-5813
Fax: (416) 447-2819
E-mail: phcinfo.pubcanada@pearsoned.com

Want to PASS or EXCEL in economics?

Don't Throw This Out!

This is your Online Resource Access Code for
EconomicsCentral

Welcome to **EconomicsCentral**, *Pearson Education Canada's online resource for economics students! You'll want to bookmark this site, because you'll find **actual past exams**, **tutorials** for difficult topics, an **online tutor** to help you with those tough questions, dynamic **Weblinks**, and much more, all right here.*

What do you

do with this

access code?

1. **Locate the Site:**
   Launch your web browser and type **www.pearsoned.ca/economics** into the location area.

2. **Use your Pearson Education Canada access code:**
   The first time you access the site, you will be required to register using this access code. Type in the access code on this page (one word per box) and follow the steps indicated. During registration, you will choose a personal User ID and password for logging into the site. Your access code can be used only once to establish your subscription, which is non-transferable. Once your registration has been confirmed, you need to enter only your personal User ID and password each time you enter the site. **This code is valid for 4 months of access to *EconomicsCentral*.**

   Warning: Once you enter your access code, registration processing may take up to 3 minutes to complete. If you do not wait for confirmation before proceeding, the access code will become invalid.

3. **Log onto the site:**
   Once your registration is confirmed, follow the **EconomicsCentral** link to log on with your newly-established User ID and Password.

CSBY-CHAFF-THOLE-PICON-AGENT-PASSE

Pearson Education Canada

This pincode is only valid with the purchase of a new book.
For help using this access code, please e-mail us at

online.support@pearsoned.com

PART ONE

What Is Economics?

Have you ever noticed that, when you go to a store to buy something, the product you seek is almost always available? Or, have you noticed that you rarely see either large numbers of people lined up waiting to buy goods or large amounts of unsold goods with nobody to buy them? What is it about a modern market economy that produces these remarkably coordinated outcomes in which the amount of something available is roughly equal to the amount that people want? What is the study of economics all about, and why will it help you to understand how today's economies function? How do economists do their job of analysing and explaining economic outcomes? What are economic models, and why are some models more sensible than others? Why is it that economists appear to disagree so much, or is this just an illusion? These are questions that you will be able to answer after reading the following two chapters.

Chapter 1 begins by talking about the self-organizing economy, and introduces Adam Smith's famous idea of an invisible hand. Here we see why markets made up of self-interested consumers and producers automatically produce the sort of coordination that we observe. We then examine the important concepts of scarcity, choice, and opportunity cost, three ideas that are central to all economic systems. We then introduce the various decision-makers in a typical market economy, including individual consumers, producers, and governments, and we see how their interactions can be represented by a circular flow of income and expenditure. Finally, we consider alternative economic systems, ranging from a pure market system to a centrally planned system in which a government planning authority makes all the decisions regarding who produces what and who consumes what. Canada, like all economies, is a mixed system, containing elements of both free markets and government intervention.

Chapter 2 discusses the study of economics itself. We consider the distinction between positive and normative statements, a distinction upon which the progress of economics as a social science is based. We then examine the role of theory in economics, and why economists—like physicists or chemists—build models to help them think about the complex world they are trying to understand. Finally, we will explain the way economists test their theories by confronting the predictions of their theories with the available evidence. Here we will also discuss graphing—a central tool for economists and one that is used extensively throughout this book—and you will see how different types of graphs can be used to present very different types of information.

CHAPTER 1

Economic Issues and Concepts

LO LEARNING OBJECTIVES

1 View the market economy as a self-organizing entity in which order emerges from a large number of decentralized decisions.

2 Understand the importance of scarcity, choice, and opportunity cost, and how all three concepts are illustrated by the production possibilities boundary.

3 Explain the circular flow of income and expenditure.

4 Recognize that there are several types of pure economic systems, but that all actual economies are mixed systems, having elements of free markets, tradition, and government intervention.

If you want a litre of milk, you go to your local grocery store and buy it. It probably does not occur to you that farmers may have stopped producing milk or that dairies may have stopped delivering it to stores. When the grocer needs more milk, he orders it from the distributor, who in turn gets it from the dairy, which in its turn gets it from the dairy farmer. The dairy farmer buys cattle feed and electric milking machines, and gets power to run all his equipment by putting a plug into a wall outlet where the electricity is supplied as he needs it. The milking machines are made from parts manufactured in several different places in Canada, the United States, and overseas. The parts themselves are made from materials mined and smelted in a dozen or more different countries.

As it is with the milk you drink, so it is with everything else that you buy. When you go to the appropriate store, what you want is normally on the shelf. Those who make these products find that all the required components and materials are available when they need them—even though these things typically come from many different parts of the world and are made by people who have no direct dealings with each other.

The Complexity of the Modern Economy

The sales and purchases in which you are involved are only a small part of the remarkably complex set of transactions that take place every day in a modern society. Shipments arrive daily at our ports, railway terminals, and airports. These shipments include raw materials, such as iron ore, logs and oil; parts, such as automobile engines, transistors, and circuit boards; tools, such as screwdrivers, lathes, and digging equipment; perishables, such as fresh flowers, coffee beans, and fruits; and all kinds of manufactured goods, such as washing machines, personal computers, and TV sets. Railways and trucking lines receive and dispatch these goods to thousands of different destinations within Canada. Some go directly to consumers. Others are used by local firms to manufacture their products—some of which will be sold domestically and some exported.

Most people who want to work can find work. They spend their working days engaging in the activities just described. In doing so, they earn incomes which they then spend on what they, and others like them, produce. Other people own firms that employ workers to assist in the many activities described above, such as importing, making, transporting, and selling things. They earn their incomes as profits from these enterprises.

The Self-Organizing Economy

Economics began when thoughtful observers asked themselves how such a complex set of dealings gets organized. Who coordinates the whole set of efforts? Who makes sure that all the activities fit together, providing jobs to produce the things that people want and delivering those things to where they are wanted? The answer is no one!

The great insight of the early economists was that an economy based on free-market transactions is *self-organizing*.

By following their own self-interest, doing what seems best and most profitable for themselves, and responding to the incentives of prices determined in open markets, people produce a spontaneous social order. In that order, literally thousands of millions of transactions and activities fit together to produce the things that people want within the constraints set by the resources that are available to the nation.

The great Scottish economist and political philosopher Adam Smith (1723-1790)[1], who was the first to develop this insight fully, put it this way:

> *It is not from the benevolence of the butcher, the brewer, or the baker, that we expect our dinner, but from their regard to their own interest. We address ourselves, not to their humanity but to their self-love, and never talk to them of our own necessities but of their advantages.*

Smith is not saying that benevolence is unimportant. Indeed, he praises it in many passages. He is saying, however, that the massive number of economic interactions that characterize a modern economy cannot all be motivated by benevolence. Although benevolence does motivate some of our actions, often the very dramatic ones, the vast majority of our everyday actions are motivated by self-interest. Self-interest, not benevolence, is therefore the foundation of economic order.

Efficient Organization

Another great insight, which was hinted at by Smith and fully developed over the next century and a half, was that this spontaneously generated social order is relatively *efficient*. Loosely speaking, efficiency means that the resources available to a nation are organized in such a way as to produce the maximum possible total output.

---

[1]Throughout this book we encounter many great economists from the past whose ideas shaped the discipline of economics. At the back of the book you will find a timeline, beginning in the 1600s, that contains brief discussions of many of these thinkers and places them in their historical context.

Smith said that a society whose economy is organized by free markets produces ordered behaviour that makes it appear as if people are guided by an *invisible hand*. He did not literally mean that a supernatural presence guides economic affairs. Instead, he referred to the amazing order that emerges out of so many independent decisions. The key to the explanation is that all individuals respond to the same set of prices, which are determined in markets that respond to overall conditions of national scarcity or plenty. Much of economics is devoted to a detailed elaboration of how this market order is generated.

A Planned Alternative

A century after Adam Smith, another great economist and political philosopher, Karl Marx (1818–1883), argued that although such a market system would produce high total output, it would distribute that output in such a way that, over time, the rich would get richer and the poor poorer. He went on to argue that when societies became rich enough, they should dispense with the spontaneous social order. They should then replace it by a consciously created system, called a *command economy*, or *communism*, in which the government plans all of the transactions we have just described and, in so doing, creates a more equal and socially just distribution of the total output.

Beginning with the Soviet Union in the early 1920s, many nations listened to Marx and established systems in which conscious government *central planning* largely replaced the spontaneous order of the free market. For much of the twentieth century two systems, the centrally planned and the market, competed with each other for the favour of undecided governments. Then, within the last two decades of the century, governments of one communist country after another abandoned their central planning apparatus. More and more economic transactions and activities were then left to be regulated by the self-organizing system of the market.

Lessons From History 1-1 elaborates on some of the reasons for the failure of the centrally planned economies. We hasten to add that Marx was right about many things, including the importance of technological change in raising living standards over the centuries (which is also a theme we discuss in this book). Where experience has shown him wrong, however, was in believing that central planning could successfully replace the market as a way of organizing all of a nation's economic activities.

In contrast to the failures of the command economies, the performance of the largely free-market economies is impressive. One theme of this book is *market success*—how the price system works to coordinate with relative efficiency the decentralized decisions made by private consumers and producers. However, doing things better does not necessarily mean doing things perfectly. Another theme of this book is *market failure*—how and why the unaided price system sometimes fails to produce efficient results and fails to take account of social values that cannot be expressed through the marketplace.

Today, as in the time of Adam Smith, economists seek to understand the self-organizing forces of a market economy, how well they function, and how governments may intervene to improve (but not to replace) their workings in specific situations.

Main Characteristics of Market Economies

What then are the main characteristics of market economies that produce this spontaneous self-ordering?

- Individuals pursue their own self-interest, buying and selling what seems best for themselves and their families.
- People respond to incentives. Other things being equal, sellers seek high prices and buyers seek low prices.
- Prices are determined in open markets in which would-be sellers compete to sell their wares to would-be buyers.
- People earn their incomes by selling their labour services, things they have produced, the services of the land, or buildings that they own to those who wish to buy them.
- All of these activities are governed by a set of institutions largely created by the state. The most important are private property and freedom of contract. The nature of private property and contractual obligations are defined by the legislature and enforced by the police and the courts.

Resources and Scarcity

All of the issues discussed so far would not matter much if we lived in an economy of such plenty that there was enough to satisfy all of everyone's wants. "Ask and you shall receive" would be the motto of such an imaginary world. In contrast, the motto of any real economy is closer to "Work for it and you may get at least some of it."

Why is the economy of plenty impossible? The short answer is "Because we live in a world of scarcity." Compared to the known desires of individuals for such products as better food, clothing, housing, education, holidays, health care, and entertainment, the existing supplies of resources are clearly inadequate. They are sufficient to produce only a small fraction of the goods and services that people desire. This gives rise to the basic economic problem of choice under conditions of scarcity. If we cannot have everything we want, we must choose what we will and will not have.

One definition of *economics* comes from the great economist Alfred Marshall (1842–1924), whom we will encounter at several points in this book: "Economics is a study of mankind in the ordinary business of life." A more penetrating definition is the following:

Economics is the study of the use of scarce resources to satisfy unlimited human wants.

Scarcity is inevitable and is central to economic problems. What are society's resources? Why is scarcity inevitable? What are the consequences of scarcity?

Resources

A society's resources consist of natural endowments such as land, forests, and minerals; human resources, both mental and physical; and manufactured aids to production such as tools, machinery, and buildings. Economists call such resources **factors of production** because they are used to produce the outputs that people desire. We divide these outputs into goods and services. **Goods** are tangible (e.g., cars and shoes), and **services** are intangible (e.g., haircuts and education).

People use goods and services to satisfy many of their wants. The act of making them is called **production**, and the act of using them to satisfy wants is called **consumption**. Goods are valued for the services they provide. An automobile, for example, helps to satisfy its owner's desires for transportation, mobility, and possibly status.

factors of production Resources used to produce goods and services; frequently divided into the basic categories of land, labour, and capital.

goods Tangible commodities, such as cars or shoes.

services Intangible commodities, such as haircuts or medical care.

production The act of making goods or services.

consumption The act of using goods or services to satisfy wants.

LESSONS FROM HISTORY 1-1

The Failure of Central Planning

In 1989, communism collapsed throughout Central and Eastern Europe, and the economic systems of formerly communist countries began the transition from centrally planned to market economies. Although political issues surely played a role in these events, the economic changes generally confirmed the superiority of a market-oriented price system over central planning as a method of organizing economic activity. The failure of central planning had many causes, but four were particularly significant.

The Failure of Coordination

In centrally planned economies, a body of planners tries to coordinate all the economic decisions about production, investment, trade, and consumption that are likely to be made by producers and consumers throughout the country. Without the use of prices to signal relative scarcity and abundance, central planning generally proved impossible to do with any reasonable degree of success. Bottlenecks in production, shortages of some goods, and gluts of others plagued the Soviet economy for decades. For example, for years there was an ample supply of black-and-white television sets but severe

shortages of toilet paper and soap. In 1989, much of a bumper harvest rotted because of shortages of storage and transportation facilities.

The fall of the Berlin Wall in November 1989 was the beginning of the end of the Soviet system of central planning.

Scarcity

For each of the world's six billion people, scarcity is real and ever present. As we said above, relative to people's desires, existing resources are inadequate; there are enough to produce only a fraction of the goods and services that are wanted.

But are not the advanced industrialized nations rich enough that scarcity is nearly banished? After all, they have been characterized as affluent societies. Whatever affluence may mean, however, it does not mean the end of the problem of scarcity. Most households that earn $100 000 per year (a princely amount by world standards) have no trouble spending it on things that seem useful to them and they would certainly have no trouble convincing you that their resources are scarce relative to their desires.

Choice

Because resources are scarce, all societies face the problem of deciding what to produce and how much each person will consume. Societies differ in who makes the choices and how they are made, but the need to choose is common to all. Just as scarcity implies the need for choice, so choice implies the existence of cost. A decision to have

Failure of Quality Control

Central planners can monitor the number of units produced by any factory and reward plants that exceed their production targets and punish ones that fall short. Factory managers operating under these conditions will meet their quotas by whatever means are available, and once the goods pass out of their factory, what happens to them is someone else's headache.

In market economies, poor quality is punished by low sales, and retailers soon give a signal to factory managers by shifting their purchases to other suppliers. The incentives that obviously flow from such private-sector purchasing discretion are generally absent from command economies, where purchases and sales are planned centrally and prices and profits are not used to signal customer satisfaction or dissatisfaction.

Misplaced Incentives

In market economies, relative wages and salaries provide incentives for labour to move from place to place, and the possibility of losing one's job provides an incentive to work diligently. This is a harsh mechanism that punishes losers with loss of income (although social programs provide floors to the amount of economic punishment that can be suffered). In planned economies, workers usually have complete job security. Industrial unemployment is rare, and even when it does occur, new jobs are usually found for all who lose theirs. Although the high level of security is attractive to many people, it proved impossible to provide sufficient incentives for reasonably hard and efficient work under such conditions. In the words of Oxford historian Timothy Garton Ash, who wrote eyewitness chronicles of the developments in Eastern Europe from 1980 to 1990, the social contract between the workers and the government in the Eastern European countries was "We pretend to work, and you pretend to pay us."

Environmental Degradation

Fulfilling production plans became the all-embracing goal in planned economies, to the exclusion of most other considerations, including the environment. As a result, environmental degradation occurred in the Soviet Union and the countries of Eastern Europe on a scale unknown in advanced Western nations. A particularly disturbing example (only one of many) occurred in central Asia where high quotas for cotton output led to indiscriminate use of pesticides and irrigation. Birth defects are now found in nearly one child in three, and the vast Aral Sea has been half drained, causing major environmental effects.

This failure to protect the environment stemmed from the pressure to fulfill production plans and the absence of a "political marketplace" where citizens could express their preferences for the environment versus economic gain. Imperfect though the system may be in democratic market economies—and in some particular cases it has been quite poor—their record of environmental protection has been vastly better than that of the command economies.

more of something requires a decision to have less of something else. The less of "something else" can be thought of as the cost of having the more of "something."

Scarcity implies that choices must be made, and making choices implies the existence of costs.

Opportunity Cost

To see how choice implies cost, we look first at a trivial example and then at one that vitally affects all of us; both examples involve precisely the same fundamental principles.

Consider the choice that must be made by your little sister who has 50 cents to spend and who is determined to spend it all on candy. For your sister there are only two kinds of candy in the world: bubblegums, which sell for 5 cents each, and lollipops, which sell for 10 cents each. Your sister would like to buy 10 bubblegums and 10 lollipops but soon discovers that this is not possible: It is not an *attainable combination,* given her scarce resources. However, several combinations are attainable: 8 bubblegums and 1 lollipop, 4 bubblegums and 3 lollipops, 2 bubblegums and 4 lollipops, and so on. Some of these combinations leave money unspent, and she is not interested in them. Only six combinations, as shown in Figure 1-1, are both attainable and use the entire 50 cents.

FIGURE 1-1 A Choice Between Bubblegums and Lollipops

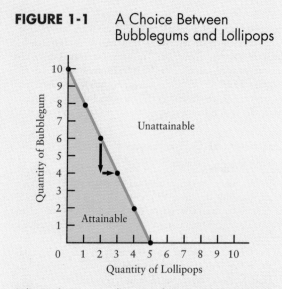

A limited amount of money forces a choice among alternatives. Six combinations of bubblegums and lollipops are attainable and use all of the child's money. The negatively sloped line provides a boundary between attainable and unattainable combinations. The arrows show that the opportunity cost of 1 more lollipop is 2 bubblegums.

After careful thought, your sister has almost decided to buy 6 bubblegums and 2 lollipops, but at the last moment she decides that she simply must have 3 lollipops. What will it cost to get this extra lollipop? One answer is 2 bubblegums. As seen in the figure, this is the number of bubblegums the child must forgo to get the extra lollipop. Economists describe the 2 bubblegums as the *opportunity cost* of the third lollipop.

Another answer is that the cost of the third lollipop is 10 cents. But this answer is less revealing than the first one. Though the real choice is one between more of this and more of that, the cost of "this" is usefully viewed in terms of what one cannot have of "that."

The idea of opportunity cost is one of the central insights of economics. Here is a precise definition. The **opportunity cost** of using resources for a certain purpose is defined to be *the benefit given up by not using them in the best alternative way.* That is, it is the cost measured in terms of other goods and services that could have been obtained instead. If, for example, resources that could have produced 20 km of road are best used instead to produce two small hospitals, the opportunity cost of a hospital is 10 km of road; looked at the other way round, the opportunity cost of 1 km of road is one-tenth of a hospital.

opportunity cost
The cost of using resources for a certain purpose, measured by the benefit given up by not using them in their best alternative use.

Every time a choice is made, opportunity costs are incurred.

See *Applying Economic Concepts 1-1* for an example of opportunity cost that should seem quite familiar to you—the opportunity cost of getting a university degree.

Production Possibilities

Although your sister's choice between bubblegums and lollipops may seem to be a trivial consumption decision, the essential nature of the decision is the same whatever the choice being made. Consider, for example, the choice that any country must face between producing military and civilian goods.

If resources are fully and efficiently employed, it is not possible to have more of both. However, as the government cuts defence expenditures, resources needed to produce civilian goods will be freed up. The opportunity cost of increased civilian goods is therefore the forgone military output. (Or, if we were considering an increase in military output, the opportunity cost of military output would be the forgone civilian goods.)

The choice is illustrated in Figure 1-2. Because resources are limited, some combinations—those that would require more than the total available supply of resources for their production—cannot be attained. The negatively sloped curve on the graph divides the combinations that can be attained from those that cannot. Points above and to the right of this curve cannot be attained because there are not enough resources; points below and to the left of the curve can be attained without using all of the available resources; and points on the curve can just be attained if all the available resources are used efficiently. The

APPLYING ECONOMIC CONCEPTS 1-1

The Opportunity Cost of Your University Degree

As discussed in the text, the opportunity cost of choosing one thing is what must be given up as the best alternative. Computing the opportunity cost of a college or university education is a good example to illustrate which factors are included (and which are excluded) from the computation of opportunity cost. You may also be surprised to learn how expensive your university degree really is!*

Suppose that a Bachelor's degree requires four years of study and that each year you spend $3500 for tuition fees—approximately the average at Canadian universities in 2000—and a further $1500 per year for books and materials. Does this mean that the cost of a university education is only $20 000? Unfortunately not; the true cost of a university degree is much higher.

The key point is that the opportunity cost of a university education does not just include the out-of-pocket expenses on tuition and books. You must also take into consideration *what you are forced to give up* by choosing to attend university. Of course, if you were not studying you could have been doing any one of a number of things, but the relevant one is *the one you would have chosen instead*—your best alternative to attending university.

Suppose that your best alternative to attending university was to get a job. In this case, the opportunity cost of your university degree must include the earnings that you would have received had you taken that job. Suppose that your (after-tax) annual earnings would have been $18 000 per year, for a total of $72 000 if you stayed at that job for four years. To the direct expenses of $20 000, we must therefore add $72 000 for the earnings that you gave up by not taking a job. This brings the true cost of your university degree—the opportunity cost—up to $92 000!

Notice that the cost of food, lodging, clothing, and other living expenses did not enter the calculation of the opportunity cost in this example. The living expenses must be incurred in either case—whether you attend uni-

versity or get a job. Of course, it is possible that your total living expenses as a student are different from what they would have been had you taken the job. In this case, the calculation of opportunity cost would need to be adjusted. For example, perhaps the job you would have taken *required* you to spend $3000 for clothes (over the 4 years) so that you could look presentable to customers. In contrast, you find that your university classmates and professors are pretty relaxed about fashion and that your old jeans are more than adequate. In this case, the opportunity cost of your university degree would be only $89 000 because by attending university you "saved" $3000 that you otherwise would have had to spend on clothes.

If the opportunity cost of a degree is so high, why do students choose to go to university? The simple answer is that they believe that they are better off by going to university than by not going (otherwise they would not go). Maybe the students simply enjoy learning, and thus are prepared to incur the high cost to be in the university environment. Or maybe they believe that a university degree will significantly increase their future earning potential. In this case, they are giving up four years of earnings at one salary so that they can invest in their own skills in the hopes of enjoying many more years in the future at a considerably higher salary.

Whatever the case, the recognition that a university degree is very expensive should convince students to make the best use of their time while they are there. Read on!

The opportunity cost to an individual completing a university degree in Canada is very large. It includes the direct cost of tuition and books as well as the earnings forgone while attending university.

---

* This box considers only the cost *to the student* of a university degree. For reasons that will be discussed in detail in Part 6 of this book, the government heavily subsidizes post-secondary education in Canada. Because of this subsidy, the cost *to society* of a university degree is generally much higher than the cost to an individual student.

curve is called the **production possibility boundary** or *production possibility curve*. It has a negative slope because when all resources are being used efficiently, producing more of one kind of good requires producing less of the other kind.

A production possibility boundary illustrates three concepts: scarcity, choice, and opportunity cost. Scarcity is indicated by the unattainable combinations outside the boundary; choice, by the need to choose among the alternative attainable points along the boundary; and opportunity cost, by the negative slope of the boundary.

The shape of the production possibility boundary in Figure 1-2 implies that an increasing amount of civilian production must be given up to achieve equal successive increases in military production. This shape, referred to as *concave* to the origin, indicates that the opportunity cost of either good increases as we increase the amount of it that is produced. A straight-line boundary, as in Figure 1-1, indicates that the opportunity cost of one good in terms of the other stays constant, no matter how much of it is produced.

The concave shape in Figure 1-2 is the way that economists usually draw a country's production possibilities boundary. The shape occurs because each factor of production is not equally useful in producing all goods. To see why differences among factors of production are so important, suppose we begin at a point where all resources are devoted to the production of military goods, and then consider gradually shifting more and more resources toward the production of civilian goods. The first resources we shift might be, just to take an example, nutrient-rich land that is particularly well suited to growing wheat. This land may not be very useful for making military equipment, but it is very useful for making certain civilian goods (like bread). This shift of resources will therefore lead to a very small reduction in military output but a substantial increase in civilian output. Thus the opportunity cost of producing the first unit of civilian goods, which is equal to the forgone military output, is very small. But as we shift more and more resources toward the production of civilian goods, we must shift more and more resources that are actually quite well suited to the production of military output, like aerospace engineers or the minerals needed to make gunpowder. As we produce more and more civilian goods (by having more and more resources devoted to producing them), the amount of military output that must be forgone to produce one *extra* unit of civilian goods rises. That is, the opportunity cost of producing one good rises as more of that good is produced.

FIGURE 1-2   A Production Possibility Boundary

(Quantity of Civilian Goods on vertical axis; Quantity of Military Goods on horizontal axis. Points a, d at top; c inside; b at lower right. Labels: Unattainable combinations, Production possibility boundary, Attainable combinations.)

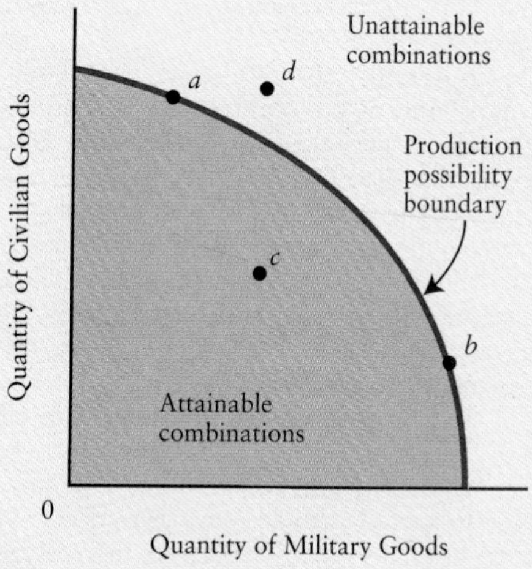

The negatively sloped boundary shows the combinations that are just attainable when all of the society's resources are efficiently employed. The production possibility boundary separates the attainable combinations of goods, such as *a*, *b*, and *c*, from unattainable combinations, such as *d*. Points *a* and *b* represent full and efficient use of society's resources. Point *c* represents either inefficient use of resources or failure to use all the available resources.

Four Key Economic Problems

Modern economies involve thousands of complex production and consumption activities. Although this complexity is important, many of the basic kinds of decisions that must be made are not very different from those made in primative economies in which people work with few tools and barter with their neighbours. Whatever the economic system, most problems studied by economists can be grouped under four main headings.

What Is Produced and How?

The allocation of scarce resources among alternative uses, called **resource allocation,** determines the quantities of various goods that are produced. What determines which goods get produced? Choosing to produce a particular combination of goods means choosing a particular allocation of resources among the industries or regions producing the goods.

Further, because resources are scarce, it is desirable that they be used efficiently. Hence it matters which of the available methods of production is used to produce each of the goods. What determines which methods of production get used and which ones do not?

In terms of Figure 1-2, these questions relate to where the economy will produce. Will the economy be inside the production possibility boundary because resources are used inefficiently? If resources are used efficiently, then at which point on the boundary will production take place?

resource allocation
The allocation of an economy's scarce resources of land, labour, and capital among alternative uses.

What Is Consumed and by Whom?

What is the relationship between an economy's production of goods and the consumption enjoyed by its citizens? Economists seek to understand what determines the distribution of a nation's total output among its people. Who gets a lot, who gets a little, and why?

If production takes place on the production possibility boundary, then how about consumption? Will the economy consume exactly the same goods that it produces? Or will the country's ability to trade with other countries permit the economy to consume a different combination of goods?

Questions relating to what is produced and how, and what is consumed and by whom, fall within the realm of microeconomics. Microeconomics is the study of the allocation of resources as it is affected by the workings of the price system and government policies that seek to influence it.

Why Are Resources Sometimes Idle?

When an economy is in a recession, many workers who would like to have jobs are unable to find employers to hire them. At the same time, the managers and owners of offices and factories would like to operate at a higher level of activity—that is, they would like to produce more goods and services. Similarly, during recessions raw materials are typically available in abundance. For some reason, however, these resources—labour, factories and equipment, and raw materials—are idle. Thus, in terms of Figure 1-2, the economy is operating within its production possibility boundary.

Why are resources sometimes idle? Should governments worry about such idle resources, or is there some reason to believe that such occassional idleness is appropriate in a well-functioning economy? Is there anything that the government can do to reduce such idleness?

Is Productive Capacity Growing?

The capacity to produce goods and services grows rapidly in some countries, expands slowly in others, and actually declines in others. Growth in productive capacity can be represented by an outward shift of the production possibility boundary, as shown in

FIGURE 1-3 The Effect of Economic Growth on the Production Possibility Boundary

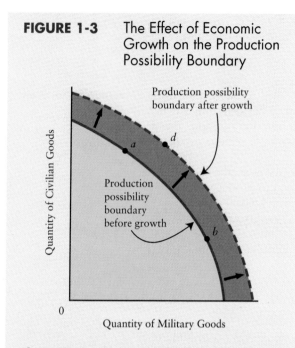

Economic growth shifts the boundary outward and makes it possible to produce more of all products. Before growth in productive capacity, points *a* and *b* were on the production possibility boundary and point *d* was an unattainable combination. After growth, as shown by the dark shaded band, point *d* and many other previously unattainable combinations are attainable.

Figure 1-3. If an economy's capacity to produce goods and services is growing, combinations that are unattainable today will become attainable tomorrow. Growth makes it possible to have more of all goods. What are the determinants of growth? Can governments do anything to increase economic growth?

Questions relating to the idleness of resources during recessions, and the growth of productive capacity, fall within the realm of macroeconomics. Macroeconomics is the study of the determination of economic aggregates such as total output, total employment, the price level, and the rate of economic growth.

Who Makes the Choices and How?

So choices have to be made, but who makes them and how are they made?

The Flow of Income and Expenditure

Figure 1-4 shows the basic decision makers and the flows of income and expenditure that they set up. Individuals own factors of production, including themselves. They sell the services of these factors to producers and receive payments in return. These are their incomes. Producers use the factor services that they buy to make goods and services for consumption. They sell these to individuals, receiving payments in return. These are the incomes of producers. These basic flows of income and expenditure pass through markets. Individuals sell the services of the factor that they own in what are collectively called *factor markets*. Producers sell their outputs of goods and services in what are collectively called *goods markets*.

The prices that are determined in these markets determine the incomes that are earned and the purchasing power of those incomes. People who get high prices for their factor services earn high incomes; those who get low prices earn low incomes. The income each person earns expressed as a fraction of all incomes that are earned in the nation shows the share of total income that each person can command. The *distribution of income* refers to how the nation's total production is distributed among its citizens. This is largely determined by the price that each type of factor service can command in factor markets.

Maximizing Decisions

The basic decision makers in a market economy are individual consumers and producers. To these two groups we will shortly add a third, the government. The most important thing about how these two groups make their decisions is that everyone tries to do as well as possible for themselves. In the jargon of economics, they are *maximizers*.

When individuals decide how many factor services to sell to producers and how many products to buy from them, they make choices designed to maximize their well-being, or *utility*. When producers decide how many factor services to buy from individuals and how many goods to produce and sell to them, they make choices designed to maximize their profits.

Marginal Decisions

The second key point about these choices is that they are all made *at the margin*. Let us see what this means. When you vote in a Canadian federal election, you have only one vote and you must support one party over the others. When you do, you vote for everything that party stands for, even though you may prefer to pick and choose elements from that party's political platform. You cannot say "I vote for the Liberals on issue A and for the Conservatives on issue B." You must make a total choice.

In contrast, when you spend your income, you do not have to decide which product to spend your entire income on. You can, and do, decide to spread your expenditure among many products. Furthermore, having decided to buy some CDs, you do not have to buy a large number or none at all. You can buy any number you wish and, as your circumstances change, you can vary the number you buy each month, raising it or lowering it a bit. These are *marginal* decisions—decisions to buy a bit more or a bit less.

FIGURE 1-4   The Circular Flow of Income and Expenditure

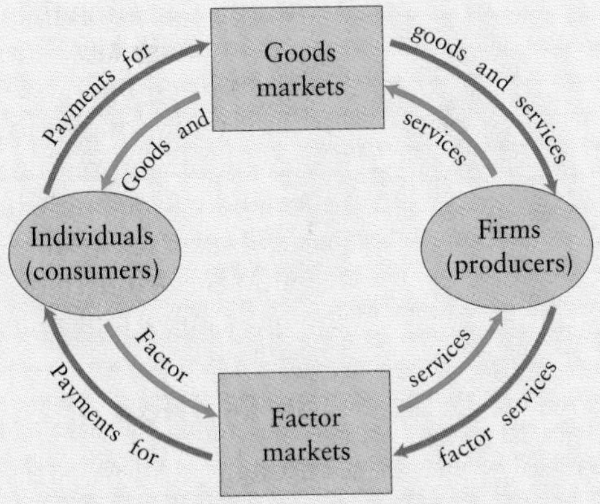

The green line shows the flows of goods and services while the blue line shows the payments made to purchase these. Factor services flow from individuals who own the factors (including their own labour) through factor markets to firms that use them to make goods and services. These goods and services then flow through goods markets to those who consume them. Money payments flow from firms to individuals through factor markets. These payments become the income of individuals. When they spend this income buying goods and services, money flows through goods markets back to producers.

Maximizing consumers and producers are constantly making marginal decisions, whether to buy or sell a bit more or less of each of the things that they buy and sell.

Production Choices

Producers decide what to produce and how to produce it. Production is a very complex process in any modern economy. A typical car manufacturer assembles a product out of thousands of individual parts. It makes some of these parts itself. Most are subcontracted to parts manufacturers and many of the major parts manufacturers subcontract some of their work out to smaller firms. This kind of production displays two characteristics noted long ago by Adam Smith—*specialization* and the *division of labour*.

Specialization

In ancient hunter–gather societies, and in modern subsistence economies, most people make most of the things they need for themselves. However, from the time that people first engaged in settled agriculture and some of them began to live in towns, people have specialized in doing particular jobs. Artisans, soldiers, priests, and government officials were some of the earliest specialized occupations. Economists call this allocation of different jobs to different people the **specialization of labour**. There are two fundamental reasons why specialization is extraordinarily efficient compared with universal self-sufficiency.

specialization of labour   The specialization of individual workers in the production of particular goods or services.

First, individual abilities differ, and specialization allows each person to do what he or she can do relatively well while leaving everything else to be done by others. Even when people's abilities are unaffected by the act of specializing, production is greater with specialization than with self-sufficiency. This is one of the most fundamental principles in economics. It is called the principle of *comparative advantage*. A much fuller discussion of comparative advantage is found in Chapter 34 where we discuss the gains from international trade.

The second reason concerns changes in people's abilities that occur *because* they specialize. A person who concentrates on one activity becomes better at it than could a jack-of-all-trades. This is called *learning by doing*. It was a factor much stressed by early economists. Modern research into what are called *learning curves* shows that learning by doing is important in many modern industries.

The Division of Labour

division of labour
The breaking up of a production process into a series of specialized tasks, each done by a different worker.

Throughout most of history each artisan who was specialized in making some product made the whole of that product. Over the last several hundred years many technical advances in production methods have made it efficient to organize agriculture and manufacturing into large-scale firms organized around what is called the **division of labour.** This term refers to specialization *within* the production process of a particular product.

Mass Production.   In a mass-production factory work is divided into highly specialized tasks using specialized machinery. Each individual repeatedly does one small task that is a small fraction of those necessary to produce any one product. This is an extreme case of the division of labour.

Artisans and Flexible Manufacturing.   Two very recent changes have significantly altered the degree of specialization found in many modern production processes. First, individual artisans have recently reappeared in some lines of production. They are responding to a revival in the demand for individually crafted, rather than mass-produced, products. Second, many manufacturing operations are being reorganized along new lines called "lean production" or "flexible manufacturing," which was pioneered by Japanese car manufacturers in the mid 1950s. It has led back to a more craft-based form of organization within the factory. In this technique employees work as a team; each employee is able to do every team member's job rather than one very specialized task at one point on the assembly line.

Globalization

Market economies constantly change, largely as a result of the development of new technologies. Many of the recent changes are referred to as *globalization*, a term often used very loosely to mean the increased importance of international trade. International trade, however, is an old phenomenon—just think of the ancient trading routes created largely by the spice trade. But the usual pattern over most of the last two hundred years was manufactured goods being sent from Europe and North America to the rest of the world, with raw materials and primary products being sent in return. What is new in the last few decades is the globalization of manufacturing.

Underlying the modern notion of globalization is the rapid reduction in transportation costs and the revolution in information technology that have occurred in the last half of the twentieth century. The cost of moving products around the world has fallen greatly in recent decades owing to containerization and the increasing size of ships. Our ability to transmit and to analyze data has been increasing even more dramatically, while the costs of doing so have been decreasing, equally dramatically. For example, today $2000 buys a computer that fits into a briefcase and has the same computing power as one that in 1970 cost $10 million and filled a large room. This revolution in information and communication technology (ICT) has made it possible to coordinate economic transactions around the world in ways that were difficult and costly fifty years ago and quite impossible a hundred years ago.

Fifty years ago, if a car was to be assembled in Oshawa, all the parts had to be made nearby. Today it is possible to make parts anywhere in the world and get them to Oshawa just as they are required. As a result, manufacturing, which was formerly concentrated in the advanced industrial countries of Europe and North America, now takes place all over the world. A typical CD player, TV set, or car contains components made in dozens of different countries. We still know where a product is assembled, but it is becoming increasingly difficult to say where it is *made*.

Globalization is as important for consumers as it is for producers. For example, as some tastes become universal to young people, spread by ever-increasing access to foreign television stations and global internet chat lines, we can see the same clothes and hear the same music in virtually all big cities. And as tastes become more universal, many *corporations* are globalizing, as they become what economists call **transnational corporations**. These are massive firms with a physical presence in many countries and an increasingly decentralized management structure. McDonald's restaurants are as visible in Moscow or Beijing as in London, New York, Vancouver, or Montreal. Many other brands are also known around the world, such as Calvin Klein, Nike, Coca Cola, Kelloggs, Heinz, Nestlé, Molson, Toyota, Rolls-Royce, Sony, and Mitsubishi.

The revolution in computer technology has drastically reduced communication and transportation costs. This reduction in costs lies at the heart of globalization.

Today no country can take an isolationist economic stance and hope to take part in the global economy where an increasing share of jobs and incomes are created.

transnational corporations (TNCs) Firms that have operations in more than one country. Also called *multinational enterprises (MNEs)*.

Markets and Money

People who specialize in doing only one thing, whether they are artisans, factory workers, or computer programmers, must satisfy most of their wants by consuming things made by other people. In early societies the exchange of goods and services took place by simple mutual agreement among neighbours. In the course of time, however, trading became centred on particular gathering places called *markets*. For example, the French markets or trade fairs of Champagne were well-known throughout Europe as early as the eleventh century AD. Even now, many small towns in Canada have regular market days. Today, however, the term *market* has a much broader meaning. We use the term *market economy* to refer to a society in which people specialize in productive activities and meet most of their material wants through exchanges voluntarily agreed upon by the contracting parties.

Specialization must be accompanied by trade. People who produce only one thing must trade most of it to obtain all of the other things they require.

barter   An economic system in which goods and services are traded directly for other goods and services instead of for money.

Early trading was by means of **barter,** the trading of goods directly for other goods. But barter is costly in terms of time spent searching out satisfactory exchanges. If a farmer has wheat but wants a hammer, he must find someone who has a hammer and wants wheat. A successful barter transaction thus requires what is called a *double co-incidence of wants.*

Money eliminates the cumbersome system of barter by separating the transactions involved in the exchange of products. If a farmer has wheat and wants a hammer, he does not have to find someone who has a hammer and wants wheat. He merely has to find someone who wants wheat. The farmer takes money in exchange. Then he finds a person who wishes to sell a hammer and gives up the money for the hammer.

Money greatly facilitates specialization and trade.

Is There an Alternative to the Market Economy?

The answer to the question in the above heading is no in one sense and yes in another. We answer no because the modern economy has no *practical* alternative to reliance on market determination. We answer yes because it is possible to identify other types of economic systems.

An economic system is a distinctive method of providing answers to the basic economic questions discussed above, such as who produces what, and who consumes what. All such systems are complex. They include producers of every sort—public and private, domestic and foreign. They include consumers of every sort—young and old, rich and poor, working and nonworking. They include laws—such as those relating to property rights—rules, regulations, taxes, subsidies, and everything else that governments use to influence what is produced, how it is produced, and who gets it. They also include customs of every conceivable kind and the entire range of contemporary mores and values.

Types of Economic Systems

Although every economy is in some ways unique, it is helpful to distinguish three pure types, called *traditional, command,* and *market* economies. These economies differ in the way in which economic decisions are coordinated. But no actual economy fits neatly into one of these three categories—all real economies contain some elements of each type.

Traditional Systems

traditional economy   An economy in which behaviour is based mostly on tradition, custom, and habit.

A **traditional economy** is one in which behaviour is based primarily on tradition, custom, and habit. Young men follow their fathers' occupations. Women do what their mothers did. There is little change in the pattern of goods produced from year to year, other than those imposed by the vagaries of nature. The techniques of production also follow traditional patterns, except when the effects of an occasional new invention are felt. Finally, production is allocated among the members according to long-established traditions. In short, the answers to the economic questions of what to produce, how to produce, and how to distribute are determined by traditions.

Such a system works best in an unchanging environment. Under such static conditions, a system that does not continually require people to make choices can prove effective in meeting economic and social needs.

Traditional systems were common in earlier times. The feudal system, under which most people in medieval Europe lived, was a largely traditional society. Peasants, artisans, and most others living in villages inherited their positions in that society. They also usually inherited their specific jobs, which they handled in traditional ways.

Command Systems

In command systems, economic behaviour is determined by some central authority, usually the government, which makes most of the necessary decisions on what to produce, how to produce it, and who gets it. Such economies are characterized by the *centralization* of decision making. Because centralized decision makers usually lay down elaborate and complex plans for the behaviour that they wish to impose, the terms **command economy** and *centrally planned economy* are usually used synonymously.

command economy
An economy in which the decisions of a centralized planning authority exert the major influence over the allocation of resources.

The sheer quantity of data required for central planning of an entire economy is enormous, and the task of analysing it to produce a fully integrated plan can hardly be exaggerated. Moreover, the plan must be continually changing to take account not only of current data but also of future trends in labour supplies, technological developments, and people's tastes for various goods and services. Doing so involves the planners in *forecasting*. This is a notoriously difficult exercise, not least because of the unavailability of all essential, accurate, and up-to-date information.

Fifteen years ago, more than one third of the world's population lived in countries that relied heavily on central planning to deal with the basic economic questions. Today, the number of such countries is small. Even in countries where planning is the proclaimed system, as in China or Cuba, increasing amounts of market determination are being quietly permitted.

Free-Market Systems

In the third type of economic system, the decisions about resource allocation are made without any central direction. Instead, they result from innumerable independent decisions made by individual producers and consumers. Such a system is known as a **free-market economy** or, more simply, a *market economy*. In such an economy, decisions relating to the basic economic issues are *decentralized*. Despite the absence of a central plan, these many decentralized decisions are nonetheless coordinated. The main coordinating device is the set of market-determined prices—which is why free-market systems are often called *price systems*.

free-market economy
An economy in which the decisions of individual households and firms exert the major influence over the allocation of resources.

In a pure market economy, all of these decisions, without exception, are made by buyers and sellers acting through unhindered markets. The state provides the background of defining property and protecting rights against foreign and domestic enemies but, beyond that, markets determine all resource allocation and income distribution.

Mixed Systems

Economies that are fully traditional or fully centrally planned or wholly free-market are pure types that are useful for studying basic principles. When we look in detail at any real economy, however, we discover that its economic behaviour is the result of some mixture of central control and market determination, with a certain amount of traditional behaviour as well.

mixed economy   An economy in which some decisions about the allocation of resources are made by firms and households and some by the government.

In practice, every economy is a **mixed economy** in the sense that it combines significant elements of all three systems in determining economic behaviour.

Furthermore, within any economy, the degree of the mix varies from sector to sector. For example, in some planned economies, the command principle was used more often to determine behaviour in heavy-goods industries, such as steel, than in agriculture. Farmers were often given substantial freedom to produce and sell what they wished in response to varying market prices.

When economists speak of a particular economy as being centrally planned, we mean only that the degree of the mix is weighted heavily toward the command principle. When we speak of one as being a market economy, we mean only that the degree of the mix is weighted heavily toward decentralized decision making in response to market signals. It is important to realize that such distinctions are always matters of degree and that almost every conceivable mix can be found across the spectrum of the world's economies.

Although no country offers an example of either system working alone, some economies, such as those of Canada, the United States, France, and Hong Kong, rely much more heavily on market decisions than others, such as the economies of China, North Korea, and Cuba. Yet even in Canada, the command principle has some sway. Crown corporations, legislated minimum wages, rules and regulations for environmental protection, quotas on some agricultural outputs, and restrictions on the import of some items are the obvious examples.

See Chapter 1 of www.pearsoned.ca/lipsey for an excellent discussion of Cuba's recent economic reforms: Archibald Ritter, "Is Cuba's Economic Reform Process Paralysed?" *World Economic Affairs.*

Ownership of Resources

We have seen that economies differ as to the principle used for coordinating their economic decisions. They also differ as to *who owns* their productive resources. Who owns a nation's farms and factories, its coal mines and forests? Who owns its railways, streams, and golf courses? Who owns its houses and hotels?

In a private-ownership economy, the basic raw materials, the productive assets of the society, and the goods produced in the economy are predominantly privately owned. By this standard, Canada has primarily a private-ownership economy. However, even in Canada, public ownership extends beyond the usual basic services such as schools and local transportation systems to include other activities such as housing projects, forest and range land, and electric power utilities.

In contrast, a public-ownership economy is one in which the productive assets are predominantly publicly owned. This was true of the former Soviet Union, and it is true to a significant extent in present-day China and in Cuba. In China, however, private ownership exists in many sectors, including the rapidly growing part of the manufacturing sector that is foreign owned, mainly by Japanese and by Chinese from Taiwan and Singapore.

Command Versus Market Determination

For over a century, a great debate raged on the relative merits of the command principle versus the market principle for coordinating economic decisions. The former Soviet Union, the countries of Eastern Europe, and China were command economies for much of this century. Canada, the United States, and most of the countries of Western Europe were, and still are, primarily market economies. The apparent successes of the Soviet Union and China in the early stages of industrialization suggested to many observers that the command principle was at least as good for organizing economic behaviour as the market principle, if not better. Over the long run, however, planned economies proved a failure of such disastrous pro-portions that they seriously depressed the living standards of their citizens. (Some of the reasons for this failure were examined in *Lessons from History 1-1*.)

Still Room for Disagreement

The failure of centrally planned economies suggests the superiority of decentralized mar-kets over centrally planned ones as mechanisms for allocating an economy's scarce re-sources. Put another way, it demonstrates the superiority of mixed economies with substantial elements of market determination over fully planned command economies. However, it does *not* demonstrate, as some observers have asserted, the superiority of com-pletely free-market economies over mixed economies.

There is no guarantee that completely free markets will, on their own, handle such urgent matters as controlling pollution or providing public goods (like national defence). Indeed, as we shall see in later chapters, much economic theory is devoted to explaining why free markets often fail to do these things. Mixed economies, with significant elements of government intervention, are needed to do these jobs.

Furthermore, acceptance of the free market over central planning does not provide an excuse to ignore a country's pressing social issues. Acceptance of the benefits of the free market still leaves plenty of scope to debate the kinds, amounts, and directions of gov-ernment interventions into the workings of our market-based economy that will help to achieve social goals.

It follows that there is still considerable room for disagreement about the degree of the mix of market and government determination in any modern mixed economy—room enough to accommodate such divergent views as could be expressed by conserv-ative, liberal, and modern social democratic parties. People can accept the free market as an efficient way of organizing economic affairs and still disagree about many things. A partial list includes: the optimal amount and types of government regulation of vari-ous parts of the economy; the types of measures needed to protect the environment; whether health care should be provided by the public or the private sector; and the op-timal amount and design of social services and other policies intended to redistribute income from more to less fortunate citizens.

So, the first answer to the question posed at the outset of this section is no. There is no practical alternative to a mixed system with major reliance on markets but a sub-stantial government presence in most aspects of the economy. The second answer is yes. Within the framework of a mixed economy there are substantial alternatives among many different and complex mixes of free-market and government determination of economic life.

Government in the Modern Mixed Economy

Market economies in today's advanced industrial countries are based primarily on vol-untary transactions between individual buyers and sellers. Private individuals have the right to buy and sell what they wish, to accept or refuse work that is offered to them, and to move to where they want when they want.

Key institutions are private property and freedom of contract, both of which must be maintained by active government policies. The government creates laws of ownership and contract and then provides the institutions to enforce these laws.

In modern mixed economies governments go well beyond these important basic functions. They intervene in market transactions to correct what economists call *market failures*. These are well-defined situations in which free markets do not work well. Resources such as fishing grounds and common pastureland tend to be overexploited to the point of destruction under free-market conditions. Some products, called *public goods*, are not provided at all by markets because, once produced, no one can be prevented from using them. So their use cannot be restricted to those who are willing to pay for them. Defence and police protection are public goods. In other cases private transactors impose costs called *externalities* on those who have no say in the transaction. This is the case when factories pollute the air and rivers. The public is harmed but has no part in the producer's decisions about what to make and how to make it. These are some of the reasons why free markets sometimes fail to function as we would like them to. They explain why citizens wish governments to intervene and alter the allocation of resources that would otherwise result from leaving everything to the market.

Also, there are important equity issues that arise from letting free markets determine people's incomes. Some people lose their jobs because firms are reorganizing to become more efficient in the face of new technologies. Others keep their jobs, but the market places so little value on their services that they face economic deprivation. The old and the chronically ill may suffer if their past circumstances did not allow them to save enough to support themselves. For many reasons of this sort we accept government intervention to redistribute income by taking from the "haves" and giving to the "have-nots." Almost everyone supports some redistribution of incomes. Care must be taken, however, not to kill the goose that lays the golden egg. By taking too much from the haves, we risk eliminating their incentive to work hard and produce income, some of which is to be redistributed to the have-nots.

Governments also play a part in influencing the overall level of prices and in attempting to stabilize the economy against extreme fluctuations in income and employment. A stable price level and full employment are two major goals of the government's *macroeconomic* policy. These are dealt with in the second half of this book.

These are some of the reasons all modern economies are mixed economies. Throughout most of the twentieth century in advanced industrial societies the mix had been altering towards more and more government participation in decisions about the allocation of resources and the distribution of income. In the last two decades of the century, however, there has been a worldwide movement to reduce the degree of government participation. The details of this shift in the market/government mix, and the reasons for it, are some of the major issues that will be studied in this book.

S U M M A R Y

The Complexity of the Modern Economy   LO❶

- A market economy is self-organizing in the sense that when individual consumers and producers act independently to pursue their own self-interest, responding to prices determined in open markets, the collective outcome is coordinated and relatively efficient.

- An alternative economic system requires a central planning authority to make the decisions of who consumes and who produces which goods. The experience of those countries that adopted central planning was that such planning was extremely difficult and quite inefficient in allocating resources.

Resources and Scarcity ⓛⓄ②

- Scarcity is a fundamental problem faced by all economies. Not enough resources are available to produce all the goods and services that people would like to consume. Scarcity makes it necessary to choose. All societies must have a mechanism for choosing what goods and services will be produced and in what quantities.
- The concept of opportunity cost emphasizes the problem of scarcity and choice by measuring the cost of obtaining a unit of one product in terms of the number of units of other products that could have been obtained instead.

- A production possibility boundary shows all of the combinations of goods that can be produced by an economy whose resources are fully and efficiently employed. Movement from one point to another along the boundary shows a shift in the amounts of goods being produced, which requires a reallocation of resources.
- Four basic questions must be answered in all economies: What is produced and how? What is consumed and by whom? Why are resources sometimes idle? Is productive capacity growing?

Who Makes the Choices and How? ⓛⓄ③

- The interaction of consumers and producers through goods and factor markets is illustrated by the circular flow of income and expenditure. Individual consumers sell factor services to producers and, by doing so, earn their income. Similarly, producers earn their income by selling goods and services to individual consumers.
- Individual consumers make their decisions in an effort to maximize their well-being or utility. Producers' decisions are designed to maximize their profits.

- Modern economies are based on the specialization and division of labour, which necessitate the exchange (trade) of goods and services. Exchange takes place in markets and is facilitated by the use of money.
- Driven by the ongoing revolution in transportation and communications technology, the world economy is rapidly globalizing. National and regional boundaries are becoming less important with the rise of transnational corporations.

Is There an Alternative to the Market Economy? ⓛⓄ④

- We can distinguish three pure types of economies: traditional, command, and free-market. In practice, all economies are mixed economies in that their economic behaviour responds to mixes of tradition, government command, and price incentives.
- In the late 1980s, events in Eastern Europe and the Soviet Union led to the general acceptance that the system of fully centrally planned economies had failed to produce minimally acceptable living standards for its citizens. All of these

countries are now moving toward greater market determination and less state command in their economies.
- Governments play an important role in modern mixed economies. They create and enforce important background institutions such as private property and freedom of contract. They intervene to correct situations where markets do not effectively perform their coordinating function. They also redistribute income and wealth in the interests of equity.

K E Y   C O N C E P T S

The self-organzing economy
Scarcity and the need for choice
Choice and opportunity cost
Production possibility boundary
Resource allocation

Growth in productive capacity
Specialization
Comparative advantange
The division of labour
Globalization

Traditional economies
Command economies
Pure market economies
Mixed economies

STUDY EXERCISES

For Questions 1-4, consider the following description of a mythical economy called Choiceland.

Choiceland has 250 workers and produces only two goods, X and Y. Labour is the only factor of production, but some workers are better suited to producing X than Y (and vice versa). The table below shows the maximum levels of output of each good possible from various levels of labour input.

Number of Workers Producing X	Annual Production of X	Number of Workers Producing Y	Annual Production of Y
0	0	250	1300
50	20	200	1200
100	45	150	900
150	60	100	600
200	70	50	350
250	75	0	0

1. Draw the production possibility boundary for Choiceland on a scale diagram.

2. Explain why the PPB is shaped concave to the origin.

3. Compute the opportunity cost of producing an extra 10 units of X if the economy is initially producing 60 units of X and 600 units of Y. How does this compare to the opportunity cost if the economy were initially producing 70 units of X?

4. Suppose now that the technology associated with producing good Y improves, so that the maximum level of Y that can be produced from any given level of labour input increases by 10 percent. Explain (or show in a diagram) what happens to the production possibilities curve.

5. Explain why a technological improvement in the production of one good means that a country can now produce more of *other* goods than it did previously.

6. Consider the decision you face when deciding whether to go skiing for the weekend. Suppose that transportation, lift tickets, and accommodation for the weekend costs $300. Suppose also that restaurant food for the weekend will cost $75. Finally, suppose that you have a weekend job that you will have to miss if you go skiing, a job that pays you $120 (after tax) for the one weekend day that you work. What is the opportunity cost of going skiing? Is there any other information that you need before computing the opportunity cost?

7. Suppose that you and a friend go wilderness camping for a week and must find your own food to survive. From past experience, you know that you and your friend have different abilities in fishing and hunting. If each of you were to work for one day either catching fish or trapping rabbits, the number of fish and rabbits that you could catch is given in the following table:

	Fish	Rabbits
You	6	3
Your friend	8	2

You and your friend decide that you should allocate the duties so that you get the most food for the least amount of work effort.

a. What is the opportunity cost for you to catch an additional rabbit? What is your friend's opportunity cost for catching an extra rabbit?

b. What is the allocation of tasks that maximizes total output for the least amount of work effort?

c. Suppose that you both decide to work for two days according to the allocation in part **b**. What is the total amount of output? What would it have been if you had decided the reverse allocation of tasks?

DISCUSSION QUESTIONS

1. What is the difference between scarcity and poverty? If everyone in the world had enough to eat, could we say that food was no longer scarce?

2. Evidence accumulates that the use of chemical fertilizers, which increases agricultural production greatly, damages water quality. Analyse the choice between more food and cleaner water involved in using such fertilizers. Use a production possibility curve with agricultural output on the vertical axis and water quality on the horizontal axis. In what ways does this production possibility curve reflect scarcity, choice, and opportunity cost? How would an improved fertilizer that increased agricultural output without further worsening water quality affect the curve? Suppose that a pollution-free fertilizer were developed; would this mean that there would no longer be any opportunity cost in using it?

3. Discuss the following statement by a leading U.S. economist: "One of the mysteries of semantics is why the government-managed economies ever came to be called planned and the market economies unplanned. It is the former that are in chronic chaos, in which buyers stand in line hoping to buy some toilet paper or soap. It is the latter that are in reasonable equilibrium—where if you want a cake of soap or a steak or a shirt or a car, you can go to the store and find that the item is magically there for you to buy. It is the liberal economies that reflect a highly sophisticated planning system, and the government-managed economies that are primitive and unplanned."

4. Consider the market for physicians' services. In what way has this market taken advantage of the specialization of labour?

5. "It is not from the benevolence of the butcher, the brewer, or the baker, that we expect our dinner, but from their regard to their own interest. We address ourselves, not to their humanity but to their self-love, and never talk to them of our own necessities but of their advantages." Do you agree with this quotation from Adam Smith's classic, *The Wealth of Nations*? How are "our dinner" and "their self-interest" related to the price system? What does Smith assume to be the motives of firms and households?

CHAPTER 2

How Economists Work

(LO) *LEARNING OBJECTIVES*

❶ Recognize the difference between positive and normative statements.

❷ Understand how theorizing and model-building help economists think about the economy.

❸ Explain the interaction between economic theories and empirical observation.

❹ Understand why testing theories about human behaviour usually requires studying large numbers of individuals.

❺ Recognize several types of economic data, including index numbers, time-series and cross-section data, and scatter diagrams.

❻ Understand that economic theories involve relations between variables and that such relations can be expressed in words, equations, or graphs.

❼ Recognize that the slope of a relation between X and Y is interpreted as the marginal response in Y to a unit change in X.

In Chapter 1 we discussed the basic question whose answer gave rise to the study of economics. How do millions of producers and consumers, acting independently in their own self-interest, somehow become organized into a coherent system that delivers the goods and services where and when they are wanted and in the approximate quantities they are wanted? Economists study how this is done by the mixed market economies in which we live. Economists also identify situations in which markets fail to perform as well as they might. In such cases they ask whether specific markets may be able to perform more effectively. Usually this involves government intervention of one form or another. Economists then seek to evaluate the efficiency with which governments achieve their goals.

Having sought to understand what is happening in the mixed economy, the next step is often to give policy advice. Indeed, economists give advice on a wide variety of policy topics. If you read a newspaper, watch television, or listen to the radio you will often notice some economist's opinions being reported. Perhaps it is on unemployment, the exchange rate, or interest rates; on some new tax; on the case for privatization or regulation of an industry; or on the possible reforms to Canada's health-care system.

Economics is regarded as a social science. Unlike a training in chemsitry or physics, however, many economists would say that a training in economics provides the student more with a "way of thinking" than with a collection of facts. This does not mean that facts are unimportant to the economist—quite the contrary. It means only that facts are typically harder to establish in economics than in the "hard" sciences and often economists do not know which facts are important without first having a way to organize their thinking.

Central to the economist's way of thinking is the distinction between *positive statements* and *normative statements*. Also of crucial importance to the economist is the role of *theory* and, in particular, the use of economic *models* to provide a framework for thinking about complex issues. Such models can be used to generate *testable hypotheses*.

In this chapter, we explore what it means to be "scientific" in the study of human behaviour and to establish criteria for evaluating how well economics succeeds in meeting that goal.

Positive and Normative Advice

Economists give two broad types of advice, called *normative* and *positive*. They sometimes advise that the government ought to try harder to reduce unemployment or to preserve the environment. When they say such things they are giving normative advice. They may be using their expert knowledge to come to conclusions about the costs of various unemployment-reducing or environment-saving schemes. But when they say that the government *ought* to do something, they are making judgements about the value of the various things that the government could do with its limited resources. Advice that depends on a value judgement is normative—it tells others what they *ought* to do.

Another type of advice is illustrated by the statement "If the government wants to reduce unemployment, reducing unemployment-insurance benefits is an effective way of doing so." This is positive advice. It does not rely on a judgement about the value of reducing unemployment. Instead the expert is saying, "If this is what you want to do, here is a way to do it."

The distinction between positive and normative is fundamental to any rational inquiry. Much of the success of modern science depends on the ability of scientists to separate their views on *what does happen* in the world, from their views on *what they would like to happen*. For example, until the eighteenth century almost everyone believed that the Earth was only a few thousand years old. Evidence then began to accumulate that the Earth was billions of years old. This evidence was hard for most people to accept since it ran counter to a literal reading of many religious texts. Many did not want to believe the evidence. Nevertheless, scientists, many of whom were religious, continued their research because they refused to allow their feelings about what they wanted to believe to affect their scientific search for the truth. Eventually, all scientists came to accept that the Earth is about 4 billion years old.

Distinguishing what is true from what we would like to be, or what we feel ought to be, requires distinguishing between positive and normative statements.

Normative statements depend on value judgements. They involve issues of personal opinion, which cannot be settled by recourse to facts. In contrast, **positive statements** do not involve value judgements. They are statements about what is, was, or will be—that is, statements that are about matters of fact.

Examples of both types of statement are given in Table 2-1. All five positive statements in the table assert things about the nature of the world in which we live. In contrast, the five normative statements involve value judgements.

Notice two things about the positive/normative distinction. First, positive statements need not be true. Statement D is almost certainly false. Yet it is positive, not normative. Second, the inclusion of a value judgement in a statement does not necessarily make the statement normative. Statement E is about the value judgements that people

normative statement
A statement about what ought to be as opposed to what actually is.

positive statement
A statement about what actually is (was or will be), as opposed to what ought to be.

TABLE 2-1   Positive and Normative Statements

Positive	Normative
A Raising interest rates encourages people to save.	F People should be encouraged to save.
B High rates of income tax encourage people to evade paying taxes.	G Governments should arrange taxes so that people cannot avoid paying them.
C Raising wage rates causes people to work harder.	H Firms should raise wage rates to provide a just reward for hard work.
D Lowering the price of tobacco causes people to smoke less.	I The government should raise the tax on tobacco to discourage people from smoking.
E The majority of the population would prefer a policy that reduced unemployment to one that reduced inflation.	J The government ought to be more concerned with reducing unemployment than inflation.

hold. We could, however, check to see if people really do prefer low unemployment to low inflation. We can ask them and we can observe how they vote. There is no need for the economist to introduce a value judgement in order to check the validity of the statement itself.

We leave you to analyse the remaining eight statements to decide precisely why each is either positive or normative. Remember to apply the two tests. First, is the statement only about actual or alleged facts? If so, it is a positive one. Second, are value judgements necessary to assess the truth of the statement? If so, it is normative.

Economic Theories and Models

Economists seek to understand the world by developing *theories* and *models* that explain some of the things that have been seen and to predict some of the things that will be seen. What is a theory and what is a model?

Theories

Theories are constructed to explain things. For example, what determines the number of eggs sold in Winnipeg in a particular week? As part of the answer to this question and ones like it, economists have developed theories of demand and supply—theories that we will study in detail in the next three chapters. Any theory is distinguished by its definitions, assumptions, and predictions.

Definitions

variable   Any well-defined item, such as the price or quantity of a commodity, that can take on various specific values.

The basic elements of any theory are its variables. A **variable** is a magnitude that can take on different possible values.

In our theory of the egg market, the variable *quantity of eggs* might be defined as the number of cartons of 12 grade-A eggs. The variable *price of eggs* is the amount of money that must be given up to purchase each carton of eggs. The particular values taken on by those two variables might be 2000 cartons at a price of $1.80 on July 1, 1998; 1800 cartons at a price of $1.95 on July 1, 1999; and 1950 cartons at a price of $1.85 on July 1, 2000.

For a theory of the egg market we define the variable *demand* as the number of cartons of eggs consumers wish to purchase over a particular time-period. We define the variable *supply* as the number of cartons of eggs producers want to sell over the same time-period.

There are two broad categories of variables that are important in any theory. An **endogenous variable** is one whose value is determined within the theory. An **exogenous variable** influences the endogenous variables but is itself determined by factors outside the theory. To illustrate the difference, the quantity of eggs is an endogenous variable in our theory of the egg market—our theory is designed to explain it. The state of the weather, however, is an exogenous variable. It may well affect the number of eggs consumers demand or producers supply but we can safely assume that the state of the weather is not influenced by the market for eggs.[1]

Assumptions

A theory's assumptions concern motives, physical relations, directions of causation, and the conditions under which the theory is meant to apply.

Motives.   The theories we study in this book make the fundamental assumption that everyone pursues their own self-interest when making economic decisions. People are assumed to know what they want, and to know how to go about getting it within the constraints set by the resources at their command.

Physical Relations.   If egg producers buy more chicks and use more labour, land, and chicken feed, they will produce more eggs. This is an example of one of the most important physical relations in the theory of markets. It concerns assumptions about how the amount of output is related to the quantities of factors of production used to produce it. This relation is specified in what is called a *production function*.

Conditions of Application.   Assumptions are often used to specify the conditions under which a theory is meant to hold. For example, a theory that assumes there is "no government" usually does not mean literally the absence of government, but only that the theory is meant to apply when governments are not significantly affecting the situation being studied.

Direction of Causation.   When economists assume that one variable is related to another, they are assuming some causal link between the two. For example, when the amount of eggs that producers want to supply is assumed to increase when the cost of their chicken feed falls, the causation runs from the price of chicken feed to the supply of eggs. Producers supply more eggs because the price of chicken feed has fallen; they do not get cheaper chicken feed because of their decision to supply more eggs.

Although assumptions are an essential part of all theories, students are often concerned about those that seem unrealistic. An example will illustrate some of the issues involved. Much of the theory that we are going to study in this book uses the assumption that owners of firms attempt to maximize their profits. The assumption of profit maximization allows economists to make predictions about the behaviour of firms. They

endogenous variable
A variable that is explained within a theory. Sometimes called an *induced variable* or a *dependent variable*.

exogenous variable
A variable that influences endogenous variables but is itself determined by factors outside the theory. Sometimes called an *autonomous variable* or an *independent variable*.

---

[1]Other words are sometimes used to make the same distinction. One frequently used pair is *induced* for endogenous and *autonomous* for exogenous. Another pair is *dependent* for endogenous and *independent* for exogenous.

A key assumption in economics is that firms make decisions with the goal of maximizing their profits.

study how firms' profits are affected by the choices firms make. They then predict that the alternative that produces the most profits will be the one selected.

Profit maximization may seem like a rather crude assumption. Surely, for example, the managers of firms sometimes choose to protect the environment rather than pursue certain highly polluting but profitable opportunities. Does this not discredit the assumption of profit maximization by showing it to be unrealistic?

The answer is no; to make successful predictions, the theory does not require that managers be solely and unwaveringly motivated by the desire to maximize profits. All that is required is that profits be a sufficiently important consideration that a theory based on the assumption of profit maximization will lead to explanations and predictions that are substantially correct.

This illustration shows that it is not always appropriate to criticize a theory because its assumptions seem unrealistic.

All theory is an abstraction from reality. If it were not, it would merely duplicate the world in all its complexity and would add little to our understanding of it.

A good theory abstracts in a useful way; a poor theory does not. If a theory has ignored some genuinely important factors, its predictions will be contradicted by the evidence—at least where an ignored factor exerts an important influence on the outcome.

Predictions

A theory's predictions are the propositions that can be deduced from it. They are often called *hypotheses*. For example, a prediction from our theory of the demand and supply for eggs is that "if the price of chicken feed falls, producers will supply more eggs." A prediction concerning a different market, the market for labour services, is "if the hourly wage paid to workers increases, the amount of labour employed will fall."

Models

economic model
A term used in several related ways: sometimes as a synonym for theory, sometimes for a specific quantification of a general theory, sometimes for the application of a general theory to a specific context, and sometimes for an abstraction designed to illustrate some point but not meant as a full theory on its own.

Economists often proceed by constructing what they call **economic models**. This term has several different but related meanings.

Sometimes the term "model" is used as a synonym for a theory, as when economists speak of the model of the determination of national income. Sometimes it may refer to a particular subset of theories, such as the Keynesian model or the Neoclassical model of income determination.

More often, a model means a specific quantitative formulation of a theory. In this case, specific numbers are attached to the mathematical relationships defined by the theory, the numbers often being derived from observations of the economy. The specific form of the model can then be used to make precise predictions about, say, the behaviour of prices in the potato market, or the course of national income and total employment. Forecasting models used by the Bank of Canada and the International Monetary Fund (IMF) are of this type.

The term "model" is often used to refer to an application of a general theory in a specific context. So if we take the theory of consumer demand and apply it to the egg market in Winnipeg we might speak of a model of the Winnipeg egg market.

Finally, a model may be an illustrative abstraction, not meant to be elaborate enough to generate testable hypotheses. The circular flow of income and expenditure in Chapter 1 is a model of this sort. By illustrating how income and payments flow between consumers and producers, it helps us to understand how decisions of these two groups influence each other through factor markets and goods markets. However, the actual flows in any real economy are vastly more complex than the simple flows shown in the figure. The model helps us to understand what is going on without being detailed enough to yield specific testable predictions about real-world behaviour. In some ways, a model of this sort is like a political caricature. Its value is in the insights it provides that help us to understand key features of a complex world.

Testing Theories

Economists make much use of evidence or, as they usually call it, empirical observation. Such observations can be used to test a specific prediction of some theory and to provide observations to be explained by theories.

A theory is tested by confronting its predictions with evidence. Are events of the type contained in the theory followed by the consequences predicted by the theory? For example, is a decrease in the price of chicken feed followed by an increase in the amount of eggs producers want to sell? Generally, theories tend to be abandoned when they are no longer useful. A theory ceases to be useful when it cannot predict better than an alternative theory. When a theory consistently fails to predict better than an available alternative, it is either modified or replaced.

The old question, "Which came first: the chicken or the egg?", is often raised when discussing economic theories. In the first instance, it was observation that preceded economic theories. People were not born with economic theories embedded in their minds; instead, economic theories first arose when people observed the coordination of market behaviour and asked themselves how such coordination occurred. But, once economics was established, theories and evidence interacted with each other. It has now become impossible to say that one precedes the other. In some cases, empirical evidence may suggest inadequacies that require the development of better theories. In other cases, an inspired guess may lead to a theory that has little current empirical support but is subsequently found to explain many observations. This interaction between theory and empirical observation is illustrated in Figure 2-1.

Theories About Human Behaviour

So far we have talked about theories in general. But what about theories that purport to explain and predict human behaviour? A scientific study of human behaviour is only possible if humans respond in predictable ways to things that affect them. Is it reasonable to expect such predictability? After all, we humans have free will and can behave in capricious ways if the spirit moves us.

Think, however, of what the world would be like if human behaviour were really unpredictable. Neither law, nor justice, nor airline timetables would be more reliable than the outcome of a single spin of a roulette wheel. A kind remark could as easily provoke fury as sympathy. Your landlady might evict you tomorrow or let you off the rent. One cannot really imagine a society of human beings that could work like this. In fact, we live

FIGURE 2-1   The Interaction Between Theory and Empirical Observation

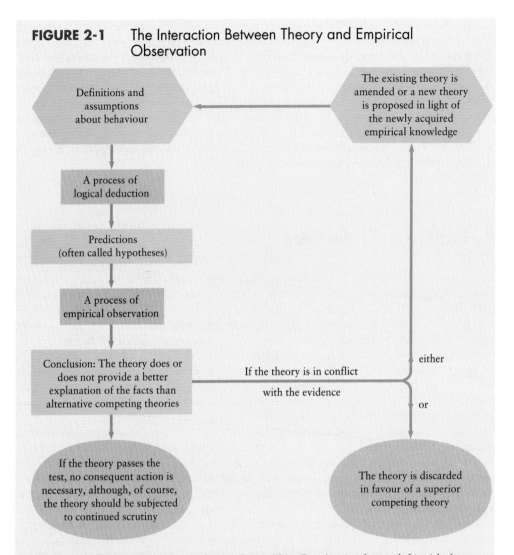

Theory and observation are in continuous interaction. Starting (at the top left) with the assumptions of a theory and the definitions of relevant terms, the theorist deduces by logical analysis everything that is implied by the assumptions. These implications are the predictions or the hypotheses of the theory. The theory is then tested by confronting its predictions with evidence. If the theory is in conflict with facts, it will usually be amended to make it consistent with those facts (thereby making it a better theory); or it will be discarded, to be replaced by a superior alternative. The process then begins again: The new or amended theory is subjected first to logical analysis and then to empirical testing.

in a world that is a mixture of the predictable for "most of the people most of the time" with the haphazard or random.

How is it that human behaviour can show stable responses even though we can never be quite sure what one individual will do? Successful predictions about the behaviour of large groups are made possible by the statistical "law" of large numbers. Very roughly, this "law" asserts that random movements of a large number of items tend to offset one another.

For example, we might wonder if there is a relationship between highway speed limits and road accidents. When the speed limit is actually lowered, it will be almost impossible to predict in advance what changes will occur in any single individual's driving record. One individual whose record had been good may have a series of accidents after the speed limit is lowered because of deterioration in his physical or emotional health. Another person may have an improved accident record for reasons not associated with the change in the speed limit—for example, because she purchases a more reliable car. Yet others may have altered driving records for no reasons that we can discern—we may have to put it down to an exercise of unpredictable free will.

If we study only a few individuals, we will learn nothing about the effects of the altered speed limit, since we will not know the importance of all the other causes that are at work. But, if we observe 1,000 individuals, the effects of the change in the speed limit— if such effects do exist—will tend to show up in the *average* responses. If a reduced speed limit does discourage accidents, the group as a whole will have fewer accidents even though some individuals have more. Individuals may do peculiar things that, as far as we can see, are inexplicable, but the group's behaviour will nonetheless be predictable, precisely because the odd things that one individual does will tend to cancel out the odd things that some other individual does.

Testing theories about human behaviour requires studying large numbers of people—to take advantage of the "law" of large numbers.

Because the unusual behaviour of one individual often offsets the unusual behaviour of someone else, it is much easier to accurately predict the average behaviour in large groups of people.

Why Economists Disagree

When all their theories have been constructed and all their evidence has been collected, economists still disagree with each other on many issues. If you hear a discussion among economists on the evening news or if you read about their debates in the daily press or weekly magazines, you will find that economists frequently disagree with each other. What should we make of this disagreement? Here are five of the many possible sources of disagreement.

First, different economists may be using different benchmarks. For example, inflation may be up compared with last year but down compared with 1990. When this sort of thing happens the disagreement is more apparent than real, although it can be confusing to observers.

Second, economists often fail to make it clear to their audience whether they are talking about short-term or long-term consequences. For example, one economist may be noting that a tax cut will stimulate consumption at the cost of lowering saving in the short run while another is pointing out that it will stimulate investment and saving in the long run. Here, again, the disagreement is more apparent than real, since both these short-run and long-run effects command much agreement among economists.

Third, economists often fail to acknowledge the full extent of their ignorance. There are many things on which economists know little, and even more on which the evidence is far from conclusive. Informed judgements are then required before an economist takes a position on even a purely positive question. If two economists' judgements differ, the disagreement is real. Evidence is not sufficient, and different people can come to different conclusions on the basis of a given set of evidence. What a responsible economist will do in such cases is to make clear the extent to which informed judgement is involved in any position he or she is taking.

Fourth, different economists have different values, and these normative views play a large part in most public discussions of policy. Many economists stress the importance of individual responsibility, while others stress the need for collective action to deal with certain issues. Different policy advice may stem from such differences in value judgements about what is socially important. The responsible economist will make it clear which part of her advice is normative and which part is positive.

A fifth reason for disagreement lies in the desire of the media to cover both sides of any contentious issue. As a result the public will usually hear one or two economists on each side of a debate, regardless of whether the profession is divided right down the middle or is nearly unanimous in its support of one side. Thus, the public will not know that in one case a reporter could have chosen from dozens of economists to present each side, whereas in another case the reporter had to spend three days finding someone willing to take a particular side because nearly all the economists supported the other side. In their desire to show both sides of all cases, however, the media tend to present the public with the appearance of a profession equally split over all matters.

Anyone seeking to discredit some particular economist's advice by showing that there is disagreement among economists will have no trouble finding evidence of some disagreement. But those who wish to know if there is a majority view, or even a strong consensus, will find one on a surprisingly large number of issues.

Because the world is complex and because no issue can be settled beyond any doubt, economists are never in unanimous agreement on any issue. Nonetheless, the methods we have been discussing in this chapter have produced an impressive amount of agreement on many aspects of how the economy works and what happens when governments intervene to alter its workings. A survey published in the *American Economic Review*, perhaps the most influential economics journal, showed strong agreement among economists on many propositions, including "Rent control leads to a housing shortage" (85 percent yes), "tariffs usually reduce economic welfare" (93 percent yes), and "large government budget deficits have adverse effects on the economy" (83 percent yes). Other examples of these areas of agreement will be found in countless places throughout this book.

Economic Data

For data on the Canadian economy and many other aspects of Canadian life, see Statistics Canada's website: www.statcan.ca.

Economists seek to explain events that they see in the world. Why, for example, did the price of wheat rise last year even though the wheat crop increased? Explaining such observations typically requires an understanding of how the economy works, an understanding based in part on the insights economists derive from their models.

Economists also use real-world observations to test their theories. For example, did the amount that people saved last year rise—as the theory predicts it should have—when a large tax cut increased after-tax incomes? To test this prediction we need reliable data for people's incomes and their savings.

Political scientists, sociologists, anthropologists, and psychologists all tend to collect the data they use to formulate and test their theories. Economists are unusual among social scientists in mainly using data collected by others, often government statisticians. In economics there is a division of labour between collecting data and using it to generate and test theories. The advantage is that economists do not need to spend much of their scarce research time collecting the data they use. The disadvantage is that they are often not as well informed about the limitations of the data collected by others as they would be if they collected the data themselves.

Once data are collected they can be displayed in various ways, many of which we will see later in this chapter. They can be laid out in tables. They can be displayed in various types of graphs. And where we are interested in relative movements rather than absolute ones, the data can be expressed in index numbers. We begin with a discussion of index numbers.

index number An average that measures change over time of such variables as the price level and industrial production; conventionally expressed as a percentage relative to a base period, which is assigned the value 100.

Index Numbers

The top part of Table 2-2 shows how the prices of gold and silver varied over an eight-year period from 1992 to 1999. How do these two sets of prices compare in volatility? It is difficult to tell from the table because the two prices fluctuate around different levels. It is easier to compare the series if we concentrate on relative rather than absolute price changes. (The absolute change is the dollar value of the change in price; the relative change is the change in the price expressed in relation to some base price.)

Index Numbers as Relative Magnitudes

Comparisons of relative changes can be made by expressing each price series as a set of **index numbers**. To do this we take the price at some point of time as the base to which prices in other periods will be compared. We call this the base period. In the present example we choose 1992 as the base period for both series. The price in that year is given a value of 100. We then take the price of gold in each subsequent year, called the given year, and divide it by the price in the base year, and then multiply the result by 100. This gives us an index number of gold prices. We then do the same for silver. The details of the calculations for gold are shown in the middle part of Table 2-2.

The results, which are shown in the bottom part of Table 2-2, allow us to compare the relative fluctuations in the two series, even though their absolute values are quite different. It is apparent from the figures that silver prices have shown significantly more percentage variability than have gold prices.

The formula of any index number is:

$$\text{Value of index in given period} = \frac{\text{absolute value at given period}}{\text{absolute value in base period}} \times 100$$

An index number merely expresses the value of some series in any given period as a percentage of its value in the base period. Thus, the 1999 index of gold prices of 81.0 tells us that the 1999 price of gold was 81.0 percent of the 1992 price. By subtracting 100 from any index we get the change from the base to the given year, expressed as a percentage of the base year. So, in the above case, the price of gold in 1999 was 19.0 percent lower than in 1992. To take a second example, the silver index

TABLE 2-2 Indexes for Gold and Silver Prices

Average January Price, US dollars per troy ounce

Year	Gold	Silver
1992	$354.83	$4.13
1993	329.78	3.68
1994	386.21	5.10
1995	378.81	4.78
1996	400.28	5.50
1997	351.01	4.78
1998	290.51	5.90
1999	287.41	5.16

Constructing an Index of Gold Prices (Base Year 1992)

Year	Procedure	Index
1992	(354.83/354.83) × 100	= 100.0
1993	(329.78/354.83) × 100	= 92.9
1994	(386.21/354.83) × 100	= 108.8
1995	(378.81/354.83) × 100	= 106.8
1996	(400.28/354.83) × 100	= 112.8
1997	(351.01/354.83) × 100	= 98.9
1998	(290.51/354.83) × 100	= 81.9
1999	(287.41/354.83) × 100	= 81.0

Index numbers are calculated by dividing the given price by the base-year price and multiplying the result by 100. For example, the given price of gold in 1998 of $290.51 is divided by the base-year price of $354.83 and multiplied by 100 to yield an index value for 1998 of 81.9.

Constructed Indexes of Gold and Silver Prices

Year	Gold	Silver
1992	100.0	100.0
1993	92.9	89.1
1994	108.8	123.5
1995	106.8	115.7
1996	112.8	133.2
1997	98.9	115.7
1998	81.9	142.9
1999	81.0	124.9

(*Source:* The BCA Research Group.)

of 124.9 in 1999 tells us that the 1999 price of silver was 124.9 percent of the 1992 price—or, the price had increased by 24.9 percent between those two years.

Index Numbers as Average Magnitudes

Practise with Study Guide Chapter 2, Exercise 3.

Index numbers are particularly useful if we wish to combine several different series into some average. Say, for example, that we want an index of precious metal prices and gold and silver are the only two commodities we need to worry about.

An Unweighted Index.   For any one year we could add the price indexes for gold and silver and average them. This would give us a precious metals index. But the index would give the two prices equal weight in determining the value of the overall index. Such an index is often called an unweighted index, but that name is misleading. Actually, it is an equal-weight index. It would be sheer luck if this were the appropriate thing to do.

A Proportional-Weights Index.   In practice, we need to weight each price by some measure of its relative importance, letting the more important prices have more weight than the less important prices in determining what happens to the overall index. In the present example, we take the value of the outputs of each metal as the appropriate weights. In the base year, gold and silver outputs were $25.4 billion and $2.6 billion respectively. In order to make the new index still have a value in the base period equal to 100, the weights are all expressed as decimal fractions that sum to 1. To do this we express each value as a fraction of the total value of $28.0 billion. This gives us weights of 0.907 for gold and 0.093 for silver. In other words, since the value of silver is only about one-tenth of the value of gold, silver prices will be given only one-tenth the influence of gold prices in determining the overall index of precious metal prices. To get our weighted index of precious metal prices, we multiply each index value in the bottom part of Table 2-2 by that metal's weight and sum the two to obtain the final index. The results are shown in Table 2-3. The quite different behaviour of the two indexes shows the importance of the choice of weights. When both prices are given equal weight, the index rises in 1998, reflecting the sharp rise in the price of silver that year. But when gold is weighted by its importance in production, the precious metals index falls in that year (because the price of gold fell in that year).

An index that averages changes in several series is the weighted average of the indexes for the separate series, where the weights should reflect the relative importance of each series.

Price Indexes.   Economists make frequent use of indexes of the price level which cover a broad group of prices across the whole economy. One of the most important of these is the consumer price index, CPI, which covers goods and services that individuals buy. This is described in detail in Chapter 19.

All price indexes are calculated using the same procedure. First, the relevant prices are collected. Then a base year is chosen. Then each price series is converted into index numbers, just as was done in Table 2-2. Finally, the index numbers are combined to create a weighted average index series where the weights indicate the relative im-

Table 2-3	Two Indexes of Precious Metals Prices	
	Equal Weights	Proportional Weights
1992	100.0	100.0
1993	91.0	92.6
1994	116.2	110.2
1995	111.3	107.6
1996	123.0	114.7
1997	107.3	100.5
1998	112.4	87.5
1999	103.0	85.1

Weights really matter! The equal-weight index is calculated for each year by adding the gold and silver price indexes from Table 2-2 and dividing by two (a simple average). The proportional-weights index is calculated for each year by taking a weighted average of the price indexes from Table 2-2, where the weights are .907 for gold and .093 for silver. These weights reflect the proportion of the total value of sales of gold and silver (in the base year) accounted for by each precious metal.

portance of each price series, as done in Table 2-3. For example, in any consumer price index the price of sardines would be given a much smaller weight than the price of living accommodation, because what happens to the price of accommodation is much more important to consumers, all of whom spend much more on accommodation than on sardines.

Graphing Economic Data

A single economic variable such as unemployment or GDP can come in two basic forms.

Cross-Section and Time-Series Data

The first is called **cross-sectional data**, which means a number of different observations on one variable all taken in different places at the same point in time. Figure 2-2 shows an example. The variable in the figure is unemployment as a percentage of the labour force. It is shown for each of the ten Canadian provinces in September 1999.

The second type of data is called **time-series data**. It refers to observations taken on one variable at successive points in time. The data in Figure 2-3 show the unemployment rate for Canada from 1978 to 1999. (Note that the Canadian unemployment

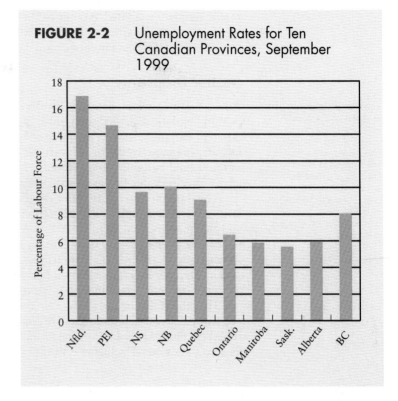

FIGURE 2-2   Unemployment Rates for Ten Canadian Provinces, September 1999

cross-sectional data A set of measurements or observations made at the same time across several different units (such as households, firms, or countries).

time-series data A set of measurements or observations made repeatedly at successive periods (or moments) of time.

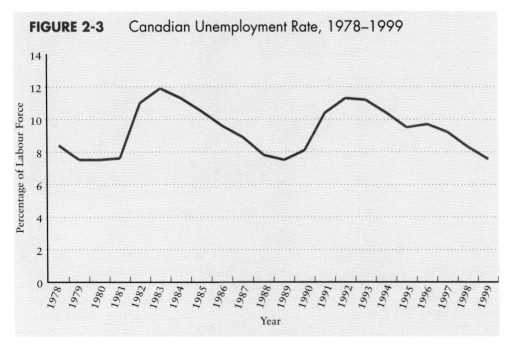

FIGURE 2-3   Canadian Unemployment Rate, 1978–1999

rate is simply a weighted average of the ten provincial unemployment rates, where the weight for each province is the size of that province's labour force expressed as a fraction of the total Canadian labour force.)

Scatter Diagrams

Another way in which data can be presented is in a **scatter diagram**. This type of chart is more analytical than those above. It is designed to show the relation between two different variables, such as the price of eggs and the quantity of eggs purchased. To plot a scatter diagram, values of one variable are measured on the horizontal axis and values of the second variable are measured on the vertical axis. Any point on the diagram relates a specific value of one variable to a corresponding specific value of the other.

The data plotted on a scatter diagram may be either cross-sectional data or time-series data. An example of a cross-sectional scatter diagram is a scatter of the price of eggs and the quantity sold in July 1999 at two dozen different places in Canada. Each dot refers to a price–quantity combination observed in a different place at the same time. An example of a scatter diagram using time-series data is the price and quantity of eggs sold in Thunder Bay for each month over the last ten years. Each of the 120 dots refers to a price–quantity combination observed at the same place in one particular month.

The table in Figure 2-4 shows data for the income and the savings of ten households in one particular year and these data are plotted on a scatter diagram. Each point in the figure represents one household, showing its income and its saving. The positive relation between the two stands out. The higher is the household's income, the higher its saving tends to be.

Graphing Economic Theories

Theories are built on assumptions about relationships between variables. For example, the quantity of eggs demanded is assumed to fall as the price of eggs rises. Or, the total amount an individual saves is assumed to rise as his or her income rises. How can such re-

Figure 2-4   A Scatter Diagram of Income and Saving

Household	Annual Income	Annual Saving
1	$70 000	$10 000
2	30 000	2 500
3	100 000	12 000
4	60 000	3 000
5	80 000	8 000
6	10 000	500
7	20 000	2 000
8	50 000	2 000
9	40 000	4 200
10	90 000	8 000

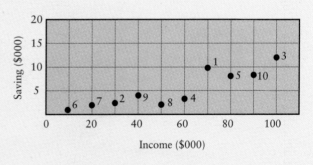

Saving tends to rise as income rises. The table shows the amount of income earned by ten selected households together with the amount they saved during the same year. The figure plots the income and saving for the ten households listed in the table. The number on each dot refers to the household in the corresponding row of the table. (Note that the scales are not the same on the two axes.)

lations be expressed? Here we introduce the concept of a *function* which is really just a special type of relation. When one variable, *X*, is related to another variable, *Y*, in such a way that to every value of *X* there is only one possible value of *Y*, we say that *Y* is a *function* of *X*.[2] When we write this relation down, we are expressing a *functional relation* between the two variables.

A functional relation can be expressed in words, in a numerical schedule, in mathematical equations, or in graphs.

To illustrate, we take a specific example of a relation between a family's annual income, which we denote by the symbol *Y*, and the total amount it spends on goods and services during that period, which we denote by the symbol *C*.

Verbal Statement.   When income is zero, the family will spend $800 a year (either by borrowing the money or by consuming past savings), and for every $1 of income that it obtains it will increase its expenditure by 80 cents.

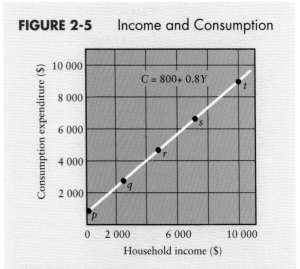

FIGURE 2-5   Income and Consumption

Consumption expenditure rises as income rises. The figure graphs the schedule and the equation for the consumption function discussed in the text.

Schedule.   This shows selected values of the family's income and the amount it spends on consumption.

Annual income	Consumption	Reference letter
$ 0	$ 800	*p*
2 500	2 800	*q*
5 000	4 800	*r*
7 500	6 800	*s*
10 000	8 800	*t*

Mathematical (Algebraic) Statement.   *C* = $800 + 0.8*Y* is the equation of the relation just described in words. As a check, you can first see that when *Y* is zero, *C* is $800. Then you can substitute any two values of *Y* that differ by $1, multiply each by 0.80, and add 800, and see that the corresponding two values of consumption differ by $0.80.

Graphical Statement.   Figure 2-5 shows both the points from the preceding schedule and the line representing the equation given in the previous paragraph.

Comparison of the values on the graph with the values in the schedule, and with the values derived from the equation just stated, shows that these are alternative expressions of the same relation between *C* and *Y*. All four of these modes of expression refer to the same relation between total consumption expenditure and total income.

---

[2]For those who find this statement difficult to understand, here is a more detailed explanation. When a relationship between two variables, *X* and *Y*, is such that for any value of *X* there is one and only one value of the variable *Y*, then *Y* is said to be a function of *X*. For example, in the relation, $Y = a + bX + cX^2$, *Y* is a function of *X* because each value of *X* gives rise to one and only one value of *Y*. It is worth noting that *Y* being a function of *X* does not necessarily imply that *X* is a function of *Y*. For example, in the equation given in this footnote, *X* cannot be expressed as a *function* of *Y* because to many values of *Y* there correspond not one but two values of *X*. Though this distinction between relations and functions (a specific type of relation) is important in much of mathematics, it is not a distinction that will play a role in this book, where we confine ourselves to functions.

Functions

Let us look in a little more detail at the algebraic expression of this relation between income and consumption expenditure. To state the expression in general form, detached from the specific numerical example above, we use a symbol to express the dependence of one variable on another. Using "f" for this purpose, we write

$$C = f(Y) \qquad\qquad (2\text{-}1)$$

This is read, "C is a function of Y." Spelling this out more fully, we would say, "The amount of consumption expenditure depends upon the household's income."

The variable on the left-hand side is the dependent variable, since its value depends on the value of the variable on the right-hand side. The variable on the right-hand side is the independent variable, since it can take on any value. The letter "f" tells us that a functional relation is involved. This means that a knowledge of the value of the variable (or variables) within the parentheses on the right-hand side allows us to determine the value of the variable on the left-hand side. Although in this case we have used "f" (as a memory-aid for "function"), any convenient symbol can be used to denote the existence of a functional relation.

Functional notation can seem intimidating to those who are unfamiliar with it. But it is helpful. Since the functional concept is basic to all science, the notation is worth mastering.

Functional Forms

The equation $C = f(Y)$ states that C is related to Y. It says nothing about the *form* that this relation takes. The term *functional form* refers to the specific nature of the relation between the variables in the function. The example above gave one specific functional form for this relation:

$$C = \$800 + 0.8Y \qquad\qquad (2\text{-}2)$$

Equation 2-1 expresses the general assumption that consumption expenditure depends on the consumer's income. Equation 2-2 expresses the more specific assumption that C rises by 80 cents for every \$1 that Y rises. An alternative form for the function in Equation 2-1 would be $C = \$600 + 0.9Y$. You should be able to say in words the behaviour implied in this relation. There is no reason why either of these assumptions must be true; indeed, neither may be consistent with the facts. But that is a matter for testing. What we do have in each equation is a concise statement of a particular assumption.

Practise with Study Guide Chapter 2, Exercise 4.

Graphing Functional Relations

Different functional forms have different graphs, and we will meet many of these in subsequent chapters. Figure 2-5 is an example of a relation in which the two variables move together. When income goes up consumption goes up. In such a relation the two variables are *positively related* to each other.

Figure 2-6 gives an example of variables that move in opposite directions. As the amount spent on abating smoke pollution goes up, the amount of pollution goes down. In such a relation the two variables are *negatively related* to each other.

Both of these graphs are straight lines. In such cases the variables are *linearly related* to each other (either positively or negatively).

The Slope of a Straight Line

Slopes are important in economics. They show you how much one variable changes as the other changes. The slope is defined as the amount of change in the variable measured on the vertical or y-axis per unit change in the variable measured on the horizontal or x-axis. In the case of Figure 2-6 it tells us how many tons of smoke pollution, symbolized by P, are removed per dollar spent on pollution control, symbolized by E. As the figure shows, if we spend $2000 more we get 1000 tons less pollution. This is 0.5 tons per dollar spent. On the graph the extra $2000 is indicated by ΔE, the arrow indicating that E rises by 2000. The 1000 tons of pollution reduction is indicated by ΔP, the arrow showing that pollution falls by 1000. (The Greek uppercase letter delta, Δ, stands for a change in something.) To get the amount of abatement per dollar of expenditure we merely divide one by the other. In symbols this is $\Delta P/\Delta E$.

If we let X stand for whatever variable is measured on the horizontal axis and Y for whatever variable is measured on the vertical axis, the slope of a straight line is $\Delta Y/\Delta X$. [1][3]

In Figure 2-5 the two variables change in the same direction, so both changes will always be either positive or negative. As a result their ratio, which is the slope of this line, is positive. In Figure 2-6 the two variables change in opposite directions; when one increases the other decreases. So the two Δs will always be of opposite sign. As a result their ratio, which is the slope of the line, is always negative.

Notice also that straight lines have the same slope no matter where on the line you measure that slope. This tells us what inspection of the chart reveals: that the change in one variable in response to a unit change in the other is the same anywhere on the line. We get 0.5 tons of additional pollution abatement for every additional $1 that we spend on abatement no matter how much we are already spending.

Nonlinear Functions

Although it is sometimes convenient to simplify a real relation between two variables by assuming them to be linearly related, this is seldom the case over their whole range. Nonlinear relations are much more common than linear ones. In the case of pollution abatement

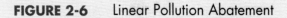

FIGURE 2-6 Linear Pollution Abatement

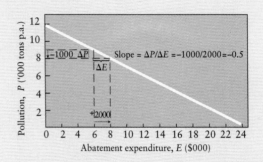

Pollution falls linearly as expenditure on abatement rises. The slope of the line indicates the marginal reduction in pollution for every increase of $1 of abatement expenditure. It is constant at -0.5, indicating that every extra $1 spent on abatement reduces pollution by half a ton.

FIGURE 2-7 Nonlinear Pollution Abatement

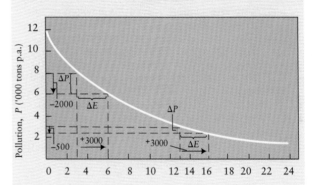

Pollution falls nonlinearly as abatement expenditure rises. When pollution is 8000 tons per year, an additional expenditure of $3000 reduces pollution by 2000 tons. The marginal return for $1 additional expenditure is $\Delta P/\Delta E$ or $-2000/3000$, which is two-thirds of a ton of pollution reduced per $1 spent on abatement. However, when pollution has already been reduced to 3000 tons, an extra $3000 spent on abatement reduces pollution by only 500 tons. The marginal return for $1 of additional expenditure, $\Delta P/\Delta E$, is now only $-500/3000$ or one-sixth of a ton of pollution reduced per $1 spent.

---

[3]Numbers in square brackets indicate mathematical notes that are found in a separate section at the back of the book.

FIGURE 2-8 Navigation Aids

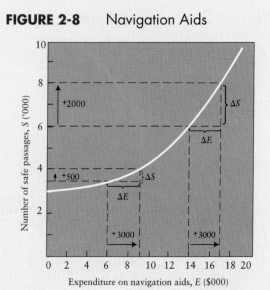

Safe passages increase at an increasing rate as naviga-tion aids are increased. The figure shows the number of safe passages varying positively with the amount spent on navigation aids. Because of network exter-nalities, the number of safe passages increases at an increasing rate as more is spent on navigation aids. An increase in expenditure on navigation aids by $3000 when expenditure is $6000 raises safe passages by 500 from 3500 to 4000. The marginal return to $1 extra spent on navigation aids is then 500/3000 or 0.167. In other words it takes $6 to get one more safe passage (3000/500). When $14 000 is already being spent, a further increase of $3000 increases safe pas-sages by 2000 from 6000 to 8000. The marginal re-turn from $1 spent on aids is now 2000/3000 or 0.667. In other words, it takes only $1.50 extra spending to get one more safe passage (3000/2000).

it is usually quite cheap to eliminate the first units of pollution. Then, as the smoke gets cleaner and cleaner, the cost of further abatement tends to increase be-cause more and more sophisticated and expensive methods need to be used. As a result, the graph re-lating expenditure on abatement and amount of pol-lution usually looks more like Figure 2-7 than Figure 2-6. Inspection of Figure 2-7 shows that as more and more is spent, the benefit in terms of extra abatement for an additional $1 of abatement expenditure gets smaller and smaller. This is shown by the diminishing slope of the curve as we move rightward along it. As the figure shows, an extra $1 of expenditure yields two-thirds of a ton of pollution reduction when pol-lution is 8000 tons ($\Delta Y/\Delta X = -2000/3000$) but only one-sixth of a ton of pollution reduction when pol-lution is 3000 tons ($\Delta Y/\Delta X = -500/3000$).

Economists call the change in abatement when a bit more or a bit less is spent on abatement the *marginal* change. The figure shows that the slope of the curve at each point measures this marginal change. It also shows that, in the type of curve il-lustrated, the marginal return per dollar spent is di-minishing as abatement proceeds. There is always a payoff to more expenditure over the range shown in the figure, but the return diminishes as more is spent. This relation can be described as *diminishing mar-ginal response*. We will meet such relations many times in what follows, so we emphasize now that di-minishing marginal response does not mean that the *total* response is diminishing. In the figure the total amount of pollution continues to fall as more and more is spent on abatement. But diminishing mar-ginal response does mean that the amount of abate-ment obtained for each additional unit of expense is diminishing as more and more pollution is abated.

Figure 2-8 shows a graph where the marginal return is increasing. It relates ex-penditure on navigational aids to the number of safe passages. At low levels of expen-diture the curve is nearly flat. An additional unit of expenditure does not yield much additional protection. But as more and more is spent, it becomes possible to employ more efficient navigation aids that work together as a whole system. Each extra unit of ex-penditure yields more additional protection than each previous unit. In this case we have what economists call increasing marginal response. The reason is that navigation aids encounter what are called *network externalities*. They are most effective not as single stand-alone bits, such as one lighthouse, but as an integrated whole. Each aid becomes more effective the more complex and interrelated is the whole system of which it is a part.

Functions with Maxima and Minima

So far, all the graphs we have shown have had either a positive or negative slope over their entire range. But many relations change direction as the independent variable increases. Figures 2-9 and 2-10 extend our navigation and pollution examples over a larger range of the independent variables. We find that as more and more is spent on navigation aids, not only does the marginal contribution of each additional $1 spent begin to decline, but eventually the *total* safety begins to decline. The reason is that the signals begin to interfere with each other and confuse rather than aid navigators. So, as expenditure on navigation aids increases, eventually the safety reaches a maximum and then begins to decline.

At the maximum point the curve is flat—it has a zero slope. Up to that point each $1 spent does increase safety—it has a positive marginal contribution. But after that point each additional $1 spent reduces safety—it has a negative marginal contribution. At the maximum point the marginal contribution is zero.

Now look at Figure 2-10, which extends the pollution abatement example. Here we see that each $1 spent on pollution control adds to abatement up to the amount E_1, but after that abatement begins to decline. The reason in this case may be that the regulations become so costly that firms find ways of evading them and total enforcement gets less effective. Pollution reaches a minimum when E_1 is spent but rises thereafter. Notice that up to E_1 the curve has a negative slope, indicating that more expenditure is associated with less pollution, but that after E_1 the curve has a positive slope, indicating that more expenditure is associated with more pollution. At the point of minimum pollution the tangent to the curve shown by the line T has a slope of zero.

These two cases illustrate an important point, which we will see over and over in what follows:

At either a minimum or a maximum value of a function, its marginal value is zero.

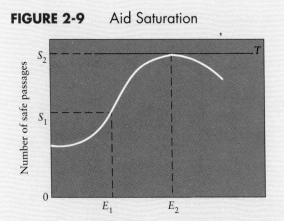

FIGURE 2-9   Aid Saturation

Increases in expenditure on navigation aids eventually serve to reduce the number of safe passages. Up to E_1, expenditure on navigation aids encounters increasing marginal returns. Each additional $1 of expenditure allows a larger increase in safe passages than each previous $1 of expenditure. As expenditure approaches E_2, it encounters decreasing marginal returns. Each additional $1 spent increases the number of safe passages by less than the previous $1 of expenditure. At E_2, safe passages reach a maximum of S_2. Further expenditure encounters negative marginal returns. Each additional $1 spent lowers the number of safe passages. At the maximum point the slope of the tangent T (the straight line that just touches the curve at that point) is zero. At that point the number of safe passages shows no response to small changes in expenditure on navigation aids.

A Final Word

We have done much in this chapter. We have discussed why economists use theory and how they build economic models. We have discussed how they test their theories and how there is a continual back-and-forth process between empirical testing of predictions and refining the theoretical model. Finally, we have devoted considerable time and space to exploring the many ways that data can be displayed in graphs and how economists use graphs to illustrate their theories.

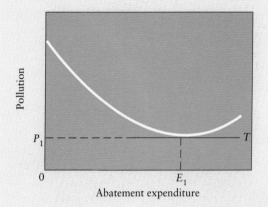

FIGURE 2-10 Abatement Saturation

Beyond a certain point additional abatement expenditure increases pollution. Up to E_1, each additional \$1 of expenditure reduces pollution, but at a diminishing amount for each \$1. At expenditure E_1, pollution reaches a minimum of P_1. If further amounts are spent, pollution actually rises. At the minimum point the slope of the tangent line T is zero. At that point, pollution shows no response to small changes in abatement expenditure.

Many students find themselves intimidated when they are first confronted with all of the details about graphing. But try not to worry. You may not yet be a master of all the graphing techniques that we have discussed in this chapter, but you will be surprised at how quickly it all falls into place. And, as is true for most skills, there is no substitute for practice. In the next three chapters we will encounter many graphs. But we will start simply and then slowly attempt more complicated cases. We are confident that in the process of learning some basic economic theories you will get enough practice in graphing that you will very soon look back at this chapter and realize how straightforward it all is.

SUMMARY

Positive and Normative Advice   ⓁⓄ❶

- A key to the success of scientific inquiry lies in separating positive questions about the way the world works from normative questions about how one would like the world to work.

Economic Theories and Models   ⓁⓄ❷

- Theories are designed to explain and predict what we see. A theory consists of a set of definitions of the variables to be employed, a set of assumptions about how things behave, and the conditions under which the theory is meant to apply.
- A theory provides conditional predictions of the type "if one event occurs, then another event will also occur."

- The term "model" has a number of meanings, including (a) a synonym for theory, (b) a precise realization of a general theory, with a specific numerical relation in place of each general relation posited by the theory, (c) an application of a general theory to a specific case, and (d) a simplified set of relations designed to study one specific force in isolation.

Testing Theories   LO ❸ ❹

- Theories are tested by checking their predictions against evidence. In some sciences, these tests can be conducted under laboratory conditions in which only one thing changes at a time. In economics, testing must be done using the data produced by the world of ordinary events.
- The fact that people sometimes act strangely, even capriciously, does not destroy the possibility of scientific study of group behaviour. The odd and inexplicable things that one person does will tend to cancel out the odd and inexplicable things that another person does. The law of large numbers thus means that group behaviour is often easier to predict than individual behaviour.
- The progress of any science lies in finding better explanations of events than are now available. Thus in any developing science, one must expect to discard some existing theories and replace them with demonstrably superior alternatives.

Economic Data   LO ❺

- Index numbers express economic series in relative form. Values in each period are expressed in relation to the value in the base period, which is given a value of 100.
- Economic data may be graphed in three different ways. Cross-section graphs show observations taken at the same time. Time-series graphs show observations on one variable taken over time. Scatter diagrams show many points, each one of which refers to specific observations on two different variables.

Graphing Economic Theories   LO ❻ ❼

- A functional relation can be expressed in words, in a schedule giving specific values, in a mathematical equation, or in a graph.
- A graph of two variables has a positive slope when they both increase or decrease together and a negative slope when they move in opposite directions.
- The marginal value of a variable gives the amount it changes in response to a change in a second variable. When the variable is measured on the vertical axis of a diagram, its marginal value at a specific point on the curve is measured by the slope of the line tangent to that point.

K E Y   C O N C E P T S

Positive and normative statements
Endogenous and exogenous variables
Theories and models
Variables, assumptions, and predictions

Economic data
Functional relations
Positive and negative relations between variables

Positive and negatively sloped curves
Marginal values
Maximum and minimum values

S T U D Y   E X E R C I S E S

1. Suppose that the relationship between the government's tax revenue (T) and national income (Y) is represented by the following equation: $T = 10 + 0.25Y$. Plot this relationship on a scale diagram, with Y on the horizontal axis and T on the vertical axis. Interpret the equation.

2. Consider the following three specific functional forms for a functional relation between X and Y:
   i) $Y = 50 + 2X$
   ii) $Y = 50 + 2X + 0.05X^2$
   iii) $Y = 50 + 2X - 0.05X^2$

a. For the values of X of 0, 10, 20, 30, 40 and 50, plot X and Y on a scale diagram for each specific functional form. Connect these points with a smooth line.

b. For each functional form, state whether the slope of the line is constant, increasing or decreasing as the value of X increases.

c. Describe for each functional form how the marginal change in Y depends on the value of X.

3. Suppose you want to create a price index for the price of pizza across several Canadian university campuses, as of March 1, 2000. The data are as follows:

University	Price per Pizza
Dalhousie	$6.50
Laval	5.95
McGill	6.00
Queen's	8.00
Waterloo	7.50
Manitoba	5.50
Saskatchewan	5.75
Calgary	6.25
UBC	7.25
Victoria	7.00

a. Using Calgary as the "base university," construct the Canadian university pizza price index.

b. At which university is pizza the most expensive, and by what percentage is the price higher than in Calgary?

c. At which university is pizza the least expensive, and by what percentage is the price lower than in Calgary?

d. Are the data listed above time-series or cross-section data? Explain why.

4. For each of the functional relations listed below, plot the relations on a scale diagram (with X on the horizontal axis and Y on the vertical axis) and compute the slope of the line.

i) $Y = 10 + 3X$
ii) $Y = 20 + 4X$
iii) $Y = 30 + 5X$
iv) $Y = 10 + 5X$

5. Suppose we divide Canada into three regions—the West, the Centre, and the East. Each region has an unemployment rate, defined as the number of people unemployed, expressed as a fraction of that region's labour force. The table that follows shows each region's unemployment rate and the size of its labour force.

Region	Unemployment Rate	Labour Force
West	5.5%	5.3 million
Centre	7.2%	8.4 million
East	12.5%	3.5 million

a. Compute an unemployment rate for Canada using a simple (equal weights) average of the rates in the three regions. Is this the "right" unemployment rate for Canada as a whole? Explain why or why not.

b. Now compute an unemployment rate for Canada using weights which reflect the size of that region's labour force as a proportion of the overall Canadian labour force. Explain the difference in this unemployment rate from the one in part **a**. Is this a "better" measure of Canadian unemployment? Explain why.

6. Draw three graphs in which the dependent variable increases at an increasing rate, at a constant rate, and at a diminishing rate. Then draw three graphs in which it decreases at an increasing, constant, and diminishing rate. For each of these graphs state a real relation that might be described by it—other than the ones given in the text of this chapter.

DISCUSSION QUESTIONS

1. What are some of the positive and normative issues that lie behind the disagreements in the following cases?

a. Economists disagree on whether the Government of Canada should try to stimulate the economy in the next six months.

b. European and North American negotiators disagree over the desirability of reducing European farm subsidies.

c. Economists argue about the merits of a voucher system that allows parents to choose the schools their children will attend.

d. Economists debate the use of a two-tier medical system in Canada (whereby health care continues to be publicly provided, but individuals are permitted to be treated by doctors who bill the patient directly—"extra billing").

2. Much recent public debate has centred on the pros and cons of permitting continued unrestricted sale of cigarettes. Proposals for the control of cigarettes range from increasing excise taxes to the mandatory use of plain packaging to an outright ban on their sale. Discuss the positive and normative assumptions that underlie the national mood to reduce the consumption of tobacco products.

3. Economists sometimes make each of the following assumptions when they construct models. Discuss some situations in which each of these assumptions might be a useful simplification in order to think about some aspect of the real world.

   a. The earth is flat.
   b. There are no differences between men and women.
   c. There is no tomorrow.
   d. There are only two periods—this year and next year.
   e. A country produces only two types of goods.
   f. People are wholly selfish.

4. What may at first appear to be untestable statements can often be reworded so that they can be tested by an appeal to evidence. How might you do this for each of the following assertions?

   a. Free-market economic systems are the best in the world.
   b. Unemployment insurance is eroding the work ethic and encouraging people to become wards of the state rather than productive workers.
   c. Robotics ought to be outlawed because it will destroy the future of working people.
   d. Laws requiring equal pay for work of equal value will make women better off.
   e. Free trade improves the welfare of a country's citizens.

5. There are hundreds of eyewitnesses to the existence of flying saucers and other UFOs. There are films and eyewitness accounts of Nessie, the Loch Ness monster. Are you convinced of their existence? If not, what would it take to persuade you? If so, what would it take to make you change your mind?

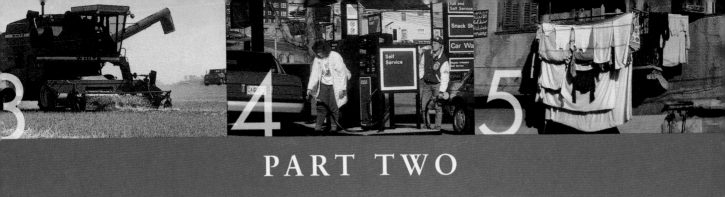

PART TWO

An Introduction to Demand and Supply

In January 1998, a massive ice storm hit Quebec and parts of Ontario and the northeastern United States, causing unprecedented stoppages in electric power. Did the ice storm cause the increase in price of portable electric generators that happened within a few days, or was this just a coincidence? In the summer of 1994, Brazil experienced a frost that severely damaged that country's coffee crop. Did it cause the large increase in the price of coffee that occurred almost immediately, or was that also a coincidence? Is the current housing shortage in Toronto related to the Ontario government's policy of rent controls, and if so, what is the connection? What determines the prices of specific products? What determines whether there will be a lot produced or only a little? These are the types of questions that you will be able to answer after reading the next three chapters.*

Chapter 3 introduces the basic concepts of demand and supply. We will see that the prices of goods in free markets are determined by the interaction of demand and supply. We will learn the meaning of equilibrium, and how equilibrium prices and quantities change in response to changes to either demand or supply. With this apparatus in place, we will look briefly at the 1998 ice storm and at Brazil's damaged coffee crop (the price increases were not coincidences!).

Chapter 4 then introduces the important idea of elasticity—the sensitivity of one variable to a change in some other variable. This concept is central to an understanding of whether a change in the demand or supply of some commodity primarily affects quantity or price. As an application of the concept of elasticity, we will examine the important policy issue of who bears the burden of commodity taxes. Do firms pay such taxes, or do consumers, or do both? How does elasticity affect the answer?

In Chapter 5 you get some practice in using what you learned in Chapters 3 and 4. We start with a discussion of how various markets interact with each other, so that events in one market lead not only to changes in that market but to changes in other markets as well. We then go on to explore two examples of government-controlled prices. The first is rent controls—you will see that the policy of rent controls produces some unusual outcomes in the rental-housing markets of Toronto, New York, and many other cities. The second is agricultural price-support policies—you will see what effects such policies have, both on farmers' incomes and on the allocation of resources.

---

*Chapter 5 does not appear in *Macroeconomics*.

CHAPTER 3

Demand, Supply, and Price

 LEARNING OBJECTIVES

1 Understand what determines "quantity demanded," the amount of some product that households want to purchase.

2 Distinguish between a shift in a demand curve and a movement along a demand curve.

3 Understand what determines "quantity supplied," the amount of some product that firms want to sell.

4 Distinguish between a shift in a supply curve and a movement along a supply curve.

5 Recognize the forces that drive market price to equilibrium.

6 Understand the four "laws" of demand and supply.

How do individual markets work? We are now ready to study this important question. The answer leads us to what are called the laws of supply and demand. And though there is much more to economics than just demand and supply (as many following chapters will illustrate), this is an essential starting point for understanding how a market, and thus a market economy, functions.

As a first step, we need to understand what determines the demand for and the supply of particular products. Then we can see how demand and supply together determine the prices of products and the quantities that are bought and sold. Finally, we examine how the price system allows the economy to respond to the many changes that impinge on it. Demand and supply help us to understand the price system's successes and failures, and the consequences of many government policies.

This chapter deals with the basic elements of demand, supply and price. In the next two chapters we use the demand-and-supply apparatus to discuss such issues as cigarette taxes, legislated minimum wages, price controls on rental housing, the burden of payroll taxes, and agricultural income-support policies.

Demand

What determines the demand for any given product? How did Canadian consumers react to the large increases in fuel prices in the 1970s? How did they respond to the more recent declines in the prices of personal computers and cellular telephones? We start by developing a theory designed to explain the demand for some typical product.

What Is "Quantity Demanded"?

The total amount of any particular good or service that consumers wish to purchase in some time period is called the **quantity demanded** of that product. It is important to notice two things about this concept.

First, quantity demanded is a *desired* quantity. It is the amount that consumers wish to purchase when faced with a particular price of the product, other prices, their incomes, their tastes, and everything else that might matter. It may be different from the amount that consumers actually succeed in purchasing. If sufficient quantities are not available, the amount that consumers wish to purchase may exceed the amount that they actually purchase. To distinguish these two concepts, the term *quantity demanded* is used to refer to desired purchases, and a phrase such as *quantity actually bought* or *quantity exchanged* is used to refer to actual purchases.

Second, quantity demanded refers to a *flow* of purchases. It must therefore be expressed as so much per period of time: 1 million units per day, 7 million per week, or 365 million per year. For example, being told that the quantity of new television sets demanded (at current prices) in Canada is 50 000 means nothing unless you are also told the period of time involved. Fifty thousand TVs demanded per day would be an enormous rate of demand; 50 000 per year would be a very small rate. The important distinction between *stocks* and *flows* is discussed in *Extensions in Theory 3-1.*

The amount of some product that consumers wish to buy in a given time period is influenced by the following important variables: [2]

- Product's own price
- Average household income
- Prices of other products
- Tastes
- Distribution of income
- Population
- Expectations about the future

It is difficult to determine the separate influence of each of these variables if we consider what happens when everything changes at once. Instead, we consider the influence of the variables one at a time. To do this, we hold all but one of them constant. Then we let the selected variable vary and study how it affects quantity demanded. We can do the same for each of the other variables in turn, and in this way we can come to understand the importance of each. We can then combine the separate influences of the variables to discover what happens when several things change at the same time—as they often do.

Holding all other influencing variables constant is often described by the expressions "other things being equal," "other things given," or the equivalent Latin phrase, *ceteris paribus.* When economists speak of the influence of the price of eggs on the quantity of eggs demanded, *ceteris paribus,* they refer to what a change in the price of eggs would do to the quantity of eggs demanded *if all other variables that influence the demand for eggs did not change.*

quantity demanded
The amount of a commodity that consumers wish to purchase in some time period.

Quantity Demanded and Price

We are interested in developing a theory of how prices are determined. To do this, we need to study the relationship between the quantity demanded of each product and that product's price. This requires that we hold all other influences constant and ask, "How will the quantity demanded of a product change as its price changes?"

EXTENSIONS IN THEORY 3-1

The Distinction Between Stocks and Flows

One important conceptual issue that arises frequently in economics is the distinction between stock and flow variables. Economic theories use both, and it takes a little practice to keep them straight.

As noted in the text, a flow variable has a time dimension—it is so much *per unit of time*. For example, the quantity of Grade A large eggs purchased in Edmonton is a flow variable. No useful information is conveyed if we are told that the number purchased was 2000 dozen eggs unless we are also told the period of time over which these purchases occurred. Two thousand dozen eggs per hour would indicate a much more active market in eggs than would 2000 dozen eggs per month.

In contrast, a stock variable is a variable whose value has meaning *at a point in time*. Thus the number of eggs in the egg producer's warehouse on a particular day— for example, 20 000 dozen eggs on September 3, 1999— is a stock variable. All those eggs are there at one time, and they remain there until something happens to change the stock held in the warehouse. The stock variable is just a number at a point in time, not a rate of flow of so much per unit of time.

The terminology of stocks and flows can be understood in terms of an analogy to a bathtub. At any moment, the tub holds so much water. This is the *stock*, and it can be measured in terms of the volume of water, say, 100 litres. There might also be water flowing into the tub from the tap; this *flow* is measured as so much water per unit time, say, 500 litres per hour.

The distinction between stocks and flows is important. Failure to keep them straight is a common source of confusion and even error. Note, for example, that because they have different dimensions, a stock variable and a flow variable cannot be added together without specifying some time period for which the flow persists.

We cannot add the stock of 100 litres of water in the tub to the flow of 500 litres per hour to get 600 litres. The new stock of water will depend on how long the flow persists; if it lasts for half an hour, the new stock will be 350 litres; if the flow persists for two hours, the new stock will be 1100 litres (or the tub will overflow!).

The amount of income earned is a flow; there is so much per year or per month or per hour. The amount of a consumer's expenditure is also a flow—so much spent per week or per month or per year. The amount of money in a bank account or a miser's hoard (earned, perhaps, in the past but unspent) is a stock—just so many thousands of dollars. The key test is always whether a time dimension is required to give the variable meaning. Other variables are neither stocks nor flows, but just numbers; for example, the price of one dozen eggs.

The amount of water behind the dam at any time is the stock of water; the amount moving through the gate is the flow, which is measured per unit of time.

A basic economic hypothesis is that the price of a product and the quantity demanded are related negatively, other things being equal. That is, the lower the price, the higher the quantity demanded; and the higher the price, the lower the quantity demanded.

The British economist Alfred Marshall (1842–1924) called this fundamental relation the "law of demand." In Chapter 6, we will derive the law of demand as a prediction that follows from more basic assumptions about consumer behaviour. For now, let's simply ask "why might this be so?" Products are used to satisfy desires and needs, and there is almost always more than one product that will satisfy any desire or need. Hunger may be alleviated by meat or vegetables; a desire for green vegetables can be satisfied by broccoli or spinach. The desire for a vacation may be satisfied by a trip to the ocean or to the mountains; the need to get there may be satisfied by different airlines, a bus, a car, or a train. For any general desire or need, there are many different products that will satisfy it.

Now consider what happens if income, tastes, population, and the prices of all other products remain constant and the price of only one product changes. As the price goes up, that product becomes an increasingly expensive way to satisfy a desire. Some consumers will stop buying it altogether; others will buy smaller amounts; still others may continue to buy the same quantity. Because many consumers will switch wholly or partly to other products to satisfy the same desire, less will be demanded of the product whose price has risen. As meat becomes more expensive, for example, consumers may to some extent switch to meat substitutes; they may also forgo meat at some meals and eat less meat at others.

Conversely, as the price goes down, the product becomes a cheaper method of satisfying a desire. Households will demand more of it. Consequently, they will buy less of similar products whose prices have not fallen and as a result have become expensive *relative* to the product in question. When the price of tomatoes falls, shoppers switch to tomatoes and cut their purchases of many other vegetables that now look relatively more expensive.

Demand Schedules and Demand Curves

A **demand schedule** is one way of showing the relationship between quantity demanded and the price of a product, other things being equal. It is a numerical tabulation showing the quantity that is demanded at certain prices.

The table in Figure 3-1 shows a hypothetical demand schedule for carrots. It lists the quantity of carrots that would be demanded at various prices, given the assumption that all other variables are held constant. We should note in particular that average

demand schedule
A table showing the relationship between the quantity of a commodity that buyers wish to purchase (per period of time) and the price of that commodity, other things being equal.

FIGURE 3-1   The Demand for Carrots

	Price Per Ton ($)	Quantity Demanded When Average Household Income Is $50 000 Per Year (thousands of tons per year)
U	20	110.0
V	40	90.0
W	60	77.5
X	80	67.5
Y	100	62.5
Z	120	60.0

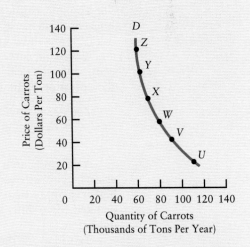

Both the table and the graph show the quantity of carrots that would be demanded at various prices, *ceteris paribus.* For example, row *W* indicates that if the price of carrots were $60 per ton, consumers would desire to purchase 77 500 tons of carrots per year, given the values of the other variables that affect quantity demanded. The demand curve, labelled *D*, relates quantity of carrots demanded to the price of carrots; its negative slope indicates that quantity demanded increases as price falls.

household income is fixed at $50 000 because later we will want to see what happens when income changes. The table gives the quantities demanded for six selected prices, but in fact a separate quantity would be demanded at each possible price from 1 cent to several hundreds of dollars.

A second method of showing the relationship between quantity demanded and price is to draw a graph. The six price-quantity combinations shown in the table are plotted in Figure 3-1. Price is plotted on the vertical axis, and quantity is plotted on the horizontal axis.

demand curve The graphical representation of the relationship between the quantity of a commodity that buyers wish to purchase (per period of time) and the price of that commodity, other things being equal.

The smooth curve drawn through these points is called a **demand curve.** It shows the quantity that purchasers would like to buy at each price. The negative slope of the curve indicates that the quantity demanded increases as the price falls. Each point on the demand curve indicates a single price-quantity combination. The demand curve as a whole shows something more.

The demand curve represents the relationship between quantity demanded and price, other things being equal.

When economists speak of demand in a particular market, they are referring not just to the particular quantity being demanded at the moment (i.e., not just to one point on the demand curve) but to the entire demand curve—to the relationship between desired purchases and all the possible prices of the product.

demand The entire relationship between the quantity of a commodity that buyers wish to purchase (per period of time) and the price of that commodity, other things being equal.

Thus, the term **demand** refers to the entire relationship between the quantity demanded of a product and the price of that product (as shown, for example, by the demand curve in Figure 3-1). In contrast, a single point on a demand schedule or curve is the quantity demanded at that point. This distinction between "demand" and "quantity demanded" is an extremely important one and we will examine it more closely later in this chapter.

Shifts in the Demand Curve

The demand schedule is drawn with the assumption that everything except the product's own price is being held constant. But what if other things change, as surely they do? For example, consider an increase in household income while price remains constant. If households increase their purchases of the product, the new quantity demanded cannot be represented by a point on the original demand curve. It must be represented on a new demand curve that is to the right of the old curve. Thus, the rise in consumer income shifts the demand curve to the right, as shown in Figure 3-2. This shift illustrates the operation of an important general rule.

A demand curve is drawn with the assumption that everything except the product's own price is held constant. A change in any of the variables previously held constant will shift the demand curve to a new position.

A demand curve can shift in two important ways. In the first case, more is bought at each price—the demand curve shifts rightward so that each price corresponds to a higher quantity than it did before. In the second case, less is bought at each price—the demand curve shifts leftward so that each price corresponds to a lower quantity than it did before.

We can assess the influence of changes in variables other than price by determining how changes in each variable shift the demand curve. Any change will shift the demand curve to the right if it increases the amount that households wish to buy, other things remaining equal. It will shift the demand curve to the left if it decreases the amount that households wish to buy, other things remaining equal.

FIGURE 3-2   An Increase in the Demand for Carrots

Price Per Ton ($)	Quantity Demanded When Average Household Income Is $50 000 Per Year (thousands of tons per year)		Quantity Demanded When Average Household Income Is $60 000 Per Year (thousands of tons per year)	
p	D_0		D_1	
20	110.0	U	140.0	U'
40	90.0	V	116.0	V'
60	77.5	W	100.8	W'
80	67.5	X	87.5	X'
100	62.5	Y	81.3	Y'
120	60.0	Z	78.0	Z'

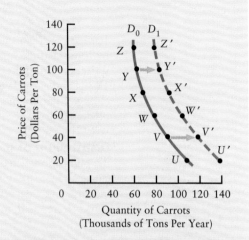

An increase in average household income increases the quantity demanded at each price. This is shown by the rightward shift in the demand curve, from D_0 to D_1. When average income rises from $50 000 to $60 000 per year, quantity demanded at a price of $60 per ton rises from 77 500 tons per year to 100 800 tons per year. A similar rise occurs at every other price.

Average Household Income.   If consumers receive more income on average, they can be expected to purchase more of most products even though product prices remain the same.[1] We therefore expect that a rise in average consumer income shifts the demand curve for most products to the right, indicating that more will be demanded at any given price. Such a shift is illustrated in Figure 3-2.

Prices of Other Goods.   We saw that the negative slope of a product's demand curve occurs because the lower its price, the cheaper the product becomes relative to other products that can satisfy the same needs or desires. These other products are called **substitutes.** Another way for the same change to come about is that the price of the substitute product rises. For example, carrots can become cheap relative to broccoli either because the price of carrots falls or because the price of broccoli rises. Either change will increase the amount of carrots that consumers wish to buy as consumers substitute away from broccoli and toward carrots. Thus a rise in the price of a substitute for a product shifts the demand curve for the product to the right. More will be demanded at each price.

substitutes   Goods that can be used in place of another good to satisfy similar needs or desires.

Complements are products that tend to be used jointly. Cars and gasoline are complements; so are CD players and speakers, golf clubs and golf balls, electric stoves and electricity, and airplane flights to Calgary and ski-lift tickets in Banff. Because complements tend to be consumed together, a fall in the price of one will increase the quantity demanded of *both* products. Thus, a fall in the price of a complement for a product will shift that product's demand curve to the right. More will be demanded at each price.

complements   Goods that tend to be used jointly.

---

[1]Such products are called *normal goods*. Products for which the quantity demanded falls as income rises are called *inferior goods*. These concepts are defined and discussed in Chapter 4.

For example, a fall in the price of airplane trips to Calgary will lead to a rise in the demand for ski-lift tickets in Banff, even though the price of those lift tickets is unchanged. (So the demand curve for ski-lift tickets will shift to the right.)

Tastes.   Tastes have an effect on people's desired purchases. A change in tastes may be long-lasting, such as the shift from fountain pens to ballpoint pens or from typewriters to computers; or it may be a short-lived fad such as CB radios (a fad in the late 1970s and early 1980s) and many toys such as Pogs and Beanie Babies. In either case, a change in tastes in favour of a product shifts the demand curve to the right. More will be demanded at each price.

Distribution of Income.   If a constant total of income is distributed differently among the population, demands may change. A change in the distribution of income, therefore, will cause an increase in the demand for products bought most by households whose incomes increase and a decrease in the demand for products bought most by households whose incomes decrease. If, for example, the government increases the deductions that may be taken for children on income-tax returns and compensates by raising basic tax rates, income will be transferred from households without children to households with children. Demands for products more heavily bought by childless persons will decline, while demands for products more heavily bought by households with children will increase.

Population.   Population growth does not create new demand unless the additional people have the means to purchase goods—that is, unless they have purchasing power. If there is an increase in population with purchasing power—for example, the immigration of wealthy foreigners—the demands for all the products purchased by the new people will rise. Thus, we expect that an increase in population will shift the demand curves for most products to the right, indicating that more will be demanded at each price.

Expectations about the Future.   Our discussion has so far focused on how changes in the current value of variables may change demand. But it is also true that changes in people's *expectations about future values* of variables may change demand. For example, suppose that you are thinking about buying a house in a small town in Nova Scotia and you have learned that in the near future a large high-tech firm will be moving its head office and several hundred employees to this same small town. Since their future movement into your town will surely increase the demand for housing and thus will drive up the *future* price of houses, this expectation will lead you (and others like you) to increase your demand *today* so as to make the purchase before the price rises. Thus, the demand curve for houses will shift to the right today in anticipation of a future event.

Figure 3-3 summarizes the reasons that demand curves shift.

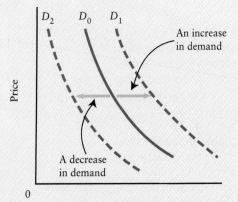

FIGURE 3-3   Shifts in the Demand Curve

A rightward shift in the demand curve from D_0 to D_1 indicates an increase in demand; a leftward shift from D_0 to D_2 indicates a decrease in demand. An increase in demand means that more is demanded at each price. Such a rightward shift can be caused by a rise in income, a rise in the price of a substitute, a fall in the price of a complement, a change in tastes that favours that product, an increase in population, a redistribution of income toward groups that favour the product, or the anticipation of a future event that will increase the price.

A decrease in demand means that less is demanded at each price. Such a leftward shift can be caused by a fall in income, a fall in the price of a substitute, a rise in the price of a complement, a change in tastes that disfavours the product, a decrease in population, a redistribution of income away from groups that favour the product, or the anticipation of a future event that will decrease the price.

Movements Along the Curve Versus Shifts of the Whole Curve

Suppose that you read in today's newspaper that a sharp increase in the price of carrots has been caused by an increased demand for carrots. Then tomorrow you read that the rising price of carrots is reducing the typical consumer's purchases of carrots, as shoppers switch to potatoes, yams, and peas. The two stories appear to contradict each other. The first associates a rising price with rising demand; the second associates a rising price with declining demand. Can both statements be true? The answer is yes—because they refer to different things. The first describes a shift in the demand curve; the second describes a movement along a demand curve in response to a change in price.

Consider first the statement that the increase in the price of carrots has been caused by an increased demand for carrots. This statement refers to a shift in the demand curve for carrots—in this case, a shift to the right, indicating more carrots demanded at each price. This shift, as we will see later in this chapter, will increase the price of carrots.

Now consider the second statement—that fewer carrots are being bought because carrots have become more expensive. This refers to a movement along the new demand curve and reflects a change between two specific quantities demanded, one before the price increased and one afterward.

Possible explanations for the two stories are:

1. A change in tastes is shifting the demand curve for carrots to the right as more carrots are demanded at each price. This, in turn, raises the price of carrots (for reasons we will soon study in detail). This was the first newspaper story.

2. The rising price of carrots is causing each individual household to cut back on its purchase of carrots. The cutback is represented by an upward movement to the left along any particular demand curve for carrots. This was the second newspaper story.

To prevent the type of confusion caused by our two newspaper stories, economists use a specialized vocabulary to distinguish between shifts of curves and movements along curves.

We have seen that demand refers to the *entire* demand curve, whereas quantity demanded refers to the quantity that is demanded at a specific price, as indicated by a particular *point* on the demand curve. In Figure 3-1, for example, demand is given by the curve *D*; at a price of $40 per ton, the quantity demanded is 90 000 tons, as indicated by the point *V*.

Economists reserve the term **change in demand** to describe a change in the quantity demanded at *every* price. That is, a change in demand refers to a shift of the entire demand curve. The term **change in quantity demanded** refers to a movement from one point on a demand curve to another point, either on the same demand curve or on a new one.

A change in quantity demanded can result from a shift in the demand curve with the price constant; from a movement along a given demand curve due to a change in the price; or from a combination of the two. [3]

We consider these three possibilities in turn.

An increase in demand means that the whole demand curve shifts to the right; a decrease in demand means that the whole demand curve shifts to the left. At a given price, an increase in demand causes an increase in quantity demanded, whereas a decrease in demand causes a decrease in quantity demanded. For example, in Figure 3-2, the shift in the demand curve from D_0 to D_1 represents an increase in demand, and at a price of $40 per ton, quantity demanded increases from 90 000 tons to 116 000 tons, as indicated by the move from *V* to *V'*.

change in demand
A change in the quantity demanded at each possible price of the commodity, represented by a shift in the whole demand curve.

change in quantity demanded   A change in the specific quantity of the good demanded, represented by a change from one point on a demand curve to another point, either on the original demand curve or on a new one.

FIGURE 3-4   Shifts of and Movements Along the Demand Curve

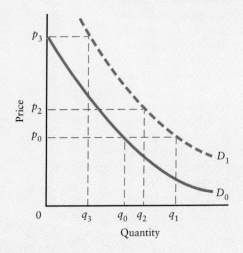

An increase in demand means that the demand curve shifts to the right, and hence quantity demanded will be higher at each price. A rise in price causes an upward movement to the left along the demand curve, and hence quantity demanded will fall. The demand curve is originally D_0 and price is p_0, which means that quantity demanded is q_0. Suppose that demand increases to D_1, which means that at any particular price, there is a larger quantity demanded; for example, at p_0, quantity demanded is now q_1. Now suppose that the price rises above p_0. This causes a movement up and to the left along D_1, and quantity demanded falls below q_1.

The net effect of these two changes can be either an increase or a decrease in the quantity demanded. In this figure, a rise in price to p_2 means that the quantity demanded q_2 is still in excess of the original quantity demanded q_0; a rise in price to p_3 means that the final quantity demanded q_3 is below the original quantity demanded q_0.

A movement down and to the right along a demand curve represents an increase in quantity demanded; a movement up and to the left along a demand curve represents a decrease in quantity demanded. For example, in Figure 3-2, with demand given by the curve D_1, an increase in price from $40 to $60 per ton causes a movement along D_1 from V' to W', and quantity demanded decreases from 116 000 tons to 100 800 tons.

When there is a change in demand *and* a change in the price, the overall change in quantity demanded is the net effect of the shift in the demand curve and the movement along the new demand curve. Figure 3-4 shows the combined effect of an increase in demand, shown by a rightward shift in the whole demand curve, and an upward movement to the left along the new demand curve due to an increase in price. The increase in demand causes an increase in quantity demanded at the initial price, whereas the movement along the demand curve causes a decrease in the quantity demanded. Whether quantity demanded rises or falls overall depends on the relative magnitudes of these two changes.

Supply

What determines the supply of any given product? Why do Canadian oil producers extract and market more oil when the price of oil is high? Why do Canadian cattle ranchers sell more beef when the price of cattle-feed (mostly grain) falls? We start by developing a theory designed to explain the supply of some typical product.

What Is "Quantity Supplied"?

quantity supplied
The amount of a commodity that producers wish to sell in some time period.

The amount of a product that firms wish to sell in some time period is called the **quantity supplied** of that product. Quantity supplied is a flow; it is so much per unit of time. Note also that quantity supplied is the amount that firms are willing to offer for sale; it is not necessarily the amount that they succeed in selling, which is expressed by *quantity actually sold* or *quantity exchanged*.

The quantity supplied of a product is influenced by the following variables: [4]

- Product's own price
- Prices of inputs
- Technology
- Number of suppliers

The situation with supply is the same as that with demand: There are several influencing variables, and we will not get far if we try to discover what happens when they all change at the same time. Again, we use the convenient *ceteris paribus* assumption to study the influence of the variables one at a time.

Quantity Supplied and Price

We begin by holding all other influences constant and ask, "How do we expect the quantity of a product supplied to vary with its own price?"

A basic hypothesis of economics is that the price of the product and the quantity supplied are related *positively,* other things being equal. That is, the higher the product's own price, the more its producers will supply; and the lower the price, the less its producers will supply.

In later chapters we will derive this hypothesis as a prediction from more basic assumptions about the behaviour of firms. But now we simply ask "why might this be so?" Firms will supply more because the profits that can be earned from producing a product will increase if the price of that product rises, whereas the costs of inputs used to produce it will remain unchanged. As a result, firms, which are in business to earn profits, will wish to produce more of the product whose price has risen.

Supply Schedules and Supply Curves

A rise in the price of wheat, other things being equal, will lead farmers to plant less of other crops and plant more wheat.

The general relationship just discussed can be illustrated by a **supply schedule,** which shows the relationship between quantity supplied of a product and the price of the product, other things being equal. A supply schedule is analogous to a demand schedule; the former shows what producers would be willing to sell, whereas the latter shows what households would be willing to buy, at alternative prices of the product. The table in Figure 3-5 presents a hypothetical supply schedule for carrots.

A **supply curve,** the graphical representation of the supply schedule, is illustrated in Figure 3-5. Each point on the supply curve represents a specific price-quantity combination; however, the whole curve shows something more.

The supply curve represents the relationship between quantity supplied and price, other things being equal; its positive slope indicates that quantity supplied increases when price increases.

When economists make statements about the conditions of supply, they are not referring just to the particular quantity being supplied at the moment—that is, not to just one point on the supply curve. Instead, they are referring to the entire supply curve, to the complete relationship between desired sales and all possible prices of the product.

Supply refers to the entire relationship between the quantity supplied of a product and the price of that product, other things being equal. A single point on the supply curve refers to the *quantity supplied* at that price.

supply schedule
A table showing the relationship between the quantity of some commodity that producers wish to sell (per period of time) and the price of that commodity, other things being equal.

supply curve   The graphical representation of the relationship between the quantity of some commodity that producers wish to sell (per period of time) and the price of that commodity, other things being equal.

supply   The entire relationship between the quantity of some commodity that producers wish to sell (per period of time) and the price of that commodity, other things being equal.

FIGURE 3-5   The Supply of Carrots

	Price Per Ton ($)	Quantity Supplied (thousands of tons per year)
u	20	5.0
v	40	46.0
w	60	77.5
x	80	100.0
y	100	115.0
z	120	122.5

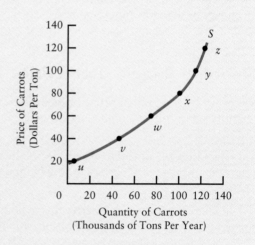

Both the table and the graph show the quantities that producers wish to sell at various prices, *ceteris paribus.* For example, row *w* indicates that if the price of carrots were $60 per ton, producers would want to sell 77 500 tons per year. The supply curve, labelled *S*, relates quantity of carrots supplied to the price of carrots; its positive slope indicates that quantity supplied increases as price increases.

Shifts in the Supply Curve

A shift in the supply curve means that at each price a quantity different from the previous one will be supplied. An increase in the quantity supplied at each price is shown in Figure 3-6. This change appears as a rightward shift in the supply curve. In contrast, a decrease in the quantity supplied at each price appears as a leftward shift. For supply, as for demand, there is an important general rule:

A change in any of the variables (other than the product's own price) that affects the quantity supplied will shift the supply curve to a new position.

Let's consider the effect of changes in several variables.

Price of Inputs.   All things that a firm uses to produce its outputs, such as materials, labour, and machines, are called the firm's *inputs.* Other things being equal, the higher the price of any input used to make a product, the less will be the profit from making that product. We expect, therefore, that the higher the price of any input used by a firm, the less the firm will produce and offer for sale at any given price of the product. A rise in the price of inputs therefore shifts the supply curve to the left, indicating that less will be supplied at any given price; a fall in the cost of inputs shifts the supply curve to the right.

Technology.   At any time, what is produced and how it is produced depend on what is known. Over time, knowledge changes; so do the quantities of individual products supplied. The enormous increase in production per worker that has been going on in industrial societies for about 200 years is due largely to improved methods of production. The Industrial Revolution is more than a historical event; it is a present reality. Discoveries in chemistry have led to lower costs of production for well-established products, such as

FIGURE 3-6   An Increase in the Supply of Carrots

Price Per Ton ($) p	Quantity Supplied Before Cost-Saving Innovation (thousands of tons per year) S_0		Quantity Supplied After Innovation (thousands of tons per year) S_1	
20	5.0	u	28.0	u'
40	46.0	v	76.0	v'
60	77.5	w	102.0	w'
80	100.0	x	120.0	x'
100	115.0	y	132.0	y'
120	122.5	z	140.0	z'

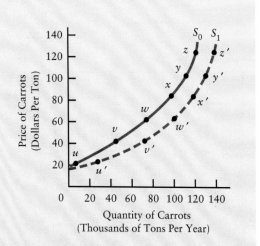

A cost-saving innovation increases the quantity supplied at each price. This is shown by the rightward shift in the supply curve, from S_0 to S_1. As a result of a cost-saving innovation, the quantity that is supplied at a price of $100 per ton rises from 115 000 to 132 000 tons per year. A similar rise occurs at every price.

paints, and to a large variety of new products made of plastics and synthetic fibers. Such inventions as silicon chips have radically changed products such as computers, televisions, and telephones, and the consequent development of smaller computers has revolutionized the production of countless other nonelectronic products.

Any technological innovation that decreases production costs will increase the profits that can be earned at any given price of the product. Because increased profitability leads to increased willingness to produce, this change shifts the supply curve to the right.

Number of Suppliers.   For given prices and technology, the total amount of any product supplied depends on the number of firms producing that product and offering it for sale. For example, in Chapter 9 we will examine the situation where profits made by existing firms producing a particular good attract other firms to enter the industry in pursuit of those profits. The effect of this increase in the number of suppliers is to shift the supply curve to the right. Similarly, if the existing firms are losing money, they will eventually leave the industry; such a reduction in the number of suppliers shifts the supply curve to the left.

Movements Along the Curve Versus Shifts of the Whole Curve

As with demand, it is important to distinguish movements along supply curves from shifts of the whole curve. Economists reserve the term **change in supply** to describe a shift of the whole supply curve—that is, a change in the quantity that will be supplied at every price. The term **change in quantity supplied** refers to a movement from one point on a supply curve to another point, either on the same supply curve or a new one. In other words, an increase in supply means that the whole supply curve has shifted to the right, so that the quantity supplied at any given price has increased; a movement up and to the right along a supply curve indicates an increase in the quantity supplied in response to an increase in the price of the product.

Practise with Study Guide Chapter 3, Exercise 6.

change in supply
A change in the quantity supplied at each possible price of the commodity, represented by a shift in the whole supply curve.

change in quantity supplied   A change in the specific quantity supplied, represented by a change from one point on a supply curve to another point, either on the original supply curve or on a new one.

A change in quantity supplied can result from a change in supply, with the price constant; from a movement along a given supply curve due to a change in the price; or from a combination of the two.

The Determination of Price

So far we have considered demand and supply separately. We now come to a key question: how do the two forces of demand and supply interact to determine price?

The Concept of a Market

Originally the term "market" designated a physical place where products were bought and sold. We still use the term this way to describe places such as Granville Island Market in Vancouver, Kensington Market in Toronto, or Jean Talon Market in Montreal. Once developed, however, theories of market behaviour were easily extended to cover products such as wheat or oil, which can be purchased anywhere in the world at a price that tends to be uniform the world over. The concepts of "the wheat market" or "the oil market" extend our viewpoint well beyond the idea of a single place to which the consumer goes to buy something.

market Any situation in which buyers and sellers can negotiate the exchange of goods or services.

For present purposes a **market** may be defined as existing in any situation (a physical place or an electronic medium) in which buyers and sellers negotiate the exchange of some product or related group of products. It must be possible, therefore, for buyers and sellers to communicate with each other and to make meaningful deals over the whole market.

Individual markets differ in the degree of *competition* among the various buyers and sellers. In the next few chapters we will confine ourselves to examining markets in which the number of buyers and sellers is sufficiently large that no one of them has any appreciable influence on the market price. This is a very rough definition of what economists call *perfectly competitive markets*. Starting in Chapter 10, we will consider the behaviour of markets in which there are small numbers of either sellers or buyers. But our initial theory of markets will actually be a very good description of the markets for such things as wheat, pork, newsprint, coffee, copper, and many other commodities.

Graphical Analysis of a Market

The table in Figure 3-7 brings together the demand and supply schedules from Figure 3-1 and 3-5. The quantities of carrots demanded and supplied at each price may now be compared.

excess demand A situation in which, at the given price, quantity demanded exceeds quantity supplied.

excess supply A situation in which, at the given price, quantity supplied exceeds quantity demanded.

There is only one price, $60 per ton, at which the quantity of carrots demanded equals the quantity supplied. At prices less than $60 per ton, there is a shortage of carrots because the quantity demanded exceeds the quantity supplied. This is a situation of **excess demand**. At prices greater than $60 per ton, there is a surplus of carrots because the quantity supplied exceeds the quantity demanded. This is a situation of **excess supply**. This same story can also be told in graphical terms. The quantities demanded and supplied at any price can be read off the two curves; the excess supply or excess demand is shown by the horizontal distance between the curves at each price.

FIGURE 3-7   Determination of the Equilibrium Price of Carrots

Price Per Ton ($) p	Quantity Demanded (thousands of tons per year) D	Quantity Supplied (thousands of tons per year) S	Excess Demand (+) or Excess Supply (−) (thousands of tons per year) D − S
20	110.0	5.0	+105.0
40	90.0	46.0	+44.0
60	77.5	77.5	0.0
80	67.5	100.0	−32.5
100	62.5	115.0	−52.5
120	60.0	122.5	−62.5

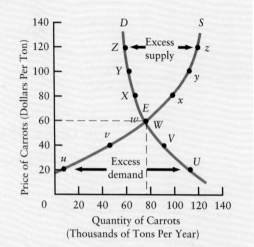

The equilibrium price corresponds to the intersection of the demand and supply curves. Equilibrium is indicated by E, which is point W on the demand curve and point w on the supply curve. At a price of $60, quantity demanded equals quantity supplied. At prices above equilibrium, there is excess supply and downward pressure on price. At prices below equilibrium, there is excess demand and upward pressure on price.

To examine the determination of market price, let's suppose first that the price is $100 per ton. At this price, 115 000 tons are offered for sale, but only 62 500 tons are demanded. There is an excess supply of 52 500 tons per year. Sellers are then likely to cut their prices to get rid of this surplus. And purchasers, observing the stock of unsold carrots, will begin to offer less money for the product. In other words, *excess supply causes downward pressure on price*.

Now consider the price of $20 per ton. At this price, there is excess demand. The 5000 tons produced each year are snapped up quickly, and 105 000 tons of desired purchases cannot be made. Rivalry between would-be purchasers may lead them to offer more than the prevailing price to outbid other purchasers. Also, sellers may begin to ask a higher price for the quantities that they do have to sell. In other words, *excess demand causes upward pressure on price*.

Finally, consider the price of $60. At this price, producers wish to sell 77 500 tons per year, and purchasers wish to buy that same quantity. There is neither a shortage nor a surplus of carrots. There are no unsatisfied buyers to bid the price up, nor are there unsatisfied sellers to force the price down. Once the price of $60 has been reached, therefore, there will be no tendency for it to change.

Equilibrium implies a state of rest, or balance, between opposing forces. The **equilibrium price** is the one toward which the actual market price will tend. It will persist, once established, unless it is disturbed by some change in market conditions which shifts the demand curve, the supply curve, or both.

The price at which the quantity demanded equals the quantity supplied is called the equilibrium price, or the market-clearing price. [5]

equilibrium price
The price at which quantity demanded equals quantity supplied. Also called the market-clearing price.

disequilibrium price
A price at which quantity demanded does not equal quantity supplied.

disequilibrium
A situation in a market in which there is excess demand or excess supply.

Any price at which the market does not "clear"—that is, quantity demanded does not equal quantity supplied—is called a **disequilibrium price.** Whenever there is either excess demand or excess supply in a market, that market is said to be in a state of **disequilibrium,** and the market price will be changing.

Figure 3-7 makes it clear that the equilibrium price occurs where the demand and supply curves intersect. Below that price, there is excess demand and hence upward pressure on the existing price. Above that price, there is excess supply and hence downward pressure on the existing price.

The Laws of Demand and Supply

Changes in any of the variables, other than price, that influence quantity demanded or supplied will cause a shift in the supply curve, the demand curve, or both. There are four possible shifts: an increase in demand (a rightward shift in the demand curve), a decrease in demand (a leftward shift in the demand curve), an increase in supply (a rightward shift in the supply curve), and a decrease in supply (a leftward shift in the supply curve).

comparative statics
The derivation of predictions by analysing the effect of a change in some exogenous variable on the equilibrium.

To discover the effects of each of the possible curve shifts, we use the method known as **comparative statics.**[2] With this method, we derive predictions by analysing the effect on the equilibrium of some change in which we are interested. We start from a position of equilibrium and then introduce the change to be studied. We then determine the new equilibrium position and compare it with the original one. The difference between the two positions of equilibrium must result from the change that was introduced because everything else has been held constant.

Each of the four possible curve shifts causes changes that are described by one of the four "laws" of demand and supply. Each of the laws summarizes what happens when an initial position of equilibrium is disturbed by a shift in either the demand curve or the supply curve. By using the term "law" to describe what happens, economists do not mean that they are absolutely certain of the outcome. The term "law" in science is used to describe a theory that has stood up to substantial testing. The laws of demand and supply are thus hypotheses that predict certain kinds of behaviour in certain situations, and the predicted behaviour occurs sufficiently often that economists continue to have confidence in the underlying theory.

The four laws of demand and supply are derived in Figure 3-8. Study the figure carefully. Previously, we had given the axes specific labels, but because it is now intended to apply to any product, the horizontal axis is simply labelled "Quantity." This means quantity per period in whatever units output is measured. "Price," the vertical axis, means the price measured as dollars per unit of quantity for the same product.

The four laws of demand and supply are as follows:

1. An increase in demand causes an increase in both the equilibrium price and the equilibrium quantity exchanged.

2. A decrease in demand causes a decrease in both the equilibrium price and the equilibrium quantity exchanged.

---

[2]The term *static* is used because we are not concerned with the actual path by which the market goes from the first equilibrium position to the second or with the time taken to reach the second equilibrium. Analysis of these movements would be described as *dynamic analysis*.

FIGURE 3-8   The Four "Laws" of Demand and Supply

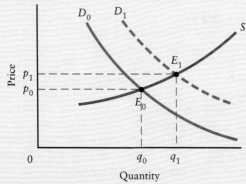

(i) The effect of shifts in the demand curve

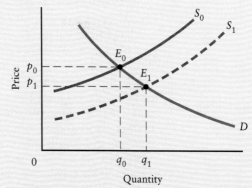

(ii) The effect of shifts in the supply curve

The effects on equilibrium price and quantity of shifts in either demand or supply are known as the laws of demand and supply.

A rise in demand. In part (i), suppose that the original demand and supply curves are D_0 and S, which intersect to produce equilibrium at E_0, with a price of p_0 and a quantity of q_0. An increase in demand shifts the demand curve to D_1, taking the new equilibrium to E_1. Price rises to p_1 and quantity rises to q_1.

A fall in demand. In part (i), the original demand and supply curves are D_1 and S, which intersect to produce equilibrium at E_1, with a price of p_1 and a quantity of q_1. A decrease in demand shifts the demand curve to D_0, taking the new equilibrium to E_0. Price falls to p_0, and quantity falls to q_0.

A rise in supply. In part (ii), the original demand and supply curves are D and S_0, which intersect to produce equilibrium at E_0, with a price of p_0 and a quantity of q_0. An increase in supply shifts the supply curve to S_1, taking the new equilibrium to E_1. Price falls to p_1, and quantity rises to q_1.

A fall in supply. In part (ii), the original demand and supply curves are D and S_1, which intersect to produce equilibrium at E_1, with a price of p_1 and a quantity of q_1. A decrease in supply shifts the supply curve to S_0, taking the new equilibrium to E_0. Price rises to p_0, and quantity falls to q_0.

3. An increase in supply causes a decrease in the equilibrium price and an increase in the equilibrium quantity exchanged.

4. A decrease in supply causes an increase in the equilibrium price and a decrease in the equilibrium quantity exchanged.

Demonstrations of these laws are given in the caption to Figure 3-8. The intuitive reasoning behind each is as follows:

1. An increase in demand creates a shortage at the initial equilibrium price, and the unsatisfied buyers bid up the price. This rise in price causes a larger quantity to be supplied with the result that at the new equilibrium, more is exchanged at a higher price.

2. A decrease in demand creates a glut at the initial equilibrium price, and the unsuccessful sellers bid the price down. As a result, less of the product is supplied and offered for sale. At the new equilibrium, both price and quantity exchanged are lower than they were originally.

3. An increase in supply creates a glut at the initial equilibrium price, and the unsuccessful suppliers force the price down. This drop in price increases the quantity demanded, and the new equilibrium is at a lower price and a higher quantity exchanged.

4. A decrease in supply creates a shortage at the initial equilibrium price that causes the price to be bid up. This rise in price reduces the quantity demanded, and the new equilibrium is at a higher price and a lower quantity exchanged.

Practise with Study Guide Chapter 3, Exercise 3.

In this chapter, we have studied many forces that can cause demand or supply curves to shift. By combining this analysis with the four laws of demand and supply, we can link many real-world events that cause demand or supply curves to shift with changes in market prices and quantities. *Applying Economic Concepts 3-1* shows how we can use demand-and-supply analysis to examine two real-world shocks: the effects of Brazil's 1994 coffee-crop failure and the effects of the 1998 ice storm in Eastern Canada. *Applying Economic Concepts 3-2* examines the effect of ongoing technological improvement on the price of computer chips.

The theory of the determination of price by demand and supply is beautiful in its simplicity. Yet as we shall see throughout this book, it is powerful in its wide range of applications.

Prices and Inflation

The theory we have developed explains how individual prices are determined by the forces of demand and supply. To facilitate matters, we have made *ceteris paribus* assumptions. Specifically, we have assumed the constancy of all prices except the one we are studying. Does this mean that our theory is inapplicable to an inflationary world in which all prices are rising at the same time? Fortunately, the answer is no.

The price of a product is the amount of money that must be spent to acquire one unit of that product. This is called the **absolute price** or *money price*. A **relative price** is the ratio of two absolute prices; it expresses the price of one good in terms of (relative to) another.

absolute price   The amount of money that must be spent to acquire one unit of a commodity. Also called *money price*.

We have been reminded several times that what matters for demand and supply is the price of the product in question *relative to the prices of other products;* that is, what matters is the relative price.

In an inflationary world, we are often interested in the price of a given product as it relates to the average price of all other products. If, during a period when all prices were increasing by an average of 10 percent, the price of oranges rose by 30 percent, then the price of oranges rose relative to the prices of other goods as a whole. Oranges became *relatively* expensive. However, if oranges had risen in price by 30 percent when other prices increased by 40 percent, then the relative price of oranges would have fallen. Although the money price of oranges rose substantially, oranges became *relatively* cheap.

relative price   The ratio of the money price of one commodity to the money price of another commodity; that is, a ratio of two absolute prices.

It has been convenient in this chapter to analyse changes in particular prices in the context of a constant price level. We can easily extend the analysis to an inflationary period by remembering that any force that raises the price of one product when other prices remain constant will, given general inflation, raise the price of that product faster than the price level is rising. For example, a change in tastes in favour of carrots that would raise their price by 5 percent when other prices were constant would raise their price by 8 percent if, at the same time, the general price level were rising by 3 percent. In each case, the price of carrots rises 5 percent *relative to the average of all prices.*

In microeconomics, whenever we refer to a change in the price of one product, we mean a change in that product's relative price; that is, a change in the price of that product relative to the prices of all other goods.

If the price level is constant, an increase in the product's relative price requires only a rise in the money price of the product. If the price level itself is rising, an increase in the product's relative price requires that the money price of the product rise faster than the price level.

APPLYING ECONOMIC CONCEPTS 3-1

Ice Storms, Droughts, and Economics

Here are two simple examples of the demand and supply apparatus in action. Both examples show how the weather—something that changes in unpredictable and often dramatic ways—can have significant effects on either the demand or the supply of various products, with obvious implications for the observed market price.

The Weather and a Demand Shock

In January of 1998, Quebec, eastern Ontario, and parts of the northeastern United States were hit by a massive ice storm. So unprecedented was this storm in its magnitude that many electric power systems were devastated. Homes and businesses in the Montreal area went without power for as long as four weeks.

This electric power shortage had many economic effects, including lost factory production, damage to much capital stock, the death of farm livestock, and the displacement of thousands of people, especially elderly people, into shelters where they could be fed and cared for. Another effect of the power shortage, as soon as it became clear that it would last for more than just a few hours, was a sudden and substantial increase in the demand for portable gas-powered electric generators. Within just a couple of days, all stores in the greater Montreal area were sold out of such generators, and the prices for newly ordered units had increased.

Furthermore, the shortages and price increases for electric generators were not confined to the area directly hit by the ice storm. As it became clear that there was an excess demand for generators in Quebec, sellers in other parts of the country began to divert their supply toward Quebec. This reduction in supply caused shortages, and thus price increases, in other parts of the country, as far away as Edmonton.

The Weather and a Supply Shock

Brazil, which produces one-third of the world's coffee, experienced unusually severe weather in 1994. Two killing frosts in June and July and a period of drought thereafter severely damaged the next year's crop. Some experts estimated that the frosts had destroyed as much as 45 percent of Brazil's 1995 harvest.

This crop damage meant that the world's supply curve of coffee shifted in—upward and to the left. Without a change in price, there would have been excess demand for coffee, with more people wanting to buy than wanting to sell. Predictably, the market forces reacted swiftly, and coffee prices soared by nearly 100 percent on the wholesale commodity market on July 14. Consumers also felt the impact of the supply shock, with retail prices climbing by about $5 per kilogram.

This severe weather hurt coffee growers in Brazil, reducing their incomes considerably. But coffee growers elsewhere—such as Colombia, Costa Rica and Kenya—actually benefited from Brazil's misfortune. They sold their normal-size crop at the elevated world price and thus enjoyed unusually high incomes.

The Quebec ice storm in January 1998 decimated the electricity distribution system. The demand for portable electricity generators (and many other emergency products) increased sharply as a result.

APPLYING ECONOMIC CONCEPTS 3-2

Technological Progress and the Market for Computer Chips

According to a June 1996 article in the *Financial Times*,

It is only nine months since the world semiconductor industry was forging ahead. Demand for chips was so great that there was a shortage, analysts were forecasting record growth and manufacturers were unveiling plans for dozens of $1 billion chip factories....

The euphoria has been short-lived. The shortage rapidly turned into surplus, and the price of dynamic random access memory (D-RAM) chips—the basic memory chips for PCs—has dropped by about 65 percent over the past six or seven months....

Commodity chip prices normally fall by 20 percent to 30 percent each year as manufacturing costs fall. But with manufacturers scrambling to protect market share, international spot market prices have fallen below the break-even point of some Asian manufacturers.

The newspaper story points to key aspects of this market. First, the technology of producing computer chips is evolving rapidly. This causes the market supply curve to shift continually to the right. Second, the demand curve has a negative slope, and shifts in some periods.

The trend decline of "20 percent to 30 percent each year" is clearly shown in the accompanying figure. So is the abnormal period between 1992 and 1995 when chip prices actually rose slightly before falling back sharply in 1996, as discussed above. What is the explanation?

In "normal" times the primary influence is that the ongoing technological improvement causes the supply curve to shift to the right along a nearly stationary demand curve. Chip prices fall and quantity demanded increases. In the 1992–95 period, however, the demand curve shifted sharply to the right. This increase in demand was due to the increased availability (and reduced prices) of such complementary software products as multimedia games and educational programs. By 1996, the demand curve had stopped shifting to the right but the supply curve had continued to shift, since the technolog-

ical improvements continued to occur. Hence prices returned to their "usual" downward trend.

Notice that the price rises associated with the temporary boom in demand between 1992 and 1995 would have increased the quantity supplied on each rightward-shifting supply curve because the high profitability of chip production encouraged higher production at each level of capacity. The fall in price in 1996 no doubt reduced the quantity supplied along the supply curve that existed at the time. However, despite the fall in price, the supply curve continued to shift to the right in successive periods as technological progress continued to reduce the costs of production.

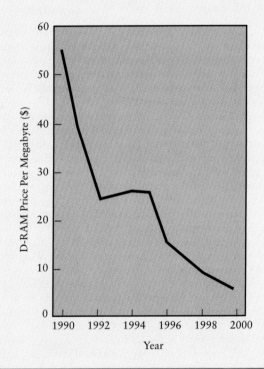

S U M M A R Y

Demand
ⓁⓄ①②

- The amount of a product that consumers wish to purchase is called *quantity demanded*. It is a flow expressed as so much per period of time. It is determined by tastes, average household income, the product's own price, the prices of other products, the size of the population, the distribution of income among consumers, and expectations about the future.
- The relationship between quantity demanded and price is represented graphically by a demand curve that shows how much will be demanded at each market price. Quantity demanded is assumed to increase as the price of the product falls, other things held constant. Thus, demand curves are downward sloping.

- A shift in a demand curve represents a change in the quantity demanded at each price and is referred to as a *change in demand*. The demand curve shifts to the right (an increase in demand) if average income rises, if population rises, if the price of a substitute rises, if the price of a complement falls, or if there is a change in tastes in favour of the product. The opposite changes shift the demand curve to the left (a decrease in demand).
- It is important to make the distinction between a movement along a demand curve (caused by a change in the product's price) and a shift of a demand curve (caused by a change in any of the other determinants of demand).

Supply
ⓁⓄ③④

- The amount of a product that firms wish to sell is called *quantity supplied*. It is a flow expressed as so much per period of time. It depends on the product's own price, the costs of inputs, the number of suppliers, and the state of technology.
- The relationship between quantity supplied and price is represented graphically by a supply curve that shows how much will be supplied at each market price. Quantity supplied is assumed to increase as the price of the product increases, other things held constant. Thus, supply curves are upward sloping.

- A shift in the supply curve indicates a change in the quantity supplied at each price and is referred to as a *change in supply*. The supply curve shifts to the right (an increase in supply) if the costs of producing the product fall or if, for any reason, producers become more willing to produce the product. The opposite changes shift the supply curve to the left (a decrease in supply).
- It is important to make the distinction between a movement along a supply curve (caused by a change in the product's price) and a shift of a supply curve (caused by a change in any of the other determinants of supply).

The Determination of Price
ⓁⓄ⑤⑥

- The *equilibrium price* is the price at which the quantity demanded equals the quantity supplied. At any price below equilibrium, there will be excess demand; at any price above equilibrium, there will be excess supply. Graphically, equilibrium occurs where the demand and supply curves intersect.

- Price rises when there is excess demand and falls when there is excess supply. Thus the actual market price will be pushed toward the equilibrium price. When it is reached, there will be neither excess demand nor excess supply, and the price will not change until either the supply curve or the demand curve shifts.

- Using the method of *comparative statics,* we can determine the effects of a shift in either demand or supply. An increase in demand raises both equilibrium price and equilibrium quantity; a decrease in demand lowers both. An increase in supply raises equilibrium quantity but lowers equilibrium price; a decrease in supply lowers equilibrium quantity but raises equilibrium price. These are called the laws of demand and supply.

- The absolute price of a product is its price in terms of money; its relative price is its price in relation to other products. In an inflationary period, a rise in the *relative price* of one product means that its absolute price rises by more than the price level; a fall in its relative price means that its absolute price rises by less than the price level.

K E Y   C O N C E P T S

"Ceteris paribus" or "other things being equal"

Quantity demanded and quantity actually bought

Demand schedule and demand curve

Change in quantity demanded versus change in demand

Quantity supplied and quantity actually sold

Supply schedule and supply curve

Change in quantity supplied versus change in supply

Equilibrium, equilibrium price, and disequilibrium

Comparative statics

Laws of supply and demand

Relative price

S T U D Y   E X E R C I S E S

1. Consider households' demand for chicken meat. For each of the events listed below, state and explain the likely effect on the demand for chicken. How would each event be illustrated in a diagram?

   a. A medical study reports that eating chicken meat reduces the likelihood of suffering from particular types of heart problems.
   b. A widespread bovine disease leads to an increase in the price of beef.
   c. An increase in average household income.

2. Consider the world market for a particular quality of coffee beans. The following table shows the demand and supply schedules for this market.

Price (per kg)	Quantity Demanded	Quantity Supplied
	(millions of kg per year)	
$2.00	28	10
$2.40	26	12
$3.10	22	13.5
$3.50	19.5	19.5
$3.90	17	22
$4.30	14.5	23.5

   a. Plot the demand and supply schedules on a scale diagram.
   b. Identify the amount of excess demand or supply associated with each price.
   c. Identify the equilibrium price in this market.
   d. Suppose that government (or a collection of national governments) were somehow able to set a minimum price for coffee equal to $3.90 per kg. Explain the outcome in the world coffee market.

3. Consider the supply for grade-A beef. As the price of beef rises, ranchers will tend to sell more cattle to the slaughter houses. Yet, a central prediction from the supply-and-demand model of this chapter is that an increase in the supply of beef reduces the equilibrium price. Reconcile the apparent contradiction. Use a diagram to do so.

4. Consider the world market for wheat. Suppose there is a major failure in Russia's wheat crop due to a severe drought. Explain the likely effect on the equilibrium price and quantity in the world wheat market. Also explain why North American wheat farmers certainly benefit from Russia's drought. Draw a diagram to carefully describe and analyse the situation.

5. The *New York Times* recently stated:

   > *While the world's appetite for chocolate grows more voracious each year, cocoa farms around the globe are failing, under siege from fungal and viral diseases and insects....Researchers predict a shortfall in beans from the cacao tree, the raw material from which chocolate is made, in as little as five to ten years.*

   Describe in terms of the supply-and-demand apparatus what is described in the quote. What is the implied prediction for the equilibrium price of chocolate? What is the implied prediction for the equilibrium quantity of chocolate?

6. This is a challenging question intended for those students who like mathematics. It requires you to solve a supply-and-demand model as a system of *simultaneous equations* (meaning simply that both equations apply at the same time). Letting p be the price of the product, suppose the demand and supply functions for some product are given by

$$Q^D = 100 - 3p$$
$$Q^S = 10 + 2p$$

   a. Plot both the demand curve and the supply curve.
   b. What is the condition for equilibrium in this market?
   c. By imposing the condition for equilibrium, solve for the equilibrium price.
   d. Substitute the equilibrium price into either the demand or supply function to solve for the equilibrium quantity. Check to make sure you get the same answer whether you use the demand function or the supply function.
   e. Now suppose there is an increase in demand so that the new demand function is given by

   $$Q^D = 180 - 3p.$$

   Compute the new equilibrium price and quantity. Is your result consistent with the "law" of demand?
   f. Now suppose that, with the new demand curve in place, there is an increase in supply so that the new supply function is given by $Q^S = 90 + 2p$. Compute the new equilibrium price and quantity. Is your result consistent with the "law" of supply?

DISCUSSION QUESTIONS

1. Recently, a government economist predicted that this spring's excellent weather would result in larger crops of wheat and canola than farmers had expected. But the economist warned consumers not to expect prices to decrease because the cost of production was rising and foreign demand for Canadian crops was increasing. "The classic pattern of supply and demand won't work this time," the economist said. Discuss his observation.

2. What would be the effect on the equilibrium price and quantity of marijuana if its sale and consumption were legalized?

3. Classify the effect of each of the following as (i) a decrease in the demand for fish or (ii) a decrease in the quantity of fish demanded. Illustrate each diagrammatically.

   a. The government of Canada closes the Atlantic cod fishery.
   b. People buy less fish because of a rise in fish prices.
   c. The Catholic Church relaxed its ban on eating meat on Fridays.

   d. The price of beef falls and, as a result, consumers buy more beef and less fish.
   e. Fears of mercury pollution lead locals to shun fish caught in nearby lakes.
   f. It is generally alleged that eating fish is better for one's health than eating meat.

4. Predict the effect on the price of at least one product of each of the following events:

   a. Winter snowfall is at a record high in the interior of British Columbia, but drought continues in Quebec ski areas.
   b. A recession decreases employment in Oshawa automobile factories.
   c. The French grape harvest is the smallest in 20 years.
   d. The province of Ontario cancels permission for citizens to cut firewood in provincial camp grounds.

5. Are the following two observations inconsistent? (a) Rising demand for housing causes prices of new homes to soar. (b) Many families refuse to buy homes as prices become prohibitive for them.

CHAPTER 4

Elasticity

🔵 *LEARNING OBJECTIVES*

❶ Understand the measurement of price elasticity of demand, and know its determinants.

❷ Understand the measurement of price elasticity of supply, and know its determinants.

❸ Explain how an excise (or sales) tax affects the producer price and the consumer price.

❹ Recognize that the incidence of a sales tax depends on relative demand and supply elasticities.

❺ Understand the effect of income on quantity demanded, and how this elasticity defines normal and inferior goods.

❻ Recognize the difference between substitute and complement goods, and how the degree of substitutability can be measured by the cross elasticity of demand.

The laws of demand and supply predict the *direction* of changes in price and quantity in response to various shifts in demand and supply. However, it usually is not enough to know merely whether price and quantity simply rise or fall; it is also important to know by *how much* each changes.

In the previous chapter we discussed the coffee-crop failure in Brazil and how this drove up the world coffee price. But what did this crop failure do to the incomes of Brazilian coffee growers? If the world price increased by more (in percentage terms) than their crop shrank, their incomes would have actually *increased*; that is, the crop failure actually would have made them, as a group, better off. On the other hand, if the price increased by less than the crop shrank, their incomes would have fallen.

Measuring and describing the extent of the responsiveness of quantities to changes in prices and other variables are often essential if we are to understand the significance of these changes. Such measurement is accomplished with the concept of *elasticity*.

Price Elasticity of Demand

Suppose there is an increase in the supply of some farm crop—that is, a rightward shift in the supply curve. We saw in Figure 3-8 when we examined the laws of supply and demand that such an increase in supply will cause the equilibrium price to fall and the equilibrium quantity to rise. But by how much will each change? The answer depends on what is called the *price elasticity of demand*.

Loosely speaking, demand is said to be *elastic* when quantity demanded is quite responsive to changes in price. When quantity demanded is quite unresponsive to changes in price, demand is said to be *inelastic*.

The meaning of elasticity is illustrated in the two parts of Figure 4-1. The two parts of the figure have the same initial equilibrium, and that equilibrium is disturbed by the same leftward shift in the supply curve. But, because the demand curves are different in the two parts of the figure, the new equilibrium position is different, and hence the magnitude

FIGURE 4-1   The Effect of the Shape of the Demand Curve

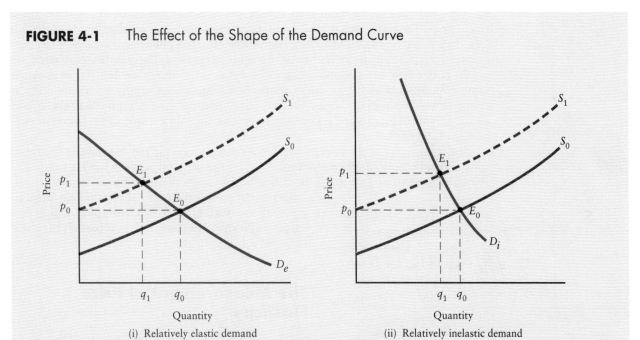

(i) Relatively elastic demand   (ii) Relatively inelastic demand

The more responsive the quantity demanded is to changes in price, the less the change in price and the greater the change in quantity resulting from any given shift in the supply curve. Both parts of the figure are drawn to the same scale. They show the same initial equilibrium and the same shift in the supply curve. In each part, initial equilibrium is at price p_0 and output q_0 and the new equilibrium is at p_1 and q_1. In part (i), the effect of the shift in supply from S_0 to S_1 is a slight rise in the price and a large decrease in quantity. In part (ii), the effect of the identical shift in the supply curve from S_0 to S_1 is a large increase in the price and a relatively small decrease in quantity.

of the effects of the increase in supply on equilibrium price and quantity are different. The demand curve in part (i) is more elastic than the demand curve in part (ii).

A shift in supply will have different quantitative effects, depending on the shape of the demand curve. The difference may be significant for government policy. Suppose the market being depicted in Figure 4-1 is the market for cigarettes, and that the government imposes a tax on each pack of cigarettes sold (as the federal government and all Canadian provincial governments do). As we will see later in this chapter, the effect of such a tax is to shift the supply curve of cigarettes upward by the amount of the tax—a reduction in supply.

Part (i) of Figure 4-1 illustrates a case in which the quantity that consumers demand is relatively responsive to price changes—that is, demand is relatively elastic. The reduction in supply pushes up the price, but, because the quantity demanded is quite responsive, only a small change in price is necessary to restore equilibrium. Thus, the effect of the government's policy is to achieve a large decrease in the production (and consumption) of cigarettes and only a small increase in price.

Part (ii) of Figure 4-1 shows a case in which the quantity demanded is relatively unresponsive to price changes—that is, demand is relatively inelastic. As before, the decrease in supply at the original price causes a shortage that increases the price. However, this time the quantity demanded by consumers does not fall much in response to the rise in price. The result is that equilibrium price rises more, and equilibrium quantity falls less, than in the first case. The effect of the government's policy is to achieve a large increase in the price of cigarettes but only a small decrease in the quantity purchased.

In both of the cases shown in Figure 4-1, the government's policy has exactly the same effectiveness as far as the producers' willingness to supply the commodity is concerned—the shifts of the supply curve are identical. The magnitude of the effects on the equilibrium price and quantity, however, is different because of the different elasticities of demand.

If the objective of the government's policy is to decrease the quantity of cigarettes consumed, the policy will be more successful if the demand curve is similar to the one shown in part (i) of Figure 4-1 than if it is similar to the one shown in part (ii). If, however, the goal of the policy is to achieve a large increase in the price of cigarettes, the policy will be less successful if demand is as shown in part (i) than if it is as shown in part (ii).

The Measurement of Price Elasticity

In Figure 4-1, we were able to say that the curve in part (i) showed a demand that was more responsive to price changes than the curve in part (ii) because two conditions were fulfilled. First, both curves were drawn on the same scale. Second, the initial equilibrium prices and quantities were the same in both parts of the figure. Let us see why these conditions matter.

First, by drawing both figures on the same scale, the curve that looked steeper actually did have the larger absolute slope. (The slope of a demand curve tells us the number of dollars by which price must change to cause a unit change in quantity demanded.)

TABLE 4-1   Price Reductions and Corresponding Increases in Quantity Demanded for Three Products

Commodity	Reduction in Price (cents)	Increase in Quantity Demanded (per month)
Cheese	40 per kilogram	7500 kilograms
T-shirts	40 per shirt	5000 shirts
CD players	40 per CD player	100 CD players

The data show, for each of the three products, the change in quantity demanded resulting from the same absolute fall in price. The data are fairly uninformative about the responsiveness of demand to price because they do not tell us either the original price or the original quantity demanded.

If we had drawn the two curves on different scales, we could have concluded nothing about the relative price changes needed to get a unit change in quantity demanded by comparing their appearances on the graph.

Second, because we started from the same price-quantity equilibrium in both parts of the figure, we did not need to distinguish between *percentage* changes and *absolute* changes. If the initial prices and quantities are the same in both cases, the larger absolute change is also the larger percentage change. However, when we wish to deal with different initial price-quantity equilibria, we need to decide whether we are interested in absolute or percentage changes. To see which is relevant, let's suppose that we have the information shown in Table 4-1. Should we conclude that the demand for portable CD players is not as responsive to price changes as the demand for cheese? After all, price cuts of 40 cents cause quite a large increase in the quantity of cheese demanded but only a small increase in the quantity demanded of CD players.

It should be obvious that a reduction in the price of 40 cents will be a large price cut for a low-priced product and an insignificant price cut for a high-priced product. All of the price reductions listed in Table 4-1 represent price reductions of 40 cents, but they are clearly different proportions of the respective prices. It is usually more revealing to know the *percentage* change in the prices of the various products. For similar reasons knowing the quantity by which demand changes is not very revealing unless the initial level of demand is also known. An increase of 7500 kilograms is quite a significant reaction to demand if the quantity formerly bought was 15 000 kilograms, but it is insignificant if the quantity formerly bought was 10 million kilograms.

Table 4-2 shows the original and new levels of price and quantity. Changes in price and quantity expressed as percentages of the *average* prices and quantities are shown in columns (1) and (2) of Table 4-3. The **price elasticity of demand,** the measure of responsiveness of quantity of a product demanded to a change in that product's price, is symbolized by the Greek letter eta, η. It is defined as follows:

price elasticity of demand (η) A measure of the responsiveness of quantity demanded to a change in the commodity's own price.

$$\eta = \frac{\text{percentage change in quantity demanded}}{\text{percentage change in price}}$$

This measure is called the price elasticity of demand, or simply *demand elasticity.* Because the variable causing the change in quantity demanded is the product's own price, the term *own-price elasticity of demand* is also used.

TABLE 4-2 Price and Quantity Information Underlying Data of Table 4-1

Product	Unit	Original Price ($)	New Price ($)	Average Price ($)	Original Quantity	New Quantity	Average Quantity
Cheese	kg	3.40	3.00	3.20	116 250	123 750	120 000
T-shirts	shirt	16.20	15.80	16.00	197 500	202 500	200 000
CD players	player	80.20	79.80	80.00	9 950	10 050	10 000

These data provide the appropriate context for the data given in Table 4-1. The table relates the 40-cent-per-unit price reduction of each product to the actual prices and quantities demanded.

TABLE 4-3   Calculation of Demand Elasticities

Product	(1) Percentage Decrease in Price	(2) Percentage Increase in Quantity	(3) Elasticity of Demand (2) ÷ (1)
Cheese	12.5	6.25	0.5
T-shirts	2.5	2.50	1.0
CD players	0.5	1.00	2.0

Elasticity of demand is the percentage change in quantity demanded divided by the percentage change in price. The percentage changes are based on average prices and quantities shown in Table 4-2. For example, the 40-cent-per-kilogram decrease in the price of cheese is 12.5 percent of $3.20. A 40-cent change in the price of CD players is only 0.5 percent of the average price per CD player of $80.00.

The Use of Average Price and Quantity in Computing Elasticity

The caption in Table 4-3 stresses that the demand elasticities are computed using changes in price and quantity measured in terms of the *average* values of each. Averages are used to avoid the ambiguity caused by the fact that when a price or quantity changes, the change is a different percentage of the original value than it is of the new value. For example, the 40-cent change in the price of cheese shown in Table 4-2 represents an 11.8 percent change of the original price of $3.40 but a 13.3 percent change of the new price of $3.00.

Using average values for price and quantity means that the measured elasticity of demand between any two points on the demand curve, call them A and B, is independent of whether the movement is from A to B or from B to A. In the example of cheese in Tables 4-2 and 4-3, the 40-cent change in the price of cheese is unambiguously 12.5 percent of the average price of $3.20, and that percentage applies to a price increase from $3.00 to $3.40 or for a price decrease from $3.40 to $3.00.

The implications of using average values for price and quantity for calculating elasticity are as follows. Consider a change from an initial price of p_0 and quantity of q_0 to a new price of p_1 and quantity of q_1. The formula for elasticity is then

$$\eta = \frac{(q_1 - q_0)/q}{(p_1 - p_0)/p} \tag{4-1}$$

where p and q are the average price and average quantity, respectively. Thus

$$p = (p_1 + p_0)/2 \quad \text{and} \quad q = (q_1 + q_0)/2.$$

We can substitute these expressions for p and q in Equation 4-1 and, after dividing out the factors of 2, we get

$$\eta = \frac{(q_1 - q_0)/(q_1 + q_0)}{(p_1 - p_0)/(p_1 + p_0)} \tag{4-2}$$

which provides a convenient formula for calculating demand elasticity. For example, for the case of cheese in Tables 4-2 and 4-3, we have

$$\eta = \frac{7500/240\ 000}{0.40/6.40} = \frac{0.03125}{0.0625} = 0.5$$

which is as in Table 4-3. There is further discussion of the use of averages to calculate elasticity and of alternative methods in the appendix to this chapter. [6]

Interpreting Numerical Elasticities

Because demand curves have negative slopes, an increase in price is associated with a decrease in quantity demanded, and vice versa. Because the percentage changes in price and quantity have opposite signs, demand elasticity is a negative number. However, we will follow the usual practice of ignoring the negative sign and speak of the measure as a positive number, as we have done in the illustrative calculations in Table 4-3. Thus the more responsive the quantity demanded (for example, CD players relative to cheese), the greater the elasticity of demand and the higher the measure (e.g., 2.0 compared with 0.5).

The numerical value of demand elasticity can vary from zero to infinity. Elasticity is zero when quantity demanded does not respond at all to a price change. As long as the percentage change in quantity demanded is less than the percentage change in price, the elasticity of demand has a value of less than one (economists sometimes say less than *unity*). When the two percentage changes are equal, elasticity is equal to one. When the percentage change in quantity demanded exceeds the percentage change in price, the elasticity of demand is greater than one.

When the percentage change in quantity demanded is less than the percentage change in price (elasticity less than 1), there is said to be **inelastic demand**. When the percentage change in quantity is greater than the percentage change in price (elasticity greater than 1), there is said to be **elastic demand**. This important terminology is summarized in part A of *Extensions in Theory 4-1*, which is found toward the end of the chapter.

A demand curve need not, and usually does not, have the same elasticity over every part of the curve. Figure 4-2 shows that a negatively sloped straight-line demand curve does not have a constant elasticity, even though it does have a constant slope. A straight-line demand curve has constant elasticity only when it is vertical or horizontal. Figure 4-3 illustrates these two cases, in addition to a third case of a particular *nonlinear* demand curve that also has a constant elasticity.

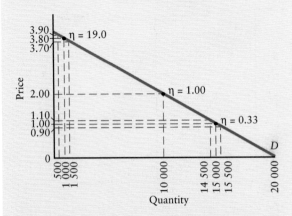

FIGURE 4-2 Elasticity Along a Straight-Line Demand Curve

Moving down a straight-line demand curve, elasticity falls continuously. On this straight-line demand curve, a reduction in price of $0.20 always leads to the same increase (1000 units) in quantity demanded.

Near the upper end of the curve, where price is $3.80 and quantity demanded is 1000 units, a reduction in price of $0.20 (from $3.90 to $3.70) is just slightly more than a 5 percent reduction, but the 1000-unit increase in quantity demanded is a 100 percent increase. Here, elasticity is 19.

Near the lower end, at a price of $1.00 and a quantity of 15 000 units, a price reduction of $0.20 (from $1.10 to $0.90) leads to the same 1000-unit increase in quantity demanded. However, the $0.20 price reduction represents a 20 percent fall, whereas the 1000-unit increase in quantity demanded represents only a 6.67 percent increase. Here, elasticity is 0.33.

inelastic demand
The situation in which, for a given percentage change in price, there is a smaller percentage change in quantity demanded; elasticity less than one.

elastic demand The situation in which, for a given percentage change in price, there is a greater percentage change in quantity demanded; elasticity greater than one.

What Determines Elasticity of Demand?

The main determinant of demand elasticity is the availability of substitutes. Some products, such as margarine, broccoli, lamb, and Toyota cars, have quite close substitutes—butter, other green vegetables, beef, and Mazda cars. A change in the prices of these products, *with the prices of the substitutes remaining constant,* can be expected to cause much substitution. A fall in price leads consumers to buy more of the product and less of the substitutes, and a rise in price leads consumers to buy less of the product and more of the substitutes. Products defined more broadly, such as *all* foods or *all* clothing or *all* methods of transportation, have many fewer satisfactory substitutes. A rise in their prices can be expected to cause a smaller fall in quantities demanded than would be the case if close substitutes were available.

A product with close substitutes tends to have an elastic demand; a product with no close substitutes tends to have an inelastic demand.

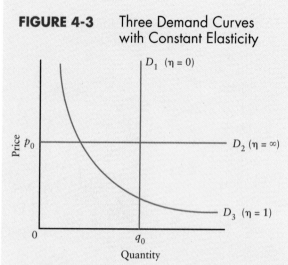

FIGURE 4-3   Three Demand Curves with Constant Elasticity

Each of these demand curves has a constant elasticity. D_1 has zero elasticity: The quantity demanded is equal to q_0, independent of the price. D_2 has infinite elasticity at the price p_0: A small price increase from p_0 decreases quantity demanded from an indefinitely large amount to zero. D_3 has unit elasticity: A given percentage increase in price brings an equal percentage decrease in quantity demanded at all points on the curve; it is a rectangular hyperbola for which price times quantity demanded is a constant.

Demand elasticity depends on the availability of substitutes. The availability of a product's substitutes, in turn, depends on how the product is defined and on the time period being considered. We explore these aspects next.

Definition of the Product

For food taken as a whole, demand is inelastic over a large price range. It does not follow, however, that any one food, such as white bread or peanut butter, is a necessity in the same sense. Individual foods can have quite elastic demands, and they frequently do.

Clothing provides a similar example. Clothing as a whole has a less elastic demand than do individual kinds of clothes. For example, when the price of wool sweaters rises, many households may buy cotton sweaters or down vests instead of buying an additional wool sweater. Thus, although purchases of wool sweaters fall, total purchases of clothing do not.

Any one of a group of related products will have a more elastic demand than the group as a whole.

Short Run and Long Run

Because it takes time to develop satisfactory substitutes, a demand that is inelastic in the short run may prove to be elastic when enough time has passed. Perhaps the most dramatic example of this principle occurred in 1973 when the Organization of Petroleum Exporting Countries (OPEC) shocked the world with its sudden and large increase in the price of oil. At that time, the short-run demand for oil proved to be highly inelastic. Large price increases were met in the short run by very small reductions in quantity demanded. In this case, the short run lasted for several years. Gradually, however, the high price of petroleum products led to such adjustments as the development of smaller, more fuel-efficient cars, economizing on heating oil by installing more efficient insulation, and replacement of fuel oil in many industrial processes with such other power sources as coal and hydroelectricity. The long-run elasticity of demand, relating the change in price to the change in quantity demanded after all adjustments were made, turned out to have an elasticity of well over unity, although the long-run adjustments took as much as a decade to work out.

The response to a price change, and thus the measured price elasticity of demand, will tend to be greater the longer the time span.

For such products as cornflakes and pillowcases, the full response to a price change occurs quickly, and there is little reason to make the distinction between short-run and long-run effects. But other products are typically used in connection with highly durable appliances or machines. A change in the price of, say, electricity and gasoline may not have its major effect until the stock of appliances and machines using these products has been adjusted. This adjustment may take several years to occur.

For products for which substitutes are developed over a period of time, it is helpful to identify two kinds of demand curves. A *short-run demand curve* shows the response of quantity demanded to a change in price for a given structure of the durable goods that use the product and for the existing sets of substitute products. A different short-run demand curve will exist for each such structure. The *long-run demand curve* shows the response of quantity demanded to a change in price after enough time has passed to ensure that all adjustments to the changed price have occurred.

The long-run demand for a product is more elastic than the short-run demand.

Figure 4-4 shows the short-run and long-run effects of an increase in supply. In the short run, the supply increase leads to a movement down the relatively inelastic short-run demand curve; it thus causes a large fall in price but only a small increase in quantity. In the long run, demand is more elastic; thus long-run equilibrium has price and quantity above those that prevailed in short-run equilibrium.

This pattern is often referred to as *overshooting* of the price. The overshooting of price that is evident in the figure is the way in which markets clear when demand is less elastic in the short run than in the long run. Note also that there is *undershooting* of quantity—that is, the equilibrium quantity rises by less in the short run than in the long run.

Because most people cannot easily or quickly change their method of transportation, the demand for gasoline is much less elastic in the short run than in the long run.

Elasticity and Total Expenditure

We know that quantity demanded increases as price falls, but what happens to the total expenditure on that product? It turns out that the response of total expenditure depends on the price elasticity of demand.

To see the relationship between the elasticity of demand and total expenditure, we begin by noting that total expenditure is equal to price times quantity:

$$\text{Total Expenditure} = \text{Price} \times \text{Quantity}$$

Because price and quantity move in opposite directions along a demand curve, one falling when the other rises, the change in total expenditure appears to be ambiguous. It is easily shown, however, that the direction of change in total expenditure depends on the relative percentage changes in the price and quantity. If the percentage change in price exceeds the percentage change in quantity, the price change will dominate, and total expenditure will change in the same direction as the price changes; this is the case where elasticity is less than unity. If the percentage change in the price is less than the percentage change in the quantity demanded (elasticity exceeds unity), the quantity change will dominate, and total expenditure will

FIGURE 4-4   Short-Run and Long-Run Equilibrium Following an Increase in Supply

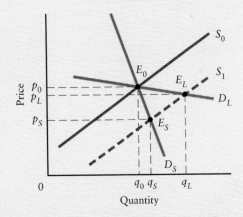

The magnitude of the changes in the equilibrium price and quantity following a shift in supply depends on the time allowed for demand to adjust. The initial equilibrium is at E_0, with price p_0 and quantity q_0. Supply then increases such that the supply curve shifts from S_0 to S_1.

On impact, the relevant demand curve is the short-run curve D_S, and the new equilibrium immediately following the supply shock is E_S. Price falls sharply to p_S, and quantity rises only to q_S. In the long run, the demand curve is the more elastic one given by D_L, and equilibrium is at E_L. The long-run equilibrium price is p_L (greater than p_S), and quantity is q_L (greater than q_S).

FIGURE 4-5   Total Expenditure and Quantity Demanded

Price ($)	Quantity Demanded	Expenditure ($)
3.80	1 000	3 800
3.00	5 000	15 000
2.50	7 500	18 750
2.00	10 000	20 000
1.50	12 500	18 750
1.00	15 000	15 000

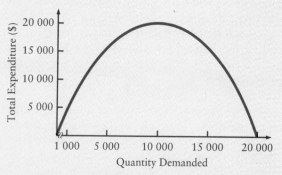

The change in total expenditure on a product in response to a change in price depends on the elasticity of demand. The table and graph are based on the demand curve shown in Figure 4-2. For quantities demanded that are less than 10 000, elasticity of demand is greater than one, and hence any increase in quantity demanded will be proportionately larger than the fall in price that caused it. In that range, total expenditure is increasing. For quantities greater than 10 000, elasticity of demand is less than one, and hence any increase in quantity demanded will be proportionately smaller than the fall in price that caused it. In that range, total expenditure is decreasing. The maximum of total expenditure occurs where the elasticity of demand equals one.

Practise with Study Guide Chapter 4, Exercises 3 and 5.

For information on OPEC and its activities, see www.opec.org.

change in the same direction as quantity changes. If the two percentage changes are equal, total expenditure is unchanged—this is the case of unit elasticity.

Figure 4-5 illustrates the relationship between elasticity of demand and total expenditure; it is based on the straight-line demand curve in Figure 4-2. Total expenditure at each of a number of points on the demand curve is calculated in the table, and the general relationship between total expenditure and quantity demanded is shown by the plotted curve. In the figure we see that expenditure reaches its maximum when elasticity is equal to 1. [7]

The following example uses this relationship between elasticity, price and total expenditure. When a bumper potato crop recently sent prices down 50 percent (a rightward shift in the supply curve), the quantity purchased increased by only 15 percent. Demand was clearly inelastic, and the result of the bumper crop was that total expenditure on potatoes *fell* sharply. Potato farmers, therefore, experienced a sharp fall in income.

A second example relates to the OPEC oil shock in the early 1970s. As the OPEC countries acted together to restrict supply and push up the world price of oil, quantity demanded fell, but only by a small percentage—much smaller than the percentage increase in price. World demand for oil (at least in the short run) was very inelastic, and the result was that total expenditure on oil *increased* dramatically. The OPEC oil producers, therefore, experienced an enormous increase in income.

Price Elasticity of Supply

price elasticity of supply (η_S)   A measure of the responsiveness of quantity supplied to a change in the commodity's own price.

The concept of elasticity can be applied to supply as well as to demand. **Price elasticity of supply** measures the responsiveness of the quantity supplied to a change in the product's price. It is denoted η_S and defined as follows:

$$\eta_s = \frac{\text{percentage change in quantity supplied}}{\text{percentage change in price}}$$

This is often called *supply elasticity.* The supply curves considered in this chapter all have positive slopes: An increase in price causes an increase in quantity supplied. Such supply curves all have positive elasticities because price and quantity change in the same direction.

There are important special cases. If the supply curve is vertical—the quantity supplied does not change as price changes—then elasticity of supply is zero. A horizontal supply curve has an infinite elasticity of supply: A small drop in price will reduce the quantity that producers are willing to supply from an indefinitely large amount to zero. Between these two extremes, elasticity of supply varies with the shape of the supply curve. Loosely speaking, steeper supply curves imply a smaller quantity response for a given change in price, and thus a lower elasticity.

Note, however, that a steeper supply curve does *not always* reflect less elastic supply. There is an important special case worth remembering. Students are quite often surprised to learn that straight-line supply curves *that pass through the origin* have a particular characteristic.

Any positively sloped straight-line supply curve through the origin has a price elasticity equal to one.

Such a supply curve is shown in Figure 4-6. To see that the price elasticity is equal to one, consider two triangles in the figure. The first has the sides p, q, and the S curve; the second has the sides Δp, Δq, and the S curve. These are similar triangles. It follows that the ratios of their sides are equal. That is,

$$p/q = \Delta p/\Delta q$$

From our earlier discussion, elasticity of supply is defined as

$$\eta_s = (\Delta q/\Delta p)\times(p/q)$$

which, by substitution, gives

$$\eta_s = (q/p)\times(p/q) = 1$$

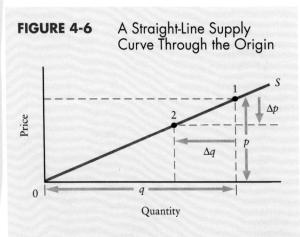

FIGURE 4-6   A Straight-Line Supply Curve Through the Origin

At every point on the supply curve, p/q equals $\Delta p/\Delta q$; hence supply elasticity equals unity at every point.

Determinants of Supply Elasticity

Because much of the treatment of demand elasticity carries over to supply elasticity, we can cover the main points quickly.

Substitution and Production Costs

The ease of substitution can vary in production as well as in consumption. If the price of a product rises, how much more can be produced profitably? This depends in part on how easy it is for producers to shift from the production of other products to the one whose price has risen. If agricultural land and labour can be readily shifted from one crop to another, the supply of any one crop will be more elastic than if they cannot. Or, if machines used to produce coats can be easily modified to produce pants (and vice versa), then the supply of both pants and coats will be more elastic than if the machines cannot be so easily modified.

Supply elasticity depends to a great extent on how costs behave as output is varied. If the costs of producing a unit of output rise rapidly as output rises, then the stimulus to expand production in response to a rise in price will quickly be choked off by increases in costs. In this case, supply will tend to be rather inelastic. If, however, the costs of producing a unit of output rise only slowly as production increases, a rise in price that raises profits will elicit a large increase in quantity supplied before the rise in costs puts a halt to the expansion in output. In this case, supply will tend to be rather elastic.

Short Run and Long Run

As with demand, length of time for response is important. It may be difficult to change quantities supplied in response to a price increase in a matter of weeks or months but easy to do so over a period of years. An obvious example is the planting cycle of crops. An increase in the price of wheat that occurs in mid-summer may lead wheat farmers to be more careful (and less wasteful) in their harvesting this fall, but it occurs too late to influence how much wheat gets planted for this years' crop. But if the high price persists, it will surely influence how much wheat gets planted next spring. Also, new oil fields can be discovered, wells drilled, and pipelines built over a period of years but not in just a few months. Thus the elasticity of oil supply is much greater over five years than over one year.

As with demand, it is useful to make the distinction between the short-run and the long-run supply curve. The *short-run supply curve* shows the response of quantity supplied to a change in price given producers' current capacity to produce the good. The *long-run supply curve* shows the response of quantity supplied to a change in price after enough time has passed to allow producers to adjust their productive capacity.

The long-run supply for a product is more elastic than the short-run supply.

Figure 4-7 illustrates the short-run and long-run effects of an increase in demand. The short-run overshooting of price and the undershooting of quantity that are evident in the figure are analogous to that shown in Figure 4-4 when we examined the short-run and long-run effects following a shift in supply. Here it arises following a shift in demand and is the market-clearing response when supply is less elastic in the short run than in the long run.

FIGURE 4-7   Short-Run and Long-Run Equilibrium Following an Increase in Demand

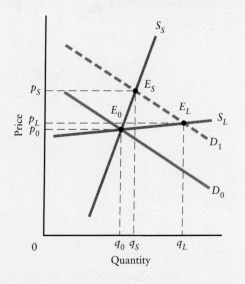

The size of the changes in the equilibrium price and quantity following a shift in demand depends on the time frame of the analysis. The initial equilibrium is at E_0, with price p_0 and quantity q_0. Demand then increases such that the demand curve shifts from D_0 to D_1.

On impact, the relevant supply curve is the short-run curve S_S, so that the new equilibrium immediately following the demand shock is at E_S. Price rises sharply to p_S, and quantity rises only to q_S. In the long run, the supply curve is the more elastic one given by S_L. The long-run equilibrium is at E_L; price is p_L (less than p_S) and quantity is q_L (greater than q_S).

An Important Example Where Elasticity Matters

So far, this chapter has been fairly tough going. We have spent much time examining price elasticity (of both demand and supply) and how to measure it. But who cares? In this section we explore the important concept of *tax incidence* and show that elasticity is crucial to determining whether consumers or producers (or both) end up being harmed by excise taxes.

The federal and provincial governments levy special sales taxes (called **excise taxes**) on many goods such as cigarettes, alcohol, and gasoline. All such taxes work in the following way. At the point of sale of the product, the sellers collect the tax on behalf of the government and then periodically remit the tax collections.

When the sellers write their cheques to the government, these firms feel—with some justification—that they are the ones paying the tax. Consumers, however, argue—again, with some justification—that *they* are the ones who are shouldering the burden of the tax because the tax causes the price of the product to rise.

The question of who *bears the burden* of a tax is called the question of **tax incidence**. A straightforward application of demand-and-supply analysis will show that tax incidence has nothing to do with whether the government collects the tax directly from consumers or from firms.

The burden of a sales (or excise) tax is distributed between consumers and sellers in a manner that depends on the relative elasticities of supply and demand.

At the beginning of this chapter we considered a government that taxed the sale of cigarettes. Let's examine that possibility again in a little more detail. We begin with Figure 4-8. To simplify the problem, we analyse the case where there is initially no tax. The equilibrium without taxes is illustrated by the solid supply and demand curves. What happens when a sales tax of t per pack of cigarettes is introduced? A sales tax means that the price paid by the consumer, called the *consumer price*, and the price received by the seller, called the *seller price*, must now differ by the amount of the tax, t.

In terms of the figure, we can analyse the effect of the tax by considering a new supply curve S' that is above the original supply curve S by the amount of the tax, t. To understand this new curve, let's consider the firm's situation at the original equilibrium quantity q_0. To supply that quantity, producers must receive p_0 per pack of cigarettes sold. However, for producers to receive p_0 when there is a tax on cigarettes, the consumer must pay a total price of $p_0 + t$—whether the consumer "pays the tax directly" by giving p_0 to the firm and t to the government or whether the consumer pays the total $p_0 + t$ to the firm and the firm then remits the tax t to

excise tax   A tax on the sale of a particular commodity.

tax incidence   The location of the burden of a tax; that is, the identity of the ultimate bearer of the tax.

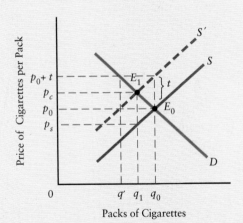

FIGURE 4-8   The Effect of a Cigarette Excise Tax

The burden of an excise tax is shared by consumers and producers. The original supply and demand curves for cigarettes are given by the solid lines S and D; equilibrium is at E_0 with price p_0 and quantity q_0. When a sales tax of t per pack is imposed, the supply curve shifts up to the dashed line S', which lies above the original supply curve by the amount of the tax t. The tax increases the consumer price and reduces the seller price. It also reduces the equilibrium quantity exchanged.

the government. Either way, the total amount that consumers must pay to obtain a given quantity from firms has increased by the amount of the tax t.

This upward shift in the supply curve for cigarettes is depicted in Figure 4-8 as the dashed curve, S'. This shift in the supply curve, caused by the tax, will generally also cause a movement *along* the demand curve, reducing the equilibrium quantity.

Consider the situation at the consumer price of $p_0 + t$. Firms will still be willing to sell the original quantity, but households will demand less because the price has risen; there is excess supply and hence pressure for the consumer price to fall.

The new equilibrium after the imposition of the sales tax occurs at the intersection of the original demand curve D with the tax-shifted supply curve S'. At this new equilibrium, E_1, the consumer price rises to p_c (greater than p_0), the seller price falls to p_s (less than p_0), and the equilibrium quantity falls to q_1.

Note that the quantity demanded *at the consumer price* is equal to the quantity supplied *at the seller price*, a condition that is required for equilibrium. As shown in the figure, compared to the original equilibrium, the consumer price is higher and the seller price is lower, although in each case the change in price is less than the full extent of the sales tax.

After the imposition of a sales tax, the difference between the consumer and seller prices is equal to the tax. In the new equilibrium, the quantity exchanged is less than that exchanged prior to the imposition of the tax.

The role of the relative elasticities of supply and demand in determining the incidence of the sales tax is illustrated in Figure 4-9. In part (i), demand is inelastic relative to

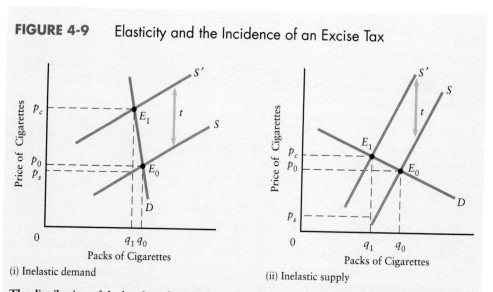

FIGURE 4-9   Elasticity and the Incidence of an Excise Tax

(i) Inelastic demand

(ii) Inelastic supply

The distribution of the burden of a sales tax between consumers and producers depends on the relative elasticities of supply and demand. In both parts of the figure, the initial supply and demand curves are given by S and D; the initial equilibrium is at E_0 with equilibrium price p_0 and quantity q_0. A tax of t per pack of cigarettes is imposed, causing the supply curve to shift up by the amount of the tax to S'. The new equilibrium is at E_1. The consumer price rises to p_c, the seller price falls to p_s, and the quantity falls to q_1. Sellers bear little of the burden of the tax in the first case (and consumers bear a lot), whereas consumers bear little of the burden in the second case (and sellers bear a lot).

supply; as a result, the fall in quantity is quite small, whereas the price paid by consumers rises by almost the full extent of the tax. Because neither the price received by sellers nor the quantity sold changes very much, sellers bear little of the burden of the tax. In part (ii), supply is inelastic relative to demand; in this case, consumers can more easily substitute away from cigarettes. There is little change in the price, and hence they bear little of the burden of the tax, which falls mostly on suppliers. Notice in Figure 4-9 that the size of the upward shift in supply is the same in the two cases, indicating the same tax increase in both cases.

When demand is inelastic relative to supply, consumers bear most of the burden of excise taxes. When supply is inelastic relative to demand, producers bear most of the burden.

Now we can examine who really pays for cigarette tax increases (or tax increases on gasoline and alcohol). The demand for cigarettes is inelastic both overall and relative to supply, suggesting that a cigarette-tax increase would be borne more by consumers than by producers. Thus, the large *reductions* in cigarette taxes which took place in the summer of 1994 in Ontario and Quebec benefited consumers more than producers. The demand for gasoline is also inelastic, but much more so in the short run than in the long run. (In the long run, drivers can change their driving routines and improve the efficiency of their vehicles, but in the short run such changes are very costly.) The supply of gasoline, given world trade in petroleum and petroleum products, is elastic relative to demand. The relatively inelastic demand and elastic supply imply that the burden of gasoline taxes falls mostly on consumers.

Applying Economic Concepts 4-1 discusses another important example of the issue of tax incidence—this time involving the burden of payroll taxes, such as the premiums that firms and workers pay for employment insurance and the Canada Pension Plan.

Practise with Study Guide Chapter 4, Exercise 9.

Other Demand Elasticities

The price of the product is not the only important variable determining demand for that product. Income and other prices also matter, and elasticity is a useful concept in measuring their effects.

Income Elasticity of Demand

One of the most important determinants of demand is the income of the customers. The responsiveness of demand to changes in income is termed the **income elasticity of demand** and is symbolized η_Y.

$$\eta_Y = \frac{\text{percentage change in quantity demanded}}{\text{percentage change in income}}$$

For most goods, increases in income lead to increases in demand—their income elasticity is positive. These are called **normal goods.** Goods for which demand decreases in response to a rise in income have negative income elasticities and are called **inferior goods.**

The income elasticity of normal goods can be greater than unity (elastic) or less than unity (inelastic), depending on whether the percentage change in the quantity

income elasticity of demand (η_Y)
A measure of the responsiveness of quantity demanded to a change in income.

normal good
A good for which quantity demanded rises as income rises—its income elasticity is positive.

inferior good
A good for which quantity demanded falls as income rises—its income elasticity is negative.

APPLYING ECONOMIC CONCEPTS 4-2

Who Really Pays for Payroll Taxes?

Some social programs in Canada are financed by **payroll taxes**—taxes collected from both firms and workers, computed as a proportion of workers' earnings. For example, the Employment Insurance program (formerly known as Unemployment Insurance) is financed by premiums paid by both firms and workers. The Canada Pension Plan is financed the same way.

When the federal government determines that such payroll taxes need to be increased (for reasons that we will discuss in Chapter 18 when we examine many aspects of Canadian social policy), an immediate question comes to the fore of the public debate: Should workers or firms be required to pay the extra taxes? There appears to be a great deal at stake in the resolution of this question. After all, neither workers nor firms want to bear the burden of extra taxes. Strikingly, however, *there is no economic difference between imposing payroll taxes on firms and imposing them on workers*. This proposition can be established by using the

same supply-and-demand analysis that we used to examine the incidence of sales taxes.

The accompanying figure illustrates a model of the labour market. The figure shows a standard demand-and-supply apparatus except that the axes have been relabelled as "Employment" and "Hourly Wage Rate."* Firms represent the demand for labour services. As the wage falls, it is profitable for firms to hire more workers (and to produce more output). Thus the demand curve for labour has a negative slope. Workers represent the supply of labour services. As the wage rises, the opportunity cost of *not working* rises, and thus workers substitute away from other activities and supply more labour services. Thus the supply curve for labour has a positive slope. The supply curve is shown to be relatively inelastic, in keeping with a considerable amount of empirical evidence showing that the quantity of labour supplied to the economy is quite unresponsive to changes in the wage rate. In the absence of any payroll taxes, the equilib-

---

payroll taxes Taxes paid by the firm and worker, computed as a percentage of the worker's total earnings.

demanded is greater or less than the percentage change in income that brought it about. It is also common to use the terms *income-elastic* and *income-inelastic* to refer to income elasticities of greater or less than unity. (See *Extensions in Theory 4-1* for a summary of the different elasticity concepts.)

The reaction of demand to changes in income is extremely important. We know that in most Western countries, economic growth caused the level of income to double every 20 to 30 years over a sustained period of at least a century. This rise in income has been shared to some extent by most citizens. As they found their incomes increasing, they increased their demands for most products, but the demands for some products, such as food and basic clothing, did not increase as much as the demands for other products. In developing countries the demand for durable goods is increasing most rapidly as household incomes rise, while in North America and Western Europe, the demand for services has risen most rapidly. The uneven impact of the growth of income on the demands for different products has important economic effects, which are studied at several points in this book.

What Determines Income Elasticity of Demand?

The variations in income elasticities shown in Table 4-4 suggest that the more basic a product, the lower its income elasticity. Food as a whole has an income elasticity of 0.2, consumer durables of 1.8. In Canada, starchy roots such as potatoes are inferior goods; their quantity demanded falls as income rises.

rium wage is w_0 and the equilibrium level of employment is E_0.

As in the analysis of excise taxes, the effect of the payroll tax is to drive a wedge between the wage paid by the firm (w_F) and the wage received by the worker (w_W). With a payroll tax of t dollars per hour, w_F rises above w_0 and w_W falls below w_0. Employment falls from E_0 to E_1. As the supply curve is drawn in the figure, however, almost all of the burden of the tax falls on workers. The lower right-hand bracket shows the amount by which the workers' take-home wage falls. The upper right-hand bracket shows the amount by which the employers' total payment per worker rises. Together, these add up to the payroll tax, shown by the left-hand bracket. Were the supply curve *perfectly* inelastic, the entire burden would fall on workers.

Quite apart from how the burden of the tax is apportioned between workers and firms, the figure also shows why many economic commentators refer to payroll taxes as "job killers"—by increasing the total cost that firms must pay for each unit of labour services, payroll taxes naturally lead firms to hire fewer workers.

The burden of payroll taxes would be shared more by firms if the supply of labour were more elastic (or if the demand were less elastic). But, as is the case with excise taxes that we discussed in the text, it is the shapes of the supply and demand curves that determine who bears the burden of payroll taxes.

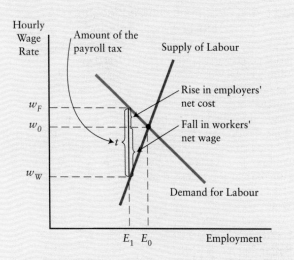

---

* This analysis assumes that the labour market is reasonably competitive—meaning that there are a large number of both workers and firms, none of which have the power to influence the market wage. Though this is usually a good description of the labour market, there are some situations that are not well modelled by a simple supply-and-demand apparatus. We discuss the role of labour unions, for example, in Chapter 14.

The more basic is an item in the consumption pattern of consumers, the lower is its income elasticity.

Income elasticities for any one product also vary with the level of a consumer's income. When incomes are low, consumers may eat almost no green vegetables and consume lots of starchy foods such as bread and potatoes; when incomes are higher, they may eat cheap cuts of meat and more green vegetables along with their bread and potatoes; when incomes are higher still, they are likely to eat higher quality and prepared foods of a wide variety.

The distinction between luxuries and necessities helps to explain differences in income elasticities. The case of restaurant meals is one example. Such meals are almost always more expensive, calorie for calorie, than meals prepared at home. It would thus be expected that at lower ranges of income, restaurant meals would be regarded as an expensive luxury but that the demand for them would expand substantially as consumers became richer. This is actually what happens.

What is true of individual consumers is also true of countries. Empirical studies show that for different countries at comparable stages of economic development, income elasticities are similar. However, the countries of the world are at various stages of economic development and thus have widely different income elasticities for the same products. Notice in Table 4-4 the different income elasticity of poultry in the United States, where it is a standard item of consumption, and in Sri Lanka, where it is a luxury good.

TABLE 4-4 Some Estimated Income Elasticities of Demand	
Inferior goods (η_Y less than zero)	
Whole milk	−0.5
Pig products	−0.2
Starchy roots	−0.2
Inelastic normal goods (η_Y between zero and one)	
Wine (France)	0.1
All food	0.2
Poultry	0.3
Elastic normal goods (η_Y greater than one)	
Gasoline	1.1
Wine	1.4
Consumer durables	1.8
Poultry (Sri Lanka)	2.0
Restaurant meals (U.K.)	2.4

Income elasticities vary widely across commodities and sometimes across countries. The basic source of food estimates by country is the Food and Agriculture Organization of the United Nations, but many individual studies have been made. (For the United States except where noted.)

Another example of the luxury-necessity distinction is shown in Table 4-4 by the different income elasticities for wine in France and the United States. In France, wine is a much more basic part of the meal than is the case in the United States, where wine is regarded as more of a luxury. As a result, increases in income lead to much smaller increases in the demand for wine in France than in the United States.

Graphical Representation of Income Elasticity

Increases in income shift the demand curve to the right for a normal good and to the left for an inferior good. Figure 4-10 shows a different kind of graph, an *income-consumption curve*. The curve resembles an ordinary demand curve in one respect: It shows the relationship of quantity demanded to one other variable, *ceteris paribus*. The other variable is not price, however, but household income. (An increase in the price of the product, holding income constant, would shift the curves in Figure 4-10 downward.)[1]

The figure shows three different patterns of income elasticity. Goods that consumers regard as necessities will generally have income elasticities that fall as income rises. The obvious reason is that as incomes rise, it becomes possible for consumers to devote a smaller proportion of their incomes to meeting basic needs and a larger proportion to buying things that they previously could not afford. At high levels of income some of the necessities may even become inferior goods. So-called luxury goods will not tend to be purchased at low levels of income but will have high income elasticities once incomes rise enough to permit consumers to sample the better things of life now available to them.

Cross Elasticity of Demand

cross elasticity of demand (η_{XY})
A measure of the responsiveness of the quantity of one commodity demanded to changes in the price of another commodity.

The responsiveness of demand to changes in the price of *another* product is called the **cross elasticity of demand.** It is denoted η_{XY} and defined as follows:

$$\eta_{XY} = \frac{\text{percentage change in quantity demanded of good } X}{\text{percentage change in price of good } Y}$$

The change in the price of good Y causes the *demand curve* for good X to shift. If X and Y are substitutes, an increase in the price of Y leads to an increase in the demand for

---

[1]In Figure 4-10, in contrast to the ordinary demand curve, quantity demanded is on the vertical axis. This placement follows the usual practice of putting the variable to be explained (the dependent variable) on the vertical axis and the explanatory variable (the independent variable) on the horizontal axis. It is the ordinary demand curve that has the axes "backward." The explanation is buried in the history of economics and dates to Alfred Marshall's *Principles of Economics* (1890). [8] For better or worse, Marshall's scheme is now used by everybody, although mathematicians never fail to wonder at this example of the odd ways of economists.

FIGURE 4-10 Income-Consumption Curves of Different Products

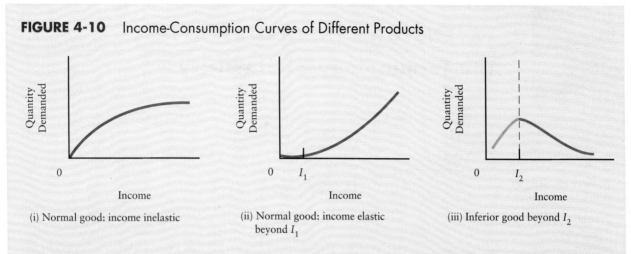

(i) Normal good: income inelastic

(ii) Normal good: income elastic beyond I_1

(iii) Inferior good beyond I_2

Different shapes of the curve relating quantity demanded to income correspond to different ranges of income elasticity. Normal goods have upward-sloping curves; inferior goods have downward-sloping curves. The good in part (i) is a typical normal good that is a necessity (the income elasticity declines as income rises). The good in part (ii) is a luxury good that is income elastic beyond income I_1. The good in part (iii) is a necessity (normal) at low incomes but becomes an inferior good at incomes beyond I_2.

X. If X and Y are complements, an increase in the price of Y leads to a reduction in demand for X. In either case, we are holding the price of X constant. We therefore measure the change in the quantity demanded of X (at its unchanged price) by measuring the shift of the demand curve for X.

Cross elasticity can vary from minus infinity to plus infinity. Complementary products, such as cars and gasoline, have negative cross elasticities. A large rise in the price of gasoline will lead to a decline in the demand for cars, as some people decide to do without a car and others decide not to buy an additional car. Substitute products, such as cars and public transport, have positive cross elasticities. A large rise in the price of cars (relative to public transport) will lead to a rise in the demand for public transport as some people shift from cars to public transport. (See *Extensions in Theory 4-1* for a summary of elasticity terminology.)

The positive or negative sign of cross elasticities tell us whether goods are substitutes or complements.

Measures of cross elasticity sometimes prove helpful in defining whether producers of similar products are in competition with each other. For example, glass bottles and tin cans have a high cross elasticity of demand. The producer of bottles is thus in competition with the producer of cans. If the bottle company raises its price, it will lose substantial sales to the can producer. In contrast, men's shoes and women's shoes have a low cross elasticity and thus a producer of men's shoes is not in close competition with a producer of women's shoes. If the former raises its price, it will not lose many sales to the latter. Knowledge of cross elasticity can be important in matters of *competition policy* in which the issue is whether a firm in one industry is or is not competing with firms in another industry. We discuss competition policy in more detail in Chapter 12.

Substitute products have a positive cross elasticity; an increase in the price of one leads to an increase in demand for the other.

EXTENSIONS IN THEORY 4-1

The Terminology of Elasticity

Term	Symbol	Numerical Measure of Elasticity	Verbal Description
A. Price elasticity of demand (supply)	η (η$_S$)		
Perfectly or completely inelastic		Zero	Quantity demanded (supplied) does not change as price changes.
Inelastic		Between zero and one	Quantity demanded (supplied) changes by a smaller percentage than does price.
Unit elastic		One	Quantity demanded (supplied) changes by exactly the same percentage as does price.
Elastic		Greater than one but less than infinity	Quantity demanded (supplied) changes by a larger percentage than does price
Perfectly, completely, or infinitely elastic		Infinity	Purchasers (sellers) are prepared to buy (sell) all they can at some price and none at all at a higher (lower) price.
B. Income elasticity of demand	η$_Y$		
Inferior good		Negative	Quantity demanded decreases as income increases.
Normal good		Positive	Quantity demanded increases as income increases:
Income-inelastic		Less than one	Less than in proportion to income increase
Income-elastic		Greater than one	More than in proportion to income increase
C. Cross elasticity of demand	η$_{XY}$		
Substitute		Positive	Price increase of a substitute leads to an increase in quantity demanded of this good.
Complement		Negative	Price increase of a complement leads to a decrease in quantity demanded of this good.

Practise with Study Guide Chapter 4, Exercise 1.

S U M M A R Y

Price Elasticity of Demand ⓛⓞ①

- *Price elasticity of demand,* also called *elasticity of demand,* is a measure of the extent to which the quantity demanded of a product responds to a change in its price. Represented by the symbol η, it is defined as

$$\eta = \frac{\text{percentage change in quantity demanded}}{\text{percentage change in price}}$$

  The percentage changes are usually calculated as the change divided by the *average* value. Elasticity is defined to be a positive number, and it can vary from zero to infinity.

- When the numerical measure of elasticity is less than unity, demand is *inelastic*—the percentage change in quantity demanded is less than the percentage change in price that brought it about. When the numerical measure exceeds unity, demand is *elastic*—the percentage change in quantity demanded is greater than the percentage change in price that brought it about.

- The main determinant of the price elasticity of demand is the availability of substitutes for the product. Any one of a group of close substitutes will have a more elastic demand than will the group as a whole. Items that have few substitutes in the short run tend to develop many substitutes when consumers and producers have time to adapt.

- Since price elasticities are larger in the long run than in the short run, a shift in supply will lead to a larger change in price and a smaller change in quantity in the short run than in the long run.

- Elasticity and total expenditure are related in the following way: If elasticity is less than unity, total expenditure is positively related with price; if elasticity is greater than unity, total expenditure is negatively related with price; and if elasticity is unity, total expenditure does not change as price changes.

Price Elasticity of Supply ⓛⓞ②

- *Elasticity of supply* measures the extent to which the quantity supplied of some product changes when the price of that product changes. Represented by the symbol η_S, it is defined as

$$\eta_S = \frac{\text{percentage change in quantity supplied}}{\text{percentage change in price}}$$

- Supply tends to be more elastic in the long run than in the short run because it usually takes time for producers to alter their productive capacity in response to price changes.

An Important Example Where Elasticity Matters ⓛⓞ③④

- The distribution of the burden of a sales tax between consumers and producers is independent of who actually remits the tax to the government. Rather, it depends on the relative elasticities of the supply and the demand for the product.

- The less elastic that demand is relative to supply, the more of the burden of an excise tax falls on the consumers.

Other Demand Elasticities

LO 5 6

- *Income elasticity of demand* is a measure of the extent to which the quantity demanded of some product changes as income changes. Represented by the symbol η_Y, it is defined as

$$\eta_Y = \frac{\text{percentage change in quantity demanded}}{\text{percentage change in income}}$$

The income elasticity of demand for a product will usually change as income varies. For example, a product that has a high income elasticity at a low income (because increases in income bring it within reach of the typical household) may have a low or negative income elasticity at higher incomes (because with further rises in incomes, it is gradually replaced by a superior substitute).

- *Cross elasticity of demand* is a measure of the extent to which the quantity demanded of one product changes when the price of a different product changes. Represented by the symbol η_{XY}, it is defined as

$$\eta_{XY} = \frac{\text{percentage change in quantity demanded of good } X}{\text{percentage change in price of good } Y}$$

It is used to define products that are substitutes for one another (positive cross elasticity) and products that are complements for one another (negative cross elasticity).

KEY CONCEPTS

Price elasticity of demand
Inelastic and perfectly inelastic demand
Elastic and infinitely elastic demand
Relationship between demand elasticity and total expenditure
The burden of a sales (or excise) tax

Consumer price and seller price
Income elasticity of demand
Income-elastic and income-inelastic demands
Normal goods and inferior goods

Cross elasticity of demand
Substitutes and complements
Elasticity of supply
Short-run and long-run responses to shifts in demand and supply

STUDY EXERCISES

1. What would you predict about the *relative* price elasticity of demand for each of the following items? Explain your reasoning.

   a. food
   b. vegetables
   c. leafy vegetables (such as spinach and lettuce)
   d. leafy vegetables sold at your local supermarket
   e. leafy vegetables sold at your local supermarket on Wednesdays

2. Suppose a stamp collector buys the only two existing copies of a stamp at an auction. After the purchase, the collector goes to the front of the room and burns one of the stamps in front of the shocked audience. What must the collector believe in order for this to be a wealth-maximizing action? Explain with a demand-and-supply diagram.

3. For each of the following events, state the relevant elasticity concept. Then compute the measure of elasticity. Where appropriate, use average prices and quantities in your calculations. In all cases, assume that these are *ceteris paribus* changes.

   a. When the price of theatre tickets is reduced from $14.00 to $11.00, ticket sales increase from 1200 to 1350.

   b. As average household income in Canada increases by 10 percent, annual sales of Toyota Camrys increase from 56 000 to 67 000.

   c. After a major failure of Brazil's coffee crop sent coffee prices up from $3.00 per kg to $4.80 per kg, sales of tea in Canada increased from 7500 kg per month to 8000 kg per month.

   d. An increase in the world demand for pulp (used in producing newsprint) increases the price by 14 percent. Annual Canadian production increases from 8 million tons to 11 million tons.

4. The following table shows the demand schedule for denim jeans.

	Price (per unit)	Quantity Demanded (per year)	Total Expenditure
A	$30	400 000	
B	35	380 000	
C	40	350 000	
D	45	320 000	
E	50	300 000	
F	55	260 000	
G	60	230 000	
H	65	190 000	

a. Compute total expenditure for each row in the table.
b. Plot the demand curve and the total expenditure curve.
c. Compute the price elasticity of demand between points A and B, B and C, C and D, and so on.
d. Over what range of prices is the demand for denim jeans elastic? Explain.
e. Over what range of prices is the demand for denim jeans inelastic? Explain.

5. Consider the following straight-line supply curves. In each case, p is the price (measured in $ per unit) and Q^S is the quantity supplied of the product (measured in thousands of units per month).

i) $p = 2Q^S$
ii) $p = 4Q^S$
iii) $p = 5Q^S$
iv) $p = 10Q^S$

a. Plot each supply curve on a scale diagram. In each case, plot point A (which corresponds to price equal to $20) and point B (which corresponds to price equal to $40).
b. For each supply curve, compute the price elasticity of supply between points A and B.
c. Explain why the *slope* of a supply curve is not the same as the *elasticity* of supply.

6. This is a challenging question intended for those students who like mathematics. It will help you work through the issue of tax incidence. Consider the market for gasoline. Suppose the market demand and supply curves are as given below. In each case, quantity refers to millions of litres of gasoline per month; price is the price per litre (in cents).

Demand: $p = 80 - 5Q^D$

Supply: $p = 24 + 2Q^S$

a. Plot the demand and supply curves on a scale diagram.
b. Compute the equilibrium price and quantity.
c. Now suppose the government imposes a tax of 14 cents per litre. Show how this affects the market equilibrium. What is the new "consumer price" and what is the new "producer price"?
d. Compute the total revenue raised by the gasoline tax. What share of this tax revenue is "paid" by consumers, and what share is "paid" by producers? (Hint: if the consumer price were unchanged from the pre-tax equilibrium, we would say that consumers pay none of the tax.)

DISCUSSION QUESTIONS

1. From the following quotations, what, if anything, can you conclude about elasticity of demand?

a. "Good weather resulted in record wheat harvests and sent wheat prices tumbling. The result has been disastrous for many wheat farmers."

b. "Ridership always went up when bus fares came down, but the increased patronage never was enough to prevent a decrease in overall revenue."

c. "As the price of CD players fell, producers found their revenues soaring."

d. "Coffee to me is an essential good—I've just gotta have it no matter what the price."

e. "The soaring price of condominiums does little to curb the strong demand in Vancouver."

2. Home computers were a leader in sales appeal through much of the 1990s. But per capita sales are much lower in Mexico than in Canada, and lower in Newfoundland than in Alberta. Manufacturers are puzzled by the big differences. Can you offer an explanation in terms of elasticity?

3. What elasticity measure or measures would be useful in answering the following questions?

a. Will cheaper transport into the central city help to keep downtown shopping centres profitable?

b. Will raising the bulk postage rate increase or decrease the revenues for Canada Post?

c. Are producers of toothpaste and mouthwash in competition with each other?

d. What effect will rising gasoline prices have on the sale of cars that use propane gas?

4. Interpret the following statements in terms of the relevant elasticity concept.

a. "As fuel for tractors has become more expensive, many farmers have shifted from plowing their fields to no-till farming. No-till acreage increased dramatically in the past 20 years."

a. "Fertilizer makers brace for dismal year as fertilizer prices soar."

c. "When farmers are hurting, small towns feel the pain."

d. "The development of the Hibernia oil field may bring temporary prosperity to Newfoundland merchants."

5. When the New York City Opera faced a growing deficit, it cut its ticket prices by 20 percent, hoping to attract more customers. At the same time, the New York Transit Authority raised subway fares to reduce its growing deficit. Was one of these two opposite approaches to reducing a deficit necessarily wrong?

More Details About Demand Elasticity

The definition of elasticity used in the text may be written symbolically in the following form:[1]

$$\eta = \frac{\Delta q}{\text{average } q} \div \frac{\Delta p}{\text{average } p}$$

where the averages are over the range, or *arc*, of the demand curve being considered. Rearranging terms, we can write

$$\eta = \frac{\Delta q}{\Delta p} \times \frac{\text{average } p}{\text{average } q}.$$

This is called *arc elasticity*, and it measures the average responsiveness of quantity to price over an interval of the demand curve.

Most theoretical treatments use a slightly different concept called *point elasticity*. This is the measure of responsiveness of quantity demanded to price *at a particular point* on the demand curve. The precise definition of point elasticity uses the concept of a derivative, which is drawn from differential calculus.

In this appendix, we first study arc elasticity, which we can regard as an approximation of point elasticity. Then we study point elasticity.

Before proceeding, we should note one further change. In the text of Chapter 4, we reported our price elasticities as positive values and thus implicitly multiplied all our calculations by −1. In theoretical work, it is more convenient to retain the concept's natural sign. Hence, normal demand elasticities have negative signs, and statements about "more" or "less" elasticity refer to the absolute, not the algebraic, value of demand elasticity.

---

[1]The following notation is used throughout this appendix.
$\eta \equiv$ elasticity of demand
$q \equiv$ initial quantity
$\Delta q \equiv$ change in quantity
$p \equiv$ initial price
$\Delta p \equiv$ change in price

Arc Elasticity as an Approximation of Point Elasticity

Point elasticity is a precise measure of elasticity at a particular price-quantity point. Without using calculus, however, we can only approximate this point elasticity. We do this by measuring the responsiveness of quantity demanded to a change in price *over a small range* of the demand curve, starting from that price-quantity point. For example, in Figure 4A-1, we can measure the elasticity at point 1 by the responsiveness of quantity demanded to a change in price that takes price and quantity from point 1 to point 2. The algebraic formula for this elasticity concept is

$$\eta = \frac{\Delta q}{\Delta p} \times \frac{p}{q} \qquad (4A-1)$$

This is similar to the definition of arc elasticity above except that, because elasticity is being measured at a

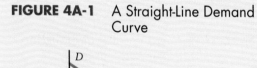

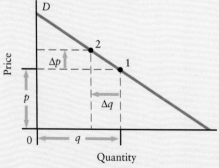

FIGURE 4A-1   A Straight-Line Demand Curve

Because p/q varies with $\Delta q/\Delta p$ constant, the elasticity varies along this demand curve; it is high at the left and low at the right.

point, the p and q corresponding to that point are used (rather than the average p and q over an arc of the curve).

Equation 4A-1 splits elasticity into two parts. The first part, $\Delta q/\Delta p$, is related to the *slope* of the demand curve. In fact, it is the *reciprocal* of the slope. The second part, p/q, is related to the *point* on the curve at which the measurement is made.

Although point elasticity of demand refers to a price-quantity point on the demand curve, the first term in Equation 4A-1 still refers to changes over an arc of the curve. This is the part of the formula that involves approximation, and, as we shall see, it has some unsatisfactory results. Nonetheless, we can derive some interesting results by using this formula as long as we confine ourselves to straight-line demand curves.

The elasticity of a downward-sloping straight-line demand curve varies from zero at the quantity axis to infinity at the price axis.

First, notice that because a straight line has a constant slope, the ratio $\Delta p/\Delta q$ is the same everywhere on the line. Therefore, its reciprocal, $\Delta q/\Delta p$, must also be constant. The changes in η can now be inferred by inspecting the ratio p/q. Where the line cuts the quantity axis, price is zero, so the ratio p/q is zero; thus $\eta = 0$. Moving up the line, p rises and q falls, so the ratio p/q rises; thus elasticity rises. Approaching the top of

the line, q approaches zero, so the ratio becomes very large. Thus elasticity increases without limit as the price axis is approached.

Where there are two straight-line demand curves of the same slope, the one farther from the origin is less elastic at each price than the one closer to the origin.

Figure 4A-2 shows two parallel straight-line demand curves. Compare the elasticities of the two curves at any price, say, p_0. Because the curves are parallel, the ratio $\Delta q/\Delta p$ is the same on both curves. Because elasticities at the same price are being compared on both curves, p is the same, and the only factor left to vary is q. On the curve farther from the origin, quantity is larger (i.e., $q_1 > q_0$) and hence p_0/q_1 is smaller than p_0/q_0; thus η is smaller.

It follows that parallel shifts of a straight-line demand curve reduce elasticity (at each price) when the line shifts outward and increase elasticity when the line shifts inward.

For two intersecting straight-line demand curves the steeper curve is the less elastic.

In Figure 4A-3, there are two intersecting curves. At the point of intersection, p and q are common to both curves, and hence the ratio p/q is the same. Therefore, η varies only with $\Delta q/\Delta p$. On the steeper

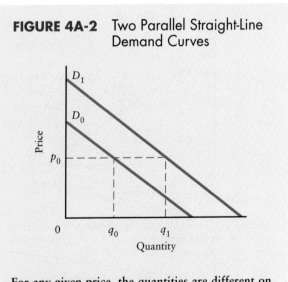

FIGURE 4A-2   Two Parallel Straight-Line Demand Curves

For any given price, the quantities are different on these two parallel curves; thus the elasticities are different, being higher on D_0 than on D_1.

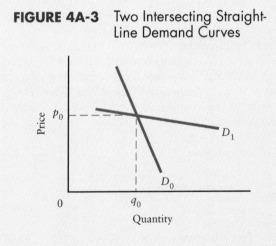

FIGURE 4A-3   Two Intersecting Straight-Line Demand Curves

Elasticities are different at the point of intersection of these demand curves because the slopes are different, being higher on D_0 than on D_1. Therefore, D_1 is more elastic than D_0 at p_0.

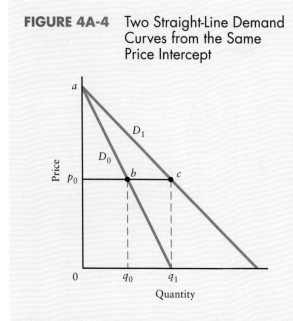

FIGURE 4A-4 Two Straight-Line Demand Curves from the Same Price Intercept

The elasticity is the same on D_0 and D_1 at any given price. This situation occurs because the steeper slope of D_0 is exactly offset by the smaller quantity demanded at any price.

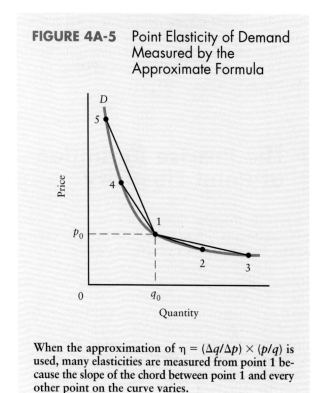

FIGURE 4A-5 Point Elasticity of Demand Measured by the Approximate Formula

When the approximation of $\eta = (\Delta q/\Delta p) \times (p/q)$ is used, many elasticities are measured from point 1 because the slope of the chord between point 1 and every other point on the curve varies.

curve, $\Delta q/\Delta p$ is smaller than on the flatter curve, so elasticity is lower.

If the slope of a straight-line demand curve changes while the price intercept remains constant, elasticity at any given price is unchanged.

This case is interesting for at least two reasons. First, when more customers having similar tastes to those already in the market enter the market, the demand curve pivots outward in this way. Second, when more firms enter a market that is shared proportionally among all firms, each firm's demand curve shifts inward in this way.

Consider in Figure 4A-4 the elasticities at point b on demand curve D_0 and at point c on demand curve D_1. We shall focus on the two triangles abp_0 on D_0 and acp_0 on D_1 formed by the two straight-line demand curves emanating from point a and by the price p_0. The price p_0 is the line segment $0p_0$. The quantities q_0 and q_1 are the line segments $p_0 b$ and $p_0 c$, respectively. The slope of D_0 is $\Delta p/\Delta q = ap_0/p_0 b$, and the slope of D_1 is $\Delta p/\Delta q = ap_0/p_0 c$. From Equation 4A-1 we can

represent the elasticities of D_0 and D_1 at the points b and c, respectively, as

$$\eta \text{ at point } b = (p_0 b/ap_0) \times (0p_0/p_0 b) = (0p_0/ap_0)$$
$$\eta \text{ at point } c = (p_0 c/ap_0) \times (0p_0/p_0 c) = (0p_0/ap_0)$$

Because the distance corresponding to the quantity demanded at p_0 appears in both the numerator and the denominator and thus cancels out, the two values of the elasticity are the same. Put differently, if the straight-line demand curve D_0 is twice as steep as D_1, it has half the quantity demanded at p_0. Therefore, in Equation 4A-1 the steeper slope (a smaller Δq for the same Δp) is exactly offset by the smaller quantity demanded (a smaller q for the same p).

The demand elasticity measured from any point, according to Equation 4A-1, depends on the direction and magnitude of the change in price and quantity.

Except for a straight line (for which the slope does not change), the ratio $\Delta q/\Delta p$ will not be the same over different ranges of a curve. Figure 4A-5 shows a demand curve that is not a straight line. To measure the elasticity from point 1, the ratio $\Delta q/\Delta p$—and thus η—will vary according to the size and the direction of the price change. This result is very inconvenient; we can avoid it by using the concept of point elasticity in its exact form.

The Precise Definition of Point Elasticity

To measure the point elasticity *exactly,* it is necessary to know the reaction of quantity to a change in price *at that point,* not over a range of the curve.

The reaction of quantity to price change at a point is called dq/dp, and this is defined as the reciprocal of the slope of the straight line tangent to the demand curve at the point in question. In Figure 4A-6, the elasticity of demand at point 1 is the ratio p/q (as it has been in all previous measures), now multiplied by the ratio of $\Delta q/\Delta p$ measured along the straight line T, tangent to the curve at point 1, that is, by dq/dp. Thus the exact definition of point elasticity is

$$\eta = \frac{dq}{dp} \times \frac{p}{q} \qquad (4A\text{-}2)$$

The ratio dq/dp, as defined, is in fact the differential calculus concept of the *derivative* of quantity with respect to price.

This definition of point elasticity is the one normally used in economic theory. Equation 4A-1 is mathematically only an approximation of this expression. In Figure 4A-6, the measure of arc elasticity will come

FIGURE 4A-6   Point Elasticity of Demand Measured by the Exact Formula

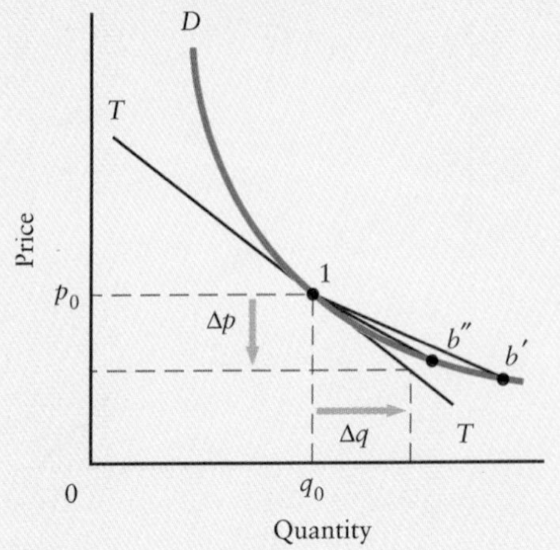

When the exact definition $\eta = (dq/dp) \times (p/q)$ is used, only one elasticity is measured from point 1 because there is only one tangent to the demand curve at that point.

closer to the measure of point elasticity as a smaller price change is used to calculate the arc elasticity. The $\Delta q/\Delta p$ in Equation 4A-1 is the reciprocal of the slope of the chord connecting the two points being compared. As the chord becomes shorter, its slope gets closer to that of the tangent T. (Compare the chords connecting point 1 to b' and b'' in Figure 4A-6.) Thus the error in using Equation 4A-1 as an approximation of Equation 4A-2 tends to diminish as the size of Δp diminishes.

CHAPTER 5

Markets in Action

LEARNING OBJECTIVES

1 Understand that individual markets do not exist in isolation, and that changes in one market typically have repercussions in other markets.

2 Understand the operation of a market that is subject to price ceilings or price floors.

3 Recognize who benefits and who loses from price controls.

4 Recognize legislated rent controls as an example of a price ceiling.

5 Understand the different short-run and long-run effects of such controls.

6 Examine various ways that governments intervene in agricultural markets in an effort to both stabilize and raise farmers' incomes.

Over the past two chapters, we have developed the model of demand and supply that you can now use to analyse individual markets. A full understanding of the basic theory, however, comes only with practice. This chapter is designed to give you such practice by examining some cases drawn from real-world experience. We explore the effects of legislated minimum wages, rent controls, and agricultural income-support policies.

Before examining these cases, however, we begin the chapter by discussing how various markets are related to each other. In Chapters 3 and 4, we used the simple demand-and-supply model to describe a single market, ignoring what was going on in other markets. For example, when we examined the market for carrots, we made no mention of the markets for inline skates, milk, or CD players. In other words, we viewed the market for carrots in isolation from all other markets. But this was only a simplification. In this chapter's opening section we note that the economy should *not* be viewed as a series of isolated markets. Rather, the economy is a complex system of interlocking markets. The implication of this complex structure is that events that lead to changes in one market typically lead to changes in other markets as well.

The Interaction Among Markets

Suppose there is an advance made in the methods for extracting natural gas. This technological improvement would be represented as a rightward shift in the supply curve for natural gas. The equilibrium price of natural gas would fall and there would be an increase in the equilibrium quantity exchanged.

How would other markets be affected? As natural-gas firms expand their production, they would increase their demand for the entire range of goods and services necessary for the extraction, processing, pumping, and distribution of natural gas. This increase in demand would raise the prices of those items, and lead the producers of those goods to devote more resources to their production. The natural-gas firms would also increase their demand for labour, since more workers would be required to drill for and extract more natural gas. The increase in demand for labour would tend to push wages up. Firms that hire similar workers in other industries would have to pay higher wages to retain their workers, and the profits of those firms would fall.

There also would be a direct effect on consumers. The reduction in the equilibrium price of natural gas would generate some substitution away from other fuels, such as oil or propane, and toward the now-lower-priced natural gas. Such reductions in demand would tend to push down the price of oil and propane, and producers of those fuels would devote fewer resources to their production.

In short, a technological improvement in the natural gas industry would have effects in many other markets. But there is nothing special about the natural gas industry. The same would be true about a change in almost any market you can think of.

No market or industry exists in isolation from the economy's many other markets.

Partial and General Equilibrium

As we have just seen, a change in one market will lead to changes in many other markets. But the induced changes in these other markets will, in turn, lead to changes in the first market. This is what economists call *feedback*. In the example of the natural gas industry, we argued that the reduction in the price of natural gas would lead consumers to reduce their demand for oil and propane, thus driving down the prices of these other fuels. But when we consider the demand and supply curves for natural gas, we assume that the *prices of all other goods are constant*. So, when the prices of oil and propane fall, the feedback effect on the natural gas market is to shift the demand curve for natural gas to the left (because natural gas is a substitute for both oil and propane).

Predicting the precise size of this feedback effect is difficult, and the analysis of the natural gas industry—or any other industry—would certainly be much easier if we could ignore it. But we cannot always ignore such feedback effects. Economists make a distinction between cases where the feedback effects are small enough that they can safely be ignored, and cases where the feedback effects are large enough that ignoring them would significantly change the analysis.

partial-equilibrium analysis The analysis of a single market in isolation, taking as given the outcomes in all other markets.

Partial-equilibrium analysis is the analysis of a single market in situations where the feedback effects from other markets are ignored. This is the type of analysis that we have used so far in this book, and it is the most common type of analysis in microeconomics. For example, when we examined the market for cigarettes at the end of Chapter 4, we ignored any potential feedback effects that could have come from the market for alcohol, coffee, or many other goods or services. In this case, we used partial-equilibrium analysis, focusing only on the market for cigarettes, because we assumed that the changes in the cigarette market would produce small enough changes on the other markets that the feedback effects from the other markets would, in turn, be sufficiently diffused that we could safely ignore them. This suggests the general rule for when partial-equilibrium analysis is a legitimate method of analysis.

If a specific market is quite small relative to the entire economy, changes in the market will have relatively small effects on other markets. The feedback effects on the original market will, in turn, be very diffuse. In such cases, partial-equilibrium analysis can successfully be used to analyse the original market.

When economists study all markets together, rather than a single market in isolation, they use what is called **general-equilibrium analysis**. This is naturally more complicated than partial-equilibrium analysis because the economist must consider not only what is happening in each individual market but also must take into account how events in each market affect all the other markets.

General-equilibrium analysis is the study of how all markets function together, taking into account the various relationships and feedback effects between individual markets.

If you go on to take advanced courses in economics, especially at the graduate level, you will study general-equilibrium analysis in considerable detail. In this section of the chapter, however, we limit the discussion to one simple but important message: when events lead to changes in one market, there are typically changes caused in other markets as well. We examine three broad reasons that markets may be connected—*regional* linkages, *input-output* linkages, and linkages through a *resource constraint*.

general-equilibrium analysis The analysis of all the economy's markets simultaneously, recognizing the interactions among the various markets.

Regional Linkages

How are geographically separate markets connected? We examine two different linkages. In the first, *mobile supply* is what links the markets; in the second, the linkage is provided by *mobile demand*.

Mobile Supply

By mobility of supply we mean the ease with which suppliers can move their products from one market to another. This mobility depends on the product in question and the distance between the two markets. If the product is very costly to transport (like gravel or cement) and the markets are far apart (like British Columbia and Nova Scotia) then the two markets will be separate. But if the product is inexpensive to transport (like computer chips or leather gloves) and the markets are close together (like Ottawa and Toronto) then the two markets will be closely linked. Consider the following example that illustrates how mobile supply can link regional markets.

In August 1992, Hurricane Andrew struck the Florida coast and caused a great deal of damage to buildings and houses. As soon as the hurricane was over, the process of rebuilding began. This caused a sharp increase in the demand for plywood for rebuilding roofs and covering windows. The predicted excess demand and price increase occurred in Florida almost immediately.

But the economic effects of the hurricane were not confined to Florida. As the price of plywood soared in Florida, suppliers from other regions of the country directed their plywood shipments toward high-price Florida. This reduction in supply in the other regions caused shortages and led to price increases. Builders across the country were forced to adjust to more expensive plywood—prices increased by 18 percent in just two weeks. This situation is illustrated in Figure 5-1.

Mobile Demand

Now consider a situation in which it is prohibitively expensive to transport a product (immobile supply) but demand can move relatively easily. This would be the case, for example, in the housing market in two residential neighbourhoods that are close together.

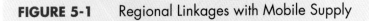

FIGURE 5-1   Regional Linkages with Mobile Supply

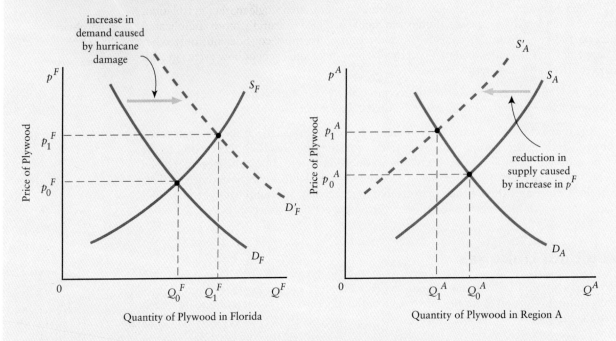

Quantity of Plywood in Florida

Quantity of Plywood in Region A

When the supply of a product is mobile between regions, prices in regional markets tend to move together. The initial equilibrium in Florida is p_0^F and Q_0^F; in some other region, denoted Region A, it is p_0^A and Q_0^A. The hurricane leads to an increase in demand for plywood in Florida and thus drives prices in Florida up to p_1^F. The supply curve in Region A, however, is drawn *for a given price of plywood in Florida* since supplying to Florida is a substitute to supplying Region A. The increase in p^F therefore reduces the supply in Region A. This reduction in supply (the shift from S_A to S'_A) shows up as part of the increase in quantity supplied in Florida (the movement along S_F). The supply reduction in Region A increases price to p_1^A. The two markets are linked through the mobility of supply, and the prices in the two markets move together.

Practise with Study Guide Chapter 5, Exercise 1.

It is obviously very expensive to move a house from one neighbourhood to another, and it is not easy to build new houses in the short run. So we can think of these two neighbourhoods as each having very inelastic short-run supplies of housing. Demand, in contrast, may be relatively mobile between the two neighbourhoods since living in one neighbourhood may be viewed as a reasonable substitute to living in the other.

Suppose that Neighbourhood A experiences a substantial increase in demand for housing, perhaps because its schools are widely reported to be of very high quality. Further, suppose that the increase in demand for housing in Neighbourhood A comes from families currently living in faraway neighbourhoods. This increase in demand will naturally create an excess demand and thus raise housing prices in Neighbourhood A. As prices rise there, however, some of the potential homeowners get crowded out by the price increases and they begin to look more favourably at houses in nearby Neighbourhood B, where prices are not rising. The shift in demand toward Neighbourhood B then creates excess demand and so prices rise there as well. Figure 5-2 illustrates this example.

The Role of Substitution

In both of the previous examples, *substitution* plays a key role in linking the regional markets. Indeed, substitution is just another word for the *mobility* of demand and supply. In

FIGURE 5-2   Regional Linkages with Mobile Demand

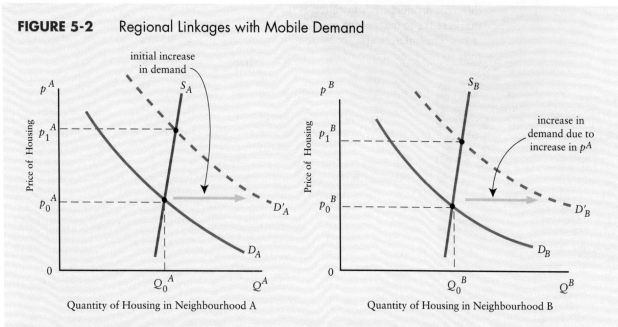

Quantity of Housing in Neighbourhood A

Quantity of Housing in Neighbourhood B

When demand for a product is mobile between regions, prices in regional markets tend to move together. The initial equilibrium in Neighbourhood A is Q_0^A and p_0^A; the equilibrium in Neighbourhood B is Q_0^B and p_0^B. Demand increases in Neighbourhood A to D'_A (coming from faraway neighbourhoods, not including B) and raises the price to p_1^A. As price increases in Neighbourhood A, some of the new demand gets crowded out and switches over to the houses in nearby Neighbourhood B. The reduction in quantity demanded along D'_A becomes the increase in Neighbourhood B's demand curve to D'_B. The regional markets are linked and the prices in the two markets move together.

the plywood example, firms viewed selling plywood in Florida as a substitute for selling plywood in other regions. In the housing example, consumers viewed buying houses in Neighbourhood B as a substitute for buying houses in Neighbourhood A.

Linkages between regional markets are determined by substitutability, either in demand or supply. The degree of substitutability, in turn, is determined by transport costs and the nature of the products.

In the plywood example, the degree of substitutability of supply—and thus the extent of the linkage between markets—is determined by the cost of transporting the plywood relative to its price. The more costly it is to transport, the less willing firms will be to move the plywood between regions. At some high level of transport costs, it will no longer pay suppliers to move the plywood, and the regional markets will not be linked together.

In the housing example, the degree of substitutability of demand—and thus the extent of the linkage between markets—is determined by the attributes of the housing in each neighbourhood (and by the characteristics of the neighbourhoods themselves). If living in Neighbourhood A is viewed by consumers as being very similar to living in Neighbourhood B, then the markets will be linked. If the two neighbourhoods are viewed as offering completely different living experiences, the markets will not be linked together.

Input-Output Linkages

We have considered cases where regional markets of the same product are linked through the mobility of supply or demand. Now think about linkages between markets of very different products. For instance, is the market for anchovies linked in any way to the beef market? Is the market for glass linked to the market for cars? The answer in both cases is yes. The linkages arise because some products (like anchovies and glass) are used as *inputs* to the production of other products (like beef and cars, respectively).

Anything that significantly increases the price of cattle feed will also increase the price of beef.

Changes in the price of one product lead to similar changes in the prices of goods that use that product as an input.

Consider the following example dealing with anchovies and cattle that is illustrated in Figure 5-3. One important use of anchovies (besides being used in Caesar salads and as a topping for pizza) is as a protein supplement for livestock, especially beef cattle. In 1973, partly as a result of the unusual weather associated with the cyclical recurrence of El Niño, there was a sharp reduction in the Peruvian anchovy catch. Since Peru was a large producer of anchovies, the decline in Peru's catch led to a significant decline in the world's supply of anchovies, which then pushed up anchovy prices. The higher price of anchovies, in turn, sharply increased the price of cattle-feed. The increased cost of the cattle-feed then led to a reduction in the supply of beef cattle. Prices for beef increased. The anchovy market and beef markets were linked, with the prices of the two products moving together.

FIGURE 5-3   Input-Output Market Linkages

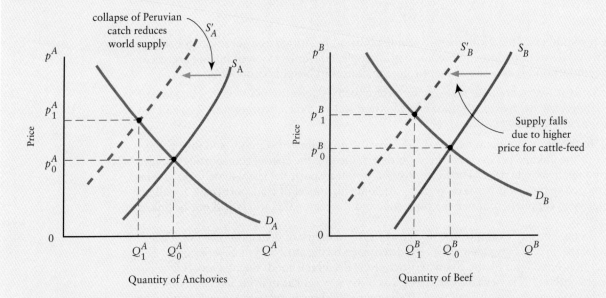

Quantity of Anchovies

Quantity of Beef

Changes in the price of inputs lead to similar changes in the prices of outputs. The initial equilibrium is Q_0^A and p_0^A in the anchovy market, and Q_0^B and p_0^B in the beef market. When El Niño leads to a reduction in the Peruvian anchovy catch, the world supply of anchovies shifts from S_A to S'_A. The shortage pushes anchovy prices up to p_1^A. The supply curve for beef is drawn for a given price of cattle-feed. As the price of cattle-feed rises (because it includes anchovies), the supply of beef shifts from S_B to S'_B. This reduction in the supply of beef causes beef shortages and price increases.

This example may seem like an unusual one but the principle involved is very general. An increase in the price of one product generally leads to price increases for all goods using that product as an input. Through such input-output linkages, we can better understand co-movements in the prices of many products, including electricity and aluminum, wheat and poultry, rubber and running shoes, fertilizer and agricultural crops, and steel and automobiles.

Linkages Through Resource Constraints

Are the markets for restaurant meals and clothing linked in any way? How about the markets for corporate jets and automobiles? In both cases, the products are clearly different and there are no obvious input-output linkages. Even though there may be none of the obvious regional or input-output linkages that we have been discussing, these seemingly unrelated markets are indeed linked, though the nature of the linkage is subtle.

Even seemingly unrelated markets are linked through resource constraints.

There are two ways to think of the resource constraints linking markets. The first is a demand-side constraint, the second is a supply-side constraint.

Demand-Side Resource Constraints

Consumers have only so much income they can spend. Even if they decide to borrow (so that they can spend in excess of their income) they must divide their total expenditure between housing, food, clothing, education, travel, entertainment, and so on. Thus, an extra $100 spent on restaurant meals must imply a reduction in spending on something else. As we saw in Chapter 1, this need for the consumer to make choices exists because of scarcity.

The scarcity faced by consumers implies that many apparently unrelated markets are actually linked together. If consumers with a constant amount of income increase their demand for chicken, they are probably decreasing their demand for beef or pork. If they increase their demand for movie tickets, they are probably reducing their demand for concerts or other forms of entertainment. If they increase their demand for airplane tickets, they are likely reducing their demand for railway or bus tickets. These linked demand changes will have effects on prices and resource allocation that you should by now be able to analyse.

Supply-Side Resource Constraints

Restaurants and theatres compete against each other for the consumer's entertainment dollar. But how about products that are arguably not in competition with each other? Surely consumers do not view corporate jets as a substitute for automobiles, or hospitals as a substitute for bridges. Though it may be true that consumers view the degree of substitutability between such products as negligible, the markets for these goods are still linked through supply-side resource constraints.

In an economy with fully employed resources, devoting more resources to producing one product must imply devoting fewer resources to producing other products.

In other words, for a given level of technology and a given amount of resources, an increase in the supply of one product must imply a reduction in the supply of some other product. This is nothing more than a restatement of what we first encountered in Chapter 1 when we described a country's production possibilities boundary. But it is surprising how often this fundamental point is either ignored or forgotten in public debate.

One of the best examples of how this supply-side constraint is ignored in public debate is the often-heard government claim that a specific program in one industry—such as a subsidy or a tax incentive—has "created jobs." The alleged proof of the claim is that the level of employment in the assisted industry is higher after the subsidy than before. But where did these new jobs come from?

Figure 5-4 shows how this situation can be analysed. The basic story is as follows. Suppose the government chooses to subsidize firms in the aerospace industry (as they have in Canada for many years). A government subsidy to aerospace firms leads those firms to expand production and increase their demand for workers. Employment in the aerospace industry will therefore increase. But those workers must come from somewhere. In particular, those workers must be drawn away from other industries, and the way this happens is through an increase in wages. The increase in demand for labour in the subsidized aerospace industry drives up the wage in that industry. As the wage rises, workers in other industries are attracted to the aerospace industry (this is the movement along the labour supply curve for the aerospace industry). But as these workers move toward the aerospace industry, there is a reduction in the supply of labour to all other industries. Thus the "created jobs" in the subsidized aerospace industry are only possible

FIGURE 5-4   Supply-Side Resource Constraints

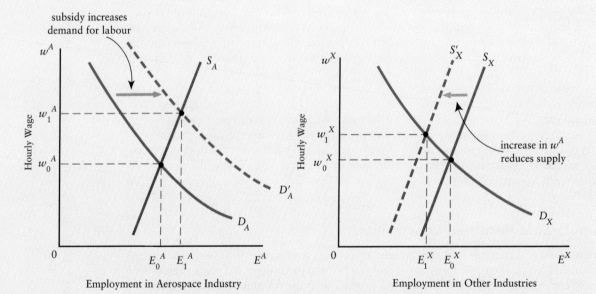

With given total supply of labour, an increase in employment in one industry must be matched by a decrease in other industries. The figure shows the two labour markets, one for the aerospace industry and the other for all other industries combined. The initial equilibrium is E_0^A and w_0^A in the aerospace industry and E_0^X and w_0^X in the other industries. When the government subsidizes firms in the aerospace industry, the demand for labour increases from D_A to D'_A. This pushes up wages in the aerospace industry and attracts workers from other industries. But, as workers move to the aerospace industry, the supply of labour to other industries falls from S_X to S'_X. This raises wages and leads to a reduction in employment in other industries. The jobs that are "created" in the aerospace industry are matched by "destroyed" jobs in other industries.

because of the "destroyed jobs" in other industries. Jobs do get created in the aerospace industry, but no new jobs get created *in the economy as a whole*.

We have just suggested that government efforts to stimulate total employment by assisting particular industries are ineffective, since the economy's resource constraint implies that any job gains in one part of the economy must be matched by job losses elsewhere. Keep in mind, however, that we have been considering an economy in which resources are fully employed, so that the economy is on the production possibility boundary. But this is not always the case. When you go on to study macroeconomics, you will learn that the economy is sometimes *inside* the production possibilities boundary because it has idle resources, the most important of which is probably unemployed labour. In such cases, government efforts to "create jobs" might have the intended effect since some of the newly employed workers in the assisted industry could come from the pool of unemployed workers. But even in such cases, this supply-side resource constraint is important. Except in extreme situations, the increase in employment in the assisted industries will overstate the increase in *total* employment because *some* of the new workers will come from other industries.

See Chapter 5 of www.pearsoned.ca/lipsey for an interview with Laurent Beaudoin, the Chairman of Bombardier, Canada's leading aerospace firm: "Trade and Subsidies in the Air," *World Economic Affairs.*

A Final Word

We began this section of the chapter by noting the difference between *partial-equilibrium analysis*, which is the study of one market in isolation, and *general-equilibrium analysis*, which is the study of all markets together. We then went on to examine how markets are linked together. By this point you should be fairly comfortable thinking about how various markets might relate to each other. Though we did not go all to way to developing formal general-equilibrium analysis, the basic point of this section has been both useful and simple: when changes occur in one market, there are generally related changes occurring in other markets.

As you go on to learn more microeconomics in this and later chapters, you will encounter mostly partial-equilibrium analysis. The book is written this way intentionally—it is easier to learn about the basic ideas of monopoly, competition policy, labour unions, and environmental policy (as well as many other topics) by restricting our attention to a single market. But keep in mind what we have seen in this section—there are many other markets "behind the scenes" that are linked in various ways to the individual markets we choose to study.

We now go on to examine the effects of government-controlled prices. These appear prominently in labour markets, rental housing markets, and agricultural markets.

Government-Controlled Prices

In a number of important cases, governments fix the price at which a product must be bought and sold in the domestic market. Here we examine the general consequences of such policies. Later, we look at some specific examples.

The equilibrium price in a free market occurs at the price at which quantity demanded equals quantity supplied. Government *price controls* are policies that attempt to hold the price at some disequilibrium value. Some controls hold the market price below its equilibrium value, thus creating a shortage at the controlled price. Other controls hold price above the equilibrium price, thus creating a surplus at the controlled price.

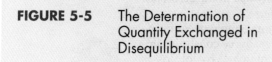

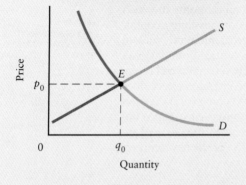

In disequilibrium, quantity exchanged is determined by the lesser of quantity demanded and quantity supplied. At p_0, the market is in equilibrium, with quantity demanded equal to quantity supplied. For prices below p_0, the quantity exchanged will be determined by the supply curve. For prices above p_0, the quantity exchanged will be determined by the demand curve. Thus the darker portions of the S and D curves show the actual quantities exchanged at different disequilibrium prices.

FIGURE 5-6   A Binding Price Floor

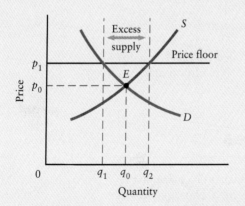

A binding price floor leads to excess supply. The free-market equilibrium is at E, with price p_0 and quantity q_0. The government now establishes an effective (binding) price floor at p_1. The result is excess supply equal to q_1q_2.

Disequilibrium Prices

When controls hold price at some disequilibrium value, what determines the quantity *actually traded* on the market? This is not a question we have to ask when examining a free market because the price adjusts to equate quantity demanded with quantity supplied. But this adjustment cannot take place if the government is controlling the price. So, in this case, what determines the quantity actually exchanged?

The key to the answer is the fact that any *voluntary* market transaction requires both a willing buyer and a willing seller. So, if quantity demanded is less than quantity supplied, demand will determine the amount actually exchanged, while the rest of the quantity supplied will remain in the hands of the unsuccessful sellers. Conversely, if quantity demanded exceeds quantity supplied, supply will determine the amount actually exchanged, while the rest of the quantity demanded will represent unsatisfied demand of unsuccessful buyers. This argument is spelled out in more detail in Figure 5-5, which establishes the following general conclusion:

At any disequilibrium price, quantity exchanged is determined by the *lesser* of quantity demanded or quantity supplied.

Price Floors

Governments sometimes establish a *price floor,* which is the minimum permissible price that can be charged for a particular good or service. A price floor that is set at or below the equilibrium price has no effect because the free-market equilibrium remains attainable. If, however, the price floor is set above the equilibrium, it will raise the price, in which case it is said to be *binding* or *effective.*

Price floors may be established by rules that make it illegal to sell the product below the prescribed price, as in the case of a legislated minimum wage. Or the government may establish a price floor by announcing that it will guarantee a certain price by buying any excess supply. Such guarantees are a feature of many agricultural support policies.

The effects of a binding price floor are illustrated in Figure 5-6, which establishes the following key result:

Effective price floors lead to excess supply. Either an unsold surplus will exist, or someone (usually the government) must enter the market and buy the excess supply.

The consequences of excess supply differ from product to product. If the product is labour, subject to a minimum wage, excess supply translates into people without jobs (unemployment). If the product is wheat, and more is produced than can be sold to consumers, the surplus wheat will accumulate in grain elevators or government warehouses. These consequences may or may not be worthwhile in terms of the other goals achieved. But worthwhile or not, these consequences are inevitable whenever a price floor is set above the market-clearing equilibrium price.

Why might the government wish to incur these consequences? One reason is that the people who succeed in selling their products at the price floor are better off than if they had to accept the lower equilibrium price. Workers and farmers are among the politically active, organized groups who have gained much by persuading the government to establish price floors that enable them to sell their goods or services at prices above free-market levels. The losses are spread across the large and diverse set of purchasers, each of whom suffers only a small loss (although the *total* loss can be considerable).

Applying Economic Concepts 5-1 examines the case of a legislated minimum wage in more detail, and explains the basis of the often-heard claim that minimum wages increase unemployment. We discuss the effects of minimum wages in greater detail in Chapter 14 when we examine various labour-market issues.

For information on various labour-market policies in Canada, see HRDC's website: www.labour-travail.hrdc-drhc.gc.ca. Then click on "Labour Program."

Price Ceilings

A *price ceiling* is the maximum price at which certain goods and services may be exchanged. Price controls on oil, natural gas, and rental housing have been frequently imposed by federal and provincial governments. If the price ceiling is set above the equilibrium price, it has no effect because the free-market equilibrium remains attainable. If, however, the price ceiling is set below the free-market equilibrium price, the price ceiling lowers the price and is said to be *binding* or *effective*. The effects of binding price ceilings are shown in Figure 5-7, which establishes the following conclusion:

Effective price ceilings lead to excess demand, with the quantity exchanged being less than in the free-market equilibrium.

Allocating a Product in Excess Demand

The free market eliminates excess demand by allowing prices to rise, thereby allocating the available supply among would-be purchasers. Because this adjustment cannot happen in the presence of a binding price ceiling, some other method of allocation must be adopted. Experience suggests what we can expect.

If stores sell their available supplies on a *first-come, first-served* basis, then people will rush to stores that are said to have stocks of the product. Buyers may wait hours to get into the store, only to find that supplies are exhausted before they can be served. This is why standing in lines became a way of life in the command economies of the Soviet Union and Eastern Europe in which price controls were pervasive.

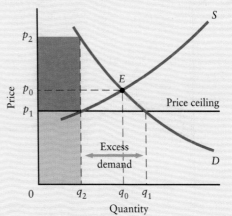

FIGURE 5-7   A Price Ceiling and Black-Market Pricing

An effective price ceiling causes excess demand and invites a black market. Equilibrium price is at p_0. If a price ceiling is set at p_1, the quantity demanded will rise to q_1 and the quantity supplied will fall to q_2. Quantity actually exchanged will be q_2. But if all the available supply of q_2 were sold on a black market, the price to consumers would rise to p_2, with black marketeers earning receipts shown by the two shaded areas. Because they buy at the ceiling price of p_1 and sell at the black-market price of p_2, profits of the black marketeers are represented by the dark shaded area.

APPLYING ECONOMIC CONCEPTS 5-1

Minimum Wages and Unemployment

All Canadian governments, provincial and federal, have legislated minimum wages. For those industries covered by provincial legislation (which includes most industries except banking, airlines, trucking, and railways), the minimum wage in 1999 ranged from a low of $5.40 per hour in Prince Edward Island to a high of $7.20 per hour in the Yukon. This box examines the effects of implementing a minimum wage in a competitive labour market, and provides a basis for understanding the often-heard claim that minimum wages lead to an increase in unemployment.

The accompanying figure shows the demand and supply curves for labour services, with "Employment" on the horizontal axis and "Hourly Wage Rate" on the vertical axis. In the absence of any legislated minimum wage, the equilibrium in the labour market would be a wage equal to w_0 and a level of employment equal to E_0.

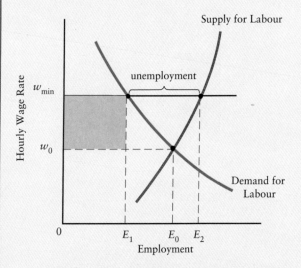

Now suppose the government introduces a minimum wage equal to w_{min} which is greater than w_0. The increased wage has two effects. First, by increasing the cost of labour services, the minimum wage reduces the level of

employment to E_1. The second effect is to increase the quantity supplied of labour services to E_2. Thus, the clear effect of the binding minimum wage, as seen in the figure, is to generate unemployment—workers that want a job but are unable to get one—equal to the amount E_1E_2.

Who does this policy benefit? And who does it harm? Firms are clearly made worse off since they are now required to pay a higher wage than before the minimum wage was imposed. They respond to this increase in costs by reducing their use of labour. On the other hand, some—but not all—workers are made better off. The workers who are lucky enough to keep their jobs—E_1 workers in the figure—get a higher wage than before. The shaded area shows the redistribution of income away from firms and toward these fortunate workers. But some workers are also harmed by the policy—the ones who lose their jobs as a result of the wage increase, shown in the figure as the quantity E_1E_0. Even though some people are made better off while others are harmed by the legislated minimum wage, the overall effect is to make the economy as a whole *worse off*. Unfortunately, to understand this overall effect we must wait until Chapter 12 when we introduce the notion of *allocative efficiency*.

We have discussed here the effects of minimum wages in a *competitive* labour market—one in which there are many firms and many workers, none of whom have the power to influence the market wage. In Chapter 14 we will examine minimum wages in more detail, and will see that if there are a small number of firms in the labour market using their "market power" to reduce the wage, then a binding minimum wage may actually increase employment and improve economic efficiency. This different behaviour of competitive and non-competitive markets in the presence of minimum wages probably accounts for the disagreements among economists and policymakers regarding the desirability of minimum-wage legislation. Until we proceed to that more advanced discussion, however, the analysis of a competitive labour market in this box provides an excellent example of the economic effects of a binding price floor in specific circumstances.

In market economies, "first-come, first-served" is often the basis for allocating tickets to concerts and sporting events when promoters set a price at which demand exceeds the supply of available seats. In these cases, an illegal market often develops, in which ticket "scalpers" resell tickets at market-clearing prices. Storekeepers (and some ticket sellers) often respond to excess demand by keeping goods "under the counter" and selling only to customers of their own choosing. When sellers decide to whom they will and will not sell their scarce supplies, allocation is said to be by **sellers' preferences.**

If the government dislikes these allocation systems, it can choose to ration the product. To do so, it prints only enough ration coupons to match the quantity supplied at the price ceiling and then distributes the coupons to would-be purchasers, who then need both money and coupons to buy the product. The coupons may be distributed equally among the population or on the basis of some criterion such as age, family status, or occupation. Rationing of this sort was used by Canada and many other countries during both the First and Second World Wars.

Black Markets

Price ceilings usually give rise to black markets. A **black market** is any market in which goods are sold illegally at prices that violate a legal price control.

Effective price ceilings create the potential for a black market because a profit can be made by buying at the controlled price and selling at the black-market price.

Figure 5-7 illustrates the extreme case in which all the available supply is sold on a black market. We say this case is extreme because there are law-abiding people in every society and because governments ordinarily have at least *some* power to enforce their price ceilings. Although some of a product subject to an effective price ceiling will be sold on the black market, it is unlikely that all of that product will be.

Does the existence of a black market mean that the goals sought by imposing price ceilings have been thwarted? The answer depends on what the goals are. A government might have three main goals for imposing a price ceiling.

1. To restrict production (perhaps to release resources for other uses, such as wartime military production)

2. To keep specific prices down

3. To satisfy notions of equity in the consumption of a product that is temporarily in short supply

When price ceilings are accompanied by a black market, only the first objective is achieved. Black markets clearly frustrate the second objective. Effective price ceilings on manufacturers in addition to an extensive black market at the retail level may produce the opposite of the third goal. There will be less to go around than if there were no controls, and the available quantities will tend to go to the people with the most money or the least social conscience.

Rent Controls: A Case Study of Price Ceilings

For long periods over this century, rent controls have existed in London, Paris, New York, and many other large cities. In Sweden and Britain, where rent controls on apartments existed for decades, shortages of rental accommodations were chronic. When rent controls were initiated in Ontario in 1975 and Rome in 1978, severe housing shortages developed, especially in those areas where demand was rising.

Rent controls provide a vivid illustration of the short- and long-term effects of this type of market intervention. Note, however, that the specifics of rent-control laws vary

sellers' preferences
Allocation of commodities in excess demand by decisions of the sellers.

black market
A situation in which goods are sold illegally at prices that violate a legal price control.

Practise with Study Guide Chapter 5, Exercise 3.

greatly and have changed significantly since they were first imposed many decades ago. In particular, current laws often permit exemptions for new buildings and allowances for maintenance costs and inflation. Moreover, in many countries rent controls have evolved into a "second generation" of legislation that focuses more on *regulating* the rental housing market than simply *controlling the price* of rental accommodation.

In this section, we confine ourselves to an analysis of rent controls that are aimed primarily at holding the price of rental housing below the free-market equilibrium value. It is this "first generation" of rent controls which produced serious results in cities like London, Paris, New York, and Toronto.

The Predicted Effects of Rent Controls

Binding rent controls are a specific case of price ceilings and therefore Figure 5-7 can be used to predict some of their effects:

1. There will be a housing shortage in the sense that quantity demanded will exceed quantity supplied. Since rents are held below their free-market levels, the available quantity of rental housing will be less than if free-market rents had been charged.

2. The shortage will lead to alternative allocation schemes. Landlords may allocate by sellers' preferences, or the government may intervene, often through security-of-tenure laws, which protect tenants from eviction and thereby give them priority over prospective new tenants.

3. Black markets will appear. For example, landlords may require large "entrance fees" from new tenants, which reflect the difference in value between the free-market and the controlled rents. In the absence of security-of-tenure laws, landlords may force tenants out when their leases expire in order to extract a large entrance fee from new tenants.

The unique feature of rent controls, however, as compared to price controls in general, is that they are applied to a highly *durable good* that provides services to consumers for a long period of time. Once built, an apartment can be used for decades. As a result, the immediate effects of rent control are typically quite different from the long-term effects.

The short-run supply response to the imposition of rent controls is quite limited. Some conversions of apartment units to condominiums (that are not covered by the rent-control legislation) may occur but the quantity of apartments does not change much. The short-run supply curve for rental housing is therefore quite *inelastic*.

In the long run, however, the supply response to rent controls can be quite dramatic. If the expected return from building new rental housing falls significantly below what can be earned on comparable investments, funds will go elsewhere. New construction will be halted, and old buildings will be converted to other uses, or will simply be left to deteriorate. Thus the long-run supply curve of rental accommodations is highly *elastic*.

Figure 5-8 illustrates the housing shortage that worsens as time passes under rent control. Because the short-run supply of housing is inelastic, the controlled rent causes only a moderate housing shortage in the short run. Indeed, most of the shortage comes from an increase in the quantity demanded rather than from a reduction in quantity supplied. As time passes, however, fewer new apartments are built, more conversions take place, and older buildings are not replaced (and not repaired) as they wear out. As a result, the quantity supplied shrinks steadily.

Along with the growing housing shortage comes an increasingly inefficient use of rental accommodation space. Existing tenants will have an incentive to stay where they are even though their family size, location of employment, or economic circumstances may change. Since they cannot move without giving up their low-rent accommodation, some may accept lower-paying jobs nearby to avoid the necessity for moving. Thus a situation will arise in which existing tenants will hang on to accommodation even if it is poorly suited to their needs while new individuals and families will be unable to find any rental accommodation except at black-market prices.

The province of Ontario instituted rent controls in 1975 and tightened them on at least two subsequent occasions. The controls permitted significant increases in rents only where these were needed to pass on cost increases. As a result, the restrictive effects of rent controls were felt mainly in areas where demand was increasing rapidly (as opposed to areas where only costs were increasing rapidly).

During the mid and late 1990s, the population of Ontario grew substantially but the stock of rental housing did not keep pace. A shortage developed in the rental-housing market, and was especially acute in Metro Toronto. This growing housing shortage led the Ontario government in 1997 to loosen rent controls, in particular by allowing landlords to increase the rent as much as they saw fit *but only as tenants vacated the apartment.* Not surprisingly, this policy had both critics and supporters. Supporters argued that a loosening of controls would encourage the construction of apartments and thus help to reduce the housing shortage. Critics argued that landlords would harass existing tenants, forcing them to move out so that rents could be increased for incoming tenants. (Indeed, this exact behaviour happened in rent-controlled New York City where a landlord pleaded guilty in January 1999 to hiring a "hit man" to kill tenants and set fires to scare them out so that rents could be increased!)

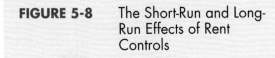

FIGURE 5-8 The Short-Run and Long-Run Effects of Rent Controls

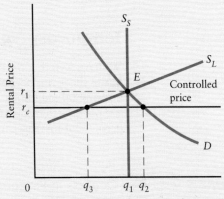

Rent control causes housing shortages that worsen as time passes. The controlled rent of r_c forces rents below their free-market equilibrium value of r_1. The short-run supply of housing is shown by the perfectly inelastic curve S_S. Thus quantity supplied remains at q_1 in the short run, and the housing shortage is q_1q_2. Over time, the quantity supplied shrinks, as shown by the long-run supply curve S_L. In the long run, there are only q_3 units of rental accommodations, fewer than when controls were instituted. The long-run housing shortage of q_3q_2 is larger than the initial shortage of q_1q_2.

Who Gains and Who Loses?

Existing tenants in rent-controlled accommodations are the principal gainers from a policy of rent control. As the gap between the controlled and the free-market rents grows, those who are lucky enough to be tenants gain more and more.

Landlords suffer because they do not get the return that they had expected on their investments. Some landlords are large companies, and others are wealthy individuals. Neither one of these groups attracts great public sympathy, even though the rental companies' stockholders are not all rich. But some landlords are people of modest means who have put their retirement savings into a small apartment block or a house or two. They find that the value of their savings is diminished, and sometimes they find themselves in the ironic position of subsidizing tenants who are far better off than they are.

The other important group of people who suffer from rent controls are *potential future* tenants. The housing shortage hurts them because the rental housing they will require will not exist in the future. These people, who wind up living elsewhere, farther from their places of employment and study, are invisible in debates over rent control because they cannot obtain housing in the rent-controlled jurisdiction. Thus rent control is often stable politically even when it causes a long-run housing shortage. The current tenants benefit, and the potential tenants, who are harmed, are nowhere to be seen or heard.

Temporary Versus Permanent Increases in Demand

We have seen that the effects of binding rent controls are more serious in the long run than in the short run because it is only over the long run that the quantity supplied of rental housing falls significantly. This suggests that a policy of rent controls *imposed only for a short time* may have few costs. Here we consider the distinction between temporary and permanent increases in housing demand, and the effects of rent controls in each case.

When Rent Controls Can Work: Short-Term Shortages

Pressure for rent controls is strongest when prices are rising most rapidly. The case for stemming the rapid rise of rents is strongest when the forces causing the rent increase are short-lived, as would be the case, for example, when people move temporarily into an area in response to a major construction project or significant international event, such as a World Exposition or the Olympic Games. When a temporary population floods in, market rents will rise. New construction of apartments will not occur, however, because investors recognize that the rise in demand for rental accommodation is only temporary. In such a situation, rent controls may stop existing landlords from making large profits and may result in few harmful supply effects because a long-run supply response is not expected in any case. After the boom is over, demand will fall, and free-market equilibrium rents will fall. Rent controls may then be removed with little further effect. This situation is illustrated in Figure 5-9.

Although the rent controls have no long-run adverse effect under these circumstances, they will still have some disadvantages. At controlled rents, there will be a severe housing shortage but no *price incentive* for existing tenants to economize on housing or for potential suppliers to find ways to convert existing space into short-run accommodations, as would occur if rents were allowed to rise. Even though the supply of permanent apartments does not change, the supply of temporary accommodations can increase (mobile homes, and the renting of bedrooms, for example). Such reactions are encouraged by the signal of rising rents but are inhibited by rent controls.

FIGURE 5-9   Rent Controls in Response to Increasing Demand

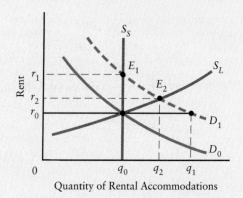

Quantity of Rental Accommodations

Rent controls prevent a temporary skyrocketing of rents when demand rises but also prevent the long-term supply adjustment where it is required.

Temporary demand fluctuations. The short-run supply curve S_S applies. In the free market, a temporary shift in demand from D_0 to D_1 and then back to D_0 will change rents from r_0 to r_1 and back to r_0. Rent control would hold rents at r_0 throughout. There would be a housing shortage of q_0q_1 because of excess demand, as long as demand was D_1, but rent control would not affect the quantity of housing supplied.

Permanent changes in demand. The long-run supply curve S_L applies. A permanent rise in demand from D_0 to D_1 would cause free-market rents to rise temporarily from r_0 to r_1 and then to fall to r_2 as the quantity of accommodations supplied grows from q_0 to q_2. But controlling the rent at r_0 produces a *permanent* housing shortage of q_0q_1.

When Rent Controls Fail: Long-Term Shortages

Now consider what happens when there is a long-term increase in the demand for rental accommodations. This has occurred most recently in Vancouver, Calgary, and Toronto where rapidly increasing populations have created local housing shortages and have forced rents to increase. Such increases in rents give the signal that apartments are highly profitable investments. A consequent building boom will lead to increases in the quantity supplied, and it will continue as long as profits can be earned on rental housing.

If rent controls are imposed in the face of such long-term increases in demand, they will prevent landlords from earning (temporarily) high profits, but they will also prevent the needed long-run construction boom from occurring. Thus, binding controls will convert a temporary shortage into a permanent one, as shown in Figure 5-9.

Policy Alternatives

Most rent controls today are meant to protect lower-income tenants, not only against "profiteering" by landlords in the face of severe local shortages but also against the steadily rising cost of housing. The market solution is to let rents rise sufficiently to cover the rising costs. If people decide that they cannot afford the market price of apartments and will not rent them, construction will cease. Given what we know about consumer behaviour, however, it is more likely that people will make agonizing choices, both to economize on housing and to spend a higher proportion of total income on it, which mean consuming less housing and less of other things as well.

If governments do not wish to accept this market solution, there are many things they can do, but they cannot avoid the fundamental fact that the opportunity cost of good housing is high. Binding rent controls create housing shortages. The shortages can be removed only if the government, at taxpayer expense, either subsidizes housing production or produces public housing directly.

Alternatively, the government can make housing more affordable to lower-income households by providing income-assistance to these households, allowing them access to higher-quality housing than they could otherwise afford. Whatever policy is adopted, it is important to recognize that providing greater access to rental accommodations has a resource cost. The costs of providing additional housing cannot be voted out of existence; all that can be done is to transfer the costs from one set of persons to another.

Perhaps the most striking effect of rent control is the long-term decline in the quality of rental housing.

Agriculture and the Farm Problem

For over 80 years, policymakers in many western countries, including Canada, have been challenged and frustrated by what is often called the "farm problem." There are actually two separate farm problems, and supply-and-demand analysis can help to make it clear why they are so challenging.

Long-Term and Short-Term Problems

The first problem is that there is a long-run tendency for farm incomes to fall below urban incomes. The second problem is that agricultural prices fluctuate substantially from year to year, causing a great deal of variability in farm incomes. The farm policies implemented by most Western countries are nominally directed at *stabilizing* farm incomes. However, the underlying long-term trend of declining farm incomes also puts pressure on governments to implement policies that *raise* farm incomes.

Long-Term Trends

Agriculture's long-term problems arise from both the demand and the supply sides of agricultural markets.

Increasing Supply.   Since 1900, the output per worker in Canadian agriculture has increased tenfold, roughly twice as much as the increase in manufacturing productivity. In 1900, one farm worker could produce enough food to feed about $2^{1}/_{2}$ people. Currently, the figure is approximately 65 people! Similar growth in farm productivity has occurred in Europe and the United States. Moreover, increases in supply—especially in Europe—have resulted from very generous agricultural subsidies under the European Union's Common Agricultural Policy (CAP). The combination of productivity growth and aggressive subsidization has caused the supply curves for agricultural products—both in Canada and abroad—to shift rapidly to the right.

Lagging Demand.   The overall growth of output throughout the entire Canadian economy has resulted in a rising trend for the real income of the average Canadian family during the last 150 years. However, at the levels of income existing in Canada and in other advanced industrial nations, most foodstuffs have low income elasticities of demand because most people are already well fed. Thus as incomes in Canada and other countries grow, the demand for agricultural goods also grows, but less rapidly.

Explosive growth of world population in the past half century has provided an expanding demand for foodstuffs, which, over much of the period, translated into a growing export market for North American produce. This tended to alleviate somewhat the domestic pressures just discussed. Beginning in the 1970s, however, many developing countries succeeded in dramatically increasing their own food production, thus reducing their demand for other countries' agricultural products.

Excess Supply.   Both the demand and the supply curves in typical agricultural markets have been shifting to the right over the whole of this century, with the demand curve shifting more slowly than the supply curve. As a result, there is a continuing tendency for an excess supply of agricultural produce to develop at existing market prices. This naturally tends to depress world prices for agricultural products.

To see the significance of these developments, note the change in the *real* crop prices received by North American farmers over the past two decades. Between 1975 and 1998, average crop prices in Canada and the United States increased by just over 27 percent. But over the same period, average prices in the economy increased by over 200 percent. This difference represents an enormous decline in the real prices received by farmers (roughly a 60 percent decline). And since most agricultural products tend to have price elasticities of demand less than one, the decline in prices tends to depress agricultural incomes.

Resource Reallocation.   Depressed prices, wages, and farm incomes signal the need for resources to move out of agriculture and into other sectors. However necessary they may be, adjustments of this kind prove to be painful to those who live and work on farms, especially when resources move slowly in response to depressed incomes. It is one thing for farmers' sons and daughters to move to the city; it is quite another for existing farmers and their parents to be displaced.

The magnitude of the required supply response has been enormous. In 1900, over 45 percent of the Canadian labour force worked in agriculture; by 1930 it was down to 29 percent, and by 1998 the number had fallen below 3 percent.

Short-Term Fluctuations

The second part of the farm problem is the short-term price volatility that is typical of many agricultural markets. Such volatility occurs for two basic reasons, both of which are beyond the farmers' control.

First, in markets that are mainly domestic, such as some fresh fruit and vegetables, changes in growing conditions—mostly due to changes in weather—can lead to sharp changes in the supply of these products. Such changes in supply, combined with a typically inelastic domestic demand, lead to large fluctuations in price. As we learned in Chapter 4, price fluctuations with inelastic demand imply that income and price fluctuate in the same direction. Thus, large supply fluctuations in such markets generate large fluctuations in farmers' incomes.

Second, in markets that are mainly international, such as wheat and other grains, changes in the *world* demand and supply lead to changes in the world price of these products. Such changes in the world price lead to significant fluctuations in the income of Canadian farmers. For example, in 1997 several countries in Southeast Asia entered into a significant recession. As incomes in these countries fell sharply, so too did their demand for many commodities, including agricultural products. This reduction in demand contributed to an ongoing decline in the world prices of such products. The implication for Canadian farmers was severe; total Canadian farm income fell by 53 percent from 1996 to 1997, even though growing conditions within Canada were approximately normal.

We discuss these two general situations and others in more detail in the next section, in which we examine the effects of agricultural stabilization and income-support policies.

The Theory of Agricultural Policy

Because of the long-term trends and the short-term fluctuations that we have just discussed, governments throughout the world intervene in agricultural markets in attempts both to stabilize agricultural incomes and to raise average farm incomes. We deal with three cases that are relevant to much of Canadian agriculture. The first two cases deal purely with the stabilization of farm income—first, the production of commodities mainly for export and, second, the production of commodities mainly for domestic consumption. The third case deals with price supports above the free-market equilibrium price. In what follows, we assume that all supply curves refer to *planned* production per year but that actual production fluctuates around that level for reasons beyond the control of farmers.

Production for Export Markets

When Canadian production is sold on world markets, the prices are largely independent of the amount sold by Canadian producers because they contribute only a small proportion of total world supply. In these markets, domestic producers face a perfectly

FIGURE 5-10   Production at a Given World Price

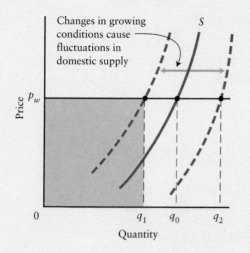

A country that exports only a small portion of the world's supply of some product faces a perfectly elastic demand because the world price is not affected by its own sales. The given world price is p_w. The domestic supply curve shows that planned output is q_0 at that price. Unplanned fluctuations cause output between q_1 and q_2. When output is q_1 (a partial crop failure), farm income is given by the shaded area. When output is q_2 (a bumper crop), farm income is given by the total of the bordered areas.

elastic demand curve, indicating that they can sell all that they wish at the given world price. A government stabilization policy then faces two key problems: first, how to cope with short-term supply fluctuations at home and, second, how to react to fluctuations in world prices.

Output Fluctuations at Given World Prices. Figure 5-10 illustrates sales at a given world price when domestic output fluctuates. In years of bumper crops, sales will rise and thus incomes will rise. In years of poor crops, sales will fall and thus incomes will fall. In neither case do the fluctuations in domestic output affect the world price.

When domestic farmers sell at a given world price, their incomes fluctuate in the same direction as their short-term fluctuations in output.

The incomes of farmers who produce nonperishable crops could be stabilized if the government developed a scheme allowing farmers to store their outputs in years of bumper crops and to sell from their accumulated stocks in years of poor crops. Effectively, sales would always be equal to planned output (q_0 in Figure 5-10). Any unplanned excess of production would be stored, and any shortfall would be made up out of sales from stocks. But storage costs money and postpones the receipt of revenue until the sales occur. A simpler alternative would be for the farmer to sell all the crop each year and then save the extra money received in good years to spend in bad years. This is something that farmers can do on their own without assistance from the government.

Fluctuations in World Prices.   Now consider a situation in which domestic supply curve is stable but the world price is fluctuating. When the domestic farmers see an increase in the world price they will increase production, though the quantity response is quite limited in the short run. Domestic farmers benefit from increases in the world price since they sell all of their output at a higher price. On the other hand, a decrease in the world price harms them because they sell all of their output at a lower price.

When domestic farmers sell their products at the world price, their incomes fluctuate in the same direction as the fluctuations in the world price.

For example, in the late summer of 1998 the Russian economy began a significant recession. As Russia is the world's largest importer of meat, its recession had a dramatic effect on the world price of meat. This contributed to the already low meat prices—especially pork—that were driven by the reductions in demand from the recession-hit Southeast Asian economies (which consume large amounts of pork). The result was a 60 percent fall in hog prices over just a few months, with the expected dramatic effect on the incomes of Canadian hog farmers. In some reported cases, farmers were losing so much money on each animal sold that it made more sense to slaughter the animals simply to get rid of them rather than to keep feeding them at considerable expense.

To stabilize farmers' incomes when the world price fluctuates, the government could create a scheme whereby they effectively guarantee farmers a price for their product equal to the *average* of the fluctuating world price. In low-price years, farmers would receive the low world price plus a supplement from the government. In high-price years, the farmers would receive the high world price but would make a payment to the government. The guaranteed price could be computed so that over time there would be a net balance between the government and the farmers—payments received by farmers in low-price years could balance the payments made by farmers in high-price years. In this way, farmers would have a smooth income stream; their income would be *as if* the world price were constant.

One problem with such a policy involves the computation of the guaranteed price. If the guaranteed price actually does equal the average of the fluctuating world price, then the payments from the farmers in the high-price years will indeed finance their income supplements in the low-price years. But if the guaranteed price is set too high, then the scheme will incur losses that must be financed from general tax revenues. Such financing, of course, involves a redistribution from taxpayers to farmers.

Production for Domestic Markets

Quite a few Canadian agricultural goods are sold mainly on the domestic market. The difference between this case and the one just considered is that the demand curve facing domestic producers is now negatively sloped and typically inelastic. In this case, increases in domestic supply (bumper crops) lead to large price reductions and declines in farm incomes, whereas decreases in supply (crop failures) lead to large price increases and increases in farm incomes. Can farm income be stabilized in this case?

Price Stabilization. Suppose that the government enters the market, buying and thereby adding to its own stocks when there is a bumper crop, and selling and thereby reducing its stocks when there is a crop failure. If it had enough storage facilities, and if its support price were set at a realistic level, the government could stabilize *prices* indefinitely. But this action would not stabilize farmers' incomes, which would be high with bumper crops and low with poor crops. In effect, the government policy that we just described imposes a demand curve that is perfectly elastic (horizontal) at the support price. The situation is then analogous to the one analysed in Figure 5-10: The product can be sold at a given price, and income fluctuates in the same direction as output.

When domestic supply is fluctuating, a policy that stabilizes farm prices will not stabilize farm incomes.

Income Stabilization. When the government does not intervene at all in domestic agricultural markets, farm income fluctuates in the *opposite* direction as farm output (because of inelastic demand). If the government intervenes to stabilize price, then farm income fluctuates in the *same* direction as farm output. This line of argument suggests that there must exist *some* government buying-and-selling policy that is able to stabilize farmers' incomes. What are the characteristics of such a policy? As has been seen, too much price stability causes incomes to vary directly with production, and too little price stability causes receipts to vary inversely with production. Thus it appears that the government could aim at some intermediate degree of price stability to stabilize farmers' incomes. If the government allows prices to vary in inverse proportion to variations in production, incomes will be stabilized. A 10 percent rise in production could be met by a 10 percent fall in price, and a 10 percent fall in production by a 10 percent rise in price.

FIGURE 5-11   Price Supports with Government Purchase of Surplus

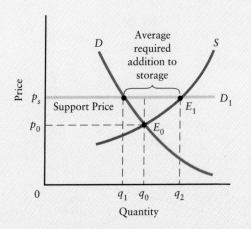

The price support becomes a price floor, and the government must purchase the excess supply at that price. *Average* annual demand and supply are D and S, respectively. The free-market equilibrium is at E_0. If the government will buy any quantity at p_s, the demand curve becomes the light blue curve D_1 and equilibrium changes to E_1. The *average* addition to storage is the quantity $q_1 q_2$. The government's purchases, financed by the taxpayer, add to farmers' incomes, but also add to the stocks of unsold output.

To stabilize farmers' incomes, the government must make the effective demand curve unit elastic. It must buy in periods of high output and sell in periods of low output, but only enough to let prices change in inverse proportion to farmers' output.

Supporting Prices Above Equilibrium

Actual stabilization plans, whether they fix prices completely or merely dampen free-market fluctuations, often maintain an average price above the average free-market equilibrium level. This is because stabilization is not the only goal; governments aim to *raise* farm incomes as well as stabilize them.

The government buys in periods of high output and sells in periods of low output, but, as shown in Figure 5-11, it buys much more on average than it sells, with the result that unsold surpluses accumulate. Taxpayers will generally be paying farmers for producing goods that no one is willing to purchase—at least, not at prices that come near to covering costs.

We have just seen that when the government directly supports the price above the free-market equilibrium there is an accumulation of unsold output. An alternative method of supporting the price that partially avoids this problem is through the use of output *quotas*. Under this system, no one can produce the product without having a government-issued quota. Sufficient quotas are issued to hold production at any desired level below the free-market output. This action drives prices above their free-market level. A quota system, which is analysed in Figure 5-12, has the advantage of not causing the accumulation of massive unsold surpluses. It is widely used in Canada.

The quota system, which is called *supply management* in Canada, affects both the short-term and the long-term behaviour of agricultural markets. Consider short-term fluctuations first. There will still be natural disturbances, such as outbreaks of crop disease, that will cause short-term reductions in output. A shortfall of output below the quota will drive price upward. Farmers with no crop to sell will lose, but farmers whose outputs fall proportionally less than the price rise will gain. Since most agricultural products have inelastic demands, the typical farmer's income must increase—the percentage increase in market price will exceed the percentage fall in the aggregate crop.

What about bumper crops that result from favourable conditions? The farmer is allowed to sell only the amount covered by the quota. The rest must be either destroyed or sold on some secondary market not covered by the quota system.

A quota system guarantees that farmers will receive income at least equal to the quota output times the market price at that restricted level of output. In bad years, when output is less than the quota amount, inelastic demand ensures that farmers' incomes will be even higher.

Now let's consider the long term. We have seen that the quota drives price above its free-market level by restricting output. For purposes of illustration, let's suppose that the quota is for milk. Those who are producing milk when the quota system is first instituted must gain. Since production falls, total costs must fall; since demand is inelastic, total revenue must rise. Therefore, milk producers find their profits rising, since they spend less to earn more revenue. No wonder quotas are popular among the original producers!

But do quotas really increase the profitability of farming in the long run? Because people leave the industry for such reasons as death and retirement and new people must enter to replace them, existing quota holders are allowed to transfer their quotas to new would-be milk producers. But the quota is valuable, since it confers the right to produce milk and earn a large profit as a result of the supply restriction. Therefore, the quota commands a market price that naturally reflects the current value of the extra future profits that ownership of the quota allows.

The free-market price of a quota to produce any good will be such that the profitability of that good's production will, after deducting the cost of the quota, be no more than the profitability of other lines of activity carrying similar risks.

In other words, the entire extra profitability created by the quota system becomes embodied in the price of the quota. The extra profits created by the quota will just provide an acceptable return on the money invested in buying the quota—if it provided more, the price of the quota would be bid up; if it provided less, the price of the quota would fall.

For this reason, *new entrants* to the industry will earn no more than the return available in other lines of production. Since that would also be the case under market-determined prices and outputs, the quota does not raise the long-run profitability of farm production. What it does do is reduce some of the uncertainty due to unexpected short-term fluctuations of output. Farming becomes a somewhat less risky operation than before.

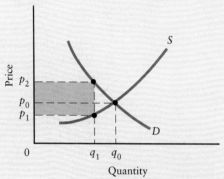

FIGURE 5-12   Price Support Through the Use of Quotas

The quota below the free-market equilibrium quantity maintains the price above the free-market equilibrium level without generating surpluses. If the total quota of q_1 is enforced, the price will rise to p_2. Since the supply curve indicates that in a free market producers would be willing to sell the quantity q_1 at the price p_1, the effect of the quota is to increase the revenues (by the shaded area) to those producers who hold quota.

Practise with Study Guide Chapter 5, Exercise 5.

Agricultural Policy in Canada

The main tools of agricultural stabilization in Canada are marketing boards and income supplement programs. Sales through marketing boards account for about half of all farm cash receipts.

Marketing Boards

There are essentially two types of government marketing boards. The first seeks to influence prices by controlling supply. The second takes prices as given and acts as a selling agency for producers.

Supply Management.   The supply-management schemes typically are provincially administered systems that restrict output of commodities sold in the Canadian market through quotas issued by provincial marketing boards. They vary from province to province but often cover milk, eggs, cheese, butter, and poultry. The farm profits created by these schemes are enormous and are reflected by the high prices farmers must pay to purchase quotas.

Schemes of this type, analysed in Figure 5-12, are successful in reducing short-term fluctuations. However, they also greatly increase the cost of becoming a producer, because a quota must be purchased in addition to the physical capital needed for production. The schemes are popular among farmers because they reduce risk in the short term and because the value of the quotas often rises over the long term. The gains to farmers and food importers are paid for by consumers in the form of higher prices.

The high domestic prices caused by supply management would normally lead to a flood of lower-priced imports. To prevent this, the federal government used to impose quotas on imports of goods subject to supply management. Under the Uruguay Round of the General Agreement on Tariffs and Trade (the GATT), Canada agreed to replace these quotas in 1994 with tariffs which had an equivalent effect. In some cases the tariff rates exceeded 300 percent! The slow speed at which these tariff rates are to be reduced under the GATT will allow the effects of supply management to persist for many years. Consumers will have to wait for future tariff reductions before they get real relief from the high-price effects of Canadian marketing boards.

Marketing Agencies.   The prime example of a marketing agency is the Canadian Wheat Board, which sells Canadian wheat at prices set on the world wheat market. Canadian wheat farmers are *required* to sell their crops to the Wheat Board at a pre-specified price. Each year, the Board estimates the average price at which it expects the wheat crop to be sold. Seventy-five percent of that price is then paid to each farmer on delivery of the wheat. After the Board sells the wheat, any proceeds in excess of the initial payments are distributed to the producers in proportion to the amount of wheat supplied by each.

The primary goal of the Wheat Board is not to influence world prices (since even the large amount of wheat sold by the Board is small relative to the total size of the world wheat market). Instead, by paying farmers 75 percent of the estimated average selling price over the year, the Board provides farmers with a secure cash flow early in the selling period. The Board also serves to secure farmers' incomes against intrayear fluctuations in wheat prices. It does this by pooling all of its receipts and paying them out to farmers according to the amount of wheat delivered by each farmer but irrespective of the date within the year of that delivery. So the farmer is relieved of worry about what the spot price of wheat may be on the day of delivery.

All wheat grown in Canada must be marketed through the Canadian Wheat Board.

In the last few years, the Canadian Wheat Board has come under attack by many prairie wheat farmers who see little value in their being restricted to sell their crops to the Board. They prefer to have the flexibility to sell their own crops to whomever they choose. Other critics of the Wheat Board point out that in recent years taxpayers have actually been supporting wheat farmers through the Board because the final selling price has been below the initial price paid to farmers (in which case, the Wheat Board does not require repayments from the farmers). Defenders of the Board argue that it is an effective means of reducing the costs associated with finding buyers and completing transactions, and that there is no evidence that the Wheat Board receives lower prices than those available to farmers acting individually.

For information on the Canadian Wheat Board, go to www.cwb.ca.

Income Supplements

The current system of income supplements to farmers includes the Net Income Stabilization Account (NISA) and the Gross Revenue Insurance Plan (GRIP). These two programs, combined with a system of crop insurance (and other companion programs) make up what might be called the "safety net programs" for Canadian farmers.

NISA is a voluntary program designed to help producers set aside money in good years to be used in bad years; producers' contributions of up to 2 percent of their net sales are matched by contributions from the federal and relevant provincial governments. Thus, although part of this program involves the individual producers saving their own financial resources, there is also a considerable portion of taxpayers' money being used to supplement farmers' incomes.

GRIP offers producers protection from revenue loss due to output or price changes beyond their control. It provides producers with a guaranteed target revenue. Though GRIP is essentially just an insurance program, it also has an income-support component. This comes from the fact that two-thirds of the insurance premiums are paid by the federal and relevant provincial governments.

All in all, the level of direct financial assistance to farmers is quite considerable, especially when seen relative to total farm income. In 1994 (an approximately typical year in the 1990s for Canadian farming), net cash income to Canadian farmers totalled $5.9 billion. In that same year, direct cash payments to farmers equalled $1.7 billion; thus direct financial assistance to farmers represented roughly 30 percent of their net cash income.

For information on Canada's agricultural sector, and Canadian agricultural policy, go to Agriculture Canada's website: www.agr.ca. Click on "Finances and Economics in Agriculture."

The Future of Agricultural Policy

A central dilemma arises whenever government intervention is designed to protect some people from economic hardship created by long-run shifts in demand and supply. Canadian farm policy reflects this dilemma. By intervening in the market—either with price supports or quotas— government farm policy impedes the reallocation of resources that is required in a changing economy. Most economists—and many politicians—believe that Canadian farm policies have been unnecessarily expensive and wasteful and that they have impeded the long-run adjustments required by changing tastes and technology.

The full benefit of increases in agricultural productivity, that permit the same farm output to be produced with fewer resources, will be felt only when resources flow out of the agricultural sector and begin producing valuable goods and services in other sectors.

Most economists believe that a more efficient system would assist farm workers to change occupations and farm producers to change products rather than subsidize them to stay where they are not needed and to produce products that cannot be marketed profitably. Such assistance would require significant outlays—as do the present schemes— but would allow the market to do the job of allocating resources to agriculture.

There is no doubt that a policy of allowing agricultural prices and outputs to be determined on free markets would avoid surplus production, but the human and political costs of this policy have been judged to be unacceptable. The challenge has been to respond to the real hardships of the farm population without intensifying the long-term problems. Canadian farm policy has not always succeeded in doing so; the economic analysis in the previous sections helps us to understand why.

S U M M A R Y

Linkages Between Markets   (LO) 1

- Partial-equilibrium analysis is the study of a single market in isolation, ignoring events in other markets. General-equilibrium analysis is the study of all markets together.
- Even markets that appear to be separate from each other are usually linked in one of three ways. Regional markets of the same product are linked, as long as there is mobile demand or supply.
- Markets for different products often have input-output linkages. In such cases, a change in the price of one product leads to a similar change in the prices of all goods that use that product as an input.
- Seemingly unrelated markets are also linked through resource constraints. Consumers have only so much income to spend, so an increase in demand for one product must be matched by a decrease in demand for another product. Furthermore, if the economy's resources are fully employed, an increase in the supply of one product must imply a reduction in supply of some other product.

Government-Controlled Prices   (LO) 2 3

- Government price controls are policies that attempt to hold the price of some good or service at some disequilibrium value—a value that could not be maintained in the absence of the government's intervention. A binding price floor is set above the equilibrium price; a binding price ceiling is set below the equilibrium price.
- Effective price floors lead to excess supply. Either the potential seller is left with quantities that cannot be sold, or the government must step in and buy the surplus. Effective price ceilings lead to excess demand and provide a strong incentive for black marketeers to buy at the controlled price and sell at the higher free-market (illegal) price.

Rent Controls: A Case Study of Price Ceilings   (LO) 4 5

- Rent controls are a widespread form of price ceiling. The major consequence of effective rent controls is a shortage of rental accommodations that gets worse over time because of a decline in the quantity of rental housing supplied.
- Rent controls can be an effective response to temporary situations in which there is a ban on building or a transitory increase in demand. They usually fail when they are introduced as a response to a long-run increase in demand.

Agriculture and the Farm Problem   (LO) 6

- Agricultural markets are subject to wide fluctuations that cause variability in farmers' incomes. They occur because of year-to-year unplanned fluctuations in supplies combined with inelastic demands (domestic markets), and because of fluctuations in prices (world markets).
- To stabilize farm incomes, the government should not stabilize prices. Instead, it should buy and sell just enough to allow prices to vary in proportion to changes in quantity, thus causing the elasticity of demand for the product to be unity.

- Agricultural prices and incomes are depressed by chronic surpluses in agricultural markets. Government policies to protect farm incomes have included buying farmers' output at above free-market prices, limiting production and acreage through quotas, and paying farmers to leave crops unproduced. Such policies tend to inhibit the reallocation mechanism.

- Canadian farm policy illustrates that government intervention to prevent the working of the market mechanisms affects resource allocation and requires alternative allocative mechanisms. Although farm policy has protected farmers from certain hardships, it has slowed the required outflow of resources that would otherwise solve the problem of chronic excess supply.

K E Y   C O N C E P T S

Partial-equilibrium analysis
General-equilibrium analysis
Regional linkages between markets
Input-output linkages between markets
Linkages through resource constraints
Price controls: floors and ceilings

Allocation by sellers' preferences and by black markets
Rent controls
Short-run and long-run supply curves of rental accommodations

The farm problem: short-run fluctuations and long-run trends
Price stabilization versus income stabilization
Quotas and price-support schemes

S T U D Y   E X E R C I S E S

1. Consider the market for some product X that is represented below in the demand-and-supply diagram.

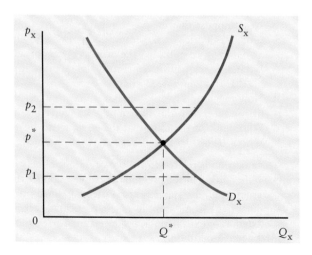

a. Suppose the government decides to impose a price floor at p_1. Describe how this affects the market equilibrium.
b. Suppose the government decides to impose a price floor at p_2. Describe how this affects the market equilibrium.
c. Suppose the government decides to impose a price ceiling at p_1. Describe how this affects the market equilibrium.
d. Suppose the government decides to impose a price ceiling at p_2. Describe how this affects the market equilibrium.

2. Consider the market for rental housing in Yourtown. The demand and supply schedules for rental housing are given in the table.

Price ($ per month)	Quantity Demanded (thousands of units)	Quantity Supplied (thousands of units)
1100	40	80
1000	50	77
900	60	73
800	70	70
700	80	67
600	90	65
500	100	60

a. In a free market for rental housing, what is the equilibrium price and quantity?
b. Now suppose that the government in Yourtown decides to impose a ceiling on the monthly rental price. What is the highest level that such a ceiling could be, in order to have any effect on the market? Explain your answer.
c. Suppose that the maximum rental price is set equal to $500 per month. Describe the effect on the rental-housing market.
d. Suppose that a black market develops in the presence of these rent controls. What is the black-market price that would exist if all of the quantity supplied were supplied on the black market?

3. Explain and show in a diagram why the short-run effects of rent control are likely to be much less significant than the long-run effects.

4. Consider the situation faced by Canadian oil producers. The price of oil is determined in world markets and Canadian oil producers take that price as given. Letting p be the world price of oil (in dollars per barrel) and Q^S be the number of barrels (in millions per month) supplied by Canadian producers, suppose the domestic supply curve is given by:

Domestic Supply: $Q^S = 20 + 8p$

a. Plot the domestic supply curve for oil (between $p = 8 and $p = 18).
b. Explain why the supply curve is upward sloping. (That is, what are firms doing to increase quantity supplied in response to an increase in price?)

c. Now suppose that the world price is volatile. For simplicity, suppose it varies between a high value of $16 per barrel and a low value of $9 per barrel. How does such volatility affect the revenue of Canadian oil producers? Show this in a diagram.

5. Consider the situation of Canadian barley farmers, who face weather conditions largely independent of those faced by barley growers in other countries. The incomes earned by the Canadian farmers, however, are affected by what happens to barley farmers in other countries. The key point is that Canadian barley farmers sell their barley on the same *world market* as all other barley farmers.

a. Show in a diagram how a bumper crop of European barley will push down the world barley price.
b. Show in a diagram how a reduction in the world price of barley, *ceteris paribus*, will reduce the incomes of Canadian barley farmers.
c. Explain why Canadian barley farmers are made better off when there are crop failures in other parts of the world.

6. This is a challenging question designed for those students who like mathematics. Consider the market for milk in Saskatchewan. If p is the price of milk (cents per litre) and Q is the quantity of litres (in millions per month), suppose that the demand and supply curves for milk are given by:

Demand: $p = 225 - 15Q^D$
Supply: $p = 25 + 35Q^S$

a. Assuming there is no government form of price support in this market, what is the equilibrium price and quantity?
b. Now suppose that the government guarantees milk producers a price of $2 per litre and promises to buy any amount of milk that the producers cannot sell. What are the quantity demanded and quantity supplied at this guaranteed price?
c. How much milk would the government be buying (per month) with this system of price supports?
d. Who pays for the milk that the government buys? Who is helped by this policy and who is harmed?

7. This question is related to the use of output quotas in the milk market in the previous question. Suppose the government used a quota system instead of direct price supports to assist milk producers. In particular, they issued quotas to existing milk producers for 1.67 million litres of milk per month.

a. If milk production is exactly equal to the amount of quotas issued, what price do consumers pay for milk?

b. Compared to the direct price controls in the previous question, whose income is higher under the quota system? Whose is lower?

8. In 1994, the Quebec and Ontario governments significantly reduced their excise taxes on cigarettes, but Manitoba and Saskatchewan left theirs in place. This led to cigarette smuggling between provinces that linked the provincial markets.

a. Draw a simple demand-and-supply diagram for the "Eastern" market and a separate one for the "Western" market.

b. Suppose that cigarette taxes are reduced in the Eastern market. Show the immediate effects.

c. Now suppose that the supply of cigarettes is (illegally) mobile. Explain and show what happens.

d. What limits the extent of smuggling that will take place in this situation?

DISCUSSION QUESTIONS

1. "When an item is vital to everyone, it is easier to start controlling the price than to stop controlling it. Such controls are popular with consumers, regardless of their harmful consequences." Explain why it may be inefficient to have such controls, why they may be popular, and why, if they are popular, the government might nevertheless choose to decontrol these prices.

2. It is sometimes asserted that the rising costs of construction are putting housing out of the reach of ordinary citizens. Who bears the heaviest cost when rentals are kept down by (a) rent controls, (b) a subsidy to tenants equal to some fraction of their rent payments, and (c) low-cost public housing?

3. "This year the weather smiled on us, and we made a crop," says a wheat farmer near Minedosa in Manitoba. "But just as we made a crop, the economic situation changed." This quotation brings to mind the old saying, "If you are a farmer, the weather is always bad." Discuss the sense in which this saying might be true.

4. During the summer of 1993, severe floods swept through the American Midwest. Although many homes that flooded that year do not typically flood, for many people this was only one in a long string of floods. However, after the waters receded, most people rebuilt their homes, generally with low-interest loans and disaster relief grants from the federal government. Discuss how the policy of subsidizing the reconstruction of property following floods affects the market for real estate in flood-prone areas. Is the outcome more or less efficient in the long run with such government intervention?

5. Gary Storey, a professor of agricultural economics at the University of Saskatchewan, made the following statement: "One of the sad truths of the agricultural policies in Europe and the United States is that they do very little for the future generations of farmers. Most of the subsidies get capitalized into higher land prices, creating windfall gains for current landowners (i.e., gains that they did not expect). It creates a situation where the next generation of farmers require, and ask for, increased government support."

a. Explain why subsidies to farmers increase land values and generate windfall gains to current landowners.

b. As we have seen in this chapter, some Canadian agricultural policies are based on supply management, which involves the use of production quotas. Do such quota systems avoid the problem described by Professor Storey?

6. Soon after the Liberal government was elected in 1993, an "infrastructure" program was implemented that involved spending several billion dollars on bridges, highways, sewer systems, and so on. One of the alleged benefits of this program was to create thousands of jobs, not only in the construction industry but also elsewhere in the economy as construction workers spent their now-higher income on cars, clothing, entertainment, and so on. Discuss how such spending would create jobs in the construction industry. Is such a program likely to create jobs in the economy as a whole?

PART THREE

Consumers and Producers

Why does water, which is essential to life and which we all value dearly, have such a low price? And why do diamonds, a more-or-less unnecessary part of life, have such a high price? Does this paradox mean that the demand-and-supply apparatus that we have just studied is all wrong? What determines the cost of specific products, and why does the cost sometimes depend on how many units are produced? For example, why is the production cost of a widely used textbook significantly less than a similar textbook used only by a few universities? Why has the declining cost of computer-related equipment led some firms to reduce their number of employees? These are the sort of questions you will be able to answer after reading the next three chapters.

In Part 2, we saw that demand and supply are important for determining market prices and quantities. We also saw that the shapes of demand and supply curves influence the way prices and quantities respond to changes in income, technology, or excise taxes. In the next three chapters, we go "behind the scenes" of demand and supply to examine in more detail the behaviour of consumers and the behaviour of firms. This detail will give us a deeper understanding of what demand and supply are all about.

In Chapter 6, we explore the theory of consumer behaviour. There we see how economists think about the way consumers make decisions. We introduce the important concept of utility, as well as the distinction between marginal and total utility. It is this distinction that explains why water has a lower price than diamonds even though it is clearly more "valuable." We will also see how demand curves are derived from the underlying consumer behaviour, and that (except in some very unusual cases) demand curves are indeed negatively sloped.

Chapters 7 and 8 explore the theory of the firm. We consider profits and costs, and how these terms are used differently in economics than in everyday life. The important concepts of average cost and marginal cost will be developed, at which point it will be clear why 50,000 textbooks can be produced at a lower cost per book than can 10,000 textbooks. We will see how firms follow the principle of substitution, and how this explains why the falling cost of computers has led some firms to reduce their workforces (and increase their use of computers). Finally, we explore how changes in technology lead to changes in firms' behaviour.

CHAPTER 6

Consumer Behaviour

🔵 LEARNING OBJECTIVES

❶ Understand why marginal utility falls as the consumption of a product rises.

❷ Recognize that maximizing utility requires consumers to adjust expenditure until the marginal utility per dollar spent is equalized across all products.

❸ View consumer surplus as the "bargain" the consumer gets by paying less for the product than he or she was willing to pay.

❹ Understand the distinction between total value, marginal value, and market value.

❺ Explain how any change in price generates both an income and a substitution effect on quantity demanded.

Imagine that you are walking down the aisle of a supermarket looking for something for your late-night snack (to have while you are studying!). With only a $5 bill in your pocket, you must choose how to divide this $5 between frozen burritos and cans of Coke. How do you make this decision? In this chapter, we see the way economists think about such problems—the theory of consumer behaviour. Not surprisingly, economists (being consumers themselves) think about consumers as caring both about the prices of the goods and the satisfaction they get from the goods.

▌ Marginal Utility and Consumer Choice

Consumers make all kinds of decisions—they choose to drink coffee or tea (or neither), to go to the movies, to dine out, to buy excellent (or not so good) stereo equipment. As we discussed in Chapter 1, economists assume that in making their choices, consumers are motivated to maximize their **utility,** the total satisfaction that they derive from the goods and services that they consume.

Utility cannot be measured directly. But our inability to measure something does not mean it is not real. You know that you derive satisfaction—or utility—from a good meal, listening to a CD, or taking a bicycle ride through a park. And even though we can-

utility The satisfaction or well-being that a consumer receives from consuming some good or service.

not measure the utility you derive from these things, we need some way to think about how you as a consumer make your decisions. As we will see in this chapter, it is possible to construct a useful theory of consumer behaviour based on utility maximization even though we cannot directly measure utility.

In developing our theory of consumer behaviour we begin by considering the consumption of a single product. It is useful to distinguish between the consumer's **total utility,** which is the full satisfaction resulting from the consumption of that product by a consumer, and the consumer's **marginal utility,** which is the *additional* satisfaction resulting from consuming one more unit of that product. For example, the total utility of consuming seven Cokes per week is the total satisfaction that those seven Cokes provide. The marginal utility of the seventh Coke consumed is the additional satisfaction provided by the consumption of that Coke.[1]

total utility   The total satisfaction resulting from the consumption of a given commodity by a consumer in a period of time.

marginal utility   The additional satisfaction obtained by a consumer from consuming one unit more of a good or service.

Diminishing Marginal Utility

The central hypothesis of utility theory, often called the *law of diminishing marginal utility,* is as follows:

The utility that any consumer derives from *successive* units of a particular product diminishes as total consumption of the product increases (if the consumption of all other products is unchanged).

Consider your utility from using clean water, either for drinking, bathing, washing your dishes or clothes, or some other purpose. Some minimum quantity is very important and you would, if necessary, give up a considerable sum of money to obtain that quantity of water. Thus, your marginal utility of that basic quantity of water is very high. You will, of course, consume more than this bare minimum, but your marginal utility of successive litres of water used over a period of time will decline steadily.

We will consider evidence for this hypothesis later, but you can convince yourself that it is at least reasonable by asking a few questions. How much money would be needed to induce you to reduce your consumption of water by one litre per week? The answer is: very little. How much would induce you to reduce it by a second litre? By a third litre? To only one litre consumed per week? The answer to the last question is: quite a bit. The fewer litres you are already using, the higher the marginal utility of one more litre of water.

Utility Schedules and Graphs

The hypothetical schedule in the table in Figure 6-1 illustrates the assumptions that have been made about utility, using Alison's movie attendance as an example. The table shows that Alison's total utility rises as she attends more movies per month. However, the utility that she gets from each *additional* movie per month is less than that of the previous one—that is, her marginal utility declines as the quantity she consumes rises. [10] The data are graphed in the two parts of Figure 6-1.

---

[1]Technically, *incremental* utility is measured over a discrete interval, such as from 6 to 7, whereas *marginal* utility is a rate of change measured over an infinitesimal interval. However, common usage applies the word marginal when the last unit is involved, even if a one-unit change is not infinitesimal. [9]

FIGURE 6-1   Alison's Total and Marginal Utility

Number of Movies Alison Attends Per Month	Alison's Total Utility	Alison's Marginal Utility
0	0	
		30
1	30	
		20
2	50	
		15
3	65	
		10
4	75	
		8
5	83	
		6
6	89	
		4
7	93	
		3
8	96	
		2
9	98	
		1
10	99	

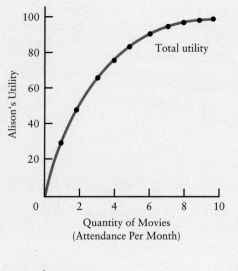

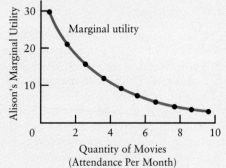

Total utility rises, but marginal utility declines, as consumption increases. The marginal utility of 20, shown as the second entry in the third column, arises because Alison's total utility increases from 30 to 50—a difference of 20—with attendance at the second movie. To indicate that the marginal utility is associated with the change from one level of consumption to another, the figures in the third column are recorded between the rows of the figures in the second column.

Maximizing Utility

Economists assume that consumers try to make themselves as well off as they possibly can in the circumstances in which they find themselves. In other words, the members of a household seek to maximize their total utility.

The Consumer's Decision

How can a consumer adjust expenditure so as to maximize total utility? A simple answer is that the consumer should consume such that the marginal utility of each product is the same—that is, such that the last unit of each product consumed is valued equally. But this would make sense only if each product had the same price per unit. Suppose Alison is buying two goods that have prices per unit of $3 and $1. The first product would represent a poor use of money if the marginal utility of the two goods were equal.

Alison would be spending $3 to get utility equal to what she could have acquired for only $1 by buying the other good.

A consumer who is maximizing utility will allocate expenditures so that the utility obtained from the last dollar spent on each product is equal.

Imagine that Alison's utility from the last dollar spent on cashews is three times her utility from the last dollar spent on toffee. In this case, Alison can increase her total utility by switching a dollar of expenditure from toffee to cashews and by gaining the difference between the utilities of a dollar spent on each.

Alison will continue to switch her expenditure from toffee to cashews as long as her last dollar spent on cashews yields more utility than her last dollar spent on toffee. This switching, however, reduces the quantity of toffee consumed and, given the law of diminishing marginal utility, raises the marginal utility of toffee. At the same time, switching increases the quantity of cashews consumed and thereby lowers the marginal utility of cashews.

Eventually, the marginal utilities will have changed enough so that the utility of Alison's last dollar spent on cashews is just equal to the utility of her last dollar spent on toffee. At this point, she gains nothing from further switches. (In fact, switching further would *reduce* her total utility.)

So much for the simple example. Now, what can we say more generally about utility maximization? Suppose we denote the marginal utility of the last unit of product X by MU_X and its price by p_X. Let MU_Y and p_Y refer, respectively, to the marginal utility of a second product Y and its price. The marginal utility per dollar spent on X will be MU_X/p_X. For example, if the last unit of X increases utility by 30 and costs $2, its marginal utility per dollar is $30/2 = 15$.

The condition required for a consumer to be maximizing utility, for any pair of products, is

$$\frac{MU_X}{p_X} = \frac{MU_Y}{p_Y} \qquad (6\text{-}1)$$

This equation says that the consumer will allocate expenditure so that the utility gained from the last dollar spent on each product is equal.

This is the fundamental equation of marginal utility theory. A consumer demands each good up to the point at which the marginal utility per dollar spent on it is the same as the marginal utility per dollar spent on every other good. When this condition is met for all goods, the consumer cannot increase utility further by reallocating expenditure. That is, utility will be maximized.

Notice from our example that when Alison is deciding how much of a given product to purchase, she compares the utility from that product to the utility she could derive from spending the same money on other things. Thus, the idea of *opportunity cost* is central to our theory of consumer behaviour.

When expenditure is adjusted to maximize utility, the value to the consumer of consuming the marginal unit of some good is just equal to the opportunity cost—the value to the consumer of the money used to make the purchase.

An Alternative Interpretation

If we rearrange the terms in Equation 6-1, we can gain additional insight into consumer behaviour.

$$\frac{MU_X}{MU_Y} = \frac{p_X}{p_Y} \qquad\qquad (6\text{-}2)$$

The right side of this equation is the *relative* price of the two goods. It is determined by the market and is beyond Alison's control. She reacts to these market prices but is powerless to change them. The left side is the *relative* ability of the two goods to add to Alison's utility. This is within her control because in determining the quantities of different goods to buy, she also determines their marginal utilities. (If you have difficulty seeing why, look again at Figure 6-1.)

If the two sides of Equation 6-2 are not equal, Alison can increase her total utility by rearranging purchases. To see this, suppose that the price of a unit of X is twice the price of a unit of Y ($p_X/p_Y = 2$) and that the marginal utility of a unit of X is three times that of a unit of Y ($MU_X/MU_Y = 3$). Under these conditions, it is worthwhile for Alison to buy more of X and less of Y. For example, if she reduces purchases of Y by two units, enough purchasing power is freed for her to buy one unit of X. Because one extra unit of X yields 1½ times the utility of two units of Y forgone, the switch is worth making. What about a further switch of X for Y? As Alison buys more of X and less of Y, the marginal utility of X falls and the marginal utility of Y rises. Alison will go on rearranging purchases, reducing Y and increasing X, until (in this example) the marginal utility of X is only twice that of Y. At this point, Alison's total utility cannot be increased further by rearranging purchases between the two products.

Consider what Alison is doing. She is faced with a set of prices that she cannot change. She responds to these prices and maximizes her utility by adjusting the things that she *can* change—the quantities of the various goods that she purchases—until Equation 6-2 is satisfied for all pairs of products.

The Consumer's Demand Curve

To derive the consumer's demand curve for a product, it is only necessary to ask what happens when there is a change in the price of that product. As an example, let us derive Alison's demand curve for cashews. Consider Equation 6-2 and let X represent cashews and Y represent *all other products taken together*. In this case, the price of Y is interpreted as the average price of all other products. What will Alison do if, with all other prices remaining constant, there is an increase in the price of cashews? When the price of cashews rises, the right side of Equation 6-2 increases. But, until Alison adjusts consumption, the left side is unchanged. Thus, after the price changes but before Alison reacts, she will be in a position in which the following circumstance prevails:

$$\frac{MU \text{ of cashews}}{MU \text{ of } Y} < \frac{\text{price of cashews}}{\text{price of } Y}$$

What does Alison do to restore the equality? The hypothesis of diminishing marginal utility tells us that as she buys fewer cashews, the *marginal* utility of cashews will rise and thereby increase the ratio on the left side. Thus, in response to an increase in the price of cashews, with all other prices constant, Alison reduces her consumption of cashews until the marginal utility of cashews rises sufficiently that Equation 6-2 is restored.

This analysis leads to the basic prediction of demand theory:

A rise in the price of a product (with income and the prices of all other products held constant) leads each consumer to reduce the quantity demanded of the product.

Practise with Study Guide Chapter 6, Exercise 2.

If this is what each consumer does, it is also what all consumers taken together do. Thus the theory of consumer behaviour that we have considered here predicts a negatively sloped market demand curve in addition to a negatively sloped demand curve for each individual consumer. *Extensions in Theory 6-1* shows how we can obtain a market demand curve by adding up the demand curves of individual consumers.

Consumer Surplus

An instinctive appreciation for the difference between *total* utility and *marginal* utility is important for understanding the theory of consumer behaviour. The concept of *consumer surplus* helps make this difference clear.

EXTENSIONS IN THEORY 6-1

Market and Individual Demand Curves

Market demand curves show how much is demanded by all purchasers. For example, in Figure 3-1, the market demand for carrots is 90 000 tons when the price is $40 per ton. This 90 000 tons is the sum of the quantities demanded by millions of different consumers. The demand curve in Figure 3-1 also tells us that when the price rises to $60, the total quantity demanded falls to 77 500 tons per year. This quantity, too, can be traced back to individual consumers. Notice that we have now identified two points not only on the market demand curve but also on the demand curves of each of the millions of individual consumers.

The market demand curve is the horizontal sum of the demand curves of individual consumers. It is the horizontal sum because we wish to add quantities demanded at a given price, and quantities are measured in the horizontal direction on a conventional demand curve.

The figure illustrates aggregation over two consumers, Alison and Brenda. At a price of $3, Alison purchases 2 units and Brenda purchases 4 units; thus together they purchase 6 units, yielding one point on the market demand curve. No matter how many consumers are involved, the process is the same: Add the quantities demanded by all consumers at each price, and the result is the market demand curve.

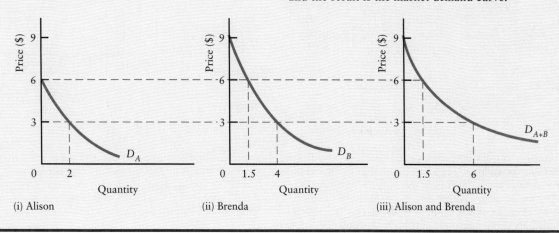

(i) Alison   (ii) Brenda   (iii) Alison and Brenda

The Concept

Imagine yourself facing an either-or choice concerning some particular product, say, ice cream: You can have the amount you are now consuming, or you can have none of it. Suppose that you would be willing to pay as much as $100 per month for the 8 litres of gourmet ice cream that you now consume, rather than do without it. Further suppose that you actually buy those 8 litres for only $40 instead of $100. What a bargain! You have paid $60 less than the most you were willing to pay. Actually this sort of bargain occurs every day in any economy in which prices do the rationing. Indeed, it is so common that the $60 "saved" in this example has been given a name: *consumer surplus*. **Consumer surplus** is the difference between the total value that consumers place on all the units consumed of some product and the payment they must make to purchase that amount of the product.

consumer surplus
The difference between the total value that consumers place on all units consumed of a commodity and the payment that they must make to purchase that amount of the commodity.

Consumer surplus is a direct consequence of negatively sloped demand curves. To illustrate this connection, suppose that we have interviewed Mr. Jean Aulait and displayed the information from the interview in the table in Figure 6-2. Our first question to Jean is, "If you were getting no milk at all, how much would you be willing to pay for one glass per week?" With no hesitation he replies, "$3.00." We then ask, "If you had already consumed that one glass, how much would you be willing to pay for a second glass per week?" After a bit of thought, he answers, "$1.50." Adding one glass per

FIGURE 6-2   Jean's Consumer Surplus on Milk Consumption

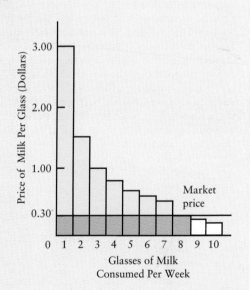

Glasses of Milk Jean Consumes Per Week	Amount Jean Is Willing to Pay to Obtain This Glass	Jean's Consumer Surplus on Each Glass if Milk Costs 30 Cents Per Glass
First	$3.00	$2.70
Second	1.50	1.20
Third	1.00	0.70
Fourth	0.80	0.50
Fifth	0.60	0.30
Sixth	0.50	0.20
Seventh	0.40	0.10
Eighth	0.30	0.00
Ninth	0.25	—
Tenth	0.20	—

Consumer surplus on each unit consumed is the difference between the market price and the maximum price that the consumer is willing to pay to obtain that unit. The table shows the value that Jean puts on successive glasses of milk consumed each week. His negatively sloped demand curve shows that he would be willing to pay progressively smaller amounts for each additional unit consumed. If the market price is 30 cents per glass, Jean will buy eight glasses of milk per week and pay the amount in the dark shaded area. The total value he places on these eight glasses is the entire shaded area. His consumer surplus is the light shaded area.

week with each question, we discover that he would be willing to pay $1.00 to get a third glass per week and 80, 60, 50, 40, 30, 25, and 20 cents for successive glasses from the fourth to the tenth glass per week.

The sum of the values that he places on each glass of milk gives us the *total value* that he places on all 10 glasses. In this case, Jean Aulait values 10 glasses of milk per week at $8.55. This is the amount he would be willing to pay if he faced the either-or choice of 10 glasses or none. This is also the amount he would be willing to pay if he were offered the milk one glass at a time and charged the maximum he was willing to pay for each.

However, Jean does not have to pay a different price for each glass of milk he consumes each week; he can buy all he wants at the prevailing market price. Suppose that the price is 30 cents per glass. He will buy eight glasses per week because he values the eighth glass just at the market price but all earlier glasses at higher amounts. He does not buy a ninth glass because he values it at less than the market price.

Because Jean values the first glass at $3.00 but gets it for 30 cents, he makes a "profit" of $2.70 on that glass. Between his $1.50 valuation of the second glass and what he has to pay for it, he clears a "profit" of $1.20. He clears a "profit" of 70 cents on the third glass, and so on. This "profit," which is shown in the third column of the table, is Jean's consumer surplus on each glass.

We can calculate Jean's total consumer surplus of $5.70 per week by summing his surplus on each glass; we can calculate the same total by first summing what he would be willing to pay for all eight glasses, which is $8.10, and then subtracting the $2.40 that he actually does pay.

Consumer surplus is the difference between what the consumer is willing to pay for the product and what the consumer actually pays.

The value placed by each consumer on the total consumption of some product can be estimated in two ways: The valuation that the consumer places on each successive unit may be summed, or the consumer may be asked how much he or she would be willing to pay to consume the amount in question if the alternative were to have none of that product.

Although other consumers would put different numerical values into the table in Figure 6-2, the negative slope of the demand curve implies that the values in the second column would be declining for every consumer. Because any consumer will go on buying additional units until the value placed on the last unit equals the market price, it follows that there will be consumer surplus on every unit consumed except the last one.

The data in the first two columns of the table give Jean's demand curve for milk. It is his demand curve because he will go on buying glasses of milk as long as he values each glass at least as much as the market price he must pay for it. When the market price is $3.00 per glass, he will buy only one glass; when it is $1.50, he will buy two glasses; and so on. The total valuation is the area below his demand curve, and consumer surplus is the part of the area that lies above the price line. These areas are shown in Figure 6-2.

Figure 6-3 shows that the same relationship holds for the smooth market demand curve that indicates the total amount that all consumers would buy at each price. Figure 6-2 is a bar chart because we only allowed Jean Aulait to vary his consumption in discrete units of one glass at a time. Had we allowed him to vary his consumption of milk one drop at a time, we could have traced out a continuous curve similar to the one shown in Figure 6-3.

Practise with Study Guide Chapter 6, Extension Exercise E-1.

Consumer surplus for the entire market is equal to the area under the market demand curve but above the price line.

Applications

Consumer surplus is an important and useful concept. It will prove useful in later chapters when we evaluate the performance—the *efficiency*—of the market system. For now, however, we discuss two examples where the concept of consumer surplus helps us to understand apparently paradoxical market outcomes. Central to both examples is the distinction between total value and marginal value.

The Paradox of Value

Early economists, struggling with the problem of what determines the relative prices of products, encountered what they called the *paradox of value*. Many necessary products, such as water, have prices that are low compared to the prices of luxury products, such as diamonds. Water is necessary to our existence, whereas diamonds are used mostly for frivolous purposes and could disappear from the face of the earth tomorrow without causing any real hardship. Does it not seem odd, then, that water is so cheap and diamonds are so expensive? As it took a long time to resolve this apparent paradox, it is not surprising that even today, analogous confusions cloud many policy discussions.

The key to resolving this apparent paradox lies in the important distinction between the total and marginal value of any product. We have seen already that the area under the demand curve is a measure of the *total value* placed on all of the units that the consumer consumes. For all consumers together, the total value of q_0 units is the entire shaded area (light and dark) under the demand curve in Figure 6-3.

What about the *marginal value* that each consumer places on one additional unit? This is given by the product's market price, which is p_0 in Figure 6-3. Facing a market price of p_0, each consumer buys all the units that he or she values at p_0 or greater but does not purchase any units valued at less than p_0. It follows that each consumer values the last unit consumed of any product at that product's price.

Now look at the total *market* value of the product. This is the amount that everyone spends to purchase it. It is price multiplied by quantity. In Figure 6-3, this is the dark shaded rectangle.

Because the market demand curve is negatively sloped, the total value that consumers place on a given amount of a product, as measured by the relevant area under the demand curve, is different from the total market value of a product, as given by the product's price multiplied by the quantity consumed. Not only are the two values different, but they are generally unrelated, except that the total area under the demand curve is always greater than the total market value. Figure 6-4 illustrates a case in which a good—like clean

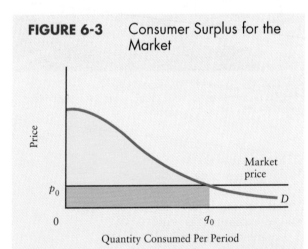

FIGURE 6-3   Consumer Surplus for the Market

Quantity Consumed Per Period

Total consumer surplus is the area under the demand curve and above the price line. The area under the demand curve shows the total valuation that consumers place on all units consumed. For example, the total value that consumers place on q_0 units is the entire shaded area under the demand curve up to q_0. At a market price of p_0, the amount paid for q_0 units is the dark shaded area. Hence consumer surplus is the light shaded area.

FIGURE 6-4 Total Value Versus Market Value

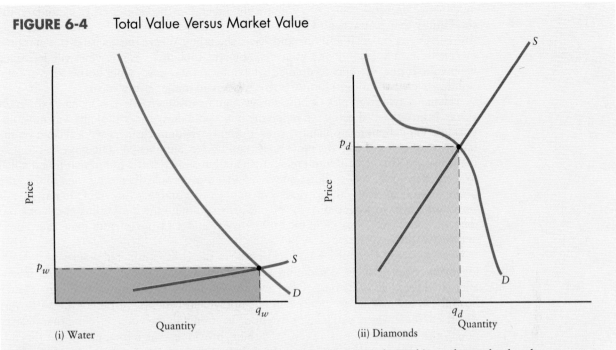

(i) Water

(ii) Diamonds

The market value of the amount of some product bears no necessary relationship to the total value that consumers place on that amount. The graph presents hypothetical demand curves for water and diamonds that are meant to be stylized versions of the real curves. The total value that consumers place on water, as shown by the area under the demand curve, is great. The total value that consumers place on diamonds is shown by the area under the demand curve for diamonds. This is clearly less than the total value placed on water.

The large supply of water makes water plentiful and makes water low in price, as shown by p_w in part (i) of the figure. Thus the total *market* value of water consumed, indicated by the dark shaded area, is low. The low supply of diamonds makes diamonds scarce and keeps diamonds high in price, as shown by p_d in part (ii) of the figure. Thus the total *market* value of diamonds sold, indicated by the light shaded area, is high.

water—has a high total value but a low market value, whereas a different good—like diamonds—has a low total value but a high market value.

The resolution of the paradox of value is that a good that is very plentiful, such as water, will have a low price and will thus be consumed to the point where all consumers place a low value on the last unit consumed, whether or not they place a high value on their *total* consumption of the product. By contrast, a product that is relatively scarce will have a high market price, and consumption will therefore stop at a point where consumers place a high value on the last unit consumed, regardless of the value that they place on their total consumption of the good.

Because the market price of a product depends on both demand and supply, there is nothing paradoxical in there being a product on which consumers place a high *total* value (such as water) selling for a low price and hence having a low *marginal* value.

Attitude Surveys

Attitude surveys often ask people which of several alternatives they prefer. Such questions reveal *total* rather than *marginal* utilities. Where the behaviour being predicted involves an either-or decision, such as to vote for the Liberal or the Conservative candidate, the total utility that is attached to each party or candidate will indeed be what matters, because the voter must choose one and reject the other. Where the decision is a marginal one regarding a little more or a little less, however, total utility is not what will determine behaviour. If one attempts to predict behaviour in these cases from knowledge of total utilities, even if the information is correct, one will make serious errors.

Here are two examples of how surveys can be misinterpreted. A Canadian market research survey asked people to name the household device they thought was most important. Though many appliances ranked highly, vacuum cleaners were judged by the most households as being the most important device. Suppliers of a new version of vacuum cleaner used the survey to predict demand but subsequently found that it had failed to accurately do so. A post-mortem revealed that most people did not respond to the sales promotion because they already had a vacuum cleaner and were unwilling to pay the advertised price for a second one. In other words, although the *total* utility they got from their vacuum cleaner was high, the utility they would get from an additional one—their *marginal* utility—was low.

For a second example, a political party in the U.K. conducted a survey to determine what types of public expenditure people thought most valuable. Unemployment benefits rated very high. The party was subsequently surprised when it aroused great voter hostility by advocating an increase in unemployment benefits. Although the party was surprised, there was nothing inconsistent or irrational in the voters' feeling that protection of the unemployed was a very good thing, providing a high total utility, but that additional payments were unnecessary, and therefore had a low marginal utility.

Income and Substitution Effects of Price Changes

In the first section of this chapter, we examined the relationship between the *law of diminishing marginal utility* and the slope of the consumer's demand curve for some product. In this section, we will consider an alternative method for thinking about the slope of an individual's demand curve. From the discussion in *Extensions in Theory 6-1*, this alternative method can also be used to think about the slope of a market demand curve.

Let's consider Tony, a college student who loves to eat ice cream. A fall in the price of ice cream affects Tony in two ways. First, it provides an incentive to buy more ice cream because it is cheaper. Second, because the price of ice cream has fallen, Tony has more *purchasing power* available to spend on all products. Suppose that the price of premium ice cream fell from $5.00 to $4.00 per litre and Tony was in the habit of eating half a litre of ice cream a day. In the course of a 30-day month, Tony could keep his ice cream habit unchanged but save $15.00, money that would be available for any purpose—more ice cream, video rentals, or photocopies of your economics notes.

real income   Income expressed in terms of the purchasing power of money income, that is, the quantity of goods and services that can be purchased with the money income. It can be calculated as money income deflated by a price index.

The price fall generates an increase in Tony's **real income**, which is defined as the quantity of goods and services that can be purchased with a given amount of money income. This rise in real income in turn provides an incentive to buy more of all normal goods. (Recall from Chapter 4 that when real income rises, the consumer buys more of all normal goods and less of all inferior goods.)

In general, the *extent* of the rise in real income depends on the share of total expenditures that the consumer spends on each good. For example, consider the extreme case in which Tony spends all of his income on ice cream. If the price of ice cream falls by half, he would find that his real income has doubled because he can buy twice as much as before. At the other extreme, if Tony spent none of his income on ice cream and all of it on other things, he would find that his consumption opportunities are unchanged—he can still buy exactly what he bought before the price of ice cream fell. For intermediate cases where both ice cream and other goods are purchased, there will be some positive effect on real income when the price of ice cream falls.

The Substitution Effect

To isolate the effect of the change in relative price when the price of ice cream falls, we can consider what would happen if we also reduce Tony's money income to restore the original purchasing power. Suppose that Tony's uncle sends him a monthly allowance for ice cream, and that when the price of ice cream falls, the allowance is reduced so that Tony can buy just as much ice cream—and everything else—as he could before. Tony's purchasing power will be unchanged. If his behaviour remains unchanged, however, he will not be maximizing his utility. Recall that utility maximization requires that the ratio of marginal utility to price be the same for all goods. In our example, with no change in behaviour, the quantities (and hence marginal utilities) and the prices of all goods other than ice cream are unchanged. The quantity of ice cream is also unchanged, but the price has fallen. To maximize his utility, Tony must therefore increase his consumption (reduce his marginal utility) of ice cream and reduce his consumption of all other goods.

When purchasing power is held constant, the change in the quantity demanded of a good whose relative price has changed is called the **substitution effect** of the price change.[2]

> **substitution effect** The change in the quantity of a good demanded resulting from a change in its relative price (holding real income constant).

The substitution effect increases the quantity demanded of a good whose price has fallen and reduces the quantity demanded of a good whose price has risen.

The Income Effect

To examine the substitution effect, we reduced Tony's *money* income following the price reduction so that we could see the effect of the relative price change, holding purchasing power constant. Now we want to see the effect of the change in purchasing power, *holding relative prices constant at their new value*. To do this, suppose that after Tony has adjusted his purchases to the new price and his reduced income, he then calls his uncle and pleads to have his allowance restored to its original (higher) amount. Tony's uncle agrees, and Tony's money income is returned to its original level. If we assume that ice cream is a normal good, Tony will increase his consumption of ice cream. The change in the quantity of ice cream demanded as a result of Tony's reaction to increased real income is called the **income effect**.

> **income effect** The change in the quantity of a good demanded resulting from a change in real income (holding relative prices constant).

---

[2]This measure, which isolates the substitution effect by holding the consumer's purchasing power constant, is known as the *Slutsky Effect*. A related but slightly different measure that holds the consumer's level of utility constant is discussed in the appendix to this chapter.

The income effect leads consumers to buy more of a product whose price has fallen, provided that the product is a normal good.

Notice that the size of the income effect depends on the amount of income spent on the good whose price changes and on the amount by which the price changes. In our example, if Tony were initially spending half of his income on ice cream, a reduction in the price of ice cream from $5 to $4 would be equivalent to a 10 percent increase in income (20 percent of 50 percent). Now consider a different case: The price of gasoline falls by 20 percent. For a consumer who was spending only 5 percent of income on gas, this is equivalent to only a 1 percent increase in purchasing power (20 percent of 5 percent).

The Slope of the Demand Curve

We have now divided Tony's reaction to a change in the price of ice cream into a substitution effect and an income effect. Of course, when the price changes, Tony moves directly from the initial consumption pattern to the final one; we do not observe any "halfway" consumption pattern. By breaking this movement into two parts for analytical purposes, however, we are able to study Tony's total change in quantity demanded as a response to a change in relative prices plus a response to a change in real income.

What is true for Tony is also true, in general terms, for all consumers. The substitution effect leads consumers to increase their demand for goods whose prices fall. The income effect leads consumers to buy more of all normal goods whose prices fall.

Putting the income and substitution effects together gives the following statement of the law of demand:

Because of the combined operation of the income and substitution effects, the demand curve for any normal commodity will be negatively sloped. Thus a fall in price will increase the quantity demanded.

For most inferior goods, the demand curve also has a negative slope. The theoretical possibility that demand curves might not have a negative slope is considered in *Extensions in Theory 6-2*.

Finally, note that the logic of breaking down a price change into the separate income and substitution effects is not limited to the analysis of demand. The same logic applies to supply. A particularly important example involves the labour market: How does a change in the market wage affect the quantity of work effort supplied by individuals? *Applying Economic Concepts 6-1* addresses the issue of how a change in income-tax rates—and thus a change in the after-tax wage—alters individuals' incentives to work.

EXTENSIONS IN THEORY 6-2

Can Demand Curves Have a Positive Slope?

The law of demand asserts that, other things being constant, the price and quantity demanded of a product are negatively related; that is, demand curves have a negative slope. Challenges to the law have taken various forms, focusing on Giffen goods and "conspicuous consumption" goods.

Giffen Goods

Great interest was attached to the apparent refutation of the law of demand by the English economist Sir Robert Giffen (1837–1910). He is alleged to have observed that when a rise in the price of imported wheat led to an increase in the price of bread, members of the British working class *increased* their consumption of bread, suggesting that their demand curve for bread was positively sloped.

Two things must be true in order for a good to be a so-called **Giffen good**. First, the good must be an inferior good, meaning that a reduction in real income leads households to purchase *more* of that good. Second, the good must take a large proportion of total household expenditure. Bread was indeed a dietary staple of the British working classes during the nineteenth century. A rise in the price of bread would therefore cause a large reduction in their real income. This could lead people to eat more bread (and less meat) in order to consume enough calories to stay alive. Though possible, such cases are all but unknown in the modern world, for in all but the poorest societies, typical households do not spend large proportions of their incomes on any single inferior good.

Conspicuous Consumption Goods

Thorstein Veblen (1857–1929), in *The Theory of the Leisure Class,* noted that some products were consumed not for their intrinsic qualities but because they had "snob appeal." He suggested that the more expensive such a commodity became, the greater might be its ability to confer status on its purchaser.

Consumers might value diamonds, for example, precisely because everyone knows they are expensive. Thus a fall in price might lead them to stop buying diamonds and to switch to a more satisfactory object of conspicuous consumption. They may behave in the same way with respect to luxury cars, buying them *because* they are expensive.

Two comments are in order. First, in a case where individuals appear to buy more goods at a higher price *because of the high price*, there is actually something else going on that explains the apparent violation of the law of demand. What really appeals to such individuals is that *other people think* they paid a high price—this is the basis for the "snob appeal." But such snobs would still buy more at a lower price (and hence still have negatively sloped demand curves) as long as they were absolutely sure that other people *thought* they had paid the high price. As one advertising slogan for a discount department store puts it: "Only you know how little you paid."

Second, even if such conspicuous consumers do exist, it is very unlikely that the *market* demand curve is positively sloped. The reason is easy to discover. The fact that countless lower-income consumers would be glad to buy diamonds or Cadillacs only if these commodities were sufficiently inexpensive suggests that positively sloped demand curves for a few individual wealthy households are much more likely than a positively sloped *market* demand curve for the same commodity.

Market Demand Curves

Even if some individual consumers exhibited one or both of the "exceptions" to the law of demand discussed here, in most cases their actions would be swamped by those of the many more consumers whose behaviour conformed to the law of demand. Thus the *market* demand curve would still be negatively sloped.

All in all, the mass of accumulated evidence confirms that demand curves generally have a negative slope. Exceptions are extremely rare.

Giffen good   An inferior good for which the negative income effect outweighs the substitution effect so that the demand curve is positively sloped.

APPLYING ECONOMIC CONCEPTS 6-1

Do Taxes Discourage Work Effort?

Although they sound highly abstract and "theoretical" when you first encounter them, the income and substitution effects turn out to be very useful tools. They help a great deal when thinking about many economic issues. One particularly important issue involves the effect that income taxes have on individuals' incentive to work. Would cutting the income-tax rate lead individuals to work more?

Policymakers frequently face such questions, and they are often surprised at the results produced by the market. In several countries, increases in income-tax rates (within a moderate range) have been found to be associated with people working more hours, rather than fewer. The surprise in such cases was the same. Simple intuition suggests that if you pay people a higher wage, they will work more hours. Experience, however, shows that the result is often the opposite.

The explanation of this surprising behaviour lies in distinguishing the income effect from the substitution effect of a change in the after-tax wage. Consider Luke starting with an endowment of 24 hours per day and deciding to consume some of that time as "leisure" (including sleep) and to trade the rest of the time for income by working. If Luke works 9 hours a day at an after-tax wage of $10 per hour, he earns $90. He is then "consuming" 15 hours a day of leisure and can use the $90 worth of income to buy goods and services.

Now suppose the government reduces the rate of income tax so that Luke's after-tax wage rises from $10 to $12. What does Luke do? His response to the increase in the after-tax wage will be made up by the income effect and the substitution effect.

The substitution effect works in the same away as does the simple intuition above. With a higher after-tax wage, Luke's opportunity cost of leisure increases. That is, Luke must now give up more income (and thus more other goods and services) for each hour of leisure that he enjoys. This simple change in relative prices (the price of leisure in terms of other goods) leads Luke to substitute toward work and away from leisure. If the substitution effect were all that mattered, then the reduction in taxes would lead people to work harder.

But there is also an income effect, and this is where the surprise comes in. The rise in the after-tax wage increases Luke's purchasing power in the sense that Luke can now afford to have more goods and more leisure. For example, he could choose to reduce his daily work time from 9 hours to 8 hours and still increase his earnings from $90 (9 hours × $10 per hour) to $96 (8 hours × $12 per hour). In this case, Luke would have more leisure and he could purchase more goods and services. In fact, if leisure is a normal "good"—meaning that Luke demands more of it when his income rises—then the income effect taken by itself would lead Luke to work less in response to the tax reduction.

What is the total effect on Luke's work effort? We simply add together the income effect and the substitution effect. If the substitution effect dominates, then the tax reduction will lead Luke to work more hours. But if the income effect dominates, then the tax reduction will lead Luke to work fewer hours.

In general, we don't know exactly how any given individual will respond to such a tax reduction. If leisure is an *inferior* good, then the substitution and income effects work in the same direction, in which case a reduction in income-tax rates will surely lead people to work more. But most economists think that leisure is a normal good. Thus the substitution and income effects work in opposite directions; in this more likely case, the net effect depends on the individual's circumstances and preferences.

Given the possibilities, policymakers should not be surprised if they find that increases in income-tax rates sometimes lead people to work more. This result is not guaranteed, but it is certainly possible. The simple explanation is that leisure is a normal good and that the income effect of the tax change is stronger than the substitution effect.

S U M M A R Y

Marginal Utility and Consumer Choice

- Marginal utility theory distinguishes between the total utility from the consumption of *all units* of some product and the incremental (or marginal) utility derived from consuming *one more unit* of the product.
- The basic assumption in marginal utility theory is that the utility that consumers derive from the consumption of successive units of a product diminishes as the number of units consumed increases.
- Consumers are assumed to make their decisions in a way that maximizes their utility. They thus make their choices such that the utility derived from the last dollar spent on each product is equal. For two goods X and Y, utility will be maximized when

$$\frac{MU_X}{p_X} = \frac{MU_Y}{p_Y}$$

- Demand curves have negative slopes because when the price of one product, X, falls, each consumer responds by increasing purchases of X sufficiently to restore the ratio of that product's marginal utility to its now lower price (MU_X/p_X) to the same level achieved for all other products.

Consumer Surplus

- The total value that consumers place on some quantity of a product consumed is given by the area under the demand curve up to that quantity. The market value is given by an area below the market price up to that quantity. Consumer surplus is the difference between the two. In other words, consumer surplus is the difference between what the consumers would be *willing to pay* for some quantity of the good and what the consumers *actually pay* for that quantity of the good.
- Consumer surplus arises because a consumer can purchase every unit of a product at a price equal to the value placed on the last unit purchased. The negative slope of demand curves implies that the value that consumers place on all other units purchased exceeds the value of the last unit purchased and hence that all but the last unit purchased yields consumer surplus.
- It is important to distinguish between total and marginal values because choices concerning a bit more and a bit less cannot be predicted from a knowledge of total values. The paradox of value involves a confusion between total value and marginal value.
- Price is related to the *marginal* value that consumers place on having a bit more or a bit less of some product; it bears no necessary relationship to the *total* value that consumers place on all of the units consumed of that product.

Income and Substitution Effects of Price Changes

- A change in the price of a product generates both an income effect and a substitution effect. The substitution effect is the reaction of the consumer to the change in relative prices, with purchasing power held constant. The substitution effect leads the consumer to increase purchases of the product whose relative price has fallen.
- The income effect is the reaction of the consumer to the change in purchasing power that is caused by the price change, holding relative prices constant. A fall in one price will lead to an increase in the consumer's purchasing power and thus to an increase in purchases of all normal goods.
- The combined income and substitution effects ensure that the quantity demanded of any normal good will increase when its money price falls, other things being equal. Normal goods, therefore, have negatively sloped demand curves.

KEY CONCEPTS

Total utility and marginal utility
Utility maximization
Equality of MU/p across different
   goods

Slope of the demand curve
Consumer surplus
The paradox of value

Income effect and substitution effect
Giffen goods and conspicuous
   consumption goods

STUDY EXERCISES

1. The table below shows how Brett's utility increases as the number of avocados he consumes (each month) increases. Brett's utility is measured in *utils*, a name that economists invented to describe units of utility.

Avocados	Total Utility (in utils)	Marginal Utility (in utils)
Zero	0	
First	100	____
Second	185	____
Third	245	____
Fourth	285	____
Fifth	315	____
Sixth	335	____
Seventh	345	____
Eighth	350	

a. Plot Brett's total utility on a scale diagram, with utils on the vertical axis and the number of avocados (per month) on the horizontal axis.

b. Compute the marginal utility for each avocado and fill in the table.

c. Plot the marginal utility on a scale diagram, with utils on the vertical axis and the number of avocados (per month) on the horizontal axis. (Make sure to plot marginal utility at the midpoints between units.)

d. Explain why it is reasonable that Brett's utility increases by smaller and smaller amounts for each successive avocado consumed.

2. In each of the cases listed below, identify how Claudia's expenditure should be changed to maximize her utility.

Case	Price of X ($)	Marginal Utility of X (units of utility)	Price of Y ($)	Marginal Utility of Y (units of utility)
A	10	2	5	3
B	12	4	4	2
C	3	1	6	2
D	4	2	4	2
E	8	4	4	3

3. Rupert really loves pizza, but he eventually tires of it. The table below shows the highest price that Rupert is willing to pay for each successive pizza per week.

Pizza	Rupert's Willingness to Pay
First	$18
Second	$16
Third	$13
Fourth	$9
Fifth	$4
Sixth	$0

a. Suppose Rupert were to eat five pizzas per week. What is the total value Rupert would place on his five weekly pizzas?

b. If the market price is $10 per pizza, how many pizzas will Rupert eat per week?

c. If the market price is $10 per pizza, what is the weekly consumer surplus that Rupert gets from eating pizza?

d. Can you state a generalization about the relationship between market price and consumer surplus?

4. Suppose there is a 10 percent increase in the prices of the following products. Explain whether you think the income effect in each case would be small or large, and why.

a. salt
b. blue jeans
c. canned vegetables
d. gasoline
e. mini-vans
f. rental apartments
g. luxury cars

5. Consider the following supply-and-demand diagrams depicting the markets for X and Y, respectively. In the market for good X, supply is perfectly elastic, indicating that producers are prepared to supply any amount of X at price p_0.

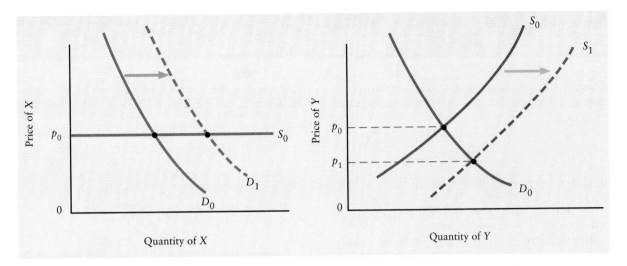

a. In the market for X, demand increases from D_0 to D_1. Explain what happens to the *total* value that consumers place on X.

b. Explain how the increase in demand for X alters the *marginal* value that consumers place on X.

c. In the market for Y, a technological improvement causes supply to increase from S_0 to S_1, causing price to fall from p_0 to p_1. Explain what happens to the total value that consumers place *on a given quantity* of Y.

d. Explain why the increase in supply leads consumers to reduce their *marginal* value of Y even though there has been no change in their preferences regarding Y (and thus no shift in the demand curve).

6. Consider the market for some product, X. The demand and supply curves for X are given by:

Demand: $p = 30 - 4Q^D$
Supply: $p = 6 + 2Q^S$

a. Plot the demand and supply curves on a scale diagram. Compute the equilibrium price (p^*) and quantity (Q^*).

b. Show in the diagram the total value that consumers place on Q^* units of the good.

c. What is the value that consumers place on an *additional* unit of the good?

d. Now suppose that production costs fall and so the market supply curve shifts to a new position given by: $p = 2 + 2Q^S$. How do consumers now value an additional unit of the good?

e. Explain why consumers' marginal value has fallen even though there has been no change in their preferences (and thus no change in the demand curve).

DISCUSSION QUESTIONS

1. Describe the difference in behaviour at a party at which drinks are free between someone who imbibes up to the point where the *marginal* value of more alcohol consumed is zero and someone who imbibes up to the point where the *average* value of alcohol consumed is zero.

2. Compare the consequences of the income effect of a drastic fall in food prices with the consequences of a rise in incomes when prices are constant.

3. Two U.S. economics professors, Jeff Biddle and Daniel Hamermesh, recently estimated that a 25 percent increase in wages will cause the average individual to reduce the time that he or she spends sleeping by about 1 percent. Interpret this finding in terms of the income and substitution effects of a wage change.

4. Consider the following common scenario. An economist is attending a conference in an unfamiliar city. She is in the mood for a high-quality dinner and wanders through the centre of the city looking for a restaurant. After narrowing her search to two establishments, she ultimately selects the restaurant with the higher prices. Because she is an economist, we know that she is rational. What might account for this behaviour?

5. Medical and hospital services in Canada are provided at zero cost to all Canadians and are paid for out of general government revenues. What will be the *marginal value* of such services consumed by each Canadian if the government provides funds to meet all demand?

Indifference Curves

In Chapter 6, we covered some basic material concerning the theory of demand; here we extend the treatment of demand theory by considering in more detail the assumptions about consumer behaviour that underlie the theory of demand.

The history of demand theory has seen two major breakthroughs. The first was *marginal utility theory*, which we used in Chapter 6. By distinguishing total and marginal values, this theory helped to explain the so-called paradox of value. The second breakthrough came with *indifference theory*, which showed that all that is required to develop demand theory is to assume that consumers can always say which of two consumption bundles they prefer without having to say *by how much* they prefer it.

Indifference Curves

Suppose Hugh currently has available some specific bundle of goods, say, 18 units of clothing and 10 units of food. Now offer him an alternative bundle of, say, 13 units of clothing and 15 units of food. This alternative combination of goods has 5 fewer units of clothing and 5 more units of food than the first one. Whether Hugh prefers this new bundle depends on the relative valuation that he places on 5 more units of food and 5 fewer units of clothing. If he values the extra food more than the forgone clothing, he will prefer the new bundle to the original one. If he values the extra food less than the forgone clothing, he will prefer the original bundle. If Hugh values the extra food the same as the forgone clothing, he is said to be *indifferent* between the two bundles.

Suppose that after much trial and error, we have identified several bundles between which Hugh is indifferent. In other words, each bundle gives him equal satisfaction or utility. They are shown in the table in Figure 6A-1.

Of course, there are combinations of the two products other than those enumerated in the table that will give Hugh the same level of utility. All of these combinations are shown in Figure 6A-1 by the smooth curve that passes through the points plotted from the table.

This curve, called an *indifference curve*, shows all combinations of products that yield Hugh the same utility.

The consumer is indifferent between the combinations indicated by any two points on one indifference curve.

Any points above the curve show combinations of food and clothing that Hugh prefers to points on the curve. Consider, for example, the combination of 20 units of food and 18 units of clothing, represented by point g in Figure 6A-1. Although it may not be obvious that this bundle must be preferred to bundle a (which has more clothing but less food), it is obvious that it will be preferred to bundle c because both less clothing and less food are represented at c than at g. Inspection of the graph shows that any point above the curve will be superior to some points on the curve in the sense that it will contain both more food and more clothing than those points on the curve. However, because all points on the curve are equal in Hugh's eyes, any point above the curve must be superior to all points on the curve. By a similar argument, all points below and to the left of the curve represent bundles that are inferior to bundles represented by points on the curve.

Any point above an indifference curve is preferred to any point along that same indifference curve; any point below an indifference curve is inferior to any point along the indifference curve.

Diminishing Marginal Rate of Substitution

How much clothing would Hugh be prepared to give up to get one more unit of food? The answer to this question measures what is called Hugh's marginal rate of substitution of clothing for food. The *marginal rate of substitution (MRS)* is the amount of one product that a consumer is prepared to give up to get one more unit of another product.

The first basic assumption of indifference theory is that the algebraic value of the *MRS* between two goods is always negative.

FIGURE 6A-1   Hugh's Indifference Curve

Alternative Bundles Giving Hugh Equal Utility

Bundle	Clothing	Food
a	30	5
b	18	10
c	13	15
d	10	20
e	8	25
f	7	30

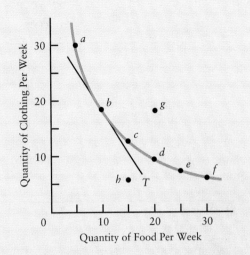

This indifference curve shows combinations of food and clothing that yield equal utility and between which Hugh is indifferent. The smooth curve through the points is an indifference curve; each combination on it gives Hugh equal utility. Point g above the line is a preferred combination to any point on the line; point h below the line is an inferior combination to any point on the line. The slope of the line T gives the marginal rate of substitution at point b. Moving down the curve from b to f, the slope flattens, showing that the more food and the less clothing Hugh has, the less willing he is to sacrifice further clothing to get more food.

A negative *MRS* means that to increase consumption of one product, Hugh is prepared to decrease consumption of a second product. The negative value of the marginal rate of substitution is indicated graphically by the negative slope of indifference curves. (See, for example, the curve in Figure 6A-1.)

The second basic assumption of indifference theory is that the marginal rate of substitution between any two goods depends on the amounts of the goods currently being consumed.

Consider a case in which Hugh has a lot of clothing and only a little food. Common sense suggests that he might be willing to give up quite a bit of plentiful clothing to get one more unit of scarce food. It suggests as well that if Hugh had little clothing and a lot of food he would be willing to give up only a little scarce clothing to get one more unit of already plentiful food.

This example illustrates the hypothesis of *diminishing marginal rate of substitution.* The less of one product, A, and the more of a second product, B, that the consumer has already, the smaller the amount of A

that the consumer will be willing to give up to get one additional unit of B. The hypothesis says that the marginal rate of substitution changes when the amounts of two products consumed change. The graphical expression of this hypothesis is that any indifference curve becomes flatter as the consumer moves downward and to the right along the curve. In Figure 6A-1, a movement downward and to the right means that Hugh is consuming less clothing and more food. The decreasing steepness of the curve means that Hugh is willing to sacrifice less and less clothing to get each additional unit of food. [11]

The hypothesis of diminishing marginal rate of substitution is illustrated in Table 6A-1, which is based on the example in Figure 6A-1. The last column of the table shows the rate at which Hugh is prepared to sacrifice units of clothing per unit of food obtained. At first, Hugh will sacrifice 2.4 units of clothing to get 1 unit more of food, but as his consumption of clothing diminishes and his consumption of food increases, Hugh becomes less and less willing to sacrifice further clothing for more food.

TABLE 6A-1	Hugh's Marginal Rate of Substitution Between Clothing and Food		
	(1)	(2)	(3) Marginal Rate of Substitution (1) ÷ (2)
Movement	Change in Clothing	Change in Food	
From a to b	−12	5	−2.4
From b to c	−5	5	−1.0
From c to d	−3	5	−0.6
From d to e	−2	5	−0.4
From e to f	−1	5	−0.2

The marginal rate of substitution of clothing for food declines (in absolute value) as the quantity of food increases. This table is based on Figure 6A-1. When Hugh moves from a to b, he gives up 12 units of clothing and gains 5 units of food; he remains at the same level of overall utility. At point a Hugh is prepared to sacrifice 12 units of clothing for 5 units of food (i.e., 12/5 = 2.4 units of clothing per unit of food obtained). When he moves from b to c, he sacrifices 5 units of clothing for 5 units of food (a rate of substitution of 1 unit of clothing for each unit of food).

The Indifference Map

So far, we have constructed only a single indifference curve for Hugh. However, starting at any other point in Figure 6A-1, such as g, there will be other combinations that will give Hugh equal utility. If the points indicating all of these combinations are connected, they will form another indifference curve. This exercise can be repeated many times, and we can thereby generate many indifference curves for Hugh. The farther any indifference curve is from the origin, the higher will be the level of Hugh's utility given by any of the points on the curve.

A set of indifference curves is called an *indifference map*, an example of which is shown in Figure 6A-2. It specifies the consumer's tastes by showing his rate of substitution between the two products for every possible level of current consumption of these products.

When economists say that a consumer's tastes are given, they do not mean that the consumer's current consumption pattern is given; rather, they mean that the consumer's entire indifference map is given.

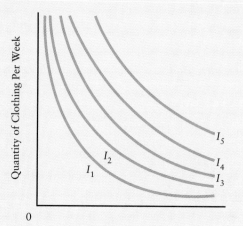

FIGURE 6A-2   Hugh's Indifference Map

An indifference map consists of a set of indifference curves. All points on a particular curve indicate alternative combinations of food and clothing that give Hugh equal utility. The farther the curve is from the origin, the higher is the level of utility it represents. For example, I_5 is a higher indifference curve than I_4, which means that all the points on I_5 give Hugh a higher level of utility than do the points on I_4.

The Budget Line

Indifference curves illustrate consumers' tastes. To develop a complete theory of their choices, we must also illustrate the alternatives available to them. These are shown as the solid line *ab* in Figure 6A-3. That line, called a *budget line*, shows all the combinations of food and clothing that Hugh can buy if he spends a fixed amount of money, in this case his entire money income of $720 per week, at fixed prices of the products (in this case, $12 per unit for clothing and $24 per unit for food).

Properties of the Budget Line

The budget line has several important properties:

1. Points on the budget line indicate bundles of products that use up the consumer's entire income. (Try, for example, the point 20C, 20F.)

FIGURE 6A-3 Hugh's Budget Line

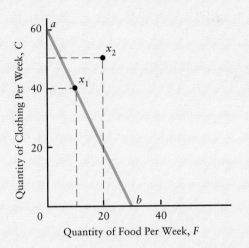

The budget line shows the quantities of goods available to a consumer given money income and the prices of goods. Any point in this diagram indicates a combination (or bundle) of so much food and so much clothing. Point x_1, for example, indicates 40 units of clothing and 10 units of food per week.

With an income of $720 a week and prices of $24 per unit for food and $12 per unit for clothing, Hugh's budget line is *ab*. This line shows all the combinations of F and C available to him. He could spend all of this money income on clothing and obtain 60 units of clothing and zero food each week. Or he could go to the other extreme and purchase only food, buying 30 units of F and zero units of C. Hugh could also choose an intermediate position and consume some of both goods—for example, spending $240 to buy 10 units of F and $480 to buy 40 units of C (point x_1). Points above the budget line, such as x_2, are not attainable.

2. Points between the budget line and the origin indicate bundles of products that cost less than the consumer's income. (Try, for example, the point 20*C*, 10*F*.)

3. Points above the budget line indicate combinations of products that cost more than the consumer's income. (Try, for example, the point 30*C*, 40*F*.)

The budget line shows all combinations of products that are available to the consumer given his money income and the prices of the goods that he purchases.

We can also show Hugh's alternatives with an equation that uses symbols to express the information contained in the budget line. Let E stand for Hugh's money income, which must be equal to his total expenditure on food and clothing. If p_F and p_C represent the money prices of food and clothing, respectively, and F and C represent the quantities of food and clothing that Hugh chooses, then his spending on food is equal to p_F times F, and his spending on clothing is equal to p_C times C. Thus the equation for the budget line is

$$E = p_F \times F + p_C \times C$$

The Slope of the Budget Line

Look again at Hugh's budget line in Figure 6A-3. The vertical intercept is 60 units of clothing, and the horizontal intercept is 30 units of food. Thus the slope is equal to -2. The minus sign means that increases in Hugh's purchases of one of the goods must be accompanied by decreases in his purchases of the other. The numerical value of the slope indicates how much of one good must be given up to obtain an additional unit of the other; in our example, the slope of -2 means that Hugh must forgo the purchase of 2 units of clothing to acquire 1 extra unit of food.

Recall that in Chapter 3 we contrasted the *absolute*, or *money*, price of a product with its *relative* price, which is the ratio of its absolute price to that of some other product or group of products. One important point is that the relative price determines the slope of the budget line. In terms of our example of food and clothing, the slope of the budget line is determined by the relative price of food in terms of clothing, p_F/p_C; with the price of food (p_F) at $24 per unit and the price of clothing (p_C) at $12 per unit, the slope of the budget line (in absolute value) is 2. [12]

The significance of the slope of Hugh's budget line for food and clothing is that it reflects his *opportunity cost* of food in terms of clothing. To increase food consumption while maintaining expenditure constant, Hugh must move along the budget line and therefore consume less clothing; the slope of the budget line determines how much clothing he must give up to obtain an additional unit of food.

The opportunity cost of food in terms of clothing is measured by the (absolute value of the) slope of the budget line, which is equal to the relative price ratio, p_F/p_C.

In the example, with fixed income and with the relative price of food in terms of clothing (p_F/p_C) equal to 2, Hugh must forgo the purchase of 2 units of clothing to acquire 1 extra unit of food. The opportunity cost of a unit of food is thus 2 units of clothing. Notice that the relative price (in our example, $p_F/p_C = 2$) is consistent with an infinite number of absolute prices. If $p_F = \$40$ and $p_C = \$20$, it is still necessary to sacrifice 2 units of clothing to acquire 1 unit of food.[1] Thus relative, not absolute, prices determine opportunity cost.

The Consumer's Utility-Maximizing Choice

An indifference map describes the preferences of a consumer, and a budget line describes the possibilities available to a consumer. To predict what a consumer will actually do, both sets of information must be combined, as is done in Figure 6A-4. Hugh's budget line is shown by the straight line, and the curves from the indifference map are also shown. Any point on the budget line is attainable, but which point will Hugh actually choose?

Because Hugh wishes to maximize utility, he wishes to reach the highest attainable indifference curve. Inspection of Figure 6A-4 shows that if Hugh purchases any bundle on the budget line at a point cut by an indifference curve, he can reach a higher indifference curve. Only when the bundle purchased is such that the indifference curve is tangent to the budget line is it impossible for Hugh to reach a higher curve by altering his purchases.

The consumer's utility is maximized at the point where an indifference curve is tangent to the budget line. At that point, the consumer's marginal rate of substitution for the two goods is equal to the relative prices of the two goods.

The intuitive explanation for this result is that if Hugh values goods differently from the way the market does, there is room for profitable exchange. Hugh

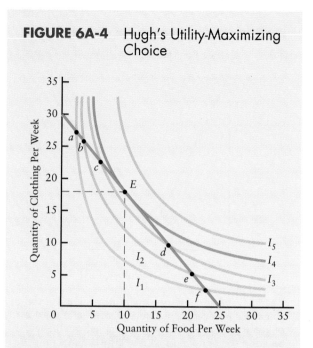

FIGURE 6A-4   Hugh's Utility-Maximizing Choice

The consumer's utility is maximized at E, where an indifference curve is tangent to the budget line. Hugh has a money income of $750 per week and faces money prices of $25 per unit for clothing and $30 per unit for food. A combination of units of clothing and food indicated by point a on I_1 is attainable but, by moving along the budget line, Hugh can reach higher indifference curves. The same is true at b on I_2 and at c on I_3. At E, however, where an indifference curve (I_4) is tangent to the budget line, Hugh cannot reach a higher curve by moving along the budget line.

can give up some of the good that he values relatively less than the market does and take in return some of the good that he values relatively more than the market does. When he is prepared to exchange goods at the same rate as they can be traded on the market, there is no further opportunity for him to raise utility by substituting one product for the other.

The theory thus proceeds by supposing that Hugh is presented with market prices that he cannot change and then analysing how he adjusts to these prices by choosing a bundle of goods such that, at the margin, his own subjective evaluation of the goods coincides with the valuations given by market prices.

We will now use this theory to predict the typical consumer's response to a change in income and in prices.

---

[1]Of course, with a given income, Hugh can afford much less of each at these higher money prices, but the opportunity cost of food in terms of clothing remains unchanged.

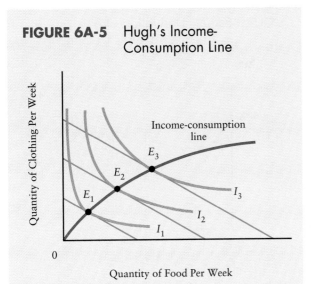

FIGURE 6A-5   Hugh's Income-Consumption Line

The income-consumption line shows how the consumer's purchases react to a change in money income with relative prices being held constant. Increases in Hugh's money income cause a parallel outward shift of his budget line, moving his utility-maximizing point from E_1 to E_2 to E_3. By joining all the utility-maximizing points, Hugh's income-consumption line is traced out.

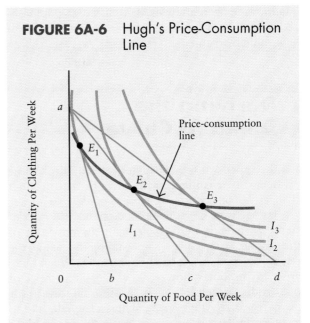

FIGURE 6A-6   Hugh's Price-Consumption Line

The price-consumption line shows how the consumer's purchases react to a change in one price with money income and other prices being held constant. Decreases in the price of food (with money income and the price of clothing held constant) pivot Hugh's budget line from ab to ac to ad. Hugh's utility-maximizing bundle moves from E_1 to E_2 to E_3. By joining all the utility-maximizing points, a price-consumption line is traced out, showing that Hugh purchases more food and less clothing as the price of food falls.

The Consumer's Reaction to a Change in Income

A change in Hugh's money income will, *ceteris paribus*, shift his budget line. For example, if Hugh's income doubles, he will be able to buy twice as much of both food and clothing compared with any combination on his previous budget line. His budget line will therefore shift out parallel to itself to indicate this expansion in his consumption possibilities. (The fact that it will be a parallel shift is established by the previous demonstration that the slope of the budget line depends only on the relative price of the two products.)

For each level of Hugh's income, there will be a utility-maximizing point at which an indifference curve is tangent to the relevant budget line. Each such utility-maximizing position means that Hugh is doing as well as possible at that level of income. If we move the budget line through all possible levels of income and if we join up all the utility-maximizing points, we will trace

out what is called an *income-consumption line*, an example of which is shown in Figure 6A-5. This line shows how Hugh's consumption bundle changes as his income changes, with relative prices being held constant.

The Consumer's Reaction to a Change in Price

We already know that a change in the relative price of the two goods changes the slope of the budget line. Given the price of clothing, for each possible price of food there is a different utility-maximizing consumption bundle for Hugh. If we connect these bundles, at a given money income, we will trace out a *price-consumption line*, as shown in Figure 6A-6. Notice that in this example, as the relative prices of food and clothing change, the relative quantities of food and clothing that Hugh purchases also change. In particular, as the price of food falls, Hugh buys more food and less clothing.

Deriving the Demand Curve

What happens to the consumer's demand for some product, say, gasoline, as the price of that product changes, *holding constant the prices of all other goods?*

If there were only two products purchased by consumers, we could derive a demand curve for one of the products from the price-consumption line like the one we showed for Hugh in Figure 6A-6. When there are many products, however, a change in the price of one product generally causes substitution toward (or away from) *all other goods.* Thus we would like to have a simple way of representing the individual's tastes in a world of many products.

In part (i) of Figure 6A-7, a new type of indifference map is plotted in which litres of gasoline per month are measured on the horizontal axis and the *value* of all other goods consumed per month is plotted on the vertical axis. We have in effect used "everything but gasoline" as the second product. The indifference curves in this figure then show the rate at which the consumer is prepared to substitute gasoline for money (which allows him to buy all other goods) at each level of consumption of gasoline and of all other goods.

To illustrate the derivation of demand curves, we use the numerical example shown in Figure 6A-7. The consumer is assumed to have an after-tax money income of $4000 per month. This level of money income is plotted on the vertical axis, showing that if the consumer consumes no gasoline, he can consume $4000 worth of other goods each month. When gasoline costs $1.50 per litre, the consumer could buy a maximum of 2667 litres per month. This set of choices gives rise to the innermost budget line. Given the consumer's tastes, utility is maximized at point E_0, consuming 600 litres of gasoline and $3100 worth of other products.

Next, let the price of gasoline fall to $1.00 per litre. Now the maximum possible consumption of gasoline is 4000 litres per month, giving rise to the middle budget line in the figure. The consumer's utility is maximized, as always, at the point where the new budget line is tangent to an indifference curve. At this point, E_1, the consumer is consuming 1200 litres of gasoline per month and spending $2800 on all other goods. Finally, let the price fall to 50 cents per

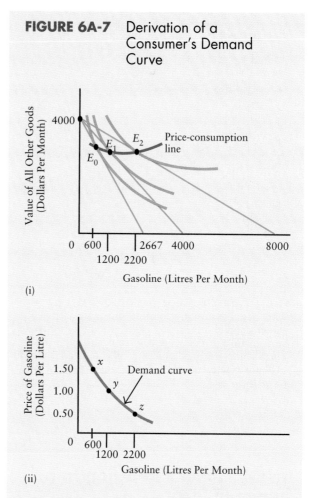

FIGURE 6A-7 Derivation of a Consumer's Demand Curve

(i)

(ii)

Every point on the price-consumption line corresponds to both a price of the product and a quantity demanded; this is the information required for a demand curve. In part (i), the consumer has a money income of $4000 and alternatively faces prices of $1.50, $1.00, and $0.50 per litre of gasoline, choosing positions E_0, E_1, and E_2 at each price. The information for litres demanded at each price is then plotted in part (ii) to yield the consumer's demand curve. The three points x, y, and z in part (ii) correspond to the points E_0, E_1, and E_2 in part (i).

litre. The consumer can now buy a maximum of 8000 litres per month, giving rise to the outermost of the three budget lines. The consumer maximizes utility by consuming 2200 litres of gasoline per month and spending $2900 on other products.

If we let the price vary over all possible amounts, we will trace out a complete price-consumption line, as shown in Figure 6A-7. The points derived in the preceding paragraph are merely three points on this line.

We have now derived all that we need to plot the consumer's demand curve for gasoline, now that we know how much the consumer will purchase at each price. To draw the curve, we merely replot the data from part (i) of Figure 6A-7 onto a demand graph, as shown in part (ii) of Figure 6A-7.

Like part (i), part (ii) has quantity of gasoline on the horizontal axis. By placing one graph under the other, we can directly transcribe the quantity determined on the upper graph to the lower one. We first do this for the 600 litres consumed on the innermost budget line. We now note that the price of gasoline that gives rise to that budget line is $1.50 per litre. Plotting 600 litres against $1.50 in part (ii) produces the point x, derived from point E_0 in part (i). This is one point on the consumer's demand curve. Next we consider the middle budget line, which occurs when the price of gasoline is $1.00 per litre. We take the figure of 1200 litres from point E_1 in part (i) and transfer it to part (ii). We then plot this quantity against the price of $1.00 to get the point y on the demand curve. Doing the same thing for point E_2 yields the point z in part (ii): price 50 cents, quantity 2200 litres.

Repeating the operation for all prices yields the demand curve in part (ii). Note that the two parts of Figure 6A-7 describe the same behaviour. Both parts measure the quantity of gasoline on the horizontal axes; the only difference is that in part (i) the price of gasoline determines the slope of the budget line, whereas in part (ii) the price of gasoline is plotted explicitly on the vertical axis.

Income and Substitution Effects

The price-consumption line in part (i) of Figure 6A-7 indicates that as price decreases, the quantity of gasoline demanded increases, thus giving rise to the negatively sloped demand curve in part (ii). As we saw in Chapter 6, the key to understanding the negative slope of the demand curve is to distinguish between the income effect and the substitution effect of a change in price. We can make this distinction more precisely, and somewhat differently, using indifference curves.

In Chapter 6, we examined the substitution effect of a reduction in price by eliminating the income effect. We did this by reducing money income until the consumer could just purchase the original bundle of goods. We then examined how the change in relative prices affected the consumer's choices. In indifference theory, however, the income effect is removed by changing money income until the *original level of utility*—the original indifference curve—can just be achieved. This method results in a slightly different measure of the income effect, but the principle involved in separating the total change into an income

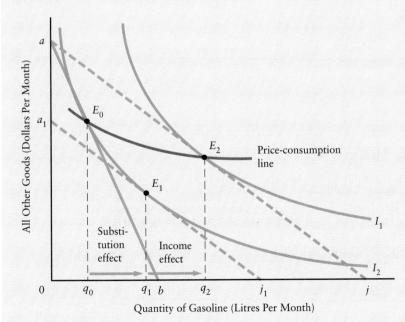

FIGURE 6A-8   The Income and Substitution Effects of a Price Change

The substitution effect is defined by sliding the budget line around a fixed indifference curve; the income effect is defined by a parallel shift of the budget line. The original budget line is at ab, and a fall in the price of gasoline takes it to aj. The original utility-maximizing point is at E_0 with q_0 of gasoline being consumed, and the new utility-maximizing point is at E_2 with q_2 of gasoline being consumed. To remove the income effect, imagine reducing the consumer's money income until the original indifference curve is just attainable. We do this by shifting the line aj to a parallel line nearer the origin a_1j_1 that just touches the indifference curve that passes through E_0. The intermediate point E_1 divides the quantity change into a substitution effect q_0q_1 and an income effect q_1q_2.

effect and a substitution effect is exactly the same as in Chapter 6.

The separation of the two effects according to indifference theory is shown in Figure 6A-8. The figure shows in greater detail part of the price-consumption line first drawn in Figure 6A-7. Points E_0 and E_2 are on the price-consumption line for gasoline; E_0 is the consumer's utility-maximizing point at the initial price, whereas E_2 is the consumer's utility maximizing point at the new price.

We can think of the separation of the income and substitution effects as occurring in the following way. After the price of the good has fallen, we reduce money income *until the original indifference curve can just be obtained.* The consumer moves from point E_0 to an intermediate point E_1, and this response is defined as the substitution effect. Then, to measure the income effect, we restore money income. The consumer moves from the point E_1 to the final point E_2, and this response is defined as the income effect.

SUMMARY

Indifference Curves

- Indifference curves describe consumers' tastes or preferences. A single indifference curve joins combinations of products that give consumers equal utility and among which they are therefore indifferent. An indifference map is a set of indifference curves.

- The basic hypothesis about tastes is that of *diminishing marginal rate of substitution.* This hypothesis states that the less of one good and the more of another the consumer has, the less willing she will be to give up some of the first good to get an additional unit of the second. Thus indifference curves are downward sloping and convex to the origin.

The Budget Line

- The budget line shows all combinations of products that are available to a consumer with a given amount of money income who faces given prices of the products.

- The slope of the budget line is determined by the relative prices of the products; the position of the budget line is determined by both prices and income.

The Consumer's Utility-Maximizing Choice

- Given the constraint of the budget line, the consumer's utility is maximized by consuming a bundle of goods such that the indifference curve through that bundle is tangent to the budget line.
- The income-consumption line shows how quantity consumed changes as income changes with relative prices being held constant.

- The price-consumption line shows how quantity consumed changes when the price of one product changes. When prices change, the consumer will consume more of the product whose relative price falls.

Deriving the Demand Curve

- The price-consumption line relating the purchases of one particular product to all other products contains the same information as a conventional demand curve. The horizontal axis measures quantity, and the slope of the budget line measures price. Transferring this price-quantity information to a diagram whose axes represent price and quantity yields a demand curve.

- The effect of a change in price of one product, all other prices and money income being held constant, changes not only relative prices but also real incomes. A change in price affects consumption through both the substitution effect and the income effect.

STUDY EXERCISES

1. Consider Katie's preferences for videos and ice-cream cones. Several "consumption bundles" are shown in the table below.

Bundle	Ice-Cream Cones	Videos
a	9	0
b	7	2
c	6	2
d	5	3
e	4	4
f	4	3
g	3	4
h	2	6
i	0	6

   a. On a scale diagram with the quantity of ice-cream cones on the vertical axis and the quantity of videos on the horizontal axis, plot the various bundles.
   b. Suppose that Katie is indifferent between bundles c and i. She is also indifferent between bundles d, g, and h, but all three of these are preferred to c or i. Finally, suppose that, of the bundles shown in the table, bundle e is Katie's favourite. Draw three indifference curves showing this information.
   c. Consider bundles e, f, and g. What can you conclude about how Katie would rank these bundles?

2. Continue with Katie from the previous question. Katie has a monthly allowance of $18 that she chooses to divide between rental videos and ice-cream cones. Videos rent for $3 each and ice-cream cones cost $2 each.

   a. For each of the consumption bundles shown in the table, compute the total cost. Which ones can Katie afford, and which ones can't she afford?

   b. Draw Katie's budget line. What is the slope of the line?
   c. Given Katie's monthly budget constraint, which bundle does she choose to maximize her utility?

3. Debra travels to Mexico and enjoys both burritos and Coronas. The diagram shows her utility-maximizing choices.

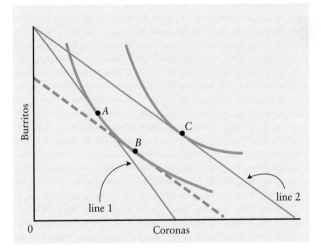

   a. If the budget line is Line 1, describe why point A is Debra's utility-maximizing choice.
   b. What event can explain why the budget line moves to Line 2?
   c. What is the meaning of point B in the figure?
   d. Suppose Coronas are a normal good for Debra. What does this restriction imply about the location of point C? Is this restriction satisfied in the diagram?

DISCUSSION QUESTIONS

1. We have all seen people who consume too much alcohol at parties. Often, even though these individuals are quite sick, they continue to drink. Draw an indifference curve for alcohol for a person who has begun to get ill but still continues to drink. Explain your representation.

2. Figure 6A-5 shows the behaviour of a hypothetical consumer as income increases. Do you think that such responses would hold globally? How might the response differ if the individual has $10 000 in income versus $1 million in income? Would there ever be a time when a person might exhibit no response to an increase in income? If so, what would the indifference map look like in that case?

3. Consider your sets of indifference curves for

   i) Coke and chips
   ii) Coke and Pepsi.

   Explain why these sets of indifference curves are likely to look different. Illustrate with a diagram. What does this difference imply about the magnitude of the substitution effects in response to changes in the price of Coke?

CHAPTER 7

Producers in the Short Run

LEARNING OBJECTIVES

1 Know the different forms of business organization and understand the various ways that firms can be financed.

2 Explain why firms sometimes make goods or services "in house" but other times purchase them from other firms.

3 Distinguish between accounting profits and economic profits.

4 Understand the relationships between total product, average product, and marginal product.

5 Explain the law of diminishing marginal returns.

6 Recognize that short-run production relationships have their counterparts in terms of short-run costs.

7 Understand the differences between fixed and variable costs, and know the relationships between total costs, average costs, and marginal costs.

In Chapter 6 we went behind the demand curve to understand how it is determined by the behaviour of consumers. In this chapter and the next we go behind the supply curve to understand how it is determined by the behaviour of firms.

We begin by comparing the firms that we see in the real world with those that appear in economic theory. Next we introduce the concepts of costs, revenues, and profits and outline the key role that profits play in determining the allocation of the nation's resources. To determine the most profitable amount for a firm to produce and supply to the market, we need to see how its costs vary with its output.

When examining the relationship between output and cost, *time* plays an important role. In this chapter, the focus is on the short run, where a firm can change only some of its inputs, and output is governed by the famous "law of diminishing returns." In the next chapter we examine the firm's behaviour in the long run—when all the firm's factors are variable—and in the very long run—when the state of technology changes. There we encounter scale economies and firms' incentives for research and development.

Firms as Agents of Production

We start by taking a brief look at the basic unit of production, the firm. After briefly studying firms as we see them in the real world, we go on to see how firms are treated in economic theory.

Firms in Practice

How are firms organized? How are firms financed? What are their goals?

Organization

A firm can be organized in any one of five different ways. A **single proprietorship**, or sole trader, has one owner-manager who is personally responsible for everything that is done. An **ordinary partnership** has two or more joint owners, each of whom is personally responsible for all of the parternship's debts. The **limited partnership**, which is less common than ordinary partnerships, provides for two types of partner. *General partners* take part in the running of the business and are liable for all the firm's debts. *Limited partners* take no part in the running of the business, and their liability is limited to the amount they actually invest in the enterprise. A **corporation** is a firm regarded in law as having an identity of its own; its owners are not personally responsible for anything that is done in the name of the firm, though its directors may be. The shares of a *private* corporation are not traded on any stock exchange (such as the Toronto or New York Stock Exchanges) whereas the shares of a *public* corporation are. A *state-owned enterprise* is set up to run a nationalized industry. It is owned by the state but is usually under the direction of a more or less independent, state-appointed board. Although its ownership differs, the organization and legal status of a state-owned enterprise are similar to those of a corporation. In Canada, such state-owned enterprises are called **crown corporations**.

A sixth method of organizing production differs from all the others in that the output is not sold. Instead, it is provided to consumers free (or at a nominal price), while costs of production are paid from tax revenue (in the case of government production) or charitable donations (in the case of private production). Important examples found in all countries are government agencies providing defence, roads, and education. In Canada we must add health-care services and post-secondary education to this list (though in recent years the prices charged for post-secondary education have been increasing significantly).

Firms that have locations in more than one country are often called *multinational enterprises (MNEs)*, although the United Nations officially designates them as **transnational corporations** (TNCs). Their numbers and importance have increased greatly over the last few decades. They are discussed in more detail in *Applying Economic Concepts 7-1*.

Financing

The money a firm raises for carrying on its business is sometimes called its financial capital, as distinct from its real capital, which is the firm's physical assets such as factories, machinery, offices, and stocks of materials and finished goods. Although the use of the term "capital" to refer to both an amount of money and a quantity of goods can be confusing, it will usually be clear from the context which sense is being used.

---

single proprietorship
A form of business organization in which the firm has one owner who makes all the decisions and is personally responsible for all of the firm's actions and debts.

ordinary partnership
A form of business organization in which the firm has two or more joint owners, each of whom takes part in the management of the firm and is personally responsible for all of the firm's actions and debts.

limited partnership
A form of business organization in which the firm has two classes of owners: general partners, who take part in managing the firm and are personally liable for all of the firm's actions and debts, and limited partners, who take no part in the management of the firm and risk only the money that they have invested.

corporation   A form of business organization in which the firm has a legal existence separate from that of the owners, and ownership and financial responsibility are divided, limited, and shared among any number of individual and institutional shareholders.

crown corporations
Firms that are owned by the government.

transnational corporations (TNCs)
Firms that have operations in more than one country. Also called multinational enterprises (MNEs).

APPLYING ECONOMIC CONCEPTS 7-1

Transnational Corporations

Over the past half century the concept of a *national* economy has become less precise as firms have produced what they require in more than one country. Such firms used to be called *multinational corporations*, but the United Nations now officially calls them *transnational corporations* (TNCs). TNCs encourage global competition as well as the transfer of technological know-how among countries. Their number has been increasing steadily over the years. Although large firms still dominate the TNC scene, the role of medium-size and small TNCs is significant and growing.

At the beginning of the 1990s there were about 37 000 TNCs in the world and they controlled about 170 000 foreign affiliates. Ninety percent of these TNCs are headquartered in developed countries; the five major home countries being France, Germany, Japan, the United Kingdom, and the United States. About 60 percent of all parent TNCs are in manufacturing, 37 percent are in services, and 3 percent are in primary production such as forestry and mining.

The main way in which firms used to develop foreign operations was foreign direct investment (FDI), which means acquiring the controlling interest in foreign production facilities either by purchasing existing facilities or by building new ones. More recently, however, other methods have become more common. The most important of these are joint ventures with domestic firms located in countries where the TNCs wish to develop an interest, and licensing arrangements whereby a domestic firm produces a TNC's product locally.

There are many reasons for a company to transfer some of its production beyond its home base (thus becoming a TNC) rather than producing everything at home and then exporting the output. First, products become more sophisticated and differentiated; locating production in large local markets allows more flexible responses to local needs than can be achieved through centralized production back home. Second, trade barriers make location in large foreign markets, such as the United States and the European Union, less risky than sending exports from the home base. Third, many TNCs are in the rapidly developing service industries such as advertising, marketing, public management, accounting, law, and financial services, where a physical presence is needed to produce a service in any country. Fourth, the computer and communications revolutions have allowed production to be "disintegrated" on a global basis. Components of any one product are often manufactured in many countries, each component being made where its production is cheapest.

Other reasons for a transnational corporation to locate production away from its home base have led some observers to be critical of TNCs. First, the TNC's internal accounting practices may allow it to report most of its revenues in low-tax countries and most of its costs in high-tax countries, thereby reducing the total tax it pays and avoiding altogether the paying of tax in some countries. Second, the TNC may threaten to remove its production away from its home base in an attempt to secure "friendly" tax policies from the government of that country. Third, the TNC may relocate its production in order to produce in countries with less stringent environmental standards.

On balance, however, most economists believe that the globalization of production—much of which has occurred through the spread of TNCs—has brought benefits to most countries. This includes developing countries, which have gained increasing employment at wages that are low by world standards but high by their own. TNCs now account for a large proportion of the foreign trade of many developed countries. As the United Nations puts it, "This dynamic aspect of the growth of TNCs is one of the major channels by which economic change is spread throughout the world."

The basic types of financial capital used by firms are *equity* and *debt*. Equity is the capital provided by the owners of the firm. Debt is the funds borrowed from creditors outside the firm.

Equity. In individual proprietorships and partnerships, one or more owners provide much of the required funds. A corporation acquires funds from its owners in return for stocks, shares, or equities (as they are variously called). These are basically ownership certificates. The money goes to the company and the shareholders become owners of the firm, risking the loss of their money, and gaining the right to share in the firm's profits. Profits that are paid out to shareholders are called **dividends.**

dividends   Profits paid out to shareholders of a corporation. Sometimes called distributed profits.

One easy way for an established firm to raise money is to retain current profits rather than paying them out to shareholders. Financing investment from such *undistributed profits* has become an important source of funding in modern times. Reinvested profits add to the value of the firm, and hence raise the market value of existing shares; they are capital provided by owners.

Debt.   The firm's creditors are not owners; they have loaned money in return for some form of loan agreement, or IOU. There is a bewildering array of such agreements, which are collectively called *debt instruments* in the business world and **bonds** in economic theory. Each has its own set of characteristics and its own name, and some types are discussed in *Applying Economics Concepts 7-2.* Two characteristics are, however, common to all debt instruments issued by firms. First, they carry an obligation to repay the

bond   A debt instrument carrying a specified amount and schedule of interest payments and (usually) a date for redemption of its face value.

APPLYING ECONOMIC CONCEPTS 7-2

Kinds of Debt Instruments

Most debt instruments can be grouped into three broad classes. First, some debt is in the form of *loans* from financial institutions such as chartered banks. These are private agreements between the firm and the bank usually calling for the periodic payment of interest and repayment of the principal, either at a stipulated future date or "on demand," meaning whenever the bank requests repayment.

Second, *bills* and *notes* are commonly used for short-term loans of up to a year. They carry no fixed interest payments, only a principal value and a redemption date. Interest arises because the borrowing firm sells the new bills that it issues at a price below their redemption value. If, for example, a bill promising to pay $1000 in one year's time is sold to a lender for $950, this gives the lender an interest payment of $50 in one year's time when the bill that he bought for $950 is redeemed for $1000. This makes an interest rate of 5.26 percent per year ((50/950) x 100). Bills are *negotiable*, which means they can be bought and sold. So if I buy a 90-day bill from some firm and want my money back 30 days later, I can sell the bill on the open market. The purchaser must be prepared to assume the loan to the firm for the 60 days that it still has to run.

The third type of instrument carries a fixed redemption date, as does a bill, and the obligation to make periodic interest payments, as do most loans. These instruments have many different details and correspondingly many different names, such as *bonds* and

debentures. They are commonly used for long-term loans—up to 20 or 30 years. A firm that issues a 7 percent 30-year instrument of this sort with redemption value of $1000 is borrowing money now and promising to pay $70 a year for 30 years and then to pay $1000 on the redemption date. All such instruments are negotiable. This is important, because few people would be willing to lend money for such long periods of time if there were no way to get it back before the redemption date.

Many large firms borrow money by issuing long-term bonds, like this one issued by MacMillan Bloedel, a large Canadian forestry products firm.

amount borrowed, called the *principal* of the loan. Second, they carry (explicitly or implicitly) an obligation to make some form of payment to the lender called *interest*. The time at which the principal is to be repaid is called the *redemption date* of the debt. The amount of time between the issue of the debt and its redemption date is called its *term*.

Goals

Firms are in business to make profits, which they do by making and selling goods and services. They must pay all their costs of production. The cost of labour includes wages, pensions, and other payments that must be made whenever labour is employed. The cost of borrowed capital is the interest they pay to those who have lent them money. The cost of intermediate goods and services covers the inputs they buy from other firms. The cost of rented inputs covers whatever they rent rather than own, often land and buildings. Firms must also *impute* costs for using their own capital equipment such as buildings, machinery, and office equipment. This cost, which is called *depreciation*, is measured by the reduction in the value of the assets that will occur if the firm uses them over the period in question. After deducting all these costs, the remainder is what firms call their profits. It is the return to their owners' capital. Some of this may be distributed to the shareholders in the form of dividends while the rest is retained for reinvestment. If the investments are sound, the value of the firm increases and this adds to the owners' capital.

Firms in Theory

In economic theory, the concept of the firm includes all types of business organization, from the single proprietorship to the corporation. It also covers the whole variety of business sizes and methods of financing, from the single investor operating in his garage and financed by whatever he can extract from a reluctant bank manager, to vast undertakings with many thousands of shareholders and customers.

The Boundaries of the Firm

If firms require something, either a specific input such as a specialized part, or a service such as cleaning their shop floor, they have two options. Either they can do it themselves—making the part and providing their own service—or they can buy what they need from some other firms. The boundary between what firms do for themselves and what they buy from outside differs among firms and changes over time. Why is is this so?

One answer was provided by British-born economist Ronald Coase, who received the 1991 Nobel Prize in economics for this, and other, path-breaking work. His analysis is based on the concept of **transaction costs**, which are the costs associated with all market transactions. For example, when a firm purchases some good or service, it must identify the market and then find what different quantities and qualities are available at what prices. This takes time and money, and it usually involves some uncertainty. When the firm decides to do the job itself "in house," it uses the *command principle*: it orders the product to be made, or the service to be performed, to its desired specifications. When the firm produces the product itself, the market transaction costs are avoided. But the advantages of buying in a competitive market are also lost.

transaction costs Costs incurred in effecting market transactions (such as negotiation costs, billing costs, and bad debts).

All firms must choose when to transact internally and when to transact through the market. For example, a car manufacturer must decide whether to purchase a certain component from an independent parts manufacturer or to produce the component itself. Most firms do both, buying many of their components from other firms and producing others for themselves.

Coase's insight was to see the firm as an institution that economizes on transaction costs. The market works best when transaction costs are low. When transaction costs are high, there is an incentive for the firm to avoid these by using the internal mechanisms of the command principle in place of market transactions.

Firms exist as an alternative to a pure market structure of transactions. Inside a firm there is a command economy. Managers of firms must decide which activities should be done inside the firm and which should be obtained in the market from other suppliers.

Changes in technology alter the relative advantages of these two types of activity. For example, the modern information and communications revolution, centred on the computer, has greatly reduced the transactions costs associated with many market activities. So the costs of obtaining things through the market have fallen relative to the costs of doing them in house. As a result, firms do many fewer things in house than they used to do. Instead, they "contract out" both the production of many parts and the performance of many services. Large firms are then able to concentrate on what they call their "core competencies," the main things they do. Smaller firms that specialize in producing single services, such as elevator maintenance, office cleaning, accounting, and product design, are often able to perform these services more efficiently than can a large multi-purpose firm.

Goals

The theory of the firm that we study in this book is called *Neoclassical*. It is based on two key assumptions. First, all firms are profit-maximizers, seeking to make as much profit for their owners as is possible. Second, each firm is regarded as a single, consistent decision-making unit.

The desire to maximize profits is assumed to motivate all decisions made within a firm, and such decisions are assumed to be unaffected by the peculiarities of the persons making the decisions and by the organizational structure in which they work.

These assumptions allow the theory to ignore the firm's internal organization and its financial structure, although the firm must still decide on the boundary between what it provides internally and what it obtains through the market. Using these assumptions, economists can predict the behaviour of firms. To do this, they first study the choices open to the firm, establishing the effect that each choice would have on the firm's profits. They then predict that the firm will select the alternative that produces the largest profits.

The appendix to this chapter considers some limitations of theories that are based on these simple but powerful assumptions. In particular, we examine why firms may in some situations choose to have an objective *other than* profit maximization. In such settings, however, a firm that is not maximizing profits becomes a potential target for takeover by other firms.

Production, Costs, and Profits

We must now specify a little more precisely the concepts of production, costs, and profits that are used by economists.

Production

In order to produce the goods or services that it sells, each firm needs inputs. Hundreds of inputs enter into the production of any specific output. Among the many inputs entering into car production, for example, are steel, rubber, spark plugs, electricity, the site of the factory, machinists, accountants, spray-painting machines, forklift trucks, painters, and managers. These can be grouped into four broad categories:

- inputs to the car firm which are outputs to some other firm, such as spark plugs, electricity, and steel;
- inputs that are provided directly by nature, such as land;
- inputs that are provided directly by people, such as the services of workers and managers; and
- inputs that are provided by the factories and machines used for manufacturing cars.

The items that make up the first group of inputs, goods and services produced by other firms, are called **intermediate products**. For example, one firm mines iron ore and sells it to a steel manufacturer. Iron ore is an intermediate product: an output of the mining firm and an input for the steel plant. These appear as inputs only because the stages of production are divided among different firms. If these intermediate products are traced back to their sources, all production can be accounted for by the services of the other three kinds of input which we first discussed in Chapter 1, and which are called *factors of production*. These are the gifts of nature, such as soil and raw materials called *land;* physical and mental efforts provided by people, called *labour;* and factories, machines, and other man-made aids to production, called *capital*.

The **production function** relates inputs to outputs. It describes the technological relationship between the inputs that a firm uses and the output that it produces. Remember that production is a flow: it is so many units per period of time. For example, when we say that production rises from 100 to 101 units, we do not mean 100 units are produced this month and 1 unit next month. Instead we mean that the rate of production has risen from 100 units each month to 101 units each month.

In terms of functional notation, a simplified production function is written as

$$q = f(L,K)$$

where q is the level of output per period, K is the flow of capital services, and L is the flow of labour services. "f" is the production function itself. Changes in the firm's technology, which alter the relationship between inputs and output, are reflected by changes in the function f.

intermediate products   All outputs that are used as inputs by other producers in a further stage of production.

production function A functional relation showing the maximum output that can be produced by each and every combination of inputs.

Costs and Profits

The production function specifies the amount of output that can be obtained from any given amounts of inputs. We have seen that firms arrive at what they call profits by taking the revenues they obtain from selling their output and deducting all the costs associated with their inputs, including depreciation of their own capital. When all costs have been correctly deducted the resulting profits are the return to the owners' capital.

Economic Profits

Compared with accountants, economists use somewhat different concepts of costs and profits. They add the opportunity cost of the owners' capital, both the pure return and the risk premium, to the firm's other costs. This is not just the depreciation of the capital, but an estimate of what the capital, and any other special advantages owned by the firm, could have earned in their best alternative uses. When this larger set of costs is deducted from revenues, the remainder is called **economic profits** (sometimes called pure profit). Where there is no room for ambiguity, economists just use the term profit.

economic profits
The difference between the revenues received from the sale of output and the opportunity cost of the inputs used to make the output. Negative economic profits are called economic losses.

What is the opportunity cost of the financial capital that the owner has tied up in a firm? The answer is best broken into two parts. First, ask what could be earned by lending this amount to someone else in a *riskless* loan. The owners could have purchased a government bond, which has no significant risk of default. Say the return on this is 6 percent per year. This amount is called the pure return, or risk-free rate of return on capital. It is clearly an opportunity cost, since the firm could close down operations, lend out its money, and earn a 6 percent return. Next, ask what the firm could earn in addition to this amount by lending its money to another firm where risk of default was equal to the firm's own risk of loss. Say this is an additional 4 percent. This is called the risk premium and it is clearly also a cost. If the firm does not expect to earn this much in its own operations, it could close down and lend its money out to some equally risky firm and earn 10 percent (6 percent pure return plus 4 percent risk premium).

Next suppose a firm owns a valuable patent or a highly desirable location, or produces a product with a popular brand name such as Kodak, Labatt, Corel, or Gap. Each of these involves an opportunity cost to the firm in production (even if it was acquired free), because if the firm did not choose to use the special advantage itself, *it could sell or lease it to others.* The firm must, therefore, charge itself for using the special advantage if it chooses to do so.

Table 7-1 compares the concepts of costs and profits as used by firms in practice and by economists in their theories. (Notice that Table 7-1 divides the firm's costs between those that vary with output, called *variable costs,* and those that do not, called *fixed costs,* a distinction that is considered in detail later in this chapter.)

What firms call profit is the return to the owners' capital. Economists deduct from this the opportunity cost of the owners' capital (and any marketable special advantages owned by the firm) to obtain their concept of economic profits.

Since there are two different concepts it would be better if two different terms were used. What firms call their profits might be referred to as the return to owners' capital. But firms do call these "profits." So when there is any possibility of confusion, economists speak of economic or pure profits. But since this is always what economists mean when they are dealing with their own theories, they usually just use the word "profits" to mean the return to the firm over and above the opportunity costs of capital.

Note that firms may have positive *accounting* profits even though they have zero *economic* profits. If a firm's profits represent a return just equal to what is available if the owner's capital were used elsewhere, then the owner's capital is earning exactly its opportunity cost. In this case, there are zero *economic* profits, even though the firm's accountant will record positive profits.

Is one of these concepts better than the other? No. Firms are interested in the return to their owners, which is what they call profits. They must also conform with tax laws which define profits the way they do. In contrast, economists are interested in how profits affect resource allocation and their definition is best for that purpose.

Practise with Study Guide Chapter 7, Exercise 4.

Profits and Resource Allocation

When resources are valued by the opportunity-cost principle, their costs show how much these resources would earn if used in their best alternative uses. If the revenues of all the firms in some industry exceed opportunity cost, the firms in that industry will be earning pure or economic profits. Hence, the owners of factors of production will want to move resources into the industry, because the earnings potentially available to them are greater there than in alternative uses. If, in some other industry, firms are incurring economic losses, some or all of this industry's resources are more highly valued in other uses, and owners of the resources will want to move them to those other uses.

Economic profits and losses play a crucial signalling role in the workings of a free-market system.

Economic profits in an industry are the signal that resources can profitably be moved into the industry. Losses are the signal that the resources can profitably be moved elsewhere. Only if there are zero economic profits is there no incentive for resources to move into or out of an industry.

Profit-Maximizing Output

To develop a theory of supply, we need to determine the level of output that will maximize a firm's profit, to which we give the symbol π (the lowercase Greek letter pi). This is the difference between the revenue each firm derives from the sale of its output, R, and the cost of producing that output, C:

$$\pi = R - C.$$

Thus, what happens to profits as output varies depends on what happens to both revenues and costs. In the rest of this chapter we develop a theory of how costs vary with output when the firm has some inputs that are fixed. In the next chapter we allow all inputs to be variable. The theory that we develop about costs and output is common to all firms. In the chapters that follow we consider how revenue varies with output. Costs and revenues are then combined to determine the profit-maximizing choices for firms in various market situations. The resulting theory can then be used to predict the outcome of changes in such things as demand, costs, taxes, and subsidies. This may seem like quite a long route to get to a theory of supply, and it is, but the payoff when we get there is in being able to understand and evaluate a great deal of economic behaviour.

TABLE 7-1   Profit and Loss Statement for XYZ Company for the Year Ending December 31, 2000

Costs		Income	
Variable Costs			
Wages	$200 000	Revenue from sales	$1 000 000
Materials	300 000		
Other	100 000		
Total VC	$600 000		
Fixed Costs			
Rent	$ 50 000		
Managerial salaries	60 000		
Interest on loans	90 000		
Depreciation allowance	50 000		
Total FC	$250 000		
Total Costs	$850 000		
Accounting Profit			$150 000

Calculation of Economic Profits	
Profit as reported by the firm	$150 000
Opportunity cost of capital	
Pure return on the firm's capital	−100 000
Risk premium	−40 000
Pure or economic profit	$ 10 000

The profit-and-loss statement shows profits as defined by the firm. The table gives a simplified version of a real profit-and-loss statement. The total revenue earned by the firm, minus what it regards as costs, yields the accounting concept of profits. To arrive at the economist's definition of profit, the opportunity cost of capital—the return on a riskless investment plus any risk premium—must be deducted from the firm's definition of profit. What is left is economic profit.

We start with inputs. Suppose that a firm wishes to increase its rate of output. To do so, it must increase the inputs of one or more factors of production. For the rest of this chapter, we consider a very simple example relating to the production of some industrial product. We can best focus on essentials by dealing with only two inputs. The first is labour, to which we give the symbol L. The second is capital, to which we give the symbol K. Thus we are ignoring land and all intermediate inputs and dealing with the simplified production function introduced earlier in this chapter:

$$q = f(L,K),$$

where q is quantity of output per period of time, L is the flow of labour services employed in production, and K is the flow of capital services used. The letter f again stands for the relation that links the inputs to the output.

Time Horizons for Decision Making

Economists organize the decisions that firms make into three classes: (1) how best to employ existing plant and equipment—the *short run*; (2) what new plant and equipment and production processes to select, given known technical possibilities—the *long run*; and (3) how to encourage, or adapt to, the development of new techniques—the *very long run*.

The Short Run

short run   A period of time in which the quantity of some inputs cannot be increased beyond the fixed amount that is available.

The **short run** is a time period in which the quantity of some inputs, called **fixed factors,** cannot be increased (or can only be increased at extremely high cost). A fixed factor is usually an element of capital (such as plant and equipment), but it might be land, the services of management, or even the supply of skilled labour. Inputs that are not fixed but instead can be varied in the short run are called **variable factors.**

fixed factor   An input whose quantity cannot be changed in the short run.

The short run does not correspond to a specific number of months or years. In some industries, it may extend over many years; in others, it may be a matter of months or even weeks. In the electric power industry, for example, it takes three or more years to acquire and install a steam turbine generator. An unforeseen increase in demand will involve a long period during which the extra demand must be met with the existing capital equipment. In contrast, a machine shop can acquire new equipment in a few weeks. An increase in demand will have to be met with the existing stock of capital for only a brief time, after which it can be adjusted to the level made desirable by the higher demand.

variable factor
An input whose quantity can be changed in the short run.

The short run is the length of time over which some of the firm's factors of production are fixed.

The Long Run

long run   A period of time in which all inputs may be varied but the basic technology of production cannot be changed.

The **long run** is a time period in which all inputs may be varied but in which the basic technology of production cannot be changed. Like the short run, the long run does not correspond to a specific length of time.

The long run corresponds to the situation the firm faces when it is planning to go into business, to expand the scale of its operations, to branch out into new products or new areas, or to change its method of production. The firm's *planning decisions* are long-run decisions because they are made from given technological possibilities but with freedom to choose from a variety of production processes that will use factor inputs in different proportions.

The long run is the length of time over which all of the firm's factors of production can be varied, but its technology is fixed.

The Very Long Run

Unlike the short run and the long run, the **very long run** is a period of time in which the technological possibilities available to a firm will change. Modern industrial societies are characterized by continuously changing technologies that lead to new and improved products and production methods.

Some of these technological advances are made by the firm's own research and development efforts. For example, much of the innovation in computer hardware and software has been made by IBM, Apple, Microsoft, and Intel. Some firms adopt technological changes developed by others. For example, liquid crystal displays and microprocessor chips have revolutionized dozens of industries that had nothing to do with developing them. Firms must regularly decide how much to spend in efforts to change technology either by developing new techniques or by adapting techniques that have been developed by others.

The very long run is the length of time over which all the firm's factors of production and its technology can be varied.

For the remainder of this chapter, we consider costs and production in the short run. We consider a simplified situation in which there are only two factors of production—labour and capital. We will assume that capital is the fixed factor whereas labour is the variable factor. In the next chapter we explore the firm's decisions in the long run and the very long run.

Production in the Short Run

Suppose that a firm starts with a fixed amount of capital and contemplates applying various amounts of labour to it. The table in Figure 7-1 shows three different ways of looking at how output varies with the quantity of the variable factor.

Total, Average, and Marginal Products

Total product *(TP)* is the total amount that is produced during a given period of time. Total product will change as more or less of the variable factor is used in conjunction with the given amount of the fixed factor. This variation is shown in columns 1 and 2 of the table in Figure 7-1. Part (i) of Figure 7-1 plots the schedule from the table. (The shape of the curve will be discussed shortly.)

Average product *(AP)* is the total product divided by the number of units of the variable factor used to produce it. If we let the number of units of labour be denoted by *L*, the average product is given by

$$AP = \frac{TP}{L}$$

very long run
A period of time that is long enough for the technological possibilities available to a firm to change.

total product (TP)
Total amount produced by a firm during some time period.

average product (AP)
Total product divided by the number of units of the variable factor used in its production.

FIGURE 7-1   Total, Average, and Marginal Products in the Short Run

Quantity of Labour (L)	Total Product (TP)	Average Product (AP) $\left(= \dfrac{TP}{L}\right)$	Marginal Product (MP) $\left(= \dfrac{\Delta TP}{\Delta L}\right)$
(1)	(2)	(3)	(4)
0	0	0	
1	43	43	43
2	160	80	117
3	351	117	191
4	600	150	249
5	875	175	275
6	1152	192	277
7	1372	196	220
8	1536	192	164
9	1656	184	120
10	1750	175	94
11	1815	165	65
12	1860	155	45

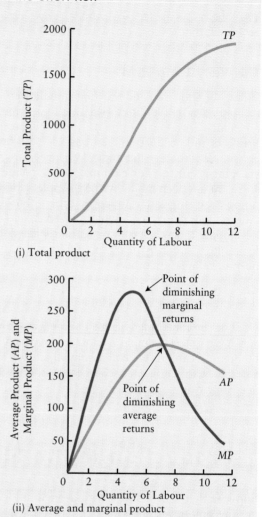

(i) Total product

(ii) Average and marginal product

The relation of output to changes in the quantity of the variable factor can be looked at in three different ways. As the quantity of labour increases, the rate of total output increases, as shown in column (2). The average product in column (3) is found by dividing the total product in column (2) by the labour requirement shown in the corresponding row of column (1). The marginal product is shown between the rows because it refers to the change in output from one level of labour input to another. The curves are plotted from the data in the table. In part (i) the *TP* curve shows the total product steadily rising, first at an increasing rate, then at a decreasing rate. This causes both the average and the marginal product curves in part (ii) to rise at first and then decline. Where *AP* reaches its maximum, *MP = AP*.

point of diminishing average productivity
The level of factor use at which average product reaches a maximum.

marginal product (MP)   The change in total output that results from using one more unit of a variable factor. Also called *incremental product* and *marginal physical product* (*MPP*).

Notice in column 3 of the table that as more of the variable factor is used, average product first rises and then falls. The level of output at which average product reaches a maximum (1372 units of output in the example) is called the **point of diminishing average productivity.** Up to that point, average product is increasing; beyond that point, average product is decreasing.

Marginal product (MP), sometimes called *incremental product* or *marginal physical product (MPP),* is the change in total product resulting from the use of one additional unit of the variable factor. [13] Recalling that the Greek letter Δ (delta) means "the change in," marginal product is given by:

$$MP = \frac{\Delta TP}{\Delta L}$$

Computed values of marginal product are shown in column 4 of the table in Figure 7-1. The values in this column are placed between the other rows of the table to stress that the concept refers to the *change* in output caused by the *change* in quantity of the variable factor. For example, the increase in labour from 3 to 4 units ($\Delta L = 1$) raises output from 351 to 600 ($\Delta TP = 249$). Thus the *MP* equals 249, and it is recorded between 3 and 4 units of labour. Note that the *MP* in the example first rises and then falls as output increases. The level of output at which marginal product reaches a maximum (between 875 and 1152 units in this example) is called the **point of diminishing marginal productivity**.

Part (ii) of Figure 7-1 plots the average product and marginal product curves from the table. Although three different curves are shown in Figure 7-1, they are all aspects of the same single relationship described by the production function. As we vary the quantity of labour, with capital being fixed, output changes. Sometimes it is interesting to look at total product, sometimes at average product, and sometimes at the marginal product.

point of diminishing marginal productivity The level of factor use at which marginal product reaches a maximum.

Diminishing Marginal Product

The variations in output that result from applying more or less of a variable factor to a given quantity of a fixed factor are the subject of a famous economic hypothesis, referred to as the **law of diminishing returns**.

The law of diminishing returns states that if increasing amounts of a variable factor are applied to a given quantity of a fixed factor, (holding the level of technology constant) eventually a situation will be reached in which the marginal product of the variable factor declines.

law of diminishing returns The hypothesis that if increasing quantities of a variable factor are applied to a given quantity of fixed factors, the marginal product and average product of the variable factor will eventually decrease.

Notice in Figure 7-1 that the marginal product curve rises at first and then begins to fall with each successive increase in the quantity of labour.

The commonsense explanation of the law of diminishing returns is that as output is increased in the short run, more and more of the variable factor is combined with a given amount of the fixed factor. As a result, each unit of the variable factor has less and less of the fixed factor to work with. When the fixed factor is capital and the variable factor is labour, each unit of labour gets a declining amount of capital to assist it as the total output grows. It is not surprising, therefore, that sooner or later, equal increases in labour eventually begin to add less and less to total output.

To illustrate the concept, consider the use of workers in a manufacturing operation. If there is only one worker, that worker must do all the tasks, shifting from one to another and becoming competent at each. As a second, third, and subsequent workers are added, each can specialize in one task, becoming expert at it. This process, as we noted in Chapter 1, is called the *division of labour*. If additional workers allow more efficient divisions of labour, marginal product will rise: Each newly hired worker will add more to total output than each previous worker did. However, according to the law of diminishing returns, the scope for such increases must eventually disappear, and sooner or later the marginal products of additional workers must decline. When the decline takes place, each additional worker will increase total output by less than did the previous worker.

Eventually, as more and more of the variable factor is employed, marginal product may reach zero and even become negative. It is not hard to see why if you consider the extreme case, in which there would be so many workers in a limited space, that additional workers would simply get in the way, thus reducing the total output.

The Average-Marginal Relationship

We have so far examined the concept of diminishing *marginal* returns; but *average* returns are also expected to diminish. The *law of diminishing average returns* states that if increasing quantities of a variable factor are applied to a given quantity of fixed factors, the average product of the variable factor will eventually decrease. [14]

Notice that in part (ii) of Figure 7-1, the *MP* curve cuts the *AP* curve at the *AP*'s maximum point. This is not a matter of luck or the way the artist just happened to draw the figure. Rather, it illustrates a fundamental property of the relationship between average and marginal product curves, one that is very important to understand.

The average product curve slopes upward as long as the marginal product curve is *above* it; whether the marginal product curve is itself sloping upward or downward is irrelevant. If an additional worker is to raise the average product of all workers, that additional worker's output must be greater than the average output of the other workers. It is immaterial whether the new worker's contribution to output is greater or less than the contribution of the worker hired immediately before; all that matters is that the new worker's contribution to output exceeds the *average* output of all workers hired previously. [15]

The relationship between marginal and average measures is very general. If the marginal is greater than the average, the average must be rising; if the marginal is less than the average, the average must be falling. For example, if you have a 3.6 cumulative grade point average (GPA) through last semester and in this (marginal) semester you get only a 3.0 GPA, your cumulative GPA will fall. To increase your cumulative GPA, you must score better in this (marginal) semester than you have on average in the past—that is, to increase the average, the marginal must be greater than the average.

The Significance of Diminishing Returns

Any batter will improve his batting average if his "marginal hit" (his next time at bat) is better than his "average hit" (his current average).

Empirical confirmation of both diminishing marginal and diminishing average returns occurs frequently. Some examples are illustrated in *Applying Economic Concepts 7-3*. But one might wish that it were not so. There would then be no reason to fear a food crisis caused by the population explosion in developing countries. If the marginal product of additional workers applied to a fixed quantity of land were constant, food production could be expanded in proportion to population growth merely by keeping a constant fraction of the population on farms. With fixed techniques, however, diminishing returns dictate an inexorable decline in the marginal product of each additional worker because an expanding population must work with a fixed supply of agricultural land.

Thus, were it not for the steady improvement in the techniques of production, continuous population growth would bring with it, according to the law of diminishing returns, declining average living standards and eventually widespread famine. This gloomy prediction of the English economist Thomas Malthus (1766–1834) is discussed further in the next chapter.

Costs in the Short Run

We now shift our attention from production to costs. The majority of firms cannot influence the prices of the inputs that they employ; instead they must pay the going market price for their inputs. For example, a shoe factory in Montreal, a metals manufacturer in

APPLYING ECONOMIC CONCEPTS 7-3

Some Examples of Diminishing Returns

- British Columbia's Campbell River, a noted sport-fishing area, has long been the centre of a thriving, well-promoted tourist trade. As sport-fishing has increased over the years, the total number of fish caught has steadily increased, but the number of fish *per person fishing* has decreased and the average hours fished for each fish caught has increased.*

- When Southern California Edison was required to modify its Mojave power plant to reduce the amount of pollutants emitted into the atmosphere, it discovered that a series of filters applied to the smoke-stacks could do the job. A single filter eliminated one-half of the discharge. Five filters in series reduced the discharge to the 3 percent allowed by law. When a state senator proposed a new standard that would permit no more than 1 percent of the pollutant to be emitted, the company brought in experts who testified that this would require at least 15 filters per stack and would triple the cost. In other words, increasing the number of filters leads to diminishing marginal returns in pollution reduction.

- Public opinion pollsters, as well as all students of statistics, know that you can use a sample to estimate characteristics of a large population. Even a relatively small sample can provide a useful estimate—at a tiny fraction of the cost of a complete enumeration of the population. However, sample estimates are subject

to sampling error. If, for example, 38 percent of a sample approves of a certain policy, the percentage of the population that approves of it is likely to be close to 38 percent, but it might well be anywhere from 36 to 40 percent. The theory of statistics shows that the size of the expected sampling error can be reduced by increasing the sample size. However, the theory also shows that successive reductions in the sampling error require ever larger increases in the sample size. Suppose that the original sample was 400; if quadrupling the sample to 1600 would halve the chance of an error of any given size from occurring, then to halve it again, the new sample would have to be quadrupled again—to 6400. In other words, increasing the sample size leads to diminishing marginal returns in terms of accuracy.

- During the early days of World War II, so few naval ships were available that each North Atlantic convoy had only a few escort vessels to protect it from German submarines. The escorts dashed about from one side of the convoy to the other and ended up sinking very few submarines. As the construction program made more ships available, the escorts could stay in one position in the convoy: some could close in on the various flanks; others could hunt farther afield. Not only did the total number of submarines sunk per convoy crossing rise, but also the number of submarines sunk per escort vessel rose. Still later in the war, as each successive convoy was provided with more and more escort vessels, the number of submarines sunk per convoy crossing continued to rise, but the number of submarines sunk *per escort vessel* began to fall sharply. Total output (submarines sunk) increased, but marginal output fell.

---

*For a *given stock of fish* and increasing numbers of boats, this example is a good illustration of the law of diminishing returns. But in recent years the story has become more complicated as overfishing has depleted the stock of fish. We examine the reasons for overfishing in Chapter 16.

Sarnia, a rancher in Red Deer, and a boat builder in Prince Rupert are each too small a part of the total demand for the factors that they use to be able to influence their prices significantly. The firms must pay the going rent for the land that they need, the going wage rate for the labour that they employ, and the going interest rate that banks charge for loans; so it is with most other firms.[1] Given these prices and the physical returns summarized by the product curves, the costs of different levels of output can be calculated.

---

[1]The firm that is a large enough employer of labour or user of land or capital to affect the prices of its factor services is the exception rather than the rule. We examine the case of such *monopsony power* in Chapter 14.

Cost Concepts Defined

The following definitions of several cost concepts are closely related to the product concepts just introduced.

total cost (*TC*)   The total cost to the firm of producing any given level of output; it can be divided into *total fixed costs* and *total variable costs*.

total fixed cost (*TFC*)   All costs of production that do not vary with the level of output.

total variable cost (*TVC*)   Total costs of production that vary directly with the level of output.

average total cost (*ATC*)   Total cost of producing a given output divided by the number of units of output; it can also be calculated as the sum of average fixed costs and average variable costs. Also called *unit cost* or *average cost*.

average fixed cost (*AFC*)   Total fixed costs divided by the number of units of output.

average variable cost (*AVC*)   Total variable costs divided by the number of units of output.

marginal cost (*MC*)   The increase in total cost resulting from raising the rate of production by one unit. Also called *incremental cost*.

Total cost *(TC)* is the full cost of producing any given level of output. Total cost is divided into two parts, *total fixed cost* and *total variable cost*. **Total fixed cost** *(TFC)* does not vary with the level of output; it is the same whether output is 1 unit or 1 million units. Such a cost is also referred to as an *overhead cost*. A cost that varies directly with output is called a **total variable cost** *(TVC)*. In the example in Figure 7-1, labour is the variable factor of production, and wages are therefore a variable cost.

Average total cost *(ATC)* is the total cost of producing any given number of units of output divided by that number of units. Average total cost is therefore the average cost *per unit of output*. ATC can be separated into **average fixed costs** *(AFC)*, fixed cost divided by the quantity of output, and **average variable costs** *(AVC)*, variable cost divided by the quantity of output.

Although average variable costs may rise or fall as production is increased, average fixed costs decline continuously as output increases. A doubling of output always leads to a halving of fixed costs *per unit of output*. This is a process known as spreading one's overhead.

Marginal cost *(MC)* is the increase in total cost resulting from increasing the level of output by one unit. Because fixed costs do not vary with output, marginal fixed costs are always zero. Therefore, marginal costs are necessarily marginal *variable* costs, and a change in fixed costs will leave marginal costs unaffected. For example, the marginal cost of producing a few more potatoes by farming a given amount of land more intensively is not affected by the rent paid for the land. [16]

See Table 7-2 for a summary of the firm's short-run cost concepts.

Short-Run Cost Curves

Using the production relationships found in Figure 7-1, suppose that the price of labour is $20 per unit and the price of capital is $10 per unit. The cost schedules that result from these values are shown in the table in Figure 7-2.

Figure 7-2 plots the cost curves for the data in the table. Notice that the MC curve cuts the ATC curve and the AVC curve at their lowest points. This is another example of the relationship between a marginal and an average curve. The ATC curve, for example, slopes downward as long as the MC curve is below it; it is upward sloping whenever MC is above it.

We consider these various cost curves one at a time.

Short-Run Average Costs

In part (ii) of Figure 7-2, the average variable cost (AVC) curve reaches a minimum and then rises. For given factor prices, when average product per worker is at a maximum, average variable cost is at a minimum. [17] Each additional worker adds the same amount to cost but a different amount to output; thus, when output per worker rises, the cost per unit of output must fall, and vice versa.

Eventually diminishing average productivity implies eventually increasing average variable costs.

Practise with Study Guide Chapter 7, Exercise 6.

The average fixed cost (*AFC*) curve in Figure 7-2 declines steadily as output rises. This decline reflects the spreading of overhead costs over more units of output.

Since average total cost is simply the sum of average variable cost and average fixed cost, it follows that the average total cost (*ATC*) curve is obtained by vertically adding the *AVC* and *AFC* curves. The result is usually a U-shaped *ATC* curve, as shown in Figure 7-2. This shape reflects the assumption that average productivity increases when output is low but that at some level of output, average productivity begins to fall fast enough so that average variable costs increase faster than average fixed costs are falling. When this happens, *ATC* increases.

Marginal Cost

In part (ii) of Figure 7-2, the marginal cost (*MC*) curve declines, reaches a minimum, and then rises. This is the reverse of the shape of the marginal product curve in part (ii) of Figure 7-1. The reason for the reversal is as follows: If extra units of a variable factor result in increasing quantities of output (marginal *product* rising), the cost per unit of extra output must be falling (marginal *cost* falling). However, if marginal product is falling, marginal cost will be rising. [18]

The law of eventually diminishing marginal product implies eventually increasing marginal cost.

Capacity

The level of output that corresponds to the minimum short-run average total cost is often called the *capacity* of the firm. In this sense, capacity is the largest output that can be produced without encountering rising average costs per unit. In part (ii) of Figure 7-2, capacity output is about 1600 units, but higher outputs can be achieved, provided that the firm is willing to accept the higher per-unit costs that accompany any level of output that is "above capacity." A firm that is producing at an output less than the point of minimum average total cost is said to have *excess capacity*.

The technical definition gives the word *capacity* a meaning that is different from the one used in everyday speech, in which it often means an upper limit that cannot be exceeded. The technical definition is, however, a useful concept in economic and business discussions.

TABLE 7-2   Short-Run Cost Concepts

Total Costs:

$$TC = TFC + TVC$$

Total Cost (*TC*) is the total cost to the firm of producing a given level of output.

Total Fixed Cost (*TFC*) is the sum of all costs of production that do not vary with the level of output. Also called overhead costs.

Total Variable Cost (*TVC*) varies directly with the level of output; it rises as more output is produced and falls as less output is produced.

Average Costs:

$$(ATC) = (AFC) + (AVC)$$

Average Total Cost (*ATC*) is the total cost per unit of output: $ATC = \dfrac{TC}{Q}$.

Average Fixed Cost (*AFC*) is the total fixed cost per unit of output: $AFC = \dfrac{TFC}{Q}$.

Average Variable Cost (*AVC*) is the total variable cost per unit of output: $AVC = \dfrac{TVC}{Q}$.

Marginal Costs:

$$MC = \dfrac{\Delta TC}{\Delta Q}$$

Marginal Cost (*MC*) is the change in total cost (ΔTC) per unit change in output (ΔQ).

FIGURE 7-2   Total, Average and Marginal Cost Curves

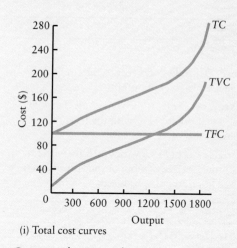

(i) Total cost curves

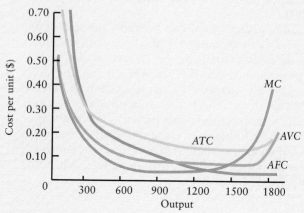

(ii) Marginal and average cost curves

Costs with Capital Fixed and Labour Variable

Inputs		Output	Total Cost			Average Cost			Marginal Cost
Capital (K) (1)	Labour (L) (2)	(q) (3)	Fixed (TFC) (4)	Variable (TVC) (5)	Total (TC) (6)	Fixed (AFC) (7)	Variable (AVC) (8)	Total (ATC) (9)	(MC) (10)
10	1	43	$100	$20	$120	$2.326	$0.465	$2.791	$0.456
10	2	160	100	40	140	0.625	0.250	0.865	0.171
10	3	351	100	60	160	0.285	0.171	0.456	0.105
10	4	600	100	80	180	0.167	0.133	0.300	0.080
10	5	875	100	100	200	0.114	0.114	0.228	0.073
10	6	1152	100	120	220	0.087	0.104	0.191	0.072
10	7	1372	100	140	240	0.073	0.102	0.175	0.091
10	8	1536	100	160	260	0.065	0.104	0.169	0.122
10	9	1656	100	180	280	0.060	0.109	0.169	0.167
10	10	1750	100	200	300	0.057	0.114	0.171	0.213
10	11	1815	100	220	320	0.055	0.121	0.176	0.308
10	12	1860	100	240	340	0.054	0.129	0.183	0.444

The relation of cost to the rate of output can be looked at in several different ways. These cost schedules are computed from the product curves of Figure 7-1, given the price of capital of $10 per unit and the price of labour of $20 per unit. Marginal cost (in column 10) is shown between the lines of total cost because it refers to the *change* in cost divided by the *change* in output that brought it about. Marginal cost is calculated by dividing the increase in costs by the increase in output when one additional unit of labour is used. This gives the increase in cost per unit of output over that range of output. For example, the MC of $0.08 is the increase in total cost of $20 (from $160 to $180) divided by the 249 unit increase in output (from 351 to 600). This tells us that when output goes from 351 to 600 (because labour inputs go from 3 to 4), the increase in costs is $0.08 per unit of output. In constructing a graph, marginal costs should be plotted midway in the interval over which they are computed. The MC of $0.08 would thus be plotted at output 475.5.

The curves are plotted from the table. Total fixed cost does not vary with output. Total variable cost and the total of all costs (TC = TVC + TFC) rise with output, first at a decreasing rate, then at an increasing rate. The total cost curves in (i) give rise to the average and marginal curves in (ii). Average fixed cost (AFC) declines as output increases. Average variable cost (AVC) and average total cost (ATC) fall and then rise as output increases. Marginal cost (MC) does the same, intersecting the ATC and AVC curves at their minimum points. Capacity output is at the minimum point of the ATC curve, which is an output of about 1600 in this example.

Shifts in Short-Run Cost Curves

So far, we have seen how costs vary as output varies, with input prices being held constant. Figure 7-3 shows the effect on a firm's cost curves of a change in the price of any variable input. A rise in the price of any input used by the firm must raise the price of producing any given quantity of output. A fall in the price of any input has the opposite effect.

A change in the price of any variable input used by the firm will shift its marginal and average cost curves—upward for a price increase and downward for a price decrease.

Thus, there is a set of average and marginal cost curves that correspond to each price of the variable factor.

A short-run cost curve shows how costs vary with output for a given quantity of the fixed factor, say, a given size of plant. But what happens when the amount of the fixed factor changes?

There is a different short-run cost curve for each given quantity of the fixed factor.

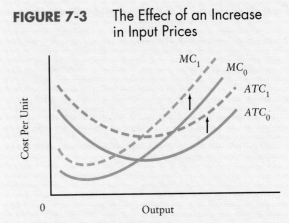

FIGURE 7-3 The Effect of an Increase in Input Prices

A change in any input price shifts the average total cost curve and the marginal cost curve. The original average total cost and marginal cost curves are shown by ATC_0 and MC_0. A rise in the price of a variable input—for example, the wage rate—raises the cost of producing each level of output. As a result, the average total cost curve and the marginal cost curve shift upward to ATC_1 and MC_1.

A small plant that manufactures nuts and bolts will have its own short-run cost curve. A medium-size plant and a large plant will each have its own short-run cost curve. If a firm expands and replaces its small plant with a medium-size plant, it will move from one short-run cost curve to another. This change from one plant size to another is a long-run change, which brings us to the next chapter, in which we discuss how short-run cost curves for plants of different sizes are related to each other.

SUMMARY

Firms as Agents of Production

- Production is organized either by private-sector firms, which take four main forms—single proprietorships, ordinary partnerships, limited partnerships, and corporations—or by state-owned enterprises.
- Modern firms finance themselves by selling shares, reinvesting their profits, or borrowing from lenders such as banks.

- A firm's profit is the difference between its total revenue and its total costs.
- The boundaries of firms are determined by the relation between the costs of making transactions in the market and the costs of producing what is required within the firm.

Production, Costs, and, Profits

LO 3

- The production function relates inputs of factor services to output.
- In addition to what firms count as their costs, economists include the opportunity costs of owners' capital. This includes the pure return (the amount that could be earned on a riskless investment) and a risk premium (the amount that could be earned over the pure return on an equally risky investment). Economic profits are the difference between revenues and all these costs.

- Economic profits play a key role in resource allocation. Positive economic profits attract resources into an industry; negative economic profits induce resources to move elsewhere.
- A firm's production decisions can be classified into three groups. The short run involves decisions in which one or more factors of production are fixed. The long run involves decisions in which all factors are variable but technology is unchanging. The very long run involves decisions in which technology can change.

Production in the Short Run

LO 4 5

- The theory of short-run costs is concerned with how output varies as different amounts of the variable factors are combined with given amounts of the fixed factors. The concepts of total, average, and marginal product represent alternative relationships between output and the quantity of the variable factors of production.

- The law of diminishing returns asserts that if increasing quantities of a variable factor are combined with given quantities of fixed factors, the marginal and the average products of the variable factor will eventually decrease. For given factor prices, this hypothesis implies that marginal and average costs will eventually rise.

Costs in the Short Run

LO 6 7

- Short-run average total cost curves are often U-shaped because average productivity increases at low levels of outputs but eventually declines sufficiently and rapidly to offset advantages of spreading overheads. The output corresponding to the minimum point of a short-run average total cost curve is called the plant's capacity.
- Changes in factor prices shift the short-run cost curves—upward when prices rise and downward when prices fall.

Thus there is a whole family of short-run cost curves, one for each set of factor prices.
- Changes in the quantity of the fixed factor also shift the short-run cost curves. An increase in the amount of capital increases the productivity of labour and thus shifts the MC and AVC curves down.

K E Y   C O N C E P T S

Forms of business organization
Methods of financing modern firms
Profit maximization
Inputs and factors of production
Alternative definitions of profits

Profits and resource allocation
Short run, long run, and very long run
Total product, average product, and marginal product
The law of diminishing returns

The relationship between productivity and cost
Total cost, marginal cost, and average cost
Short-run cost curves
Capacity

STUDY EXERCISES

1. Consider the revenues and costs in 1999 for Spruce Decor Inc., an Alberta-based furniture company entirely owned by Mr. Harold Buford.

Furniture Sales	$645 000
Catalogue Sales	$ 12 000
Labour Costs	$325 000
Materials Costs	$157 000
Advertising Costs	$ 28 000
Debt-Service Costs	$ 32 000

   a. What would accountants determine Spruce Decor's profits to be in 1999?
   b. Suppose Mr. Buford has $400 000 of capital invested in Spruce Decor. Also suppose that equally risky enterprises earn a 16% rate of return on capital. What is the opportunity cost for Mr. Buford's capital?
   c. What are the *economic* profits for Spruce Decor in 1999?
   d. If Spruce Decor's economic profits were typical of furniture makers in 1999, what would you expect to happen in this industry? Explain.

2. Consider an example of a production function that relates the monthly production of widgets to the monthly inputs of capital and labour. Suppose the production function takes the following specific algebraic form:

   $$q = KL - (0.1) L^2$$

   where q is the output of widgets, K is the input of capital services, and L is the input of labour services.

   a. Suppose that, in the short run, K is constant and equal to 10. Fill in the following table.

K	L	q
10	5	—
10	10	—
10	15	—
10	20	—
10	25	—
10	30	—
10	40	—
10	50	—

   b. Using the values from the table, plot the values of q and L on a scale diagram, with q on the vertical axis and L on the horizontal axis.
   c. Now suppose that K increases to 20 because the firm increases the size of its widget factory. Re-compute the value of q for each of the alternative values of L. Plot the values of q and L on the same diagram as in **b**.

   d. Explain why an increase in K increases the level of q (for any given level of L).

3. The following table shows how the total output of skates (per month) changes when the quantity of the variable input (labour) changes. The firm's amount of capital is fixed.

Hours of Labour	Pairs of Skates	Average Product	Marginal Product
100	200	—	—
120	260	—	—
140	350	—	—
160	580	—	—
180	720	—	—
200	780	—	—
220	800	—	—
240	810	—	—

   a. Compute the average product of labour for each level of output and fill in the table. Plot the *AP* curve on a scale diagram.
   b. Compute the marginal product of labour for each interval (that is, between 100 and 120 hours, between 120 and 140 hours, and so on). Fill in the table and plot the *MP* curve on the same diagram. Remember to plot the value for *MP* at the midpoint of the intervals.
   c. Is the "law of diminishing marginal returns" satisfied?
   d. Explain the relationship between the marginal product of labour and the average product of labour.

4. Consider the table below which shows the total fixed costs (*TFC*) and variable costs (*TVC*) for producing specialty bicycles in a small factory with a fixed amount of capital.

Output per year (thousands of bicycles)	TFC	TVC	AFC	AVC	ATC
		(thousands of dollars)			
1	200	40	—	—	—
2	200	70	—	—	—
3	200	105	—	—	—
4	200	120	—	—	—
5	200	135	—	—	—
6	200	155	—	—	—
7	200	185	—	—	—
8	200	230	—	—	—
9	200	290	—	—	—
10	200	350	—	—	—
11	200	425	—	—	—

a. Compute average fixed costs (*AFC*) for each level of output.

b. Compute average variable costs (*AVC*) for each level of output.

c. Compute average total cost (*ATC*) for each level of output. What level of output (per year) is the firm's "capacity"?

d. Plot the *AFC*, *AVC* and *ATC* curves on a scale diagram with dollars on the vertical axis and the level of output on the horizontal axis.

5. This is a challenging question that requires you to understand the relationship between total product, average product, and marginal product. Each of the diagrams below shows how total product (*TP*) changes as the quantity of the variable input (which we call *L*) changes. These reflect four *different* production functions.

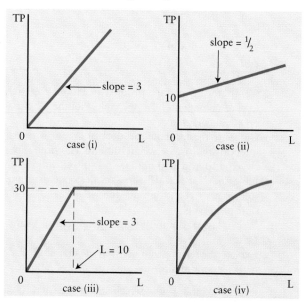

a. In each case, describe in words how total output depends on the amount of variable input.

b. In each case, draw a diagram showing the average product (*AP*) curve. (Recall that *AP* is given by total output divided by total variable input. The value of *AP* is also equal to the slope of a straight line from the origin to the *TP* curve.)

c. On the same diagram, draw the marginal product (*MP*) curve. (Recall that *MP* is given by the *change* in total output divided by the *change* in the variable input. The value of *MP* is also equal to the slope of a tangent line to the *TP* curve.)

d. Is the relationship between *AP* and *MP* discussed in the text satisfied by each of the production functions?

6. In 1921, a classic set of experiments with chemical fertilizers was performed at the Rothampsted Experimental Station, an agricultural research institute in Hertfordshire, England. Researchers applied different amounts of a particular fertilizer to 10 apparently identical quarter-acre plots of land. The results for one test, using identical seed grain, are listed in the following table. Compute the average and marginal product of fertilizer, and identify the (approximate) points of diminishing average and marginal productivity.

Plot	Fertilizer Dose	Yield Index*
1	15	104.2
2	30	110.4
3	45	118.0
4	60	125.3
5	75	130.2
6	90	131.4
7	105	131.9
8	120	132.3
9	135	132.5
10	150	132.8

* Yield without fertilizer = 100.

DISCUSSION QUESTIONS

1. Which concept of profits—accounting or economic—is implied in the following quotations?

a. "Profits are necessary if firms are to stay in business."

b. "Profits are signals for firms to expand production and investment."

c. "Accelerated depreciation allowances reduce profits and thus benefit the company's owners."

2. Does the short run consist of the same number of months for increasing output as for decreasing it? Must the short run in an industry be the same length for all firms in the industry? Under what circumstances might the short run actually involve a longer time span than the very long run for one particular firm?

3. Indicate whether each of the following conforms to the hypothesis of diminishing returns and, if so, whether it refers to marginal returns, average returns, or both.

a. "The bigger they are, the harder they fall."

b. "As more and more of the population receives chicken pox vaccinations, the reduction in the chicken pox disease rate for each additional 100 000 vaccinations becomes smaller."

c. "Five workers produce twice as much today as 10 workers did 40 years ago."

d. "Diminishing returns set in last year when the rising rural population actually caused agricultural output to fall."

4. Consider the education of a person as a process of production. Regard years of schooling as one variable factor of production. What are the other factors? What factors are fixed? At what point would you expect diminishing returns to set in? For an Einstein, would diminishing returns set in during his lifetime?

5. A carpenter quits his job at a furniture factory to open his own cabinetmaking business. In his first two years of operation, his sales average $100 000 and his operating costs for wood, workshop and tool rental, utilities, and miscellaneous expenses average $70 000. Now his old job at the furniture factory is again available. Should he take it or remain in business for himself? How would you make this decision?

6. The point of minimum average cost is referred to as the capacity of the firm. Yet we draw the average cost curve extending both to the left and to the right of this point. Obviously, a firm can operate below capacity, but how can a firm operate above capacity? Are there any types of firms for which it may be desirable to have a capacity below the level at which the firm may have to produce occasionally or even relatively frequently? Explain.

Do Firms Really Maximize Profits?

In the text, we said that the Neoclassical theory of the firm is based on two key assumptions. First, firms strive to maximize their profits. Second, firms act as if they are a single consistent decision maker. These assumptions rule out two potentially interesting questions regarding actual firm behaviour. First, do firms ever have a goal other than profit maximization? Second, doesn't it matter who is actually making the decisions inside the firm? These issues are explored in this appendix. As we will see, they are related to each other: the decisions actually made by a firm may depend on who is making them.

The Separation of Ownership From Control

One hundred years ago, the single-proprietor firm, whose manager was its owner, was common in many branches of industry. In such firms, the single-minded pursuit of profits would be expected. Today, however, ownership is commonly diversified among thousands of stockholders, and the firm's managers are rarely its owners. Arranging matters so that managers always act in the best interests of stockholders is, as we shall see, anything but straightforward. Thus there is potential for managers to maximize something other than profits.

In corporations, the stockholders elect directors, and those directors then appoint managers. Directors are supposed to represent stockholders' interests and to determine broad policies that the managers will carry out. To conduct the complicated business of running a large firm, a full-time professional management group must be given broad powers of decision making. Although managerial decisions can be reviewed from time to time, they cannot be closely monitored on a day-to-day basis. The links between the directors and the managers are typically weak enough so that top management often truly controls the corporation over long periods of time.

As long as directors have confidence in the managerial group, they accept and ratify their proposals. Stockholders in turn elect and reelect directors who are proposed to them. If the managerial group does not satisfy the directors' expectations, it may be replaced.

Within fairly broad limits, then, effective control of the corporation's activities generally resides with the managers. Although the managers are legally employed by the stockholders, they remain largely independent of them. Indeed, the management group typically asks for, and gets, the *proxies* of enough stockholders to elect directors who will reappoint it, and thus it perpetuates itself in office. (A proxy authorizes a person who is attending a stockholders' meeting to cast a stockholder's vote.) In the vast majority of cases, nearly all votes cast are in the form of proxies.

None of these factors matter unless the managers pursue different interests from those of the stockholders. Do the interests of the two groups diverge? To study this question, we need to look at what is called principal-agent theory.

Principal-Agent Theory

If you (the *principal*) hire a girl down the block (your *agent*) to mow your lawn while you are away, all you can observe is how the lawn looks when you come back. She could have mowed it every week, as you agreed, or she could have waited until two days before you were due home and mowed it only once. By prevailing on a friend or a neighbour to *monitor* your agent's behaviour, you could find out what she actually did, but only at some cost.

When you visit a doctor for a diagnosis and for treatment of your lower back pain, it is almost impossible for you to monitor the doctor's effort and diligence on your behalf. You have not been to medical school, and much of what the doctor does will be a mystery to you.

This latter situation is close to the principal-agent relationship that exists between stockholders and managers. The managers have information and expertise that the stockholders do not have—indeed, that is why they are the managers. The stockholders can observe profits, but they cannot directly observe the managers' efforts. To complicate matters further, even when the managers' behaviour can be observed, the stockholders do not generally have the expertise to evaluate whether that behaviour was the most appropriate. Everyone can see how well the firm performs, but it takes very detailed knowledge of the firm and the industry to know how well it *could have performed*.

Boards of directors, who represent the firm's stockholders, can acquire some of the relevant expertise and monitor managerial behaviour, but, again, such monitoring is costly.

These examples illustrate the *principal-agent problem*—the problem of designing mechanisms that will induce agents to act in their principals' interests. In general, unless there is close monitoring of the agent's behaviour, the problem cannot be completely solved. Hired managers (like hired gardeners) will generally wish to pursue their own goals. They cannot ignore profits because if they perform badly enough, they will lose their jobs. Just how much latitude they have to pursue their own goals at the expense of profits will depend on many things, including the degree of competition in the industry and the possibility of takeover by more profit-oriented management.

Principal-agent analysis shows that when a firm's ownership and control are separated, the self-interest of agents will tend to make profits lower than in a world in which principals act as their own agents.

Managers' Motives

In the case of firms, the principals (the stockholders) are interested in maximizing profits. What different motives might their agents (the managers) have, and what market forces might limit their ability to act on these motives?

Sales Maximization

If managers do not maximize profits, what do they do? One alternative is that they seek to maximize *sales*. Suppose that the managers need to make some minimum level of profits to keep the stockholders satisfied. Beyond this, they are free to maximize their firm's sales revenue. This might be a sensible policy on the part of management because salary, power, and prestige all rise with the size of a firm as well as with its profits. Generally, the manager of a large, normally profitable corporation will earn a salary that is considerably higher than the salary earned by the manager of a small but highly profitable corporation.

The sales-maximization hypothesis says that managers of firms seek to maximize their sales revenue, subject to a profit constraint.

Sales maximization subject to a profit constraint leads to the prediction that a firm's managers will sac-

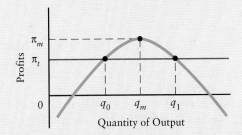

FIGURE 7A-1   Output of the Firm Under Profit Maximizing, Sales Maximizing, and Satisficing Behaviour

The "best" level of output depends on the motivation of the firm's managers. The curve shows the level of profits associated with each level of output. The shape of the curve reflects the fact that the firm generally has a unique level of output that maximizes its profits.

A profit-maximizing firm produces output q_m and earns profit π_m. A sales-maximizing firm, with a minimum profit constraint of π_t, produces the output q_1. A satisficing firm with a target level of profits of π_t is willing to produce any output between q_0 and q_1. Thus, satisficing allows a range of outputs on either side of the profit-maximizing level, whereas sales maximization results in a higher output than profit maximization.

rifice some profits by producing more output than the profit-maximizing level. Figure 7A-1 demonstrates this point.

Failure to Minimize Costs

It is also possible that firms will produce their chosen output at greater than minimum cost. Why would a firm's managers fail to minimize costs?

The most straightforward answer is that minimizing costs can demand a great deal of detailed managerial attention, and if management can avoid doing so, it would prefer not to make the necessary effort. A second reason managers may not minimize costs is that they may benefit from some higher-than-necessary expenditures. For example, lavish offices, in-house fitness centres, and subsidized cafeterias may all increase the pleasure of the job. And though *some* spending of this type may also be good for the employees' morale and productivity—and thus be good for the company overall—managers may prefer to spend much more generously than is necessary.

As with sales maximization, however, pressure from profit-minded stockholders will limit the extent to which such inefficiencies can persist. Also relevant is the threat of takeover—to which we now turn.

The Market for Corporate Control

Managers who stray too far from profit maximization face the risk that their firms will be taken over by more profit-oriented ownership. *Mergers* and *takeovers* can be interpreted as transactions in a *market for corporate control*. This market, like any other, has both buyers (people who would acquire the rights to control a firm) and sellers (the current stockholders of the firm). As in other markets, the expected outcome is that the assets being exchanged will wind up in the hands of the parties who value them most—usually those who can come closest to maximizing the firm's profits.

A takeover begins when the management of the acquiring firm makes a *tender offer* to the stockholders of the target firm. Tender offers are promises to purchase stock at a specified price for a limited period of time, during which the acquiring firm hopes to gain control of the target company. Typically, the prices offered are considerably higher than the prevailing stock-market price, reflecting the belief by the acquiring firm that the assets of the target firm would be worth more if they were better managed. A takeover is called a *hostile takeover* when the current management of the target firm opposes it.

Are takeovers beneficial for the economy as a whole? The main argument in their favour is that after a takeover, the new management can make more efficient use of the target firm's assets. The acquiring firm should be able to exploit profit opportunities that the target management is not exploiting. This can be done by such means as operating the target firm more efficiently, providing funds that the target firm could not obtain, or providing access to markets that would be too expensive for the target firm to open up on its own.

Most economists believe that the threat of takeovers provides a useful discipline that helps to restrain managers from acting in non-profit-maximizing ways. Such discipline helps to improve the allocation of resources as managers are under pressure to use the assets under their management in the most efficient way.

Nonmaximizing Theories

Many students of corporate behaviour, particularly economists based in business schools, criticize the profit-maximization assumption from a perspective different from that given by principal-agent theory. They argue that there are other reasons for doubting that modern corporations are "simple profit-maximizing computers." They believe that corporations are *profit-oriented* in the sense that, other things being equal, more profits are preferred to less profits. They do not believe, however, that corporations are profit *maximizers*.

A major group of critics of profit maximization develop their argument as follows: Firms operate in highly uncertain environments. Their long-term success or failure is determined largely by their ability to administer innovation and change. But the risks of innovation are large, and the outcomes are highly uncertain. Rational firms therefore tend to be quite risk-averse. They develop routines of behaviour that they follow as long as they are successful. Only when profits fall low enough to threaten their survival do they significantly change their course of action.

Supporters of this view argue that firms simply cannot handle the task of scrutinizing all possibilities, calculating the probable outcomes, and then choosing among these so as to maximize their expected profits. Instead, firms carry on with existing routines as long as these produce satisfactory profits, and only when profits fall to unacceptably low levels do the firms search for new ways of doing old things or new lines of activity.

One way of formalizing these views is the *theory of satisficing*. It was first put forward by Herbert Simon of Carnegie-Mellon University, who was awarded the Nobel Prize in Economics in 1978 for his work on the behaviour of firms. He wrote, "We must expect the firm's goals to be not maximizing profits but attaining a certain level or rate of profit, holding a certain share of the market or a certain level of sales." In general, a firm is said to be *satisficing* if it does not change its behaviour, provided that a *satisfactory* (rather than optimal) level of performance is achieved.

According to the satisficing hypothesis, firms could produce any one of a range of outputs that produce profits at least equal to the target level. This contrasts with the unique output that is predicted by profit-maximizing theory. Figure 7A-1 compares satisficing behaviour with sales- and profit-maximizing behaviour.

The theory of satisficing predicts not a unique level of output but a range of possible outputs that includes the profit-maximizing output.

The Importance of Nonmaximizing Behaviour

What would be the implications if nonmaximizing theories were accepted as being better theories of the behaviour of firms than the "standard model," which is based on the assumption of profit maximization?

The Implications of Nonmaximizing Behaviour

To the extent that existing non-profit-maximizing theories are accurate, the economic system does not perform with the delicate precision that follows from profit maximization. Firms will not always respond quickly and precisely to changes in market signals from either the private sector or government policy.

The nonmaximizing theories imply that in many cases, firms' responses to small changes in market signals will be of uncertain speed and direction.

According to all existing theories, maximizing and nonmaximizing, firms will tend to sell more when demand increases and less when it decreases. They will also tend to alter their prices and their input mixes when they face sufficiently large changes in input prices. (This is an aspect of firm behaviour we will examine in detail in the next chapter.) Moreover, there are limits to the extent to which the nonmaximizing behaviour can survive in the marketplace. Failure to respond to profit opportunities can lead to takeover by a more profit-oriented management. Although this threat of takeover does not mean that profits are being precisely maximized at all times, it does put real limits on the extent to which firms can ignore profits.

Profits are a potent force in the life and death of firms. The resilience of profit-maximizing theory and its ability to predict the economy's reactions to many major changes (such as the dramatic decline in computer prices that have occurred over the past two decades) suggest that firms are at least strongly motivated by the pursuit of profits.

Over the past two decades, the question of how firms behave in detail has received renewed attention from both economists and organization theorists. Almost everyone in the field agrees that firms do not *exactly* maximize profits at all times and in all places. At the same time, almost everyone agrees that firms cannot stray too far from the goal of profit maximization. Just how far is too far depends on the circumstances in which firms operate and the mechanisms that firms' owners can use to influence managers. These areas are at the frontier of current economic research.

Profit Maximization as an Evolutionary Equilibrium

U.S. economist Armen Alchian has suggested that firms will evolve over time to become profit maximizers. The basic argument is based on the principle of *survival of the fittest*. In a competitive environment, firms that pursue goals or adopt rules that are inconsistent with profit maximization will be unable to stay in business; firms that either choose or happen upon rules that are closer to profit maximization will displace those that do not. Eventually, only the profit-maximizing firms will survive in the marketplace.

A similar kind of argument can be applied to firms that operate in markets with fewer competitors (such as oligopolistic markets that we examine in Chapter 11). Here it is not competition in the product market that forces the firm toward profit maximization in the long run but competition in the market for corporate control. A firm that does not maximize profits will be less valuable than one that does maximize profits. Thus, the non-profit-maximizing firm can be bought by profit-maximizing managers, who will increase its value as they increase its profits.

Alchian's argument suggests the following conclusion:

Even if no firm starts out with the intention of maximizing profits, in the long run the firms that survive in the marketplace will tend to be the profit maximizers.

This view provides an apparent synthesis of maximizing and evolutionary theories of the firm. The distinction between the theories is not so stark as it might seem.

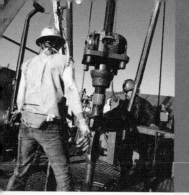

CHAPTER 8

Producers in the Long Run

LEARNING OBJECTIVES

1 Understand why cost minimization requires firms to equate the marginal product per dollar spent for all factors.

2 Explain the principle of substitution, and why it implies that firms will use more of factors whose prices have fallen (and use less of factors whose prices have increased).

3 Recognize the relationship between short-run and long-run cost curves.

4 Understand that changes in the economic environment often lead firms to innovate to improve their technology.

In the first part of this chapter, we look at the long run, in which firms are free to vary all factors of production. Picking up from the end of Chapter 7, the choice that a firm faces in the long run is *which* of the several short-run cost curves it should be on. Remember that a different short-run average total cost (*SRATC*) curve exists for each possible amount of the fixed factor. Some firms use a great deal of capital and only a small amount of labour. Others use less capital and more labour. Here we examine the effects that these choices have on firms' costs, and we look at the conditions that determine these choices.

In the second part of the chapter, we examine the very long run, in which technology changes. The discussion concerns the improvements in technology and productivity that have dramatically increased output and incomes in all industrial countries over centuries. Firms are among the most important economic actors that cause technological advances to take place. Evidence shows that the hypotheses of profit maximization and cost minimization can help us to understand technological changes. Here, as in the short and long run, firms respond to events such as changes in factor prices. But in the very long run, firms often respond by innovating—that is, by developing *new* technologies.

Throughout this chapter, we should remember that the lengths of the various runs under consideration are defined by the kinds of changes that can take place, not by calendar time. Thus we would expect actual firms in any given time period to minimize costs in the short run, as described in Chapter 7; to choose among alternative short-run cost curves in the long run, as described in the first part of this chapter; and to change technologies in the very long run as described in the latter part of this chapter.

The Long Run: No Fixed Factors

In the short run, in which at least one factor is fixed, the only way to produce a given output is to adjust the input of the variable factors. In the long run, in which all factors can be varied, there are numerous ways to produce any given output. For example, the firm could use a lot of capital and few workers, or little capital and many workers. Thus, firms in the long run must choose the type and amount of plant and equipment and the size of their labour force.

In making these choices, the firm tries to be **technically efficient** by using no more of all inputs than necessary—that is, the firm does not want to waste any of its valuable inputs. Technical efficiency is not enough, however. To be *economically* efficient, the firm must choose from among the many technically efficient options the one that produces a given level of output at the lowest possible cost. (The distinction between various types of efficiency sometimes causes confusion, particularly when engineers and economists are involved in the same decision-making process. *Applying Economic Concepts 8-1* elaborates on this important distinction.)

Long-run planning decisions are important. A firm that decides to build a new steel mill and invest in the required machinery will choose among many alternatives. Once installed, that equipment is fixed for a long time. If the firm makes a wrong choice, its survival may be threatened; if it estimates correctly, it may be rewarded with large profits.

technical efficiency
When a given number of inputs are combined in such a way as to maximize the level of output.

Profit Maximization and Cost Minimization

Any firm that is trying to maximize its profits in the long run should select the economically efficient method of production, which is the method that produces its output at the lowest possible cost. As we noted in the previous chapter, this implication of the hypothesis of profit maximization is called **cost minimization**: From the alternatives open to it, the profit-maximizing firm will choose the least costly way of producing whatever level of output it chooses.

cost minimization
An implication of profit maximization that firms choose the production method that produces any given level of output at the lowest possible cost.

Long-Run Cost Minimization

If it is possible to substitute one factor for another to keep output constant while reducing total cost, the firm is currently not using the least costly combination of factors. In such a situation, the firm should substitute one factor for another factor as long as the marginal product of the one factor *per dollar spent on it* is greater than the marginal product of the other factor *per dollar spent on it*. The firm is not minimizing its costs whenever these two magnitudes are unequal. For example, if an extra dollar spent on labour produces more output than an extra dollar spent on capital, the firm can reduce costs by spending less on capital and more on labour.

If we use K to represent capital, L to represent labour, and p_L and p_K to represent the prices per unit of the two factors, the necessary condition for cost minimization is as follows:

Oil is a very important input in many industries. Increases in the price of oil will lead profit-maximizing firms to substitute away from oil toward other factors of production.

APPLYING ECONOMIC CONCEPTS 8-1
Different Concepts of Efficiency

In popular discussion, business decision making, and government policies, three different types of efficiency concepts are encountered. These are engineering, technical, and economic efficiency. Each is a valid concept, and each conveys useful information. However, the use of one concept in a situation in which another is appropriate is a frequent source of error and confusion.

Engineering efficiency refers to the physical amount of some *single key input* that is used in production. It is measured by the ratio of that input to output. For example, the engineering efficiency of an engine refers to the ratio of the amount of energy in the fuel burned by the engine to the amount of usable energy produced by the engine. The difference is in friction, heat loss, and other unavoidable sources of waste. Saying that a steam engine is 40 percent efficient means that 40 percent of the energy in the fuel that is burned in the boiler is converted into work that is done by the engine, while the other 60 percent is lost.

Technical efficiency is related to the physical amount of *all factors* used in the process of producing some product. A particular method of producing a given level of output is technically efficient if there are no other ways of producing the output that use less of at least one input while not using more of any others.

Economic efficiency is related to the *value* (rather than the physical amounts) of all inputs used in producing a given output. The production of a given output is economically efficient if there are no other ways of producing the output that use a smaller *total value* of inputs.

What is the relationship between economic efficiency and these other two concepts? We have seen that engineering efficiency measures the efficiency with which a single input is used. Although knowing the efficiency of

any given gasoline, electric, or diesel engine is interesting, increasing this efficiency is not necessarily economically efficient because doing so usually requires the use of other valuable resources. For example, the engineering efficiency of a gas turbine engine can be increased by using more and stronger steel in its construction. Raising the engineering efficiency of an engine saves on fuel, but at the cost of using more of other inputs. To know whether this is worth doing, the firm must compare the value of the fuel saved with the value of the other inputs used.

Technical efficiency is desirable as long as inputs are costly to the firm in any way. If a technically inefficient process is replaced by a technically efficient process, there is a saving of resources. We do not need to put a precise value on the cost of inputs to make this judgement. All we need to know is that inputs have a positive cost to the firm, so that saving on these costs is desirable.

Usually, however, any given output may be produced in any one of many alternative technically efficient ways. Achieving technical efficiency is clearly a *necessary* condition for producing any output at the least cost. The existence of technical inefficiency means that costs can be reduced by reducing some inputs and not increasing any others. Achieving technical efficiency, however, is not a *sufficient* condition for producing at the lowest possible cost. The firm must still ask which of the many technically efficient methods it should use. This is where the concept of economic efficiency comes in. The appropriate method is the one that uses the smallest *total value* of inputs. This ensures that the firm spends as little as possible producing its given output; in terms of opportunity cost, the firm sacrifices the least possible value with respect to other things that it might do with those inputs.

$$\frac{MP_K}{p_K} = \frac{MP_L}{p_L} \qquad (8\text{-}1)$$

Whenever the ratio of the marginal product of each factor to its price is not equal for all factors, there are possibilities for factor substitutions that will reduce costs (for a given level of output).

To see why Equation 8-1 must be satisfied when costs are being minimized, consider an example where the equation is *not* satisfied. Suppose that the marginal product of capital is 40 units of output and the price of a unit of capital is $10, making the left side of Equation 8-1 equal to 4. Suppose also that the marginal product of labour is 20 units of output and the price of a unit of labour is $2, making the right side equal to 10. Thus the last dollar spent on capital adds only 4 units to output, whereas the last dollar spent on labour adds 10 units to output. In this case, it is possible for the firm to keep its output constant but reduce its costs by using more labour and less capital. Specifically, if the firm spent an additional $4 on labour, output would rise by 40 units; but then it could spend exactly $10 less on capital and output would fall back by 40 units. Making such a substitution of labour for capital would leave output unchanged but it would reduce costs by $6. Thus the original combination of factors was not a cost-minimizing one.[1]

By rearranging the terms in Equation 8-1, we can look at the cost-minimizing condition a bit differently.[2]

$$\frac{MP_K}{MP_L} = \frac{p_K}{p_L} \qquad (8\text{-}2)$$

The ratio of the marginal products on the left side compares the contribution to output of the last unit of capital and the last unit of labour. The right side shows how the cost of an additional unit of capital compares to the cost of an additional unit of labour. If the two sides of Equation 8-2 are the same, then the firm cannot make any substitutions between labour and capital to reduce costs (if output is held constant). However, with the marginal products and factor prices used in the example above, the left side of the equation equals 2 but the right side equals 5; the last unit of capital is twice as productive as the last unit of labour but it is five times as expensive. It will thus pay the firm to switch to a method of production that uses less capital and more labour. If, however, the ratio on the right side were less than the ratio on the left, then it would pay the firm to switch to a method of production that used less labour and more capital. Only when the ratio of marginal products is exactly equal to the ratio of factor prices does the firm have no incentive to change its production method.

Firms adjust the quantities of factors they use to the prices of the factors given by the market.

Practise with Study Guide Chapter 8, Exercise 2.

The Principle of Substitution

The preceding discussion suggests that cost-minimizing firms will react to changes in factor prices by changing their methods of production. This is referred to as the **principle of substitution.**

Suppose that a firm is currently meeting the cost-minimizing conditions and that the cost of capital decreases while the cost of labour remains unchanged. The least-cost method of producing any output will now use less labour and more capital than was required to produce the same output before the factor prices changed.

Methods of production will change if the relative prices of factors change. Relatively more of the cheaper factor and relatively less of the more expensive factor will be used.

The principle of substitution plays a central role in resource allocation because it relates to the way in which individual firms respond to changes in relative factor prices that are caused by the changing relative scarcities of factors in the economy as a whole.

principle of substitution   The principle that methods of production will change if relative prices of inputs change, with relatively more of the cheaper input and relatively less of the more expensive input being used.

---

[1]The argument in this paragraph assumes that the marginal products do not change when expenditure changes by a very small amount.
[2]The appendix to this chapter provides a graphical analysis of this condition, which is similar to the analysis of consumer behaviour in the appendix to Chapter 6.

Individual firms are motivated to use less of factors that become scarcer to the economy and more of factors that become more plentiful. Here are two examples of the principle of substitution in action.

In the past two decades, the price of both business computers and office software has fallen sharply relative to the wages of clerical workers. One result of this change has been the near demise of the form letter, beginning "Dear Sir or Madam." Nowadays, even total strangers send you letters that are customized by name and sometimes more. Twenty years ago, such customized attention would have required that a secretary look up the information in a file and type it into a letter. Now a basic mail-merge program can do the job at much lower cost, and we see the result every day. Here we see the substitution toward capital and away from labour as their relative prices change.

The principle of substitution can also explain why methods of producing the same product often differ across countries. In Canada, where labour is generally highly skilled and expensive, a farmer with a large farm may use elaborate machinery to economize on labour. In China, however, where labour is abundant and capital is scarce, a much less mechanized method of production is appropriate. The Western engineer who believes that the Chinese are inefficient because they are using methods long ago discarded in the West is missing the truth about efficiency in the use of resources: Where factor scarcities differ across nations, so will the economically efficient methods of production.

Long-Run Cost Curves

long-run average cost (LRAC) curve
The curve showing the lowest possible cost of producing each level of output when all inputs can be varied.

When all factors of production can be varied, there exists a least-cost method of producing any given level of output. Thus, with given factor prices, there is a minimum achievable cost for each level of output; if this cost is expressed in terms of dollars per unit of output, we obtain the long-run average cost of producing each level of output. When this minimum cost of producing each level of output is plotted on a graph, the result is called a **long-run average cost (LRAC) curve**. Figure 8-1 shows one such curve.

The *LRAC* cost curve is determined by the firm's current technology and by the prices of the factors of production. It is a "boundary" in the sense that points below it are unattainable; points on the curve, however, are attainable if sufficient time elapses for all inputs to be adjusted. To move from one point on the *LRAC* curve to another requires an adjustment in *all* factor inputs, which may, for example, require building a larger, more elaborate factory.

The *LRAC* curve is the boundary between cost levels that are attainable, with known technology and given factor prices, and those that are unattainable.

Just as the short-run cost curves discussed in Chapter 7 relate to the production function describing the physical relationship between factor inputs and output, so does the *LRAC* curve. The difference is that in deriving the *LRAC* curve, there are no fixed factors of production. Thus, since all costs are variable in the long run, we do not need to distinguish between *AVC, AFC,* and *ATC,* as we did in the short run; in the long run, there is only one *LRAC* for any given set of input prices.

The Shape of the Long-Run Average Cost Curve

The *LRAC* curve shown in Figure 8-1 first falls and then rises. This curve is often described as U-shaped, although empirical studies suggest it is often "saucer-shaped." Consider the three portions of any such saucer-shaped *LRAC* curve.

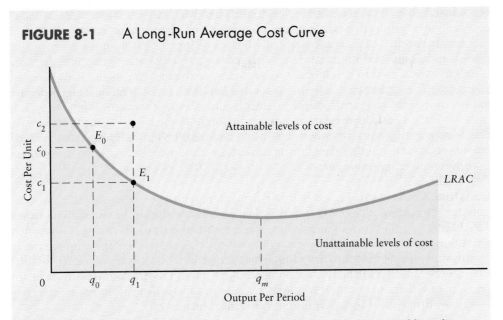

FIGURE 8-1   A Long-Run Average Cost Curve

The long-run average cost *(LRAC)* curve is the boundary between attainable and unattainable levels of costs. If the firm wishes to produce output q_0, the lowest attainable cost level is c_0 per unit. Thus, point E_0 is on the *LRAC* curve. E_1 represents the lowest possible average cost of producing q_1. Suppose that a firm is producing at q_0 and desires to increase output to q_1. In the long run, a plant optimal for output q_1 can be built, and the cost of c_1 per unit can be attained. However, in the short run, it will not be able to vary all factors, and thus costs per unit will be above c_1, say, c_2. At output q_m, the firm attains its lowest possible per unit cost of production for the given technology and factor prices.

Decreasing Costs.   Over the range of output from zero to q_m, the firm has falling long-run average costs: An expansion of output permits a reduction of costs per unit of output. Technologies with this property exhibit **economies of scale**. Because the *LRAC* curve is drawn under the assumption of constant factor prices, the decline in long-run average cost occurs because output is increasing *more than* in proportion to inputs as the scale of the firm's production expands. Over this range of output, the decreasing-cost firm is often said to enjoy long-run **increasing returns**.[3]

Increasing returns may occur as a result of increased opportunities for specialization of tasks made possible by the division of labour. Even the most casual observation of the differences in production techniques used in large and small plants will show that larger plants use greater specialization. These differences arise because large, specialized equipment is useful only when the volume of output that the firm can sell justifies employment of that equipment. For example, assembly-line techniques and body-stamping machinery in automobile production are economically efficient only when individual operations are repeated thousands of times. Use of elaborate harvesting equipment (which combines many

economies of scale Reduction of average total costs resulting from an expansion in the scale of a firm's operations so that more of all inputs are being used.

increasing returns (to scale) A situation in which output increases more than in proportion to inputs as the scale of a firm's production increases. A firm in this situation is a decreasing-cost firm.

---

[3]Economists shift back and forth between speaking in physical terms ("increasing returns") and cost terms ("decreasing costs"). As the text explains, the same relationship can be expressed either way.

individual tasks that would otherwise be done by hand and by tractor) provides the least-cost method of production on a big farm but not on one of only a few acres.

Another source of increasing returns consists of inputs that do not have to be increased as the output of a product is increased, even in the long run. For example, there are often large fixed costs in developing new products, such as a new generation of personal computers. These R&D costs have to be incurred only once for each product and hence are independent of the scale at which the product is subsequently produced. Even if the product's *production costs* increase in proportion to output in the long run, such *product development costs* per unit of output will fall as the scale of output rises. The influence of such one-time costs is that, other things being equal, they cause average total costs to be falling over the entire range of output.

constant returns (to scale)   A situation in which output increases in proportion to inputs as the scale of production is increased. A firm in this situation is a constant-cost firm.

decreasing returns (to scale)   A situation in which output increases less than in proportion to inputs as the scale of a firm's production increases. A firm in this situation is an increasing-cost firm.

Constant Costs.   In Figure 8-1, the firm's long-run average costs fall until output reaches q_m and rise thereafter. Another possibility should be noted. The firm's *LRAC* curve might have a flat portion over a range of output around q_m. With such a flat portion, the firm would be encountering constant costs over the relevant range of output, meaning that the firm's long-run average costs do not change as its output changes. Because factor prices are assumed to be fixed, the firm's output must be increasing *exactly in proportion to* the increase in inputs. When this happens, the constant-cost firm is said to be exhibiting **constant returns.**

Increasing Costs.   Over the range of outputs greater than q_m, the firm encounters rising long-run average costs. An expansion in production, even after sufficient time has elapsed for all adjustments to be made, is accompanied by a rise in average costs. If factor prices are constant, the firm's output must be increasing *less than* in proportion to the increase in inputs. When this happens, the increasing-cost firm is said to encounter long-run **decreasing returns.** Decreasing returns imply that the firm suffers some *diseconomies of scale.* As its scale of operations increases, diseconomies are encountered that increase its per-unit cost of production.

Such diseconomies may be associated with the difficulties of managing and controlling an enterprise as its size increases. For example, planning problems do not necessarily vary in direct proportion to size. At first, there may be scale economies as the firm grows and benefits from greater specialization. But, sooner or later, planning and coordination problems may multiply more than in proportion to the growth in size. If so, management costs per unit of output will rise.

Other sources of scale diseconomies are the possible alienation of the labour force as size increases; it becomes more difficult to provide appropriate supervision as more layers of supervisors and middle managers come between the person at the top and the workers on the shop floor. Control of middle-range managers may also become more difficult. As the firm becomes larger, managers may begin to pursue their own goals rather than devote all of their efforts to making profits for the firm. Much of the "reengineering" of large firms in the 1990s has been aimed at reducing the extent to which management difficulties increase with firm size, but the problem has not been, and probably cannot be, eliminated entirely.

FIGURE 8-2   *LRAC* and *SRATC* Curves

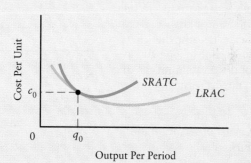

The *SRATC* curve is tangent to the *LRAC* curve at the output for which the quantity of the fixed factors is optimal. The particular *SRATC* curve shown is drawn for a plant size that minimizes costs for output q_0. For all other levels of output the plant is either too big or too small and *SRATC* therefore lies above *LRAC*. If some level of output other than q_0 is to be sustained, costs can be reduced to the level of the *LRAC* curve when sufficient time has elapsed to adjust the plant size.

Note that long-run decreasing returns differs from short-run diminishing returns. In the short run, at least one factor is fixed, and the law of diminishing returns ensures that returns to the variable factor will eventually diminish. In the long run, all factors are variable, and it is possible that physically diminishing returns will never be encountered—at least as long as it is genuinely possible to increase inputs of all factors.

The Relationship Between Long-Run and Short-Run Costs

The short-run cost curves from the previous chapter and the long-run curve studied in this chapter are all derived from the same production function. Each curve assumes given prices for all factor inputs. The long-run average cost *(LRAC)* curve shows the lowest cost of producing any output when all factors are variable. Each short-run average total cost *(SRATC)* curve shows the lowest cost of producing any output when one or more factors are fixed.

No short-run cost curve can fall below the long-run curve because the *LRAC* curve represents the lowest attainable cost for each possible output.

As the level of output is changed, a different-size plant is normally required to achieve the lowest attainable cost. Figure 8-2 shows the *SRATC* curve above the *LRAC* curve at all levels of output except q_0.

As we saw in the last chapter, any individual *SRATC* curve is just one of many such curves. The *SRATC* curve in Figure 8-2 shows how costs vary as output is varied, holding the plant size constant. Figure 8-3 shows a family of *SRATC* curves, along with a single *LRAC* curve. The *LRAC* curve is sometimes called an **envelope** because it encloses a series of *SRATC* cost curves by being tangent to them.

Practise with Study Guide Chapter 8, Exercise 4.

envelope   Any curve that encloses, by being tangent to, a series of other curves. In particular, the envelope cost curve is the *LRAC* curve, which encloses the *SRATC* curves by being tangent to each without cutting any of them.

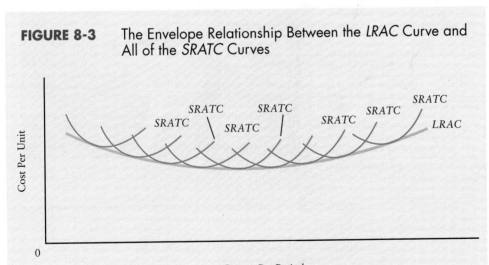

FIGURE 8-3   The Envelope Relationship Between the *LRAC* Curve and All of the *SRATC* Curves

To every point on the *LRAC* curve, there is an associated *SRATC* curve tangent at that point. Each short-run curve is drawn for a given amount of fixed factors, and shows how costs vary if output varies. The level of output at the tangency between each *SRATC* curve and the *LRAC* curve shows the level of output for which the amount of the fixed factor is optimal.

LESSONS FROM HISTORY 8-1

Jacob Viner and the Clever Draftsman

Jacob Viner (1892–1970) was born in Montreal and studied economics at McGill University under Stephen Leacock (1869–1944). Viner was clearly an outstanding student and, according to some of his McGill classmates, knew much more about economics than did Leacock, who was actually better known as a humourist than an economist. Viner was such a good economist that he was the first person to work out the relationship between a firm's long-run average costs and its short-run average costs. He went on to teach economics at the University of Chicago and at Princeton University and became one of the world's leading economic theorists.

The student who finds the relationship between *SRATC* and *LRAC* hard to understand may take some comfort from the fact that when Jacob Viner first worked out this relationship, and published it in 1931, he made a crucial mistake. In preparing a diagram like Figure 8-3, he instructed his draftsman to draw the *LRAC* curve through the *minimum points* of all the *SRATC* curves, "but so as to never lie above" the *SRATC* curves. Viner later said of the draftsman: "He is a mathematician, however, not an economist, and he saw some mathematical objection to this procedure which I could not succeed in understanding. I could not persuade him to disregard his scruples as a craftsman and to follow my instructions, absurd though they might be."

Viner's mistake was to require that the draftsman connect all of the *minimum* points of the *SRATC* curves rather than to construct the curve that would be the *lower envelope* of all the *SRATC* curves. The former curve can of course be drawn, but it *is not* the *LRAC* curve. The latter curve *is* the *LRAC* curve, and is tangent to each *SRATC* curve.

Since Viner's article was published in 1931, generations of economics students have experienced great satisfaction when they finally figured out his crucial mistake.

Viner's famous article was often reprinted, for its fame was justly deserved, despite the importance of the mistake. But Viner always rejected suggestions that he correct the error because he did not wish to deprive other students of the pleasure of feeling one up on him.

The economic sense of the fact that tangency is *not* at the minimum points of *SRATC* rests on the subtle distinction between the least-cost method of utilizing *a given plant* and the least-cost method of producing *a given level of output*. The first concept defines the minimum of any given *SRATC* curve, whereas the second defines a point on the *LRAC* curve for any given level of output. It is the second concept that interests us in the long run. If bigger plants can achieve lower average costs, there will be a gain in building a bigger plant *and underutilizing it* whenever the gains from using the bigger plant are enough to offset the costs of being inefficient in the use of the plant. If there are gains from building bigger plants (i.e., if *LRAC* is declining), some underutilization is always justified.

Montreal-born Jacob Viner taught at Princeton and Chicago and was one of the world's leading economic theorists.

Each *SRATC* curve is tangent to the long-run average cost curve at the level of output for which the quantity of the fixed factor is optimal and lies above it for all other levels of output.

The relationship between the *LRAC* curve and the many different *SRATC* curves has a famous history in economics. The economist who is credited with first working out this relationship, Jacob Viner, initially made a serious mistake that ended up being published; *Lessons From History 8-1* explains his mistake and shows how it illustrates an important difference between short-run and long-run costs.

Shifts in Cost Curves

We saw in Chapter 7 how changes in either technological knowledge or factor prices will cause the entire family of short-run cost curves to shift. The same is true for long-run cost curves. Because loss of existing technological knowledge is rare, we focus on the effects of technological improvement. Improved ways of producing existing products make lower-cost methods of production available, thereby shifting cost curves downward.

Changes in factor prices can exert an influence in either direction. If a firm has to pay more for any factor that it uses, the cost of producing each level of output will rise; if the firm has to pay less for any factor that it uses, the cost of producing each level of output will fall.

A rise in factor prices shifts short-run and long-run average cost curves upward. A fall in factor prices or a technological improvement shifts average cost curves downward.

The Very Long Run: Changes in Technology

In the long run, profit-maximizing firms do the best they can to produce known products with the techniques and the resources currently available. Firms are therefore on, rather than above, their long-run cost curves. In the very long run, however, there are changes in the available techniques and resources. Such changes cause *shifts* in long-run cost curves.

The decrease in costs that can be achieved by choosing from among available factors of production, known techniques, and alternative levels of output is necessarily limited. Improvements by invention and innovation are potentially limitless, however, and hence sustained growth in living standards is critically linked to technological change.

Technological change refers to all changes in the available techniques of production. To measure its extent, economists use the notion of **productivity,** defined as a measure of output produced per unit of resource input. Two widely used measures of productivity are output per worker and output per hour of work. The rate of increase in productivity provides a measure of technological change. The significance of productivity growth is explored in *Applying Economic Concepts 8-2.*

technological change Any change in the available techniques of production.

productivity Output produced per unit of some input; frequently used to refer to labour productivity, measured by total output divided by the amount of labour used.

Technological Change

Technological change was once thought to be mainly a random process, brought about by inventions made by crackpots and eccentric scientists working in garages and scientific laboratories. As a result of recent research by economists, we now know better.

Changes in technology are often *endogenous responses* to changing economic signals; that is, they result from responses by firms to the same things that induce the substitution of one factor for another within the confines of a given technology.

In our discussion of long-run demand curves in Chapter 4, we looked at just such technological changes in response to rising relative prices when we spoke of the development, in the 1970s, of smaller, more fuel-efficient cars in the wake of rising gasoline prices. Similarly, much of the move to substitute capital for labour in manufacturing,

APPLYING ECONOMIC CONCEPTS 8-2

The Significance of Productivity Growth

Economics used to be known as the "dismal science" because some of its predictions were grim. Thomas Malthus (1766–1834) and other Classical economists predicted that the pressure of more and more people on the world's limited resources would cause a decline in output per person due to the law of diminishing returns. Human history would see more and more people living less and less well and the surplus population, which could not be supported, dying off from hunger and disease.

This prediction has proved wrong for the developed countries, for two main reasons. First, their populations have not expanded as rapidly as predicted by early economists, who were writing before birth-control techniques were widely used. Second, technological advances have been so important during the past 150 years that output has increased faster than the population. We have experienced sustained growth in productivity that has permitted increases in output per person. As the accompanying figure shows, real output per worker in Canada increased by 264 percent between 1926 and 1998, an average annual growth rate of 1.8 percent.

Even such small annual productivity increases are a powerful force for increasing living standards over many years. Our great-grandparents would have regarded today's standard of living in most industrialized countries as unattainable. An apparently modest rate of increase in productivity of 2 percent per year leads to a doubling of per capita output every 35 years.

During the 1970s, the rate of productivity growth in most industrialized countries dropped sharply below its historical trend. This slowdown was particularly acute in Canada and the United States. In recent years, annual productivity growth rates have increased somewhat, but are still below the high rates that existed in the 1950s and 1960s.

Due to the importance of productivity growth in raising long-run living standards, it is not surprising that explaining the sources of technological progress has become a very active area of research, among both academic and government economists.

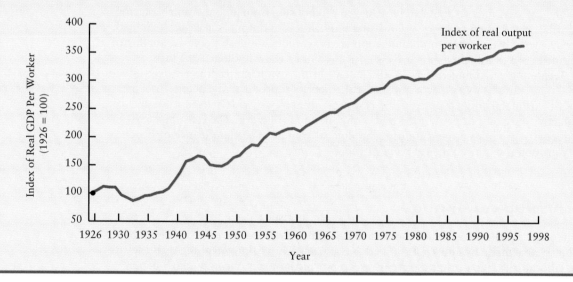

transportation, communications, mining, and agriculture in response to rising wage rates has taken the form of inventing new labour-saving methods of production.

Consider three kinds of change that influence production and cost in the very long run—*new techniques, new products,* and *improved inputs.*

New Techniques

Throughout the nineteenth and twentieth centuries, changes in the techniques available for producing existing products have been dramatic; this is called *process innovation*. About the same amount of coal is produced in North America today as was produced 50 years ago, but the number of coal miners is less than one-tenth what it was then. A century ago, roads and railways were built by gangs of workers who used buckets, spades, and draft horses. Today, bulldozers, giant trucks, and other specialized equipment have banished the workhorse completely from construction sites and to a great extent have displaced the pick-and-shovel worker.

Prior to the Second World War, electricity was generated either by burning fossil fuels or by harnessing the power of flowing water. With the rise of the atomic age immediately following the war, many countries developed large-scale nuclear generating capacity. Economies of scale in electricity production were significant. In recent years, however, the development of small-scale, gas-combustion turbines has permitted inexpensive construction of small generating stations that can produce electricity at a lower average cost than the much larger nuclear, hydro, or fossil-fuel-burning generating stations. The product—electricity—is absolutely unchanged, but the techniques of production have changed markedly over the past several decades.

New Products

New goods and services are constantly being invented and marketed; this is called *product innovation*. VCRs, personal computers, CD players, video disks, cellular phones, and many other current consumer products did not exist a mere generation ago. Other products have changed so dramatically that the only connection they have with the "same" product from the past is the name. Today's Ford automobile is very different from a 1920 Ford, and it is even different from a 1980 Ford in size, safety, and gasoline consumption. Modern jet airliners are revolutionary compared with the first passenger jet aircraft, which were in turn many times larger and faster than the DC–3, the workhorse of the airlines during the 1930s and 1940s. Beyond having wings and engines, the DC–3 itself bore little resemblance to the Wright brothers' original flying machine.

Improved Inputs

Improvements in health and education raise the quality of labour services. Today's workers and managers are healthier and better educated than their grandparents. Many of today's unskilled workers are literate and competent in arithmetic, and their managers are apt to be trained in methods of business management and computer science.

Similarly, improvements in material inputs are constantly occurring. For example, the type and quality of metals have changed. Steel has replaced iron, and aluminum substitutes for steel in a process of change that makes a statistical category such as "primary metals" seem unsatisfactory. Even for a given category, say, steel, today's product is lighter, stronger, and more flexible than the "same" product manufactured only 20 years ago.

Firms' Choices in the Very Long Run

Firms respond to signals that indicate changes in the economic environment. For example, consider the situation faced by Alcan—a major Canadian aluminum producer—when the price of electricity (a major input) increases and is expected to remain at the higher level for some time. How can Alcan respond to this change in the economic environment?

One option for Alcan is to make a long-run response by substituting away from the use of electricity by changing its production techniques within the confines of existing technology. Another option is to invest in research in order to develop new production techniques that innovate away from electricity. Of course, both responses could be adopted, but because both involve the use of costly resources, the responses are substitutes in the sense that Alcan may have to choose more of one at the cost of using less of the other.

Faced with increases in the price of an input, firms may either *substitute away* or *innovate away* from the input.

It is important to recognize that the two options can involve quite different actions and can ultimately have quite different implications for productivity.

For example, consider three different responses to an increase in Canadian labour costs. One firm reallocates its production activities to Mexico or Southeast Asia, where labour costs are relatively low and hence labour-intensive production techniques remain quite profitable. A second firm chooses to reduce its use of labour but increase its use of capital equipment. These two firms have, in different ways, chosen to *substitute away* from the higher-priced Canadian labour. A third firm devotes resources to developing new production techniques, perhaps using robotics or other new equipment. This firm has *innovated away* from higher-priced Canadian labour.

All three are possible reactions to the changed circumstances. The first two are largely well understood in advance and will lead to improved efficiency relative to continued reliance on the original production methods. The third response, depending on the often unpredictable results of the innovation, may reduce costs sufficiently to warrant the investment in research and development and may even lead to substantially more effective production techniques that allow the firm to maintain an advantage over its competitors for a number of years.

S U M M A R Y

The Long Run: No Fixed Factors

(LO)❶❷❸

- There are no fixed factors in the long run. Profit-maximizing firms choose from the available alternatives the least-cost method of producing any specific output. A long-run cost curve represents the boundary between attainable and unattainable costs for the given technology and given factor prices.
- The principle of substitution implies that, in response to changes in factor prices, firms will substitute toward the cheaper factors and substitute away from the more expensive factors.
- The shape of the *LRAC* curve depends on the relationship of inputs to outputs as the whole scale of a firm's operations changes. Increasing, constant, and decreasing returns lead, respectively, to decreasing, constant, and increasing long-run average costs.
- The *LRAC* and *SRATC* curves are related. Every long-run cost corresponds to some quantity of each factor and is thus on some short-run cost curve. The short-run cost curve shows how costs vary when that particular quantity of a fixed factor is used to produce outputs greater than or less than the output for which it is optimal.
- Cost curves shift upward or downward in response to changes in the prices of factors or changes in technology. Increases in factor prices shift cost curves upward. Decreases in factor prices and technological advances shift cost curves downward.

The Very Long Run: Changes in Technology

LO 4

- Over the very long run, the most important influence on costs of production and on standards of living has been increases in output made possible by technological improvements.
- Changes in technology are often *endogenous responses* to changing economic signals; that is, they result from responses by firms to the same things that induce the substitution of one factor for another in a given technology.

- There are three important kinds of technological change—developments of new techniques, new products, and improved inputs.
- In trying to understand any industry's response to changes in its operating environment, it is important to consider the effects of endogenous innovations in technology as well as substitution based on changes in the use of existing technologies.

KEY CONCEPTS

The implication of cost minimization

The interpretation of $MP_K/MP_L = p_K/p_L$

The principle of substitution

Increasing, decreasing, and constant returns

Economies of scale

LRAC curve as an envelope of *SRATC* curves

Technological change and productivity growth

Changes in technology as endogenous responses

STUDY EXERCISES

1. Use the principle of substitution to predict the effect in each of the following situations.

   a. During the past 10 years, technological advances in the computer industry have led to dramatic reductions in the prices of personal and business computers. At the same time, real wages have increased slowly.

   b. The ratio of land costs to building costs is much higher in big cities than in small cities.

   c. Wages of textile workers and shoe machinery operators are higher in Canada than in the southern United States.

   d. A new collective agreement results in a significant increase in wages for pulp and paper workers.

2. The following table shows the marginal product of capital and labour for each of several methods of producing 1000 kilograms of flour per day.

Production Method	MP_K	MP_L
A	14	3
B	12	6
C	10	9
D	8	12
E	6	15
F	4	18
G	2	21

   a. As we move from A to G, are the production methods becoming more or less *capital intensive*? Explain.

   b. If capital costs $8 per unit and labour costs $4 per unit, which production method minimizes the cost of producing 1000 kg of flour?

   c. For each of the methods that are not cost minimizing (with the factor prices from part **b**), describe how the firm would have to adjust its use of capital and labour to minimize costs.

d. Now suppose that the price of capital falls to $4 per unit and the price of labour rises to $6 per unit. Which method now minimizes costs?

3. Consider the following diagram of SRATC and LRAC curves.

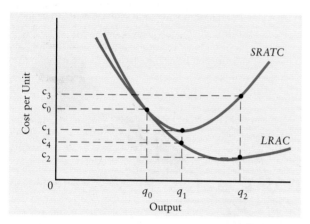

a. The SRATC curve is drawn for a given plant size. What is the level of output for which this plant size is optimal in the short run? What are unit costs in the short run at this level of output?
b. What is the level of output for which this plant size is optimal in the long run? What are unit costs in the short run at this level of output?
c. Explain the economics of why c_1 is greater than c_4.
d. Suppose the firm wants to increase output to q_2 in the short run. How is this accomplished, and what would unit costs be?
e. Suppose the firm wants to increase output to q_2 in the long run. How is this accomplished, and what would unit costs be?

4. In the text, we stated that the LRAC curve eventually slopes upward because of *diseconomies of scale*. In the previous chapter we saw that the SRATC curve eventually slopes upward because of *diminishing marginal product of the variable factor*.

a. Explain the difference between *diseconomies of scale and diminishing marginal product of the variable factor*. Why is one a short-run concept and the other a long-run concept?
b. Draw a diagram which shows short-run and long-run average cost curves that illustrates *for the same level of output* both diseconomies of scale and diminishing marginal product of the variable factor.

5. In the text, we stated that the LRAC curve initially slopes downward because of *economies of scale*. In the previous chapter we saw that the SRATC curve can initially slope downward because of *spreading overhead*.

a. Explain the difference between *economies of scale* and *spreading overhead*. Why is one a short-run concept and the other a long-run concept?
b. Draw a diagram which shows short-run and long-run average cost curves that illustrates *for the same level of output* both economies of scale and spreading overhead.

6. This question combines the various concepts from questions 4 and 5.

a. Draw a diagram which shows short-run and long-run average cost curves that illustrates *for the same level of output* economies of scale in the long run but diminishing marginal product for the variable factor in the short run.
b. Draw a diagram which shows short-run and long-run average cost curves that illustrates *for the same level of output* diseconomies of scale in the long run but falling average total costs in the short run.

7. This question relates to the material in the appendix. The following table shows several methods of producing 500 rubber tires per day. There are two factors, labour and capital, with prices per unit of $3 and $6, respectively.

Production Method	Units of Labour	Units of Capital	Total Cost
A	110	20	—--
B	90	25	—--
C	70	33	—--
D	50	43	—--
E	30	55	—--
F	10	70	—--

a. Compute the total cost for each production method and fill in the table.
b. Which production method minimizes costs for producing 500 tires?
c. Plot the isoquant for 500 tires.
d. Given the factor prices, draw the isocost line that corresponds to the cost-minimizing production method.
e. Now suppose that the price of labour rises to $5 per unit but the firm still wants to produce 500 tires per day. Explain how a cost-minimizing firm adjusts to this change (with no change in technology).

DISCUSSION QUESTIONS

1. In *The Competitive Advantage of Nations*, Michael Porter of Harvard University claimed: "Faced with high relative labor cost, . . . American consumer electronics firms moved to locate labor-intensive activities in . . . Asian countries, leaving the product and production process essentially the same. . . . Japanese rivals . . . set out instead to eliminate labor through automation. Doing so involved reducing the number of components which further lowered cost and improved quality. Japanese firms were soon building assembly plants in the United States, the place American firms had sought to avoid." Discuss these reactions in terms of changes over the long run and the very-long run.

2. Why must a profit-maximizing firm choose the least-cost method of producing any given output? Might a non-profit-maximizing organization such as a university, church, or government intentionally choose a method of production other than the least-cost one?

3. What is the interpretation of a move from one point on a long-run average cost curve to another point on the same curve? Contrast this with a movement along a short-run average total cost curve.

4. Each of the following is a means of increasing productivity. Discuss which groups in a society might oppose each one.

   a. A labour-saving invention that permits all goods to be manufactured with less labour than before
   b. Rapidly increasing population growth in the economy
   c. The removal of all government production safety rules
   d. A reduction in corporate income taxes
   e. A reduction in production of services and an increase in agricultural production

5. Policymakers and commentators often argue that the Canadian health-care system is more efficient than the U.S. health-care system. What sense of the term *efficiency* is being used in these arguments?

6. In December 1998, after a year in which Asian demand for B.C. lumber had fallen dramatically, an article in *The Globe and Mail* had the following headline: "Drastic Cost Reductions Needed to Save 13 B.C. Sawmills."

   a. Does the headline suggest that the B.C. lumber companies are not profit maximizers?
   b. If long-run unit costs are "too high," what is stopping the lumber companies from simply moving down their *LRAC* curves?

7. "Necessity is the mother of invention." Explain why this statement captures the essence of the view that firms often innovate their way around unfavourable changes in their economic environment.

The production function gives the relationship between the factor inputs that the firm uses and the output that it obtains. In the long run, the firm can choose among many different combinations of inputs that yield the same output. The production function and the long-run choices open to the firm can be represented graphically by using *isoquants*.

Isoquants

The table in Figure 8A-1 illustrates a hypothetical example in which several combinations of two inputs, labour and capital, can produce a given quantity of output. The data from the table are plotted graphically in Figure 8A-1. A smooth curve is drawn through the points to indicate that there are additional ways, which are not listed in the table, of producing the same output.

This curve is called an *isoquant*. It shows the whole set of technically efficient factor combinations for producing a given level of output. This is an example of graphing a relationship between three variables in two dimensions. It is analogous to the contour line on a map, which shows all points of equal altitude, and to an indifference curve (discussed in the Appendix to Chapter 6), which shows all combinations of products that yield the consumer equal utility.

As we move from one point on an isoquant to another, we are *substituting one factor for another* while holding output constant. If we move from point *b* to point *c,* we are substituting 1 unit of labour for 3 units of capital.

The marginal rate of substitution measures the rate at which one factor is substituted for another with output being held constant.

Sometimes the term *marginal rate of technical substitution* is used to distinguish this concept from the analogous one for consumer theory (the marginal rate of substitution) that we examined in Chapter 6.

Graphically, the marginal rate of substitution is measured by the slope of the isoquant at a particular point. We adopt the standard practice of defining the marginal rate of substitution as the negative of the

slope of the isoquant so that it is a positive number. The table in Figure 8A-1 shows the calculation of some marginal rates of substitution between various points on an isoquant. [19]

The marginal rate of substitution is related to the marginal products of the factors of production. To see how, consider an example. Suppose that at the present level of inputs of labour and capital, the marginal product of labour is 2 units of output and the marginal product of capital is 1 unit of output. If the firm reduces its use of capital and increases its use of labour to keep output constant, it needs to add only one-half unit of labour for 1 unit of capital given up. If, at another point on the isoquant with more labour and less capital, the marginal products are 2 for capital and 1 for labour, the firm will have to add 2 units of labour for every unit of capital it gives up. The general proposition is this:

The marginal rate of (technical) substitution between two factors of production is equal to the ratio of their marginal products.

Economists assume that isoquants satisfy two important conditions: They are downward sloping, and they are convex when viewed from the origin. What is the economic meaning of these conditions?

The downward slope indicates that each factor input has a positive marginal product. If the input of one factor is reduced and that of the other is held constant, output will be reduced. Thus if one input is decreased, production can be held constant only if the other factor input is increased.

To understand the convexity of the isoquant, consider what happens as the firm moves along the isoquant of Figure 8A-1 downward and to the right. Labour is being added and capital reduced to keep output constant. If labour is added in increments of exactly 1 unit, how much capital can be dispensed with each time? The key to the answer is that both factors are assumed to be subject to the law of diminishing returns. Thus the gain in output associated with each additional unit of labour added is *diminishing*, whereas the loss of output associated with each additional unit of capital forgone is *increasing*. Therefore, it takes ever-smaller reductions in capital to compensate for equal increases in labour. Viewed from the origin, therefore, the isoquant is convex.

FIGURE 8A-1   An Isoquant

Alternative Methods of Producing a Given Level of Output

Method	K	L	ΔK	ΔL	Marginal Rate of Substitution (absolute value of ΔK/ΔL)
a	18	2			
			−6	1	6.00
b	12	3			
			−3	1	3.00
c	9	4			
			−3	2	1.50
d	6	6			
			−2	3	0.67
e	4	9			
			−1	3	0.33
f	3	12			
			−1	6	0.17
g	2	18			

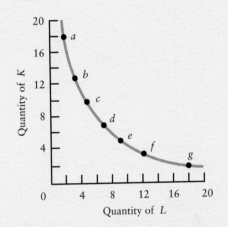

An isoquant describes the firm's alternative methods for producing a given level of output. Method *a* uses a great deal of capital *(K)* and very little labour *(L)*. As we move down the table, labour is substituted for capital in such a way as to keep output constant. Finally, at the bottom, most of the capital has been replaced by labour. The marginal rate of substitution between the two factors is calculated in the last three columns of the table. Note that as we move down the table, the marginal rate of substitution declines.

When the isoquant is plotted it is downward sloping and convex. The downward slope reflects the requirement of technical efficiency: keeping the level of output constant, a reduction in the use of one factor requires an increase in the use of the other factor. The convex shape of the isoquant reflects a diminishing marginal rate of (technical) substitution.

An Isoquant Map

The isoquant of Figure 8A-1 is for a given level of output. Suppose it is for 6 units. In this case, there is another isoquant for 7 units, another for 7000 units, and a different one for every other level of output. Each isoquant refers to a specific level of output and connects combinations of factors that are technically efficient methods of producing that output. If we plot a representative set of these isoquants from the same production function on a single graph, we get an *isoquant map* like that in Figure 8A-2. The higher the level of output along a particular isoquant, the farther the isoquant is from the origin.

Cost Minimization

Finding the *economically efficient* way of producing any output requires finding the least-cost factor com-

bination. To do this requires knowledge of the factor prices. Suppose that capital is priced at $4 per unit and labour at $1 per unit. An *isocost line* shows alternative combinations of factors that a firm can buy for a given total cost. Four different isocost lines appear in Figure 8A-3. The slope of each isocost line reflects *relative* factor prices. For given factor prices, a series of parallel isocost lines will reflect the alternative levels of expenditure on factor purchases that are available to the firm. The higher the level of expenditure, the farther the isocost line is from the origin.

In Figure 8A-4, the isoquant and isocost maps are brought together. Recall that economic efficiency requires any given level of output to be produced at minimum possible cost. Thus, the economically efficient method of production must be a point on an isoquant that just touches (is tangent to) an isocost line. If the isoquant cuts the isocost line, it is possible to move along the isoquant and reach a lower level of cost. Only at a point of tangency is a movement in either direction along the isoquant a movement to a higher cost level.

FIGURE 8A-2   An Isoquant Map

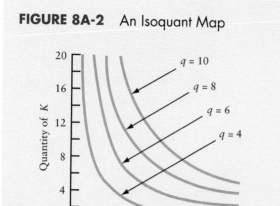

An isoquant map shows a set of isoquants, one for each level of output. Each isoquant corresponds to a specific level of output and shows factor combinations that are technically efficient methods of producing that output.

FIGURE 8A-3   Isocost Lines

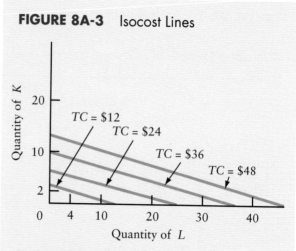

Each isocost line shows alternative factor combinations that require the same expenditure. The graph shows the four isocost lines that result when labour costs $1 per unit and capital $4 per unit and when expenditure (total cost, TC) is held constant at $12, $24, $36, and $48, respectively.

As shown in Figure 8A-4, the lowest attainable cost of producing 6 units is $24. This cost level can be achieved only by operating at point A, where the $24 isocost line is tangent to the 6-unit isoquant.

The least-cost position is given graphically by the tangency point between the isoquant and the isocost lines.

The slope of the isocost line is given by the ratio of the prices of the two factors of production. The slope of the isoquant is given by the ratio of their marginal products. When the firm reaches its cost-minimizing position, it has equated the price ratio (which is given to it by the market) with the ratio of the marginal products (which it can adjust by changing its usage of the factors). In symbols,

$$\frac{MP_L}{MP_K} = \frac{p_L}{p_K}$$

This is the same condition that we derived in the text (see Equation 8-2), but here we have derived it by using the isoquant analysis of the firm's decisions. [20]

Note the similarity of this condition for a cost-minimizing firm to Equation 6-2 where we saw how utility maximization for a consumer requires that the ratio of marginal utilities of consuming two products must equal the ratio of the two product prices. Both conditions reveal the basic principle that the decision makers (consumers or producers) face market prices beyond their control and so adjust quantities (consumption or factor inputs) until they are achieving their objective (utility maximization or cost minimization).

The Principle of Substitution

Suppose that with technology unchanged (that is, for a given isoquant map), the price of one factor changes. In particular, suppose that with the price of capital unchanged at $4 per unit, the price of labour rises from $1 to $4 per unit. Originally, the efficient factor combination for producing 6 units of output was 12 units of labour and 3 units of capital. Total cost was $24. To produce that same output in the same way would now cost $60 at the new factor prices. Figure 8A-5 shows why this is not economically efficient. The slope of the isocost line has changed, which makes it efficient to substitute the now relatively cheaper capital for the relatively more expensive labour. The change in slope of the isocost line illustrates the principle of substitution.

FIGURE 8A-4   Cost Minimization

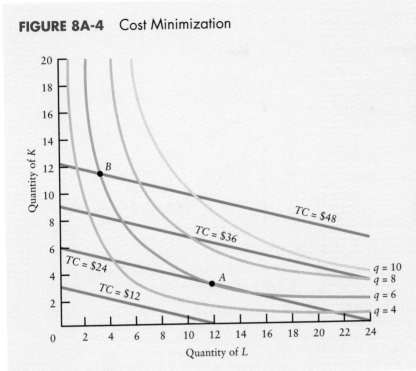

Cost minimization occurs at points of tangency between isoquant and isocost lines. The isoquant map of Figure 8A-2 and the isocost lines of Figure 8A-3 are brought together. Consider point A. It is on the 6-unit isoquant and the $24 isocost line. Thus it is possible to achieve the output $q = 6$ for a total cost of $24. There are other ways to achieve this output, for example, at point B, where $TC = \$48$. Moving along the isoquant from point A in either direction increases cost. Similarly, moving along the isocost line from point A in either direction lowers output. Thus either move would raise cost per unit.

Changes in relative factor prices will cause a partial replacement of factors that have become relatively more expensive by factors that have become relatively cheaper.

Of course, substitution of capital for labour cannot fully offset the effects of a rise in the cost of labour, as Figure 8A-5(i) shows. Consider the output attainable for $24. In the figure, there are two isocost lines representing $24 of outlay—at the old and new prices of labour. The new isocost line for $24 lies inside the old one (except where no labour is used). The $24 isocost line must therefore be tangent to a lower isoquant. Thus, if production is to be held constant, higher costs must be accepted. However, because of substitution, it is not necessary to accept costs as high as those that

would accompany an unchanged factor proportion. In the example, 6 units can be produced for $48 rather than the $60 that would be required if no change in factor proportions were made.

This analysis leads to the following predictions:

A rise in the price of one factor with all other factor prices held constant will (1) shift the cost curves of products that use that factor upward and (2) lead to a substitution of factors that are now relatively cheaper for the factor whose price has risen.

Both of these predictions were stated in Chapter 8; now they have been derived formally by the use of isoquants and isocost lines.

FIGURE 8A-5   The Effects of a Change in Factor Prices on Costs and Factor Proportions

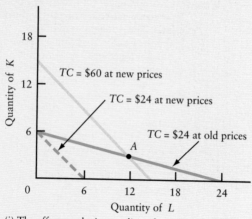

(i) The effect on the isocost line of an increase in the price of labour

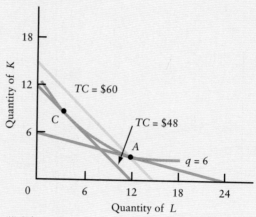

(ii) Substitution of capital for labour resulting from an increase in the price of labour

An increase in the price of labour pivots the isocost line inward, increasing its slope. This changes the cost-minimizing method of producing any level of output. In part (i), the rise in the price of L from \$1 to \$4 per unit (with the price of K being held constant at \$4) pivots the \$24 isocost line inward to the dashed line. Any output previously produced for \$24 will cost more at the new prices if it uses any labour. The new cost of using the factor combination at A rises from \$24 to \$60. In part (ii), the steeper isocost line is tangent to the $q = 6$ isoquant at C, not A, so that more capital and less labour is used. Costs at C are \$48, higher than they were before the price increase but not as high as they would be if the factor substitution had not occurred.

PART FOUR

Markets, Pricing, and Efficiency

Do wheat farmers in Saskatchewan and Manitoba compete with each other in the same way that Nike competes with Reebok? How would the Saskatchewan farmer respond to an improvement in techniques used by the Manitoba farmer? How would Nike respond to a price reduction by Reebok? Why do some firms, such as airlines, charge different prices to different consumers for the same product? Why did the Canadian government prevent the merger of the Royal Bank and the Bank of Montreal in 1998? These are the types of questions you will be able to answer after reading the next four chapters.

Chapter 9 discusses the theory of perfect competition. This theory describes markets in which a very large number of firms produce very similar products, like the wheat farmers in Saskatchewan and Manitoba. The chapter introduces the important concept of price taking. We will discuss how the existence of profits in such an industry leads to the entry of new firms, and why such entry leads to the dissipation of those profits. Similarly, we will see why losses lead existing firms to exit, and why this increases the profits of the remaining firms.

Chapter 10 examines monopoly—a situation in which there is only a single seller of a product. We will see that monopolies typically produce less output and have higher prices than do firms under perfect competition. We will discuss why several firms often try to join together to form a cartel, in which case they act as if they were a monopoly seller. We will also see why such cartels often break down.

Imperfect competition, which describes markets that are between the polar cases of perfect competition and monopoly, is discussed in Chapter 11. We will learn about industries with many firms but differentiated products, and also about industries with very few firms, in which strategic behaviour between the firms is important. It is here that you will see how economists use simple game theory to think about Nike's likely response to Reebok's price reduction.

The concept of allocative efficiency is examined in Chapter 12. We will consider why perfectly competitive markets are more efficient than monopolized markets. This difference in efficiency explains economists' long-held wariness of monopoly and why economists typically advocate competition over monopoly. Canadian competition policy, as we will see, is designed to encourage competition and discourage monopoly.

CHAPTER 9

Competitive Markets

LO LEARNING OBJECTIVES

① Distinguish between competitive markets and competitive firm behaviour.

② Know the key assumptions of the theory of perfect competition.

③ Explain the difference between an individual firm's demand curve and the industry demand curve for a perfectly competitive market.

④ Understand the rules for profit-maximizing behaviour.

⑤ Identify whether firms are making losses or profits in the short run.

⑥ Explain the role that entry and exit play in a competitive industry's long-run equilibrium.

⑦ Understand how competitive industries respond to long-run changes in demand.

Does PetroCanada compete with Esso in the sale of gasoline? Does American Express compete with Visa? Does a wheat farmer from Biggar, Saskatchewan compete with a wheat farmer from Brandon, Manitoba? If we use the ordinary meaning of the word compete, the answer to the first two questions is plainly yes, and the answer to the third question is no.

PetroCanada and Esso both advertise extensively to persuade consumers to buy their products. All sorts of things, from free dishes to performance-enhancing gasoline additives, are used to tempt drivers to buy one brand of gasoline rather than another. A host of world travellers in various tight spots attest on television or in magazines to the virtues of American Express, while other happy faces advise us that only with a Visa card can their pleasures be ours.

When we shift our attention to wheat farmers, however, we see that there is nothing that the Saskatchewan farmer can do to affect either the sales or the profits of the Manitoba farmer. Even if the Saskatchewan farmer could do something to influence the profits of the Manitoba farmer, there would be no point in doing so, since changes in the profits of the Manitoba farmer would not affect the Saskatchewan farmer.

To sort out the questions of who is competing with whom and in what sense, it is useful to distinguish between the behaviour of individual firms and the type of market in which they operate. Economists are interested in two different concepts—*competitive behaviour* and *competitive market structure*.

Market Structure and Firm Behaviour

The term **market structure** refers to all the features that may affect the behaviour and performance of the firms in a market, such as the number of firms in the market or the type of product that they sell.

Competitive Market Structure

The competitiveness of the market is the extent to which individual firms have power to influence market prices or the terms on which their product is sold.

The less power an individual firm has to influence the market in which it sells its product, the more competitive is that market's structure.

The extreme form of competitive market structure occurs when each firm has zero market power. In such a case, there are so many firms in the market that each must accept the price set by the forces of market demand and market supply. The firms perceive themselves as being able to sell as much as they choose at the prevailing market price and as having no power to influence that price. If the firm charged a higher price, it would make no sales; so many other firms would be selling at the market price that buyers would take their business elsewhere.

This extreme is called a *perfectly competitive market structure* or, more simply, a *perfectly competitive market*. In such a market there is no need for individual firms to compete actively with one another because none has any power over the market. One firm's ability to sell its product does not depend on the behaviour of any other firm. For example, the Saskatchewan and Manitoba wheat farms operate in a perfectly competitive market over which they have no power. Neither can change the market price for its wheat by altering its own behaviour.

Competitive Behaviour

In everyday language, the term *competitive behaviour* refers to the degree to which individual firms actively vie with one another for business. For example, PetroCanada and Esso clearly engage in competitive behaviour. It is also true, however, that both companies have some real power over their market. Each has the power to decide the price that people will pay for their gasoline and oil, within limits set by buyers' tastes and the prices of competing products. Either firm could raise its prices and still continue to attract some customers. Even though they actively compete with each other, they do so in a market that does not have a perfectly competitive structure.

In contrast, the Saskatchewan and Manitoba wheat farmers do not engage in competitive behaviour because the only way they can affect their profits is by changing their own outputs of wheat or their own production costs.

The distinction that we have just made between behaviour and structure explains why firms in perfectly competitive markets (e.g., the Saskatchewan and Manitoba wheat producers) do not compete actively with each other, whereas firms that do compete actively with each other (e.g., PetroCanada and Esso) do not operate in perfectly competitive markets.

The Significance of Market Structure

When the managers of a firm make their production and sales decisions, they need to know what quantity of a product their firm can sell at various prices. That is, they need to know the demand curve for their *own firm's* output. If they know the demand curve that their own firm faces, they know the sales that their firm can make at each price it might charge, and thus they know its potential revenues. If they also know their firm's costs for producing the product, they can calculate the profits that would be associated with each rate of output. With this information, they can choose the output that maximizes profits.

Note that the demand curve for the firm's output may not be the same as the demand curve for the industry as a whole. Indeed, this is where *market structure* enters the picture. Recall that economists define market structure as the characteristics that affect the behaviour and performance of firms that sell in that market. These characteristics determine, among other things, the relationship between the market demand curve for the industry's product and the demand curve that each firm in that industry faces. One thing that we will see in this chapter is that in a perfectly competitive market, an individual firm faces a very different demand curve than that faced by the industry as a whole.

To reduce the analysis of market structure to manageable proportions, economists focus on four theoretical market structures that cover most actual cases: *perfect competition, monopoly, monopolistic competition,* and *oligopoly*. Perfect competition will be dealt with in the rest of this chapter, the other structures in the chapters that follow.

The Theory of Perfect Competition

The perfectly competitive market structure—usually referred to simply as **perfect competition**—applies directly to a number of markets. It also provides an important benchmark for comparison with other market structures.

The Assumptions of Perfect Competition

The theory of perfect competition is built on a number of key assumptions relating to each firm and to the industry as a whole.

1. All the firms in the industry sell an identical product. Economists say that the firms sell a **homogeneous product.**

2. Customers know the nature of the product being sold and the prices charged by each firm.

3. The level of a firm's output at which its long-run average cost reaches a minimum is small relative to the *industry's* total output. (This is the precise way of saying that the firm is small relative to the size of the industry.)

4. The industry is characterized by *freedom of entry and exit;* that is, any new firm is free to enter the industry and start producing if it so wishes, and any existing firm is free to cease production and leave the industry. Existing firms cannot bar the entry of new firms, and there are no legal prohibitions or other artificial barriers to entering or exiting the industry.

perfect competition A market structure in which all firms in an industry are price takers and in which there is freedom of entry into and exit from the industry.

homogeneous product In the eyes of purchasers, every unit of the product is identical to every other unit.

The first three assumptions imply that each firm in a perfectly competitive industry is a **price taker.** This means that the firm can alter its rate of production and sales without affecting the market price of its product. Thus a firm operating in a perfectly competitive market has no power to influence that market through its own individual actions. It must passively accept whatever happens to be the market price, but it can sell as much as it wants at that price.

The Saskatchewan and Manitoba wheat farmers we considered earlier provide us with good illustrations of firms that are operating in a perfectly competitive market. Because each individual wheat farmer is just one of a very large number of producers who are all growing the same product, one firm's contribution to the industry's total production is a tiny drop in an extremely large bucket. Each firm will correctly assume that variations in its output have no significant effect on the price of wheat. Thus, each firm, knowing that it can sell as much or as little as it chooses at that price, adapts its behaviour to a given market price of wheat. Furthermore, there is nothing that any one farmer can do to stop another farmer from growing wheat, and there are no legal deterrents to becoming a wheat farmer. Anyone who has enough money to buy or rent the necessary land, labour, and equipment can become a wheat farmer.

The difference between the wheat farmers and PetroCanada is the *degree of market power.* Each firm that is producing wheat is an insignificant part of the whole market and thus has no power to influence the price of wheat. PetroCanada does have power to influence the price of gasoline because its own sales represent a significant part of the total Canadian sales of gasoline.

> **price taker** A firm that can alter its rate of production and sales without significantly affecting the market price of its product.

The Demand Curve for a Perfectly Competitive Firm

A major distinction between firms in perfectly competitive markets and firms in any other type of market is the shape of the firm's own demand curve.

Each firm in a perfectly competitive market faces a horizontal demand curve because variations in the firm's output have no noticeable effect on price.

The horizontal (perfectly elastic) demand curve does not indicate that the firm could actually sell an infinite amount at the going price. It indicates, rather, that the variations in production *that it will normally be possible for the firm to make* will leave price unchanged because their effect on total industry output will be negligible.

Figure 9-1 contrasts the market demand curve for the product of a competitive industry with the demand curve that a single firm in that industry faces. *Applying Economic Concepts 9-1* provides an example of the important difference between the firm's demand curve and the market demand curve. It shows a detailed calculation of why the demand curve facing any individual wheat farmer is very nearly perfectly elastic, even though the *market* demand for wheat is quite inelastic.

Total, Average, and Marginal Revenue

To study the revenues that firms receive from the sales of their products, economists define three concepts called *total, average,* and *marginal revenue.* These are the revenue counterparts of the concepts of total, average, and marginal cost that we considered in Chapter 7.

Total revenue *(TR)* is the total amount received by the seller from the sale of a product. If q units are sold at p dollars each, $TR = p \times q$.

> **total revenue (TR)** Total receipts from the sale of a product; price times quantity.

FIGURE 9-1   The Demand Curve for a Competitive Industry and for One Firm in the Industry

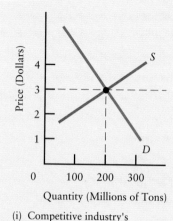

(i) Competitive industry's
demand curve

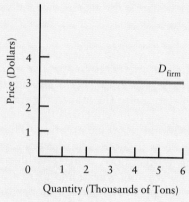

(ii) Competitive firm's
demand curve

The industry's demand curve is nega-tively sloped; the firm's demand curve is virtually horizontal. Notice the dif-ference in the quantities shown on the horizontal scale in each part of the fig-ure. The competitive industry has an output of 200 million tons when the price is $3. The individual firm takes that market price as given and consid-ers producing up to, say, 6000 tons. The firm's demand curve in part (ii) is horizontal because any change in out-put that this single firm could manage would leave price virtually unchanged at $3. The firm's output variation has only a tiny percentage effect on indus-try output.

Average revenue (AR) is the amount of revenue per unit sold. It is equal to total revenue divided by the number of units sold, and is thus equal to the price at which the product is sold: $AR = (p \times q)/q = p$.

Marginal revenue (MR), sometimes called *incremental revenue*, is the change in a firm's total revenue resulting from a change in its sales by 1 unit. Whenever output changes by more than 1 unit, the change in revenue must be divided by the change in out-put to calculate marginal revenue. For example, if an increase in output of 3 units is accompanied by an increase in revenue of $1500, the marginal revenue is $1500/3, or $500. [21]

To illustrate each of these revenue concepts, consider a firm that is selling barley in a perfectly competitive market at a price of $3 per bushel. Total revenue rises by $3 for every bushel sold. Because every bushel brings in $3, the average revenue per bushel sold is clearly $3. Furthermore, because each *additional* bushel sold brings in $3, the marginal revenue of an extra bushel sold is also $3. The table in Figure 9-2 shows calculations of these revenue concepts for a range of outputs between 10 and 13 bushels.

The important point illustrated in the table is that as long as the firm's own level of output cannot affect the price of the product it sells, then the firm's marginal revenue is equal to its average revenue (which is *always* equal to price). Thus, for a price-taking firm, $AR = MR = $ price. Graphically, as shown in part (i) of Figure 9-2, average revenue and marginal revenue are the same horizontal line drawn at the level of market price. Because the firm can sell any quantity it chooses at this price, the horizontal line is also the *firm's demand curve*; it shows that any quantity the firm chooses to sell will be associated with this same market price.

If the market price is unaffected by variations in the firm's output, then the firm's demand curve, its average revenue curve, and its marginal revenue curve all coincide in the same horizontal line.

This result can be stated in a slightly different way that turns out to be important for our later study:

For a firm in perfect competition, price equals marginal revenue.

It follows, of course, that total revenue rises in direct proportion to output, as shown in part (ii) of Figure 9-2.

APPLYING ECONOMIC CONCEPTS 9-1

Demand Under Perfect Competition: Firm and Industry

Consider an individual wheat farmer and the market for wheat. Since products have negatively sloped market demand curves, any increase in the industry's output (caused by a shift in supply) will cause some fall in the market price. However, as the calculations made below show, any conceivable increase that one wheat farm could make in its output has such a negligible effect on the industry's price that the farmer correctly ignores it—the individual wheat farmer is thus a price taker. Although the arithmetic used in reaching this conclusion is unimportant, it is crucial to understand why an individual wheat farmer is a price taker.

Here is the argument that the calculations summarize. The *market* elasticity of demand for wheat is approximately 0.25. Thus, if the quantity of wheat supplied in the world were to increase by 1 percent, the price of wheat would have to fall by roughly 4 percent to induce the world's wheat buyers to purchase the extra wheat.

Even huge farms produce a very small fraction of the total world crop. In a recent year, one large farm produced 1750 metric tons of wheat. This was only 0.000 35 percent of that year's world production of 500 million metric tons. Suppose that the farmer decided in one year to produce nothing and in another year managed to produce twice the normal output of 1750 metric tons. This is an extremely large variation in one farm's output.

The increase in output from zero to 3500 metric tons represents a 200 percent variation measured around the farm's average output of 1750 metric tons. Yet the percentage increase in world output is only (3500 / 500 million) × 100 = 0.0007 percent. Given the demand elasticity of 0.25, this increase in output would lead to a decrease in the world price of 0.0028 percent. This price change, together with the 200 percent change in the farm's *own* output, implies that the farm's own demand curve has an elasticity of over 71 000. This enormous elasticity of demand means that the farm would have to increase its output by over 71 000 percent to bring about a 1 percent decrease in the price of wheat. Because the farm's output cannot be varied this much, it is not surprising that the farmer regards the price of wheat as unaffected by any change in output that he or she could conceiv-

ably make. For all intents and purposes, the individual farmer faces a perfectly elastic demand curve for its product and is thus a *price taker*.

Calculation of the Firm's Demand Elasticity

We begin by taking as given the world elasticity of demand ($\eta = 0.25$) and world output (500 million metric tons). A large farm with an average output of 1750 metric tons varies its output between 0 and 3500 tons. The variation of 3500 tons represents 200 percent of the farm's average output of 1750 metric tons. This causes world output to vary by only 0.0007 percent.

Step 1: Find the percentage change in world price. We know that the market elasticity is 0.25. This means that the percentage change in price must be *four* times as big as the percentage change in *quantity*. Since world quantity changes by 0.0007 percent, world price must change by 0.0028 percent.

Step 2: Find the firm's elasticity of demand. This is the percentage change in its *own output* divided by the resulting percentage change in the world price: 200 percent divided by 0.0028 percent. Clearly, the percentage change in quantity vastly exceeds the percentage change in price, making elasticity very high. Its precise value is 200 / 0.0028 = 71 429.

The demand for wheat is quite inelastic. But the demand for an individual farmer's wheat is almost perfectly elastic.

FIGURE 9-2   Revenue Curves for a Price-Taking Firm

Price p	Quantity q	$TR = p \times q$	$AR = TR/q$	$MR = \Delta TR/\Delta q$
$3	10	$30	$3	
3	11	33	3	$3
3	12	36	3	3
3	13	39	3	3

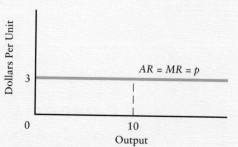

(i) Average and marginal revenue

When the firm is a price taker, $AR = MR = p$. Because price does not change as a result of the *firm* changing its output, neither marginal revenue nor average revenue varies with output. In the table, marginal revenue is shown between the rows because it represents the *change* in total revenues in response to a *change* in quantity. When price is constant, total revenue (which is price times quantity) is an upward-sloping straight line starting from the origin.

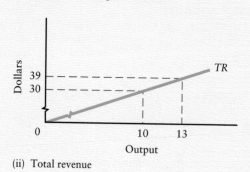

(ii) Total revenue

Short-Run Decisions

We learned in Chapters 7 and 8 how each firm's costs vary with its output. In the short run, the firm has one or more fixed factors, and the only way it can change its output is by using more or less of its variable factor inputs. Thus, the firm's short-run cost curves are relevant to its output decision.

Rules for All Profit-Maximizing Firms

We have just learned how the revenues of each price-taking firm vary with its output. The next step is to combine information about the firm's costs and revenues to determine the level of output that will maximize its profits. We start by stating two rules that apply to *all* profit-maximizing firms, whether or not they operate in perfectly competitive markets. The first rule determines whether the firm should produce at all, and the second determines how much it should produce.

Should the Firm Produce at All?

The firm always has the option of producing nothing. If it exercises this option, it will have an operating loss that is equal to its fixed costs. If it decides to produce, it will add the variable cost of production to its costs and the receipts from the sale of its product to its revenue. Therefore, since it must pay its fixed costs in any event, it will be worthwhile for the firm to produce as long as it can find some level of output for which revenue exceeds *variable* cost. However, if its revenue is less than its variable cost at every level of output, the firm will actually lose more by producing any level of output than by not producing at all.

Rule 1: A firm should not produce at all if for all levels of output, the total variable cost of producing that output exceeds the total revenue derived from selling it or, equivalently, if the average variable cost of producing the output exceeds the price at which it can be sold. [22]

The price at which the firm can just cover its average variable cost, and so is indifferent between producing and not producing, is called the **shut-down price**. Such a price is shown in part (i) of Figure 9-5. (We will return in a moment to Figures 9-3 and 9-4.) At the price of $2, the firm can just cover its average variable cost by producing q_0 units. At this price, any other output would not produce enough revenue to cover variable costs. For any price below $2, there is no output at which variable costs can be covered, and thus the firm will shut down. The price of $2 in part (i) is therefore the shut-down price.

shut-down price
The price that is equal to the minimum of a firm's average variable costs. At prices below this, a profit-maximizing firm will produce no output.

How Much Should the Firm Produce?

If a firm decides that, according to Rule 1, production is worth undertaking, it must then decide *how much* to produce. The key to understanding how much the firm should produce is to think about it on a unit-by-unit basis. If any unit of production adds more to revenue than it does to cost, producing and selling that unit will increase profits. However, if any unit adds more to cost than it does to revenue, producing and selling that unit will decrease profits. According to the terminology introduced earlier, a unit of production raises profits if the *marginal* revenue obtained from selling it exceeds the *marginal* cost of producing it; it lowers profits if the marginal revenue (*MR*) obtained from selling it is less than the marginal cost (*MC*) of producing it.

Now let a firm with some existing rate of output consider increasing or decreasing that output. If a further unit of production will increase the firm's revenues by *more* than it increases costs (*MR>MC*), the firm should expand its output. However, if the last unit produced increases revenues by *less* than it increases costs (*MR<MC*), the firm should reduce its output. From this it follows that the only time the firm should leave its output unaltered is when the last unit produced adds the same amount to revenues as it does to costs (*MR = MC*).

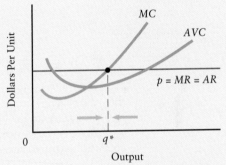

FIGURE 9-3 Profit-Maximization for a Competitive Firm

The firm chooses the output for which $p = MC$ above the level of *AVC*. When $p = MC$, as at q^*, the firm would decrease its profits if it changed its output. At any point to the left of q^*, price is greater than the marginal cost, and it is worthwhile for the firm to increase output (as indicated by the arrow on the left). At any point to the right of q^*, price is less than the marginal cost, and it is worthwhile for the firm to reduce output (as indicated by the arrow on the right).

Rule 2: If it is worthwhile for the firm to produce at all, the firm should produce the output at which marginal revenue equals marginal cost. [23]

The two rules that we have stated refer to each firm's own costs and revenues, and they apply to all profit-maximizing firms, whatever the market structure in which they operate.

FIGURE 9-4 Profit-Maximization Using Total Cost and Revenue Curves

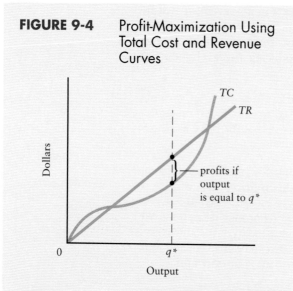

The firm chooses the output for which the gap between the total revenue and the total cost curves is the largest. At each output, the vertical distance between the *TR* and the *TC* curves shows the amount by which total revenue exceeds total cost. In the figure, the gap is largest at output q^*, which is thus the profit-maximizing output.

Practise with Study Guide Chapter 9, Exercise 1.

Rule 2 Applied to Price-Taking Firms

Rule 2 tells us that any profit-maximizing firm that produces at all will produce at the point where marginal cost equals marginal revenue. However, we have already seen that for price-taking firms, marginal revenue is the market price. Combining these two results gives us an important conclusion:

A firm that is operating in a perfectly competitive market will produce the output that equates its marginal cost of production with the market price of its product (as long as price exceeds average variable cost).

In a perfectly competitive industry, the market determines the price at which the firm sells its product. The firm then picks the quantity of output that maximizes its profits. We have seen that this is the output for which price equals marginal cost. When the firm has reached a position where its profits are maximized, it has no incentive to change its output. Therefore, unless prices or costs change, the firm will continue to produce this output because it is doing as well as it can do, given the market situation. This profit-maximizing behaviour is illustrated in Figures 9-3 and 9-4.

The perfectly competitive firm adjusts its level of output in response to changes in the market-determined price.

Figure 9-3 shows the profit-maximizing choice of the firm using average cost and revenue curves. We can, if we wish, show the same result using total cost and revenue curves, as in Figure 9-4. Figure 9-4 combines the total cost curve first drawn in Figure 7-2 with the total revenue curve first shown in Figure 9-2. It shows the profit-maximizing output as the output with the largest positive difference between total revenue and total cost. This, of course, is the same output as the one we located in Figure 9-3 by equating marginal cost and marginal revenue.

Short-Run Supply Curves

We have seen that in a perfectly competitive market, the firm responds to a price that is set by the forces of demand and supply. By adjusting the quantity it produces in response to the current market price, the firm helps to determine the market supply. The link between the behaviour of the firm and the behaviour of the competitive market is provided by the market supply curve. But, before we can derive the supply curve for the market, we need to derive the supply curve for each of the firms in that market.

The Supply Curve for One Firm

The competitive firm's supply curve is derived in part (i) of Figure 9-5, which shows a firm's marginal cost curve and four alternative prices. The horizontal line at each price is the firm's demand curve when the market price is at that level. The firm's marginal cost curve gives the marginal cost corresponding to each level of output. What we are trying

FIGURE 9-5   The Derivation of the Supply Curve for a Competitive Firm

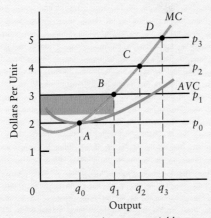
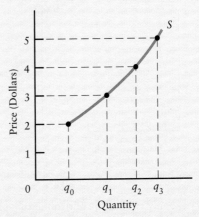

(i) Marginal cost and average variable cost curves

(ii) Supply curve

The supply curve of the competitive firm, shown in part (ii), is the same as its MC curve, shown in part (i). For prices below $2, output is zero because there is no output at which AVC can be covered. The point A, where the price of $2 is just equal to AVC, is the point at which the firm will shut down. As price rises to $3, $4, and $5, the profit-maximizing point changes to B, C, and D, taking output to q_1, q_2, and q_3. At any of these prices, the firm's revenue exceeds its variable costs of production. An example of the excess is shown in part (i) of the figure by the shaded area associated with price p_1 and output q_1. This amount is available to help cover fixed costs and, once these are covered, to provide a profit.

to derive is a supply curve that shows the quantity of output that the firm will supply at each price. For prices below average variable cost, the firm will supply zero units (Rule 1). For prices above average variable cost, the competitive firm will equate price and marginal cost (Rule 2). This behaviour leads to the following conclusion:

A competitive firm's supply curve is given by its marginal cost curve for those levels of output for which marginal cost exceeds average variable cost.

The Supply Curve for an Industry

Figure 9-6 shows the derivation of an industry supply curve for an industry containing only two firms. The general result is as follows:

In perfect competition, the industry supply curve is the horizontal sum of the marginal cost curves (above the level of average variable cost) of all firms in the industry.

Each firm's marginal cost curve shows how much that firm will supply at each given market price, and the industry supply curve is the sum of what each firm will supply.

This supply curve, based on the short-run marginal cost curves of all the firms in the industry, is the industry's supply curve that we first encountered in Chapter 3. We have now established the profit-maximizing behaviour of individual firms that lies behind that curve. It is sometimes called a **short-run supply curve** because it is based on the short-run, profit-maximizing behaviour of all the firms in the industry. It should not be confused with the long-run industry supply curve, which relates quantity supplied to the price that exists *when the industry is in long-run equilibrium* (which we will study later in this chapter).

Practise with Study Guide Chapter 9, Exercise 4.

short-run supply curve   A curve showing the relationship between quantity supplied and market price, with one or more fixed factors; it is the horizontal sum of marginal cost curves (above the level of average variable costs) of all firms in a perfectly competitive industry.

FIGURE 9-6   The Derivation of the Supply Curve of a Competitive Industry

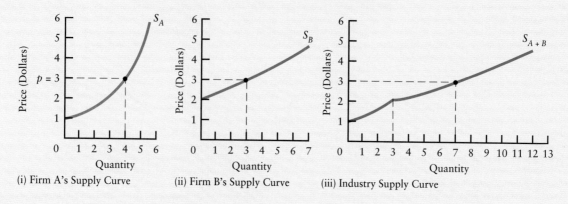

(i) Firm A's Supply Curve

(ii) Firm B's Supply Curve

(iii) Industry Supply Curve

The industry's supply curve is the horizontal sum of the supply curves of each of the firms in the industry. At a price of $3, Firm A would supply 4 units and Firm B would supply 3 units. Together, as shown in part (iii), they would supply 7 units. If there are hundreds of firms, the process is the same. In this example, because Firm B does not enter the market at prices below $2, the supply curve S_{A+B} is identical to S_A up to price $2 and is the horizontal sum of S_A and S_B above $2.

Short-Run Equilibrium in a Competitive Market

The price of a product sold in a perfectly competitive market is determined by the interaction of the industry's short-run supply curve and the market demand curve. Although no single firm can influence the market price significantly, the collective actions of all firms in the industry (as shown by the industry supply curve) and the collective actions of households (as shown by the market demand curve) together determine the equilibrium price. This occurs at the point where the market demand and supply curves intersect.

When a perfectly competitive industry is in **short-run equilibrium,** each firm is producing and selling a quantity for which its marginal cost equals price. No firm is motivated to change its output in the short run. Because total quantity demanded equals total quantity supplied, there is no reason for market price to change in the short run.

When an industry is in short-run equilibrium, quantity demanded equals quantity supplied, and each firm is maximizing its profits given the market price.

However, we do not know *how large* these profits are. It is one thing to know that a firm is doing as well as it can, given its particular circumstances; it is another thing to know *how well* it is doing.

Figure 9-7 shows three possible positions for a firm when the industry is in short-run equilibrium. In all cases, the firm is maximizing its profits by producing where price equals marginal cost, but in part (i) the firm is suffering losses, in part (ii) it is just covering all of its costs (breaking even), and in part (iii) it is making profits because price exceeds average total cost. In all three cases, the firm is doing as well as it can, given its costs and the market price.

short-run equilibrium For a competitive industry, the price and output at which industry demand equals short-run industry supply, and all firms are maximizing their profits. Either profits or losses for individual firms are possible.

FIGURE 9-7   Alternative Short-Run Profits of a Competitive Firm

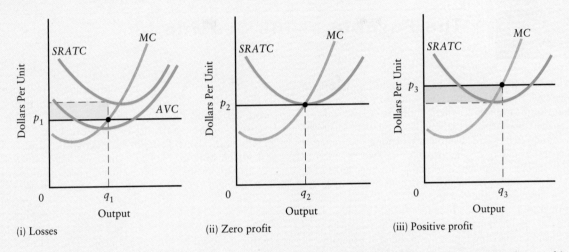

(i) Losses   (ii) Zero profit   (iii) Positive profit

When the industry is in short-run equilibrium, a competitive firm may be suffering losses, breaking even, or making profits. The diagrams show a firm with given costs that faces three alternative prices p_1, p_2, and p_3. In each part of the figure, $MC = MR =$ price. Because in all three cases price exceeds AVC, the firm produces positive output in each case.

   In part (i), price is p_1 and the firm is suffering losses, shown by the shaded area, because price is below average total cost. Because price exceeds average variable cost, it is worthwhile for the firm to keep producing, but it is not worthwhile for it to replace its capital equipment as it wears out. In part (ii), price is p_2 and the firm is just covering its total costs. It is worthwhile for the firm to replace its capital as it wears out, since it is covering the full opportunity cost of its capital. In part (iii), price is p_3 and the firm is earning profits, shown by the shaded area.

Applying Economic Concepts 9-2 discusses an interesting example of a firm that remains in operation even though it is not covering its full costs—that is, even though it is making losses as in part (i) of Figure 9-7. You have probably seen many firms like this one as you drive through small towns in any part of Canada.

Long-Run Decisions

Although Figure 9-7 shows three possible positions for a typical firm when the industry is in short-run equilibrium, not all of them are possible outcomes in the long run.

Entry and Exit

The key difference between a perfectly competitive industry in the short run and in the long run is the entry or exit of firms. We have seen that firms may be making profits, suffering losses, or just breaking even when the industry is in short-run equilibrium. Because costs include the opportunity cost of capital, firms that are just breaking even are doing as well as they could do by investing their capital elsewhere. Hence there will be no incentive

APPLYING ECONOMIC CONCEPTS 9-2

The Parable of the Seaside Inn

Why do some resort hotels stay open during the off-season, even though to do so they must offer bargain rates that do not even cover their "full costs"? Why do the managers of other hotels allow them to fall into disrepair even though they are able to attract enough customers to stay in business? Are the former being overly generous, and are the latter being irrational penny-pinchers?

To illustrate what is involved, consider an imaginary resort hotel called the Seaside Inn. Its revenues and costs of operating during the four months of the high-season and during the eight months of the off-season are shown in the accompanying table. When the profit-maximizing price for its rooms is charged in the high-season, the hotel earns revenues of $58 000 and incurs variable costs equal to $36 000. Thus there is an "operating profit" of $22 000 during the high-season. This surplus goes toward meeting the hotel's annual fixed costs of $24 000. Thus, $2000 of the fixed costs are not yet paid.

If the Seaside Inn were to charge the same rates during the off-season, it could not attract enough customers even to cover its costs of maids, bellhops, and managers. However, the hotel discovers that by charging lower rates during the off-season, it can rent some of its rooms and earn revenues of $20 000. Its costs of operating (variable costs) during the off-season are $18 000. So, by operating at reduced rates in the off-season, the hotel is able to contribute another $2000 toward its annual fixed costs, thereby eliminating the shortfall.

Therefore, the hotel stays open during the whole year by offering off-season bargain rates to grateful guests. Indeed, if it were to close during the off-season, it would not be able to cover its total fixed and variable costs solely through its high-season operations.

We have not yet discussed firms' long-run decisions in the chapter, but you can get a feel for the issues by considering the following situation. Suppose that the off-season revenues fall to $19 000 (everything else remaining the same). The short-run condition for staying open, that total revenue *(TR)* must exceed total variable cost *(TVC)*, is met both for the high-season and for the off-season. However, since the *TR* over the whole year of $77 000 is less than the total costs of $78 000, the hotel is now making losses for the year as a whole. The hotel will remain open as long as it can do so with its present capital—it will produce in the short run. However, it will not be worthwhile for the owners to replace the capital as it wears out.

If the reduction in revenues persists, the hotel will become one of those run-down hotels about which guests ask, "Why don't they do something about this place?"—but the owners are behaving quite sensibly. They are operating the hotel as long as it covers its variable costs, but they are not putting any more investment into it because it cannot cover its fixed costs. Sooner or later, the fixed capital will become too old to be run, or at least to attract customers, and the hotel will be closed.

Hotels and other resorts often charge low prices in the off-season, low enough that they do not cover their total costs, but as long as the price covers the variable costs, it is better than shutting down during the off-season.

The Seaside Inn: Total Costs and Revenues ($)

Season	Total Revenue (TR)	Total Variable Cost (TVC)	Contribution to Fixed Costs (TR-TVC)	Total Fixed Costs
High-Season	58 000	36 000	22 000	
Off-Season	20 000	18 000	2 000	
Total	78 000	54 000	24 000	24 000

for such firms to leave the industry. Similarly, if new entrants expect just to break even, there will be no incentive for firms to enter the industry, because capital can earn the same return elsewhere in the economy. If, however, existing firms are earning revenues in excess of all costs, including the opportunity cost of capital, new capital will enter the industry to share in these profits. Conversely, if existing firms are suffering losses, capital will leave the industry because a better return can be obtained elsewhere in the economy. Let us now consider this process in a little more detail.

An Entry-Attracting Price

First, suppose that there are 100 firms in a competitive industry, all making positive profits like the firm shown in part (iii) of Figure 9-7. New firms, attracted by the profitability of existing firms, will enter the industry. Suppose that in response to the high profits, 20 new firms enter. The market supply curve that formerly added up the outputs of 100 firms must now add up the outputs of 120 firms. At any price, more will be supplied because there are more producers. This entry of new firms into the industry implies a rightward shift in the industry supply curve.

With an unchanged market demand curve, this shift in the short-run industry supply curve means that the previous equilibrium price will no longer prevail. The shift in supply will reduce the equilibrium price, and both new and old firms will have to adjust their output to this new price, as illustrated in Figure 9-8. New firms will continue to enter, and the equilibrium price will continue to fall, until all firms in the industry are just covering their total costs. All firms will then be in the position of the firm shown in part (ii) of Figure 9-7, which is called a *zero-profit equilibrium*. The entry of new firms then ceases.

Profits in a competitive industry are a signal for the entry of new firms; the industry will expand, pushing price down until profits fall to zero.

An Exit-Inducing Price

Now suppose that all of the firms in the industry are making losses, like the firm shown in part (i) of Figure 9-7. Although the firms are covering their variable costs, the return on their capital is less than the opportunity cost of capital. They are not covering their total costs. This is a signal for the exit of firms. Old plants and equipment will not be replaced as they wear out. As a result, the industry's short-run supply curve eventually shifts leftward, and the market price rises. Firms will continue to exit, and the market price will continue to rise, until the remaining firms can cover their total costs—that is, until they are all in the zero-profit equilibrium illustrated in part (ii) of Figure 9-7. The exit of firms then ceases.

Losses in a competitive industry are a signal for the exit of firms; the industry will contract, driving the market price up until the remaining firms are just covering their total costs.

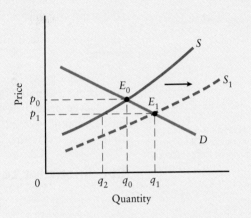

FIGURE 9-8   The Effect of New Entrants

New entrants shift the supply curve to the right and reduce the equilibrium price. Initial equilibrium is at E_0. The entry of new firms shifts the supply curve to S_1. Equilibrium price falls to p_1, while output rises to q_1. Before the entry of new firms, only q_2 would have been produced had the price been p_1. The extra output is supplied by the new firms.

Practise with Study Guide Chapter 9, Exercise 5.

Long-Run Equilibrium

Because firms exit when they are making losses and enter in pursuit of profits, we get the following conclusion:

The long-run equilibrium of a competitive industry occurs when firms are earning zero profits.

When a perfectly competitive industry is in long-run equilibrium, each firm will be like the firm in part (ii) of Figure 9-7. For such firms, the price p_2 is sometimes called the **break-even price**. It is the price at which all costs, including the opportunity cost of capital, are being covered. The firm is just willing to stay in the industry. It has no incentive to leave, nor do other firms have an incentive to enter.

break-even price
The price at which a firm is just able to cover all of its costs, including the opportunity cost of capital.

Conditions for Long-Run Equilibrium

The previous discussion suggests four conditions for a competitive industry to be in long-run equilibrium.

1. Existing firms must be maximizing their profits, given their existing capital. Thus short-run marginal costs of production must be equal to market price.

2. Existing firms must not be suffering losses. If they are suffering losses, they will not replace their capital and the size of the industry will decline over time.

3. Existing firms must not be earning profits. If they are earning profits, then new firms will enter the industry and the size of the industry will increase over time.

4. Existing firms must not be able to increase their profits by changing the size of their production facilities. Thus each existing firm must be at the minimum point of its *long-run* average cost (*LRAC*) curve.

This last condition is new to our discussion. Figure 9-9 shows that if the condition does not hold—that is, if the firm is *not* at the minimum of its *LRAC* curve—a firm can increase its profits. Although the firm is maximizing its profits with its existing production facilities, there are unexploited economies of scale. By building larger plants, the firm can move down its *LRAC* curve and reduce its average cost. Because in its present position, average cost is just equal to the market price, any reduction in average cost must yield profits.

For a competitive firm to be maximizing its long-run profits, it must be producing at the minimum point on its *LRAC* curve.

FIGURE 9-9   Short-Run Versus Long-Run Profit Maximization for a Competitive Firm

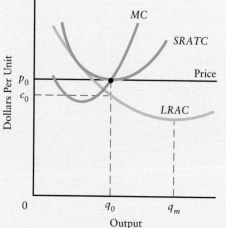

A competitive firm that is not at the minimum point on its *LRAC* curve is not maximizing its long-run profits. A competitive firm with short-run cost curves *SRATC* and *MC* faces a market price of p_0. The firm produces q_0, where *MC* equals price and total costs are just being covered. However, the firm's long-run average cost curve lies below its short-run curve at output q_0. The firm could produce output q_0 at cost c_0 by building a larger plant so as to take advantage of economies of scale. Profits would rise, because average total costs of c_0 would then be less than price p_0. The firm cannot be maximizing its long-run profits at any output below q_m because, with any such output, average total costs can be reduced by building a larger plant. The output q_m is the *minimum efficient scale* of the firm.

The level of output at which *LRAC* reaches a minimum is known as the firm's **minimum efficient scale (MES)**.

When each firm in the industry is producing at the minimum point of its long-run average cost curve and just covering its costs, as in Figure 9-10, the industry is in long-run equilibrium. Because marginal cost equals price, no firm can improve its profits by varying its output in the short run. Because each firm is at the minimum point on its *LRAC* curve, there is no incentive for any existing firm to alter the scale of its operations. Because there are neither profits nor losses, there is no incentive for entry into or exit from the industry.

In long-run competitive equilibrium, each firm's average cost of production is the lowest attainable, given the limits of known technology and factor prices.

The Long-Run Industry Supply Curve

Consider a competitive industry that is in long-run equilibrium. Now suppose that the market demand for the industry's product increases. The reactions to this demand shift should by now be a familiar story. First, price will rise and, in response, existing firms will increase their outputs and earn profits. New firms then enter the industry, attracted by the profits. As new firms enter the industry, the industry supply curve will shift to the right, driving down the market price. This process continues until profits have been eliminated. At that time, existing firms once again will be just covering their full costs. Note that in *both* of the long-run equilibrium positions just discussed—the one before and the one after the change in demand—all firms in the industry are producing at the lowest point on their *LRAC* curves.

This is now familiar ground, but there is one further question that we could ask. When all the dust has settled, will the new long-run equilibrium price be higher than, lower than, or the same as the price at the initial long-run equilibrium? We could make a similar analysis for a fall in demand, and could ask the same question.

The adjustment of a competitive industry to the types of changes that we have just discussed is shown by what is sometimes called the **long-run industry supply (LRS) curve**. This curve shows the relationship between the market price and the quantity produced in a competitive industry *when it is in long-run equilibrium*. Note that the curve is drawn on the assumption that technological knowledge is constant. Figure 9-11 shows the derivation of this curve and its possible shapes.

Horizontal Long-Run Supply Curve. In part (i) of the figure, the *LRS* curve is horizontal. An industry with a horizontal *LRS* curve is said to be a **constant-cost industry**. This situation occurs when the long-run expansion of the industry, due to the entry of new firms, leaves the long-run cost curves of existing firms unchanged. Because new firms have access to the same technology and face the same factor prices as existing firms, their cost curves will be the same as those of existing firms. It follows that the cost curves of all firms, new or old, will be unaffected by expansion or contraction of the

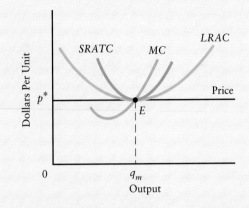

FIGURE 9-10 A Typical Competitive Firm When the Industry is in Long-Run Equilibrium

In long-run competitive equilibrium, each firm is operating at the minimum point on its *LRAC* curve. In long-run equilibrium, each firm must be (1) maximizing short-run profits, $MC = p$; (2) earning profits of zero on its existing plant, $SRATC = p$; and (3) unable to increase its profits by altering the scale of its operations. These three conditions can be met only when the firm is at *E*, the minimum point on its *LRAC* curve, with price p^* and output q_m.

minimum efficient scale (MES) The smallest output at which long-run average cost reaches its minimum; all available economies of scale in production and distribution have been realized at this point.

long-run industry supply (LRS) curve A curve showing the relationship between the market price and the quantity supplied by a competitive industry when all the firms in that industry are at the minimum of their *LRAC* curves.

constant-cost industry An industry in which costs of the most efficient size firm remain constant as the entire industry expands or contracts in the long run.

FIGURE 9-11   Long-Run Industry Supply Curves

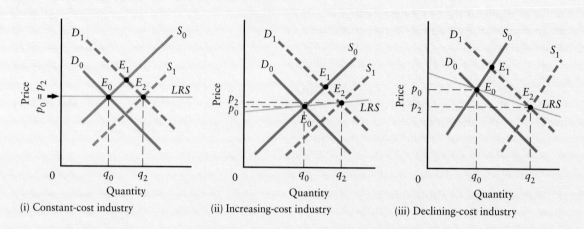

(i) Constant-cost industry   (ii) Increasing-cost industry   (iii) Declining-cost industry

The long-run industry supply curve may be horizontal, positively sloped, or negatively sloped. In all three parts, the initial curves are at D_0 and S_0, yielding equilibrium at E_0, with price p_0 and output q_0. A rise in demand shifts the demand curve to D_1, taking the short-run equilibrium to E_1. New firms now enter the industry, shifting the supply curve to the right, pushing down price until profits are no longer being earned. At this point, the supply curve is S_1 and the new equilibrium is E_2, with price at p_2 and output q_2.

In part (i), price returns to its original level, making the long-run industry supply curve horizontal. In part (ii), a new long-run equilibrium is achieved at a price higher than p_0. This gives the LRS curve a positive slope. In part (iii), the price falls below its original level before profits are eliminated, giving the LRS curve a negative slope.

industry. Thus long-run equilibrium can be reestablished only when price returns to its original level. In other words, because cost curves are unaffected by the expansion or contraction of the industry, each firm must start from, and return to, the long-run position shown in Figure 9-10—*which means that market price must also do the same.*

Upward-Sloping Long-Run Supply Curve.

When an increase in demand for an industry's product leads that industry to expand, more of its inputs will be needed. The increase in demand for these inputs tends to bid up their prices.

If costs rise with increasing levels of industry output, so too must the price at which the producers are able to cover their costs. As the industry expands, the short-run supply curve shifts outward, but the firms' $SRATC$ curves shift upward because of rising factor prices. The expansion of the industry comes to a halt when price is equal to minimum $LRAC$ for existing firms. Because costs have risen, this new equilibrium must occur at a higher price than prevailed before the expansion began, as illustrated in part (ii) of Figure 9-11. A competitive industry with an upward-sloping LRS curve is called an **increasing-cost industry**.

increasing-cost industry An industry in which costs of the most efficient size firm rise as the entire industry expands in the long run.

Downward-Sloping Long-Run Supply Curve.

So far in our discussion the long-run supply curve has been flat or upward sloping. Could it ever be downward sloping, thereby indicating that higher outputs are associated with lower prices in long-run equilibrium?

It is tempting to answer yes because of the opportunities of more efficient scales of operation using greater mechanization and more effective specialization of labour.

However, this answer would not be correct for perfectly competitive industries because in long-run equilibrium each firm must already be at the lowest point on its *LRAC* curve. If a firm could lower its costs by building a larger, more mechanized plant, it would be profitable to do so without waiting for an increase in demand.

The scale economies that we have just considered are within the control of the firm; they are said to be **internal economies of scale.** A perfectly competitive industry might, however, have a downward-sloping long-run supply curve if industries that supply its inputs have increasing returns to scale. Such effects are outside the control of the perfectly competitive firm and are called **external economies of scale.** Whenever expansion of an industry leads to a fall in the prices of some of its inputs, the individual firms will find their cost curves shifting downward.

As an illustration of how the expansion of one industry could cause the prices of some of its inputs to fall, consider the early stages of the growth of the automobile industry. As the output of automobiles increased, the industry's demand for tires grew greatly. This increased the demand for rubber and tended to raise its price, but it also provided the opportunity for tire manufacturers to build larger plants that exploited the scale economies available in tire production. These economies were large enough to offset any factor price increases, and tire prices charged to automobile manufacturers fell. Thus automobile costs fell because of lower prices of an important input. This case is illustrated in part (iii) of Figure 9-11. An industry that has a downward-sloping *LRS* curve is called a **declining-cost industry.**

Notice in this example that although the economies of scale were *external* to the automobile industry, they were *internal* to the tire industry. This, in turn, requires that the tire industry *not* be perfectly competitive; if it were, all of its scale economies would already have been exploited as firms locate at the minimum of their *LRAC* curves in the long run. So this case refers to a perfectly competitive industry that uses an input produced by a non-perfectly-competitive industry whose own scale economies have not yet been fully exploited because demand is insufficient.

We can now use our long-run theory to understand the behaviour of firms in two commonly encountered but often misunderstood situations—changes in technology and declining industries.

internal economies of scale Scale economies that result from the firm's own actions and hence are available to it by raising its own output.

external economies of scale Scale economies that cause the firm's costs to fall as industry output rises but are external to the firm and so cannot be obtained by the firm's increasing its own output.

declining-cost industry An industry in which costs of the most efficient size firm decline as the entire industry expands in the long run.

Changes in Technology

Consider a competitive industry in long-run equilibrium. Because the industry is in long-run equilibrium, each firm must be earning zero profits. Now suppose that some technological development lowers the cost curves *of newly built plants.* Because price is just equal to the average total cost *for the existing plants,* new plants will be able to earn profits, and some of them will now be built. The resulting expansion in capacity shifts the short-run supply curve to the right and drives price down.

The expansion in industry output and the fall in price will continue until price is equal to the short-run average total cost of the *new* plants. At this price, old plants will not be covering their long-run costs. As long as price exceeds their average variable cost, however, such plants will continue in production. As the outmoded plants wear out, they will gradually be closed. Eventually, a new long-run equilibrium will be established in which all plants will use the new technology.

New plants are usually built with the latest technology. This often results in new plants having lower unit costs (and thus higher profits) than the existing plants built with older technology.

FIGURE 9-12   Plants of Different Vintages in an Industry with Continuous Technological Progress

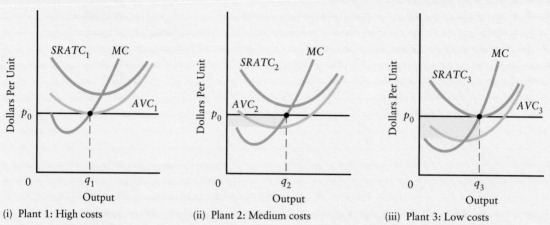

(i) Plant 1: High costs   (ii) Plant 2: Medium costs   (iii) Plant 3: Low costs

Entry of progressively lower-cost firms forces price down, but older plants with higher costs remain in the industry as long as price covers average variable cost. Plant 3 is the newest plant with the lowest costs. Long-run equilibrium price will be determined by the average total costs of plants of this type because entry will continue as long as the owners of the newest plants expect to earn profits from them. Plant 1 is the oldest plant in operation. It is just covering its AVC, and if the price falls any further, it will be closed down. Plant 2 is a plant of intermediate age. It is covering its variable costs and earning some contribution toward its fixed costs. In parts (ii) and (iii), profits are shown by the shaded area.

What happens in a competitive industry in which technological change does not occur as a single isolated event but instead happens more or less continuously? Plants built in any one year will tend to have lower costs than plants built in any previous year. This common occurrence is illustrated in Figure 9-12.

Industries that are subject to continuous technological change have three common characteristics. The first is that plants of different ages and with different costs exist side by side. This characteristic is dramatically illustrated by the many different vintages of farm equipment found in the agricultural sector; some farms have much newer and better equipment than others. Indeed, even any individual farm that has been established for a long time will have various vintages of equipment, all of which are in use. Older models are not discarded as soon as a better model comes on the market.

Critics who observe the continued use of older, higher-cost plants and equipment often urge that something be done to "eliminate these wasteful practices." These critics miss the point of economic efficiency. If the plant or piece of equipment is already there, it can be profitably operated as long as its revenues more than cover its *variable* costs. As long as a plant or equipment can produce goods that are valued by consumers at an amount above the value of the resources currently used up for their production (variable costs), the value of society's total output is increased by using it.

In industries with continual technological improvement, low-cost firms will exist side by side with older high-cost firms. The older firms will continue operating as long as their revenue covers their variable costs.

A second characteristic of a competitive industry that is subject to continuous technological improvement is that price is eventually governed by the minimum ATC of the *lowest-cost* plants. Firms will enter the industry until plants of the newest vintage are just expected to earn normal profits over their lifetimes. The benefits of the new technology are passed on to consumers because all of the units of the product, whether produced by new or old plants, are sold at a price that is related solely to the *ATCs* of the new plants. Owners of older plants find that their returns over variable costs fall steadily as newer plants drive the price of the product down.

A third characteristic is that old plants are discarded (or "mothballed") when the price falls below their *AVCs*. This may occur well before the plants are physically worn out. In industries with continuous technological progress, capital is usually discarded because it is *economically obsolete,* not because it is physically worn out. Old capital is obsolete when the market price of output does not even cover its average variable cost of production. Thus a steel mill that is still fully capable of producing top-quality steel may be shut down for perfectly sensible reasons; if the price of steel cannot cover the average variable cost of the steel produced, then profit-maximizing firms will shut down the plant.

Declining Industries

What happens when a competitive industry in long-run equilibrium experiences a continual decrease in the demand for its product? One example of this might be a long-term change in tastes that leads households to substitute away from red meat and toward fish and poultry. As market demand for red meat declines, market price falls, and firms that were previously covering average total costs are no longer able to do so. They find themselves suffering losses instead of breaking even; the signal for the exit of capital is given, but exit takes time.

The Response of Firms

The economically efficient response to a steadily declining demand is to continue to operate with existing equipment as long as its variable costs of production can be covered. As equipment becomes obsolete because the firm cannot cover even its variable cost, it will not be replaced unless the new equipment can cover its total cost. As a result, the capacity of the industry will shrink. If demand keeps declining, capacity must keep shrinking.

Declining industries typically present a sorry sight to the observer. Revenues are below long-run total costs and, as a result, new equipment is not brought in to replace old equipment as it wears out. The average age of equipment in use thus rises steadily. The untrained observer, seeing the industry's plight, is likely to blame it on the old equipment.

The antiquated equipment in a declining industry is often the effect rather than the cause of the industry's decline.

The Response of Governments

Governments are often tempted to support declining industries because they are worried about the resulting job losses. Experience suggests, however, that propping up genuinely declining industries only delays their demise—at significant national cost. When the government finally withdraws its support, the decline is usually more abrupt and, hence, the required adjustment is more difficult than it would have been had the industry been allowed to decline gradually under the natural market forces.

Once governments recognize the decay of certain industries and the collapse of certain firms as an inevitable aspect of economic growth, a more effective response is to provide retraining and income-support schemes that cushion the impacts of change. These can moderate the effects on the incomes of workers who lose their jobs and make it easier for them to transfer to expanding industries. Intervention that is intended to increase mobility while reducing the social and personal costs of mobility is a viable long-run policy; trying to freeze the existing industrial structure by shoring up an inevitably declining industry is not.

SUMMARY

Market Structure and Firm Behaviour

LO 1

- A competitive market structure is one in which individual firms have no power to influence the market in which they sell their product.

- Competitive behaviour exists when firms actively compete against one another, responding directly to other firms' actions. Perfectly competitive firms *do not* have competitive behaviour.

The Theory of Perfect Competition

LO 2 3

- Four key assumptions of the theory of perfect competition are as follows:

  1. All firms produce a homogeneous product.
  2. Purchasers know the nature of the product and the price charged for it.
  3. Each firm's minimum efficient scale occurs at a level of output that is small relative to the industry's total output.
  4. The industry displays freedom of entry and exit.

- Any profit-maximizing firm will produce at a level of output at which (a) price is at least as great as average variable cost and (b) marginal cost equals marginal revenue. In perfect competition, firms are price takers, so marginal revenue is equal to price. Thus, a profit-maximizing competitive firm equates marginal cost to price.

Short-Run Decisions

LO 4 5

- If a profit-maximizing firm is to produce at all, it must be able to cover its variable costs. However, such a firm may be suffering losses (price is less than average total cost), making profits (price is greater than average total cost), or just breaking even (price is equal to average total cost).

- Under perfect competition, each firm's short-run supply curve is identical to its marginal cost curve above average variable cost. The perfectly competitive industry's short-run supply curve is the horizontal sum of the supply curves of the individual firms.

Long-Run Decisions

LO 6 7

- In the long run, profits or losses will lead to the entry or the exit of firms into or out of the industry. This pushes any competitive industry to a long-run, zero-profit equilibrium and moves production to the level that minimizes average cost.

- The long-run response of an industry to steadily changing technology is the gradual replacement of less efficient plants by more efficient ones. Older plants will be discarded and replaced by more modern ones only when price falls below average variable cost.

- The long-run response of a declining industry will be to continue to satisfy demand by employing its existing plants as long as price exceeds short-run average variable cost. Despite the antiquated appearance that results, this response is the correct one.

KEY CONCEPTS

Competitive behaviour and competitive market structure
Perfect competition
Price taking and a horizontal demand curve

Average revenue, marginal revenue, and price under perfect competition
Rules for maximizing profits
The relationship of supply curves to marginal cost curves
Short-run and long-run equilibrium of competitive industries

Entry and exit in achieving long-run equilibrium
Long-run industry supply curves
Constant, increasing, and decreasing cost industries

STUDY EXERCISES

1. In Figure 9-1 in the chapter, we explain the difference between the demand curve for a competitive industry and the demand curve facing an individual firm in that industry. Review that figure now and then answer the following questions.

   a. Explain what would happen if the individual firm tried to charge a higher price for its product.
   b. Explain why the individual firm has no incentive to charge a lower price for its product.
   c. Explain why the demand curve for an individual firm is horizontal at the current market price.

2. Consider the following table showing the various revenue concepts for DairyTreat Inc., a perfectly competitive firm that sells milk by the litre. Suppose the firm faces a constant market price of $2 per litre.

Price (p)	Quantity	Total Revenue (TR)	Average Revenue (AR)	Marginal Revenue (MR)
$2	150	—	—	—
2	175	—	—	—
2	200	—	—	—
2	225	—	—	—
2	250	—	—	—

   a. Compute total revenue for each level of output. Fill in the table.
   b. Compute average and marginal revenue for each level of output. Fill in the table. (Remember to compute marginal revenue *between* successive levels of output.)
   c. Explain why for a perfectly competitive firm, $AR = MR = p$.
   d. Plot the TR, MR, and AR curves on a scale diagram. What is the slope of the TR curve?

3. The diagram below shows the various short-run cost curves for a perfectly competitive firm.

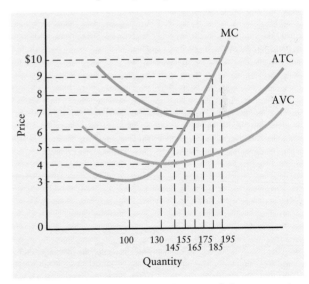

   a. Based on the diagram above, and the assumption that the firm is maximizing its profit, fill in the following table. The last three columns require only a "yes" or "no."

Market Price ($)	Firm's Output	Is price >ATC?	Is price >AVC?	Are Profits Positive?
$3	—	—	—	—
4	—	—	—	—
5	—	—	—	—
6	—	—	—	—
7	—	—	—	—
8	—	—	—	—
9	—	—	—	—
10	—	—	—	—

b. At which price will this firm shut down? Explain.

c. What is this firm's supply curve? Explain.

4. Consider the table below showing the supply schedules for three competitive firms, each producing honey by the kilogram. These three firms make up the entire industry.

Market Price ($ per kg)	Firm A	Firm B	Firm C	Industry
2.50	100	0	0	—-
3.00	125	0	0	—-
3.50	150	100	0	—-
4.00	175	150	0	—-
4.50	200	200	100	—-
5.00	225	250	175	—-
5.50	250	300	250	—-
6.00	275	350	325	—-

a. Compute the total industry supply at each price and fill in the table.

b. On a scale diagram similar to Figure 9-6, plot the supply curve for each firm and for the industry as a whole.

c. Explain the economics of why Firm B produces no output at prices $3 and lower (or for why Firm C produces no output at prices $4 and lower).

5. Consider the perfectly competitive barley industry. It is initially in long-run equilibrium at quantity Q_0 and price p_0.

a. Draw a supply-and-demand diagram for the barley market, showing the initial long-run equilibrium.

b. Draw a diagram for a typical firm when the industry is in its initial long-run equilibrium, showing its MC, ATC, *and* LRAC curves. Are there any profits being earned by the typical barley farmer?

c. Now suppose there is an increase in demand (caused by an increase in demand for beer, which uses barley as an input). Price rises to p_1. In your diagram, show the typical firm's response to the increase in market price from p_0 to p_1. Show the typical firm's profits at this new price.

d. Explain how this industry adjusts to its new long-run equilibrium. Illustrate this adjustment both in the demand-and-supply diagram and in the diagram of the typical firm. (You may assume that the barley industry is a constant-cost industry.)

6. A major theme of this chapter is the role that *free entry and exit* play in determining a competitive industry's long-run equilibrium. Keeping this theme in mind, think of the following statement:

In industry X, demand and supply do determine price in the short run, but in the long run, only supply matters.

a. Assuming that Industry X is a constant-cost industry, use a demand-and-supply diagram to illustrate why the statement is exactly correct.

b. Now, assuming that Industry X is an increasing-cost industry, show in a demand-and-supply diagram why the statement is not quite correct.

DISCUSSION QUESTIONS

1. Discuss the common allegation that when all firms in an industry are charging the same price, this indicates the absence of competition and the presence of some form of price-setting agreement.

2. Which of the following observed facts about an industry are inconsistent with its being a perfectly competitive industry?

a. Different firms use different methods of production.

b. The industry's product is extensively advertised by a trade association.

c. Individual firms devote a large fraction of their sales receipts to advertising their own product brands.

d. There are 24 firms in the industry.

e. The largest firm in the industry makes 40 percent of the sales, and the next largest firm makes 20 percent of the sales, but the products are identical, and there are 61 other firms.

   f. All firms made large profits last year.

3. In which of the following sectors of the Canadian economy might you expect to find competitive behaviour? In which might you expect to find industries that are classified as operating under perfectly competitive market structures?

   a. Manufacturing
   b. Agriculture
   c. Transportation and public utilities
   d. Wholesale and retail trade
   e. Illegal drugs

4. Today's typical office contains personal computers of various vintages, with the newest machines having the largest output per unit of cost. There are also old machines that, though still able to function, are not in use at all. What determines the secondhand price of the older machines? What is the economic value of the machines that are no longer used?

5. What, if anything, does each one of the following tell you about ease of entry into or exit from an industry?

   a. Profits have been very high for two decades.
   b. No new firms have entered the industry for 20 years.
   c. The average age of the firms in the 40-year-old industry is less than 7 years.
   d. Most existing firms are using obsolete equipment alongside newer, more modern equipment.
   e. Profits are low or negative; many firms are still producing, but from steadily aging equipment.

6. Explain why perfectly competitive agricultural industries may have external economies of scale—and thus may be declining-cost industries—arising from the behaviour of the farm machinery industry. Is it relevant that the farm machinery industry is dominated by a small number of very large firms?

CHAPTER 10

Monopoly

LO *LEARNING OBJECTIVES*

1 Explain why marginal revenue is less than price for a profit-maximizing monopolist.

2 Recognize the importance of entry barriers in allowing monopolists to maintain positive profits in the long run.

3 Understand how firms can form a cartel in which they restrict industry output and increase price and profits.

4 Explain the different forms and consequences of price discrimination.

monopoly A market containing a single firm.

monopolist A firm that is the only seller in a market.

Perfect competition is at one end of the spectrum of market structures. At the other end is **monopoly**. Economists say that a monopoly occurs when the output of an entire industry is produced and sold by a single firm, called a **monopolist** or a *monopoly firm*. Examples of monopoly are rare at the national level but are much more common for smaller geographical areas. The company that supplies electric power to your home is almost certainly a monopoly, as is the firm that provides local (but not long-distance) telephone service and cable television. Because monopoly is the market structure that allows for the maximum possible exercise of market power on the part of the firm, monopoly markets and perfectly competitive markets provide two extremes of behaviour that are useful for economists in their study of market structure.

In this chapter we examine how a profit-maximizing monopolist determines its price and quantity. We begin by considering a monopolist that sells all of its output at a single price. We then consider *cartels*—the attempt by several firms to band together and behave like a monopolist. We end the chapter by examining situations in which a firm is able to charge different prices to its different customers—something you have probably observed with airlines, movie theatres, and even your local grocery store.

A Single-Price Monopolist

We look first at a monopolist that charges a single price for its product. This firm's profits, like those of all firms, will depend on the relationship between its production costs and its sales revenues.

Cost and Revenue in the Short Run

We saw in Chapter 7 that U-shaped short-run cost curves are a consequence of the law of diminishing returns. Because this law applies to the conditions under which goods are produced rather than to the market structure in which they are sold, monopolists have U-shaped short-run cost curves for the same reasons as do perfectly competitive firms.

Because a monopolist is the sole producer of the product that it sells, its demand curve is simply the market demand curve for that product. The market demand curve, which shows the total quantity that buyers want to purchase at each price, also shows the quantity that the monopolist will be able to sell at each price.

The monopolist, unlike the perfectly competitive firm, faces a negatively sloped demand curve.

A monopolist therefore faces a tradeoff between the price it charges and the quantity it sells. For a monopolist, sales can be increased only if price is reduced, and price can be increased only if sales are reduced.

Average Revenue

Starting with the market demand curve, we can readily derive the monopolist's average and marginal revenue curves. When the monopolist charges the same price for all units sold, its total revenue (*TR*) is simply equal to the single price times the quantity sold,

$$TR = p \times q$$

Since average revenue is total revenue divided by quantity, it follows that average revenue is equal to the price,

$$AR = TR/q = (p \times q)/q = p$$

And since the price is given by the position of the demand curve, it follows that the demand curve is also the monopolist's average revenue curve.

Marginal Revenue

Now let's consider the monopolist's *marginal revenue*—the revenue resulting from the sale of an additional (or marginal) unit of production. Because its demand curve is negatively sloped, the monopolist must reduce the price that it charges on *all* units in order to sell an extra unit. It follows that the addition to its revenue resulting from the sale of an extra unit is less than the price that it receives for that unit. It is less by the amount that it loses as a result of cutting the price on all the units that it was selling already.

The monopolist's marginal revenue is less than the price at which it sells its output. Thus the monopolist's *MR* curve is below its demand curve. [24]

The relationship between marginal revenue and price for an example is shown in detail in Figure 10-1. Consider the table first. Notice that the numbers in columns (4) and (5) are plotted between the rows that refer to specific prices, because the figures refer to what happens when the price is changed between the amounts shown in two adjacent

FIGURE 10-1   A Monopolist's Average and Marginal Revenue Curves

(1) Price (Average Revenue)	(2) Quantity Sold	(3) Total Revenue $(p \times q)$	(4) Change in Total Revenue (ΔTR)	(5) Marginal Revenue $(\Delta TR/\Delta q)$
10	0	0		
9	10	90	90	9
8	20	160	70	7
7	30	210	50	5
6	40	240	30	3
5	50	250	10	1
4	60	240	−10	−1
3	70	210	−30	−3
2	80	160	−50	−5
1	90	90	−70	−7
0	100	0	−90	−9

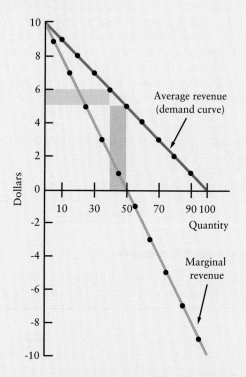

Marginal revenue is less than price because the price at which existing units are sold must be reduced in order to sell more units. The data show that every time the firm lowers its price by $1, its sales increase by 10 units. Column 3 gives the total revenue associated with each price, which is that price multiplied by the quantity sold. Column 4 gives the change in total revenue as the price is altered by $1. To calculate the change in revenue associated with a unit change in quantity, we must divide the change in column 4 by 10 to get the change in revenue *per unit change in quantity*. The result is recorded in column 5, which is the marginal revenue.

rows. The method of calculating marginal revenue shown in the table involves subtracting the total revenue associated with one price from the total revenue associated with another price and then dividing this change by the change in the number of units sold.

Now look at the figure. It plots the entire demand curve that gave rise to the individual figures for price and quantity shown in the table. It also plots the entire marginal revenue curve and locates the specific points on it that were calculated in the table. For purposes of illustration, a straight-line demand curve has been chosen.[1]

Notice that marginal revenue is positive up to 50 units of sales, indicating that reductions in price between $10 and $5 increase total revenue. Notice also that marginal revenue is negative for sales greater than 50 units, indicating that reductions in price below $5 cause total revenue to fall.

The figure also illustrates the two opposing forces that are present whenever the price is changed. As an example, consider the reduction in price from $6 to $5. First, the

---

[1]When drawing these curves, note that if the demand curve is a negatively sloped straight line, the *MR* curve also has a negative slope but is twice as steep. Its price intercept (where $q = 0$) is the same as that of the demand curve, and its quantity intercept (where $p = 0$) is one-half that of the demand curve. [25]

40 units that the firm was already selling bring in less money at the new lower price than at the original higher price. This loss in revenue is the amount of the price reduction multiplied by the number of units already being sold (40 units × $1 per unit = $40). This is shown as the green shaded area in the figure. The second force, operating in the opposite direction, is that new units are sold, which brings in more revenue. This gain in revenue is given by the number of new units sold multiplied by the price at which they are sold (10 units × $5 = $50). This is shown as the purple shaded area. The *net change* in total revenue is the *difference* between these two amounts ($10). In the example shown in the figure, the increase resulting from the sale of new units exceeds the decrease resulting from existing sales now being made at a lower price. Marginal revenue is thus positive. Furthermore, the change in total revenue is $10 whereas the change in the number of units sold is 10 units. Thus marginal revenue, given by $\Delta TR/\Delta q$, is equal to $10/10 = $1.

The proposition that marginal revenue is always less than price provides an important contrast with perfect competition. Recall that in perfect competition, the firm's marginal revenue from selling an extra unit of output is equal to the price at which that unit is sold. The reason for the difference is not difficult to understand. The perfectly competitive firm is a price taker; it can sell all it wants at the given market price. In contrast, the monopolist faces a negatively sloped demand curve; it must reduce the market price to increase its sales.

If you plot the data on *TR* from Figure 10-1 you will notice that *TR* rises (*MR* is positive) as price falls, reaching a maximum where $p = 5 and $MR = 0$. Then, as price continues to fall, *TR* falls (*MR* is negative). Using the relationship between elasticity and total revenue that we first saw in Chapter 4, it follows that demand is elastic ($\eta > 1$) when *MR* is positive and demand is inelastic ($\eta < 1$) when *MR* is negative. The value of η declines steadily as we move down the demand curve. As we will see shortly, a profit-maximizing monopolist will always produce on the elastic portion of its demand curve (that is, where *MR* is positive).

Short-Run Profit Maximization

To show the profit-maximizing position of a monopolist, we bring together information about its revenues and its costs and then apply the two rules developed in Chapter 9: (1) The firm should not produce at all unless there is some level of output for which price is at least equal to average variable cost, and (2) if the firm does produce, its output should be set at the point where marginal cost equals marginal revenue.

When the monopolist equates marginal cost with marginal revenue, its situation is as shown in Figure 10-2. The profit-maximizing level of output is where marginal cost equals marginal revenue. The price is read off the demand curve, which shows the price corresponding to that output.

Notice that because marginal revenue is always less than price for the monopolist, when marginal revenue is equated with marginal cost, both are less than price.

When a monopolist is maximizing its profit, its marginal cost is always less than the price it charges for its output.

Monopoly Profits

The fact that a monopolist produces the output that maximizes its profits tells us nothing about *how large* these profits will be or even whether there will be any profits at all. The monopolist may earn positive profits or may suffer losses, depending on the position of the *ATC* curve. Figure 10-2 shows the possibilities. Nothing guarantees that

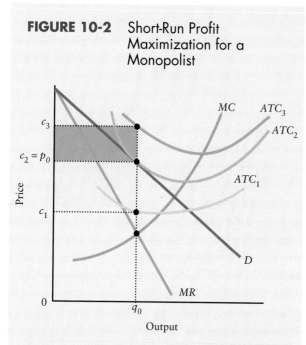

FIGURE 10-2 Short-Run Profit Maximization for a Monopolist

The profit-maximizing output is q_0, where $MR = MC$; price is p_0, which is above MC at that output. The rules for profit maximization require $MR = MC$ and $p > AVC$. (AVC is not shown in the graph, but it must be below ATC.) Whether profits at q_0 are positive or negative (or zero) depends on the position of the ATC curve. If average total cost is ATC_1, then unit costs at q_0 are given by c_1 and the monopolist makes positive profits shown by the light shaded area. If average cost is ATC_2, the monopolist breaks even because the price p_0 exactly equals average total costs, c_2. If average total cost is ATC_3, unit costs at q_0 are given by c_3 and the monopolist makes losses shown by the dark shaded area.

a monopolist will make profits in the short run, but if it suffers persistent losses, it will eventually go out of business.

No Supply Curve for a Monopolist

In describing the monopolist's profit-maximizing behaviour, we did not introduce the concept of a supply curve, as we did in the discussion of perfect competition. In perfect competition, the industry short-run supply curve depends only on the marginal cost curves of the individual firms, because under perfect competition, profit-maximizing firms equate marginal cost with price. Given marginal costs, it is possible to know how much will be supplied at each price. This is not the case, however, with a monopolist.

For a monopolist, there is no unique relationship between market price and quantity supplied.

To prove this point to yourself, draw a monopolist's marginal cost curve and any marginal revenue curve to intersect the MC curve at some output that you call q^*. Now draw as many other different MR curves as you like, all of which intersect MC at q^*. All of these curves give rise to profit-maximizing output of q^*, but because each MR curve is different, each must be associated with a different demand curve and hence a different price at which q^* is sold. This exercise shows that a given quantity may be associated with many different prices, depending on the slope of the demand curve that the monopolist faces.

Firm and Industry

Because the monopolist is the only producer in an industry, there is no need for separate theories about the firm and the industry, as is necessary with perfect competition. The monopolist *is* the industry. Thus, the short-run, profit-maximizing position of the firm, as shown in Figure 10-2, is also the short-run equilibrium of the industry.

Competition and Monopoly Compared

The comparison of monopoly with perfect competition is important. For a perfectly competitive industry, the equilibrium is determined by the intersection of the industry demand and supply curves. Since the industry supply curve is simply the sum of the individual firms' marginal cost curves, the equilibrium output in a perfectly competitive industry is such that price equals marginal cost. For the monopolist, in contrast, equilibrium output is such that price is greater than marginal cost. And since demand curves are downward sloping and MC curves are typically upward sloping, the gap between price and marginal cost implies one thing: the level of output in a monopolized industry is less than the level of output that would be produced if the industry were instead made up of many price-taking firms.

A perfectly competitive industry produces a level of output such that price equals marginal cost. A monopolist produces a lower level of output, with price exceeding marginal cost.

In Chapter 12 we will discuss the important concept of *allocative efficiency* and will see that a perfectly competitive industry achieves allocative efficiency whereas a monopolist does not. The full explanation is fairly involved, but for now a simple explanation will suffice. Since price exceeds marginal cost for a monopolist, society as a whole would benefit by reallocating resources so as to produce more of the monopolist's product—because the gain to society of additional output, as reflected in the marginal value (price) of the product, exceeds the marginal cost of producing the additional output. In contrast, a perfectly competitive industry has price equal to marginal cost. Thus the marginal value (price) to society of additional output is equal to the marginal cost of producing it, and there is no scope to improve the outcome.

We will return in detail to the topic of allocative efficiency in Chapter 12, where we will compare perfect competition, monopoly, and other market structures. For now, we go on to discuss the long-run equilibrium for monopoly.

Long-Run Equilibrium

In a monopolized industry, as in a perfectly competitive one, losses and profits provide incentives for exit and entry. If the monopoly is suffering losses in the short run, it will continue to operate as long as it can cover its variable costs. In the long run, however, it will leave the industry unless it can find a scale of operations at which its full opportunity costs can be covered. If the monopoly is making profits, other firms will wish to enter the industry in order to earn more than the opportunity cost of their capital. If such entry occurs, the monopoly's position will change and the firm will cease to be a monopoly. Instead of facing the entire market demand curve, the (former) monopolist will have to compete with the new firms and thus will capture only part of the overall market demand.

In order for positive monopoly profits to lead to the entry of new firms into the industry, however, these new firms must *be able* to enter the industry. This observation leads us to a discussion of *entry barriers*.

Entry Barriers

Impediments that prevent entry are called **entry barriers**; they may be either natural or created.

If monopoly profits are to persist in the long run, the entry of new firms into the industry must be prevented by effective entry barriers.

entry barrier Any natural barrier to the entry of new firms into an industry, such as a large minimum efficient scale for firms, or any firm-created barrier, such as a patent.

Natural Entry Barriers.   Natural barriers most commonly arise as a result of economies of scale. When the long-run average cost curve is negatively sloped over a large range of output, big firms have significantly lower average total costs than small firms.

Recall from Chapter 9 that the *minimum efficient scale (MES)* is the smallest-size firm that can reap all of the economies of large-scale production. It occurs at the level of output where the firm's long-run average cost curve reaches a minimum.

To see how economies of scale can act as an entry barrier, suppose that the technology of an industry is such that one firm's *MES* would be 10 000 units per week at an average total cost of $10 per unit. Further suppose that at a price of $10, the quantity demanded in the entire market is 11 000 units per week. Under these circumstances,

natural monopoly
An industry characterized by economies of scale sufficiently large that one firm can most efficiently supply the entire market demand.

only one firm can operate at or near its *MES*. Any potential entrant would have unit costs higher than those of the existing firm and so could not compete successfully.

A **natural monopoly** occurs when the industry's demand conditions allow no more than one firm to cover its costs while producing at its minimum efficient scale. Electrical power transmission is a natural monopoly—with current technology it is cheaper to have only one set of power lines (rather than two or more) serving a given region.

Another type of natural barrier is *setup cost*. If a firm could be catapulted fully grown into the market, it might be able to compete effectively with the existing monopolist. However, the cost to the new firm of entering the market, developing its products, and establishing such things as its brand image and its dealer network may be so large that entry would be unprofitable.

Created Entry Barriers.   Many entry barriers are created by conscious government action. Patent laws, for instance, may prevent entry by conferring on the patent holder the sole legal right to produce a particular product for a specific period of time.

Patent protection has led to a major and prolonged battle among nations fought out in international organizations that seek to enforce conditions for fair trade and investment. The major developed countries, where much of the research and development is done, have sought to extend patent rights to other countries. They argue that without the temporary monopoly profits that a patent creates, the incentive to develop new products will be weakened. The developing countries have sought to maintain weak or nonexistent patent laws. This allows them to produce new products under more competitive conditions and thus to avoid paying monopoly profits to the original patent holders in developed countries.

A firm may also be granted a charter or a franchise that prohibits competition by law. Canada Post, for example, has a government-sanctioned monopoly on the delivery of first-class mail. In other cases the regulation and/or licensing of firms severely restricts entry. Professional organizations for dentists or engineers, for example, might restrict the number of places in accredited dental or engineering schools, and thus restrict entry into those industries.

Other barriers can be created by the firm or firms already in the market. In extreme cases, the threat of force or sabotage can deter entry. The most obvious entry barriers of this type are encountered in organized crime, where operation outside of the law makes available an array of illegal but potent barriers to new entrants. But law-abiding firms must use legal tactics in an attempt to increase a new entrant's setup costs. Such tactics range from the threat of price cutting—designed to impose unsustainable losses on a new entrant—to heavy brand-name advertising. (These and other created entry barriers will be discussed in more detail in Chapter 11.)

The Significance of Entry Barriers

Because there are no entry barriers in perfect competition, profits cannot persist in the long run. In monopolized industries, however, profits can persist in the long run whenever there are effective barriers to entry.

In competitive industries, profits attract entry, and entry erodes profits. In monopolized industries, entry barriers permit positive profits to remain in the long run.

Applying Economic Concepts 10-1 discusses an interesting example from Ireland where government regulations, by restricting entry, have led local pubs to have considerable monopoly power. At a time when Irish pubs are becoming a popular trend in many countries, it is ironic to see how a booming Irish economy combined with government regulation has caused a shortage of Irish pubs in Ireland itself!

APPLYING ECONOMIC CONCEPTS 10-1

The Economics of Irish Pubs

In recent years, the Irish economy has been booming—so much that many economists refer to it as the "Celtic Tiger," putting it in the same category as the Asian tigers of Taiwan, Singapore, Hong Kong, and South Korea. As the Irish economy has boomed, however, line-ups and prices in many Irish pubs have skyrocketed. The shortage of pubs has been so severe that some pub operators have implemented their own rationing schemes by turning away young people, bachelor parties, and sloppy dressers. In some cases, publicans have even threatened to expel anyone who starts to sing, a long-standing tradition in Irish pubs.

So what is going on in the pub industry in Ireland? Ordinarily, as demand increases and profits rise, new pubs would be established. This entry of new pubs would keep the existing pubs from earning high profits.

The problem in Ireland is that the issuance of pub licences is governed by a 1902 law that froze the number of licences at the level in place at that time. As incomes grew over time and the demand for pubs increased, the entry of new pubs was prevented. It is therefore no surprise that prices in pubs have been rising and that existing pubs are extremely profitable. This profitability is reflected in the high purchase prices of the pubs themselves. Currently, pubs sell for about two and a half times their annual sales. Twenty years ago, well before the shortages developed, pubs sold for a price roughly equal to their annual sales.

Another aspect of the 1902 legislation that has caused local pub shortages is that pub owners are prevented from transferring licences across county lines. As the population has increasingly moved from small towns to larger cities over the past several decades, small towns are left with too many pubs while neighbourhoods in the larger cities have far too few. The legislation therefore acts as *both* a barrier to entry and a barrier to exit (though closing down the pub is still permitted).

Who gains from this legislation, and who loses? The clear losers are the pubs' customers (especially in growing towns and cities) who are faced with higher prices and longer lineups. The clear gainers are the current owners of the pubs in areas where demand is strong. It is no surprise, therefore, that Ireland's powerful pub lobby continues to fight efforts by the government to review pub legislation.

Government legislation in Ireland has restricted the entry of new pubs and has therefore permitted existing pubs to earn high profits without the threat of competition.

Based on "Barred: Ireland Faces a Shortage of Pubs" in *The Globe and Mail*, March 17, 1999.

The Very Long Run and Creative Destruction

In the very long run, technology changes. New ways of producing old products are invented, and new products are created to satisfy both familiar and new wants. These are related to the concept of entry barriers; a monopoly that succeeds in preventing the entry of new firms capable of producing its product will sooner or later find its barriers circumvented by innovations. One firm may be able to use new processes that avoid some patent or other barrier that the monopolist relies on to bar entry of competing firms. Another firm may compete by producing a somewhat different product that satisfies the same need as the monopolist's product. Yet another firm might get around a natural monopoly by inventing a technology that produces at a low minimum efficient scale and ultimately allows several firms to enter the market and still cover costs.

The distinguished economist, Joseph Schumpeter (1883–1950), took the view that entry barriers were not a serious problem in the very long run. He argued that monopoly profits provide one of the major incentives for people who risk their money by financing inventions and innovations. In his view, the short-run profits of a monopoly provide a strong incentive for others to try to usurp some of these profits for themselves. If a frontal attack on the monopolist's entry barriers is not possible, the barriers will be circumvented by such means as the development of similar products against which the monopolist will not have entry protection.

Schumpeter called the replacement of one monopolist by another through the invention of new products or new production techniques the *process of creative destruction*. "Creative" referred to the rise of new products; "destruction" referred to the demise of the existing monopoly. Some everyday examples of creative destruction are presented in *Applying Economic Concepts 10-2*.

Schumpeter argued that this process of creative destruction reflects new firms' abilities to circumvent entry barriers that would otherwise permit monopolists to earn profits in the long run. He also argued that because creative destruction thrives on innovation, the existence of monopoly profits is a major incentive to economic growth. A key part of his argument appears in the following words:

> *What we have got to accept is that it [monopoly] has come to be the most powerful engine of progress and in particular of the long-run expansion of total output not only in spite of, but to a considerable extent through, this strategy [of creating monopolies], which looks so restrictive when viewed in the individual case and from the individual point of time.*[2]

Schumpeter was writing at a time when the two dominant market structures studied by economists were perfect competition and monopoly. His argument easily extends, however, to any market structure that allows profits to exist in the long run. Today, pure monopolies are few, but there are many industries in which profits can be earned for long periods of time. Such industries, which are called *oligopolies,* are candidates for the operation of the process of creative destruction. We study these industries in detail in Chapter 11.

Cartels as Monopolies

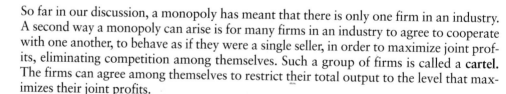

To learn more about OPEC, see its website at www.opec.org.

cartel   An organization of producers who agree to act as a single seller in order to maximize joint profits.

So far in our discussion, a monopoly has meant that there is only one firm in an industry. A second way a monopoly can arise is for many firms in an industry to agree to cooperate with one another, to behave as if they were a single seller, in order to maximize joint profits, eliminating competition among themselves. Such a group of firms is called a **cartel**. The firms can agree among themselves to restrict their total output to the level that maximizes their joint profits.

The most famous example of a successful cartel is the Organization of Petroleum Exporting Countries (OPEC), which successfully raised the world price of oil in 1973 and again in 1979. In recent years, however, its members have had difficulty agreeing among themselves regarding the appropriate level of output restrictions.

A less well-known example, but one that has been more successful over many years, is the diamond cartel, controlled by the South African company, DeBeers. DeBeers produces roughly half of the world's annual production of diamonds but also purchases a

---

[2]Joseph Schumpeter, *Capitalism, Socialism, and Democracy*, 3rd ed. (New York: Harper & Row, 1950), p. 106.

APPLYING ECONOMIC CONCEPTS 10-2

Some Everyday Examples of Creative Destruction

Creative destruction, the elimination of one product by a superior product or one production process by a superior process, is a major characteristic of all advanced countries. It eliminates the strong market position of the firms and workers who make the threatened product or operate the threatened process.

The steel-nibbed pen eliminated the quill pen with its sharpened bird's feather nib. The fountain pen eliminated the steel pen and its accompanying ink well. The ballpoint pen virtually eliminated the fountain pen. Who knows what will come next in writing implements?

The silent films eliminated vaudeville. The talkies eliminated silent films and colour films have all but eliminated black and white. Television seriously reduced the demand for films (and radio) while not eliminating either of them. Cable greatly reduced the demand for direct TV reception by offering better pictures and a more varied selection. The satellite is threatening to eliminate cable by offering much more selection.

For long-distance passenger travel by sea, the steamship eliminated the sailing vessel around the beginning of the twentieth century. The airplane eliminated the ocean liner in the 1950s and 1960s. For passenger travel on land, the train eliminated the stage coach while the bus competed with the train without eliminating it. The airplane wiped out the passenger train in most of North America while leaving the bus still in a low-cost niche used mainly for short and medium distances.

The above examples all involve the elimination of a product by the development of a new, better product. But creative destruction also occurs with the development of better *processes*. The laborious hand-setting of metal type for printing was replaced by the linotype that allowed the type to be set by a keyboard operator but that still involved a costly procedure for making corrections. The linotype was swept away by computer typesetting and much of the established printing shop operations have been replaced by desktop publishing.

Masses of assembly-line workers, operating highly specialized and inflexible machines, replaced craftsmen when Henry Ford perfected the techniques of mass production. A smaller number of less specialized flexible manufacturing workers, operating sophisticated and less specialized machinery, have replaced the assembly line workers who operated the traditional factory.

These cases all illustrate the same general message. Technological change transforms the products we consume, how we make those products, and how we work. It continually sweeps away positions of high income and economic power established by firms that were in the previous wave of technological change and by those who work for them. It is an agent of dynamism in our economy, an agent of change and economic growth, but it is not without its dark side in terms of the periodic loss of privileged positions on the part of the replaced firms and their workers.

---

considerable amount from smaller producers worldwide. The result is that roughly 70 percent of the world's annual diamond supply is marketed through the DeBeers-controlled Central Selling Organization (CSO). In years when demand is slack, DeBeers restricts the output of diamonds through the CSO to keep prices from falling.

Notice in both examples that there are firms *outside* of the cartel. There are many oil producers that are not part of OPEC; similarly, there are many diamond mines that are not owned or controlled by DeBeers (one of which is Canada's first diamond mine, the Ekati mine in the North West Territories). Indeed, this type of cartel is much more common than the type in which *all* firms successfully band together to form a cartel.

In this chapter, however, we simplify the analysis by considering the case in which *all* firms in the industry form a cartel. This is the easiest setting in which to see the central point—that cartels are inherently unstable.

DeBeers controls 70 percent of the world's supply of diamonds through its Central Selling Organization.

FIGURE 10-3   The Effect of Cartelizing a Competitive Industry

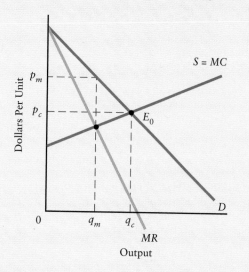

Cartelization of a competitive industry can always increase that industry's profits. Equilibrium for a competitive industry occurs at E_0, where the supply and the demand curves intersect. Equilibrium price and output are p_c and q_c. Because the industry demand curve is negatively sloped, marginal revenue is less than price.

If the industry is cartelized, profits can be increased by reducing output. All units between q_m and q_c add less to revenue than to cost—the MR curve lies below the MC curve. (Recall from Figure 9-6 that the industry's supply curve is the sum of the supply curves, and hence of the marginal cost curves, of each of the firms in the industry.) If the units between q_m and q_c are not produced, output is reduced to q_m and price rises to p_m. This price-output combination maximizes the industry's profits because it is where industry marginal revenue equals industry marginal cost.

The Effects of Cartelization

Because perfectly competitive firms are price takers, they accept the market price as given and increase their output until their marginal cost equals price. In contrast, a monopolist knows that increasing its output will depress the market price. Taking account of this, the monopolist increases its output only until marginal cost equals marginal revenue. If all the firms in a competitive industry form a cartel, they too will be able to take account of the effect of their *joint output* on price. They can agree to restrict industry output to the level that maximizes their joint profits (where the industry's marginal cost is equal to the industry's marginal revenue). The incentive for firms to form a cartel lies in the cartel's ability to restrict output, thereby raising price and increasing profits.

When a competitive industry is cartelized, the firms can agree to restrict their joint output to the joint-profit-maximizing level. One way to do this is to establish a quota for each firm's output. For example, suppose that the joint-profit-maximizing output is two-thirds of the perfectly competitive output. When the cartel is formed, each firm could be given a quota equal to two-thirds of its competitive output.

The cartelization of a competitive industry will reduce output and raise price from the perfectly competitive levels.

The effect of cartelizing a competitive industry is shown in more detail in Figure 10-3.

Problems That Cartels Face

Cartels encounter two characteristic problems. The first is ensuring that members follow the behaviour that will maximize the cartel members' *joint* profits. The second is preventing these profits from being eroded by the entry of new firms.

Enforcement of Output Restrictions

The managers of any cartel want the industry to produce its profit-maximizing output. Their job is made more difficult if individual firms either stay out of the cartel or join the cartel and then cheat on their output quotas. Any one firm, however, has an incentive to do just this—to be either the one that stays out of the organization or the one that enters and then cheats on its output quota. For the sake of simplicity, assume that all firms enter the cartel; thus enforcement problems are concerned strictly with cheating by its members.

If Firm X is the only firm to cheat, it is then in the best of all possible situations. All other firms restrict output and hold the industry price up near its monopoly level. They earn profits but only by restricting output. Firm X can then reap the full benefit of the other firms' output restraint and sell some additional output at the high price that has been set by the cartel's actions. However, if all of the firms cheat, the price will be pushed back to the competitive level, and all of the firms will return to their competitive position.

This conflict between the interests of the group as a whole and the interests of each individual firm is the cartel's main dilemma. Provided that enough firms cooperate in restricting output, all firms are better off than they would be if the industry remained perfectly competitive. Any one firm, however, is even better off if it remains outside or if it enters and cheats. However, if all firms act on this incentive, all will be worse off than if they had joined the cartel and restricted output.

Cartels tend to be unstable because of the incentives for individual firms to violate the output quotas needed to sustain the monopoly price.

The conflict between the motives for cooperation and for independent action is analysed in more detail in Figure 10-4. In Chapter 11, we will consider an explicit theory, called *game theory*, that economists use to analyse conflicts of this kind.

Cartels and similar output-restricting arrangements have a long history. For example, schemes to raise farm incomes by limiting crops bear ample testimony to the accuracy of the predicted instability of cartels. Industry agreements concerning crop restriction

Practise with Study Guide Chapter 10, Exercise 5.

FIGURE 10-4   A Cartel Member's Incentive to Cheat

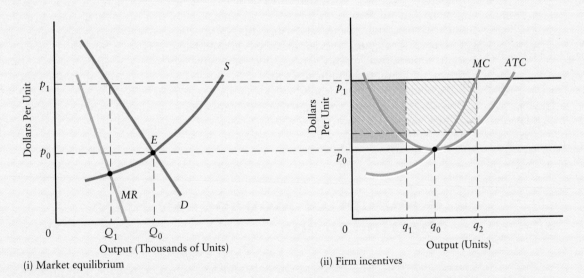

(i) Market equilibrium

(ii) Firm incentives

Cooperation leads to the monopoly price, but individual self-interest leads to production in excess of the monopoly output. Market conditions are shown in part (i), and the situation of a typical firm is shown in part (ii). (The change of scale between the two graphs is reflected by the upper case Q in part (i) and the lower case q in part (ii).) Initially, the market is in competitive equilibrium with price p_0 and quantity Q_0. The individual firm is producing output q_0 and is just covering its total costs.

The cartel is formed and then enforces quotas on individual firms that are sufficient to reduce the industry's output to Q_1, the output where industry MR equals industry MC. Q_1 is thus the output that maximizes the joint profits of the cartel members. Price rises to p_1 as a result. The typical firm's quota in part (ii) is q_1. The firm's profits rise from zero to the amount shown by the gray shaded area in part (ii). Once price is raised to p_1, however, the individual firm would like to increase output to q_2, where marginal cost is equal to the price set by the cartel. This would allow the firm to earn profits, shown by the diagonally striped area. However, if all firms increase their outputs above their quotas, industry output will increase beyond Q_1, and the resulting fall in price will reduce the joint profits of the cartel.

often break down, and prices fall as individual farmers exceed their quotas. This is why most crop restriction plans are now operated by governments rather than by private cartels. Government marketing boards of the type discussed in Chapter 5, backed by the full coercive power of the state, can force monopoly behaviour on existing producers and can effectively bar the entry of new ones.

Restricting Entry

A cartel must not only police the behaviour of its members but must also be able to prevent the entry of new producers. An industry that is able to support a number of individual firms presumably has no overriding natural entry barriers. Thus, if it is to maintain its profits in the long run, a cartel of many separate firms must create barriers that prevent the entry of new firms that are attracted by the cartel's profits. Successful cartels are often able to license the firms in the industry and to control entry by restricting the number of licences. This practice is often used by professionals, from physicians to beauticians. At other times, the government has operated a quota system and has given it the force of law. If no one can produce without a quota and the quotas are allocated among existing producers, entry is successfully prevented.

As we mentioned earlier, DeBeers has been somewhat successful at preventing the entry of new diamond producers and has been able to control 70 percent of the world's annual diamond sales through its Central Selling Organization (CSO). But recently, restricting entry into the diamond industry has been a bit more challenging. In the diamond industry, of course, "entry" means the development of new diamond mines. In 1998, Canada's first diamond mine (the Ekati mine in the North West Territories) began production. At production levels of roughly $500 million per year, the Ekati mine alone accounts for roughly 7 percent of the world's total annual production. The owners of the Ekati mine, however, have stated that they will market the diamonds independently rather than going through the CSO. With entries such as this, combined with some Russian and Australian producers leaving the CSO to sell their diamonds independently, DeBeers is faced with the challenge of keeping diamond prices supported above competitive levels. Time and further developments will determine how successful DeBeers will be in maintaining their dominant position in the industry.

A Multiprice Monopolist: Price Discrimination

So far in this chapter, we have assumed that the monopolist charges the same price for every unit of its product, no matter where or to whom it sells that product. But as we shall soon see, a monopolist finds it profitable to sell different units of the same product at different prices whenever it gets the opportunity. Because this practice is prevalent both for monopoly and for markets in which there are a few large sellers, the range of examples we will discuss cover both types of market structure.

Airlines often charge less to people who stay over a Saturday night than to those who come and go within the week. Raw milk is often sold at one price when it is to be used as fluid milk but at a lower price when it is to be used to make ice cream or cheese. In countries where medical services are provided by the market, physicians in private practice often charge for their services according to the incomes of their patients. Movie theatres often have lower admission prices for children than for adults, and typically also have lower prices for seniors. Electric companies sell electricity at one rate to homes and at a different rate to firms.

Price discrimination occurs when a producer charges different prices for different units of the same product *for reasons not associated with differences in cost.* Not all price differences represent price discrimination. Quantity discounts, differences between wholesale and retail prices, and prices that vary with the time of day or the season of the year may not represent price discrimination because the same product sold at a different time, in a different place, or in different quantities may have different costs. An excellent example is electricity. If an electric power company has unused capacity at certain times of the day, it may be cheaper for the company to provide service at those hours than at peak demand hours.

price discrimination
The sale by one firm of different units of a commodity at two or more different prices for reasons not associated with differences in cost.

If price differences reflect cost differences, they are not discriminatory. When a price difference is based on different buyers' valuations of the same product, it is discriminatory.

It does not cost a movie-theatre operator less to fill seats with children than with adults, but it is worthwhile for the movie theatre to let the children in at a discriminatory low price if few of them would attend at the full adult fare and if they take up seats that would otherwise be empty. Similarly, it does not cost an airline any less to sell a ticket to a student than to a non-student. But since few students may be inclined to buy airline tickets at the full price, it is profitable for the airline to attract more students with a lower price and, in that manner, fill up seats that would otherwise be empty.

Different Forms of Price Discrimination

Why should a firm want to sell some units of its output at a price that is below the price that it receives for other units of its output? The simple answer is because it is profitable to do so. Why should it be profitable?

Persistent price discrimination is profitable either because different buyers are willing to pay different amounts for the same product or because one buyer is willing to pay different amounts for different units of the same product. The basic point about price discrimination is that in either of these circumstances, sellers may be able to capture some of the consumer surplus that would otherwise go to buyers. (Review the discussion of consumer surplus in Chapter 6.) We first discuss how each type of discrimination takes place; we then examine its implications.

Discrimination Among Units of Output

Look back to Figure 6-2, which shows the consumer surplus received by one consumer when buying eight glasses of milk at a single price. If the firm could sell the consumer each glass separately, it could capture this consumer surplus. It would sell the first unit for $3.00, the second unit for $1.50, the third unit for $1.00, and so on until the eighth unit was sold for 30 cents. The firm would get total revenues of $8.10 rather than the $2.40 obtained from selling eight units at the single price of 30 cents each. In this example, the firm is able to discriminate perfectly and to extract all of the consumer surplus.

Perfect price discrimination occurs when the entire consumer surplus is obtained by the firm. This usually requires that each unit be sold at a different price. In practice, perfect discrimination is seldom possible. Suppose, however, that the firm could charge two different prices, one for the first 4 glasses sold and one for the next 4 glasses sold. If it sold each of the first 4 glasses of milk for 80 cents and each of the next 4 glasses for 30 cents, it would receive $4.40—less than it would receive if it could discriminate perfectly but more than it would receive if it sold all glasses at 30 cents.

Discrimination Among Buyers

Think of the demand curve in a market that is made up of individual buyers, each of whom has indicated the maximum price that he or she is prepared to pay for a single unit. Suppose, for the sake of simplicity, that there are only four buyers for the product; the first is prepared to pay up to $4 for one unit of the good, the second is prepared to pay up to $3, the third up to $2, and the fourth up to $1. Suppose that the product has a marginal cost of production of $1 per unit for all units. If the selling firm is limited to a single price, we know it will maximize its profits by setting marginal revenue equal to marginal cost. It will thus charge $3, sell 2 units, and earn profits of $4. (You can compute for yourself the firm's marginal revenue schedule.)

However, if the seller is able to discriminate among the buyers, it could charge the first buyer $4 and the second $3, thus increasing its profits from the first 2 units to $5. Moreover, it could also sell the third unit for $2, thus increasing its profits to $6. It would be indifferent about selling a fourth unit because the price would just cover marginal cost.

Price discrimination among buyers is quite common. Discounted prices charged for seniors at movie theatres or for students on airlines are both examples of this practice.

Discrimination Among Markets

Practise with Study Guide Chapter 10, Exercise 4.

Suppose now that the monopolist sells its product in two different markets. For example, it might be the only seller in a tariff-protected home market while in foreign markets it sells in competition with so many other firms that it is a price taker. In this case, the firm would equate its marginal cost to the price in the foreign market but to marginal revenue in the domestic market. As a result, it would charge a higher price on sales in the home market than on sales abroad.

Figure 10-5 shows in more detail how a firm might discriminate among markets. Profit maximization requires that marginal cost be set equal to marginal revenue *in each market*. Examine Figure 10-5 to see that the market with the less elastic demand will be the market with the higher price. For a very elastic demand curve, the vertical distance between the demand curve and the marginal revenue curve is small. In contrast, this distance is larger for an inelastic demand curve. Thus, when the firm equates *MC* and *MR* in each market, the price is higher in the market with inelastic demand.

Price discrimination between markets results in higher prices in those markets with less elastic demand.

FIGURE 10-5 Price Discrimination Among Markets

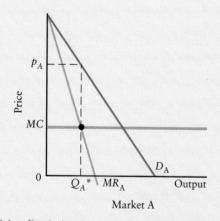

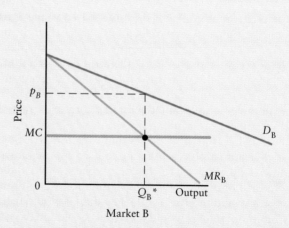

Market A

Market B

Price discrimination among markets leads firms to charge higher prices in those markets where demand is less elastic. Market A has less elastic demand than Market B. The *MC* curve for each firm is horizontal, indicating that all units have the same marginal cost. Profit maximization requires that *MC* = *MR* in each market, thus determining Q_A^* and Q_B^*. Since Market A has less elastic demand than Market B, p_A exceeds p_B.

Price discrimination is quite common among markets for the same product in different countries. In these cases, distance and transport costs or government regulation help to keep the markets separate. For example, Levi Strauss, the manufacturer of jeans, actively discriminates in its pricing of Levi 501s (and other products). The price in France is more than twice that in the United States. Ordinarily, we would expect importers in France to import inexpensive 501s from the United States and sell them in France, thus pushing down the price. In this case, however, the price discrimination is made possible by European Union legislation barring the import of less expensive brand-name goods from outside the European Union. French consumers understandably don't like this price discrimination, but their less elastic demand combined with the EU legal barriers leads Levi Strauss to sensibly charge much more in France than in the United States.

Price Discrimination in General

Demand curves have a negative slope because different units are valued differently, either by one individual or by different individuals. This fact, combined with a single price for a product, gives rise to consumer surplus.

The ability to charge multiple prices gives a seller the opportunity to capture some (or, in the extreme case, all) of the consumer surplus.

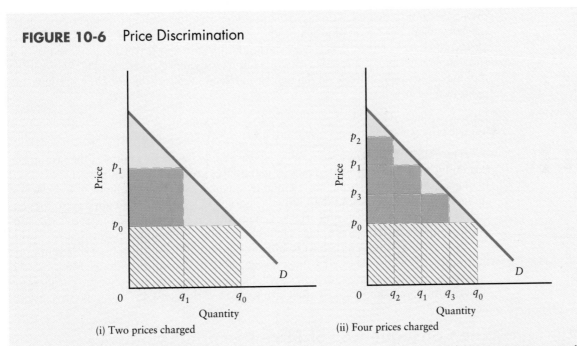

FIGURE 10-6 Price Discrimination

(i) Two prices charged

(ii) Four prices charged

Multiple prices permit a seller to capture consumer surplus. Suppose in either graph that if a single price were charged, it would be the price p_0. Quantity q_0 would be sold, and consumer surplus would be the entire area above p_0 and below the demand curve. The seller's revenue is the cross-hatched area.

Part (i) assumes that the market can be segregated in such a way that two prices are charged: p_1 for the first q_1 units and p_0 for the remaining q_1q_0 units. Consumer surplus is reduced to the two light blue triangles, and the seller's revenue is increased by the dark shaded area.

Part (ii) assumes that the market can be segregated in such a way that four prices are charged: p_2 for the first q_2 units, p_1 for the units between q_2 and q_1, and so on. Consumer surplus is reduced to the four light blue triangles, and the seller's revenue is increased by the dark shaded area. At the extreme, if a different price could be charged for each unit, producers could extract every bit of the consumer surplus, and the price discrimination would be perfect.

In general, the larger the number of different prices it can charge, the greater the firm's ability to increase its revenue at the expense of consumers. This is illustrated in Figure 10-6.

It follows that if a selling firm is able to discriminate through price, it can increase revenues received (and thus also profits) from the sale of any given quantity. However, price discrimination is not always possible, even if there are no legal barriers to its use.

When Is Price Discrimination Possible?

Discrimination *among units of output* sold to the same buyer requires that the seller be able to keep track of the units that a buyer consumes in each period. Thus the tenth unit purchased by a given buyer in a given month can be sold at a price that is different from the fifth unit *only* if the seller can keep track of each consumer's purchases. This can be done by an electric company through its meter readings or by a magazine publisher by distinguishing between renewals and new subscriptions. Another familiar example is the coffee-cards that are handed out at coffee shops such as Second Cup. For each coffee purchased, the consumer's card gets hole-punched. After 6 hole-punches, the consumer is entitled to one free coffee. The coffee-card is the way that the seller keeps track of the consumer's purchases.

Discrimination *among buyers* is possible only if the buyers who face the low price cannot resell the goods to the buyers who face the high price. However, even though the local butcher might like to charge the banker twice as much for steak as he charges the taxi driver, he cannot succeed in doing so. The banker can always shop for meat in the supermarket, where her occupation is not known. Even if the butcher and the supermarket agreed to charge her twice as much, she could hire the taxi driver to shop for her. The surgeon, however, may succeed in discriminating (especially if other reputable surgeons do the same) because it will not do the banker much good to hire the taxi driver to have her operation for her.

Price discrimination is possible if the seller can either distinguish individual units bought by a single buyer or separate buyers into groups such that resale between groups is impossible.

The ability to prevent resale tends to be associated with the nature of the product or the ability to classify buyers into readily identifiable groups. Services are less easily resold than goods; goods that require installation by the firm (e.g., heavy equipment or cable TV service) are less easily resold than movable goods such as household appliances. In general, transportation costs, tariff barriers, and import quotas are among the factors that separate groups of buyers geographically and may make discrimination possible.

Of course, it is not enough to be able to separate different buyers or different units into separate groups. The seller must also be able to control the supply going to each group. For example, there is no point in asking more than the competitive price from some buyers if they can simply go to other firms who sell the good at the competitive price.

The Consequences of Price Discrimination

The consequences of price discrimination are summarized in the following two propositions.

For any given level of output, the most profitable system of discriminatory prices will provide higher profits to the firm than the profit-maximizing single price.

This first proposition, which was illustrated in Figure 10-6, requires only that the demand curve have a negative slope. To see that the proposition is correct, remember that a monopolist with the power to discriminate could produce exactly the same quantity as a single-price monopolist and charge everyone the same price. Therefore, it need never receive less revenue, and it can do better if it can raise the price on even one unit sold, so long as the price need not be reduced on any other.

A monopolist that price discriminates among units will produce more output than will a single-price monopolist.

To understand this second proposition, remember that a monopolist that must charge a single price for a product will produce less than would all the firms in a perfectly competitive industry. It produces less because it knows that selling more depresses the price. Price discrimination allows it to reduce this disincentive. To the extent that the firm can sell its output in separate blocks, it can sell another block without spoiling the market for blocks that are already sold. In the case of perfect price discrimination, in which every unit of output is sold at a different price, the profit-maximizing monopolist will produce every unit for which the price charged is greater than or equal to its marginal cost. A perfect-price-discriminating monopolist will therefore produce the same quantity of output as would all firms combined in a perfectly competitive industry.

Normative Aspects of Price Discrimination

Two quite separate issues are involved in evaluating any particular example of price discrimination. One is the effect of price discrimination on the level of output, and the other is the effect of discrimination on the distribution of income.

As we saw in the second proposition above, a monopolist that is able to price discriminate among units will produce more output than will a single-price monopolist. This has implications for *allocative efficiency*, a concept we briefly introduced earlier in the chapter.

Recall from this earlier discussion that a single-price monopolist produces at a level of output where price exceeds marginal cost. Thus society would benefit from having more of the good produced because the marginal value of the good to society (as reflected by its price) exceeds the marginal cost of the good. This gap between price and marginal cost reflects the allocative *inefficiency* of monopoly.

For a monopolist that price discriminates among units, however, there are several prices rather than just a single price. As Figure 10-6 shows, the more prices the discriminating monopolist is able to charge, the more output is produced, and the lower the price becomes *on the marginal units*. Thus the gap between price and marginal cost is lower for a price-discriminating monopolist than for a single-price monopolist. The smaller gap between price and marginal cost implies that a price-discriminating monopolist is more efficient (or less inefficient) than a single-price monopolist.

Efficiency, however, is only one of the normative aspects of price discrimination. Often it is the effects on income distribution that lead to people's strong emotional reactions to it. But one's view will depend on who wins and who loses.

For instance, when railroads discriminate against small farmers, the results arouse public anger. It seems acceptable to many people, however, that doctors practise price discrimination in countries where medical services are provided by the market, charging lower prices to poor patients than to wealthy ones. Not everyone disapproves when airlines discriminate by giving senior citizens and vacationers lower fares than business travellers.

By increasing the seller's profits, price discrimination transfers income from buyers to sellers. When buyers are poor and sellers are rich, this transfer may seem undesirable. However, as in the case of doctor's fees and senior citizens' discounts, discrimination sometimes allows lower-income people to buy a product that they would otherwise be unable to afford if it were sold at the single price that maximized the producer's profits.

S U M M A R Y

A Single-Price Monopolist

- Monopoly is a market structure in which an entire industry is supplied by a single firm. The monopolist's own demand curve is identical to the market demand curve for the product. The market demand curve is the monopolist's average revenue curve, and its marginal revenue curve always lies below its demand curve.
- A single-price monopolist is maximizing its profits when its marginal revenue is equal to marginal costs. Since marginal costs are positive, profit maximization means that marginal revenue is positive. Thus, in turn, elasticity of demand is greater than unity at the monopolist's profit-maximizing level of output.
- A monopolist produces such that price exceeds marginal cost, whereas in a perfectly competitive industry price equals marginal cost. Output in a monopolized industry is less than if the industry were made up of many competitive price-taking firms.
- The profits that a monopoly earns may be positive, zero, or negative in the short run, depending on the relationship between demand and cost.
- For monopoly profits to persist in the long run, there must be effective barriers to the entry of other firms. Entry barriers can be natural or created.
- Monopoly power is limited by the presence of substitute products, the development of new products, and the entry of new firms. In the very long run, it is difficult to maintain entry barriers in the face of the process of creative destruction—the invention of new processes and new products to attack the entrenched position of existing monopolies.

Cartels as Monopolies

- A group of firms may form a cartel by agreeing to restrict their joint output to the monopoly level. Cartels tend to be unstable because of the strong incentives for each individual firm to cheat by producing more than its quota allows.

A Multiprice Monopolist: Price Discrimination

- A price-discriminating monopolist can capture some of the consumer surplus that exists when all of the units of a product are sold at a single price. Successful price discrimination requires that the firm be able to control the supply of the product offered to particular buyers and to prevent the resale of the product.
- A firm that discriminates between different markets will equate *MC* and *MR* in each market. The market with the less elastic demand will have the higher price.
- A profit-maximizing monopolist that can enforce discriminatory prices will produce higher output and earn larger profits than will a single-price monopolist.

K E Y   C O N C E P T S

The relationship between price and
  marginal revenue for a monopolist
Short-run monopoly profits
Natural and created entry barriers

The process of creative destruction
Cartels as monopolies
The instability of cartels
Price discrimination among units or
  buyers or markets

The causes and consequences of price
  discrimination
Perfect price discrimination

STUDY EXERCISES

1. The following table shows data for a monopolist. The first two columns provide all the data necessary to plot the monopolist's demand curve.

Price	Quantity Demanded	Total Revenue (TR)	Average Revenue (AR)	Marginal Revenue (MR)
$20	100	—	—	—
18	125	—	—	—
16	150	—	—	—
14	175	—	—	—
12	200	—	—	—
10	225	—	—	—
8	250	—	—	—
6	275	—	—	—
4	300	—	—	—

   a. Compute total and average revenue for each level of output and fill in the third and fourth columns in the table. Explain why average revenue is equal to price.
   b. Compute marginal revenue for each successive *change* in output and fill in the last column. Explain why *MR* is less than price.
   c. On a scale diagram, plot the demand (average revenue) curve and the marginal revenue curve.
   d. On a second scale diagram, with $ on the vertical axis and output on the horizontal axis, plot the *TR* curve. What is the value of *MR* when *TR* reaches its maximum?

2. The diagram below shows a monopolist's *MC* and *ATC* curves as well as the industry demand and *MR* curves.

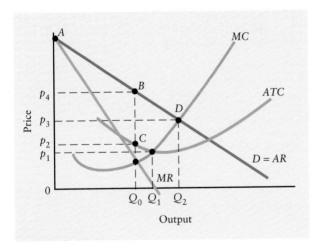

   a. What is the profit-maximizing price and level of output for the monopolist?
   b. What area in the figure shows the level of profits for the monopolist? Are profits positive or negative?
   c. What area shows consumer surplus in this case?
   d. Now suppose that the industry is made up of many small, price-taking firms (with the same technology). What are the equilibrium price and level of output in this case?
   e. What area shows consumer surplus in this case?

3. Imagine a monopolist that has fixed costs but no variable costs (thus there are no marginal costs, so $MC = 0$). For example, consider a firm that owns a spring of water that can produce indefinitely once it installs certain pipes in an area where no other source of water is available.

   a. Draw a downward-sloping demand curve for water, its associated *MR* curve, and the monopolist's *MC* curve.
   b. On your diagram, show the monopolist's profit-maximizing price and level of output.
   c. What is the marginal value of this good to society, and how does it compare to the marginal cost? What do you conclude about the *allocative efficiency* of this outcome?

4. Consider the market for corn. Suppose this is a competitive industry, made up of many price-taking farmers. We begin in a situation where market price is p_0, industry output is Q_0, and the typical farm is earning zero profit.

   a. Draw two diagrams like the ones on the next page.
   b. Now suppose that the farmers in this industry form a cartel and collectively agree to restrict the industry output of corn to the level that a monopolist would produce. Call this level of output Q^c and call the new price p^c. Show this outcome in the two diagrams.
   c. Show how the cartel raises the profits for the typical farmer.
   d. Now consider the incentives for an individual farm to cheat on its fellow cartel members. Would it be profitable to produce an extra unit and sell it at the cartel price? How is this shown in your diagram?
   e. Show how the typical farm's profits would rise if it were the only farm to cheat. What level of output would the cheating farm produce?
   f. Explain what would happen if *all* farms tried to cheat in this way.

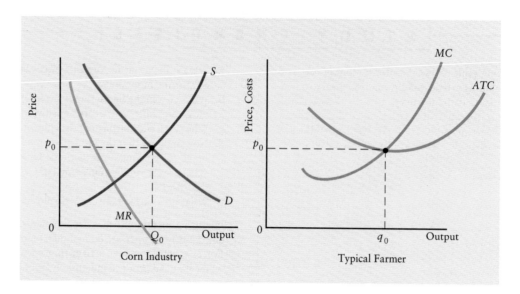

Corn Industry   Typical Farmer

5. Consider each of the following examples where a firm sells the same product to different customers at different prices. Identify in each case whether price discrimination is likely to be taking place. If there is unlikely to be price discrimination occurring, what explains the different prices?

   a. Weekend airline fares that are less than mid-week fares.

   b. Business-class airline fares that are 50% higher than economy-class fares. (Recognize that two business class seats take the same space inside the plane as three economy-class seats.)

   c. Discounts on furniture negotiated from "suggested retail price" for which sales personnel are authorized to bargain and to get as much in each transaction as the customer is prepared to pay.

   d. Higher tuition for law students than for graduate students in economics.

6. In the text we mentioned how Levi Strauss price discriminates between the European and American markets. This question is designed to help you analyse this situation. The equations below are hypothetical demand curves for Levi 501s in Europe and in America. We have expressed the price in dollars in both markets, and quantity is thousands of units per year.

European Demand:	$Q^D_E = 150 - p$
American Demand:	$Q^D_A = 250 - 4p$

   a. On two separate scale diagrams, one for Europe and one for America, plot the two demand curves.

   b. Now, recalling that a straight-line demand curve has an associated MR curve that has twice its slope, plot the two MR curves.

   c. Now suppose that Levi Strauss has a constant marginal cost of $15 per unit. Plot the MC curve in both diagrams.

   d. What is the profit-maximizing price in each market? Explain why profit maximization requires that MC be equated to MR *in each market.*

   e. Compute the price elasticity of demand (at the profit-maximizing points) in each market. (You may want to review Chapter 4 on elasticity at this point.) Does the market with less elastic demand have the higher price?

DISCUSSION QUESTIONS

1. Suppose that only one professor teaches economics at your university. Would you say that this professor is a monopolist who can exact any "price" from students in the form of readings assigned, tests given, and material covered? Suppose now that two additional professors have been hired. Has the original professor's market power been decreased? What if the three professors form a cartel agreeing on common reading lists, workloads, and the like?

2. Which of these industries—licorice candy, copper wire, outboard motors, coal, or the local newspaper—would it be most profitable to monopolize? Why? Does your answer depend on several factors or on just one or two? Which would you as a consumer least like to have monopolized by someone else? If your answers to the two questions are different, explain why.

3. Aristotle Murphy owns movie theatres in two towns of roughly the same size, 100 kilometres apart. In Monopolia, he owns the only chain of theatres; in Competitia, there is no theatre chain, and he is only one of a number of independent theatre operators. Would you expect movie prices to be higher in Monopolia or in Competitia in the short run? In the long run? If differences occur in his prices, would Murphy be discriminating in price?

4. Airline fares to Europe are higher in summer than in winter. Some railroads charge lower fares during the week than on weekends. Electric companies charge consumers lower rates the more electricity they use. Are these all examples of price discrimination? What additional information would you like to have before answering this question?

5. Acme Department Store has a sale on luggage. It is offering $30 off any new set of luggage to customers who trade in an old suitcase. Acme has no use for the old luggage and throws it away at the end of each day. Is this price discrimination? Why or why not? Which of the conditions necessary for price discrimination are or are not met?

6. The world price of coffee has declined in real terms over the past 40 years. In 1950, coffee was priced at just under $3 per pound (in 1994 U.S. dollars), whereas by 1995 the world price had fallen to just over $1 per pound. On July 29, 1995, *The Economist* magazine reported that,

   > On July 26 the Association of Coffee Producing Countries agreed in New York to limit exports to 60m bags for 12 months. The current level is 70m bags. . . . Coffee prices rallied a bit on the news, but few expect the pact to last: some big coffee producers such as Mexico have not signed up, and even those who have will probably cheat.

   Explain why "few expect the pact to last," keeping in mind the two characteristic problems for cartels that were discussed in this chapter.

CHAPTER 11

Imperfect Competition

🔟 *LEARNING OBJECTIVES*

① Recognize that most industries in Canada have either a large number of small firms or a small number of large firms.

② Understand that imperfectly competitive firms distinguish their products from those of their competitors and often engage in non-price competition.

③ Explain the key elements of the theory of monopolistic competition.

④ Recognize how free entry drives profits to zero in the long run.

⑤ Understand why strategic behaviour is a key feature of oligopoly.

⑥ Use the basic tools of game theory to explain the difference between cooperative and noncooperative oligopoly outcomes.

The two market structures that we have studied so far—perfect competition and monopoly—are polar cases; they define the two extremes of a firm's market power over an industry. Under perfect competition, firms are price takers, price is equal to marginal cost, and economic profits in the long run are zero. Under monopoly, the firm is a price setter, it sets price above marginal cost, and it may earn positive profits in the long run.

Although they provide important insights, these two polar cases are insufficient for understanding the behaviour of *all* firms. Indeed, most of the products that we easily recognize—computers, breakfast cereals, automobiles, cameras and fast food, to name a few—are produced by firms that have some market power but are neither perfect competitors nor monopolists.

This chapter is devoted to the discussion of industries that are neither perfectly competitive nor monopolistic. Before discussing the theory, however, we turn to a brief discussion of how prevalent this "intermediate" market structure is in the Canadian economy.

The Structure of the Canadian Economy

Along the spectrum of market structures, we can divide Canadian industries into two broad groups—those with a large number of relatively small firms and those with a small number of relatively large firms.

Industries with Many Small Firms

About two-thirds of Canada's gross domestic product is produced by industries made up of firms that are small relative to the size of the market in which they sell.

The perfectly competitive model does quite well in explaining the behaviour of some of these industries. These are the ones in which individual firms produce more-or-less identical products and so are price takers. Forest and fish products provide many examples. Agriculture also fits fairly well in most ways since individual farmers are clearly price takers. Many basic raw materials, such as iron ore, tin, and copper, are sold on world markets where most individual firms lack significant market power.

Other industries, however, are not well described by the perfectly competitive model, even though they contain many small firms. In retail trade and in services, for example, most firms have some influence over prices. Your local grocery stores, clothing shops, night clubs, and restaurants spend a good deal of money advertising on television and in newspapers—something they would not have to do if they faced perfectly elastic demand curves. Moreover, each store in these industries has a unique location that may give it some local monopoly power over nearby customers.

Industries with many relatively small firms can therefore be divided into two categories. In one category, the firms' behaviour can be explained by the perfectly competitive model; in the other category, the perfectly competitive model does not apply because the firms, though small, are not price takers. It is this second group of industries that we examine in this chapter.

Industries with a Few Large Firms

About one third of Canada's gross domestic product is produced by industries that are dominated by either a single firm or a few large ones.

The most striking cases of single-firm monopolies in today's economy are the electric utilities and the firms which provide local telephone and cable TV services. In the first case they are typically owned by provincial governments; in the second they are subject to government regulation (which we examine in Chapter 12). Other than these and similar cases in which government ownership or regulation play an important role, cases of single-firm monopoly are very rare in Canada today. However, there are some notable examples of monopoly (or near monopoly) from many years ago. For example, the Eddy Match Company was virtually the sole producer of wooden matches in Canada between 1927 and 1940, and Canada Cement Limited produced nearly all of the output of cement until the 1950s.

This type of market dominance by a single large firm is now a thing of the past. Most modern industries that are dominated by large firms contain several firms. Their names are part of the average Canadian's vocabulary: Canadian National and Canadian Pacific; Canadian Airlines and Air Canada; Banque National, Royal Bank, and Scotiabank; Imperial Oil, Petro Canada, and Irving; Stelco, Dofasco, and Alcan; Falconbridge and INCO; Abitibi-Consolidated and MacMillan Bloedel; Ford, Toyota, and GM; Sony, Mitsubishi, and Toshiba; and Nortel, Newbridge, and Corel. Many service industries that used to be dominated by small independent producers have in recent decades seen the development of large firms operating on a world-wide basis. In accounting, firms such as PricewaterhouseCoopers are enormous and clearly have some market power. SNC-Lavalin and Acres are two examples of very large engineering firms that have business contracts all over the world. In management consulting, McKinsey & Co., Boston Consulting Group, and Monitor are also very large firms with market power.

Industrial Concentration

An industry with a small number of relatively large firms is said to be highly *concentrated*. An industry with a large number of relatively small firms is less concentrated. A formal measure of such industrial concentration is given by the *concentration ratio*.

Concentration Ratios

concentration ratio
The fraction of total market sales (or some other measure of market occupancy) controlled by a specified number of the industry's largest firms.

When we measure whether an industry has power concentrated in the hands of only a few firms or dispersed over many, it is not sufficient to count the number of firms. For example, an industry with one enormous firm and 29 very small ones is more concentrated in any meaningful sense than an industry with only five equally sized firms. One approach to this problem is to calculate what is called a **concentration ratio,** which shows the fraction of total market sales controlled by the largest sellers. Common types of concentration ratios cite the share of total market sales made by the largest four or eight firms.

Figure 11-1 shows the four-firm concentration ratios in several Canadian manufacturing industries. As is clear, the degree of concentration is quite varied across these industries. In the tobacco and petroleum industries, for example, the largest four firms account for over 80 percent of total sales. At the other extreme, the largest four firms in the furniture industry account for a paltry 7 percent of sales. These largest furniture firms may be large in some absolute sense, but the low concentration ratios suggest that they have quite limited market power.

Defining the Market

The main problem associated with using concentration ratios is to *define the market* with reasonable accuracy. On the one hand, the market may be much smaller than the whole country. For example, concentration ratios in national cement sales are low, but they understate the market power of cement companies because high transportation costs divide the cement *industry* into a series of regional *markets*, with each having relatively few firms. On the other hand, the market may be larger than one country. This is a particularly important consideration in a small trading country such as Canada.

Indeed, the globalization of competition brought about by the falling costs of transportation and communication has been one of the most significant developments in the world economy in recent decades. As the world has "become smaller" through the advances in communication technologies, the nature of domestic markets has changed dramatically. The presence of only a single firm in one industry in Canada in no way implies monopoly power when it is in competition with five foreign firms that can easily sell in the Canadian market. *Applying Economic Concepts 11-1* discusses how the communication revolution that has taken place in the past two decades has altered the nature of production and competition in Canada and around the world.

FIGURE 11-1   Concentration Ratios in Selected Canadian Industries

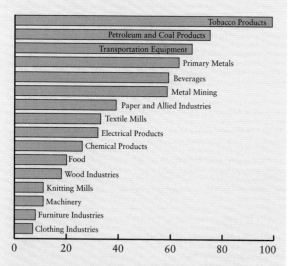

Concentration ratios vary greatly among manufacturing industries. These data show the share of total shipments (in dollar terms) accounted for by the four largest firms in the industry.

(*Source*: Douglas West, *Modern Canadian Industrial Organization*, HarperCollins 1994, p. 37.)

APPLYING ECONOMIC CONCEPTS 11-1

Globalization and the Communication Revolution

A mere 150 years ago, people and news travelled by sailing ship, and it took months to communicate across various parts of the world. Advances in the first 60 years of the twentieth century sped up both communications and travel. In the past few decades, the pace of change in communication technology has accelerated. The world has witnessed a communication revolution that has dramatically changed the speed with which business decisions are made and implemented.

Four decades ago, telephone links were labouriously and unreliably connected by operators, satellites were newfangled and not especially useful toys for rocket scientists, photocopying and telecopying were completely unknown, mail was the only way to send hard copy and getting it to overseas destinations often took weeks, computers were in their infancy, and jets were just beginning to replace the much slower and less reliable propeller aircraft. Today, direct dialing is available worldwide at a fraction of what long-distance calls cost 40 years ago. Faxes, satellite links, jet travel, computer networks, cheap courier services, and a host of other developments have made communication that is reliable and often instantaneous available throughout the world.

The communication revolution has been a major contributor to the development of what has become known as the "global village," a term first used by Canadian author Marshall McLuhan in his writing about the social implications of changes in communication technology. Three important characteristics of the global village are a globalization of production, an increase in competition, and a decline in the power of the nation-state.

Production

The communication revolution has allowed many large international companies, known as *transnational corporations (TNCs),* to decentralize their production processes. They are now able to locate their research and development (R&D) where the best scientists are available. They can produce various components in dozens of places, locating each activity in a country where costs are cheapest for that type of production. They can then ship all the parts, as they are needed, to an assembly factory where the product is "made."

The globalization of production has brought employment, and rising real wages, to people in many developing countries. At the same time, it has put less-skilled labour in the developed countries under strong competitive pressures.

Competition

The communication revolution has also caused a globalization of competition in almost all industries. National markets are no longer protected for local producers by high costs of transportation and communication or by the ignorance of foreign firms. Walk into a local supermarket or department store today and you will have no trouble finding products representing most nations of the world.

Consumers gain by being able to choose from an enormous range of well-made, low-priced goods and services. Firms that are successful gain worldwide sales. Firms that fall behind even momentarily may, however, be wiped out by competition coming from many quarters. Global competition is fierce, and firms need to be fast on the uptake—of other people's new ideas or their own—if they are to survive.

Economic Policy

The international character of TNCs means that national economic policies have been seriously constrained. Much international trade takes place between segments of single TNCs. This gives them the opportunity, through their accounting practices, to localize their profits in countries where corporate taxes are lowest and to localize their costs in countries where cost write-offs are highest.

The globalization of production also allows TNCs to shift production around the world. Tough national policies in one country may lead firms to move production elsewhere. Generous policies that seek to attract production may succeed in attracting only small and specialized parts of it.

Globalization of production, and consequently of competition, places constraints on the way countries design and implement policies. In particular, government policies must take into account the heightened international mobility of labour and capital. Such mobility does not make governments powerless, but it forces them to recognize that policies implemented today may have different effects than the same policies would have had a mere generation ago.

However, the use of concentration ratios, adjusted appropriately to correctly define the relevant market, can give us useful information about the degree to which production in a given market is concentrated in the hands of a few firms.

The industries shown in Figure 11-1 are not monopolies, because there are several firms in the industry, and these firms engage in rivalrous behaviour. But neither do these firms operate in perfectly competitive markets. Often there are only a few major rival firms in an industry, but even when there are many, they are not price takers. Virtually all consumer goods are differentiated products, and any one firm will typically have several lines of a product that differ more or less from one another and from competing lines produced by other firms. To explain and predict behaviour in these markets, we must go beyond simple concentration ratios; we need to develop theories of the behaviour of firms in market structures other than monopoly and perfect competition.

Imperfectly Competitive Market Structures

The market structures that we are now going to study are called *imperfectly competitive*. The word *competitive* emphasizes that we are not dealing with monopoly, and the word *imperfect* emphasizes that we are not dealing with perfect competition (in which firms are price takers). What is referred to, then, is rivalrous competitive behaviour among firms that have some amount of market power.

Let's begin by noting a number of important characteristics of behaviour that are typical of imperfectly competitive firms. To help organize our thoughts, we classify these under two main headings. First, firms choose the *variety* of the product that they produce and sell. Second, firms choose the *price* at which they will sell that product.

Firms Choose Their Products

differentiated product A group of commodities that are similar enough to be called the same product but dissimilar enough so that all of them do not have to be sold at the same price.

If a new farmer enters the wheat industry, the full range of products that the farmer can produce is already in existence. In contrast, if a new firm enters the snack food industry, that firm must decide on the characteristics of the new snacks that it is to produce. It will not produce snacks that are identical to those already in production. Rather, it will develop variations on existing snack foods or even a totally new food. Each of these will have its own distinctive characteristics. As a result, firms in the snack food industry sell an array of differentiated products, no two of which are identical.

The term **differentiated product** refers to a group of commodities that are similar enough to be called the same product but dissimilar enough that they can be sold at different prices. For example, although one brand of face soap is similar to most others, soaps differ from each other in chemical composition, colour, smell, softness, brand name, packaging, reputation, and a host of other characteristics that matter to customers. All face soaps taken together can be regarded as one differentiated product.

Most firms in imperfectly competitive markets sell differentiated products. In such industries, the firm itself must decide on what characteristics to give the products that it will sell.

These breakfast cereals are different enough that they can each have their own price, but they are similar enough to be called the same product – they are a differentiated product.

Firms Choose Their Prices

Because firms in perfect competition sell an identical product, they face a market price that they are unable to influence. In all other market structures, firms have negatively sloped demand curves and thus face a tradeoff between the price that they charge and the quantity that they sell.

Whenever different firms' products are not identical, each firm must decide on a price to set. For example, no market sets a single price for razor blades or television sets by equating overall demand with overall supply. What is true for razor blades and for television sets is true for virtually all consumer goods and many capital goods. Any one manufacturer will typically have several product lines that differ from each other and from the competing product lines of other firms. Each product has a price that must be set by its producer.

In such circumstances, economists say that firms *administer* their price. An **administered price** is a price set by the conscious decision of an individual firm rather than by impersonal market forces. Firms that administer their prices are said to be **price setters**.

Each firm has expectations about the quantity it can sell at each price that it might set. Unexpected demand fluctuations then cause unexpected variations in the quantities that are sold at the administered prices.

In market structures other than perfect competition, firms set their prices and then let demand determine sales. Changes in market conditions are signaled to the firm by changes in the firm's sales.

The changed sales may or may not then lead firms to change their prices.

One striking contrast between perfectly competitive markets and markets for differentiated products concerns the behaviour of prices. In perfect competition, prices change continually in response to changes in demand and supply. In markets where differentiated products are sold, prices often change less frequently. Manufacturers' prices for automobiles, TVs, and men's suits do not change with anything like the frequency that prices change in markets for wheat, oil, copper, and newsprint.

Modern firms that sell differentiated products typically have hundreds of distinct products on their price lists. Changing such a long list of administered prices at the same frequency that competitive market prices change would be extremely costly if not impossible. Even changing them only occasionally involves costs. These include the costs of printing new list prices and notifying all customers, the difficulty of keeping track of frequently changing prices for purposes of accounting and billing, and the loss of customer and retailer goodwill due to the uncertainty caused by frequent changes in prices.

Thus transitory fluctuations in demand may be met by changing output with prices constant, while changes in costs that accompany inflation are typically passed on through price increases. Because few firms expect inflationary price increases to be reversed, they know that they must raise their prices to cover them. Even in these cases, however, they do so periodically, rather than continuously, because of the costs incurred in making such changes.

administered price A price set by the conscious decision of the seller rather than by impersonal market forces.

price setter A firm that faces a downward sloping demand curve for its product. It chooses which price to set.

Non-price Competition

Several other important aspects of the observed behaviour of firms in imperfect competition could not occur under either perfect competition or monopoly.

First, many firms spend large sums of money on advertising. They do so in an attempt both to shift the demand curves for the industry's products and to attract customers from competing firms. A firm in a perfectly competitive market would not engage in advertising because the firm faces a perfectly elastic demand curve at the market price and so advertising would involve costs but would not increase the firm's revenues. A monopolist would see no benefit in advertising because it has no competitors in the industry. However, in some cases a monopolist will still advertise in an attempt to convince consumers to shift their spending away from other goods and toward the monopolist's product. An example is when DeBeers, the giant near-monopoly diamond producer, has lavish advertisements claiming that "A diamond is forever."

Second, many firms engage in a variety of other forms of non-price competition, such as offering competing standards of quality and product guarantees.

Third, firms in many industries engage in activities that appear to be designed to hinder the entry of new firms, thereby preventing existing pure profits from being eroded by entry. We will consider these activities in more detail later in the chapter.

Monopolistic Competition

monopolistic competition Market structure of an industry in which there are many firms and freedom of entry and exit but in which each firm has a product somewhat differentiated from the others, giving it some control over its price.

The theory of **monopolistic competition** was originally developed to deal with the phenomenon of product differentiation. This theory was first developed by the U.S. economist Edward Chamberlin in his 1933 pioneering book, *The Theory of Monopolistic Competition.*

This market structure is similar to perfect competition in that the industry contains many firms and exhibits freedom of entry and exit. It differs, however, in one important respect: Whereas firms in perfect competition sell an identical product and are price takers, firms in monopolistic competition sell a differentiated product and thus have some power over setting price.

Product differentiation leads to, and is enhanced by, the establishment of brand names and advertising, and it gives each firm a degree of monopoly power over its own product. Each firm can raise its price, even if its competitors do not, without losing all its sales. This is the *monopolistic* part of the theory. However, each firm's monopoly power is severely restricted in both the short run and the long run. The short-run restriction comes from the presence of similar products sold by many competing firms; this causes each firm's demand curve to be very elastic. The long-run restriction comes from free entry into the industry, which permits new firms to compete away the profits being earned by existing firms. These restrictions comprise the *competition* part of the theory.

The Assumptions of Monopolistic Competition

The theory of monopolistic competition is based on three key assumptions.

1. Each firm produces one specific variety, or brand, of the industry's differentiated product. Each firm thus faces a demand curve that, although negatively sloped, is highly elastic because competing firms produce many close substitutes.

2. The industry contains so many firms that each one ignores the possible reactions of its many competitors when it makes its own price and output decisions. In this re-

spect, firms in monopolistic competition are similar to firms in perfect competition. They make decisions based on their own demand and cost conditions and do not consider interdependence between their own decisions and those of the other firms in the industry.

3. There is freedom of entry and exit in the industry. If profits are being earned by existing firms, new firms have an incentive to enter. When they do, the demand for the industry's product must be shared among more brands.

Predictions of the Theory

Product differentiation, which is the *only* thing that makes monopolistic competition different from perfect competition, has important consequences for behaviour in both the short and the long run.

The Short-Run Decision of the Firm

In the short run, a firm that is operating in a monopolistically competitive market structure is similar to a monopoly. It faces a negatively sloped demand curve and maximizes its profits by equating marginal cost with marginal revenue. If the demand curve cuts the average total cost curve as shown in part (i) of Figure 11-2, the firm makes positive profits.

FIGURE 11-2   Profit Maximization for a Firm in Monopolistic Competition

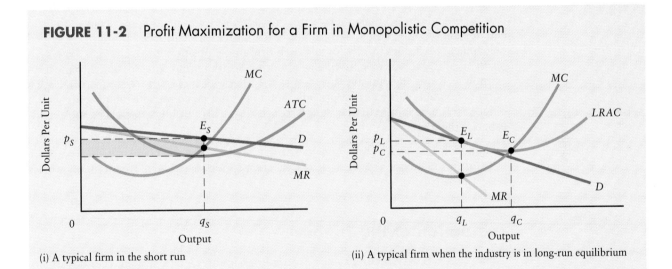

(i) A typical firm in the short run

(ii) A typical firm when the industry is in long-run equilibrium

The short-run position for a monopolistically competitive firm is similar to that of a monopolist. In the long run, firms in a monopolistically competitive industry have zero profits and excess capacity. Note the very elastic demand curve—this reflects the fact that each firm produces a good for which there are many close (but not perfect) substitutes. Short-run profit maximization occurs in part (i) at E_S, the output for which $MR = MC$. Price is p_S and quantity is q_S. Profits may exist; in this example they are shown by the shaded area. Starting from the short-run position shown in part (i), entry of new firms shifts the firm's demand curve to the left and eliminates profits. In part (ii), point E_L, where demand is tangent to $LRAC$, is the position of each firm when the industry is in long-run equilibrium. Price is p_L and quantity is q_L. Price is greater and quantity is less than would exist in the long run if the industry were perfectly competitive (p_C and q_C). When the industry is in long-run equilibrium, each monopolistically competitive firm has excess capacity of $q_L q_C$.

Practise with Study Guide Chapter 11, Exercises 1 and 2.

The Long-Run Equilibrium of the Industry

Profits, as shown in part (i) of Figure 11-2, provide an incentive for new firms to enter the industry. As they do so, the total demand for the industry's product must be shared among this larger number of firms; thus, each gets a smaller share of the total market. Such entry shifts the demand curve for each existing firm's product to the left. Entry, and the consequent leftward shifting of the existing firms' demand curves, continues until profits are eliminated. When this has occurred, each firm is in the position shown in part (ii) of Figure 11-2. Its demand curve has shifted to the left until the curve is *tangent* to the average total cost curve. At this output, the firm is just covering all of its costs. At any other output, it would be suffering losses because average total costs would exceed average revenue.

To see why this "tangency solution" provides the only possible long-run equilibrium for the industry, consider the two possible alternatives. First, suppose that the firm's demand curve *nowhere touched* the ATC curve. There would then be no output at which costs could be covered, and exit would occur. The exit of firms from the industry would then lead each *remaining* firm's demand curve to shift to the right, until it eventually touched the ATC curve. Second, suppose that the demand curve *cut* the ATC curve. There would then be a range of output over which profits could be earned. These profits would lead firms to enter the industry, and this entry would shift each *remaining* firm's demand curve to the left until it was just tangent to the ATC curve.

The Excess-Capacity Theorem

Part (ii) of Figure 11-2 makes it clear that monopolistic competition results in a long-run equilibrium of zero profits, even though each individual firm faces a negatively sloped demand curve. It does this by forcing each firm into a position in which it has *excess capacity;* that is, each firm is producing an output less than that corresponding to the lowest point on its long-run average cost (*LRAC*) curve. If the firm were to increase its output, it would reduce its cost per unit, but it does not do so because selling more would reduce revenue by more than it would reduce cost. This result is often called the **excess-capacity theorem.**

excess-capacity theorem   The property of long-run equilibrium in monopolistic competition that firms produce on the falling portion of their long-run average cost curves. This results in excess capacity, measured by the gap between present output and the output that coincides with minimum average cost.

In monopolistic competition, goods are produced at a point where average total costs are not at their minimum, in contrast to perfect competition, where they are produced at their lowest possible cost.

Evaluation of the Theory

The excess-capacity theorem once aroused passionate debate among economists because it seemed to show that all industries that sell differentiated products would produce them at a higher cost than was necessary. Because product differentiation is a characteristic of virtually all modern consumer goods industries, this theorem suggested that modern market economies were systematically inefficient.

Subsequent analysis by economists has shown that the charge of inefficiency has not been proved. The excess capacity of monopolistic competition does not necessarily indicate a waste of resources because some benefits accrue to consumers from the greater choice and variety of products.

Saying that consumers value variety is not saying that *each* consumer necessarily values variety. You might like only one of the many brands of tooth paste and be better off if only that one brand were produced and the price were lower. But other consumers would prefer one of the other brands. Thus, it is the differences in tastes *across many consumers* that gives rise to the social value of variety, and the price of that greater variety is the higher price per unit.

From society's point of view, there is a tradeoff between producing more brands to satisfy diverse tastes and producing fewer brands at a lower cost per unit.

Monopolistic competition produces a wider range of products but at a somewhat higher cost per unit than perfect competition. As consumers clearly value variety, the benefits of variety must be matched against the extra cost that variety imposes in order to find the *socially optimal* amount of product differentiation. Product differentiation is wasteful only if the costs of providing variety exceed the benefits conferred by providing that variety. Depending on consumers' tastes and firms' costs, monopolistic competition may result in too much, too little, or the optimal amount of product variety.

Empirical Relevance

A controversy raged for several decades as to the empirical relevance of monopolistic competition. Of course, product differentiation is pervasive in many industries. Nonetheless, many economists maintained that the monopolistically competitive market structure was almost never found in practice.

To see why, we need to distinguish between products and firms. Single-product firms are extremely rare in manufacturing industries. Typically, a vast array of differentiated products is produced by each of the few firms in the industry. Most of the vast variety of breakfast cereals, for example, is produced by only three firms (Kellogg's, Nabisco, and General Foods). Similar circumstances exist in soap, chemicals, cigarettes, and numerous other industries where many competing products are produced by a few very large firms. These industries are clearly not perfectly competitive and neither are they monopolies. Are they monopolistically competitive? The answer is no because they contain few enough firms for each to take account of the others' reactions when determining its own behaviour. Furthermore, these firms often earn large profits without attracting new entry (thereby violating the third assumption of monopolistic competition). In fact, they operate under the market structure called *oligopoly*, which we consider in the next section.

Although monopolistic competition is not applicable to differentiated products produced in industries with high concentration, some economists think that the theory is useful for analysing industries where concentration ratios are low and products are differentiated, as in the cases of restaurants, clothing stores, gas stations, dry cleaners, hair salons, and landscaping services. Indeed, many of the small stores and services that are located in or near your neighbourhood are monopolistically competitive firms.

Oligopoly

Industries that are made up of a small number of large firms have a market structure called *oligopoly*, from the Greek words *oligos polein*, meaning "few to sell." An **oligopoly** is an industry that contains two or more firms, at least one of which produces a significant portion of the industry's total output. Whenever there is a high concentration ratio for the firms that are serving one particular market, that market is oligopolistic. The market structures of oligopoly, monopoly, and monopolistic competition are similar in that firms in all of these markets face negatively sloped demand curves.

oligopoly   An industry that contains two or more firms, at least one of which produces a significant portion of the industry's total output.

strategic behaviour
Behaviour designed to
take account of the
reactions of one's rivals to
one's own behaviour.

**nonstrategic
behaviour**   Behaviour
that does not take account
of the reactions of rivals to
one's own behaviour.

See Chapter 11 of
www.pearsoned.ca/lipsey for a
discussion of business strategy by
Hugh Courtney, "What Is Business
Strategy?" *World Economic Affairs.*

In contrast to a monopoly (which has no competitors) and to a monopolistically competitive firm (which has many competitors), an oligopolistic firm faces only a few competitors. The number of competitors is small enough for each firm to realize that its competitors may respond to anything that it does and that it should take such possible responses into account. In other words, *oligopolists are aware of the interdependence among the decisions made by the various firms in the industry.*

Economists say that oligopolists exhibit **strategic behaviour,** which means that they take explicit account of the impact of their decisions on competing firms and of the reactions they expect competing firms to make. In contrast, firms in perfect competition or monopolistic competition engage in **nonstrategic behaviour,** which means they make decisions based on their own costs and their own demand curves without considering any possible reactions from their large number of competitors. Monopolists also do not engage in strategic behaviour—simply because they have no competitors to worry about.

In oligopolistic industries, prices are typically administered. Products are usually differentiated. The intensity and the nature of rivalrous behaviour vary greatly from industry to industry and from one period of time to another. This variety has invited extensive theorizing and empirical study.

Why Bigness?

There are several reasons why so many industries are dominated by a few large firms. Some are based on technology and some are based on firms' behaviour.

Economies of Scale

Much factory production uses the principle of the division of labour that we first studied in Chapter 1. The production of a commodity is broken up into hundreds of simple tasks. This type of division of labour is the basis of the assembly line, which revolutionized the production of many goods in the early twentieth century, and still underlies economies of large-scale production in many industries. Such division of labour is, as Adam Smith observed long ago, dependent on the size of the market. If only a few units of a product can be sold each day, there is no point in dividing its production into a number of tasks, each of which can be done in a few minutes. So big firms with large sales have an advantage over small firms with small sales whenever there are opportunities for economies based on an extensive division of labour.

Modern industries produce many differentiated products that give rise to a different type of scale economies. It is costly to develop and market a new product, and it may be only a matter of a few years before it is replaced by some superior version of the same basic product. These *fixed costs* of product development and marketing must be recovered in the revenues from sales of the product. The larger the firm's sales, the lower the fixed cost that has to be recovered from each unit sold and thus the lower the market price can be. With the enormous development costs of some of today's high-tech products, firms that can sell a large volume have a distinct pricing advantage over firms that sell a smaller volume.

Where size confers a cost advantage through economies of scale, there may be room for only a few firms, even when the total market is quite large. This cost advantage of size will dictate that the industry be an oligopoly unless government regulation prevents the firms from growing to their efficient size.

Firm-Created Causes of Bigness

The number of firms in an industry may be decreased while the average size of the survivors rises because of strategic behaviour of the firms themselves. Firms may grow by buying out rivals or merging with them or by driving rivals into bankruptcy through extreme competitive practices. This process increases the size and market shares of the survivors and may, by reducing competitive behaviour, allow them to achieve larger profit margins.

The surviving firms must then be able to create and sustain barriers to entry where natural ones—based on economies of scale—do not exist. The industry will then be dominated by a few large firms only because they are successful in preventing the entry of new firms that would otherwise reduce the industry's concentration ratio.

Is Bigness Natural or Firm-Created?

Most observers would agree that bigness results from a mix of both natural and firm-created causes. Some industries have high concentration ratios because the efficient size of the firm is large relative to the overall size of the industry's market. Other industries may have high concentration ratios mainly because the firms are seeking enhanced market power through entry restriction. The issue that is debated is the relative importance of these two forces, the one coming from economies of scale and the other coming from the desire of firms to create market power by growing large. In Chapter 12 we will see that this debate lies at the heart of *competition policy*—the set of laws designed to promote competition among firms.

The Basic Dilemma of Oligopoly

Oligopoly behaviour is often strategic behaviour. It is dangerous for an oligopolist to neglect how its rivals might react to its actions. In deciding on strategies, oligopolists face a basic dilemma between *competing* and *cooperating*.

Oligopolistic firms will make more profits as a group if they cooperate; any one firm, however, may make more profits for itself if it defects while the others cooperate.

This result is similar to the one established in Chapter 10 for the incentives of an individual firm within a cartel. In a competitive industry with many firms, a cooperative outcome cannot be reached unless some central governing body is formed, by either themselves or the government, to force the necessary behaviour on all firms. In contrast, the few firms in an oligopolistic industry will themselves recognize the possibility of cooperating to avoid the loss of profits that will result from competitive behaviour.

Cooperative and Noncooperative Outcomes

If the firms in an oligopolistic industry cooperate to produce among themselves the monopoly output, they can maximize their joint profits. If they do this, they will reach what is called a **cooperative outcome**, which is the position that a single monopoly firm would reach if it owned all the firms in the industry.

If all the firms in an oligopolistic industry are at the cooperative outcome, it will usually be worthwhile for any one of them to cut its price or to raise its output, so long as the others do not do so. However, if everyone does the same thing, they will be worse off as a group and may all be worse off individually. An industry outcome that is reached

cooperative outcome
A situation in which existing firms cooperate to maximize their joint profits.

noncooperative outcome   An industry outcome reached when firms calculate their own best policy without considering competitors' reactions.

game theory   The theory that studies rational decision making in situations in which one must anticipate the reactions of one's competitors to the moves that one makes.

duopoly   An industry that contains only two firms.

Practise with Study Guide Chapter 11, Exercises 3 and 4.

Nash equilibrium   An equilibrium that results when each firm in an industry is currently doing the best that it can, given the current behaviour of the other firms in the industry.

when firms proceed by calculating only their own gains, without considering the reactions of others, is called a **noncooperative outcome.**

An Example from Game Theory

Game theory is used to study decision making in situations in which a number of players compete, each knowing that others will react to their actions and each taking account of others' expected reactions when making moves. For example, suppose that a firm is deciding whether to raise, lower, or maintain its price. Before arriving at an answer, it asks: "What will the other firms do in each of these cases, and how will their actions affect the profitability of whatever decision I make?"

When game theory is applied to oligopoly, the players are firms, their game is played in the market, their strategies are their price or output decisions, and the payoffs are their profits.

An illustration of the basic dilemma of oligopolists, to cooperate or to compete, is shown in Figure 11-3 for the case of a two-firm oligopoly, called a **duopoly.** In this simplified game there are only two strategies for each firm: to produce an output equal to either one-half of the monopoly output or two-thirds of the monopoly output. Even this simple game, however, is sufficient to illustrate several key ideas in the modern theory of oligopoly.

Figure 11-3 presents what is called a *payoff matrix.* The data in the matrix show that if both firms cooperate, *each* producing one-half of the monopoly output, they achieve the cooperative outcome and jointly earn the monopoly profits by *jointly* producing the output that a monopolist would produce. As a group, they can do no better.

Once the cooperative outcome is attained, the data in the figure show that if A cheats and produces more, its profits will increase. However, B's profits will be reduced: A's behaviour drives the industry's price down, so B earns less from its unchanged output. Because A's cheating takes the firms away from the joint-profit-maximizing monopoly output, their joint profits must fall. Thus B's profits fall by more than A's rise.

Similar considerations also apply to B. It is worthwhile for B to depart from the joint-profit-maximizing output, so long as A does not do so. Thus both A and B have an incentive to agree to cooperate to jointly produce the monopoly output and then to privately cheat by departing from that level of output.

Finally, Figure 11-3 shows that when either firm does depart from the cooperative outcome, the other has an incentive to do so as well. When each follows this "selfish" strategy, both reach the noncooperative outcome at which they jointly produce 1⅓ times as much as the monopolist would. Each then has lower profits than at the cooperative outcome.

Nash Equilibrium.   The noncooperative outcome shown in Figure 11-3 is called a **Nash equilibrium,** after the U.S. mathematician John Nash, who developed the concept in the 1950s and received the Nobel Prize in Economics in 1994 for this work. In a Nash equilibrium, each firm's best strategy is to maintain its present behaviour *given the present behaviour of the other firms.*

It is easy to see that there is only one Nash equilibrium in Figure 11-3. In the bottom-right cell, the best decision for each firm, given that the other firm is producing two-thirds of the monopoly output, is to produce two-thirds of the monopoly output itself. Between them, they produce a joint output of 1⅓ times the monopoly output. Neither firm has an incentive to depart from this position (except through cooperation with the other). In any other cell, each firm has an incentive to change its output *given the output of the other firm.*

The basis of a Nash equilibrium is rational decision-making in the absence of cooperation. Its particular importance in oligopoly theory is that it is the only type of self-policing equilibrium. It is self-policing in the sense that there is no need for group behaviour to enforce it. Each firm has a self-interest to maintain it because no move will improve its profits, given what other firms are currently doing.

If a Nash equilibrium is established by any means whatsoever, no firm has an incentive to depart from it by altering its own behaviour.

Strategic Behaviour.   We have seen how the Nash equilibrium in Figure 11-3 can be arrived at when both firms cheat on an agreement to reach the cooperative outcome. The same equilibrium will be attained if each firm behaves strategically by choosing its optimal strategy taking into account what the other firm may do. Let's see how this works.

Suppose that Firm A reasons as follows: "B can do one of two things; what is the best thing for me to do in each case? First, what if B produces one-half of the monopoly output? If I do the same, I receive a profit of 20, but if I produce two-thirds of the monopoly output, I receive 22. Second, what if B produces two-thirds of the monopoly output? If I produce one-half of the monopoly output, I receive a profit of 15, whereas if I produce two-thirds, I receive 17. Clearly, in either case my best strategy is to produce two-thirds of the monopoly output."

Firm B will reason in the same way. As a result, they end up producing 1⅓ times the monopoly output between themselves, and each earns a profit of 17. This type of game, in which the noncooperative equilibrium makes *both* players worse off than if they were able to cooperate, is called a *prisoners' dilemma*. The reason for this curious name is discussed in *Extensions in Theory 11-1.*

Cooperation or Competition?

We have seen that although oligopolists have an incentive to cooperate, they may be driven, through their own individual decisions, to produce more and earn less than they would if they cooperated. Our next step is to look in more detail at the types of cooperative and competitive behaviour that oligopolists may adopt. We can then go on to study the forces that influence the balance between cooperation and competition in actual situations.

FIGURE 11-3   The Oligopolist's Dilemma: To Cooperate or to Compete?

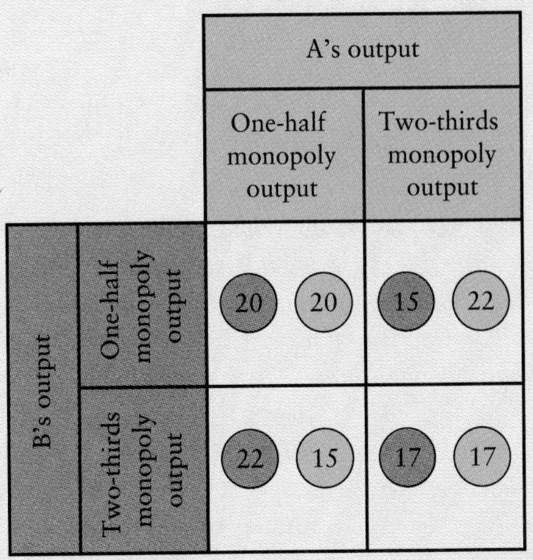

Cooperation to determine the overall level of output can maximize joint profits, but it leaves each firm with an incentive to cheat. The figure gives what is called a payoff matrix for a two-firm game. Only two levels of production are considered in order to illustrate the basic problem. A's production is indicated across the top, and its payoffs (profits in millions of dollars) are shown in the green circles within each square. B's production is indicated down the left side, and its payoffs are shown in the red circles within each square. For example, the top right square tells us that if B produces one-half while A produces two-thirds of the output that a monopolist would produce, A's profits will be 22, while B's will be 15.

If A and B cooperate, each produces one-half the monopoly output and receives a payoff of 20, as shown in the upper left box. However, at that position, known as the cooperative outcome, each firm can raise its profits by producing two-thirds of the monopoly output, provided that the other firm does not do the same.

Now suppose that A and B make their decisions noncooperatively. A reasons that whether B produces either one-half or two-thirds of the monopoly output, A's best output is two-thirds. B reasons similarly. In this case, they reach the noncooperative outcome, where each produces two-thirds of the monopoly output, and each makes less than it would if the two firms cooperated. In this example, the noncooperative outcome is a Nash equilibrium.

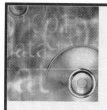

EXTENSIONS IN THEORY 11-1
The Prisoners' Dilemma

The game shown in Figure 11-3 is often known as a prisoners' dilemma game. This is the story that lies behind the name:

Two men, John and William, are arrested for jointly committing a crime and are interrogated separately. They know that if they both plead innocence, they will get only a light sentence, and if they both admit guilt they will both receive a medium sentence. Each is told, however, that if either protests innocence while the other admits guilt, the one who claims innocence will get a severe sentence while the other will be released with no sentence at all.

Here is the payoff matrix for that game:

		John's Plea	
		Innocent	Guilty
William's Plea	Innocent	J light sentence / W light sentence	J no sentence / W severe sentence
	Guilty	J severe sentence / W no sentence	J medium sentence / W medium sentence

John reasons as follows: William will plead either guilty or innocent. First assume that he pleads innocent. I get a light sentence if I also plead innocent but no sentence at all if I plead guilty, so guilty is my better plea. Now assume that he pleads guilty. I get a severe sentence if I plead innocent and a medium sentence if I plead guilty. So once again guilty is my preferred plea. William reasons in the same way and, as a result, they both plead guilty and get a medium sentence. Note, however, that if they had been able to communicate and coordinate their pleas, they could both have agreed to plead innocent and get off with a light sentence.

The prisoners' dilemma also arises in many situations of firm rivalry. Consider the case where two firms are making sealed bids on a contract. For simplicity, suppose that only two bids are permitted, either a high or a low price. The high price yields a profit of $10 million, whereas the low price yields a profit of $7 million. If the two firms put in the same price, they share the job, and each earns half the profits. If they give different bids, the firm submitting the lower bid gets the job and all the profits. You should have no trouble in drawing up the payoff matrix and determining the outcomes under noncooperative and cooperative behaviour. (See Study Exercises #5 at the end of the chapter for an example of this type.)

Types of Cooperative Behaviour

When firms agree to cooperate in order to restrict output and raise prices, their behaviour is called **collusion**. Collusive behaviour may occur with or without an explicit agreement to collude. Where explicit agreement occurs, economists speak of *overt* or *covert collusion*, depending on whether the agreement is open or secret. Where no explicit agreement actually occurs, economists speak of *tacit collusion*. In this case, all firms behave cooperatively without an explicit agreement to do so. They merely understand that it is in their mutual interest to restrict output and to raise prices.

collusion An agreement among sellers to act jointly in their common interest, for example, by agreeing to raise prices. Collusion may be overt or covert, explicit or tacit.

Explicit Collusion.   The easiest way for firms to ensure that they will all maintain their joint-profit-maximizing output is to make an explicit agreement to do so. Such collusive agreements have occurred in the past, although they have been illegal among privately owned firms in Canada for a long time. When they are discovered today, they are rigorously prosecuted. We shall see, however, that such agreements are not illegal everywhere in the world, particularly when they are supported by national governments.

We saw in Chapter 10 that when a group of firms get together to act in this way, they create a *cartel*. Cartels show in stark form the basic conflict between cooperation and competition that we just discussed. Cooperation among cartel members allows them to restrict output and raise prices, thereby increasing the cartel members' profits. But it also presents each cartel member with the incentive to cheat. The larger the number of firms, the greater the temptation for any one of them to cheat. After all, cheating by one small firm may not be noticed because it will have a negligible effect on price. Conversely, a cartel made up of a small number of firms is more likely to persist because cheating by any one member is more difficult to conceal from the other members.

DeBeers is an example of a firm that has been able to assemble a cartel in the world's diamond industry. Through their own Central Selling Organization (CSO), DeBeers markets roughly 70 percent of the world's annual diamond production. With such influence over the market, they are able to manage the flow of output, in response to changes in world demand, to keep prices high. Another example of a cartel is the Association of Coffee Producing Countries, a collection of Central American countries that have attempted to restrict output in order to raise coffee prices in recent years.

But surely the most famous example of a cartel—and the one that has had the most dramatic effect on the world economy—is the Organization of Petroleum Exporting Countries (OPEC). OPEC's explicit cooperation is discussed in *Lessons from History 11-1*.

For information on DeBeers and the diamond industry, see DeBeers' website: www.adiamondisforever.com.

For more information on OPEC, check out their website: www.opec.org.

Tacit Collusion.   Although collusive behaviour that affects prices is illegal, a small group of firms that recognize the influence that each has on the others may act without any explicit agreement to achieve the cooperative outcome. In such tacit agreements, the two forces that push toward cooperation and competition are still evident.

First, firms have a common interest in cooperating to maximize their joint profits at the cooperative solution. Second, each firm is interested in its own profits, and any one of them can usually increase its profits by behaving competitively.

Types of Competitive Behaviour

Although the most obvious way for a firm to violate the cooperative solution is to produce more than its share of the joint-profit-maximizing output, there are other ways in which rivalrous behaviour can occur.

Competition for Market Shares.   Even if *joint* profits are maximized, there is the problem of market shares. How is the profit-maximizing level of sales to be divided among the colluding firms? Competition for market shares may upset the tacit agreement to hold to joint-profit-maximizing behaviour. Firms often compete for market shares through various forms of non-price competition, such as advertising and variations in the quality of their product. Such costly competition may reduce industry profits.

Covert Cheating.   In an industry that has many differentiated products and in which sales are often by contract between buyers and sellers, covert rather than overt cheating may seem attractive. Secret discounts and rebates can allow a firm to increase its sales at the expense of its competitors while appearing to hold to the tacitly agreed price.

LESSONS FROM HISTORY 11-1

Explicit Cooperation in OPEC

The experience of the Organization of Petroleum Exporting Countries (OPEC) in the 1970s and 1980s illustrates the power of cooperative behaviour to create short-run profits, as well as the problems of trying to exercise long-run market power in an industry without substantial entry barriers.

OPEC did not attract worldwide attention until 1973, when its members voluntarily restricted their output by negotiating quotas among themselves. In that year, OPEC countries accounted for about 70 percent of the world's supply of crude oil. Although it was not a complete monopoly, the cartel came close to being one. By reducing output, the OPEC countries were able to drive up the world price of oil and to earn massive profits both for themselves and for non-OPEC producers, who obtained the high prices without having to limit their output. After several years of success, however, OPEC began to experience the typical problems of cartels.

Entry

Entry became a problem for the OPEC countries. The high price of oil encouraged the development of new supplies, and within a few years, new productive capacity was coming into use at a rapid rate in non-OPEC countries. The development of North Sea oil by the UK and the development of the Athabasca Tar Sands in Alberta, both in the late 1970s, are two examples of this new productive capacity.

Long-Run Adjustment of Demand

The short-run demand for oil proved to be highly inelastic. Over time, however, adaptations to reduce the demand for oil were made within the confines of existing technology. Homes and offices were insulated more efficiently, and smaller, more fuel-efficient cars became popular. This is an example of the distinction between the short-run and long-run demand for a commodity first introduced in Chapter 4.

Innovation further reduced the demand for oil in the very long run. Over time, technologies that were more efficient in their use of oil, as well as alternative energy sources, were developed. Had the oil prices stayed up longer than they did, major breakthroughs in solar and geothermal energy would surely have occurred.

This experience in both the long run and the very long run shows the price system at work, signaling the need for adaptation and providing the incentives for that adaptation. It also provides an illustration of Schumpeter's concept of creative destruction, which we first discussed in Chapter 10. To share in the profits generated by high energy prices, new technologies and new substitute products were developed, and these destroyed much of the market power of the original cartel.

Cheating

At first, there was little incentive for OPEC countries to violate quotas. Members found themselves with such undreamed-of increases in their incomes that they found it difficult to use all of their money productively. As the output of non-OPEC oil grew, however, OPEC's output had to be reduced to hold prices high. Furthermore, as the long-run adjustments in demand occurred, even larger output restrictions by OPEC were required to prop up the price of oil. Incomes in OPEC countries declined as a result.

Many OPEC countries had become used to their enormous incomes, and their attempts to maintain them in the face of falling output quotas brought to the surface the instabilities inherent in all cartels. In 1981, oil prices reached their peak of U.S. $35 per barrel. In real terms, this was about five times as high as the 1972 price, but production quotas were less than one-half of OPEC's capacity. Eager to increase their oil revenues, many individual OPEC members gave in to the pressure to cheat and produced in excess of their production quotas. In 1984, Saudi Arabia indicated that it would not tolerate further cheating by its partners and demanded

Very-Long-Run Competition. As we first discussed in Chapter 10, very-long-run considerations may also be important. When technology and product characteristics change constantly, there may be advantages to behaving competitively. A firm that behaves competitively may be able to maintain a larger market share and earn larger profits than it would if it cooperated with the other firms in the industry, even though all the firms' joint profits are lower. In our world of constant change, a firm that thinks it can keep ahead of its rivals through innovation has an incentive to compete even if that

that others share equally in reducing their quotas yet further. However, agreement proved impossible. In December 1985, OPEC decided to eliminate production quotas and let each member make its own decisions about output.

After the Collapse

OPEC's collapse as an output-restricting cartel led to a major reduction in world oil prices. Early in 1986, the downward slide took the price to $20 per barrel, and it fell to $11 per barrel later in the year. Allowing for inflation, this was around the price that had prevailed just before OPEC introduced its output restrictions in 1973. Prices have been volatile since then, oscillating between about $10 per barrel, which is close to the perfectly competitive price, and $20 per barrel, which seems to be all that can be sustained under the modest output restrictions that can currently be obtained.

The Role of Politics

OPEC is also an excellent example of how politics affects economic outcomes. Especially during the 1990s, OPEC's inability to significantly restrict oil production has been largely a result of political frictions among the various OPEC members.

In OPEC's March 1999 meetings, for example, Iran was pushing for reductions in Saudi Arabia's oil production to compensate for Iraq's production increases. Iran argued that when Iraq's oil exports were prevented by a United Nations sanction (following the Persian Gulf War in 1990), Saudi Arabia received the lion's share of Iraq's production quota. Thus, in Iran's view, Iraq's subsequent increases in production should have been matched by a reduction in Saudia Arabia's. Saudia Arabia argued that their large share of OPEC production (roughly 30 percent) was justified on the grounds that it spent a lot of money in the Gulf War and invested considerably in production capacity when the war disrupted oil production.

Political frictions like these will not end anytime soon. Along with the basic economic incentives that individual OPEC members have to cheat on any output-restricting agreement, such political frictions only add to the already difficult task of forming and maintaining a cartel. Only time will tell if OPEC will be able to repeat their spectacular successes of the 1970s. By early in 2000, OPEC had succeeded in driving the world price of oil up to $30 per barrel. But will it last?

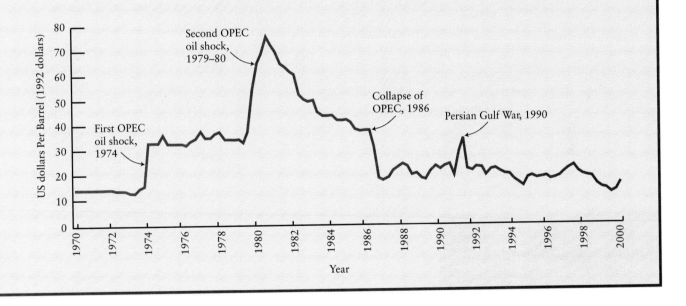

competition lowers the joint profits of the whole industry. Such competitive behaviour contributes to the long-run growth of living standards and may provide social benefits over time that outweigh any losses due to the restriction of output at any one point in time.

For these and other reasons, there are often strong incentives for oligopolistic firms to compete rather than to maintain the cooperative outcome, even when they understand the inherent risks to their joint profits.

The Importance of Entry Barriers

Suppose that firms in an oligopolistic industry succeed in raising prices above long-run average costs and earn substantial profits that are not completely eliminated by non-price competition. In the absence of significant entry barriers, new firms will enter the industry and erode the profits of existing firms, as they do in monopolistic competition. Natural barriers to entry were discussed in Chapter 10. They are an important part of the explanation of the persistence of profits in many oligopolistic industries.

Where such natural entry barriers do not exist, however, oligopolistic firms can earn profits in the long run only if they can *create* entry barriers. To the extent this is done, existing firms can move toward joint profit maximization without fear that new firms, attracted by the high profits, will enter the industry. We now discuss some types of *firm-created* entry barriers.

See Chapter 11 of www.pearsoned.ca/lipsey for an interesting discussion of how simple game theory can be used by managers: Hugh Courtney, "Games Managers Should Play," *World Economic Affairs*.

Brand Proliferation

By altering the characteristics of a differentiated product, it is possible to produce a vast array of variations on the general theme of that product. Think, for example, of automobiles with a little more or a little less acceleration, braking power, top speed, cornering ability, fuel efficiency, and so on, compared with existing models.

Although the multiplicity of existing brands is no doubt partly a response to consumers' tastes, it can have the effect of discouraging the entry of new firms. To see why, suppose that the product is the type for which there is a substantial amount of brand switching by consumers. In this case, the larger the number of brands sold by existing firms, the smaller the expected sales of a new entrant.

Suppose, for example, that an industry contains three large firms, each selling one brand of cigarettes, and say that 30 percent of all smokers change brands in a random fashion each year. If a new firm enters the industry, it can expect to pick up one-third of the smokers who change brands (a smoker who switches brands now has three *other* brands to choose between). The new firm would get 10 percent (one-third of 30 percent) of the total market the first year merely as a result of picking up its share of the random switchers, and it would keep increasing its share for some time thereafter. If, however, the existing three firms have five brands each, there would be 15 brands already available, and a new firm selling one new brand could expect to pick up only one-fifteenth of the brand switchers, giving it only 2 percent of the total market the first year, with smaller gains also in subsequent years. This is an extreme case, but it illustrates a general result.

Many companies spend millions of dollars annually on lavish advertising campaigns. In addition to being informative, advertising can be an effective entry barrier.

The larger the number of differentiated products that are sold by existing oligopolists, the smaller the market share available to a new firm that is entering with a single new product. Brand proliferation therefore can be an effective entry barrier.

Advertising

Advertising is one means by which existing firms can impose heavy costs on new entrants. Advertising, of course, serves purposes other than that of creating barriers to entry. Among them, it performs the useful function of informing buyers about their alternatives. Indeed, a new firm may find that advertising is essential, even when existing firms do not advertise at all, simply to call attention to its entry into an industry in which it is currently unknown.

Nonetheless, advertising can also operate as a potent entry barrier by increasing the costs of new entrants. Where heavy advertising has established strong brand images for existing products, a new firm may have to spend heavily on advertising to create its own brand images in consumers' minds. If the firm's sales are small, advertising costs *per unit* will be large, and price will have to be correspondingly high to cover those costs. Consider Nike, Reebok, and their competitors. They advertise not so much the quality of their athletic shoes as images that they wish consumers to associate with the shoes. The same is true for cosmetics, beer, cars, and many more consumer goods. The ads are lavishly produced and photographed. They constitute a formidable entry barrier for a new producer.

Figure 11-4 illustrates how heavy advertising can shift the cost curves of a firm with a low minimum efficient scale *(MES)* to make it one with a high *MES*. In essence, what happens is that a high *MES* of advertising is added to a low *MES* of production, with the result that the overall *MES* is raised.

A new entrant with small sales but large required advertising costs finds itself at a substantial cost disadvantage relative to its established rivals.

The combined use of brand proliferation and advertising as an entry barrier helps to explain one apparent paradox of everyday life—that one firm often sells multiple brands of the same product, which compete actively against one another as well as against the products of other firms. The soap and beer industries provide classic examples of this behaviour. Because all available scale economies can be realized by quite small plants, both industries have few natural barriers to entry. Both contain a few large firms, each of which produces an array of heavily advertised products. The numerous existing products make it harder for a new entrant to obtain a large market niche with a single new product. The heavy advertising, although directed against existing products, creates an entry barrier by increasing the average costs of a new product that seeks to gain the attention of consumers and to establish its own brand image.

Predatory Pricing

A firm will not enter a market if it expects continued losses after entry. One way in which an existing firm can create such an expectation is to cut prices below costs whenever entry occurs and to keep them there until the entrant goes bankrupt. The existing firm sacrifices profits while doing this, but it sends a discouraging message to potential future rivals, as well as to present ones. Even if this strategy is costly in terms of lost profits in the short run, it may pay for itself in the long run by creating *reputation effects* that deter the entry of new firms at other times or in other markets that the firm controls.

Predatory pricing is controversial. Some economists argue that pricing policies that appear to be predatory can be explained by other motives and that existing firms only hurt themselves when they engage

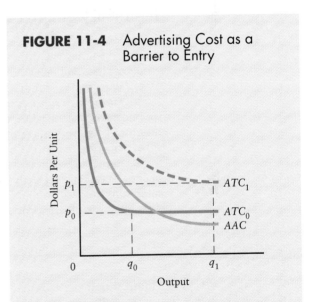

FIGURE 11-4 Advertising Cost as a Barrier to Entry

Large advertising costs can increase the minimum efficient scale *(MES)* of production and thereby increase entry barriers. The ATC_0 curve shows that the *MES* without advertising is at q_0. The curve *AAC* (for average advertising cost) shows that advertising cost per unit falls as output rises. Advertising increases average total cost to ATC_1, which is downward sloping over its entire range. The new *MES* is given by q_1. Advertising has given a scale advantage to large sellers and has thus created a barrier to entry.

in such practices instead of accommodating new entrants. Others argue that predatory pricing has been observed and that it is in the long-run interests of existing firms to punish the occasional new entrant even when it is costly to do so in the short run.

Canadian courts have taken the position that predatory pricing does indeed occur and a number of firms have been convicted of using it as a method of restricting entry.

Contestable Markets

We have been discussing the role played by entry barriers in determining the long-run characteristics of an oligopolistic industry. In general, we expect profits made by existing firms to lead new firms to enter the industry. Such entry will, in turn, reduce profits toward their competitive level. We now turn to a theory that emphasizes not the role of *actual* entry, but rather the role of *potential* entry in keeping industry profits near their competitive level.

The theory of *contestable markets* holds that markets do not have to contain many firms or experience *actual* entry for profits to be held near the competitive level. *Potential* entry can do the job just as well as actual entry, as long as (1) entry can be easily accomplished and (2) existing firms take potential entry into account when making price and output decisions.

The Theory of Contestable Markets

Entry is usually costly to the entering firm. It may have to build a plant, develop new versions of the industry's differentiated product, or advertise heavily to call attention to its product. These and many other initial expenses are often called *sunk costs of entry*. A sunk cost of entry is a cost that a firm must incur to enter the market and that *cannot be recovered if the firm subsequently exits*. For example, if an entering firm builds a product-specific factory that has no resale value, the new factory is a sunk cost of entry. However, the cost of a factory that is not product-specific and can be resold for an amount that is close to its original cost is not a sunk cost of entry.

A market in which new firms can enter and leave without incurring *any* sunk costs of entry is called a perfectly **contestable market.** But because all markets require at least some sunk costs of entry, contestability must be viewed along a continuum. The lower the sunk costs of entry, the more contestable the market.

In a contestable market, the existence of even temporary profits will attract entry. Firms will enter to gain a share of these profits and will then exit.

As an example, consider the market for air travel in the lucrative Toronto-Ottawa-Montreal triangle. This market would be quite contestable *if* counter and loading space were available to new entrants at the three cities' airline terminals. An airline that was not currently serving the cities in question could shift some of its existing planes to the market with small sunk costs of entry. Some training of personnel would be needed for them to become familiar with the route and the airport. This is a sunk cost of entry that could not be recovered if the cities in question were no longer to be served. However, most of the airline's costs are not sunk costs of entry. If it were to subsequently decide to leave a city, the rental of terminal space would stop and the airplanes and the ground equipment could be shifted to another location.

Sunk costs of entry constitute a barrier to entry, and the larger these are, the larger the profits of existing firms can be without attracting new entrants. The flip side of this argument is that firms operating in markets without large sunk costs of entry will not earn large profits. Strategic considerations will lead them to keep prices near the level that

contestable market
A market in which there are no sunk costs of entry or exit so that potential entry may hold profits of existing firms to low levels—zero in the case of perfect contestability.

would just cover their total costs. They know that if they charge higher prices, firms will enter to capture the profits while they last and then exit.

Contestability, where it is possible, is a force that can limit the profits of existing oligopolists. Even if entry does not occur, the ease with which it can be accomplished may keep existing oligopolists from charging prices that would maximize their joint profits.

Contestability is just another example, in somewhat more refined form, of the key point that the possibility of entry is the major force preventing the exploitation of market power to restrict output and to raise prices. But, in practice, the degree of contestability is something to be measured rather than simply asserted. The higher the sunk costs of entry, the less contestable the market, and the higher the profits that existing firms can earn without attracting entry. Current evidence suggests that a high degree of contestability is quite rare in practice.

Oligopoly and the Economy

Oligopoly is found in many industries and in all advanced economies. It typically occurs in industries where both perfect and monopolistic competition are made impossible by the existence of major economies of scale. In such industries, there is simply not enough room for a large number of firms all operating at or near their minimum efficient scales.

Three questions are important for the evaluation of oligopoly. First, do oligopolistic firms respond to changes in market conditions very differently from the way perfectly competitive firms do? Second, in their short-run and long-run price-output behaviour, where do oligopolistic firms typically settle between the extreme outcomes of earning zero profits and earning the profits that would be available to a monopolist? Third, how much do oligopolists contribute to economic growth by encouraging innovative activity in the very long run? We consider each of these questions in turn.

Market Adjustment Under Oligopoly

We have seen that under perfect competition, prices are set by the impersonal forces of demand and supply, whereas firms in oligopolistic markets administer their prices. The market signaling system works slightly differently when prices are administered rather than being determined by the market. Changes in market conditions are signaled to the perfectly competitive firm by changes in the price of its product. Changes in market conditions for the oligopolist, however, are typically signaled by changes in the volume of sales at administered prices.

Increases in demand will cause the sales of oligopolistic firms to rise. Firms will then respond by increasing output, thereby increasing the quantities of society's resources that are allocated to producing that output. They will then decide whether or not to alter their administered prices.

The market system adjusts to changes in demands in roughly the same way under oligopoly as it does under perfect competition.

Profits Under Oligopoly

Some firms in some oligopolistic industries succeed in coming close to joint profit maximization in the short run. In other oligopolistic industries, firms compete so intensely among themselves that they come close to achieving competitive prices and outputs.

In the long run, those profits that do survive competitive behaviour among existing firms will tend to attract entry. These profits will persist only insofar as entry is restricted either by natural barriers, such as large minimum efficient scales for potential entrants, or by barriers created, and successfully defended, by the existing firms.

Very-Long-Run Competition

Once we allow for the effects of technological change, we need to ask which market structure is most conducive to the sorts of very-long-run changes that we discussed in Chapter 8. These are the driving force of the economic growth that has so greatly raised living standards over the past two centuries. They are intimately related to Schumpeter's concept of creative destruction, which we first encountered in our discussion of entry barriers in Chapter 10.

As we saw in Chapter 10, examples of creative destruction abound. In the nineteenth century, railways began to compete with wagons and barges for the carriage of freight. In the twentieth century, trucks operating on newly constructed highways began competing with trains. During the 1950s and 1960s, airplanes began to compete seriously with both trucks and trains. In recent years, fax machines and e-mail have eliminated the monopoly of the postal service in delivering hard-copy (printed) communications.

An important defence of oligopoly relates to this process of creative destruction. Some economists have adopted Schumpeter's concept of creative destruction to develop theories in which intermediate market structures, such as oligopoly, lead to more innovation than would occur in either perfect competition or monopoly. They argue that the oligopolist faces strong competition from existing rivals and cannot afford the more relaxed life of the monopolist. At the same time, however, oligopolistic firms expect to keep a good share of the profits that they earn from their innovative activity and thus have considerable incentive to innovate.

Everyday observation provides support for this view. Leading North American firms that operate in highly concentrated industries, such as Abitibi-Consolidated, Du Pont, Kodak, General Electric, Newbridge, Nortel, and Xerox, have been highly innovative over many years.

This observation is not meant to suggest that *only* oligopolistic industries are innovative. Much innovation is also done by very small new firms; and if today's new firms are successful in their innovation, they may become tomorrow's corporate giants. For example, Hewlett-Packard, Microsoft, and Intel, which are enormous firms today, barely existed two decades ago; their rise from new start-up firms to corporate giants reflects their powers of innovation.

Oligopoly is an important market structure in modern economies because there are many industries in which the minimum efficient scale is simply too large to support many competing firms. The challenge to public policy is to keep oligopolists competing, rather than colluding, and using their competitive energies to improve products and to reduce costs, rather than merely to erect entry barriers.

S U M M A R Y

The Structure of the Canadian Economy

- Most industries in the Canadian economy lie between the two extremes of monopoly and perfect competition. Within this spectrum of market structure we can divide Canadian industries into two broad groups—those with a large number of relatively small firms and those with a small number of relatively large firms. Such intermediate market structures are called imperfectly competitive.
- When measuring whether an industry has power concentrated in the hands of only a few firms or dispersed over many, it is not sufficient to count the number of firms. Instead, economists consider the concentration ratio, which shows the fraction of total market sales controlled by the largest group of sellers.
- One important problem associated with using concentration ratios is to define the market with reasonable accuracy. Since many goods produced in Canada compete with foreign-produced goods, the national concentration ratios overstate the degree of industrial concentration.

Imperfectly Competitive Market Structures

- Most firms operating in imperfectly competitive market structures sell differentiated products whose characteristics they choose themselves. They also administer their prices, do not change their prices as often as prices change in perfectly competitive markets, engage in non-price competition, and sometimes take actions designed to prevent the entry of new firms.

Monopolistic Competition

- Monopolistic competition is a market structure that has the same characteristics as perfect competition except that the many firms each sell a differentiated product rather than all selling a single homogeneous product. Firms face negatively sloped demand curves and may earn profits in the short run.
- As in a perfectly competitive industry, the long run in monopolistic competition sees new firms enter the industry whenever profits can be made. Long-run equilibrium in the industry requires that each firm earn zero profits. But unlike perfect competition, the long-run equilibrium in monopolistic competition has each firm producing less than its minimum-cost level of output. This is the excess-capacity theorem associated with monopolistic competition.
- Excess capacity in the long-run equilibrium of monopolistic competition does not necessarily result in inefficiency. Even though each firm produces at a cost that is higher than the minimum attainable cost, the resulting product choice is valued by consumers and so may be worth the extra cost.

Oligopoly

- Oligopolies are dominated by a few large firms that usually sell differentiated products and have significant market power. They can maximize their joint profits if they cooperate to produce the monopoly output. By acting individually, each firm has an incentive to depart from this cooperative outcome.
- Strategic behaviour, in which each firm chooses its best strategy in light of other firms' possible decisions, may lead to a Nash equilibrium. Economists use game theory to study strategic behaviour.
- Tacit cooperation is possible but often breaks down as firms struggle for market share, indulge in non-price competition, and seek advantages through the introduction of new technology.
- Oligopolistic industries will exhibit profits in the long run only if there are significant barriers to entry. Natural barriers relate to the economies of scale in production, finance and marketing, and also to large entry costs. Firm-created barriers can be created by proliferation of competing brands, heavy brand-image advertising, and the threat of predatory pricing when new entry occurs.

- The theory of contestable markets holds that *potential* entry may be sufficient to hold profits down and emphasizes the importance of sunk costs as an entry barrier.
- In the presence of major scale economies, oligopoly may be the best of the feasible alternative market structures.

Evaluation of oligopoly depends on how much interfirm competition (a) drives the firms away from the cooperative, profit-maximizing solution and (b) leads to innovations in the very long run.

KEY CONCEPTS

Concentration ratios
Administered prices
Product differentiation
Monopolistic competition
The excess-capacity theorem

Oligopoly
Strategic behaviour
Cooperative and noncooperative outcomes
Game theory
Nash equilibrium

Explicit and tacit collusion
Natural and firm-created entry barriers
Contestable markets
Sunk costs of entry
The social benefits of oligopoly in the very long run

STUDY EXERCISES

1. The following table provides annual sales for the four largest firms in four hypothetical industries in Canada. Also provided are total Canadian and total world sales for the industry. (All figures are in millions of dollars.)

	Firm 1	Firm 2	Firm 3	Firm 4	Total Sales —Canada	Total Sales —World
Forestry products	185	167	98	47	550	1368
Chemicals	27	24	9	4	172	2452
Women's clothing	6	5	4	2	94	3688
Pharmaceuticals	44	37	22	19	297	2135

   a. Suppose that Canada does not trade internationally any of the goods produced in these industries. Compute the 4-firm Canadian concentration ratio for each industry.

   b. Rank the industries in order from the most concentrated to the least concentrated.

   c. Now suppose that goods in these industries are freely traded around the world. Compute a new concentration ratio for each industry based on world sales.

2. The following figure shows the revenue and cost curves for a typical monopolistically competitive firm in the short run.

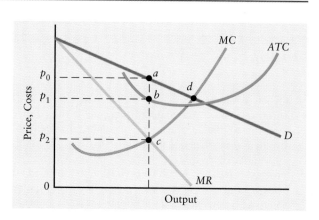

a. Note that the firm's demand curve is shown to be quite flat. Explain which assumption of monopolistic competition suggests a relatively elastic demand curve for each firm.

b. What is the profit-maximizing level of output for the firm?

c. At the profit-maximizing level of output, are profits positive or negative? What area in the diagram represents the firm's profits?

d. Will firms enter or exit the industry? Explain.

3. The diagram below shows a typical monopolistically competitive firm when the industry is in long-run equilibrium.

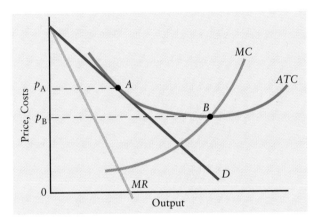

a. Explain why free entry and exit implies that the long-run equilibrium is at point A.

b. What is the significance of point B and price p_B?

c. Explain the sense in which long-run equilibrium in monopolistic competition is less efficient than in perfect competition.

4. In the text we argued that a key difference between monopolistic competition and oligopoly is that in the former firms do not behave *strategically* whereas in the latter they do. For each of the goods or services listed below, state whether the industries are likely to be best described by monopolistic competition or oligopoly. Explain your reasoning.

a. Car repair
b. Haircuts
c. Dry cleaning
d. Soft drinks
e. Breakfast cereals
f. Restaurant meals

5. The table below is the "payoff matrix" for a simple two-firm game. Firms A and B are bidding on a government contract, and each firm's bid is not known by the other firm. Each firm can bid either $10 000 or $5000. The cost of completing the project for each firm is $4000. The low-bid firm will win the contract at its stated price; the high-bid firm will get nothing. If the two bids are equal, the two firms will split the price and costs evenly. The payoffs for each firm under each situation are shown in the matrix.

	A bids $10 000	A bids $5000
B bids $10 000	Firms share the contract	A wins the contract
	Payoff to A = $3000	Payoff to A = $1000
	Payoff to B = $3000	Payoff to B = $0
B bids $5000	B wins the contract	Firms share the contract
	Payoff to A = $0	Payoff to A = $500
	Payoff to B = $1000	Payoff to B = $500

a. Recall from the text that a Nash equilibrium is an outcome in which each player is maximizing their own payoff *given the actions of the other players*. Is there a Nash equilibrium in this game?

b. Is there more than one Nash equilibrium? Explain.

c. If the two firms could cooperate, what outcome would you predict in this game? Explain.

DISCUSSION QUESTIONS

1. It is sometimes said that there are more drugstores and gasoline stations than are needed. In what sense might this be correct? Does the consumer gain anything from this plethora of retail outlets?

2. Do you think any of the following industries might be monopolistically competitive? Why or why not?

a. Textbook publishing (more than 12 elementary economics textbooks are in use on campuses in Canada this year)

b. Postsecondary education

c. Cigarette manufacturing

d. Restaurant operation

e. Automobile retailing

3. "The periods following each of the major OPEC price shocks proved to the world that there were many available substitutes for gasoline, among them bicycles, car pools, moving closer to work, cable TV, and Japanese cars." Discuss how each of these may be a substitute for gasoline.

4. Evidence suggests that the profits earned by all the firms in many oligopolistic industries are less than the profits that would be earned if the industry were monopolized. What are some reasons why this might be so?

5. What is the key difference between monopolistic competition and oligopoly? Assume that you are in an industry that is monopolistically competitive. What actual steps might you take to transform your industry into a more oligopolistic form?

6. Explain why an unregulated taxi industry is likely to be more contestable than an unregulated restaurant industry. What is the implication for prices and profits in the two industries?

CHAPTER 12

Economic Efficiency and Public Policy

LEARNING OBJECTIVES

❶ Explain the difference between productive and allocative efficiency.

❷ Understand why perfect competition is allocatively efficient, whereas monopoly is allocatively inefficient.

❸ Understand the alternative methods of regulating a natural monopoly.

❹ Gain a basic knowledge of Canadian competition policy.

Monopoly has long been regarded with suspicion. In *The Wealth of Nations,* Adam Smith (1723–1790) developed a stinging attack on monopolists. Since then, most economists have criticized monopoly and advocated competition.

In this chapter, we first consider what economic theory has to say about the relevant advantages of the two polar market structures of monopoly and perfect competition. This discussion requires an understanding of *economic efficiency*. We then examine how economic regulations and competition policy are designed to promote economic efficiency.

Economic Efficiency

Economic efficiency requires that resources not be wasted. This requires that workers, machines, and land are not lying idle. In other words, economic efficiency requires that factors of production are fully employed. However, full employment of resources is not enough to prevent the waste of resources. Even when resources are fully employed, they may be used inefficiently. Here are three examples of inefficiency in the use of fully employed resources.

1. If firms do not use the least-cost method of producing their chosen outputs, they are being inefficient. For example, a firm that produces 30 000 pairs of shoes at a resource cost of $400 000 when it could have been done at a cost of only $350 000 is using resources inefficiently. The lower-cost method would allow $50 000 worth of resources to be transferred to other productive uses.

2. If the marginal cost of production is not the same for every firm in an industry, the industry is being inefficient. For example, if the cost of producing the last ton of steel is higher for some firms than for others, the industry's overall cost of producing steel is

higher than necessary. The same amount of steel could be produced at lower total cost if the total output were distributed differently among the various producers.

3. If too much of one product and too little of another product are produced, resources are being used inefficiently. To take an extreme example, suppose that so many shoes are produced that every consumer has all the shoes he or she could possibly want and thus places a zero value on obtaining an additional pair of shoes. Further suppose that fewer coats are produced relative to demand, so that each consumer places a positive value on obtaining an additional coat. In these circumstances, each consumer can be made better off if resources are reallocated from shoe production, where the last shoe produced has a low value in the eyes of each consumer, to coat production, where one more coat produced would have a higher value to each consumer.

These three examples illustrate inefficiency in the use of resources. But the *type* of inefficiency is different in each case. The first example considers the cost for a single firm producing some level of output. The second example is closely related, but the focus is on the total cost for all of the firms in an industry. The third example relates to the level of output of one product compared to another.

Productive and Allocative Efficiency

These examples suggest that we must refine our ideas about the waste of resources beyond the simple notion of ensuring that all resources are employed.

Productive Efficiency

Productive efficiency has two aspects, one concerning production within each firm and one concerning the allocation of production among the firms in an industry.

productive efficiency for the firm When the firm chooses among all available technologies and produces a given level of output at the lowest possible cost.

Productive efficiency for the firm requires that the firm produce any given level of output at the lowest possible cost. In the short run, with only one variable factor, the choice of technique is not a problem for the firm. It merely uses enough of the variable factor to produce the desired level of output. In the long run, however, more than one method of production is available. Productive efficiency requires that the firm use the least costly of the available methods of producing any given output—that is, firms are located on, rather than above, their long-run average cost curves.

In Chapter 8, we studied the condition for productive efficiency within the firm:

Productive efficiency for the firm requires the firm to produce its given output by combining factors of production so that the ratios of the marginal products of each pair of factors equals the ratio of their prices.

If this were not so, the firm could reduce the resource costs of producing its given output by altering the quantities of each input it uses.

Any firm that is not being productively efficient is producing at a higher cost than is necessary and thus will have lower profits. It follows that any profit-maximizing firm will seek to be productively efficient no matter which market structure it operates within—perfect competition, monopoly, oligopoly, or monopolistic competition.

productive efficiency for the industry When the industry is producing a given level of output at the lowest possible cost. This requires that marginal cost be equated across all firms in the industry.

Productive efficiency for the industry requires that the industry's total output is allocated among its individual firms in such a way that the total cost is minimized. If an industry is productively *inefficient*, it is possible to reduce the industry's total cost of producing any given output by reallocating production among the industry's firms.

Productive efficiency at the level of the industry requires that the marginal cost of production must be the same for each firm.

To see why marginal costs must be equated across firms, consider a simple example that is illustrated in Figure 12-1. Aslan Shoe Company has a marginal cost of $70 for the last shoe of some standard type it produces. Digory Shoes Inc. has a marginal cost of only $50 for the same type of shoe. If Aslan were to produce one fewer pair of shoes and Digory were to produce one more pair, total shoe production would be unchanged. Total industry costs, however, would be lower by $20.

Clearly, this cost saving can go on as long as the two firms have different marginal costs. However, as Aslan produces more shoes, its marginal cost rises, and as Digory produces fewer shoes, its marginal cost falls. Once marginal cost is equated across the two firms, there are no further cost savings to be obtained by reallocating production.

Figure 12-2 shows a production possibility curve of the sort that we first saw in Chapter 1. Productive *inefficiency* implies that the economy is at some point *inside* the production possibility curve. In such a situation, it is possible to produce more of some goods without producing less of others.

Productive efficiency implies being on, rather than inside, the economy's production possibility curve.

Allocative Efficiency

Allocative efficiency concerns the relative quantities of the products to be produced. It concerns the choice between alternative points on the production possibilities curve such as points *b, c,* and *d* in Figure 12-2. When the combination of goods produced is allocatively efficient, economists say that the economy is *Pareto efficient*, in honour of

allocative efficiency
A situation in which no reorganization of production or consumption could make anybody better off without making at least one person worse off.

FIGURE 12-1   Productive Efficiency for the Industry

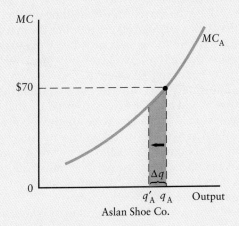
Aslan Shoe Co.

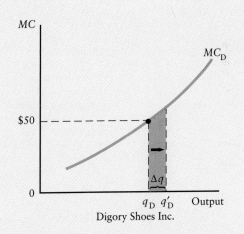
Digory Shoes Inc.

Productive efficiency for the industry requires that marginal costs be equated for all firms. At the initial levels of output, q_A and q_D, marginal costs are $70 for Aslan and $50 for Digory. If Digory increases output by Δq to q'_D and Aslan reduces output by the same amount, Δq, to q'_A, total output is unchanged. But total industry costs are lower by an amount equal to Aslan's shaded area minus Digory's shaded area. When marginal costs are equalized, no further reallocation of output can reduce costs—product efficiency will have been achieved.

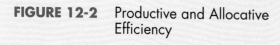

FIGURE 12-2   Productive and Allocative Efficiency

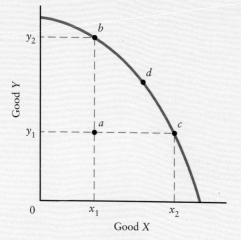

Any point on the production possibility curve is productively efficient; not all points on this curve are allocatively efficient. The curve shows all combinations of two goods X and Y that can be produced when the economy's resources are fully employed and being used with productive efficiency.

Any point inside the curve, such as *a*, is productively inefficient. If the inefficiency exists in industry X, then either some producer of X is productively inefficient or industry X as a whole is productively inefficient. In either case, it is possible to increase total production of X without using more resources, and thus without reducing the output of Y. This would take the economy from point *a* to point *c*. Similarly, if the inefficiency exists in industry Y, production of Y could be increased, moving the economy from point *a* to point *b*.

Allocative efficiency requires being at the most efficient point on the production possibility curve. Assessing allocative efficiency requires comparing various points on the curve, such as *b*, *c*, and *d*, and comparing marginal cost with price for each good. Allocative efficiency requires that *MC = p* for *each* good. Usually only one such point will be allocatively efficient (though all of them are productively efficient).

the nineteenth century Italian economist Vilfredo Pareto (1843–1923) who developed this concept of efficiency.

From an allocative point of view, resources are said to be used *inefficiently* when using them to produce a different bundle of goods makes it possible for at least one person to be better off while making no other person worse off. Conversely, resources are said to be used *efficiently* when it is impossible to produce a different bundle of goods that makes one person better off without making at least one other person worse off.

How do we find the efficient point on the production possibility curve? For example, how many shoes, dresses, and hats should be produced to achieve allocative efficiency? The answer is as follows:

The economy is allocatively efficient when, for each good produced, its marginal cost of production is equal to its price.

To understand the reasoning behind this answer, we need to recall a point that was established in our discussion of consumer surplus in Chapter 6. The price of any product indicates the value that consumers place on the last unit consumed of that product. Faced with the market price of some product, the consumer goes on buying units until the last one is valued exactly at its price. Consumer surplus arises because the consumer would be willing to pay more than the market price for all but the last unit that is bought. On the last unit bought (the marginal unit), however, the consumer only "breaks even" because the valuation placed on it is just equal to its price.

Now let us return to our shoe example. Suppose that shoes sell for $60 per pair but the marginal cost is $70. If one fewer pair of shoes were produced, the value that all households would place on the pair of shoes not produced would be $60. Using the concept of opportunity cost, however, we see that the resources that would have been used to produce that last pair of shoes could instead produce another good (say, a coat) valued at $70. If society can give up something that its members value at $60 and get in return something that its members value at $70, the original allocation of resources is inefficient. Someone can be made better off, and no one need be worse off.

This is easy to understand when the same consumer gives up the shoes and gets the coat, but the concept applies even when different consumers are involved. In this case, the market value of the gains to the household that gets the coat exceeds the market value of the loss to the household that gives up the shoes. The gaining household *could afford* to compensate the losing household and still come out ahead.

Suppose next that shoe production is cut back until the price of a pair of shoes rises from $60 to $65, while its marginal cost falls from $70 to $65. Efficiency is achieved in shoe production because $p = MC = \$65$. Now if one fewer pair of shoes were produced, $65 worth of shoes would be sacrificed, while at most, $65 worth of other products could be produced with the freed resources.

In this situation, it is not possible to change the allocation of resources to shoe production to make someone better off without making someone else worse off. If one household were to sacrifice one pair of shoes, it would give up goods worth $65 and would then have to obtain for itself all of the new production of the alternative commodity produced just to break even. It cannot gain without making another household worse off. The same argument can be repeated for every product, and it leads to the following conclusion:

The allocation of resources is efficient when each product's price equals its marginal cost of production.

There is one final point to make about allocative efficiency. Whereas an individual firm or an individual industry may be *productively efficient,* it does not make sense to say that a given firm or industry is *allocatively efficient.* Allocative efficiency is a property of the overall economy, concerning the relative outputs of its various industries, and it is achieved when price equals marginal cost in *all* industries simultaneously. Thus, if we were to observe price greater than marginal cost in an individual industry, we would know that the economy is not allocatively efficient because society as a whole would be made better off by producing more of that good and less of other goods. But if we were to see price equal to marginal cost in that one industry, we must still check *all* other industries before we know whether the economy is allocatively efficient.

Efficiency and Market Structure

We now know that for productive efficiency, marginal cost should be the same for all firms in any one industry, and that for allocative efficiency, marginal cost should be equal to price in each industry. Do the market structures that we have studied in earlier chapters lead to productive and allocative efficiency?

Perfect Competition

Productive Efficiency.   We saw in Chapter 9 that in the long run under perfect competition, each firm produces at the lowest point on its long-run average cost curve. Therefore, no one firm could reduce its costs by altering its own production. Every firm in perfect competition is therefore productively efficient.

We also know that in perfect competition, all firms in an industry face the same price of their product and they equate marginal cost to that price. It follows immediately that marginal cost will be the same for all firms. (Suppose, for example, that Aslan and Digory faced the same market price in Figure 12-1. Aslan would produce where $MC_A=p$ and Digory would produce where $MC_D=p$. It follows then that $MC_A=MC_D$.) Thus, in perfectly competitive industries, the industry as a whole is productively efficient.

Allocative Efficiency.   We have already seen that perfectly competitive firms maximize their profits by equating marginal cost to price. Thus, when perfect competition is the market structure for the whole economy, price is equal to marginal cost in each line of production, resulting in allocative efficiency.

Monopoly

Productive Efficiency.   Monopolists have an incentive to be productively efficient because their profits will be maximized when they adopt the lowest-cost production method. Hence, profit-maximizing monopolists will operate on their *LRAC* curves.

Allocative Efficiency.   Although a monopolist will be productively efficient, it will choose a level of output that is too low to achieve allocative efficiency. This result follows from what we saw in Chapter 10—that the monopolist chooses an output at which the price charged is *greater than* marginal cost. Such a choice violates the conditions for allocative efficiency because the amount that consumers pay for the last unit of output exceeds the opportunity cost of producing it.

Consumers would be prepared to buy additional units for an amount that is greater than the cost of producing these units. Some consumers could be made better off, and none need be made worse off, by shifting extra resources into production of the monopolized product, thus increasing the output of the product. From this follows the classic efficiency-based preference for competition over monopoly:

Monopoly creates allocative inefficiency because the monopolist's price always exceeds its marginal cost.

This result has important policy implications for economists and for policymakers, as we shall see later in this chapter.

Other Market Structures

Note that the result just stated extends beyond the case of a simple monopoly. Whenever a firm has any market power, in the sense that it faces a negatively sloped demand curve, its marginal revenue will be less than its price. Thus, when it equates marginal cost to marginal revenue, as all profit-maximizing firms do, marginal cost will also be less than price. This inequality implies allocative inefficiency. Thus, oligopoly and monopolistic competition are also allocatively inefficient.

Oligopoly is an important market structure in today's economy because in many industries the minimum efficient scale is simply too high to support a large number of competing firms. Although oligopoly does not achieve the conditions for allocative efficiency, it may nevertheless produce more satisfactory results than monopoly. We observed one reason why oligopoly may be preferable to monopoly in Chapter 11: Competition among oligopolists encourages very-long-run adaptations that result in both new products and cost-reducing methods of producing old ones.

An important defence of oligopoly as an acceptable market structure is that it may be the best of the available alternatives when minimum efficient scale is large. As we observed at the end of Chapter 11, the challenge to public policy is to keep oligopolists competing and using their competitive energies to improve products and to reduce costs rather than to restrict interfirm competition and to erect entry barriers. As we shall see later in this chapter, much public policy has just this purpose. What economic policymakers call *monopolistic practices* include not only output restrictions operated by firms with complete monopoly power but also anticompetitive behaviour among firms that are operating in oligopolistic industries.

Allocative Efficiency and Total Surplus

By using the concepts of price and marginal cost, we have established the basic points of productive and allocative efficiency. A different way of thinking about allocative efficiency—though completely consistent with the first approach—is to use the concepts of consumer and producer surplus.

Consumer and Producer Surplus

Recall from Chapter 6 that consumer surplus is the difference between the total value that consumers place on all the units consumed of some product and the payment that they actually make for the purchase of that product. Consumer surplus is shown once again in Figure 12-3.

    Producer surplus is analogous to consumer surplus. It occurs because all units of each firm's output are sold at the same market price whereas, given an upward-sloping MC curve, each unit except the last is produced at a marginal cost that is less than the market price.

    Producer surplus is defined as the price that producers receive for a product minus the lowest price that they would be prepared to accept for it (which is equal to the marginal cost). It is thus the difference between price and marginal cost. Since in perfect competition the industry supply curve is simply the horizontal sum of all firms' MC curves, producer surplus in a perfectly competitive market is the area above the supply curve and below the price line, as shown in Figure 12-3.

producer surplus
The difference between the amount that producers receive for a unit sold of a commodity and the marginal cost of producing that unit.

The Allocative Efficiency of Perfect Competition Revisited

Using the concepts of consumer and producer surplus, we can restate the condition for allocative efficiency.

Allocative efficiency occurs where the sum of consumer and producer surplus is maximized.

    The allocatively efficient output occurs under perfect competition where the demand curve intersects the supply curve—that is, the point of equilibrium in a competitive market. This is shown in Figure 12-4. For any output that is less than the competitive output, the demand curve lies above the supply curve; thus the value that consumers place on the last unit of production exceeds its marginal cost of production. Suppose that the current output of shoes is such that consumers value at $70 an additional pair of shoes that adds $60 to costs. If it is sold at any price between $60 and $70, both producers and consumers gain; $10 of surplus will be divided between the two groups. In contrast, the last unit produced and sold in a competitive equilibrium adds nothing to either

FIGURE 12-3   Consumer Surplus and Producer Surplus

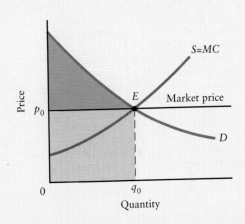

Consumer surplus is the area under the demand curve and above the market price line. Producer surplus is the area above the supply curve and below the market price line. The total value that consumers place on q_0 of the commodity is given by the sum of the three shaded areas. The amount they pay is the rectangle $p_0 q_0$. The difference, shown as the dark blue shaded area is consumer surplus.

    The receipts to producers from the sale of q_0 units are also $p_0 q_0$. The area under the supply curve, the red shaded area, is the minimum amount producers require to supply the output. The difference, shown as the light blue shaded area, is producer surplus.

FIGURE 12-4   The Allocative Efficiency of Perfect Competition

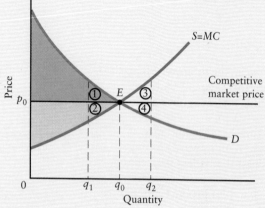

Competitive equilibrium is allocatively efficient because it maximizes the sum of consumer and producer surplus. The competitive equilibrium occurs at the price-output combination of p_0 and q_0. At this equilibrium, consumer surplus is the dark shaded area above the price line, while producer surplus is the light shaded area below the price line.

For any output that is less than q_0, the sum of the two surpluses is less than at q_0. For example, reducing the output to q_1 but keeping price at p_0 lowers consumer surplus by area 1 and lowers producer surplus by area 2.

For any output that is greater than q_0, the sum of the surpluses is also less than at q_0. For example, if producers are forced to produce output q_2 and to sell it to consumers, who are in turn forced to buy it at price p_0, producer surplus is reduced by area 3 while the amount of consumer surplus is reduced by area 4.

Practise with Study Guide Chapter 12, Exercise 4.

consumer or producer surplus because consumers value it at exactly its market price, and it adds the full amount of the market price to producers' costs.

If production were pushed beyond the competitive equilibrium, the sum of the two surpluses would fall. Suppose, for example, that firms were forced to produce and sell further units of output at the competitive market price and that consumers were forced to buy these extra units at that price. (Note that neither group would do so voluntarily.) Firms would lose producer surplus on those extra units because their marginal costs of producing the extra output would be above the price that they received for it. Purchasers would lose consumer surplus because the valuation that they placed on these extra units, as shown by the height of the demand curve, would be less than the price that they would have to pay.

The sum of producer and consumer surplus is maximized only at the perfectly competitive level of output. This is the only level of output that is allocatively efficient.

The Allocative Inefficiency of Monopoly Revisited

We have just seen in Figure 12-4 that the output in perfectly competitive equilibrium maximizes the sum of consumer and producer surplus. It follows that the lower monopoly output must result in a smaller total of consumer and producer surplus.

The monopoly equilibrium is not the outcome of a voluntary agreement between the one producer and the many consumers. Instead, it is imposed by the monopolist by virtue of the power it has over the market. When the monopolist chooses an output below the competitive level, market price is higher than it would be under perfect competition. As a result, consumer surplus is diminished, and producer surplus is increased. In this way, the monopolist gains at the expense of consumers. This is not the whole story, however.

When output is below the competitive level, there is always a *net loss* of total surplus: More surplus is lost by consumers than is gained by the monopolist. Some surplus is lost because output between the monopolistic and the competitive levels is not produced. This loss of surplus is called the *deadweight loss of monopoly*. It is illustrated in Figure 12-5.

It follows that there is a conflict between the private interest of the monopolist and the public interest of all the nation's consumers. This creates grounds for government intervention to prevent the formation of monopolies or at least to control their behaviour.

Allocative Efficiency and Market Failure

We have seen that perfect competition is allocatively efficient and that monopoly, in general, is not. Most of the remainder of the chapter presents ways in which public policy has attempted to deal with problems raised by monopoly. Before we go on, however, it is important to reemphasize that perfect competition is a theoretical ideal that exists in a small number of industries, is at best only approximated in many others, and is not even closely resembled in most. Hence, to say that perfect competition is allocatively efficient is not to say that real-world market economies are ever allocatively efficient.

In Chapter 16, we discuss the most important ways (other than monopoly) that market economies may fail to produce efficient outcomes. In Chapters 17 and 18, we discuss and evaluate the most important public policies that have been used to try to correct for these *market failures*. The most important problems arise when market transactions—production and consumption—impose costs or confer benefits on economic agents who are not involved in the transaction. Cases like these, which are called *externalities* because they involve economic effects that are external to the transaction, generally raise the possibility that market outcomes will be allocatively inefficient.

A simple example illustrates the problem. We know that markets for most agricultural commodities are highly competitive, with many relatively small producers who are unable to affect the price of the goods that they are producing. At the same time, the technology of agricultural production involves the extensive use of fertilizers that pollute nearby streams and rivers. This pollution in turn imposes costs on downstream fisheries and on households downstream who use the water for drinking and cleaning. Because these costs are not taken into account in the market for the agricultural products, they will be external to transactions in those markets. Generally, when production of a good or service causes pollution, the quantity produced in a perfectly competitive industry will exceed the efficient amount.

One of the most important issues in public policy is whether, and under what circumstances, government action can increase the allocative efficiency of market outcomes.

As we will see later in this book, there are many circumstances in which there is room to increase the efficiency of market outcomes, but there are also many cases in which the cure is worse than the disease. In the remainder of this chapter we examine economic regulation and competition policy, both of which are designed to promote economic efficiency.

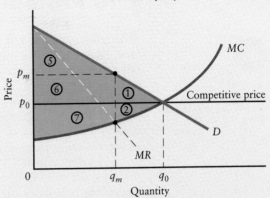

FIGURE 12-5   The Allocative Inefficiency of Monopoly

Monopoly is allocatively inefficient because it produces less than the competitive output and thus does not maximize the sum of consumer and producer surplus. If this market were perfectly competitive, price would be p_0, output would be q_0, and consumer surplus would be the sum of areas 1, 5, and 6. When the industry is monopolized, price rises to p_m and consumer surplus falls to area 5. Consumers lose area 1 because that output is not produced; they lose area 6 because the price rise has transferred it to the monopolist.

Producer surplus in a competitive equilibrium would be the sum of areas 7 and 2. When the market is monopolized and price rises to p_m, the surplus area 2 is lost because the output is not produced. However, the monopolist gains area 6 from consumers (6 is known to be greater than 2 because p_m maximizes profits).

Whereas area 6 is surplus that is transferred from consumers to producers by the price rise, areas 1 and 2 are lost altogether. They represent the deadweight loss resulting from monopoly and account for its allocative inefficiency.

Economic Regulation to Promote Efficiency

To learn about the Canadian Radio-television and Telecommunications Commission (CRTC), see their website: www.crtc.gc.ca.

Monopolies, cartels, and price-fixing agreements among oligopolists, whether explicit or tacit, have met with public suspicion and official hostility for over a century. These and other noncompetitive practices are collectively referred to as *monopoly practices*. The laws and other instruments that are used to encourage competition and discourage monopoly practices make up *competition policy*. By and large, Canadian competition policy has sought to create more competitive market structures where possible, to discourage monopolistic practices, and to encourage competitive behaviour where competitive market structures cannot be established.

Federal, provincial, and local governments also employ *economic regulations,* which prescribe the rules under which firms can do business and in some cases determine the prices that businesses can charge for their output. Electric power, local telephone, and cable TV are examples of services that are subject to this kind of regulation.

The quest for allocative efficiency provides rationales both for competition policy and for economic regulation. Competition policy is used to promote allocative efficiency by increasing competition in the marketplace. Where effective competition is not possible (as in the case of a natural monopoly, such as an electric power company), public ownership or economic regulation of privately owned firms can be used as a substitute for competition. Consumers can then be protected from the high prices and reduced output that result from the use of monopoly power.[1]

In the remainder of this chapter, we look at a variety of ways in which policy-makers have chosen to intervene in the workings of the market economy using economic regulation and competition policy.

Regulation of Natural Monopolies

natural monopoly
An industry characterized by economies of scale sufficiently large that one firm can most efficiently supply the entire market demand.

The clearest case for public intervention arises with what is called a **natural monopoly**—an industry in which scale effects are so dominant that there is room for *at most* one firm to operate at the minimum efficient scale. (Indeed, scale effects could be so important that even a single firm could satisfy the entire market demand before reaching its minimum efficient scale.) In the past, there have been many natural monopolies. Today, they are found mainly in public utilities, such as electricity transmission, cable television, and local telephone service.

crown corporations
In Canada, business concerns owned by the federal or a provincial government.

One response to natural monopoly is for government to assume ownership of the single firm. In Canada, such government-owned firms are called **crown corporations.** In these cases, the government appoints managers and directors who are supposed to set prices in the national interest. Another response to the problem of natural monopoly is to allow private ownership but to *regulate* the monopolist's behaviour. In Canada, both government ownership (e.g., Canada Post and the provincial hydro authorities) and regulation (e.g., cable television and local telephone) are used actively. In the United States, with a few notable exceptions, regulation has been the preferred alternative.

Whether the government owns or merely regulates natural monopolies, the industry's pricing policy is determined by the government. The industry is typically required to fol-

---

[1]A second kind of regulation involves the legislated rules that require firms to consider the environmental and other consequences of their behaviour. Environmental regulation is discussed in Chapter 17.

low some pricing policy that conflicts with the goal of profit max-imization. We will see that such government intervention must deal with problems that arise in the short run, the long run, and the very long run.

Short-Run Price and Output

There are three general types of pricing policies for regulated nat-ural monopolies: *marginal-cost pricing, two-part tariffs,* and *av-erage-cost pricing.* We discuss each in turn.

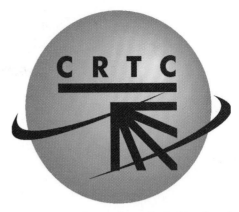

The CRTC regulates radio and television broad-casting as well as telecommunications rates and licensing.

Marginal-Cost Pricing.   Sometimes the government dictates that the natural monopoly sets prices equal to short-run marginal cost. In principle, this policy, called **marginal-cost pricing,** induces the allocatively efficient level of output. This is not, however, the profit-maximizing output, which is where marginal cost equals marginal revenue. Thus, marginal-cost pricing sets up a tension between the regulator's desire to achieve the allocatively efficient level of output and the monopolist's desire to maximize profits.

Marginal-cost pricing creates different problems in each of two cases. In the first case, when producing the allocatively efficient level of output, the natural monopoly is operating on the downward-sloping portion of its *ATC* curve. In this case, marginal cost will be less than average total cost. It follows that when price is set equal to marginal cost, price will be less than average cost, and marginal-cost pricing will lead to losses. This result is shown in part (i) of Figure 12-6.

In the second case, demand is sufficient to allow the firm to produce a level of out-put beyond its minimum efficient scale and thus to operate on the upward-sloping por-tion of its *ATC* curve. At any such level of output, marginal cost exceeds average total cost. If the firm is required to equate price with marginal cost, it is clear that price will be above average total cost. Marginal-cost pricing will therefore lead the firm to earn pos-itive profits. This result is shown in part (ii) of the figure.

When a natural monopoly with falling average costs sets price equal to marginal cost, it will suffer losses. When a natural monopoly with rising average costs sets price equal to marginal cost, it will earn positive profits.

marginal-cost pricing
Setting price equal to marginal cost so that buyers for the last unit are just willing to pay the amount that it cost to make that unit.

Two-Part Tariff.   Though marginal-cost pricing achieves allocative efficiency, a natural monopoly with declining average costs cannot be expected to incur losses indefinitely. One way of trying to cover total costs in this case is to allow the firm to charge a **two-part tariff** in which customers pay one price to gain access to the product and a second price for each unit consumed. Consider the case of a regulated cable TV company. In principle, the hook-up fee covers fixed costs, and then each unit of output can be priced at marginal cost. Indeed, most new subscribers to cable TV are surprised at how high the hook-up fee is—clearly much higher than the cost of the cable guy's half-hour to complete the job! Yet, if this fee also includes that household's share of the firm's fixed costs (spread over many thousands of households), then the large hook-up fee is more understandable.

two-part tariff
A method of charging for a good or a service in which the consumer pays a flat access fee and a specified amount per unit purchased.

Average-Cost Pricing.   Another method of regulating a natural monopoly is to set prices just high enough to cover total costs, thus generating neither profits nor losses. The firm produces to the point where average revenue equals average total cost, which is where the demand curve cuts the *ATC* curve. Part (i) of Figure 12-6 shows that for a firm with declining average costs, this pricing policy requires producing at less than the

FIGURE 12-6   Pricing Policies for Natural Monopolies

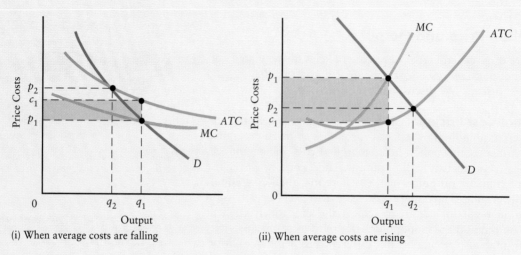

(i) When average costs are falling   (ii) When average costs are rising

Marginal-cost pricing leads to profits or losses, whereas average-cost pricing violates the efficiency condition. In each part, the output at which marginal cost equals price is q_1 and price is p_1. In part (i), average costs are falling at output q_1, so marginal costs are less than the average cost c_1. There is an average loss of c_1-p_1 on each unit, making a total loss equal to the shaded area. In part (ii), average cost c_1 is less than price at output q_1. There is an average profit of p_1-c_1 on each unit sold, making a total profit equal to the shaded area.

In each part of the diagram, the output at which average cost equals price is q_2 and the associated price is p_2. In part (i), marginal cost is less than price at q_2, so output is below its allocatively efficient level. In part (ii), marginal cost exceeds price at q_2, so output is greater than its allocatively efficient level.

Practise with Study Guide Chapter 12, Exercise 3.

allocatively efficient output. The firm's financial losses that would occur under marginal-cost pricing are avoided by producing less output than what is socially optimal. Part (ii) shows that for a firm with rising average costs, the average-cost pricing policy requires producing at more than the allocatively efficient output. The profits that would occur under marginal-cost pricing are dissipated by producing more output than what is socially optimal.

Generally, average-cost pricing will not result in allocative efficiency because price will not equal marginal cost.

On what basis do we choose between marginal-cost pricing and average-cost pricing? Marginal-cost pricing generates allocative efficiency, but the firm may incur losses. In this case, the firm will eventually go out of business unless someone is prepared to cover the firm's costs. If the government is unwilling to do so, seeing no reason why taxpayers should subsidize the users of the product in question, then average-cost pricing is probably preferable. It provides the lowest price that can be charged and the largest output that can be produced, given the requirement that sales revenue must cover the total cost of producing the product.

Long-Run Investment

So far, we have examined the implications of different pricing policies in the short run. Recall that in the short run the level of the firm's capital is fixed. The allocatively efficient pricing policy sets price equal to short-run marginal cost. The position of the short-run marginal cost curve depends, however, on the amount of fixed capital that is currently available to be combined with the variable factors. What should determine the firm's long-run capital stock? In answering this question, we begin by assuming that the demand for the product is constant.

The efficient answer follows from comparing the current market price with the *long-run* marginal cost of producing the product. The current market price reflects the value consumers place on one additional unit of output. The long-run marginal cost reflects the full resource cost (including capital costs) of providing an extra unit of output. Thus, if the current price exceeds long-run marginal cost, then the natural monopoly should increase its capacity; if current price is less than long-run marginal cost, the natural monopoly should allow its capacity to decline as its capital wears out.

The previous paragraph assumed that demand was constant and so the *current* market price was relevant to the long-run investment decision. But what if demand is expected to increase in the future, and therefore consumers' marginal value of the product will rise? In this case, the appropriate comparison is between the future price and the long-run marginal cost, and so it may be efficient to increase capacity even if the current price is below the long-run marginal cost. Similarly, if demand is expected to fall in the future, then it may be efficient to decrease capacity even though the current price is above long-run marginal cost.

For given capacity in the short run, the allocatively efficient pricing system determines output by setting price equal to the short-run marginal cost of production. It also adjusts capacity in the long run until the long-run marginal cost of production is equal to the price.

Since marginal cost is generally different from average cost, average-cost pricing will generally lead to inefficient patterns of long-run investment. For example, consider a regulated utility that is operating on the downward-sloping portion of its *ATC* curve and is required to set price equal to average cost. Since price equals average cost, the firm will be just breaking even and thus it will have no incentive to increase its amount of fixed capital. Note, however, that the price in this case must exceed the short-run marginal cost (because marginal cost must be below average cost if average cost is falling). If the price also exceeds the long-run marginal cost, society would benefit by having a larger amount of fixed capital allocated to producing this good. But the regulated utility will not undertake this socially desirable investment.

Average-cost pricing generally leads to inefficient long-run investment decisions.

Very-Long-Run Innovation

Natural monopoly is a long-run concept—that is, given *existing technology,* there is room for only one firm to operate profitably. In the very long run, however, technology changes. Not only does today's competitive industry sometimes become tomorrow's natural monopoly, but today's natural monopoly often becomes tomorrow's competitive industry.

A striking example is found in the telecommunications industry. Thirty years ago, hard-copy message transmission was close to a natural monopoly belonging to the post office. Today, technological developments such as satellite transmission, electronic mail, fax machines, and the Internet have made this activity highly competitive.

Other examples of industries that used to be natural monopolies but are now much more competitive include airlines, long-distance telephone service, and the generation of electricity (the distribution of electricity continues to be a natural monopoly).

Practical Problems

Many practical problems arise with regulations designed to prevent natural monopolies from charging profit-maximizing prices. These problems begin with the fact that regulators do not have enough data to determine demand and cost curves precisely. In the absence of accurate data, regulators have tended to judge prices according to the level of the regulated firm's profits. Regulatory agencies tend to permit price increases only when profits fall below "fair" levels and require price reductions if profits exceed such levels. What started as price regulation becomes instead profit regulation, which is often called *rate-of-return regulation*. Concepts of marginal cost and economic efficiency are typically ignored in such regulatory decisions.

If average-cost regulation is successful, only a normal rate of return will be earned; that is, economic profits will be zero. Unfortunately, the reverse is not necessarily true. Profits can be zero for any of a number of reasons, including inefficient operation and misleading accounting. Thus, regulatory commissions that rely on rate of return as their guide to pricing must monitor a number of other aspects of the regulated firm's behaviour in order to limit the possibility of wasting resources. This monitoring itself requires a considerable expenditure of resources.

Regulation of Oligopolies

Governments have from time to time intervened in industries that were oligopolies (rather than natural monopolies), seeking to enforce the type of price and entry behaviour that was thought to be in the public interest. Such intervention has typically taken two distinct forms. In many European countries, it was primarily nationalization of whole oligopolistic industries such as railways, steel, and coal mining, which were then to be run by government-appointed boards. In the United States, firms such as airlines and railways were left in private hands, but their decisions were regulated by government-appointed bodies that set prices and regulated entry. As so often happens, Canada followed a mixture of British and American practices. Many Canadian crown corporations were set up, and many firms that remained in private hands were regulated. For example, in the regulated railway industry, Canadian Pacific was privately owned while Canadian National, until it was privatized in 1995, was a crown corporation.

Scepticism About Direct Control

Policymakers have become increasingly sceptical of their ability to improve the behaviour of oligopolistic industries by having governments control the details of their behaviour through either ownership or regulation. Three main experiences have been important in developing this scepticism.

Oligopolies and Economic Growth.   Oligopolistic market structures provided much of the economic growth in the twentieth century. New products and new ways of producing old products have followed each other in rapid succession, leading to higher living standards and higher productivity. Many of these innovations have been provided by firms in oligopolistic industries such as automobiles, agricultural implements, steel, petroleum refining, chemicals, electronics, computing, and telecommunications. As long as oligopolists continue to compete with each other, rather than cooperating to produce monopoly profits, most economists see no need to regulate such things as the prices at which oligopolists sell their products and the conditions of entry into oligopolistic industries.

Cross Subsidization.   Many regulatory bodies have imposed policies in which prices are not related to the cost of each of the services being priced. These prices involved what is called *cross subsidization*, whereby profits that are earned in the provision of one service are used to subsidize the provision of another service at a price below cost. For example, when they were in control, regulators typically required that long-distance telephone calls subsidize local calls, first-class mail subsidize third-class mail, and long-haul airline rates subsidize short-haul rates. These pricing policies forced users of the profitable service to subsidize users of the unprofitable service. But cross subsidization does not increase overall welfare. It reduces the sum of producer and consumer surplus because price exceeds marginal cost in some lines of output but is less than marginal cost in others.

Protection from Competition.   The record of postwar government intervention into regulated industries seemed poorer in practice than its supporters had predicted. Research by the University of Chicago Nobel Laureate George Stigler (1911–1991) and others established that in many industries, regulatory bodies were "captured" by the very firms that they were supposed to be regulating. As a result, the regulatory bodies that were meant to ensure competition often acted to enforce monopoly practices that would have been illegal if instituted by the firms themselves.

Airline regulation in Canada and the United States provides an obvious example. When airline routes and fares were first regulated, it was possible to argue that demand was too low to permit effective competition among many firms. Whatever the validity of that argument in earlier times, by the mid 1960s the regulation was plainly protecting the industry, allowing it to charge higher fares, earn higher profits, and pay higher wages than it would under more competitive conditions. For decades, Canadian and U.S. regulation of airline prices consistently prevented price competition. For example, until recently airlines other than Air Canada and Canadian Airlines were prevented from introducing cheap fares between Canada and Europe. This regulation could not be explained as protecting the interests of passengers against the predatory behaviour of the carriers.

Why did regulatory bodies shift from protecting consumers to protecting firms? One reason is that the regulatory commissions were gradually captured by the firms they were supposed to regulate. In part, this capture was natural enough. When regulatory bodies were hiring staff, they needed people who were knowledgeable in the industries they were regulating. Where better to go than to people who had worked in these industries? Naturally, these people tended to be sympathetic to firms in their own industries. Also, because many of them aspired to go back to those industries once they had gained experience within the regulatory bodies, they were not inclined to arouse the wrath of industry officials by imposing policies that were against the firms' interests.

Deregulation and Privatization

The 1980s witnessed the beginning of a movement in many advanced industrial nations to reduce the level of government control over industry. Various experiences in these countries have been pushing in this direction:

- The realization that regulatory bodies often sought to reduce, rather than increase, competition
- The dashing of the hopes that publicly owned industries would work better than privately owned firms in the areas of efficiency, productivity growth, and industrial relations

- The realization that replacing a private monopoly with a publicly owned one would not greatly change the industry's performance and that replacing privately owned oligopolists by a publicly owned monopoly might actually worsen the industry's performance
- The awareness that falling transportation costs and revolutions in data processing and communications exposed local industries to much more widespread international competition than they had previously experienced domestically

There were two natural outcomes from these revised views. The first was deregulation—intended to leave prices and entry free to be determined by private decisions. The second was privatization of publicly owned firms.

In the United States, where regulation rather than government ownership had been the adopted policy, many industries were deregulated. In Canada, hundreds of crown corporations that the government had acquired for a variety of reasons, but were neither natural monopolies nor operating in highly concentrated industries, were sold off. Many large crown corporations operating in oligopolistic industries, such as Air Canada, Petro Canada, and Canadian National, were privatized. Also, many industries, such as airlines and gas and oil, were deregulated. Prices were freed, to be set by the firms in the industries, and entry was no longer restricted by government policy.

Canadian Competition Policy

competition policy Policy designed to prohibit the acquisition and exercise of monopoly power by business firms.

The least stringent form of government intervention is designed neither to force firms to sell at particular prices nor to regulate the conditions of entry and exit; it is designed, instead, to create conditions of competition by preventing firms from merging unnecessarily or from engaging in anticompetitive practices such as colluding to set monopoly prices. This is referred to as **competition policy**.

combine laws Laws that prevent firms either from combining into one unit or from cooperating so as to behave monopolistically.

Laws designed for the purposes of preventing anticompetitive behaviour are called **combine laws** in Canada. They have provided the main thrust of Canadian competition policy since its inception in the nineteenth century. They prohibit monopolies, attempts to monopolize, and conspiracies in restraint of trade. Throughout the history of Canadian competition policy, legislation has been directed chiefly at the misuse of market power by single firms or groups of firms and only rarely at mergers per se.

This acceptance of the need for relatively large firms in the business sector was partly a function of the small size of the Canadian economy in the days when most production was solely for the domestic market. Firms that were large enough to exploit the available economies of scale were likely to be large in relation to the total market. This meant that there would be fewer firms in Canadian industries dominated by scale effects than would be found in similar industries in such relatively large economies as the United States.

See Chapter 12 of www.pearsoned.ca/lipsey for an excellent discussion of how economic theory has played a role in competition policy: Jerry Hausman and Greg Leonard, "Achieving Competition: Antitrust Policy and Consumer Welfare," *World Economic Affairs*.

The Evolution of Canadian Policy

The first Canadian combine laws were adopted in 1889 and 1890, when legislation made it an offence to combine, to agree to lessen competition unduly, or to restrain trade. Because the proscribed behaviour was illegal, an offence was a criminal act to be handled by the criminal justice system. The laws have been changed frequently since that time, but their basic procompetition stance still prevails in current legislation.

By the 1950s, Canadian anticombine laws had evolved to make illegal three broad classes of activity:

- combinations, such as price-fixing agreements that unduly lessen competition
- mergers or monopolies that may operate to the detriment of the public interest
- unfair trade practices

Many cases of unfair trade practices were successfully pursued under these laws, but few cases were brought against mergers, and none of those that were brought were successful. The reason most often cited for this lack of success was the inability of criminal legislation to cope with complex economic issues. Under criminal law, the government must prove *beyond a reasonable doubt* that the accused party has committed the offence. As an added complication, Canadian courts have been much less willing than American courts to assess economic evidence.

A major review of Canadian legislation was undertaken in the late 1960s by the now-disbanded Economic Council of Canada. Its recommendations formed the basis of the amendments to the Combines Investigation Act that are still in force. Of the recommendations that were accepted, some were put into effect in 1976 and the remainder in 1986.

The 1976 amendments included several provisions:

- extending the Combines Investigation Act to service industries
- allowing *civil* (rather than criminal) actions to be brought for damages resulting from contravention of the act
- strengthening legislation against misleading advertising

Claims about product quality must now be based on adequate tests. Advertising a product at a bargain price when the supplier does not supply the product in reasonable quantities is prohibited. Also prohibited is the supplying of a product at a price higher than the advertised price. In 1992, the court levied a record fine against one individual of $500 000 for seriously misleading advertising.

In 1986, the final set of amendments to the Combines Investigation Act were passed. The resulting Act—now called the Competition Act—has three central themes: economic efficiency, adaptability, and international trade. The new Act creates a specialized Competition Tribunal to deal with civil matters now that competition policy has been taken out of the sphere of the criminal law. The Act also gives the role of "watchdog" to the Director of Investigations who heads the Competition Bureau. This gives the Director of Investigations the responsibility for observing developments in the economy and evaluating the likely effects on competition of mergers and various trade practices.

Perhaps the most important of the 1986 amendments was the one which placed mergers under civil (rather than criminal) law—the statutory test being whether or not the merger "substantially lessens competition." For the first time in Canada, economic considerations are stated to be directly relevant in judging the acceptability of a merger. When reviewing a merger, the Competition Bureau is obliged to consider such things as effective competition after the merger, the degree of foreign competition, barriers to entry, the availability of substitutes, and the financial state of the merging firms.

The Competition Bureau also considers any efficiency gains that a merger might generate. Even in a situation where there are considerable entry barriers to an industry, a merger may bring benefits to consumers even though it raises the industry's measured concentration. If, by merging, two firms can achieve scale economies that were not achievable separately, then reductions in average total costs may get passed on to consumers in the form of lower prices.

This possibility presents a significant challenge to competition policy. The challenge is to prevent those mergers that mostly lead to less competition, producing only small efficiency gains, but to allow those mergers that mostly lead to efficiency gains, with only small reductions in competition. The practical problem for the authorities is to identify the likely effects of each merger.

Recent Developments

This new merger legislation has had some substantial effects on business mergers for the first time in the history of Canadian competition policy. Many firms have consulted with the Competition Bureau before concluding a merger. As a result, some proposed mergers have been amended, and a few have been abandoned. Many mergers that have gone forward have been investigated, and the terms of some have been substantially modified.

To read the Competition Bureau's assessment of the proposed 1998 bank mergers, as well as other mergers, go to its website: www.ct-tc.gc.ca.

The most recent high-profile merger case in Canada occurred in the spring of 1998 when the Royal Bank and the Bank of Montreal announced their intentions to merge. This was followed almost immediately by a similar announcement by the CIBC and Toronto Dominion. These four large chartered banks argued that in order to compete effectively in the world market for financial services, they needed to achieve larger scale. In particular, they argued that the mergers would allow them to spread the enormous fixed costs of computing systems over a much larger customer base, thereby achieving cost reductions that would allow them to compete against foreign banks, especially those in the United States.

The Competition Bureau was not convinced. It concluded, after studying all relevant aspects of the financial-services industry, that the bank mergers would substantially lessen competition in many local personal banking markets, as well as in many banking markets for small and medium-sized businesses. An important part of the Competition Bureau's arguments was that, even if current legislation were changed to increase foreign firms' access to the Canadian market, the established network of bank branches represented a massive entry barrier. This barrier would permit the merged banks to have a stranglehold on the Canadian banking industry.

As it turned out, the Minister of Finance (who ultimately must make the decision on any mergers in the financial sector) disallowed the mergers. But spokespeople for Canada's banks continue to emphasize the need for mergers in order to compete successfully against foreign banks. They argue that the established network of branches is no longer a significant entry barrier in a world in which foreign banks can sell credit cards and mutual funds to Canadian households over the Internet.

The next few years will likely see some reforms in Canada's financial-services industry. The issue of bank mergers, though settled for the time being, is sure to come to the fore of public debate once again.

Another important merger is the one between Canadian Airlines and Air Canada. In April of 1999, Onex Corporation made an offer to purchase both airlines and merge them. Canadian Airlines, which had been losing money for some time, was receptive to the offer. In contrast, the management of Air Canada viewed Onex's offer as a hostile takeover attempt, and responded by making its own offer to purchase Canadian Airlines and operate it as an independent airline. In November, however, Onex withdrew its offer when a Quebec court ruled that the offer was illegal since it would result in more than 10 percent of Air Canada being owned by one party (a restriction on ownership put in place when Air Canada was privatized in the mid 1980s).

With the withdrawal of the Onex bid, however, Air Canada left its offer on the table. The Competition Bureau recommended allowing the merger provided that the Canadian market was opened up to foreign competition—the so-called open skies policy. This, in turn, would probably require that a 25 percent foreign-ownership restriction on Canadian airlines be either altered or removed altogether. As this book went to press in the late fall of 1999, the government appeared unwilling to open the doors to increased foreign ownership, but it also appeared unwilling to prevent the merger.

Without an increase in foreign competition, however, it is clear that a merger between Air Canada and Canadian Airlines will significantly lessen competition. However, there will also be some cost reductions as the two airlines consolidate their flights and, as a

APPLYING ECONOMIC CONCEPTS 12-1
The U.S. Antitrust Case Against Microsoft

In May of 1998, the U.S. Department of Justice and 20 state attorneys-general launched what may well turn out to be the most important antitrust suit of the century. The target of the suit was Microsoft, the enormous software company that has dominated the market for operating systems of personal computers, first with DOS and more recently with Windows. The head of the Justice Department, in launching the suit, stated that "What cannot be tolerated—and what the antitrust laws forbid—is the barrage of anticompetitive practices that Microsoft uses to destroy its rivals and to avoid competition."

The focus of the ongoing suit concerns the way Microsoft has responded to competition in the market for Internet browsers. Netscape is the leading supplier of Internet browsers, with its flagship product called Navigator. Microsoft has a competing browser called Internet Explorer. Central to the case is that, while Microsoft is not the leader in the Internet browser market, it is the undisputed leader in the market for PC operating systems. But, as the Internet develops along with new programming languages such as Java, access to the Internet may end up being a substitute for the PC operating system. If this happens, Microsoft would end up being the dominant producer of largely redundant operating systems. And Netscape, as the leading supplier of browsers, would then be in a position of considerable dominance.

The Justice Department alleges that Microsoft initially tried to push Netscape into colluding with it, dividing up the market for browsers. When Netscape rejected the offer, Microsoft then tried to force PC manufacturers into installing its own Internet Explorer as a condition for receiving licences for Windows 95. Such "tied selling" is illegal under U.S. antitrust law. Microsoft argues that Internet Explorer is an integral part of the Windows operating system, and thus the tying of the sales of Internet Explorer to the sales of Windows is only natural. Furthermore, Microsoft argues that if it is prohibited from tying Internet Explorer to the Windows operating system, there will be fewer innovative developments from Microsoft and the ultimate losers will be the consumers.

In November of 1999, Thomas Penfield Jackson, the judge for the case, concluded that Microsoft was a monopolist and was guilty of business practices that had the effect of reducing the amount of competition. Judge Jackson said:

Most harmful of all is the message that Microsoft's actions have conveyed to every enterprise with the potential to innovate in the computer industry. Through its conduct toward Netscape, IBM, Compaq, Intel, and others, Microsoft has demonstrated that it will use its prodigious market power and immense profits to harm any firm that insists on pursuing initiatives that could intensify competition against one of Microsoft's core products.

Microsoft's sentence was not announced in November. Instead, the judge gave Microsoft time to meet with the plaintiffs in an attempt to reach an out-of-court settlement. As this book went to press, a settlement had yet to be reached. One possibility is to break Microsoft into three separate companies, one dealing with operating systems, a second for applications, and a third for its Internet operations. Critics of this proposal point out that each of these three companies would still be huge and would possess immense power in their respective markets. Others argue that much of Microsoft's market power comes from the linkage among these three areas and that severing the links will indeed lead to more competition. Look for the final outcome in the months and years to come!

Bill Gates, chairman of Microsoft Corp., created Microsoft in the late 1970s and turned it into a multibillion-dollar company and in the process became the world's wealthiest person.

result, operate their planes with less excess capacity. Thus, while the reduction in competition will probably have the effect of raising prices, the reduction in excess capacity will reduce costs and tend to reduce prices. In this merger case, as in many others, the tradeoff between the reduction in competition and the reduction in costs is of central importance. Time will tell how this merger proceeds.

See *Applying Economic Concepts 12-1* for a brief discussion of an important antitrust case in the United States—the case against Microsoft.

Looking Forward

The 1986 Competition Act will not be the end of the evolution of Canadian competition policy, but it appears to have marked the end of a major chapter. Canadian legislation has for a long time provided substantial protection to consumers against the misuse of market power by large firms. For the first time, it now also seems to provide some substantial protection against the creation, through mergers, of market power that is not justified by gains to efficiency or international competitiveness.

What type of reforms might we expect in the years ahead? The ongoing process of globalization poses two challenges for Canadian competition policy. First, as the flow of goods and services across national boundaries increases, it becomes more important to define markets on an international basis rather than on national ones. For example, consider again the Canadian banking industry. With the continuing development of the Internet, it becomes possible for foreign-based banks to sell some financial services to Canadians without establishing a costly *physical* presence in Canada—such as a network of branches. In this case, the appropriate definition of the market (for the case of assessing the impact of a merger) is larger than just the one defined by Canada's borders.

The second challenge posed by globalization is the desirability of standardizing competition policy across countries. Firms that are mobile and have considerable market power may tend to locate their firms where competition policy is the most lax, exporting into other countries. To avoid such socially inefficient locational choices, countries have an incentive to standardize their competition policy—in this case, firms would choose their locations on the basis of economic rather than legal forces.

See Chapter 12 of www.pearsoned.ca/lipsey for an interview with the Royal Bank's John Cleghorn on the case for bank mergers: "A Case for Bank Mergers," *World Economic Affairs.*

S U M M A R Y

Economic Efficiency

- Economists distinguish two main kinds of efficiency: productive and allocative.
- Productive efficiency exists for given technology when whatever output being produced is being produced at the lowest attainable cost. This outcome requires, first, that firms be on, rather than above, their relevant cost curves and, second, that all firms in an industry have the same marginal cost.

- Allocative efficiency is achieved when it is impossible to change the mix of production in such a way as to make someone better off without making someone else worse off. The allocation of resources will be efficient when each product's price equals its marginal cost.
- Perfect competition achieves both productive and allocative efficiency. Productive efficiency is achieved because

the same forces that lead to long-run equilibrium lead to production at the lowest attainable cost. Allocative efficiency is achieved because in competitive equilibrium, with quantity demanded equalling quantity supplied, price equals marginal cost for every product.

- The economic case against monopoly rests on its allocative inefficiency, which arises because profit maximization for a monopolist implies that price exceeds marginal cost. Oligopolistic industries are also allocatively inefficient since price exceeds marginal cost. But oligopoly also produces benefits. Empirical evidence suggests that technological change and innovation can, to a measurable extent, be traced to the efforts of large firms operating in oligopolistic industries.

Economic Regulation to Promote Efficiency

- Two broad types of policies are designed to promote allocative efficiency in imperfectly competitive markets. These can be divided into *economic regulations* and *competition policy*. Economic regulation is used both in the case of a natural monopoly and in the case of an oligopolistic industry. Competition policy applies more to the latter.
- Efficient operation of natural monopolies requires that price be set equal to short-run marginal cost and that investment be undertaken whenever that price exceeds the full long-run marginal cost of production. Average-cost pricing results in too little output in the short run and too little investment in the long run in falling-cost industries; it also leads to too much output and too much investment in rising-cost industries.
- Direct control of pricing and entry conditions of some key oligopolistic industries has been common in the past, but deregulation is reducing such control. The move to deregulation is largely the result of the experiences that oligopolistic industries are a major engine of growth, as long as their firms are encouraged to compete; that direct control of such industries has produced disappointing results in the past; and that forced cross subsidization can have serious consequences for some users.

Canadian Competition Policy

- Canadian combine laws have always recognized the need for firms that are large in relation to the domestic market if economies of scale are to be exploited. Such laws seek to restrict growth in size through mergers where the size is not justified by efficiencies and seek to prevent the unwarranted exploitation of market power.
- In 1976, such laws were removed from the criminal code, where enforcement proved difficult, and placed in the civil code, where enforcement appears to be easier.
- Since 1986, the Competition Bureau has modified its approach to mergers. Whereas in early years there was generally a presumption that a merger would reduce competition and thus be undesirable, there is now a view that efficiency gains may make some mergers desirable.

K E Y   C O N C E P T S

Productive and allocative efficiency	The inefficiency of monopoly	Regulation and effects on innovation
Consumer and producer surplus	Regulation of natural monopolies	Deregulation
The efficiency of competition	Marginal- and average-cost pricing	Canadian competition policy

STUDY EXERCISES

1. Summer Tees and Fancy Tees are two firms producing T-shirts. The table below shows the average and marginal cost of producing T-shirts for the two companies.

Summer Tees				Fancy Tees			
Quantity	ATC	TC	MC	Quantity	ATC	TC	MC
5	$8	—		5	$9	—	
			—				—
10	7	—		10	7	—	
			—				—
15	6	—		15	6	—	
			—				—
20	6	—		20	5	—	
			—				—
25	7	—		25	5.50	—	
			—				—
30	9	—		30	6.50	—	
			—				—
35	11	—		35	8	—	

a. Calculate TC and MC for both companies and fill in the table.

b. Draw, in two separate scale diagrams, the ATC and MC curves for each firm.

c. Summer Tees is initially producing 30 shirts; Fancy Tees is initially producing 15 shirts. What is the total industry production cost?

d. Now suppose that Summer Tees produces 10 fewer shirts. By how much do its costs fall?

e. Now suppose that Fancy Tees produces 10 more shirts. By how much do its costs rise?

f. If the two firms are to produce 45 shirts in total, what is the cost-minimizing way to allocate production between the two firms? (Assume that production must be changed by increments of 5 shirts, as shown in the table.)

2. Assume that the market for eggs is perfectly competitive. The diagram shows the demand and supply for eggs.

a. At the free-market equilibrium, p^* and Q^*, show what areas represent consumer and producer surplus.

b. Now suppose that the egg producers organize themselves and establish a system of quotas. Each farmer's output is restricted by an amount to keep aggregate output at Q^Q. What happens to industry price?

c. In the quota system in part b, what areas now represent consumer and producer surplus? Is the quota system allocatively efficient? Explain.

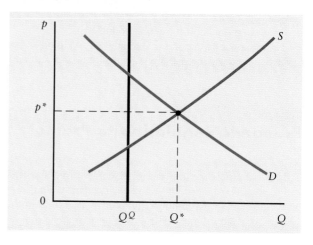

3. The diagram below shows supply and demand in the labour market.

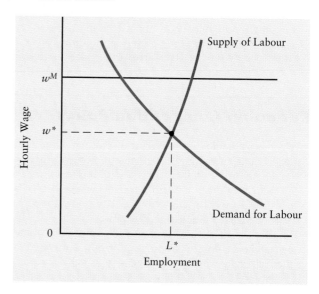

a. At the free-market equilibrium, w^* and L^*, show what areas represent consumer and producer surplus.

b. Now suppose that the government establishes a minimum wage at w^M. What is the outcome of this policy?

c. In the situation of part b, what areas now represent consumer and producer surplus? Is the outcome allocatively efficient? Explain.

4. The diagram below shows the production possibility boundary for a country that produces only two goods, limes and coconuts. Assume that resources are fully employed at points *A*, *B*, *C*, and *D*.

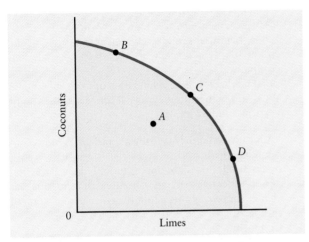

a. Suppose individual firms in the lime industry are not producing at their minimum possible cost. Which point(s) could represent this situation?

b. Suppose all firms and both industries are productively efficient. Which points could represent this situation?

c. Suppose point *B* occurs when the lime industry is monopolized but the coconut industry is perfectly competitive. Is point *B* allocatively efficient? Is it productively efficient?

d. Suppose point *D* occurs when the coconut industry is monopolized but the lime industry is perfectly competitive. Is point *D* allocatively efficient? Is it productively efficient?

e. Suppose point *C* is allocatively efficient. What do we know about each industry in this case?

5. The following diagram shows the *ATC* and *MC* curves for a natural monopoly—average costs are falling over the entire range of the demand curve.

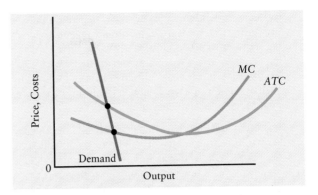

a. Identify what price and quantity would exist if the firm were required by regulators to set price equal average cost.

b. What would be the profits (or losses) in this case?

c. Would the outcome be allocatively efficient? Explain why or why not.

d. Suppose now that the firm were required by regulators to set price equal to marginal cost. What would be the price and quantity in this case?

e. In the diagram, show the profits (or losses) in this case.

f. Would the outcome be allocatively efficient? Explain why or why not.

6. One important factor that the Canadian Competition Bureau must consider when assessing the likely effects of a merger is the definition of the market. Discuss how geography is likely to affect the definition of the market for the following products:

a. fresh-baked breads and cakes

b. cement

c. gold jewellery

d. computer hardware

DISCUSSION QUESTIONS

1. Suppose that allocative inefficiency of some economy amounts to 5 percent of the value of production. What does this statement mean? If it is true, would consumers *as a whole* be better off if policy measures were successful in moving the economy to an allocatively efficient outcome? Would *every* consumer be better off if the economy moved to an allocatively efficient outcome?

2. Evaluate the wisdom of having the Competition Bureau use profits as a measure of monopoly power in deciding whether to prosecute a case. Would such a rule be expected to affect the behaviour of firms with high profits? In what ways might any changes induced by such a rule be socially beneficial, and in what ways might they be socially harmful?

3. It is often asserted that whenever a regulatory agency is established, ultimately it will become controlled by the people whom it was intended to regulate. (This argument raises the question of who regulates the regulators.) Can you identify why this phenomenon might happen? How might the integrity of regulatory boards be protected?

4. This chapter has identified several strategies for dealing with natural monopolies and their associated inefficiencies. Alternatively, assume that you are a regulator and that the monopoly you face is able to price discriminate—perhaps perfectly. Does this ability change the options you have for encouraging the efficient level of production? Would you choose to use this additional option? Why or why not?

5. "Canadian air travellers opting for U.S. carriers were [partly] responsible for Canadian airlines deregulation."
—C. D. Howe Institute.
"Canadian consumers crossing the border to buy cheap U.S. agricultural products may be responsible for the end of supply management in Canada."—Canadian economist.
What market forces lie behind each of these quotations? What difficulties do they reveal for the regulation of particular industries?

6. "Allocative efficiency is really about whether the economy 'has the quantities right'—it is not really about prices at all. Prices are important only in a discussion about allocative efficiency because *in a free market* changes in prices bring about the efficient allocation of resources."
Comment.

13 14 15

PART FIVE

Factor Markets

Why do university professors typically get paid more than elementary-school teachers? Why does an acre of land outside Kamloops rent for less than an acre of land in downtown Vancouver? Are government attempts to equalize the earnings of people in different occupations ever successful? What do unions do? What are the effects of discrimination in the labour market? What is the connection between the interest rate and firms' investment in physical capital? These are the sort of questions you will be able to answer after reading the next three chapters.

In Chapter 13, we examine the way economists think about markets for factors of production. Not surprisingly, demand and supply play a key role. We will see several reasons for factor-price differentials. It is here that we see why the acre of land in Kamloops rents for less than the one in Vancouver. We will also discuss the importance of factor mobility, and why this mobility can thwart government efforts to establish pay equity.

Chapter 14 examines labour markets in detail. We explore how working conditions and human capital can combine to explain why some workers get paid more than others. We examine the effects of legislated minimum wages, the objectives of labour unions, and the important issue of discrimination in labour markets. Finally, we will discuss whether the decline of the manufacturing sector (and the rise of the service sector) is necessarily a bad thing.

Chapter 15 begins by discussing the market for physical capital. We will see why firms choose to buy less capital when the interest rate rises (and more when the interest rate falls). We will also examine how the equilibrium interest rate is determined, and how it is affected by changes in technology. The chapter then goes on to discuss the pricing of nonrenewable resources, such as oil, natural gas, or minerals. We will discuss how the market system works as a conservation mechanism—the idea that rising prices of nonrenewable resources encourage the conservation of these scarce resources.

CHAPTER 13

Factor Pricing and Factor Mobility

LEARNING OBJECTIVES

① Understand the size and functional distributions of income.

② Explain a profit-maximizing firm's demand for a factor.

③ Understand the determinants of the elasticity of factor demand.

④ Explain the role of factor mobility in determining factor supply.

⑤ Distinguish between temporary and equilibrium factor-price differentials.

⑥ Explain the concept of economic rent, and how it is related to factor mobility.

Most people spend a considerable amount of their time working. Some of those people are fortunate enough to earn good wages, and thus have good incomes that enable them to afford many of the "good things in life." Others are not so fortunate, and earn only low wages. What determines the wages that individuals earn? What explains why professors usually are paid more than high-school teachers, or why doctors are paid more than nurses? Labour is not the only factor of production, of course. Physical capital is also important, as are land and natural resources. What determines the payments that these factors earn? Why does an acre of farm land in northern Saskatchewan rent for much less than an acre of land in downtown Toronto? Not surprisingly, understanding why different factors of production earn different payments requires us to understand both demand-side and supply-side aspects of the relevant factor markets.

In this chapter we examine the issue of factor pricing and the closely related issue of factor mobility. Understanding what determines the payments to different factors of production will help us to understand the overall distribution of income in the economy. We begin with the distribution of income.

Income Distribution

The founders of Classical economics, Adam Smith (1723–1790) and David Ricardo (1772–1823), were concerned with the distribution of income among what were then the three great social classes: workers, capitalists, and landowners. They defined three factors of production as labour, capital, and land. The return to each factor was treated as the income of the respective social class.

Smith and Ricardo were interested in what determined the income of each class relative to the total national income. Their theories predicted that as society progressed, landlords would become relatively better off and capitalists would become relatively worse off. Karl Marx (1818–1883) had a different theory which predicted that as growth occurred, capitalists would become relatively better off and workers would become relatively worse off (until the whole capitalist system collapsed).

These nineteenth-century debates focused on what is now called the **functional distribution of income,** defined as the distribution of national income among the major factors of production. Modern economists, however, emphasize the **size distribution of income.** This refers to the distribution of income among different individuals without reference to the source of the income or the "social class" of the individual.

If we want to measure and understand the income inequality between individuals, the size distribution of income is a better indicator than is the functional distribution of income. The reason is that income classes often do not coincide with "social" classes. Many capitalists, such as the owners of small retail stores, are in the lower part of the income scale. Conversely, many wage earners, such as professional athletes, are in the upper income scale. Furthermore, it is becoming increasingly difficult to distinguish "workers" from "capitalists." Through employer-sponsored pension plans, workers now own much more of the country's capital than do the richer "non-working" capitalists.

Figure 13-1 shows that even among full-time, full-year workers, there was substantial inequality in the distribution of (pre-tax) income across individuals in 1996 (the most recent year for which these data are available). Another way to show the size distribution of income is found in Figure 13-2. Each of the curves in the figure is a Lorenz curve. A **Lorenz curve** shows how much of total income is accounted for by given proportions of the nation's families. If every family had the same income, then the Lorenz curve would lie exactly along the diagonal. The farther the curve bends away from the diagonal, the less equal the distribution of income. The curve farther from the diagonal in Figure 13-2 shows, for example, that in 1995 the bottom 20 percent of all Canadian

functional distribution of income The distribution of national income among the major factors of production.

size distribution of income The distribution of income among households, without regard to source of income or social class of households.

Lorenz curve A graph showing the extent of inequality of income distribution.

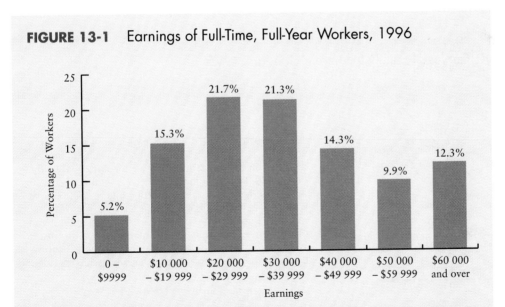

FIGURE 13-1   Earnings of Full-Time, Full-Year Workers, 1996

There is considerable inequality in the distribution of (pre-tax) earned income, even among full-time workers who work the full year. Just over 12 percent of such workers earned more than $60 000 in 1996; 20.5 percent earned less than $20 000. Average earned income in 1996 was $37 465.

(*Source:* These data are available on Statistics Canada's website: www.statcan.ca.)

families received 2.1 percent of all pre-tax income. The curve closer to the diagonal, however, shows that Canada's tax-and-transfer system is effective at redistributing income; the same 20 percent of families receive 7.7 percent of after-tax income.

To understand the size distribution of income, we must first study how individual incomes are determined. Superficial explanations of differences in income, such as "People earn according to their ability," are inadequate. Incomes are distributed much more unequally than any *measured* index of ability, be it IQ, physical strength, or typing skill. The best professional sports players may only score twice as many points as the average players, but their salary is many times more than the average salary. Something other than simple ability is at work here. However, if answers that are couched in terms of ability are easily refuted, so are answers such as "It's all a matter of luck" or "It's just the system." In this chapter, we look beyond such superficial explanations.

A Glimpse of the Theory Ahead

In this chapter, we confine ourselves to factor markets that are perfectly competitive. As a result, the firms we study face a given price of each factor that they buy. Similarly, owners of factors face a given price for the factor services that they sell.

Dealing first with competitive factor markets allows us to study the principles of factor-price determination in the simplest context. Once these principles are understood, it is relatively easy to extend the theory to more complicated settings. This is done in Chapter 14.

The income that a factor earns depends on the price charged for its services and on the quantity that is employed. To determine factor incomes, therefore, we need to ask how markets determine these prices and quantities. The answer is that factor prices and quantities are determined in just the same way as the prices and quantities of goods—by the interaction of demand and supply. What is new about factor pricing arises from the *determinants* of factor demands and factor supplies.

FIGURE 13-2   Lorenz Curves of Family Income in Canada, 1995

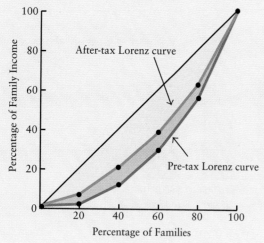

The size of the shaded area between the Lorenz curve and the diagonal is a measure of the inequality of income distribution. If there were complete income equality, the bottom 20 percent of income receivers would receive 20 percent of the income, and so forth, and the Lorenz curve would coincide with the diagonal line.

The Lorenz curve farther from the diagonal is the one for pre-tax income. That Canada's tax-and-transfer system achieves some redistribution of income is shown by the Lorenz curve for after-tax income, which is closer to the diagonal.

(*Source:* Statistics Canada #13-210-XPB, 1996)

Events in goods markets have implications for factor markets. Firms' decisions on how much to produce and how to produce it imply specific demands for the various factors of production. These demands, together with the supplies of the factors of production (which are determined by the owners of the factors), come together in factor markets. Together they determine the quantities of the various factors of production that are employed, their prices, and the incomes earned by their owners.

There is a close relationship between the production and pricing of the goods produced by firms, on the one hand, and the pricing, employment, and incomes earned by the factors of production they hire, on the other hand. This relationship leads to one of the great insights of economics:

When demand and supply interact to determine the allocation of resources among various lines of production, they also determine the incomes of the factors that are used in producing the goods.

The rest of this chapter is an elaboration of this important theme. We first study the demand for factors, then their supply, and finally how demand and supply come together to determine factor prices and quantities.

The Demand for Factors

Firms require the services of land, labour, capital, and natural resources to be used as inputs. Firms also use as inputs the products of other firms, such as steel, legal services, computer software, and electricity.

Firms require inputs not for their own sake but as a means to produce goods and services. For example, the demand for computer programmers and technicians is growing as more and more computers are used. The demand for carpenters and building materials rises and falls as the amount of housing construction rises and falls. The demand for any input is therefore *derived from the demand* for the goods and services that it helps to produce; for this reason, the demand for a factor of production is said to be a **derived demand**.

derived demand
The demand for a factor of production that results from the demand for the products that it is used to make.

Derived demand provides a link between goods markets and factor markets.

The Firm's Marginal Decision on Factor Use

What determines whether an individual firm will choose to hire one extra worker, or whether the same firm will decide to use one extra machine, or an extra kilowatt-hour of electricity? Since we are considering whether the firm will use one extra unit of some factor, we refer to this as the firm's *marginal decision* on factor use.

As we have seen in earlier chapters, any profit-maximizing firm increases its output until its marginal cost equals its marginal revenue. Since producing more output requires hiring more factors of production, we can say this another way—the firm will increase its use of any factor of production until the last unit of the factor adds as much to revenue as it does to costs.

The addition to total cost resulting from employing one more unit of a factor is that factor's price. (Recall that the firm is assumed to buy its factors in competitive markets.) So, if one more worker is hired at a wage of $15 per hour, the addition to the firm's costs is $15.

The amount that one unit of a factor adds to revenue is called the factor's **marginal revenue product (MRP)**. The factor's *MRP* has two components—a *physical* component and a *dollar* component. The physical amount by which output increases when one more unit of the factor is employed is called the factor's **marginal physical product (MPP)**. This is the concept we learned about in Chapter 7 where we simply called it the factor's *marginal product*. The dollar amount by which total revenue changes when output increases by one unit is simply the firm's marginal revenue, *MR*.

The factor's marginal revenue product is simply the combination of this physical component and this dollar component—it is the change in output (*MPP*) times the firm's marginal revenue (*MR*). [26] For example, if the factor's marginal physical product is 2 units and the firm's marginal revenue is $7.50, the factor's *MRP* is $15 ($7.50×2).

We can now restate the condition for a firm to be maximizing its profits in two ways. First:

$$\text{Marginal Cost of the Factor} = \text{Marginal Revenue Product of the Factor} \qquad (13\text{-}1)$$

This equation holds for *any* firm and any factor, no matter what market structure applies. In the special case of competitive goods and factor markets, however, we can simplify the equation. In this case, the marginal cost of the factor is simply the factor's price, which we call w. Furthermore, since the firm's *MR* is just the product's price, p, the *MRP* is equal to $MPP \times p$. Thus, the condition for profit maximization becomes

$$w = MPP \times p \qquad (13\text{-}2)$$

To check your understanding of Equation 13-2, consider an example. Suppose that the factor is available to the firm at a cost of $10 per unit ($w = \$10$). Suppose also that employing another unit of the factor adds 3 units to output ($MPP = 3$). Suppose further that any amount of output can be sold for $5 per unit ($p = \$5$). Thus, the additional unit of the factor adds $15 to the firm's revenue but only $10 to its costs. In this case, the firm will increase profits by hiring more units of the factor.

Now suppose, however, that the last unit of the factor hired by the firm has a marginal physical product of 1 unit of output—it adds only one extra unit to output—and so adds only $5 to revenue. In this case, the firm can increase profits by reducing its use of the factor.

Finally, suppose that another unit of the factor taken on or laid off changes revenue by $10. Now the firm cannot increase its profits by altering its employment of the variable factor in either direction.

To maximize its profits, any firm must hire each factor to the point where the factor's marginal revenue product equals the factor's price.

In Chapters 9 and 10, we saw the firm varying its output until the marginal cost of producing another unit was equal to the marginal revenue derived from selling that unit. Now we see the same profit-maximizing behaviour in terms of the firm's varying its inputs until the marginal cost of another unit of input is just equal to the revenue derived from selling that unit's marginal product.

marginal revenue product (MRP)   The extra revenue that results from using one unit more of a variable factor.

marginal physical product (MPP)   The extra output that results from using one unit more of a variable factor.

The Firm's Demand Curve for a Factor

We now know what determines the quantity of a variable factor a firm will buy when facing some specific price of the factor and some specific price of its output. Next we wish to derive the firm's *entire* demand curve for a factor, which tells us how much of the factor the firm will buy at *each* price.

To derive a firm's demand curve for a factor, we start by considering the right-hand side of Equation 13-1, which tells us that the factor's marginal revenue product is composed of a physical component and a dollar component. We examine these two separate components in turn.

Practise with Study Guide Chapter 13, Exercise 1.

The Physical Component of *MRP: MPP*

As the quantity of the variable factor changes, output will change. The hypothesis of diminishing returns, first discussed in Chapter 7, predicts what will happen: As the firm adds further units of the variable factor to a given quantity of the fixed factor, the additions to output will eventually get smaller and smaller. In other words, the factor's marginal physical product declines as shown in part (i) of Figure 13-3.

The Dollar Component of *MRP: MR*

To convert the marginal physical product curve of Figure 13-3(i) into a curve showing the marginal revenue product of the variable factor, we need to know the dollar value of the extra physical product. Part (ii) of Figure 13-3 shows a marginal revenue product curve for labour on the assumption that the firm sells its product in a competitive market at a price of $5 per unit. The *MRP* curve represents *MPP* × *MR* for each additional unit of the factor. Since the *MR* for a firm in perfect competition is simply equal to the price of the product, the *MRP* curve has the same shape as the *MPP* curve.

Note, however, that if the firm were not perfectly competitive, then *MR* would not be equal to price. If *MR* declined as output increases (as it would if the firm were not a price taker), then the *MRP* curve would be steeper than the *MPP* curve—because the increase in output produced by the extra unit of the factor would lead to a fall in the price of the product.

From *MRP* to the Demand Curve

Equation 13-1 states that the profit-maximizing firm will employ additional units of the factor up to the point at which the *MRP* equals the price of the factor. For example, in Figure 13-3, if the price of hiring one worker were $2000 per month, the profit-maximizing firm would employ 60 workers. (There is no point in employing a sixty-first because that worker would add less than $2000 to revenue but a full $2000 to costs.) Thus, the profit-maximizing firm hires the quantity of the variable factor that equates the marginal revenue product with the price of the variable factor.

The *MRP* curve of the variable factor is the firm's (derived) demand curve for that variable factor.

Elasticity of Factor Demand

The elasticity of demand for a factor measures the *degree* of the response of the quantity demanded to a change in its price. The preceding sections have explained the *direction* of the response; that is, that quantity demanded is negatively related to price. But you

FIGURE 13-3   From Marginal Physical Product to Demand Curve

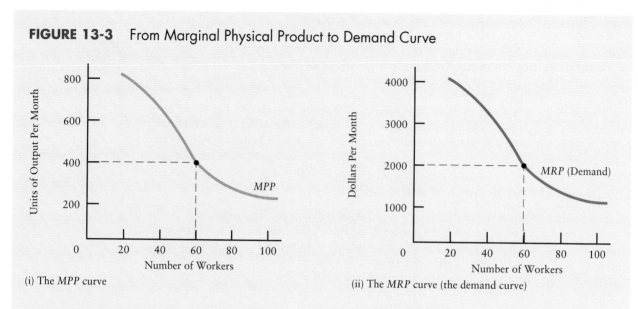

(i) The *MPP* curve

(ii) The *MRP* curve (the demand curve)

Each additional unit of the factor employed adds a certain amount to total product, as shown in part (i), and hence a certain amount to total revenue, as shown in part (ii). This determines the amount of the factor that firms will demand at each price. The firm is assumed to be a price taker in the goods market, facing a price of $5 per unit.

should not be surprised to hear that the magnitude of the response depends on the strength of various effects. For example, the extent of diminishing returns to labour, and the ability of the firm to substitute between labour and other factors of production, will both affect the firm's elasticity of demand for labour.

Diminishing Returns

The first influence on the slope of the demand curve for a factor is the diminishing marginal product of that factor. If marginal product declines rapidly as more of a variable factor is employed, a fall in the factor's price will not induce many more units to be employed. This is the case of a relatively steep *MPP* curve, and thus *MRP* curve, in Figure 13-3. Conversely, if marginal product falls only slowly as more of a variable factor is employed, there will be a large increase in quantity demanded as price falls. This is the case of a relatively flat *MPP* curve, and thus *MRP* curve, in Figure 13-3.

Substitution Between Factors

In the long run, all factors are variable. If one factor's price rises, firms will try to substitute relatively cheaper factors for it. (This is the *principle of substitution*, which we first encountered in Chapter 8.) For this reason, the slope of the demand curve for a factor is influenced by the ease with which other factors can be substituted for the factor whose price has changed.

The ease of substitution depends on the substitutes that are available and on the technical conditions of production. It is often possible to vary factor proportions in surprising ways. For example, in automobile manufacturing and in building construction, glass and steel can be substituted for each other simply by varying the dimensions of the windows. Another example is that construction materials can be substituted for maintenance labour in the case of most durable consumer goods. This is done by making the product more or less durable and more or less subject to breakdowns by using more or less expensive materials in its construction.

Importance of the Factor

Other things being equal, the more important is a factor in producing some good, the greater the elasticity of demand for that factor.

To see this, suppose that wages account for 50 percent of the costs of producing a good and raw materials account for 10 percent. A 20 percent rise in the price of labour raises the cost of producing the good by 10 percent (20 percent of 50 percent), but a 20 percent rise in the price of raw materials raises the cost of the good by only 2 percent (20 percent of 10 percent). The larger the increase in the cost of production, the larger the shift in the product's supply curve and hence the larger the decreases in quantities demanded of both the good and the factors used to produce it.

Elasticity of Demand for the Output

Other things being equal, the more elastic is the demand for the product that the factor is used to produce, the more elastic is the demand for the factor.

If an increase in the price of the product causes a large decrease in the quantity demanded—that is, if the demand for the product is highly elastic—there will be a large decrease in the quantity of a factor needed to produce it in response to a rise in the factor's price. However, if an increase in the price of a product causes only a small decrease in the quantity demanded—that is, if the demand for the product is inelastic—there will be only a small decrease in the quantity of the factor required in response to a rise in its price.

In *Extensions in Theory 13-1*, the forces affecting the elasticity of the derived demand curves are related more specifically to the market for the industry's output.

The Supply of Factors

When we consider the supply of any factor of production, we can consider supply at three different levels of aggregation:

- the amount supplied to the economy as a whole
- the amount supplied to a particular industry or occupation
- the amount supplied to a particular firm

The elasticity of supply of a factor will normally be different at each of these levels of aggregation for the simple reason that the amount of factor mobility is very different at these different levels of aggregation. A given factor of production is often very mobile between firms within a given industry, less mobile between different industries, and even less mobile from the perspective of the entire economy. As an example, an electrician may be very mobile between industries within a given city, and reasonably mobile between provinces, but it may be very difficult for that electrician to move to another country to find a job. In this section, we examine the relationship between factor mobility and the supply of factors of production. We start with the highest level of aggregation, the supply of each factor to the economy as a whole.

EXTENSIONS IN THEORY 13-1

The Principles of Derived Demand

Alfred Marshall (1842–1924) referred to the two propositions derived here as the principles of *derived demand*.

1. The larger the proportion of total costs accounted for by a factor, the more elastic the demand for it.

    Consider the figure on the left. The demand curve for the industry's product is D and, *given the factor's original price,* the industry supply curve is S_0. Equilibrium is at E_0 with output at q_0.

    Suppose that the factor's price then falls. If the factor accounts for a small part of the industry's total costs, each firm's marginal cost curve shifts downward by only a small amount. So also does the industry supply curve, as illustrated by the supply curve S_1. Output expands only a small amount to q_1, a change that implies only a small increase in the quantity of the factor demanded.

    If the factor accounts for a large part of the industry's total costs, each firm's marginal cost curve shifts downward a great deal. So also does the industry supply curve, as illustrated by the curve S_2. Output expands to q_2, a

change that implies a large increase in the quantity of the factor demanded.

2. The more elastic the demand curve for the product, the more elastic the demand for the factors that are used to make it.

    Now consider the figure on the right. The original demand and supply curves for the industry's product intersect at E_0 to produce an industry output of q_0. A fall in the price of a factor causes the industry supply curve to shift downward to S_1.

    When the demand curve is relatively inelastic, as shown by the curve D_i, industry output increases by only a small amount, to q_1. The quantity of the factor demanded increases by a correspondingly small amount.

    When demand for the product is relatively elastic, as shown by the curve D_e, industry output increases by a large amount to q_2. The quantity of the factor demanded then increases by a correspondingly large amount.

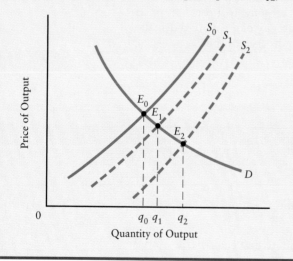

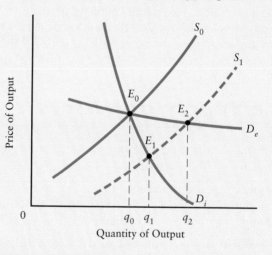

The Total Supply of Factors

At any one time, the total supply of each factor of production is given. For example, in each country, the labour force is of a certain size, so much arable land is available, and there is a given supply of discovered petroleum. However, these supplies can and do change in response to both economic and noneconomic forces. Sometimes the change is very gradual, as when a climatic change slowly turns arable land into desert or when medical advances reduce the rate of infant mortality and, hence, increase the rate of population growth, thereby eventually increasing the supply of adult labour. Sometimes the changes can be quite rapid, as when a boom in business activity brings retired persons back into the labour force or a rise in the price of agricultural produce encourages the draining of marshes to add to the supply of farmland.

Physical Capital

The supply of capital in a country consists of the stock of existing machines, plants, and equipment. Capital is a manufactured factor of production, and its total supply is in no sense fixed, although it changes only slowly. Each year, the stock of capital goods is diminished by the amount that becomes physically or economically obsolete and is increased by the amount that is newly produced. The difference between these is the net addition to (or net subtraction from) the capital stock. On balance, the trend has been for the capital stock to grow from decade to decade over the past few centuries. We will consider the determinants of investment in capital in Chapter 15.

Land

The total area of dry land in a country is almost completely fixed, but the supply of *fertile* land is not. Considerable care and effort are required to sustain the productive power of land. If farmers earn low incomes, they may not provide the necessary care, and the land's fertility may be destroyed within a short time. In contrast, high earnings from farming may provide the incentive to increase the supply of arable land by irrigation and other forms of reclamation.

Labour

The number of people willing to work is called the labour force; the total number of hours they are willing to work is called the **supply of labour**. The supply of labour depends on three influences: the size of the population, the proportion of the population willing to work, and the number of hours that each individual wishes to work. Each of these is partly influenced by economic forces.

supply of labour
The total number of hours of work that the population is willing to supply. Also called the *supply of effort*.

Population.   The population of a country varies over time, and these variations are influenced to some extent by economic forces. There is some evidence, for example, that the birthrate and the net immigration rate (immigration minus emigration) are higher in good times than in bad.

Labour-Force Participation.   The proportion of the total population that is willing to work is called the *labour-force participation rate*. Economists also define participation rates for subgroups, such as women or youths. Participation rates vary in response to many influences, including changes in attitudes and tastes. The enormous rise in female participation rates in the past four decades is one example. Another is a lowering of the retirement age, which has the effect of reducing the overall labour-force participation rate.

These new births will eventually increase the labour force and thus the country's supply of labour.

Forces other than tastes also play a role in determining the labour-force participation rate. For example, a rise in the demand for labour, and an accompanying rise in the wage, will lead to an increase in the proportion of the population willing to work. More women with children enter the labour force when wages are high. For the same reasons, the labour force tends to decline when earnings and employment opportunities decline.

Hours Worked. The wage rate not only influences the number of people in the labour force, but it also affects the number of hours worked for each person. When workers sell their labour services to employers, they are giving up leisure in order to gain income with which to buy goods. They can therefore be thought of as trading leisure for goods. A rise in the wage implies a change in the relative price of goods and leisure. An increase in the wage means that leisure becomes more expensive relative to goods, because each hour of leisure consumed is at the cost of more goods forgone.

It is not necessarily the case, however, that an increase in the wage increases the amount of hours worked. In fact, an increase in the wage generates both income and substitution effects (see Chapter 6). As the wage rises, the substitution effect leads the individual to work more hours (consume less leisure) because leisure is now relatively more expensive. The income effect of a higher wage, however, leads the individual to work fewer hours (consume more leisure). Because the two effects work in the opposite direction we are, in general, unsure how a rise in the wage will affect the number of hours an individual chooses to work.

The Supply of Factors to a Particular Use

Most factors have many uses. A given piece of land can be used to grow any one of several crops, or it can be subdivided for a housing development. A computer programmer living in the Ottawa valley can work for one of several firms, for the government, or for Carleton University. A lathe can be used to make many different products, and it requires no adaptation when it is turned for one use or another.

One industry or occupation can attract a factor away from another industry or occupation, even though the total supply of that factor may be fixed. Thus, a factor's elasticity of supply to a particular use is larger than its elasticity of supply to the entire economy.

factor mobility The ease with which factors can be transferred between uses.

When we consider the supply of a factor for a particular use, the most important concept is **factor mobility**. A factor that shifts easily between uses in response to small changes in incentives is said to be *mobile*. Its supply to any one use will be elastic because a small increase in the price offered will attract many units of the factor from other uses. A factor that does not shift easily from one use to another, even in response to large changes in remuneration, is said to be *immobile*. It will be in inelastic supply in any one use because even a large increase in the price offered will attract only a small inflow from other uses. Generally, a factor is less mobile in the short run than in the long run.

An important determinant of factor mobility is time: The longer the time interval, the easier it is for a factor to convert from one use to another.

Consider the factor mobility among particular uses of each of the three key factors of production.

Capital. Some kinds of capital equipment—lathes, trucks, and computers, for example—can be shifted readily among uses; many others are comparatively unshiftable. A great deal of machinery is specific: Once built, it must be used for the purpose for which it was designed, or it cannot be used at all. Indeed, it is the immobility of much fixed capital equipment that makes the exit of firms from declining industries the slow and difficult process described in Chapter 9.

In the long run, however, capital is highly mobile. When capital goods wear out, a firm may replace them with identical goods, it may buy a newly designed machine to produce the same goods, or it may buy machines to produce totally different goods.

Land.   Land, which is physically the least mobile of factors, is one of the *most* mobile in an economic sense. Consider agricultural land. In a given year, one crop can be harvested and a totally different crop can be planted. A farm on the outskirts of a growing city can be sold for subdivision and development on short notice. Once land is built on, however, its mobility is much reduced.

Although land is highly mobile among alternative uses, it is completely immobile as far as location is concerned. There is only so much land within a given distance of the centre of any city, and no increase in the price paid can induce further land to be located within that distance. This locational immobility has important consequences, including high prices for desirable locations and the tendency to build tall buildings to economize on the use of scarce land, as in the centre of large cities.

Labour.   The supply of labour services often requires the physical presence of the person who supplies it. Absentee landlords, while continuing to live in the place of their choice, can obtain income from land that is located in remote parts of the world. Investment can be shifted from iron mines in South Africa to mines in Labrador while the owners commute between Calgary and Hawaii. The same is true for some workers, such as designers or bookkeepers, who can work in one location and submit their work to clients in other locations. But almost all workers involved in manufacturing and most of those involved in serving the public in stores, restaurants, and so on, must actually be present to supply their labour services to an employer. When a worker who is employed by a firm producing men's ties in Montreal decides instead to supply his or her labour services to a firm producing women's shoes in Winnipeg, the worker must physically travel to Winnipeg. This has an important consequence.

Because of the need for labour's physical presence when its services are provided for the production of many goods, nonmonetary considerations are much more important for the supply of labour than for other factors of production.

People may be satisfied with or frustrated by the kind of work that they do, where they do it, the people with whom they do it, and the social status of their occupations. Because these considerations influence their decisions about what they will do with their labour services, they will not always move just because they could earn a higher wage.

Nevertheless, labour is mobile among industries, occupations, and areas in response to changes in the signals provided by wages and opportunities for employment. The ease with which such mobility occurs depends on many forces. For example, it is not difficult for a secretary to shift from one company to another in order to take a job in Red Deer, Alberta, instead of Regina, Saskatchewan, but it can be difficult for a secretary to become an editor, a model, a machinist, or a doctor within a short period of time. Workers who lack ability, training, or inclination find certain kinds of mobility difficult or impossible.

Some barriers to movement may be virtually insurmountable once a person's training has been completed. For example, it may be impossible for a farmer to become a surgeon or for a truck driver to become a professional athlete, even if the relative wage rates change greatly. However, the children of farmers, doctors, truck drivers, and athletes, when they are deciding how much education or training to obtain, are not nearly as limited in their choices as their parents, who have already completed their education and are settled in their occupations.

The role of education in helping new labour-force entrants to adapt to available jobs is important. In a society like Canada's in which university and college education is available to most people at highly subsidized rates, it is possible to achieve large increases in the supply of any needed labour skill within just a few years. These issues are discussed at greater length in the first part of Chapter 14.

The labour force as a whole is mobile, even though many individual members in it are not.

The mobility of labour may sound like a pretty abstract topic—one that is hard to get excited about. You may not think so, however, when you find that jobs for which you are trained are abundant but only at the other end of the country. One particular case of labour mobility has become hotly debated in Canada in the past few years. Some economists and policymakers are concerned about the net flow of workers, especially highly skilled ones, from Canada to the United States—what has become known as Canada's "brain drain." *Applying Economic Concepts 13-1* discusses the recent mobility of labour between Canada and the United States, and outlines some of the central issues in the debate.

The Supply of Factors to a Particular Firm

Most firms usually employ a small proportion of the total supply of each factor that they use. As a result, they can usually obtain their factors at the going market price. This is true both in the case of less-skilled workers and in the case of highly skilled workers. For example, a firm of management consultants can usually augment its clerical staff by placing an ad in the local newspaper and paying the going rate for clerks. A university which is hoping to expand its economics department can similarly place an ad in *The Economist* or in a professional journal; it would also find itself paying the going rate for economics professors. In neither case will the employer's hiring actions affect the rate of pay earned by clerks (or professors) in its area.

Individual firms generally face perfectly elastic supply curves for factors, even though the supply for the economy as a whole may be quite inelastic.

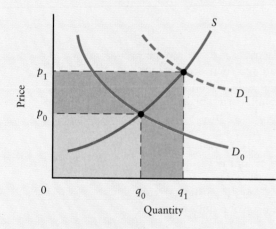

FIGURE 13-4 The Determination of Factor Price and Income in a Competitive Factor Market

In competitive factor markets, demand and supply determine factor prices, quantities of factors used, and factor incomes. With demand and supply curves D_0 and S, the price of the factor will be p_0 and the quantity employed will be q_0. The total income earned by the factor is the light gray shaded area. A shift in demand from D_0 to D_1 raises equilibrium price and quantity to p_1 and q_1, respectively. The income earned by the factor rises by an amount equal to the dark gray shaded area.

The Operation of Factor Markets

Once you have mastered the basic analysis of demand and supply in Chapters 3 through 5, the determination of the price, quantity, and income of a factor in a single market poses no new problems. Figure 13-4 shows a competitive market for a factor. The intersection of the demand and the supply curve determine the factor's price and the quantity of it that is employed. The price times quantity is the factor's total income.

In this section, we explore three issues relating to factor pricing. First, what explains the differences in payments received by different units of the same factor? For example, why do some workers get paid more than others? Second, what is the effectiveness of policies designed to reduce these differences? Can policies that promote "pay equity" eliminate these differences? Finally, we explore the important concept of *economic rent*.

Differentials in Factor Prices

Why is it that airline pilots typically get paid more than auto mechanics? Why does an acre of land in downtown Calgary rent for much more than an acre of land 150 kilometres away in the Crowsnest Pass? Are such *factor-price differentials* to be expected in well-functioning markets?

If all workers were the same, if the attractiveness of all jobs were the same, and if workers moved freely among markets, the price of labour would be the same in all uses. Workers would move from low-priced jobs to high-priced ones. The quantity of labour supplied would diminish in low-wage occupations and the resulting labour shortage would tend to force those wages up. Conversely, the quantity of labour supplied would increase in high-wage occupations and the resulting surplus would force wages down. The movement would continue until there were no further incentives to change occupations—that is, until wages were equalized in all uses.

In fact, however, wage differentials commonly occur, as is clear from even the most cursory examination of the help-wanted ads in any newspaper. As it is with labour, so it is with other factors of production. If all units of any factor of production were identical and moved freely among markets, all units would receive the same remuneration in equilibrium. In fact, however, different units of any one factor receive different payments.

Factor-price differentials can be divided into two types: those that exist only temporarily and those that exist in long-run equilibrium.

Temporary factor-price differentials lead to, and are eroded by, factor mobility. Equilibrium differentials are not eliminated by factor mobility.

Let's see why this is the case.

Temporary Differentials

Some factor-price differentials reflect temporary disturbances in factor markets. They are brought about by circumstances such as the growth of one industry and the decline of another. The differentials themselves lead to reallocation of factors, and such reallocations in turn act to eliminate the differentials.

Consider the effect on factor prices of a rise in the demand for air transport and a decline in the demand for rail transport. The airline industry's demand for factors increases while the railroad industry's demand for factors decreases. Factor prices will go up in airlines and down in railroads. The differential in factor prices causes a net movement of factors away from the railroad industry and toward the airline industry, and this movement causes the differentials to lessen and eventually to disappear. How long this process takes will depend on how easily factors can be reallocated from one industry to the other—that is, on the degree of factor mobility.

The behaviour that causes the erosion of temporary differentials is summarized in the hypothesis of the *maximization of net advantage:* The owners of factors of production will allocate those factors to uses that maximize the net advantages to themselves, taking both monetary and nonmonetary rewards into consideration. If net advantages were higher

APPLYING ECONOMIC CONCEPTS 13-1

Is Canada Suffering a "Brain Drain"?

Thousands of United Empire Loyalists left the American colonies in the late 1770s and settled in what eventually became eastern and southern Ontario. A century later, thousands of Canadians moved to work in the rapidly expanding textile factories in Massachusetts and other New England states. Indeed, workers have been flowing in both directions across the 49th parallel for centuries. The close proximity of Canada and the United States, combined with a shared language and similar culture, makes moving between the two countries relatively easy. This movement of workers is an excellent example of labour mobility.

Recent Canada–U.S. Migration

The accompanying figure shows the annual total flows of migrants between Canada and the United States between 1982 and 1996. By migration, we mean people who move permanently between countries. In 1982, the two flows were about the same—approximately 3500 workers per year migrated in each direction. More recently, however, the flows out of Canada have grown substantially whereas the flows into Canada have gradually declined. By 1996, almost 7000 Canadian workers were migrating annually to the United States whereas only 1300 were coming in the opposite direction.

Note that these migration data understate the amount of worker mobility. Many workers move temporarily between the two countries, working for several months or even a few years before returning to their home country. There is some debate about the size of these flows of temporary workers, but based on research by John Helliwell at UBC, the annual flow of temporary workers from Canada to the United States appears to be roughly 10 000.

Two questions immediately come to mind regarding these data. First, who are these mobile workers? When the migration data are examined more closely, we see a net outflow from Canada of all broad categories of worker—professionals, managers, skilled workers and unskilled workers. The greatest outflow, however, occurs among the professionals and managers. For the temporary workers, the data are less clear, but roughly half of the annual outflow have university degrees.

Second, why are these people moving? This question is more difficult to answer precisely. Here are four possible an-

swers. First, U.S. immigration policy, especially toward Canadians, has loosened since the inception of the Canada-U.S. Free Trade Agreement (FTA) in 1989 and the North American Free Trade Agreement (NAFTA) in 1994. But this only tells us that it is easier to move than before—it doesn't tell us why people want to move in the first place. Second, job prospects for certain types of workers may be more promising in the United States than in Canada. This may be especially true for university researchers and workers in the health-care sector. As government budget cuts during the 1990s have hit these publicly funded areas sharply, highly trained workers may be led to seek better prospects in the United States. A third explanation is that relatively higher personal income-tax rates in Canada have been driving Canadians southward, seeking a smaller "tax bite." A fourth reason for Canadians to move to the United States is that average real incomes in the United States are significantly higher than in Canada—the gap was approximately 30 percent in 1997.

The "Brain Drain"

Many Canadian economists and policymakers have come to see this net outflow of Canadian workers—the "brain drain"—as an important problem. They argue that the brain drain generates both short-term and long-term costs. To the extent that education and skills are an important determinant of long-run economic growth, the departure of highly trained workers will harm Canada's long-run growth potential. This is the long-run cost.

The short-run cost is the effect on the government's fiscal budget. First, the departure of highly trained workers means that the Canadian government will no longer be able to tax their higher-than-average incomes. This is a direct reduction in government revenues. Second, the education and skills acquired by people in Canada before they move to the United States have, in general, been provided at publicly funded institutions. Thus, Canadian taxpayers are financing individuals to acquire education that is then used to generate benefits accruing to those in the United States—this is a transfer from Canadian taxpayers to U.S. residents.

Many who see the brain drain as a serious economic problem advocate "doing something" to either reduce or re-

in occupation A than in occupation B, factors would move from B to A. The increased supply in A and the reduced supply in B would drive factor earnings down in A and up in B until net advantages would be equalized, after which no further movement would occur. This analysis gives rise to the prediction of *equal net advantage*: In equilibrium, units of each verse this outflow of Canadian workers. But what can be done? The Canadian tax system is a straightforward policy tool that many economists and policymakers have advocated using. They propose reducing tax rates as a way of preventing both the short-run and long-run costs that a continuing brain drain would otherwise cause. Another option that is more directed at reducing the mobility of highly trained workers is to make students pay the full cost of their university education unless they remain in Canada for a specified number of years after graduation. This would both reduce the outflow of workers and, where such an outflow still existed, reduce the cost to Canadian taxpayers.

An Important Debate

Some economists suggest several reasons why the brain drain may not be so serious. They point to the large flow of temporary workers from Canada to the United Sates and note that as long as those workers return to Canada, there will be no permanent costs for the Canadian economy. But many economists fear that a large fraction of those large annual flows of "temporary" workers will quickly choose to remain in the United States where job prospects are better and real incomes are higher.

The second point is that the mobility between Canada and the United States is only part of the story. Equally important is the mobility of workers between Canada and other countries. Canada may be suffering a brain drain to the United States, but if this is more than made up by a "brain gain" from other countries, then perhaps there is no real

problem at all. Indeed, Helliwell's data suggest that over the past fifty years, total emigration from Canada has averaged only about 35 percent of total immigration to Canada. Others point out, however, that these workers from Asia, Eastern Europe or South America tend to be slightly less skilled than the workers we lose to the United States.

Finally, note that the annual flows of workers shown in the figure are actually small compared to the total Canadian labour force. In 1996, the Canadian labour force was 15.1 million workers. Thus, the outflow of 7000 workers was only 0.0004 percent of the labour force. Even if we add the full 10 000 temporary workers, the total is still only 0.001 percent of the labour force. Other economists, however, note that while this flow is small relative to the overall Canadian labour force, it is a much larger fraction of Canada's stock of highly skilled workers. And it is the loss of these workers that is at the heart of the issue.

So what is the conclusion? Is the brain drain an important enough problem that Canadian policymakers should be worried about the tax and expenditure implications, or the effects on Canada's long-run growth? It is too early for a consensus. More research will surely be done on this issue over the next few years, and perhaps then a consensus will emerge.

The migration data in this box are from D. DeVoretz and S. Laryea, "Canadian Human Capital Transfers: The United States and Beyond," C.D. Howe Institute Commentary No. 115, October 1998. See also John Helliwell, "Checking the Brain Drain: Evidence and Implications," UBC mimeo, June 1999.

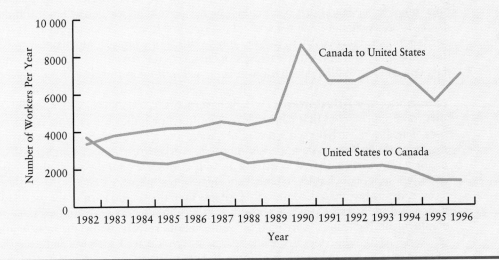

kind of factor of production will be allocated among alternative possible uses in such a way that the net advantages in all uses are equalized.

Although nonmonetary advantages are important in explaining differences in levels of pay for labour in different occupations, they tend to be fairly stable over time. As a result, monetary advantages, which vary with market conditions, lead to *changes* in net advantage.

A change in the relative price of a factor between two uses will change the net advantages of the uses. It will lead to a shift of some units of that factor to the use for which relative price has increased.

This shift implies an upward-sloping supply curve for a factor in any particular use. When the price of a factor rises in that use, more will be supplied to that use. This factor supply curve (like all supply curves) can also *shift* in response to changes in other variables. For example, an improvement in the safety record in a particular occupation improves the attractiveness of that occupation and thus shifts to the right the labour-supply curve to that occupation.

Equilibrium Differentials

Some factor-price differentials persist without generating any forces that eliminate them. These equilibrium differentials can be explained by intrinsic differences in the factors themselves and, for labour, by differences in the cost of acquiring skills and by different non-monetary advantages of different occupations. Because these factor-price differentials *compensate* for nonmonetary aspects of the job or the factor, they are commonly called **compensating differentials**; they were introduced into economics more than two hundred years ago by Adam Smith.

compensating differential
A difference in the financial payment to a factor of production (usually labour) across two jobs to compensate the factor for differences in non-monetary aspects of the two jobs.

Intrinsic Differences. If various units of a factor have different characteristics, the price that is paid may differ among these units. If dexterity is required to accomplish a task, manually dexterous workers will earn more than less dexterous workers. If land is to be used for agricultural purposes, highly fertile land will earn more than poor land. These differences will persist even in long-run equilibrium.

Acquired Differences. If the fertility of land can be increased by costly methods, then more fertile land must command a higher price than less fertile land. If it did not, landowners would not incur the costs of improving fertility. The same principle holds true for labour since it is costly to acquire most skills. For example, an engineer must train for some time, and unless the earnings of engineers remain sufficiently above what can be earned in less skilled occupations, people will not incur the cost of training.

Nonmonetary Advantages. Whenever working conditions differ among various uses for a single factor, that factor will earn different equilibrium amounts in its various uses. The difference between a test pilot's wage and a chauffeur's wage is only partly a matter of skill; the rest is compensation to the worker for facing the higher risk of testing new planes as compared to driving a car. If both were paid the same, there would be an excess supply of chauffeurs and a shortage of test pilots.

Academic researchers commonly earn less than they could earn in the world of commerce and industry because of the substantial nonmonetary advantages of academic employment. If chemists were paid the same in both sectors, many chemists would prefer academic to industrial jobs. Excess demand for industrial chemists and excess supply of academic chemists would then force chemists' wages up in industry and down in academia until the two types of jobs seemed equally attractive on balance.

Equilibrium differentials also exist in the regional earnings of otherwise identical factors. People who work in remote logging or mining areas are paid more than are people who do jobs requiring similar skills in large cities. Without higher pay, not enough people would be willing to work at sometimes dangerous jobs in unattractive or remote locations. Similarly, because many people prefer living in the Maritimes to living in the Yukon, equilibrium wages in comparable occupations are lower in the Maritimes than in the Yukon.

Pay Equity

The distinction between temporary and equilibrium factor-price differentials raises an important consideration for policy. Trade unions, governments, and other bodies often have explicit policies about earnings differentials, sometimes seeking to eliminate them in the name of equity. The success of such policies depends to a great extent on the kind of differential that is being attacked. One general lesson here is the following: Policies that attempt to eliminate *equilibrium* differentials will encounter severe difficulties.

Some government legislation attempts to impose *equal pay for work of equal value,* or **pay equity.** Such policy is designed to eliminate the wage differentials that exist between workers *in different jobs* but who are deemed to have approximately the same skills and responsibilities. For example, a policy of pay equity might require that a nurse with 10 years of experience receive the same salary as a teacher with 10 years of experience. Whatever the social value of such laws, they run into trouble whenever they require equal pay for jobs that have different nonmonetary advantages.

To illustrate the nature of the problem encountered by such legislation, consider the following example. Suppose that two jobs demand equal skills, training, and everything else that is taken into account in a decision about what constitutes work of equal value but that, in a city with an unpleasant climate, one is an outside job and the other is an inside job. If legislation requires equal pay for both jobs, there will be a shortage of people who are willing to work outside and an excess of people who want to work inside. Employers will seek ways to attract outside workers. Higher pensions, shorter hours, and longer holidays may be offered. If these are allowed, they will achieve the desired result but will defeat the original purpose of equalizing the monetary benefits of the inside and outside jobs; they will also cut down on the number of outside workers that employers will hire because the total cost of an outside worker to an employer will have risen. If the jobs are unionized or if the government prevents such "cheating," the shortage of workers for outside jobs will remain.

In Chapter 14, we discuss the effects of race and sex discrimination on wage differentials. Although these effects can be important, it remains true that many factor-price differentials are a natural market consequence of supply and demand conditions that have nothing to do with inequitable treatment of different groups in the society.

Policies that seek to eliminate factor-price differentials without consideration of what causes them or how they affect the supply of the factor often have perverse results.

Economic Rent

One of the most important concepts in economics is that of *economic rent*.

A factor must earn a certain amount in its present use to prevent it from moving to another use—Alfred Marshall called this amount the factor's **transfer earnings.** If there were no nonmonetary advantages in alternative uses, as is typically the case for land and capital, the factor would have to earn its opportunity cost (what it could earn elsewhere) to prevent it from moving elsewhere.

pay equity
A government policy designed to eliminate the wage differentials between workers in different jobs who nonetheless appear to have similar levels of skills and responsibilities.

transfer earnings
The payment required by a factor in order to prevent it from leaving to other uses. Any payment in excess of the transfer earnings is economic rent.

For labour, however, the nonmonetary advantages of various jobs are very important. Labour must earn enough in each use to equate the total advantages—both monetary and nonmonetary—among various jobs. For example, in order to accept a job that is dirty or unsafe, workers will require a higher wage so that the total advantage of the unsafe job equals the total advantage of some alternative job.

Any excess that a factor earns over the minimum amount needed to keep it at its present use is called its **economic rent**. Economic rent is analogous to economic profit as a surplus over the opportunity cost of capital. Here are three examples:

economic rent   The surplus of total earnings over what must be paid to prevent a factor from moving to another use.

1. Consider a farmer who grows wheat and earns $1000 per acre. He has calculated that if his earnings fall to $900 per acre, he will switch to growing barley instead, his next best alternative. In this case, each acre of land is earning $100 of economic rent.

2. A famous actor earns $15 million per year. She decides that her next best alternative to acting is to promote shampoo in television commercials, in which case she would earn $2.5 million per year. She is earning $12.5 million per year of economic rent.

3. An individual has invested $300 000 of capital into a restaurant, and currently earns a 20 percent annual return—investment income of $60 000 annually. The next best alternative investment (with similar risk) can earn a 15 percent return, or $45 000 annually. The $300 000 of capital is thus earning economic rent equal to $15 000 per year. In this case, rent is just another name for profit in the economist's sense of the term.

The concept of economic rent is crucial in predicting the effects that changes in earnings have on the movement of factors among alternative uses. However, the terminology is confusing because economic rent is often called simply *rent*, which can of course also mean the price paid to hire something, such as a machine, a piece of land, or an apartment. How the same term came to be used for these two very different concepts is explained in *Lessons from History 13-1*.

How Much of Factor Earnings Is Rent?

In most cases, as in the three previous examples, economic rent makes up part of the factor's total earnings. From the definitions above, however, note that total earnings for any factor are the sum of its transfer earnings and its economic rent.

A factor's transfer earnings plus its economic rent equals its total earnings.

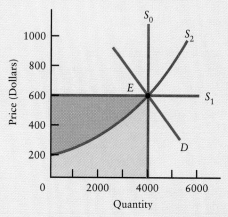

FIGURE 13-5   The Determination of Rent in Factor Payments

The amount of rent in factor payments depends on the shape of the supply curve. A single demand curve is shown with three different supply curves. In each case, the competitive equilibrium price is $600, and 4000 units of the factor are hired. The total payment ($2.4 million) is represented by the entire shaded area.

When the supply curve is vertical (S_0), the whole payment is economic rent because a decrease in price would not lead any units of the factor to move elsewhere.

When the supply curve is horizontal (S_1), none of the payment is rent because even a small decrease in price offered would lead all units of the factor to move elsewhere.

When the supply curve is positively sloped (S_2), part of the payment is rent. As shown by the height of the supply curve, at a price of $600, the 4000th unit of the factor is receiving just enough to persuade it to offer its services in this market, but the 2000th unit, for example, is earning well above what it requires to stay in this market. The aggregate of economic rents is shown by the blue shaded area, whereas the aggregate of the factor's transfer earnings is shown by the red area.

Practise with Study Guide Chapter 13, Exercises 3 and 5.

But *how much* of total earnings is economic rent? The distinction is easiest to see in two extreme examples. In the first, all of the factor's income is rent; in the second, none of the income is rent.

The possibilities are illustrated in Figure 13-5. When supply is perfectly inelastic, the same quantity is supplied whatever the price. Evidently, the quantity supplied does not decrease, no matter how low the price goes. This inelasticity indicates that the factor has no alternative use, and thus requires no minimum payment to keep it in its present use. In this case, there are no transfer earnings and so the whole of the payment is economic rent.

When supply is perfectly elastic, the factor is extremely mobile between various uses. In this case, all of the factor's income is transfer earnings and so none of it is economic rent. If any lower price is offered, nothing whatsoever will be supplied since all units of the factor will transfer to some other use.

The more usual situation is that of an upward-sloping supply curve. A rise in the factor's price serves the allocative function of attracting more units of the factor into the market in question, but the same rise provides additional economic rent to all units of the factor that are *already employed*. We know that the extra pay that is going to the units already employed is economic rent because the owners of these units were willing to

LESSONS FROM HISTORY 13-1

David Ricardo and "Economic Rent"

In the early nineteenth century, there was a public debate about the high price of wheat in England. The high price was causing great hardship because bread was a primary source of food for the working class. Some people argued that wheat had a high price because landlords were charging high rents to tenant farmers. In short, it was argued that the price of wheat was high because the rents of agricultural land were high. Some of those who held this view advocated restricting the rents that landlords could charge.

David Ricardo (1772–1823), a great British economist who was one of the originators of Classical economics, argued that the situation was exactly the reverse. The price of wheat was high, he said, because there was a shortage, caused by the Napoleonic Wars. Because wheat was profitable to produce, there was keen competition among farmers to obtain land on which to grow wheat. This competition in turn forced up the rental price of wheat land. Ricardo advocated removing the existing tariff on wheat so that imported wheat could come into the country. The increase in imports would then increase the supply of wheat in England and lower its price. This would then reduce the rent on land.

The essentials of Ricardo's argument were these: The supply of land was fixed. Land was regarded as having only one use, the growing of wheat. Nothing had to be paid to prevent land from transferring to a use other than growing wheat because it had no other use. No landowner would leave land idle as long as some return could be obtained by renting it out. Therefore, all the payment to land, that is, rent in the ordinary sense of the word, was a surplus over and above what was necessary to keep it in its present use.

Given a fixed supply of land, the price of land depended on the demand for land, which depended in turn on the demand for wheat (i.e., the demand for land was *derived from* the demand for wheat). Rent, the term for the payment for the use of land, thus became the term for a surplus payment to a factor over and above what was necessary to keep it in its present use.

Later, two facts were realized. First, land often had alternative uses, and, from the point of view of any one use, part of the payment made to land would necessarily have to be paid to keep it in that use. Second, factors of production other than land also often earned a surplus over and above what was necessary to keep them in their present use. This surplus is now called *economic rent*, whether the factor is land, labour, or a piece of capital equipment.

supply them at the lower price. The general result for a positively sloped supply curve is stated as follows.

If the demand for a factor in any of its uses rises relative to the supply available to that use, its price will rise in that use. This increase in price will serve the allocative function of attracting additional units into that use. It will also increase the economic rent to all units of the factor already in that use.

Various Perspectives on Economic Rent

The proportion of a given factor payment that is economic rent varies from situation to situation. We cannot point to a factor of production and assert that some fixed fraction of its income is always its economic rent. The proportion of its earnings that is rent depends on its alternatives.

Consider first a narrowly defined use of a given factor—say, its use by a particular firm. From that firm's point of view, the factor will be highly mobile, as it could readily move to another firm in the same industry. The firm must pay the going wage or risk losing that factor. Thus, from the perspective of the single firm, a large proportion of the payment made to a factor is needed to prevent it from transferring to another use. Thus, only a small portion of its payment is rent.

Now consider a more broadly defined use—for example, the factor's use in an entire industry. From the industry's point of view, the factor is less mobile because it would be more difficult for it to gain employment quickly outside the industry. From the perspective of the particular *industry* (rather than the specific *firm* within the industry), a larger proportion of the payment to a factor is economic rent.

From the even more general perspective of a particular *occupation*, mobility is likely to be even less, and the proportion of the factor payment that is economic rent is likely to be more. It may be easier, for example, for a carpenter to move from the construction industry to the furniture industry than to retrain to be a computer programmer.

As the perspective moves from a narrowly defined use of a factor to a broadly defined use of a factor, the mobility of the factor decreases; as mobility decreases, the share of the factor payment that is economic rent increases.

Whether Michael Jordan's immense salary with the Chicago Bulls was economic rent depends on the perspective. From the perspective of the entire NBA, most of his salary was economic rent.

Consider how this relationship applies to the often controversial large salaries that are received by some highly specialized types of labourers, such as recording stars and professional athletes. These performers have a style and a talent that cannot be duplicated, whatever the training. The earnings that they receive are mostly economic rent from the viewpoint of the occupation: These performers generally enjoy their occupations and would pursue them for much less than the high remuneration that they actually receive.

For example, Michael Jordan would probably have chosen basketball over other alternatives even at a much lower salary. However, because of Jordan's amazing skills as a basketball player, most NBA teams would have paid handsomely to have him on their rosters, and he was able to command a high salary from the team he did play for. From the perspective of the individual firm, the Chicago Bulls, most of Jordan's salary was required to keep him from switching to another team and hence was not economic rent. From the point of view of the basketball "industry," however, much of his salary was economic rent.

Notice also that Michael Jordan's salary was largely determined by the demand for his services. The supply was perfectly inelastic—no one else possessed his particular combination of skills. So the market-clearing price was determined by the position of the demand curve.

A Final Word

This chapter has examined the operation of factor markets. You should now be able to answer the questions that we posed in the opening paragraph. Here are some of the key points for two of those questions.

What explains why professors usually get paid more than high-school teachers? Part of the answer surely lies in the fact that to be a university professor typically requires nine years of university education (four for the bachelor's degree plus five for the completion of the master's degree and the doctorate) whereas to be a teacher usually requires only four or five years. Since that extra education is costly and time-consuming, it is not surprising that fewer people are willing to become university professors than teachers. This lower supply for professors, other things equal, leads to a higher wage.

Why does an acre of farm land in northern Saskatchewan rent for far less than an acre of land in downtown Toronto? To answer this, just think about the alternative uses for the farm land, and compare them to the alternative uses for the acre in downtown Toronto. The acre of farm land has very few alternative uses. Or, more correctly, it has many alternative uses, but there is little demand to use that particular piece of land to build a skyscraper, shopping mall, or baseball stadium. But one acre of land in downtown Toronto has many alternative uses—there always seems to be demand for additional space for parking garages, office buildings, retail stores, and many other things. Since the piece of farm land in Saskatchewan must stay where it is, its rental price is determined by demand. Since there is little demand for the land, its rental price is low. Similarly, the land in downtown Toronto cannot move anywhere, and so its rental price is determined by demand. And since there is lots of demand for an acre in downtown Toronto, its rental price is high.

Having learned about factor markets in general, we are now ready to examine some specific factor markets. In Chapter 14, we examine some details about labour markets, such as minimum wages, discrimination, and labour unions. In Chapter 15, we examine the pricing of physical capital and of nonrenewable resources.

S U M M A R Y

Income Distribution

LO 1

- The functional distribution of income refers to the shares of total national income going to each of the major factors of production; it focuses on sources of income. The size distribution of income refers to the shares of total national income going to various groups of households; it focuses only on the amount of income, not its source.

- Canada has considerable inequality in the distribution of income. The poorest fifth of families currently receive 2.1 percent of aggregate pre-tax income; the richest fifth receives 44.6 percent. But Canada's tax-and-transfer system reduces the extent of inequality—the poorest fifth of families earn 7.7 percent of after-tax income.

- The income of a factor of production is composed of two elements: the price paid per unit of the factor and the quantity of the factor used. The determination of factor prices and quantities is an application of the same price theory that is used to determine product prices and quantities.

The Demand for Factors

- The firm's decisions on how much to produce and how to produce it imply demands for factors of production, which are said to be derived from the demand for goods that they are used to produce.
- A profit-maximizing firm will hire units of a factor until the last unit adds as much to cost as it does to revenue. Thus, the marginal cost of the factor will be equated with that factor's marginal revenue product.
- When the firm is a price taker in input markets, the marginal cost of the factor is its price per unit. When the firm sells its output in a competitive market, the marginal revenue product is the factor's marginal physical product multiplied by the market price of the output.

- A price-taking firm's demand for a factor is negatively sloped because the law of diminishing returns implies that the marginal physical product of a factor declines as more of that factor is employed (with other inputs held constant).
- The industry's demand for a factor will be more elastic (a) the slower the marginal physical product of the factor declines as more of the factor is used, (b) the easier it is to substitute one factor for another, (c) the larger the proportion of total variable costs accounted for by the cost of the factor in question, and (d) the more elastic the demand for the good that the factor is used to produce.

The Supply of Factors

- The total supply of each factor is fixed at any moment but varies over time. The supply of labour depends on the size of the population, the participation rate, and the number of hours that people want to work.
- A rise in the wage rate has a substitution effect, which tends to induce more work, and an income effect, which tends to induce less work (more leisure consumed).

- The supply of a factor to a particular industry or occupation is more elastic than its supply to the whole economy because one industry can bid units away from other industries. The elasticity of supply to a particular use depends on factor mobility, which tends to be greater the longer the time allowed for a reaction to take place.

The Operation of Factor Markets

- Factor-price differentials often occur in competitive markets. Temporary differentials in the earnings of different units of factors of production induce factor movements that eventually remove the differentials. Equilibrium differentials reflect differences among units of factors as well as nonmonetary benefits of different jobs; they can persist indefinitely.
- Equal net advantage is a theory of the allocation of the total supply of factors to particular uses. Owners of factors will choose the use that produces the greatest net

advantage, allowing for both the monetary and non-monetary advantages of a particular employment.
- Some amount must be paid to a factor to prevent it from transferring to another use. This amount is the factor's transfer earnings. Economic rent is the difference between that amount and a factor's actual earnings. Whenever the supply curve is positively sloped, part of the total payment going to a factor is needed to prevent it from transferring to another use, and part of it is rent. The more narrowly defined the use, the larger the fraction that is transfer earnings and the smaller the fraction that is economic rent.

KEY CONCEPTS

Functional distribution and size distribution of income

Derived demand for a factor

Marginal physical product *(MPP)*

Marginal revenue product *(MRP)*

The determinants of elasticity of factor demand

Factor mobility

Temporary versus equilibrium factor-price differentials

Equal net advantage

Transfer earnings

Economic rent

STUDY EXERCISES

1. The table below shows the size distribution of income for Fantasyland.

Household Income Rank	Percentage of Aggregate Income	Cumulative Total
Lowest fifth	6.8	—
Second fifth	14.1	—
Third fifth	21.5	—
Fourth fifth	26.2	—
Highest fifth	31.4	—

   a. Compute the cumulative percentage of total income. Fill in the table.
   b. On a scale diagram, with the percentage of households on the vertical axis and the percentage of aggregate income on the horizontal axis, plot the Lorenz curve for Fantasyland.
   c. How does the diagram show the extent of income inequality in Fantasyland?
   d. Now suppose that Fantasyland introduces a system which redistributes income from higher-income households to lower-income households. How would this affect the Lorenz curve?

2. Demands for the following goods and services are increasing rapidly. In each case, list two derived demands that you predict will be increasing as a result.

   a. Demand for natural gas
   b. Demand for medical services
   c. Demand for international travel
   d. Demand for children's computer games

3. The diagram below shows the market for fast-food workers in British Columbia.

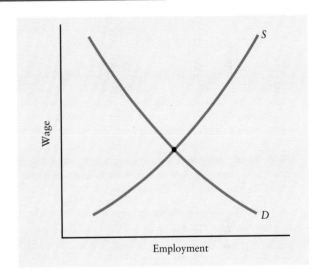

   a. The supply curve is upward sloping. If the wage in this industry rises, where do the extra workers come from?
   b. Suppose there is a significant decrease in demand for fast food. How is this likely to affect fast-food workers' earnings? Show this in the diagram.
   c. Now suppose that new legislation bans high-school students from doing any homework. As a result, more students look for jobs in the fast-food industry. How will this affect the labour market for fast-food workers? Show this in the diagram.

4. The three following diagrams show the supply of luxury ocean liners at three different levels of aggregation—the entire world, a particular country, and a particular firm.

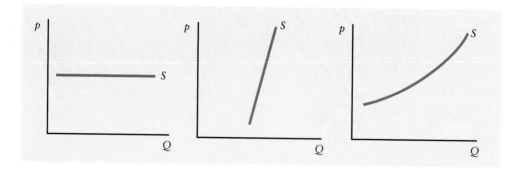

a. Which diagram shows the supply of ocean liners to the world as whole? Explain its elasticity.

b. Which diagram shows the supply of ocean liners to Canada? Explain its elasticity.

c. Which diagram shows the supply of ocean liners to an individual Canadian firm? Explain its elasticity.

d. What is the general relationship between factor mobility and the elasticity of factor supply?

5. In the text we argued that temporary factor-price differentials tend to be eroded by factor mobility. This question requires you to think about this process. Consider the two markets for sheet-iron workers and steel-pipe workers in the same region. Suppose both markets are competitive. We begin in a situation in which both sheet-iron workers and steel-pipe workers earn $20 per hour. Assume that workers can switch reasonably easily between the two jobs.

a. Draw diagrams showing the supply and demand for labour in each market.

b. Now suppose there is a sharp increase in the demand for steel pipe. Explain what happens in the market for steel-pipe workers.

c. If the employment of steel-pipe workers increased in part **b**, explain where the extra workers came from.

d. What effect does the event in part **b** have on the market for sheet-iron workers?

e. What is the long-run effect of the shock on the relative wages in the two types of jobs?

6. How much of the following payments for factor services is likely to be economic rent?

a. The $750 per month that a landlord receives for an apartment rented to students

b. The salary of the Canadian Prime Minister

c. The annual income of Tiger Woods or Shania Twain

d. The salary of a window cleaner who says, "It's dangerous work, but it beats driving a truck."

DISCUSSION QUESTIONS

1. Other things being equal, how would you expect each of the following events to affect the size distribution of after-tax income?

a. An increase in unemployment

b. Rapid population growth in an already crowded city

c. An increase in food prices relative to other prices

d. An increase in social insurance benefits and taxes

e. Elimination of the personal income-tax exemption for interest earned within an RRSP.

2. A labour dispute has broken out at a university between the faculty and the university's board of governors. One of the issues is the faculty's complaint that summer school teaching salaries are below the regional average and hence too low. The trustees argue that considering that they have more professors asking to teach summer school at the current pay than they have courses for these faculty to teach, the pay is adequate. Comment.

3. This chapter introduced the Lorenz curve, which gives a graphical representation of the equality of income distribution. Many observers criticize Canadian policy because Canada's Lorenz curve is bent significantly off the diagonal. Can you provide an economically valid defence of this criticism? If you could pick a shape for

the nation's Lorenz curve, what would it be? Defend your choice using positive economic tools.

4. A recent *Wall Street Journal* article asks, "Why do baseball players earn millions of dollars a year for their negligible contribution to society while major contributors—such as schoolteachers, policemen, firemen, and ambulance drivers—earn barely enough to survive?" Can you offer an answer based on what was discussed in this chapter?

5. For most of the years in the past two decades, the unemployment rate in the province of Quebec has been higher than the Canadian average. It has also been higher than the unemployment rate in next-door Ontario. Given that there are almost no legal restrictions on the flow of labour across Canadian provincial boundaries, provide an explanation for how such a gap in unemployment rates can persist for so long.

CHAPTER 14

Labour Markets

LO *LEARNING OBJECTIVES*

❶ Explain wage differentials in competitive labour markets.

❷ Explain the wage differentials that arise in imperfectly competitive labour markets.

❸ Understand the effects of legislated minimum wages.

❹ Recognize the tradeoff that unions face between employment and wages.

❺ Explain why the trend away from manufacturing jobs and toward service jobs is not necessarily a problem for the economy as a whole.

The competitive theory of factor-price determination, presented in Chapter 13, tells us a great deal about factor prices, factor movements, and the distribution of income. In this chapter, we apply this theory to the most important of factor markets, the labour market. In the process, we extend the theory to cover situations in which suppliers and demanders of labour have some market power in the labour market, and are thus not price takers. We also examine the effects of legislated minimum wages and the role of labour unions. The chapter closes with a discussion of the often-heard claim that Canada and other developed countries have been gaining "bad jobs" at the expense of "good jobs."

Wage Differentials

If all workers were identical, all jobs had the same working conditions, and labour markets were perfectly competitive, all workers would earn the same wage. In reality, however, wages vary enormously across workers and occupations. Generally, the more education and experience a worker has, the higher are his or her wages. Given equal education and experience, women on average earn less than men. Workers in highly unionized industries tend to get paid more than workers with similar skills and experience in nonunionized industries. Such differentials arise because workers are not all identical, jobs are not all identical, and because many important noncompetitive forces operate in labour markets. We now look more systematically at the reasons why different types of labour earn different wages.

Wage Differentials in Competitive Markets

Where there are many employers (buyers) and many workers (sellers), there is a competitive labour market of the kind discussed in Chapter 13. Under competitive conditions, the wage rate and level of employment are set by supply and demand. No worker or group of workers, and no firm or group of firms, is able to affect the market wage. In practice, however, there are many kinds of workers and many kinds of jobs. We can therefore think of a series of related labour markets rather than a single national market. Among these various labour markets, there are several reasons for wage differentials.

Working Conditions

Given identical skills, those working under relatively onerous or risky conditions earn more than those working in pleasant or safe conditions. For example, construction workers who work the "high iron," assembling the frames for skyscrapers, are paid more than workers who do similar work at ground level. The reason is simple: Risk and unpleasantness reduce the supply of labour, thus raising the wage above what it would otherwise be. Different working conditions in different jobs thus lead to wage differentials—these are equilibrium differentials as discussed in Chapter 13.

In competitive labour markets, supply and demand set the equilibrium wage, but the wage will differ according to the nonmonetary aspects of the job.

Inherited Skills

Large incomes will be earned by people who have scarce skills that cannot be taught and that are highly valued—for example, the physical ability to be an NBA basketball player. In this case, the combination of a small and inelastic supply and a large enough demand of the relevant kind of labour cause the market-clearing wage to be high. Wage differentials of this kind are equilibrium differentials.

Inherited skills, which are mostly beyond the individual's control, can have important effects on wages.

Human Capital

A machine is physical capital. It requires an investment of time and money to create it, and once created, it yields valuable services over a long time. In the same way, labour skills require an investment of time and money to acquire, and once acquired, they yield an increased income to their owner over a long time. Since investment in labour skills is similar to investment in physical capital, acquired skills are called **human capital.** The more costly it is to acquire the skill required for a particular job, the higher its pay must be to attract people to train for it.

human capital   The capitalized value of productive investments in persons; usually refers to value derived from expenditures on education, training, and health improvements.

Investment in human capital is costly, and the return is usually in terms of higher future wages.

The two main ways in which human capital is acquired are through formal education and on-the-job training.

Formal Education.   Compulsory education is an attempt to provide some minimum human capital for all citizens. Some people, either through luck or through their own efforts, acquire more human capital than others. Subsequent income differentials

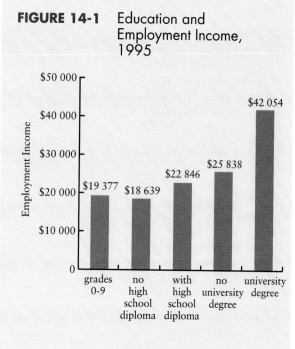

FIGURE 14-1   Education and Employment Income, 1995

There is a financial payoff to formal education, especially a university degree. The increase in employment income that can be expected from extra education is modest for levels of education below a university degree. But the payoff for completing a university degree is very substantial.

(*Source:* These data are available on Statistics Canada's website: www.statcan.ca.)

reflect these differences in human capital acquired in the early stages of education.

Those who decide to stay in school beyond the years of compulsory education, such as the people reading this book, are deciding to invest voluntarily in acquiring further human capital. The opportunity cost is measured by the income that could have been earned if the person had entered the labour force immediately, in addition to any out-of-pocket costs for such items as tuition fees and equipment. The return is measured by the higher income earned when a better job is obtained.

How large is the payoff to higher education? Figure 14-1 shows how average employment income varies with years of schooling. In 1995, the latest year for which census data are available, the average employment income for Canadians with a university degree was just over $42 000; in contrast, someone who had completed grade 9 or less had an average employment income of less than half this amount.

Evidence suggests that in recent years the demand for workers with more education has been rising relative to the demand for those with less education. As we would expect, this change in relative demand raises the relative wages of more-educated people, thereby increasing the payoff to their investment in education. Not surprisingly, students today find the completion of a university degree much more important than did students a generation ago.

Changes in demand and supply change the costs and benefits of acquiring human capital. Individuals respond according to their personal assessment of these costs and benefits.

On-the-Job Training.   Wage differentials according to experience are readily observable in most firms and occupations. To a significant extent, these differentials are a response to human capital acquired on the job. For example, a civil engineer with 20 years' experience in bridge design will generally earn more than a newly graduated civil engineer, even though they both have the same formal education.

On-the-job training is important in creating rising wages for employees and for making firms competitive. Evidence suggests that people who miss on-the-job training early in life are handicapped relative to others throughout much of their later working careers.

Wage differentials that are due to differences in human capital—either through formal education or on-the-job-training—are *temporary* differentials. In the long run, these wage differentials will affect the choices that individuals make about investing in human capital. These choices will, in turn, help to erode these differentials. For example, if university graduates earn more than high-school graduates, then more people will choose to attend university. This will eventually increase the supply of university graduates (and reduce the supply of people with only a high-school education) and thus reduce their wage relative to high-school graduates. Full adjustment in this process will clearly not occur immediately, and may take many years.

Wage differentials due to differences in human capital will eventually be eroded by the changing pattern of human-capital acquisition. But these wage differentials may persist for many years.

Gender and Race Discrimination

Crude statistics show that incomes vary by race and gender. For example, the average full-time female worker in Canada earns only about 75 percent of the wage of the average full-time male worker. More detailed studies suggest that a significant part of these differences can be explained by such considerations as the amount of human capital acquired through both formal education and on-the-job experience. When all such explanations are taken into account, however, there still appears to be some discrimination on the basis of both gender and race. The following is a simple model of labour-market discrimination.

To isolate the effects of discrimination, we begin by building a simplified picture of a nondiscriminating labour market and then introduce discrimination between two sets of equally qualified workers. The discussion here is phrased in terms of males and females but the analysis applies equally well to any situation in which workers are distinguished on grounds *other than* their ability, such as race or skin colour, citizenship, religion, sexual preference, or political beliefs.

FIGURE 14-2 The Effect of Discrimination on Wages

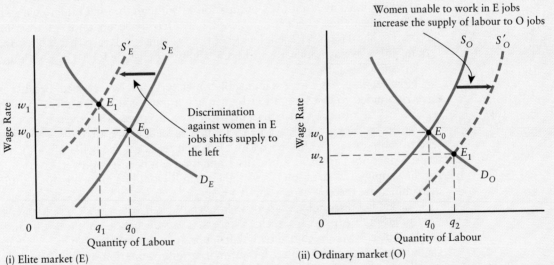

If market E discriminates against one group and market O does not, the supply curve will shift to the left in E and to the right in O. Market E requires above-average skills, while market O requires only ordinary skills. When there is no discrimination, demand and supply are D_E and S_E in market E and D_O and S_O in market O. Initially, the wage rate is w_0 and employment is q_0 in each market. (w_0 in market E will be higher than w_0 in market O because the workers in E have higher skills than those in O.) When all women are barred from E occupations, the supply curve shifts to S'_E, and the wage earned by the remaining workers, all of whom are men, rises to w_1. Women put out of work in the E occupations now seek work in the O occupations. The resulting shift in the supply curve to S'_O brings down the wage to w_2 in the O occupations. Because all women are in O occupations, they have a lower wage rate than many men. The average male wage in the economy is higher than the average female wage.

334 PART 5 FACTOR MARKETS

Suppose that half of the people are male and the other half are female. Each group has the same proportion who are educated to various levels, identical distributions of talent, and so on. Suppose also that there are two occupations. Occupation E (*elite*) requires people of above-average education and skills, and occupation O (*ordinary*) can use anyone. Finally, suppose that the nonmonetary aspects of the two occupations are the same.

In the absence of discrimination, the theory of competitive factor markets that we have developed suggests that the wages in E occupations will be bid up above those in O occupations in order that the E jobs attract the workers of above-average skills. Men and women of above-average skill will take the E jobs, while the others, both men and women, will have no choice but to seek O jobs. Because skills are equally distributed among both sexes, each occupation will employ one-half men and one-half women.

Now suppose that discrimination enters in an extreme form. All E occupations are hereafter open only to men, but O occupations are open to either men or women. The immediate effect is to reduce by 50 percent the supply of job candidates for E occupations; candidates must now be *both* men and above average. The discrimination also increases the supply of applicants for O jobs by 50 percent; this group now includes all women and the below-average men.

As shown in Figure 14-2, wages rise in E occupations and fall in O occupations.

Discrimination, by changing supply, can decrease the wages and incomes of a group that is discriminated against.

In the longer run, further changes may occur. Notice that total employment in the E jobs falls. Employers may find ways to use slightly below average labour and thus lure the next best qualified men out of O occupations. Although this will raise O wages slightly, it will also make these occupations increasingly "female occupations." If discrimination has been in place for a sufficient length of time, women will learn that it does not pay to acquire above-average skills. Regardless of ability, women are forced by discrimination to work in unskilled jobs.

Now suppose that a long-standing discriminatory policy is reversed. Because they will have responded to discrimination by acquiring fewer skills than men, many women will be locked into the O occupations, at least for a time. Moreover, if both men and women come to expect that women will have less education than men, employers will tend to look for men to fill the E jobs. This will reinforce the belief of women that education does not pay. Such subtle discrimination can persist for a very long time, making the supply of women to O jobs higher than it would be in the absence of the initial discrimination, thereby depressing the wages of women and below-average men.

The kind of discrimination that we have considered in our model is extreme. It is similar to the South African apartheid system that was dismantled in the 1980s and 1990s, in which blacks were excluded by law from prestigious and high-paying occupations. In Canada and the United States, labour-market discrimination against a specific group usually occurs in somewhat less obvious ways. First, it may be difficult (but not impossible, as in our model) for members of the group to get employment in certain jobs. Second, members of groups subject to discrimination may receive lower pay for a given kind of work than members of groups not subject to discrimination.

Wage Differentials in Noncompetitive Markets

We have examined several explanations for why wage differentials exist in competitive labour markets. Another explanation for wage differentials is that the labour market may *not* be competitive. In Chapters 9 through 11, we distinguished different *structures* for the markets in which firms sell their outputs. The inputs that firms use are also bought in markets that can have different structures. Although some markets are perfectly competitive, many show elements of market power on either the demand or the supply side.

To study the influence of different labour-market structures on wages, consider the case of an industry that employs identical workers for only one kind of job. In this way, we eliminate the possibility that any wage differentials are caused by differences between workers or differences between jobs—we thus highlight the role of market structure.

Let's examine two general cases. The first is one in which workers form a group and exercise some market power over setting the wage; the second is one in which the firm does not have to compete with other firms to hire workers.

Monopoly: A Union in a Competitive Market

For the purposes of our discussion of labour markets, a **union** (or *labour union*) is an association that is authorized to represent workers in negotiations with their employers. We examine unions in greater detail later in this chapter. For now we take the simple view that when workers are represented by a labour union, there is essentially only a single supplier of labour.

Suppose that a union enters a competitive labour market to represent all of the workers. As the single seller of labour for many buyers, the union is a monopolist, and it can establish a wage below which no one will work, thus changing the supply curve of labour. The industry can hire as many units of labour as are prepared to work at the union wage but no one at a lower wage. Thus, the industry (and each firm) faces a supply curve that is horizontal at the level of the union wage up to the maximum quantity of labour that is willing to work at that wage.

If the union uses its monopoly power, it will negotiate a wage above the competitive level. This situation is shown in Figure 14-3, in which the intersection of this horizontal supply curve and the demand curve establishes a higher wage rate and a lower level of employment than the competitive equilibrium. In this case, there will be some workers who would like to work in the unionized industry or occupation but cannot. A conflict of interest has been created between serving the interests of the union's employed and unemployed members.

An alternative way to achieve the higher wage is to shift the supply curve to the left. The union may do this by restricting entry into the occupation by methods such as lengthening the required period of apprenticeship and reducing openings for trainees.

FIGURE 14-3   A Union in a Competitive Labour Market

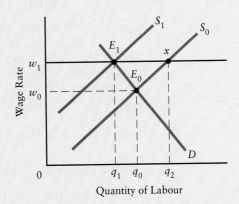

A union can raise the wages of people who continue to be employed but only by reducing the number of people employed. The competitive equilibrium is at E_0, the wage is w_0, and employment is q_0. If a union enters this market and sets a wage of w_1, a new equilibrium will be established at E_1. The supply curve has become $w_1 x S_0$. At the new wage w_1, employment will be q_1, and there will be $q_1 q_2$ workers who would like to work but whom the industry will not hire.

The wage w_1 can be achieved without generating a pool of unemployed persons. To do so, the union must restrict entry into the occupation and thus shift the supply curve to the left to S_1. Employment will again be q_1.

This figure can also be used to illustrate the effect of the government imposing a minimum wage of w_1 on the market where the competitive equilibrium is at E_0. The q_1 workers who remain employed benefit by the wage increase. The $q_1 q_0$ workers who lose their jobs in this industry suffer to the extent that they fail to find new jobs at a wage of w_0 or more.

union   An association authorized to represent workers in bargaining with employers. Also called *trade union* and *labour union*.

Practise with Study Guide Chapter 14, Exercise 1.

Alternatively, the union may shift the supply curve by persuading the government to impose restrictive licensing or certification requirements on people who wish to work.

By restricting entry into the occupation or industry, unions may drive the wage above the competitive level.

Raising wages by restricting entry is not limited to unions. It occurs, for example, with many professional groups, including doctors. Because professional standards have long been regarded as necessary to protect the public from incompetent practitioners, doctors have found it publicly acceptable to control supply by limiting entry into their profession. Physicians' incomes are among the highest of any profession partly because of barriers to entry, including the difficulties of getting into an approved medical school, the high costs of setting up new medical schools, and various certification requirements applying to students, schools, and practitioners.

Monopsony: A Single Buyer in the Market

monopsony
A market situation in which there is a single buyer.

A **monopsony** is a market in which there is only one buyer; monopsony is to the buying side of the market what monopoly is to the selling side. Although cases of monopsony are not very common, it does sometimes arise. Monopsony sometimes occurs in small towns that contain only one industry and often only one large plant or mine. For example, the towns of Iroquois Falls in Ontario and Pine Falls in Manitoba are small towns where the principal employer is a single firm (Abitibi-Consolidated) that operates a newsprint plant. Although both towns provide alternative sources of employment in retailing and service establishments, the large industrial employer has some monopsony power over the local labour market. In other cases, local labour markets may contain only a few large industrial employers. Individually, each has substantial market power, and if they all act together, either explicitly or tacitly, they can behave as if they were a single monopsonist. Our analysis applies whenever employers have substantial monopsony power, but for concreteness, we consider a case in which the few firms operating in one labour market form an employers' hiring association in order to act as a single buying unit. We therefore refer to a single monopsonist.

Monopsony Without a Union. Suppose there are many potential workers and they are not members of a union. The monopsonist can offer any wage rate that it chooses, and the workers must either accept employment at that rate or find a different job.

Suppose that the monopsonist decides to hire some specific quantity of labour. The labour supply curve shows the wage that it must offer. To the monopsonist, this wage is the *average cost* of labour. In deciding how much labour to hire, however, the monopsonist is interested in the *marginal cost* of hiring additional workers. The monopsonist wants to know how much its total costs will increase as it takes on additional units of labour.

FIGURE 14-4 Monopsony in a Labour Market

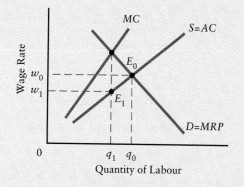

A monopsonist lowers both the wage rate and employment below their competitive levels. D and S are the competitive demand and supply curves, respectively. The competitive equilibrium is E_0. The marginal cost of labour *(MC)* to the monopsonist is above the average cost. The monopsonistic firm will maximize profits at E_1. It will hire only q_1 units of labour. At q_1, the marginal cost of the last worker is just equal to the amount that the worker adds to the firm's revenue, as shown by the demand curve. The wage that must be paid to get q_1 workers is only w_1.

Whenever the supply curve of labour slopes upward, the marginal cost of employing extra units will exceed the average cost.

The marginal cost exceeds the wage paid (the average cost) because the increased wage rate necessary to attract an extra worker must also be paid to *everyone already employed.* [27] For example, assume that 100 workers are employed at $8.00 per hour and that to attract an extra worker, the wage must be raised to $8.01 per hour. The marginal cost of the 101st worker is not the $8.01 per hour paid to the worker but $9.01 per hour—made up of the extra 1 cent per hour paid to the 100 existing workers and $8.01 paid to the new worker. Thus the marginal cost is $9.01, whereas the average cost is $8.01.

The profit-maximizing monopsonist will hire labour up to the point at which the marginal cost of labour just equals the amount that the firm is willing to pay for an additional unit of labour. That amount is determined by labour's marginal revenue product *(MRP)* and is shown by the demand curve illustrated in Figure 14-4.

Monopsony power in a labour market will result in a lower level of employment and lower wages than would exist in a competitive labour market.

The intuitive explanation is that the monopsonistic employer is aware that by trying to purchase more, it is responsible for driving up the wage. It will therefore stop short of the point that is reached when workers are hired by many separate firms, no one of which can exert a significant influence on the wage rate.

Bilateral Monopoly: Monopsony with a Union.

Suppose that the workers in this industry organize themselves under a single union so that the monopsonistic employer's organization now faces a monopoly union. This situation is often referred to as *bilateral monopoly* since both sides of the market have considerable market power. In this case, the two sides will settle the wage through a process known as *collective bargaining*. The outcome of this bargaining process will depend on each side's objective and on the skill that each has in bargaining for its objective. We have seen that, left to itself, the employer's organization will set the monopsonistic wage shown in Figure 14-4. To understand the possible outcomes for the wage after the monopoly union enters the market, let us ask what the union would do if it had the power to set the wage unilaterally. The result will give us insight into the union's objectives in the actual collective bargaining that does occur.

Suppose the union can set a wage below which its members will not work. Here, just as in the case of a wage-setting union in a competitive market, the union presents the employer with a horizontal supply curve (up to the maximum number of workers who will accept work at the union wage). As shown in Figure 14-5, if the union sets the

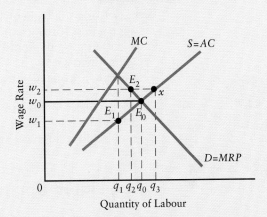

FIGURE 14-5 Bilateral Monopoly in the Labour Market

By presenting a monopsonistic employer with a fixed wage, the union can raise both wages and employment over the monopsonistic level. The monopsony position before the union enters is at E_1 (from Figure 14-4), with a wage rate of w_1 and q_1 workers hired. A union now enters and sets the wage at w_0. The supply curve of labour becomes w_0E_0S, and wages and employment rise to their competitive levels of w_0 and q_0 without creating a pool of unemployed workers. If the wage is raised further, say, to w_2, the supply curve will become w_2xS, the quantity of employment will fall below the competitive level to q_2, and a pool of unsuccessful job applicants of q_2q_3 will develop.

This figure can also be used to illustrate the effect of the government imposing a minimum wage of w_0 or w_2 on a monopsonistic labour market where the equilibrium wage was initially w_1.

Practise with Study Guide Chapter 14, Exercise 3.

wage above the monopsony wage but below the competitive wage, the union can raise *both* wages and employment above the monopsonistic level.

However, the union may not be content merely to neutralize the monopsonist's power. It may choose to raise wages further above the competitive level. If it does, the outcome will be similar to that shown in Figure 14-3. If the wage is raised above the competitive level, the employer will no longer wish to hire all the labour that is offered at that wage. The amount of employment will fall, and unemployment will develop. These changes are also shown in Figure 14-5.

We now know that the employers would like to set the monopsonistic wage (w_1) while the union would like a wage *no less than* the competitive wage (w_0). The union may target for a still higher wage, depending on how it trades off employment losses against wage gains. If the union is content with an amount of employment as low as would occur at the monopsonistic wage, it could target for a wage substantially higher than the competitive wage.

Simple demand and supply analysis can take us no further. The actual outcome will, as we have already observed, depend on such other things as what target wage the two sides actually set for themselves, their relative bargaining skills, how each side assesses the costs of concessions, and how serious a strike would be for each. We discuss unions in more detail in the next section of this chapter.

For interesting information on labour-market policies in Canada, see the website for Human Resources Development Canada: www.hrdc-drhc.gc.ca. Click on "Labour Program."

Legislated Minimum Wages

We have examined wage differentials arising in competitive and noncompetitive labour markets. Government policy can also affect observed wage differentials by legislating minimum wages. Governments in Canada and many other countries legislate specific **minimum wages,** which define the lowest wage rates that may legally be paid. In 1999, minimum wages ranged from $5.40 per hour in Newfoundland to $7.20 per hour in the Yukon.

minimum wages
Legally specified minimum rate of pay for labour.

For a large proportion of all employment covered by the law, the minimum wage is below the actual market wage, and thus in such cases the minimum wage is *not binding.* Some workers, however, are employed in industries in which the free-market wage would be below the legal minimum, and thus the legislated minimum wage is *binding.* It is only in these cases where the effects of minimum wages are of interest.

Although legislated minimum wages are now an accepted part of the labour scene in Canada and many other industrialized countries, economists are often sceptical about the benefits from such a policy. As our analysis in Chapter 5 indicated, a binding price floor in a competitive market leads to a market surplus of the product—in this case, an excess supply of labour, or unemployment. Thus, a policy that legislates minimum wages in an otherwise competitive market will benefit some workers only by hurting others.

The problem is more complicated than the analysis of Chapter 5 would suggest, however, because not all labour markets are competitive. In addition, those groups in the labour force that tend to have the lowest wages, such as youth and minorities, are affected more than the average worker by minimum wages.

Theoretical Effects of a Minimum Wage

Suppose that minimum-wage laws apply uniformly to all occupations. The occupations and the industries in which minimum wages are binding will be the lowest paying in the country; they usually involve unskilled or semiskilled labour. In most of them, the workers are not members of unions. Thus, the situations in which minimum wages are likely to be binding include competitive labour markets and those in which employers exercise some monopsony power. The effects on employment are different in the two cases.

Competitive Labour Markets. The consequences for employment of a binding minimum wage are unambiguous when the labour market is competitive. By raising the wage that employers must pay, minimum-wage legislation leads to a reduction in the quantity of labour that is demanded and an increase in the quantity of labour that is supplied. As a result, the actual level of employment falls, and unemployment rises. This situation is exactly analogous to the one that arises when a union succeeds in setting a wage above the competitive equilibrium wage, as illustrated in Figure 14-3. The excess supply of labour at the minimum wage also creates incentives for people to evade the law by working "under the table" at wages below the legal minimum wage.

Employers with Some Monopsony Power. The minimum-wage law can simultaneously increase both wages and employment in markets in which employers have some monopsony power. The circumstances in which this can occur are the same as those in which a union facing a monopsonistic employer is able to increase both the wage and the level of employment, as shown in Figure 14-5. Of course, if the minimum wage is raised above the competitive wage, employment will start to fall, as in the union case. When it is set at the competitive level, however, the minimum wage can protect workers against monopsony power and lead to *increases* in employment.

Evidence on the Effects of Minimum Wages

Empirical research on the effects of minimum-wage laws reflects these mixed theoretical predictions. There is some evidence that people who keep their jobs gain when the minimum wage is raised. There is some evidence that some groups suffer a decline in employment consistent with raising the wage in a fairly competitive market. At other times and places, there is evidence that both wages and employment rise when the minimum wage rises, consistent with labour markets in which employers have some monopsony power.

Several Canadian studies have examined the relationship between minimum wages and employment (or unemployment). Though the studies differ in their approaches and data used, there is a broad consensus that minimum wages decrease the level of employment (and raise unemployment), particularly for low-wage groups such as women and teenagers. In this sense, the Canadian results confirm the theoretical predictions of the effects of minimum wages in competitive labour markets.

Some widely discussed research in the United States, however, has produced different and hotly debated results. David Card, from Berkeley, and Alan Krueger, from Princeton University, traced the effects of minimum-wage increases in California during 1988 and New Jersey during 1992 and found that substantial rises in these states' minimum wages not only increased wages but were also associated with small employment *gains* for teenagers. Card and Krueger argue that these findings are inconsistent with a competitive labour market and thus take the results as evidence in support of the view that firms have some monopsony power in the labour market.

The Card and Krueger results, however, have come under heavy criticism from many other economists in the last few years. One criticism is that some of the data used by Card and Krueger are faulty, and that their conclusions are therefore suspect. Another relates to the short span of time covered by their study. The argument is that firms will not immediately reduce the level of employment in response to an increase in the minimum wage—they will instead choose *not to replace* workers who leave their jobs in the natural turnover process that occurs in labour markets. But workers who are receiving the minimum wage may be more reluctant to leave their job after an increase in their wage, thereby reducing this natural turnover. Thus, it is not surprising to see few employment losses (or slight gains) when one examines the labour market immediately before and

APPLYING ECONOMIC CONCEPTS 14-1

The Puzzle of Interindustry Wage Differentials in Canada

Differences in wages across industries have been observed for as long as information on wages has been collected. But only recently have economists examined carefully whether they can be explained by differences in skills, jobs, or market structure. In Canada, a study published by Surendra Gera and Gilles Grenier shows the extent of these wage differentials in 1986.*

The table shows results from their study for selected industries; for each industry, the number in the table shows the industry's *wage premium*—that is, the amount by which wages in each industry exceed the average after controlling for such factors as the worker's education, age, gender, occupation, union status, and so on. The challenge is to explain such wage premia.

Competitive Wage Differentials?

Following our discussion in the text, three possible explanations of these wage differentials are consistent with the labour market being competitive.

The first possibility is that these observed wage differentials for 1986 may reflect temporary shifts in the pattern of labour demand or supply across industries. For example, a large increase in the demand for labour in the forestry industry that occurs together with a large decline in the demand for labour in the textiles industry could account for some of the data in the table. To address this possible explanation, Gera and Grenier examine Canadian census data for 1970, 1980, and 1985. They find that the pattern of interindustry wage differentials is very similar across these three periods, suggesting that the observed wage differentials are not simply temporary phenomena.

*S. Gera and G. Grenier, "Interindustry Wage Differentials and Efficiency Wages: Some Canadian Evidence," *Canadian Journal of Economics*, 1994.

The second possibility is that the wage differentials can be explained by differences in the quality of the workers that are not observable to economists when conducting such a study. For example, they are not able to observe whether a worker is "highly motivated," "innovative," or "a good problem solver." But many of these characteristics *are* observable to potential employers, either by watching the individual work for a short period of time, or by asking previous employers who know the worker. To examine this explanation, Gera and Grenier examine the group of individuals in their sample that move from a job in one industry to a job in a different in-

Selected Industry Wage Premia in Canada
(percentage above average wage)

Tobacco Products	33.4
Mineral Fuels	25.5
Forestry	18.9
Electric Power, Gas, and Water Utilities	14.4
Paper and Allied Products	12.0
Communications	10.5
Transportation Equipment	7.0
Wholesale Trade	3.8
Electrical Products	2.6
Education and Related Services	−1.0
Food and Beverages	−3.5
Insurance and Real Estate Agencies	−4.1
Clothing	−8.1
Fishing and Trapping	−9.5
Personal Services	−16.7
Retail Trade	−11.1
Textiles	−19.0
Accommodation and Food Services	−20.3

See Chapter 14 of www.pearsoned.ca/lipsey for a discussion of the possible effects of legislating the length of the work week: Jan Olters, "Some Doubts About France's 35-Hour Week," *World Economic Affairs.*

immediately after the change in legislation. Proponents of this view argue that the total employment effects of minimum wages can only be detected by examining the data over longer periods of time.

Economists have not reached a definitive conclusion regarding the desirability or the effects of legislated minimum wages. Given its mixed economic effects, support for and opposition to the minimum wage might be understood as arising largely from political and sociological motives. Organized labour has consistently pressed for a broad, relatively high minimum wage. There is some economic reason for this, in that there is evidence that the minimum wage "trickles up" to higher-wage workers, both unionized and not. Arguably, however, the support dates back to the 1930s, when organized labour was still dustry. For example, if high wages to a particular worker in the tobacco industry are due to that worker's unobserved skills, then when that worker switches to the clothing industry, the high wage should persist. But Gera and Grenier find the opposite. A worker that moves from a high-wage industry to a low-wage industry tends to suffer a fall in wage; similarly, a worker that moves from a low-wage industry to a high-wage industry tends to experience a rise in the wage. This finding suggests that the observed wage differentials are not due mainly to unobserved labour quality.

The final possible explanation consistent with a competitive labour market is that the observed wage differentials reflect different characteristics of the *jobs*. Maybe the jobs in the high-wage industries are less pleasant jobs—longer hours, less job security, less safe—than those in the low-wage industries. Gera and Grenier offer two pieces of evidence against this explanation. First, they note that workers in *similar occupations* receive very different wages in different industries, and it is difficult to believe that working conditions for, say, a clerk are very different in the tobacco industry than in the textiles industry. Second, if the observed wage differentials reflect just different job characteristics, then in competitive equilibrium workers are indifferent between (pleasant) jobs in the low-wage industries and (unpleasant) jobs in the high-wage industries. Yet workers appear to quit jobs in the high-wage industries much less frequently than they quit jobs in the low-wage industries. In other words, workers *appear* to view the high-wage jobs as valuable relative to the low-wage jobs. This phenomenon, of course, suggests that the observed wage differentials are reflecting more than just differences in working conditions.

Other Explanations?

Maybe the explanation for these observed wage differentials lies in a noncompetitive market structure. Perhaps unions have a large presence in some industries and little or no presence in others. When Gera and Grenier examine this possibility, they find that the interindustry wage differentials are just as marked among unionized workers as they are among nonunionized workers.

If the observed wage differentials across Canadian industries cannot be explained by considering different characteristics of the workers, jobs, or market structures, what is the explanation? One possible explanation is based on the theory of *efficiency wages*. According to this theory, firms in even a competitive labour market may *pay more than the competitive wage* to their workers. Firms do this because they perceive that a higher wage will make their workers more productive. Since workers are receiving more than is required to attract their services, they are earning *economic rents* (a concept that we examined in Chapter 13). The fact that workers are receiving rents, in turn, explains why they are reluctant to leave these good jobs—and thus their quit rates from such jobs are low.

Though the efficiency-wage theory offers one possible explanation for why some workers might earn rents, it does not directly offer an explanation for why these rents might be different across industries. In order for the efficiency-wage theory to explain the observed interindustry wage differentials, it must explain why firms' incentives to pay higher wages are greater in some industries than in others. So far, proponents of the theory have not come up with convincing reasons.

The efficiency-wage theory generates considerable disagreement among economists. But there is little debate that there exist significant wage differentials across industries, even after taking account of observable characteristics of workers and jobs. As more data become available, perhaps economists will find better explanations for the observed interindustry wage differentials.

Workers in the forestry industry receive wages roughly 20 percent higher than workers of similar ages and skills in the average industry.

fighting for its position in North American society. Enactment of a minimum wage was then a great political victory, and the minimum wage still has symbolic significance.

A Final Word

We have examined several explanations for why some workers get paid more than others. The explanations include differences in workers' educations and skills, differences in job characteristics, discrimination, and differences in the structure of the various labour markets. But this apparent abundance of explanations should not

FIGURE 14-6 Union Membership in Canada, 1921-1992

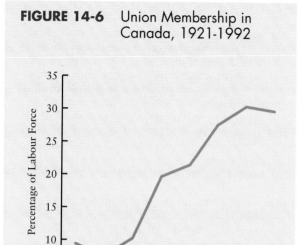

As a share of the labour force, the number of union members has increased significantly over the past century, but appears to have stabilized at around 30 percent. The large increases in Canadian unionization occurred during and after the Second World War, and during the 1960s.

(Source: Richard Chaykowski, *Modern Labour Economics,* HarperCollins 1994.)

lead you to believe that economists understand *all* wage differentials that are observed in the labour market. Recent studies, both in Canada and in the United States, have revealed significant differences in wages across industries that appear to defy explanations based on the sort of arguments we have examined. *Applying Economic Concepts 14-1* discusses the continuing puzzle of interindustry wage differentials in Canada.

Labour Unions

Unions currently represent fewer than 30 percent of the labour force in Canada. Of those workers employed in the public sector, however, approximately 80 percent are unionized. Figure 14-6 shows how union membership has changed in Canada over the past several decades. Table 14-1 shows unionization rates by industry. As is clear from the table, unionization is most common in the public and educational sectors and least common in agriculture, finance, and business services.

Despite the relatively low degree of unionization among Canada's private-sector workers, unions have a considerable influence in the private sector. One reason is the impact that union wage contracts have on other labour markets. When, for example, the Canadian Auto Workers negotiates a new contract with an automobile producer in Oshawa, its provisions set a pattern that directly or indirectly affects other labour markets, both in Ontario and in other provinces. A second reason is the major leadership role that unions have played in the past 50 years in the development of labour market practices and in lobbying for legislation that applies to all workers.

In this section, we discuss the process of *collective bargaining* and, in particular, examine the inherent conflict that unions face between striving for higher wages and for increasing employment. *Lessons from History 14-1* examines the historical development of labour unions in Canada.

Collective Bargaining

collective bargaining
The process by which unions and employers arrive at and enforce agreements.

The process by which unions and employers reach an agreement is known as **collective bargaining.** This process has an important difference from the theoretical models that we discussed in the previous section. In those models, we assumed that the union had the power to set the wage unilaterally; the employer then decided how much labour to hire. In actual collective bargaining, however, the firm and union typically bargain over the wage (as well as other aspects of the employment relationship). There is usually a substantial range over which an agreement can be reached, and the actual result in particular cases will depend on the strengths of the two bargaining parties and on the skill of their negotiators.

To see the possible outcomes, refer back to Figure 14-5. It may be that the firm wants the wage to be w_1 and the union wants the wage to be w_2. Depending on each side's market power, and on their bargaining tactics, the final agreed-upon wage may be anywhere in between. Note that while actual collective bargaining has the firm and union bargaining over the wage, it is typically the case that the firm retains the "right to manage"—meaning that the firm can decide how much labour it wants to employ at the bargained wage.

Wages Versus Employment

Unions seek many goals when they bargain with management. They may push for higher wages, higher fringe benefits, or less onerous working conditions. In recent years, unions in Canada have also emphasized the importance of "job security," meaning a commitment by the firm to not lay workers off in the event of a downturn in business conditions. Firms, however, are understandably reluctant to promise such security since reducing their workforce is an effective way to reduce costs when business conditions deteriorate.

Whatever unions' specific goals, unless they face a monopsonist across the bargaining table, they must deal with a fundamental dilemma.

There is an inherent conflict between the level of wages and the size of the union itself.

The more successful a union is in raising wages, the more management will reduce the size of its work force, substituting capital for labour. This will lead to lower union membership. However, if the union does not provide some wage improvement for its members, they will have little incentive to stay around.

TABLE 14-1 Unionization Rates by Industry

Industry	Membership as Percentage of Paid Workers
Agriculture	1.8
Forestry	58.8
Fishing & Trapping	33.4
Mining	28.4
Manufacturing	36.7
Construction	59.6
Transportation, Communication, and other Utilities	54.8
Trade	11.6
Finance, Real Estate, and Insurance	3.5
Services	
Business	3.1
Educational	77.0
Health and Social	50.8
Other	11.6
Public Administration	80.6
Total Canadian Economy	**34.7**

There is considerable variation across Canadian industries in the extent of unionization. The public sector and the educational services sector are the most unionized; agriculture, finance, and business services are the least unionized.

(*Source:* Richard Chaykowski, *Modern Labour Economics,* HarperCollins 1994.)

The Union Wage Premium

Despite the costs to unions (i.e., reduced membership) of pushing for higher wages, there is clear evidence in Canada of a *union wage premium*—that is, a higher wage attributed only to the union status of the job. It is not easy to measure this wage premium, however, because it is not appropriate simply to compare the average wage of unionized workers with the average wage of nonunionized workers. After all, unions may occur mainly in industries where workers have higher skills or where working conditions are less pleasant. And we know from the first section of this chapter that differences in skills or working conditions can lead to wage differentials. Economists have therefore been forced to use complicated statistical techniques to identify this union wage premium. The consensus appears to be that the union wage premium in Canada is somewhere between 10 and 15 percent—that is, unionized workers with a particular set of skills in particular types of jobs get paid 10 to 15 percent more than *otherwise identical workers* who are not members of unions.

For information on the Canadian labour movement, see the website for the Canadian Labour Congress: www.clc.org.

LESSONS FROM HISTORY 14-1

The Development of Unions in Canada

Early Canadian unionization was strongly dominated by the influence of international unions, which had their headquarters and an overwhelming proportion of their membership outside Canada. The creation of Canadian locals of American unions began in the 1860s. By 1911, 90 percent of Canadian workers who were union members belonged to international unions.

During the first half of the twentieth century, there was strong pressure: first, toward a single national federation; and second, to achieve autonomy from American unions. The issues became intertwined when conflicts in the United States arose between craft and industrial unions. Until the 1930s, *craft unions*—which cover persons in a particular occupation—were the characteristic form of collective action in the United States. In Canada, meanwhile, trade unionists were attracted to *industrial unions* that embraced unskilled workers as well as skilled craftsmen in one industry such as steel making.

Because of the impossibility of establishing bargaining strength by controlling the supply of unskilled workers, the rise of industrial unionism in Canada was associated with political action as an alternative means of improving the lot of the membership. In general, social and political reform were given much more emphasis by Canadian unionists than by their American counterparts. Political action here extended to the support for social democratic political parties: first, the Cooperative Commonwealth Federation (CCF), established in 1932, and later its successor, the New Democratic Party (NDP), formed in 1961.

The late Senator Eugene Forsey, a former director of research for the Canadian Labour Congress, viewed the unification of the bulk of Canadian unions under the CLC in 1956 as the beginning of virtual autonomy for Canadian locals from their U.S. head offices. Throughout the postwar period, the percentage of total Canadian union membership represented by international unions fell: In the mid 1950s, it was about 70 percent, and by the mid 1990s, it was just over 30 percent.

One factor in the increased share of national unions is the growth of membership in the two unions repre-

senting government workers, the Canadian Union of Public Employees and the Public Service Alliance. Another major component of noninternational union membership has arisen out of the distinct aspirations of French-Canadian workers. More recently, the formation of the Canadian Auto Workers, independent of the American Auto Workers, represented a significant further reduction of membership in international unions.

Rapid gains in union membership in Canada occurred in the years during World War II. This led to pressure for the rights of workers to organize and to elect an exclusive bargaining agent. These rights were established by provisions of the Wartime Labour Relations Regulations Act of 1944.

Government intervention in industrial disputes in Canada has a history dating back to the early years of the twentieth century. The earliest legislation applied only to public utilities and coal mining. It provided that before a strike or a lockout could be initiated, the parties were required to submit any dispute to a conciliation board. This system of compulsory conciliation and compulsory delay in work stoppage was extended to a much larger segment of the economy under special emergency powers adopted by the government of Canada during World War II. In the postwar period, jurisdiction over labour policy reverted to the provinces, but the principles established have been carried over into provincial legislation.

The Winnipeg General Strike of 1919 began a wave of increased unionism and militancy across Canada.

Unionized workers earn, on average, between 10 and 15 percent higher wages than nonunionized workers with similar characteristics.

There is also evidence that the size of this union wage premium differs across industries. Given that workers in different industries and with different occupations are often represented by different unions, this cross-industry difference in the union wage premium may simply reflect the differences in unions' preferences for higher wages versus higher employment.

Employment Effects of Unions

We said earlier that unions face an inherent conflict between the level of wages and the level of employment. This simply reflects the firm's profit-maximizing behaviour as embodied in its downward-sloping demand curve for labour. As the union pushes for higher wages, the firm naturally chooses to hire fewer workers.

What continues to puzzle economists, however, is how the clear evidence of a 10 to 15 percent union wage premium can be consistent with a second empirical result—the absence of any clear effect on employment. One possible explanation for the absence of an employment effect is that unions use the collective bargaining process to pressure firms to hire more workers than they otherwise would. This practice is known as *feather-bedding,* and for years was infamous in the railroads where union contracts required the railway to hire firemen (whose job it was to keep the coal fires burning) long after the widespread adoption of diesel locomotives.

If such feather-bedding is pervasive in unionized firms, it may well be the explanation for the absence of an observable union effect on employment. The employment reduction caused by the higher wage may be offset by the employment increase due to feather-bedding.

Unanswered Questions

Labour unions have played a significant role in the economies of Canada, the United States, and Europe for many years. Given this fact, it is surprising how little economists actually know about how unions influence economic outcomes and, in particular, how unions affect long-run productivity.

Unions may reduce long-run productivity through a process known as the *hold-up* of capital. Much physical capital, once it is installed, is very difficult to move or resell. For this reason, *installed* capital has a very inelastic supply and, following the discussion from Chapter 13, a large part of its factor payment takes the form of economic rent. The union may be able to extract these rents from the firm in the form of higher wages. That is, the union may be able to *hold up* the firm by forcing it to pay higher wages; the firm is stuck with its installed capital and thus pays the higher wages and, in turn, receives lower profits. If firms are forward-looking, however, they can anticipate this sort of behaviour from unions *before* making such investments in physical capital. The possibility of being held up by union wage demands reduces the expected profitability of investment and may result in a reduction in investment. This decision to invest less would likely have negative implications for productivity growth in the industry.

There is some empirical evidence that the presence of a union does reduce investment by firms. It is not yet clear, however, whether such reduced investment has long-term effects on productivity. This issue is currently unresolved.

The "Good Jobs–Bad Jobs" Debate

Figure 14-7 shows how the composition of Canadian employment has changed over the past century. In particular, the share of total employment in agriculture has fallen from 45 percent in 1891 to less than three percent today. In contrast, the share of total employment in services (including government) has increased from less than 10 percent in

FIGURE 14-7 One Hundred Years of Change in the Composition of Canadian Employment

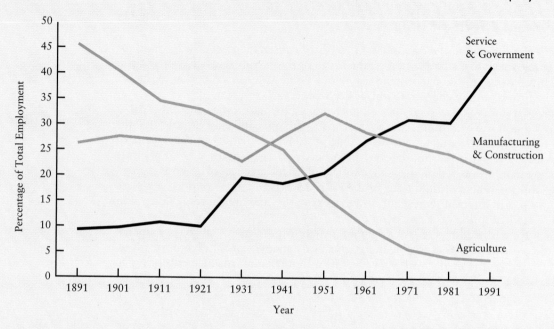

Over the past century, major shifts in employment have taken place between sectors of the economy. In 1891, over 45 percent of Canadian employment was in agriculture, and only 9 percent in services (including government). One hundred years later, agriculture accounted for only 3 percent of employment, while services had increased to 41 percent. The share of employment in manufacturing and construction increased from 26 percent in 1891 to 32 percent just after the Second World War, and then declined back to 20 percent by 1991.

(*Source: Canadian Census*, various years, authors' calculations.)

1891 to over 40 percent today. The share in manufacturing and construction has been more variable, but has been on a clear downward trend over the past half-century, falling from about 35 percent in 1951 to about 20 percent today.

Similar changes have also occurred in the United States and in many other industrialized countries. This changing composition of the labour force has led to some concerns. The specific change that has received considerable attention is the decline in the share of total employment in the manufacturing sector since the Second World War, and the simultaneous increase in the share of total employment in the service sector.

Some people fear that productivity is lower and the opportunities for growth are much more limited in some service industries than in goods-producing industries. They argue that the possibilities for using more capital per unit of labour employed, which raises labour productivity, are less in the service sector than in the manufacturing sector. Another concern is that many of the "good jobs" in the manufacturing sector appear to have been replaced by "bad jobs" in the service sector, where such "bad jobs" are characterized by lower pay and less job security.

The reduction in manufacturing employment is partly the result of that sector's dynamism – more and more output can be produced with fewer and fewer workers.

Should these dramatic changes in the composition of employment worry us? Is there something undesirable about the fact that fewer workers are now producing manufactured goods than forty years ago? Or that more workers are working in the service sector than forty years ago? Are good jobs being replaced by bad jobs? This final section of the chapter addresses this contentious issue.

Four Observations

There are four reasons why the decline in the manufacturing sector—in Canada and elsewhere—may not reflect anything "wrong" with the economy. First, we need to keep a sense of perspective about the emergence of low-paying service jobs. As is apparent in Figure 14-7, the trend toward services has been going on for over a century. Yet real income per hour worked has been rising throughout this period; as a nation, we are getting wealthier, not poorer.

Second, to a considerable extent, the decrease in the share of manufacturing in total employment is a result of that sector's dynamism. More and more manufactured goods have been produced by fewer and fewer workers, leaving more workers to produce services. This movement is analogous to the one out of agriculture earlier in the century. At the turn of the century, nearly 45 percent of the Canadian labour force worked on farms. Today that number is less than 3 percent, yet they produce more total output than did the 45 percent in 1900. This movement away from agricultural employment freed workers to move into manufacturing, raising our living standards and transforming our way of life. In like manner, the movement away from manufacturing is freeing workers to move into services, and by replacing the grimy blue-collar jobs of the smokestack industries with more pleasant white-collar jobs in the service industries, it will once again transform our way of life.

Third, to a considerable extent, the decrease in the share of manufacturing in total employment also follows from consumers' tastes. Just as consumers in the first half of the century did not want to go on consuming more and more food products as their incomes rose, today's consumers do not wish to spend all of their additional income on manufactured products. Households have chosen to spend a high proportion of their increased incomes on services, thus creating employment opportunities in that sector. This simply reflects the fact that many products of the service sector—like restaurant meals, hotel stays, and airline flights—are products that have a high income elasticity of demand. Thus, as the income of the average Canadian household increases, so too does that household's demand for these products of the service sector.

Finally, it is easy to underestimate the scope for quality, quantity, and productivity increases in services. But these changes permit us to have a higher standard of living than we would otherwise have. As just one example of productivity increases, consider your ability to make an automatic cash withdrawal, at any time of the day or night, from your bank account in Truro, Nova Scotia, while you are on vacation in Brazil. Now compare that to the apprehension your parents faced twenty years ago when they had to get to the bank before 3:00 pm on a Friday afternoon to make sure that they had enough cash for the weekend. It would have been simply impossible for them to cash a cheque in Brazil without having made elaborate prior arrangements.

Also, many quality improvements in services go unrecorded. Today's hotel room is vastly more comfortable than a hotel room of 40 years ago, yet this quality improvement does not show up in our national income statistics. Measuring such technological improvements is even more difficult when they take the form of entirely new products. Airline transportation, telecommunication, fast-food chains, and financial services are prominent examples. The resulting increase in output is not always properly captured in existing statistics.

A Mixed Blessing?

It is easy to become concerned when looking at the official statistics, which show low wages earned in some service jobs. Indeed, the shift in employment toward services is, like most changes that hit the economy, a mixed blessing. It entails a significant increase in the number of "bad" service-sector jobs with low pay or low job security. Further, such transitions often generate temporary unemployment as workers get laid off from a contracting manufacturing sector and only slowly find jobs in the expanding service sector. Such transitions suggest a role for government policy to maintain the income of those workers temporarily unemployed (we will discuss unemployment insurance and other income-support programs in Chapter 18). However, if we focus on the *overall economy,* and consider the growth in the real living standards of the *average* Canadian household, we are reminded that average real income has continued to rise, not only throughout the shift from agriculture to manufacturing, but also throughout the shift from manufacturing to services. There is little reason to think that the continued growth of the service sector will stand in the way of this slow but steady improvement in Canadians' living standards.

S U M M A R Y

Wage Differentials

- In a competitive labour market, wages are set by the forces of supply and demand. Differences in wages will arise because some skills are more valued than others, because some jobs are more onerous than others, because of varying amounts of human capital, and because of discrimination based on such factors as gender and race.
- A union entering a competitive market acts as a monopolist and can raise wages, but only at the cost of reducing employment.
- A monopsonistic employer entering a competitive labour market will reduce both the wage and the level of employment.

- A union in a monopsonistic labour market—a case of bilateral monopoly—may increase both employment and wages relative to the pure monopsony outcome. If the union sets wages above the competitive level, however, it will create a pool of workers who are unable to get the jobs that they want at the going wage.
- Governments set some wages above their competitive levels by passing minimum-wage laws. In competitive labour markets, these laws raise the incomes of many employees, and cause unemployment for some of those with the lowest levels of skills. In monopsonistic labour markets, a legislated minimum wage (as long as it is not too high) can raise both wages and employment.

Labour Unions

- Labour unions seek many goals when they bargain with management. They may push for higher wages, higher fringe benefits, more stable employment, or less onerous working conditions. Whatever their specific goals, unless they face a monopsonist across the bargaining table, they must recognize the inherent conflict between the level of wages and the size of the union itself.

- Despite the costs to unions (i.e., reduced membership) of pushing for higher wages, there is clear evidence in Canada of a union wage premium. The union wage premium is somewhere between 10 and 15 percent—that is, unionized workers with a particular set of skills in particular types of jobs get paid 10 to 15 percent more than otherwise identical workers that are not members of unions.

The "Good Jobs–Bad Jobs" Debate

- The past half-century has witnessed an increase in the share of total employment in the service sector and a decline in the share of employment in manufacturing. Some people are concerned that "good" manufacturing jobs are being replaced by "bad" service jobs.

- Though the shift away from manufacturing and toward services involves some costs during the transition period, the ongoing growth in average per capita income (plus the hard-to-measure quality improvements) suggests that the shift is not a problem for the economy as a whole.

K E Y   C O N C E P T S

Wage differentials in competitive labour markets
Effects of discrimination on wages
Labour unions as monopolists

Single employer as monopsonist
Effects of legislated minimum wages
Collective bargaining

Union goals: wages versus employment
Union wage premium
"Good jobs" vs. "bad jobs"

S T U D Y   E X E R C I S E S

1. Suppose there were only two industries in the economy. All workers have the same skills and the same preferences. But the jobs in the two industries are different. In the Pleasant industry, working conditions are desirable (quiet, safe, clean, etc.). In the Grimy industry, working conditions are awful (noisy, unsafe, dirty, etc.).

   a. Draw supply-and-demand diagrams for the labour market in each industry.
   b. In which industry are wages higher? Why?
   c. Now suppose that the Grimy industry made its working conditions just as pleasant as in the Pleasant industry? Explain what happens in *both* labour markets.

2. Suppose there are two types of basketball players—black and white. Suppose also that, on average, black players are no better and no worse than white players. Furthermore, suppose there are only two types of basketball teams—good and bad. Good teams hire only good players; bad teams will hire both good and bad

players. The two diagrams that follow show the initial outcomes in the labour markets for good teams and bad teams. Assume there is *no discrimination based on race*.

   a. As shown in the figures, the wage paid by good teams is higher than the wage paid by bad teams. What explains this wage differential?
   b. Do black players earn more or less than white players, on average? Explain.
   c. Now suppose that the good teams discriminate against white players—rightly or wrongly they *believe* that black players are better than white players. Show in your diagram what happens in both labour markets.
   d. In the situation in part c, what happens to the wage differential between good and bad teams?
   e. In the situation in part c, what happens to the average black-white wage differential?

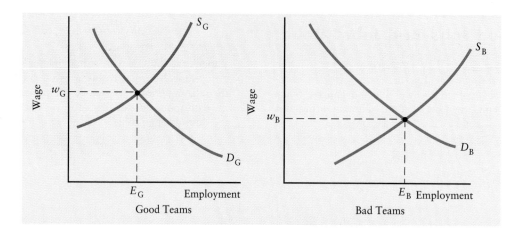

Good Teams   Bad Teams

3. Suppose *in the real world* you observe that black basketball players get paid more than white basketball players. Do you conclude that discrimination is present? Explain why or why not.

4. The table below shows how many workers are prepared to work at various hourly wages in the forestry industry. It also shows the workers' marginal revenue product (*MRP*).

Number of Workers	Wage ($)	Marginal Cost of Labour ($)	MRP ($)
50	10	—	50
100	12	14	40
150	14	18	30
200	16	—	24
250	18	—	22
300	20	—	20
350	22	—	18

a. On a scale diagram, draw the supply of labour curve and the demand for labour curve.
b. What is the equilibrium wage and level of employment if the labour market is competitive?
c. Now suppose there is only a single buyer for labour—a *monopsonist*. Compute the marginal cost of labour for each level of employment and fill in the table. (Recall that the *MC* of labour is the change in labour cost divided by the change in employment. The first two rows have been completed for you.)
d. What wage and level of employment would the monopsonist choose? Explain.

5. The diagram below shows the market for labour in a particular industry. It shows both the supply of labour (the average cost of labour) and the marginal cost of labour.

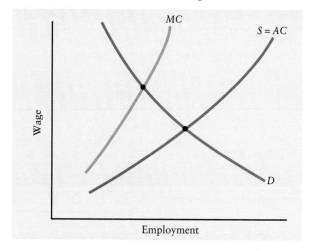

a. Suppose the labour market is competitive. What will be the equilibrium wage and level of employment (call them w^* and L^*)?
b. Now suppose the government imposes a minimum wage equal to $w^{min} > w^*$. Show what happens to wages and employment.
c. In the absence of a minimum wage, show the outcome if there is a monosony buyer of labour services. Call this wage w^p.
d. Beginning with the monopsony outcome, show what happens if the government imposes a minimum wage above w^p but lower than w^*.
e. Do minimum wages always reduce employment? Explain.

6. The following diagram shows the market for labour in a particular industry. It shows both the supply of labour

(the average cost of labour) and the marginal cost of labour. If the labour market were competitive, the outcome would be w^* and L^*.

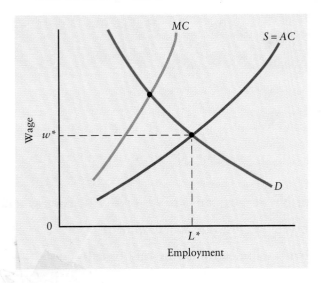

a. Suppose the workers in this industry form a union that is able to raise the wage above w^*. Show the expected outcome in the figure.
b. Now suppose there is no union, but there is a monopsony buyer of labour. Show the expected outcome in this market.
c. Now suppose there is both a union and a monopsony firm. What can you predict about the outcome in this case?

DISCUSSION QUESTIONS

1. "The great increase in the number of women entering the labour force for the first time means that relatively more women than men earn beginning salaries. It is therefore not evidence of discrimination that the average wage earned by females is less than that earned by males." Discuss.

2. Physicians are among the highest-paid of workers. However, in addition to a bachelor's degree, would-be physicians must attend four years of medical school, three years of residency, and up to seven additional years of residency to be specialists. How does this lengthy training change your perception with respect to how much physicians are paid? What additional information would you need to determine whether physicians' real pay is higher than that of other professionals?

3. In trying to measure the extent to which labour unions are responsible for increasing wages, economists use sophisticated statistical methods to compare the wages of unionized workers with those of nonunionized workers. Explain why it is not legitimate to simply compare the average wage across the two groups and attribute the difference to the effects of unionization.

4. "One can judge the presence or absence of discrimination by looking at the proportion of the population in different occupations." Does such information help? Does it suffice? Consider each of the following examples. Relative to their numbers in the total population, there are

   a. Too many blacks and too few Jews among professional athletes
   b. Too few male secretaries
   c. Too few female judges
   d. Too few female prison guards
   e. Too few male school teachers
   f. Too few female graduate students in economics.

5. "Equal pay for work of equal value" is a commonly held goal, but "equal value" is hard to define. What would be the consequences of legislation that enforces equal pay for what turns out to be work of unequal value?

6. There is clear evidence of a union wage premium of between 10 and 15 percent. There is also clear evidence that firms' demand curves are downward sloping. Reconcile these two "facts" with the third fact that there is *no* clear evidence that unions lead to employment reductions.

CHAPTER 15

Capital and Natural Resources

(LO) *LEARNING OBJECTIVES*

❶ Compute the present value of an asset that delivers a stream of future benefits.

❷ Explain why the demand for physical capital depends on the interest rate.

❸ Understand how the equilibrium interest rate is determined.

❹ Explain how competitive firms will determine the rate of extraction of a nonrenewable resource.

❺ Recognize the conservation role played by free-market prices for resources.

In this chapter, we discuss capital and nonrenewable natural resources. These are similar factors of production in that each is a stock of valuable things that gets used up in the process of producing goods and services. They are also similar in that the optimal level of capital used by firms and the optimal level of extraction of a nonrenewable resource depend on the interest rate. They are different in that capital can be replaced, whereas nonrenewable resources—by definition—cannot. A new machine can always be built to replace one that wears out, but a barrel of oil used represents a permanent reduction in the world's total stock of oil.

We begin the chapter by discussing how firms decide how much capital to purchase and how the market determines the price of capital. The interest rate plays an important role in both parts. We then go on to discuss how profit-maximizing firms decide how fast to extract a nonrenewable resource, and we also examine whether competitive markets produce the socially desirable rate of extraction. Here we see the price system behaving as a conservation mechanism, with the price of the resource rising as it becomes more scarce.

Capital and the Interest Rate

Capital is a produced factor of production. The nation's capital stock consists of all produced goods that are used in the production of other goods and services. Factories, machines, tools, computers, roads, bridges, and railroads are but a few of the many examples.

We begin our study of capital by exploring an important complication that arises because factors of production are durable—a machine lasts for years, a labourer for a lifetime, and land more or less forever. It is convenient to think of a factor's lifetime as being divided into the shorter periods that we refer to as *production periods*. The present time is the current period. Future time is one, two, three, and so on, periods hence.

The durability of factors makes it necessary to distinguish between the factor itself and the *flow of services* that it provides in a given production period. For example, we can rent a piece of land for use over some period of time, or we can buy the land outright. This distinction is just a particular instance of the general distinction between flows and stocks that we first encountered in Chapter 3.

Two Prices of Capital

If a firm hires a piece of capital equipment for use over some period of time—for example, one truck for one month—it pays a price for the privilege of using that piece of capital equipment. If the firm buys the truck outright, it pays a different (and higher) price for the purchase. Consider each of these prices in turn.

Rental Price

The *rental price of capital* is the amount that a firm pays to obtain the services of a capital good for a given period of time. The rental price of one week's use of a piece of capital is analogous to the weekly wage rate that is the price of hiring the services of labour.

A capital good may also be used by the firm that owns it. In this case, the firm does not pay out any rental fee. However, the rental price is the amount that the firm could charge if it leased its capital to another firm. The rental price is thus the *opportunity cost* to the firm of using the capital good itself. This rental price is the *implicit* price that reflects the value to the firm of the services of its own capital that it uses during the current production period.

Purchase Price

The price that a firm pays to buy a capital good is called the *purchase price of capital*. When a firm buys a capital good outright, it obtains the use of the good's services over the whole of that good's lifetime. The capital good contributes a flow of benefits over its lifetime. These benefits are the marginal revenue product (*MRP*) of capital in each production period. The price that the firm is willing to pay for the capital good, naturally enough, is related to the total value that it places now on this stream of *expected MRPs* over future time periods. The term *expected* emphasizes that the firm is usually uncertain about what the future *MRPs* will be.

In order to compute the value that the firm places on receiving a future stream of benefits, we must examine the concept of *present value*. The following discussion proceeds under the simplifying assumption that the firm knows the future *MRPs* with certainty. This allows us to develop the central insights about present value without dealing with the complications arising from uncertainty.

The distinction between the rental price and the purchase price applies to any durable factor of production, including land and labour. *Applying Economic Concepts 15-1* examines this distinction in the case of labour. We now turn to the computation of present value.

APPLYING ECONOMIC CONCEPTS 15-1

The Rental and Purchase Price of Labour

If you wish to farm a piece of land, you can buy it yourself, or you can rent it for a specific period of time. If you want to set up a small business, you can buy your office and equipment, or you can rent them. The same is true for all capital and all land; a firm often has the option of buying or renting.

Exactly the same would be true for labour if we lived in a slave society. You could buy a slave to be your assistant, or you could rent the services either of someone else's slave or of a free person. Fortunately, slavery is illegal throughout most of today's world. As a result, the labour markets that we know deal only in the *services* of labour; we do not go to a labour market to buy a worker, only to hire his or her services.

You can, however, hire the services of a labourer for a long period of time. In professional sports, multiyear contracts are common. Publishers sometimes tie up their authors in multibook contracts, and movie and television production firms often sign up their actors on long-term contracts. In all cases of such *personal-services contracts*, the person is not a slave, and his or her personal rights and liberties are protected by law. The purchaser of the long-term contract is nonetheless buying ownership of the factor's *services* for an extended period of time. The price of the contract will reflect the person's expected earnings over the contract's lifetime. If the contract is transferable, the owner can sell these services for a lump sum or rent them out for some period. As with land and capital goods, the price paid for this stock of labour services depends on the expected rental prices over the contract period.

For many years, Wayne Gretzky had a personal-service contract with Peter Pocklington, the former owner of the Edmonton Oilers.

The Present Value of Future Returns

Consider the stream of future benefits that is provided by a piece of capital equipment. How much is that stream worth *now*? How much would someone be willing to pay now to buy the right to receive that flow of future benefits? The answer is called the capital's *present value*. In general, present value (*PV*) refers to the value now of one or more payments to be received in the future.

The Present Value of a Single Future Payment

One Period in the Future.   How much would a firm be prepared to pay now to purchase a capital good that produces an *MRP* of $100 in one year's time, after which time the capital good will be useless? One way to answer this question is to ask a somewhat *opposite* question: How much would the firm have to *lend* now in order to have $100 a year from now? Suppose for the moment that the interest rate is 5 percent per annum, which means that $1.00 invested today will be worth $1.05 in one year's time.

If we use *PV* to stand for this unknown amount, we can write $PV \times (1.05) = \$100$. Thus, $PV = \$100/1.05 = \$95.24$. This tells us that the present value of $100 receivable in one year's time is $95.24 when the interest rate is 5 percent. Anyone who lends out $95.24 for one year at 5 percent interest will receive $95.24 back plus $4.76 in interest, or $100 in total. When we calculate this present value, the interest rate is used to *discount* (reduce to its present value) the $100 to be received in one year's time.

The actual present value that we have calculated depended on our assuming that the interest rate is 5 percent. What if the interest rate is 7 percent? At that interest rate, the present value of the $100 receivable in one year's time would be $100/1.07 = $93.46.

These examples are easy to generalize. In both cases, we have found the present value by dividing the sum that is receivable in the future by 1 plus the rate of interest.[1] In general, if the interest rate is *i* per year, then the present value of the *MRP* (in dollars) received one year hence is

$$PV = MRP/(1 + i)$$

Several Periods in the Future.   Now we know how to calculate the present value of a single sum that is receivable one year in the future. The next step is to ask what would happen if the sum were receivable at a later date. For example, what is the present value of $100 to be received *two* years hence when the interest rate is 5 percent? This is $100/[(1.05)(1.05)] = $90.70. We can check this by seeing what would happen if $90.70 were lent out for two years. In the first year, the loan would earn interest of (0.05)($90.70) = $4.54, and hence after one year, the firm would receive $95.24. In the second year, the interest would be earned on this entire amount; interest earned in the second year would equal (0.05)($95.24) = $4.76. Hence, in two years the firm would have $100.

In general, the present value of *MRP* dollars received *t* years in the future when the interest rate is *i* per year is

$$PV = MRP/(1 + i)^t$$

This formula simply discounts the *MRP* by the interest rate, repeatedly, once for each of the *t* periods that must pass until the *MRP* becomes available. If we look at the formula, we see that the higher is *i* or *t*, the higher is the whole term $(1 + i)^t$. This term, however, appears in the denominator, so *PV* is *negatively* related to both *i* and *t*.

The formula $PV = MRP/(1 + i)^t$ shows that the present value of a given sum payable in the future will be smaller the more distant the payment date and the higher the rate of interest.

The Present Value of a Stream of Payments

Now consider the present value of a stream of receipts that continues *forever*. This is closer to the situation we are interested in when examining the firm's decision to purchase a capital good since that capital good will typically generate a stream of benefits long into the future. At first glance, the *PV* in this case might seem very high because the total amount received grows without reaching any limit as time passes. The preceding section suggests, however, that people will not value the far-distant payments very highly.

To find the *PV* of $100 a year, payable forever, we ask: How much would you have to lend now, at an interest rate of *i* per year, to obtain $100 each year in interest earnings? This is simply $i \times PV = \$100$, where *i* is the interest rate and *PV* the sum required. Dividing through by *i* shows the present value of the stream of $100 per year forever:

$$PV = \$100/i$$

---

[1] In this type of formula, the interest rate *i* is expressed as a decimal fraction where, for example, 7 percent is expressed as 0.07, so that $1 + i$ equals 1.07.

For example, if the interest rate is 10 percent, the present value would be $1000. In other words, $1000 invested at 10 percent yields $100 of interest per year forever. Notice that, as in the preceding sections, *PV* is negatively related to the rate of interest: The higher the interest rate, the lower the present value of the stream of future payments.

Practise with Study Guide Chapter 15, Exercise 2.

Conclusions

Our discussion about present value can be summarized as follows:

1. The present value of a unit of capital is positively related to the *MRP*s it produces.

2. The present value of a unit of capital is negatively related to the interest rate.

3. The present value of a unit of capital is negatively related to the time the owner must wait to receive the future *MRP*s.

The Firm's Decision

An individual firm faces a given interest rate and a given purchase price of capital goods. The firm can vary the quantity of capital that it employs, and as a result, the marginal revenue product of its capital varies. The law of diminishing marginal returns tells us that the more capital the firm uses, the lower its *MRP*.

The Decision to Purchase a Unit of Capital

Consider a firm that is deciding whether or not to add to its capital stock and facing an interest rate of *i* at which it can borrow or lend money. The first thing the firm has to do is to estimate the expected stream of *MRP*s from the new piece of capital over its lifetime. Then it discounts this at the interest rate of *i* per year to find the present value of the stream of receipts the machine will generate. Having computed the *PV* of the stream of *MRP*s, the firm then compares this *PV* with the purchase price of the capital good. If the purchase price is less than the *PV*, then the firm buys the capital good; if *PV* is less than the purchase price, the firm will not buy the capital good.

Consider the following simple example. Suppose that a machine has an *MRP* of $1000 each period—that is, by buying this machine the firm can produce more and thereby achieve a net addition to its revenues of $1000 each period. Suppose further that the machine lasts for 3 periods—after that, the machine is completely worn out and worth nothing. Finally, suppose the interest rate is 10 percent per year. The *PV* of this stream of *MRP*s is then equal to

$$PV = \$1000 + \$1000/(1 + 0.10) + \$1000/(1 + 0.10)^2 = \$2735.53.$$

The present value, by its construction, tells us how much any flow of future receipts is worth now. If the firm can buy the machine for less than its *PV*—that is, for any amount less than $2735.53—then this machine is a good buy. If it must pay more, the machine is not worth its price.

It is worthwhile for a firm to buy another unit of capital whenever the present value of the stream of future *MRP*s provided by that unit exceeds its purchase price.

The Firm's Optimal Capital Stock

Because of the law of diminishing marginal returns, the *MRP* declines as the firm's capital stock rises. The firm will thus go on adding to its stock of capital until the present value of the stream of *MRP*s generated by the *last unit* added is equal to the purchase price of that unit.

The profit-maximizing capital stock of the firm is such that the present value of the flow of *MRP*s that is provided by the last unit of capital is equal to its purchase price.

Now suppose the firm has achieved its profit-maximizing stock of capital. What would then lead the firm to increase that stock? Given the price of the machines, anything that increases the present value of the flow of income that the machines produce will have that effect. Two things will do this. First, the *MRP*s of the capital may rise, as would happen if technological changes make capital more productive so that each unit produces more than before. (We will deal with this possibility later in the chapter.) Second, the interest rate may fall, causing an increase in the present value of any given stream of future *MRP*s. For example, suppose that next year's *MRP* is $1000. This has a *PV* of $909.09 when the interest rate is 10 percent and $952.38 when the interest rate falls to 5 percent.

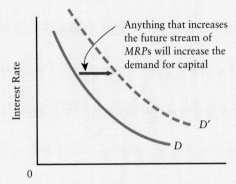

FIGURE 15-1   The Firm's Demand for Capital

Anything that increases the future stream of *MRP*s will increase the demand for capital

The lower the rate of interest, the larger is the firm's desired capital stock. The lower the interest rate, the higher is the present value of any given stream of *MRP*s and hence the more capital that the firm will wish to use.

An improvement in technology that increases the future stream of *MRP*s produced by the capital leads the firm to demand more units of capital at any interest rate—the demand curve shifts to *D′*.

Thus, when the interest rate falls, the firm will wish to add to its capital stock. It will go on doing so until the decline in the *MRP*s of successive additions to its capital stock, according to the law of diminishing marginal returns, reduces the present value of the *MRP* at the new lower rate of interest to the purchase price of the capital.

The size of a firm's desired capital stock increases when the rate of interest falls, and it decreases when the rate of interest rises.

This relationship is shown in Figure 15-1. It can be thought of as the firm's demand curve for capital where the relevant "price" is the interest rate. It shows how the desired stock of capital varies with the interest rate.

What would cause a firm's demand for capital to shift? First, suppose the firm's expectations about future demand for its product improve. This optimism leads the firm to expect an increase in the future stream of *MRP*s produced by capital. With higher expected *MRP*s, the firm is prepared to purchase more units of capital (at any interest rate). Thus the firm's demand curve for capital shifts to the right. Second, suppose an improvement in technology increases the future stream of *MRP*s. Again, the higher future *MRP*s leads to a higher demand for capital at any interest rate—a rightward shift in the firm's demand curve for capital.

Any event that increases the expected future stream of *MRP*s leads to an increase in the firm's demand for capital.

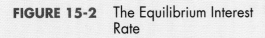

FIGURE 15-2   The Equilibrium Interest Rate

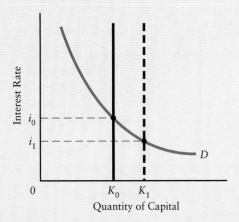

In the short run, the interest rate fluctuates to equate the demand and supply of capital; in the long run, the interest rate falls as more capital is accumulated. The economy's desired capital stock is negatively related to the interest rate, as shown by the curve D. In the short run, the aggregate capital stock is given. When the capital stock is K_0, the equilibrium interest rate is i_0. Above that rate firms will not want to hold all of the available capital; below that rate firms will want to borrow and add to their capital. In the long run, as the capital stock grows to K_1, the equilibrium interest rate falls to i_1.

The Equilibrium Interest Rate

Because the aggregate or total demand for capital goods is simply the sum of all the individual firms' demands, the analysis that we have used for a single firm also applies for the entire economy. Thus the higher is the market interest rate, the lower will be the total quantity of capital goods demanded. Also, changes in technology that make each unit of capital more productive lead to an increase in the total demand for capital goods.

The important difference between the analysis of a single firm and the analysis of the entire economy is that, whereas any individual firm takes the market interest rate as given, the interest rate is determined *in equilibrium* for the economy as a whole. This is analogous to each competitive firm taking the product price as given, whereas the product's price is determined in equilibrium in the market as a whole.

Short-Run Equilibrium

In the short run, the economy's capital stock is given. Though any single firm can change its own capital stock relatively easily—by buying or selling capital goods to or from other firms—the economy as a whole adjusts its capital stock only slowly. To reduce the aggregate capital stock, firms must either scrap their existing capital (if it is no longer profitable to keep it) or allow their capital goods to wear out, or *depreciate*. To increase the aggregate capital stock, new capital goods must be built, some of which—like buildings, bridges, and factories—take a considerable time to complete.

Figure 15-2 shows the economy's fixed short-run supply of capital as well as the total demand for capital goods, which is negatively related to the interest rate. Since the aggregate capital stock is fixed in the short run, equilibrium is achieved through changes in the interest rate, as opposed to changes in the level of capital.[2]

For the economy as a whole, the condition that the present value of the *MRP*s should equal the price of capital goods determines the equilibrium interest rate.

Let us see how this comes about. If the price of capital is less than the present value of its stream of future *MRP*s, it would be worthwhile for all firms to borrow money to purchase capital. For the economy as a whole, however, the stock of capital cannot change quickly, so the effect of this demand for borrowing would be to push up the interest rate until the present value of the *MRP*s equals the price of a unit of capital goods. Conversely, if the price of capital is above its present value, no one would

---

[2]In the macroeconomics part of this textbook, we see that if prices are inflexible in the short run, then actions taken by the central bank can also affect the interest rate. For now, we continue our assumption that all prices (for goods and factors) rise or fall quickly to clear markets, so that the short-run equilibrium interest rate is determined only by the economy's marginal product of capital.

wish to borrow money to invest in capital, and the rate of interest would fall. These points are illustrated in Figure 15-2.

Changing Capital and Technology

In the long run, the economy's capital stock is free to change, but technology is constant. If capital is accumulated over time, then the *MRP* will fall, and the equilibrium interest rate will also fall. Conversely, if the aggregate capital stock is allowed to wear out, then the *MRP* will rise and so will the equilibrium interest rate. This is shown in Figure 15-2, where the aggregate capital stock changes between K_0 and K_1, holding the demand for capital goods constant.

In the very long run, however, technology changes. As a result, the capital stock becomes more productive as the old, obsolete capital is replaced by newer, more efficient capital. The resulting outward shift of the *D* curve tends to increase the equilibrium interest rate associated with any particular size of the capital stock. In contrast, the accumulation of capital moves the economy downward to the right along any given *D* curve, which reduces the interest rate. The net effect on the interest rate of both of these changes may be to raise it, to lower it, or to leave it unchanged, as shown in Figure 15-3.

In almost all industrialized countries, there have been enormous increases in the aggregate capital stock over the past century. Yet, there *have not* been large decreases in the interest rate over the same period. We can easily understand this fact by examining Figure 15-3. Technological change has improved the marginal productivity of capital goods and has thus led to increases in the aggregate demand for capital. Taken alone, such technological improvements would lead to increases in the equilibrium interest rate. Working in the other direction, however, is the continual accumu-

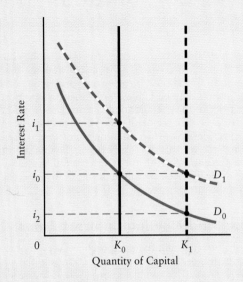

FIGURE 15-3 The Effect of Changing Technology and Capital Stock

Technological changes which increase the marginal product of capital, and changes in the capital stock itself, have opposite effects on the equilibrium interest rate. The original capital stock is K_0 and the original technology gives rise to the demand for capital given by D_0. Thus, the equilibrium interest rate is i_0. Technological changes which increase the marginal product of capital shift the demand curve to D_1 and, with a constant capital stock, would increase the interest rate to i_1. Alternatively, an increase in the capital stock to K_1, holding technology constant, lowers the interest rate to i_2. If technology improves *and* the capital stock increases, then the interest rate could rise or fall. In the figure, the two effects exactly offset each other so that the interest rate is unchanged at i_0.

lation of capital, which tends to push down the equilibrium interest rate. The observation that the aggregate capital stock has increased dramatically, combined with the absence of a clear trend in the interest rate, suggests that these forces are offsetting each other more or less equally. The very-long-run effects of changing technology, combined with a growing capital stock, are represented in greater detail in Chapter 32.

One final comment about capital and the interest rate. We have shown that changes in the interest rate lead to changes in the firm's desired capital stock. We have also said that changes in the economy's stock of capital lead to changes in the equilibrium interest rate. When you go on to study macroeconomics, however, you will learn that the presence of inflation requires economists to make a distinction between the *real* interest rate and the *nominal* interest rate. All of our discussion here has been about the real interest rate. See *Extensions in Theory 15-1* for a more detailed discussion of inflation and interest rates.

EXTENSIONS IN THEORY 15-1

Inflation and Interest Rates

Inflation means the prices of all goods in the economy are rising. More correctly, it means that the prices of goods are rising on *average*—some prices may be rising and others may be falling, but if there is inflation then the price of the average good is rising. Economists refer to the average price of all goods as the *price level*. When the price level is rising, inflation is positive; if prices are rising at a rate of 5 percent per year, the rate of inflation is 5 percent. When the price level is falling, inflation is negative. If prices are falling at a rate of 2 percent per year, the rate of inflation is −2 percent.

Real and Nominal Interest Rates

In the presence of inflation, it becomes very important to distinguish between the *real interest rate* and the *nominal interest rate*. The nominal interest rate is measured simply in dollars paid. If you pay me $7 interest for a $100 loan for one year, the nominal interest rate is 7 percent.

Consider further my one-year loan to you of $100 at the nominal rate of 7 percent. The real rate that I earn depends on what happens to the price level during the course of the year. If the price level remains constant over the year, then the real rate that I earn is also 7 percent—because I can buy 7 percent more real goods and services with the $107 that you repay me than with the $100 that I lent you. However, if the price level were to rise by 7 percent during the year, the real rate would be zero because the $107 you repay me will buy exactly the same quantity of real goods as did the $100 I gave up. If I were unlucky enough to have lent money at a nominal rate of 7 percent in a year in which prices rose by 10 percent, the real rate would be −3 percent. The real rate of interest concerns the ratio of the purchasing power of the money repaid to the purchasing power of the money initially borrowed, and it will be different from the nominal rate whenever inflation is not zero. *The real interest rate is the difference between the nominal interest rate and the rate of inflation.*

If lenders and borrowers are concerned with the real costs measured in terms of purchasing power, the nominal interest rate will be set at the real rate they require plus an amount to cover any expected rate of inflation. Consider a one-year loan that is meant to earn a real return to the lender of 3 percent. If the expected rate of inflation is zero, the nominal interest rate for the loan will also be 3 percent. If, however, a 10 percent inflation is expected, the nominal interest rate will have to be set at 13 percent in order that the real return be 3 percent.

This point is often overlooked, and as a result people are surprised at the high nominal interest rates that exist during periods of high inflation. But it is the real interest rate that matters more to borrowers and lenders. Inflation is currently quite low in Canada but it has not always been that way. For example, in 1976 the rate of inflation was 7.5 percent and the nominal interest rate to prime borrowers was 10.0 percent! The real interest rate was then 2.5 percent. By 1999, the rate of inflation had fallen to 1.5 percent and the nominal rate to prime borrowers had fallen to 6.5 percent; the real rate was then 5.0 percent. Thus, the period of higher nominal interest rates was actually the period of lower real interest rates.

Back to Capital

In this chapter, we have examined the firm's decision to buy capital stock, and we emphasized the importance of the interest rate to this decision. We also discussed how changes in the aggregate stock of capital affected the economy's equilibrium interest rate. Though the text did not say it explicitly, all of our discussion related to the *real* interest rate.

When you go on to study *macroeconomics,* you will learn more about what causes inflation, and thus what forces us to make the distinction between real and nominal interest rates. For now, however, keep in mind that in this chapter we are supposing that there is no inflation; thus, real and nominal interest rates are the same.

Nonrenewable Resources

So far, we have discussed the pricing of factors, such as labour and capital, that can be replaced as they wear out. As older people leave the labour force because of retirement or death, young persons, seeking their first jobs, enter. As an existing piece of capital equipment is retired because of depreciation or obsolescence, it is replaced by a new piece of equipment. Such resources are called **renewable resources.**

We now consider factors of production that are available in fixed amounts. For each such factor, the total stock is given, and every unit that is used today permanently reduces the stock that is available for future use. Such a factor is called a **nonrenewable resource** or an *exhaustible resource.*

In practice, few, if any, resources are completely nonrenewable. Although there is only a fixed stock of oil, coal, or iron ore that is known to exist at any given time, new discoveries add to the known stock, and extraction subtracts from it. However, it is possible to imagine exhausting all of the world's supplies of oil, natural gas, or coal. In this sense, they are nonrenewable resources.

renewable resources
Productive resources that can be replaced as they are used up.

nonrenewable resource   Any productive resource that is available as a fixed stock and cannot be replaced once it is used. Also called an *exhaustible resource.*

The Extraction Rate of a Resource

To focus on the basic issues, it is easiest to think of a resource that is completely nonrenewable. Suppose for the moment that all of the oil in existence has been discovered so that every unit that is used permanently diminishes the available stock by one unit.

Suppose that many firms own the land that contains the oil supply. They have invested money in discovering the oil, drilling wells, and laying pipelines. Their current extraction costs are virtually zero; all they have to do is turn their taps on, and the oil flows at any desired rate to the oil markets. It is obviously a simplification to assume that current production costs are actually zero. But this assumption is actually not too far from reality in the case of such a resource as oil, where the fixed costs of discovery, extraction, and distribution account for the bulk of total costs.

Profit-Maximizing Firms

What should each firm do? It could extract all of its oil in a great binge of production this year, or it could save the resource for some future rainy day and produce nothing this year. In practice, it is likely to adopt some intermediate policy, producing and selling some oil this year and holding stocks of it in the ground for extraction in future years. But *how much* should it extract this year and *how much* should it carry over for future years? What will the decision imply for the price of oil over the years?

The firms that own land with oil underneath it are holding a valuable resource. These firms have two alternatives. First, they can extract the oil now and sell it at the current market price. Second, they can leave the oil in the ground and extract it at some later date. The firms, naturally, will choose the alternative that gives them the highest return. Their choice will depend on two key variables—the interest rate and the expected rate of increase in the price of oil. To see how the firms' decisions are made, consider two cases.

First, suppose that the price of oil is expected to rise by less than the interest rate. For example, suppose the interest rate is 10 percent per year but the price of oil is expected to increase by only 5 percent per year. Oil extracted and sold now will in this case have a higher value than oil left in the ground, since revenues from current sales could be earning 10 percent in a bank account. Firms will therefore extract more oil this year. Because the demand curve for oil has a negative slope, raising the extraction rate (increasing the current supply) will reduce this year's price. Production will rise, and the current price will fall until the expected price increase between this year and next year is equal to the interest rate. The firms will then be indifferent between producing another barrel this year and holding it for production next year.

Second, suppose that the price is expected to rise by more than the interest rate. Firms will in this case prefer to leave more oil in the ground, where they earn a higher return than they could earn by selling the oil this year and investing the proceeds at the current interest rate. Thus, firms will cut their rate of production for this year, which will reduce the current supply and therefore raise this year's price. When the current price has risen so that the gap between the current price and next year's expected price is equal to the interest rate, firms will value equally a barrel of oil extracted and one left in the ground.

In a competitive industry for a nonrenewable resource, equilibrium occurs when the last unit currently produced earns just as much for each firm as it would if it had been left in the ground for future sales.

If the current interest rate is greater than the expected rate of increase in the price of oil, a profit-maximizing firm will extract the oil today.

To illustrate this important idea, suppose that next year's price is expected to be $1.05 and that the rate of interest is 5 percent. Now suppose that the current price is $1.04 per barrel. It clearly pays to extract more oil now because the $1.04 that is earned by selling a barrel now can be invested to yield approximately $1.09 ($1.04 × 1.05), which is more than the $1.05 that the oil would be worth in a year's time if it is left in the ground.

Now suppose that the current price is $.90 cents per barrel. It pays to extract less oil because oil left in the ground will be worth 16.7 percent more next year [(1.05/0.90) × 100]. Extracting it this year and investing the money will produce a gain of only 5 percent.

Finally, suppose the current price is $1.00. Now oil producers make the same amount of money whether they leave $1.00 worth of oil in the ground to be worth $1.05 next year or they sell the oil for $1.00 this year and invest the proceeds at 5 percent interest.

Market Pricing

What we have established so far determines the *rate of increase* of prices over time: If stocks are given and unchanging, prices should rise over time at a rate equal to the rate of interest. But what about the *level* of prices? Will they start low and rise to only moderate levels over the next few years, or will they start high and then rise to even higher levels? The answer depends on the total stock of the resource that is available (and, where some new discoveries are possible, on the expected additions to that stock in the future). The scarcer the resource relative to the demand for it, the higher its market price at the outset.

A resource's price tends to rise over time at a rate equal to the rate of interest; the current price will depend on current demand.

Hotelling's Rule

Oil is a scarce resource, and the value to consumers of one more barrel produced now is the price that they would be willing to pay for it, which in our example is the current $1.00 market price of the oil. If the oil is extracted this year and the proceeds are invested at the rate of interest (5 percent), they will produce $1.05 worth of valuable goods next year. If that barrel of oil is not produced this year and is left in the ground for extraction next year, its value to consumers at that time will be next year's price of oil. It is not *socially optimal*, therefore, to leave the oil in the ground unless it will be worth at least $1.05 to consumers next year.

Hotelling's rule
Determines the optimal rate of extraction of a nonrenewable resource as one such that the price rises at a rate equal to the interest rate.

The answer to the question "How much of a nonrenewable resource should be consumed now?" was provided many years ago by the U.S. economist Harold Hotelling. His answer—now referred to as **Hotelling's Rule**—is very simple, yet it specifically determines the optimal pattern of prices over the years. It is interesting that the answer applies to *all* nonrenewable resources. It does not matter whether there is a large or a small demand or whether that demand is elastic or inelastic. In all cases the answer is the same:

The socially optimal rate of extraction of any nonrenewable resource is such that its price increases at a rate equal to the interest rate.

For example, if the rate of interest is 4 percent, the price of the resource should be rising 4 percent per year. If it is rising by more, there is too much current extraction; if it is rising by less, there is not enough current extraction. We have already seen that this is the rate of extraction that will be produced by a competitive industry.

A competitive industry produces the socially optimal rate of extraction of a nonrenewable resource.

The Rate of Extraction

Hotelling's Rule does not tell us exactly how many barrels of oil should be extracted each year. Instead, it only tells us that the year's extraction rate should be such that the market price rises at a rate equal to the interest rate. What then should the actual extraction rate be if the competitive market fulfills Hotelling's Rule for optimal extraction rates? The answer to this question *does* depend on market conditions. Specifically, it depends on the position and the slope of the demand curve. If the quantity demanded at all prices is small, the rate of extraction will be small. The larger the quantity demanded at each price, the higher the rate of extraction will tend to be.

Now consider the influence of the demand elasticity. A highly inelastic demand curve suggests that there are few substitutes and that purchasers are prepared to pay large sums rather than do without the resource. This inelasticity will produce a relatively even rate of extraction, with small reductions in each period being sufficient to drive up the price at the required rate. A relatively elastic demand curve suggests that people can easily find substitutes once the price rises. This will encourage a great deal of consumption now and a rapidly diminishing amount over future years because large reductions in consumption are needed to drive the price up at the required rate.

Figure 15-4 illustrates this working of the price mechanism with a simple example in which the whole stock of oil must be consumed in only two periods, this year and next year. The general point is this:

The more inelastic the demand curve, the more even the rate of extraction (and hence the rate of use) will be over time; the more elastic the demand curve, the more uneven the rate of extraction will be over time.

An elastic demand curve will lead to large consumption now and a rapid fall in consumption over the years. An inelastic demand curve will lead to lower consumption now and a less rapid fall in consumption over the years.

Practise with Study Guide Chapter 15, Exercise 6.

Conservation Through the Price System

In this discussion, we see the price system playing its now familiar role of coordinator. By following private profit incentives, firms are led to conserve the resource in a manner that is consistent with society's needs.

The Role of Rising Prices

We have seen that, from society's viewpoint, the optimal extraction pattern of a nonrenewable resource occurs when its price rises each year at a rate equal to the interest

FIGURE 15-4 The Extraction Rate for a Nonrenewable Resource

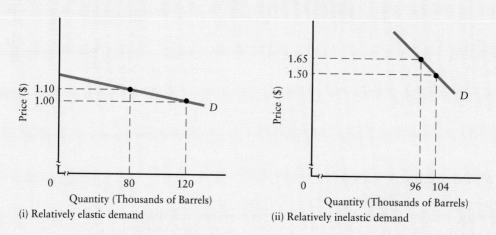

(i) Relatively elastic demand

(ii) Relatively inelastic demand

The shape of the demand curve determines the extraction pattern over time. In the example in this figure, the interest rate is assumed to be 10 percent, and there is a fixed supply of 200 000 barrels of oil that can be extracted from the ground at zero marginal cost. (All costs are fixed costs.) The oil is available for extraction either in the current period or in the next period, after which it spoils.

In part (i) of the figure, the demand curve is relatively flat. The two conditions—that the whole supply be used over two periods and that the price rise by 10 percent between the two periods—dictate that the quantities be 120 000 barrels in the first period, with a price of $1.00 per barrel, and 80 000 in the second period, with a price of $1.10 per barrel.

In part (ii), the demand curve is rather steep. The same two conditions now dictate that the quantities be 104 000 barrels in the first period, with a price of $1.50 per barrel, and 96 000 barrels in the second period, with a price of $1.65 per barrel.

rate. If the price is prevented from rising, the resource is depleted too quickly. The rising price fulfills a number of useful functions.

First, the rising price encourages conservation. As the resource becomes scarcer and its price rises, users will be motivated to be more economical in its use. Uses with low yields may be abandoned altogether, and uses with high yields will be pursued only as long as their value at the margin is enough to compensate for the high price.

Second, the rising price encourages the discovery of new sources of supply—at least in cases in which the world supply is not totally fixed and already known.

Third, the rising price encourages innovation. New products that will do the same job may be developed, as well as new processes that use alternative resources. For example, a rising price of oil encourages the development of alternative sources of energy, such as solar and wind power.

How Might the Price System Fail?

We now examine three basic ways in which the price system might fail to produce the optimal rate of resource extraction. First, private owners may not have sufficient information to determine the optimal extraction rate. Second, deficiencies in property rights may result in firms' having incentives to extract the resource too fast. Third, markets may not correctly reflect social values. We look at examples of each of these and ask if they justify government intervention. In looking at these examples in which the price system fails, we are anticipating what will be the major theme of Chapter 16.

Ignorance.   Private owners might not have enough knowledge to arrive at the best estimate of the rate at which prices will rise. If they do not know the world stocks of their commodity and the current extraction rate, they may be unable to estimate the rate of the price rise and thus will not know when to raise or lower their current rates of extraction. For example, if all firms think that prices will rise only slowly in the future, but prices actually end up rising quickly, they will all produce too much now and conserve too little for future periods.

In this situation, however, there is no reason to think that the government could do any better, unless it has access to some special knowledge that private firms do not possess. If it does have such knowledge, the government can make it public; further intervention is unnecessary if a competitive industry is maximizing profits on the basis of the best information available to it. In practice, what knowledge does exist about both the proven reserves of nonrenewable resources and their current extraction rates is usually freely and openly available.

Inadequate Property Rights.   Some nonrenewable resources have the characteristics of what is called *common property*. Such property cannot be exclusively owned and controlled by one person or firm. For example, one person's oil-bearing land may be adjacent to another person's, and the underground supplies may be interconnected. In such a case, if one firm holds off producing now, the oil may end up being extracted by the neighbour. In such cases, which are often encountered with oil, there is a tendency for a firm to extract the resource too fast because a firm's oil that has been left in the ground may not be available to that firm at a future date. (A similar issue arises with any common-property resource such as fishing grounds. We examine this further in Chapter 16.)

What is being described here is a problem of *inadequate property rights*. Because the resource will be worth more in total value when it is exploited at the optimal extraction rate than when small firms exploit it too quickly, there will be an incentive for individual owners to combine until each self-contained source of supply is owned by only one firm. After that, the problem of overexploitation will no longer arise. Government ownership is not necessary to achieve this result. What is needed, at most, is intervention to ensure that markets can work to provide the optimal size of individual units so that proper extraction management can be applied by the private owners.

Political uncertainty can be another source of inadequate property rights. For example, the owners of the resource may fear that a future election or a revolution will establish a government that will confiscate their property. They will then be motivated to exploit the resource too quickly, on the grounds that certain revenue now is more valuable than uncertain revenue in the future. The current rate of extraction will tend to increase until the expected rate of price rise exceeds the interest rate by a sufficient margin to compensate for the risks of future confiscation of supplies left in the ground.

Unequal Market and Social Values.   In a competitive world, the market interest rate indicates the rate at which it is optimal to discount the future. Society's investments are beneficial if they earn at least the market rate of return; they are not beneficial if they earn less (because the resources could be used in other ways to produce more value to consumers). In certain circumstances, however, the government may have reasons to adopt a different discount rate. It is then said that the *social rate of discount*— the discount rate that is appropriate to the society as a whole—differs from the private rate, as indicated by the market rate of interest. In such circumstances, there is reason for the government to intervene to alter the rate at which the private firms would exploit the resource.

Critics are often ready to assume that profit-hungry producers will despoil most exhaustible resources by using them up too quickly. They argue for government intervention

For good information on fossil fuels, see the website for the U.S. Department of Energy: www.doe.gov. Click on "Fossil Fuel Lessons."

to conserve the resource by slowing its rate of extraction. Yet, unless the social rate of discount is below the private rate, there is no clear social gain in investing by holding resources in the ground where they will yield only, say, a 2 percent return, when perhaps 5 percent can be gained on other investments.

Because governments must worry about their short-term popularity and their chances of reelection, they may have a discount rate higher than either the social or market rate. Thus, there is no presumption that government intervention will slow the rate of extraction. Instead, governments might extract resources *faster* than would occur by private firms in the absence of intervention.

A good example is provided by the Hybernia oil field that lies off the coast of Newfoundland. When development began in the late 1970s, the cost of developing the field and extracting the oil exceeded the market value of the oil. It would therefore not have been extracted under free-market conditions. Instead, taxpayers' money was used to produce oil whose market value was less than its full costs of production. If left beneath the ocean floor, the oil would one day have developed a value sufficient for it to be extracted by private firms, either because of increases in the price of oil or improvements in technology that reduced the costs of extraction.

Actual Price Movements

Many nonrenewable resources do not seem to have the steadily rising prices predicted by Hotelling's Rule. The OPEC cartel restricted the supply of oil in the 1970s and thereby pushed its price up dramatically. But in the mid 1980s both the rate of extraction and the real price of oil returned approximately to their pre-OPEC levels. Since then the price of oil has increased only occasionally, whenever the producing countries have succeeded in intermittently enforcing some output restrictions. The price of coal has not soared; nor has the price of iron ore. In many cases, the reason lies in the discovery of new supplies, which have prevented the total known stocks of many resources from being depleted. In the case of oil, for example, the ratio of known reserves to one year's consumption is no lower now than it was two or even four decades ago. Furthermore, most industry experts believe that large quantities of undiscovered oil exist under both the land and the sea.

In other cases, the invention of new substitute products has reduced the demand for some of these resources and has thus prevented prices from rising as quickly as they otherwise would have. For example, plastics have replaced metals in many uses, and fiber optics have replaced copper wire in many types of message transmission.

In yet other cases, the reason is to be found in government pricing policy. An important example of this type is the use of nonrenewable water for irrigation in much of the United States. Though vast underground reserves of water lie in aquifers beneath many areas of the United States, they are being used up at a rate that will exhaust them in a matter of decades. The water is often supplied by government water authorities at a price that covers only a small part of the total extraction cost and that does not rise steadily to reflect the dwindling stocks. Current U.S. water policy will have strong effects on Canada, which controls a large *renewable* supply of fresh water from rivers and lakes.

Such a constant-price policy for *any* nonrenewable resource creates three characteristic problems. First, the resource will be exhausted much faster than if the price were to rise over time. Second, since the price is not allowed to rise, no signals go out to induce conservation, innovation, and exploration. Third, when the supply of the resource is finally exhausted, the adjustment will have to come all at once. If the price had risen steadily each year under free-market conditions, adjustment would have taken place little by little each year. The controlled price, however, gives no signal of the ever-diminishing stock of the resource until all at once the supplies run out. The required adjustment will then be much more painful than it would have been if it had been spread over time in response to steadily rising prices.

When governments intervene to keep the price of a nonrenewable resource below its free-market value, the current users of the resource are essentially obtaining a subsidy from future users, who, if the policy continues, will have to make many adjustments abruptly while paying much higher prices for the resource.

For lots of good information about various forms of energy, check out the Energy Information Administration's website: www.eia.doe.gov.

Currently, several of the western U.S. states are suffering severe water shortages. In spite of the shortages, water prices are being held well below what they would be in free markets. The low prices both encourage water uses that would not even be contemplated under free-market conditions and discourage conservation, thus leading to more rapidly growing shortages than would occur under rising free-market prices. For example, about 80 percent of California's water supply goes to farmers even though agriculture accounts for only one tenth of the state's economy. Throughout California's Central Valley, sprinklers irrigate cattle pastures and fields of alfalfa, cotton, and rice—crops more suited to monsoon lands than to the valley's dry climate. Alfalfa fields alone take up more water than that used by all the people in San Francisco and Los Angeles combined.

The dwindling water supplies under much of the continent would long ago have led to price increases close to those predicted by Hotelling's theory, and hence to a series of gradual adjustments, had the price been permitted to rise to reflect the growing scarcity of the resource.

S U M M A R Y

Capital and the Interest Rate

- Because capital goods are durable, it is necessary to distinguish between the stock of capital goods and the flow of services provided by them and thus between their purchase price and their rental price. The rental price is the amount that is paid to obtain the flow of services that a capital good provides for a given period. The purchase price is the amount that is paid to acquire ownership of the capital.

- To determine the purchase price of capital, it is necessary to compute the present value of the stream of benefits produced by the unit of capital. The present value will be lower when the benefits are more distant and the interest rate is higher.

- An individual firm will purchase capital as long as the present value of the stream of future net returns that is provided by another unit of capital exceeds its purchase price. For a single firm and for the economy as a whole, the profit-maximizing size of the capital stock varies negatively with the rate of interest.

- Whereas individual firms take the market interest rate as given, the interest rate is determined in equilibrium for the economy as a whole. Long-run increases in the aggregate capital stock, holding technology constant, lead to reductions in the equilibrium interest rate. Changes in technology that increase the marginal revenue product of capital lead to increases in the equilibrium interest rate.

Nonrenewable Resources

⑩④⑤

- The socially optimal rate of extraction for a nonrenewable resource occurs when its price rises at a rate equal to the rate of interest. This is Hotelling's Rule. This rate of price increase is also the rate that will be established by profit-maximizing firms in a competitive industry.
- Resources for which the demand is highly elastic will have a high rate of extraction in the near future and a fairly rapid falloff over time. Resources for which the demand is highly inelastic will have a lower rate of extraction in the near future and a smaller falloff over time.
- Rising prices act as a conservation device by rationing consumption over time according to people's preferences.

As prices rise, conservation, discovery of new sources of supply, and innovation to reduce demand are all encouraged.
- The price system can fail to produce optimal results if (a) people lack the necessary knowledge, (b) property rights are inadequate to protect supplies left for future use by their owners, or (c) the social rate of discount differs significantly from the market rate.
- Controlling the price of an exhaustible resource at a constant level speeds up the rate of extraction and removes the price incentives to react to its growing scarcity.

K E Y   C O N C E P T S

Rental price and purchase price
  of capital
Present value

A firm's demand for capital
The interest rate and the capital stock
The equilibrium interest rate

Hotelling's Rule
The conservation role of rising prices
  of nonrenewable resources

S T U D Y   E X E R C I S E S

1. The following table shows the stream of income produced by several different assets. In each case, P_1, P_2, and P_3 are the payments made by the asset in years 1, 2 and 3.

Asset	(i)	P_1	P_2	P_3	Present Value
A	8%	$1000	$0	$0	---
B	7%	0	0	5000	---
C	9%	200	0	200	---
D	10%	50	40	60	---

   a. For each asset, compute the asset's present value. (Note that the market interest rate, i, is not the same in each situation.)
   b. In each case, what is the most a firm would be prepared to pay to acquire the asset?
   c. Suppose the listed purchase price for an asset were less than its present value. What would you expect to observe?

2. The table below shows how the present value of the future MRPs produced by each unit of capital changes as the firm's total capital stock increases.

Units of Capital	PV of future MRPs
100	$10 000
101	9 000
102	8 000
103	7 000
104	6 000
105	5 000
106	4 000
107	3 000

a. Notice that the present value of the *MRP* declines as more capital is used. What economic principle accounts for this?
b. If a unit of capital can be purchased for $5000, how many will the firm purchase? Explain.
c. Suppose the market interest rate suddenly falls. Explain what happens to the *PV* of the stream of future *MRPs*. What happens to the firm's profit-maximizing level of capital?

3. The diagram below shows an individual firm's demand curve for capital. The market interest rate is i_0.

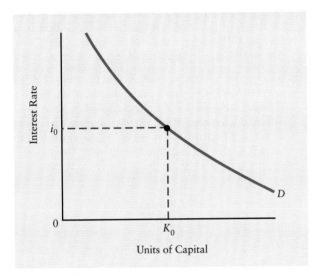

a. Explain why the firm's demand curve is downward sloping.
b. Suppose the firm now expects the market for its product to be especially good in the future. Explain what happens to its demand curve for capital.
c. Now suppose that some technical problem leads to a reduction in the future stream of *MRPs* produced by capital. How does this affect the firm's demand for capital?

4. The following diagram shows the economy's aggregate demand for capital as a function of the interest rate.

a. If the economy's stock of capital is currently K_0, what is the equilibrium interest rate? Explain.

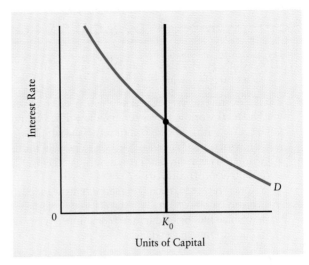

b. If firms experience an improvement in technology that increases the expected future *MRP* of each unit of capital, what is the effect on the equilibrium interest rate? Explain.

5. The table below shows a number of situations faced by Prairie Energy Inc., an Alberta-based oil company. The price of oil is given as dollars per barrel.

Case	Interest Rate (per annum)	Oil Price Now	Oil Price in One Year	Extract Now?
A	8%	$20	$25	—-
B	10%	15	18	—-
C	12%	10	8	—-
D	12%	10	12	—-
E	20%	15	18	—-

a. In each case, what rate of return would Prairie Energy earn *over the coming year* by leaving its oil in the ground and then extracting it and selling it in one years' time?
b. In each case, what rate of return would Prairie Energy earn on its alternative investment?
c. In each case, indicate whether it is beneficial for Prairie Energy to extract the oil now, or to wait until next year.

DISCUSSION QUESTIONS

1. How would you go about evaluating the present value of each of the following?

   a. The existing reserves of a relatively small oil company
   b. The total world reserves of an exhaustible natural resource with a known completely fixed supply
   c. A long-term bond, issued by a very unstable third-world government, that promises to pay the bearer $1000 per year forever
   d. A lottery ticket that your neighbour bought for $10, which was one of 1 million tickets sold for a drawing which will be held in one year's time paying $2 million to the single winner

2. Your parents argue that it makes more sense for you to take taxis and, on occasion, to rent a car while you are at university because you will be spending most of your time in the library and your need for a car should be minimal. Make an argument based on the rental price of transportation (not on the other advantages of having the car) that it may be cheaper for you to buy a car for use while you are at university.

3. Obtain annual data on the world price of oil over the past 30 years. Explain whether the observed path of prices appears to follow Hotelling's Rule. Can you explain any deviations? (For lots of energy-related data, check out www.eia.doe.gov.)

4. There are many examples of resources that are technically renewable—such as the stock of old-growth forests—but that may not be replenished within your lifetime if the current stock is depleted. Explain how you would expect the market to price such resources.

5. Species that are on the verge of extinction—beluga whales, African elephants, mountain gorillas, and the California condor—might be classified as nonrenewable resources; once they disappear, there will be no regeneration. Does the market create appropriate incentives to ensure that extinction will not occur?

16 16 17 18

PART SIX

Government in the Market Economy

When is there a role for government to intervene in the market economy? Is government action necessary to reduce sulphur dioxide emissions, or can the market economy handle that problem itself? Why doesn't the private sector provide things like national defence? What are tradable pollution permits and how do they work? How does the Canadian government raise the money it needs to finance its expenditures, and on what does the Canadian government spend? These are the kinds of questions you will be able to answer after reading the next three chapters.

Chapter 16 discusses the basic functions of governments and then reviews the case for free markets. We will see the reasons why economists often argue in favour of free markets and against government intervention. We then explore the case for government intervention based on the concept of a market failure—a situation in which the free market fails to produce the allocatively efficient outcome. It is here that we see why the free market typically cannot be relied upon to solve the problem of pollution; we will also learn why the private sector does not provide national defence. Next, we explore reasons for government intervention that are motivated by the pursuit of broad social goals. Finally, we examine the process of government intervention and the reasons for government failures.

In Chapter 17 we explore the economics of pollution. We examine the rationale for regulating pollution and various methods of pollution control, including tradable pollution permits—the most recent (and most controversial) method for dealing with pollution.

Chapter 18 then examines the taxation and expenditure patterns of Canadian governments. We discuss the Canadian tax system, and how to evaluate a tax system from the standpoints of both efficiency and equity. We then explore some of the most important spending programs and discuss some of the recent debates about reforming various elements of Canadian social programs.

CHAPTER 16

Market Failures and Government Intervention

🔵 *LEARNING OBJECTIVES*

① Recognize that two basic functions of government are the protection of individuals from others and the establishment and enforcement of property rights.

② Understand the ability of free markets to respond to change and to promote innovation.

③ Define an externality and explain why it leads to allocative inefficiency.

④ Define public goods, and explain why they will not be provided by private markets.

⑤ Understand why asymmetric information can lead to market failures.

⑥ Understand why free markets generally will not achieve some desirable social goals.

⑦ Explain the direct and indirect costs of government intervention.

⑧ Understand some of the important causes of government failure.

Most aspects of Canadian economic life are determined in free markets. Most of the goods and services that you buy are produced by privately owned profit-making firms, and the prices of those goods and services are determined in free markets. The incomes of most Canadian workers are also determined by free-market forces.

But government intervention and regulation are also pervasive. Canadian governments regulate the pricing of cable TV, local telephone service, and electricity. The Canadian government owns Canada Post, the Export Development Corporation, and many other crown corporations that sell goods or services to firms and households. And Canadian governments have extensive regulations regarding many aspects of our lives, including waste disposal, workplace safety, building codes, minimum wages, taxi service, and so on.

Which elements of the economy can be left to free markets and which elements require government intervention? Governments are necessary to provide law and order and to define and enforce property rights. But beyond these basic functions—ones that we all too often take for granted—what is the case for government intervention in otherwise free markets?

The general case for some reliance on free markets is that allowing decentralized decision making is more desirable than having all economic decisions made by a centralized planning body. The general case for some government intervention is that almost no one wants to let markets decide *everything* about our economic affairs. Most people believe that there are areas in which markets do not function well and in which government intervention can improve the general social good.

The operative choice is not between an unhampered free-market economy and a fully centralized command economy. It is rather the choice of *which mix* of markets and government intervention best suits people's hopes and needs.

In this chapter, we discuss the role of the government in market-based economies, making the case both for and against government intervention. We begin by examining the basic functions of government.

Basic Functions of Government

Governments are as old as organized economic activity. They arose shortly after the neolithic agricultural revolution turned people from hunter–gatherers into settled farmers. An institution that has survived that long must be doing something right! Over the intervening 100 centuries the functions undertaken by governments have varied enormously. But through all that time the function that has not changed is to provide what is called a *monopoly of violence*. Violent acts can be conducted by the military and the civilian police arms of government, and through its judicial system the government can deprive people of their liberty by incarcerating them or, in extreme cases, by executing them. This is a dangerous monopoly that is easily abused. For this reason satisfactory societies have systems of checks and balances designed to keep the government's monopoly directed to the general good rather than to the good of a narrow government circle.

The importance of having a monopoly of violence can be seen in those countries whose governments do not have it. Somalia in recent decades and China in the 1920s provide examples of countries in which individual warlords commanded armies that could not vanquish each other. Colombia, and to some extent Russia, provide examples of organized crime having substantial power to commit violence that the government cannot control. In extreme cases where many groups have almost equal ability to exert military violence, power struggles can create havoc with normal economic and social life. Life then becomes "nasty, brutish, and short"—to use the words of the seventeenth-century English political philosopher Thomas Hobbes (1588–1679).

The importance of having checks on the government's arbitrary use of its monopoly is seen in the disasters that ensue in the many dictatorships that misuse their power. The USSR under Stalin, Uganda under Idi Amin, Nigeria under Sanni Abacha, and Cambodia under Pol Pot are a few of the many modern-day examples.

When the government's monopoly of violence is secure and functions with restrictions against its arbitrary use, citizens can safely carry on their ordinary economic and social activities.

So governments are, as they always have been, institutions to which people accept a monopoly of violence in return for the enforcement of "law and order."

A related government activity is to provide security of property. Governments define and enforce property rights that give people a secure claim to the fruits of their own labour. These property rights include clear definition and enforcement of the rights and obligations of institutions such as corporations, banks, insurance companies, and stock exchanges.

As the founder of British classical economics, Adam Smith, put it a long time ago:

The first duty of the sovereign [is] that of protecting the society from the violence and invasion of other independent societies. . . . The second duty of the sovereign [is] that of protecting, as far as possible, every member of the society from the injustice or oppression of every other member of it.[1]

In a modern complex economy, providing these "minimal" government services is no simple task. Countries whose governments are not good at doing these things have seldom prospered economically.

The Case for Free Markets

Within a secure framework of law and order, and well-defined and enforced property rights, a modern economy can function at least moderately well without further government assistance. In this section we review the case for free markets. In subsequent sections we study government functions that arise when free markets fail to produce acceptable results.

Free markets are impressive institutions. Consumers' tastes and producers' costs help to generate price signals. These signals coordinate separate decisions taken by millions of independent agents, all pursuing their own self-interest and oblivious to national priorities. In doing so, they allocate the nation's resources without conscious central direction. Markets also determine the distribution of income by establishing prices of factors of production, which provide incomes for their owners. Furthermore, modern market economies, where firms compete to get ahead of each other by producing better goods more cheaply, generate the technological changes that have raised average living standards fairly steadily at least over the past two centuries.

In presenting the case for free markets economists have used two quite different approaches. The first of these may be characterized as the "formal defence," and is based on the concept of allocative efficiency, introduced in Chapter 12. The essence of the formal defence of free-market economies is that if all markets were perfectly competitive, and if governments allowed all prices to be determined by demand and supply, then resources would be allocated in the *optimal* manner. That is, prices would equal marginal cost for all products and thus the economy would be allocatively efficient.

The other defence of free markets—what might be called the "informal defence"—is at least as old as Adam Smith and is meant to apply to market economies whether or not they are perfectly competitive. It is based on the theme that markets are a very effective mechanism for coordinating the decisions of decentralized decision makers. The informal defence is intuitive in that it is not laid out in a formal model of an economy, but it does follow from some hard reasoning, and it has been subjected to much intellectual probing.

This informal defence of free markets is based on three central arguments.

1. Free markets provide automatic coordination of the actions of decentralized decision makers.

2. The pursuit of profits in free markets provides a stimulus to innovation and economic growth.

3. Free markets permit a decentralization of economic power.

---

[1]Adam Smith, *The Wealth of Nations* (1976; New York: Random House, 1937 edn., pp. 653, 669).

Automatic Coordination

Defenders of the market economy argue that, compared with the alternatives, the decentralized market system is more flexible and adjusts more quickly to changes.

Suppose, for example, that the price of oil rises. One household might prefer to respond by maintaining a high temperature in its house and economizing on its driving; another household might do the reverse. A third household might give up air-conditioning instead. This flexibility can be contrasted with centralized control, which would force the same pattern on everyone, say, by fixing the price, by rationing heating oil and gasoline, by regulating permitted temperatures, and by limiting air-conditioning to days when the temperature exceeded 27°C.

Furthermore, as conditions continue to change, prices in a market economy will continue to change, and decentralized decision makers can react continually. In contrast, government quotas, allocations, and rationing schemes are much more difficult to adjust. As a result, there are likely to be shortages and surpluses before adjustments are made. One great value of the market is that it provides automatic signals *as a situation develops* so that not all of the consequences of an economic change have to be anticipated and allowed for by a group of central planners. Millions of responses to millions of changes in thousands of markets are required every year, and it would be a herculean task to anticipate and plan for them all.

A market system allows for coordination *without anyone needing to understand how the whole system works.* As Professor Thomas Schelling put it:

> The dairy farmer doesn't need to know how many people eat butter and how far away they are, how many other people raise cows, how many babies drink milk, or whether more money is spent on beer or milk. What he needs to know is the prices of different feeds, the characteristics of different cows, the different prices . . . for milk . . . , the relative cost of hired labor and electrical machinery, and what his net earnings might be if he sold his cows and raised pigs instead.[2]

It is, of course, an enormous advantage that all the producers and consumers of a country collectively can make the system operate, yet not one of them, much less all of them, has to understand how it works.

Innovation and Growth

Technology, tastes, and resource availability are changing all the time, in all economies. Thirty years ago, there was no such thing as a personal computer or a digital watch. Front-wheel drive was a curiosity in North America. Students carried their books in briefcases or in canvas bags that were anything but waterproof. Manuscripts existed only as hard copy, not as electronic files in a computer. To change one word in a manuscript, one usually had to retype an entire page. Videocassettes did not exist, nor did compact discs, cell phones, or the Internet.

Digital watches, personal computers, front-wheel drive cars, and compact discs are all products that were invented or developed by individuals or firms in pursuit of profits. An entrepreneur who correctly "reads" the market and perceives that there may be a demand for some product will be inclined to develop it.

The next 20 years will also surely see changes great and small. Changes in technology may make an idea that is not practical today practical five years from now. New prod-

---

[2]Schelling, T.C. *Micro Motives and Macro Behavior* (New York: Norton, 1978).

ucts and techniques will be devised to adapt to shortages, gluts, and changes in consumer demands and to exploit new opportunities made available by new technologies.

In a market economy, individuals risk their time and money in the hope of earning profits. Though many fail, some succeed. New products and processes appear and disappear. Some are fads or have little impact; others become items of major significance. The market system works by trial and error to sort them out and allocates resources to what prove to be successful innovations.

In contrast, planners in more centralized systems have to guess which innovations will be productive and which goods will be strongly demanded. Central planning may achieve wonders by permitting a massive effort in a chosen direction, but central planners also may guess incorrectly about the direction and put too many eggs in the wrong basket or reject as unpromising something that will turn out to be vital. Perhaps the biggest failure of centrally planned economies was their inability to encourage the experimentation and innovation that have proved to be the driving forces behind long-run growth in advanced market economies. It is striking that the last decade has seen most centrally planned economies abandon their system in favour of a price system in one fell swoop while the only remaining large planned economy, China, is increasing the role of markets in most aspects of its economy.

Decentralization of Power

Another important part of the case for a free-market economy is that it tends to decentralize power and thus requires less coercion of individuals than any other type of economy. Of course, even though markets tend to diffuse power, they do not do so completely; large firms and large labour unions clearly have and exercise substantial economic power.

Though the market power of large corporations and unions is not negligible, it tends to be constrained both by the competition of other large entities and by the emergence of new products and firms. This is the process of creative destruction that was described by Joseph Schumpeter and that we examined in Chapter 10. In any case, say defenders of the free market, even such aggregations of private power are far less substantial than government power.

Governments must coerce if markets are not allowed to allocate people to jobs and goods to consumers. Not only will such coercion be regarded as arbitrary (especially by those who do not like the results), but the power creates major opportunities for bribery, corruption, and allocation according to the tastes of the central administrators. If, at the going prices and wages, there are not enough apartments or coveted jobs to go around, the bureaucrats can allocate some to those who pay the largest bribe, some to those with religious beliefs, or political views that they like, and only the rest to those whose names come up on the waiting list.

This line of reasoning has been articulated forcefully by the Nobel laureate and conservative economist Milton Friedman, who was for many years a professor of economics at the University of Chicago. Friedman argues that economic freedom—the ability to allocate resources through private markets—is essential to the maintenance of political freedom.[3] Other economists and social theorists have challenged this proposition.

---

[3]Milton Friedman, *Capitalism and Freedom* (Chicago: The University of Chicago Press: 1982).

Market Failures

Free markets do all of the good things that we have just discussed; yet there are many circumstances in which the free market does not produce the best outcomes. In these cases, economists say that markets have *failed*. The case for intervening in free markets turns in large part on identifying the conditions that lead to market failure. Much of the following discussion is devoted to this task.

We must be careful when using the expression *market failure* because the word *failure* may convey the wrong impression. Market failure does not mean that nothing good has happened. It means, instead, that the *best attainable outcome* has not been achieved. More precisely, **market failure** refers to a situation where private markets, in the absence of government intervention, fail to achieve allocative efficiency. In other words, in some market or markets, the marginal benefit of the good differs from its marginal cost.

> Market failure describes a situation in which the free market, in the absence of government intervention, fails to achieve allocative efficiency.

It is useful to recall the distinction between normative and positive statements that we first encountered in Chapter 2. The statement that the economy is allocatively efficient (or not) is a *positive* statement. We can say that the economy has or has not achieved allocative efficiency without making any value judgement—the statement uses only an observation about the economy and the definition of allocative efficiency. It is important to note, however, that the allocatively efficient outcome may not be the most desirable outcome in a normative sense. For example, the economy may be allocatively efficient even though the distribution of income is judged by some to be undesirable. As we see later in the chapter, such concerns provide another motivation for government intervention.

We now examine five situations in which the free market fails to achieve allocative efficiency—*monopoly, externalities, non-rivalrous* and *non-excludable goods, asymmetric information* and *missing markets*. All of these market failures provide a justification, at least in principle, for government intervention in markets. We then discuss other reasons for government intervention that are not based on market failure—chief among these is intervention to achieve a desirable income distribution.

market failure
Failure of the unregulated market system to achieve allocative efficiency.

Market Power

As we discussed in Chapter 10, firms that face downward-sloping demand curves—whether they are monopolistic competitors or monopolists—will maximize profits at an output where price exceeds marginal cost, leading to allocative inefficiency. Although some market power is maintained through artificial barriers to entry, such power can also arise naturally because in some industries the least costly way to produce a good or a service is to have few producers relative to the size of the market. The standard government remedies are competition policy and regulation, which, as discussed in Chapter 12, present problems of their own.

Externalities

Recall from Chapter 12 that in order for the economy to be allocatively efficient, marginal benefit must equal marginal cost for all products. But whose benefits and costs are relevant? Firms that are maximizing their *own* profits are interested only in their own costs of production—they are not interested in any costs that their actions might impose on others. Similarly, individual consumers are interested in the benefits *they* receive from any given

externality   An effect, either good or bad, on parties not directly involved in the production or use of a commodity. Also called *third-party effects*.

product—they usually ignore the benefits that might accrue to others. An **externality** occurs whenever actions taken by firms or consumers impose costs or confer benefits on *others that are not involved in the transaction*. When you smoke a cigarette in a restaurant, you might impose costs on others present; when you renovate your home, you might confer benefits on your neighbours by improving the general look of the neighbourhood. Externalities are also called *third-party effects* because parties other than the two primary participants in the transaction (the buyer and the seller) are affected.

Private and Social Costs

private cost   The value of the best alternative use of resources used in production as valued by the producer.

social cost   The value of the best alternative use of resources used in production as valued by society.

The foregoing discussion suggests the importance of the distinction between *private cost* and *social cost*. **Private cost** measures the cost faced by the private decision maker, including production costs, advertising costs, and so on. **Social cost** includes the private cost (since the decision maker is a member of society) but also includes any other costs imposed on third parties. There is a similar distinction between *private benefit* and *social benefit*. To simplify things, however, we will discuss all externalities in terms of the distinction between private and social cost. But this does not limit our discussion in any way. If we want to consider a situation where your listening to good music confers benefits to your nearby friends, we can think of your action as either increasing their benefits or, equivalently, as decreasing their costs. Similarly, your smoking of cigarettes can be viewed either as reducing their benefits or, equivalently, as increasing their costs. By expressing everything in terms of costs (rather than benefits), we merely simplify the discussion.

Discrepancies between private cost and social cost occur when there are externalities. The presence of externalities, even when all markets are perfectly competitive, leads to allocatively inefficient outcomes.

Externalities arise in many different ways, and they may be harmful or beneficial to the third parties. When they are harmful they are called *negative externalities;* when they are beneficial, they are called *positive externalities*. Figure 16-1 shows why an externality leads to allocative efficiency, even though the market is perfectly competitive. Here are two examples.

Consider the case of a firm whose production process for steel generates harmful smoke as a byproduct. Individuals who live and work near the firm bear real costs as they cope with breathing (or trying to avoid breathing) the harmful smoke. When the firm makes its decision concerning how much steel to produce, it ignores the costs that it imposes on other people. This is a negative externality. In this case, because the firm ignores those parts of social cost that are not its own private cost, the firm will produce too much steel relative to what is allocatively efficient.

Now consider what happens when an individual renovates her home and thus improves its external appearance. Such improvements enhance the neighbours' view and the value of their property. Yet the individual renovator ignores the benefits that her actions have on the neighbours. This is a positive externality. In this case, because the renovator ignores those parts of social benefits that are not her own private benefits, there will be too little home renovation done relative to what is allocatively efficient.

With a positive externality, a competitive free market will produce too little of the good. With a negative externality, a competitive free market will produce too much of the good.

The Importance of Property Rights

Economist and Nobel laureate Ronald Coase has argued that when property rights are well defined (for example, the law is clear on whether a polluter has rights to determine the emissions from a smokestack), third parties will be able to negotiate with the producers of externalities in order to ensure that the producers take all relevant valuations of their behaviour into account. In such cases, externalities would not be a source of allocative inefficiency because social marginal cost and social marginal benefit would be incorporated into the supply and demand decisions of the parties engaged in the externality-producing activity. Since social marginal cost and social marginal benefit would then be equalized, the free market would generate the allocatively efficient outcome.

An example will help to clarify this important idea—known as the **Coase Theorem.** Suppose a paper mill dumps toxic waste in a nearby river and there is a privately owned beach resort on the shore of the river downstream from the paper mill. Suppose further that for every ton of paper produced a barrel of toxic waste is dumped in the river, thereby imposing a $100 cost on the downstream resort owner. The social marginal cost per ton of paper produced is thus $100 more than the private marginal cost.

Coase's insight is that, *as long as property rights are clearly defined,* this situation need not result in allocative inefficiency. For example, if the owners of the paper mill also owned the river, then they would clearly have the "right" to dump their toxic waste there. However, the downstream resort owner would be prepared to pay $100 for every ton of paper that the paper mill *did not produce.* If the resort owner made such an offer, the paper mill would then face an incentive to reduce the output of paper. Indeed, since the paper mill would gain $100 for each ton *not produced* (in addition to the private costs not incurred), the paper mill's private marginal cost of production would equal the social marginal cost of production. The market outcome would therefore be allocatively efficient. (In terms of Figure 16-1, the offer by the downstream resort owner would shift the mill's MC curve up to MC_S^1, so the mill's output would fall.)

Note, however, that the efficient result does not require that ownership over the river is given to the paper mill. Perhaps the most striking part of the Coase Theorem is that the allocatively efficient outcome would also be achieved if the resort owner were awarded ownership over the river. To see this, note that if the resort owner owned the river, then he could force the paper mill to pay for the right to dump toxic waste in the river. If the resort owner charged the paper mill $100 per barrel of waste dumped in the river, then the paper mill would be forced to recognize the costs that its activities incur on the rest of society. That is, the paper mill's private marginal cost would now equal the social marginal cost, and hence the market outcome would be allocatively efficient. (In terms of Figure 16-1, the charge by the downstream resort owner would again shift the mill's MC curve up to MC_S^1.)

If the two sides to an externality—the one causing it and the one suffering it—can bargain together, they will produce the allocatively efficient outcome. The externality will then not become a market failure.

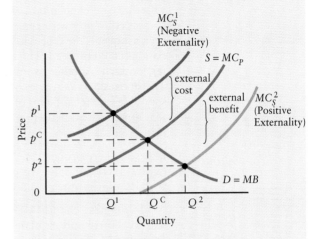

FIGURE 16-1   An Externality Leads to Allocative Inefficiency

When there is an externality, either too much or too little of the good is produced. The outcome is not allocatively efficient. If the market for this good is perfectly competitive and there is no government intervention, the equilibrium is shown by p^C and Q^C. If there is no externality, then social and private marginal cost are the same and so the outcome is allocatively efficient.

Now suppose the production or the consumption of the good imposes costs on third parties. This is a *negative* externality—social marginal costs are MC_S^1, above MC_P. The allocatively efficient quantity is now Q^1 where MB equals MC_S^1. But the free market will produce Q^C, too much of the good.

If the production or consumption of the good instead confers benefits on third parties, this is a positive externality—social marginal costs are MC_S^2, below MC_P. The allocatively efficient quantity is now Q^2 where MB equals MC_S^2. But the free market will produce Q^C, too little of the good.

Coase theorem   The idea (originally put forward by Ronald Coase) that as long as property rights are clearly assigned, externalities need not result in allocative inefficiency.

High Transactions Costs

The practical application of the Coase Theorem depends in large part on the *number* of third parties affected. In cases where there is only one (or a few), as in the example above, it is plausible that careful definition of property rights would be sufficient to permit private markets to deal efficiently with the externality. When millions of third parties are affected, however, as often is the case with air pollution in urban areas, it is hard to see how such negotiations could proceed. This is because the *transactions costs* of the negotiations would be far too high. Another example is where the externalities cross international boundaries. The smokestack industries of the U.S. industrial midwest are commonly thought to be responsible for the problems of acid rain in Canada and New England. It is difficult to believe that any practical definition of property rights could eliminate the effects of these externalities.

In cases where property rights cannot be clearly assigned or transactions costs are excessive, there are only two possibilities. We may accept the externality and learn to live with it, or governments may intervene on our behalf to deal with it.

In the next chapter we will see how governments do indeed intervene on our behalf to control and regulate pollution in order to reduce the amount of environmental degradation. As we will see there, government intervention to achieve allocative efficiency is not always easy.

Non-Rivalrous and Non-Excludable Goods

rivalrous A good or service is rivalrous if, when one person consumes one unit of it, there is one less unit available for others to consume.

excludable A good or service is excludable if its owner can prevent others from consuming it.

Economists classify goods and services into four broad categories depending on the *rivalry* for the good and the *excludability* of the good. Table 16-1 shows these four types of goods.

A good or service is said to be **rivalrous** if one person's consumption of the good means that no one else can also consume it. For example, a chocolate bar is rivalrous because if you eat the entire bar, it cannot also be eaten by your friend. In contrast, a television signal is not rivalrous. You and your friend can sit in your separate living rooms and both receive the same signal, neither of you diminishing the amount available to the other.

A good is said to be **excludable** if people can be prevented from consuming it. A chocolate bar is excludable because you cannot eat it unless you buy it first. A regular TV signal is not excludable, but some speciality channels are because only those who pay for the special receivers can view them. Your access to clean air is also not excludable since nobody can effectively prevent you from breathing.

TABLE 16-1 Four Types of Goods

	Excludable	Non-Excludable
Rivalrous	*Ordinary Goods* VCRs A seat on an airplane An hour of legal advice	*Common Property* Fisheries Rivers and streams Wildlife
Non-Rivalrous (up to capacity)	Art galleries Roads Bridges	*Public Goods* National defence Public information Public protection

Free markets cope best with rivalrous and excludable goods—what we here call "ordinary" goods. The table gives examples of goods in each of four categories, depending on whether consumption of the good is rivalrous and whether one can be excluded from consuming the good.

Ordinary Goods

Most goods and services that you consume are both rivalrous and excludable. Your consumption of food, clothing, a rental apartment, a car, gasoline, CDs, airline tickets, and textbooks are only possible because you pay the seller for the right to own those goods or services. Furthermore, your consumption of those goods reduces the amount available for others. In Table 16-1 we simply refer to these goods as ordinary goods.

Goods that are both rivalrous and excludable pose no particular problem to public policy.

Common-Property Resources

Goods that are rivalrous but non-excludable pose an interesting challenge for public policy. Note in Table 16-1 that the examples of these goods include such things as fisheries, common grazing land, wildlife, rivers and streams, and so on. These are called **common-property resources**. My consumption of clean river water reduces the amount available for you, but there is no practical way that my access to the water can be controlled. And since my access to the water cannot be controlled, there is no practical way to make me pay for it. The result is that there is a zero price. The zero price leads to the obvious result that, in the absence of government intervention, private users will tend to *overuse* common-property resources. In other words, private users will use so much of these resources that the marginal cost to society of having one more user will exceed the marginal benefit to society of having one more user. Society would thus be better off if less of these resources were used.

common-property resource   A resource that is owned by nobody and may be used by anyone.

The overuse of common-property resources is especially noticeable in such cases as the Atlantic cod and Pacific salmon fisheries where individual fishermen have a natural incentive to over-fish. After all, if they don't catch a particular fish, they will merely be leaving it to be caught by the next fisherman who comes along. It is this natural inclination to overuse the fisheries that have led the Canadian government over the years to develop a system of licences and quotas whereby individual fishermen must pay to have access to the common-property resource. *Applying Economic Concepts 16-1* examines the depletion of the world's fisheries.

Goods that are rivalrous and non-excludable are called common-property resources. They tend to be overused by private firms and consumers.

Applying Economic Concepts 16-2 examines other cases of common property, including North American buffalo a century ago and African elephants today.

For information on Canada's policies for commercial fishing, and for data on the fisheries, see the website for the Department of Fisheries and Oceans: www.dfo-mpo.gc.ca.

Excludable But Non-Rivalrous Goods

Goods that are excludable but not rivalrous are also interesting, and many of the obvious examples of these—art galleries, roads, and bridges—are typically provided by government. The non-rivalry for these goods means that the marginal cost of providing the good to one extra person is zero. To see this, just ask yourself what it costs for an extra person to walk through the Canadian Museum of Civilization in Hull, given that it is already open but not many people are there. The answer is zero. But if the marginal cost to society of providing one more unit of the good is zero, then allocative efficiency requires that the price also be zero. Any positive price would prevent some people from using it, but this would be inefficient. As long as their marginal benefit exceeds the social marginal cost of providing the good (zero in this case), it is efficient for these people to use the good.

To avoid inefficient exclusion, the government often provides non-rivalrous but excludable goods and services.

For this reason, art galleries, museums, libraries, roads, bridges, and national parks are provided by various levels of government. In some cases, like libraries and roads, the price is usually zero. In others, like national parks and art galleries, there is usually some positive price.

APPLYING ECONOMIC CONCEPTS 16-1

The World's Endangered Fish

The fish in the ocean are a common-property resource, and theory predicts that such a resource will be overexploited if there is a high enough demand for the product and suppliers are able to meet that demand. In the past centuries there were neither enough people eating fish nor efficient enough fishing technologies to endanger stocks. Over the last fifty years, however, the population explosion has added to the demand for fish and advances in technology have vastly increased the ability to catch fish. Large boats, radar detection, and more murderous nets have tipped the balance in favour of the predator and against the prey. As a result, the overfishing prediction of common property theory has been amply borne out. Today, fish are a common-property resource; tomorrow, they could become no one's resource.

Since 1950 the world's catch has increased fivefold. The increase was sustained only by substituting smaller, less desirable fish for the diminishing stocks of the more desirable fish and by penetrating ever further into remote oceans. Today, all available stocks are being exploited, and now even the total tonnage is beginning to fall. The UN estimates that the total value of the world's catch could be increased by nearly $30 billion if fish stocks were properly managed by governments interested in the total catch, rather than exploited by individuals interested in their own catch.

The developed countries have so overfished their own stocks that Iceland and the European Union could cut their fleets by 40 per cent and catch as much fish as they do today. This is because more fish would survive to spawn, allowing each boat in a smaller fleet to catch about 40 per cent more than does each boat in today's large fishing fleet.

The problem has become so acute that Canada shut down its entire Atlantic cod fishing industry in 1993 and its Pacific salmon industry in 1998. Tens of thousands of Newfoundland residents lost their livelihoods in the demise of what had been the province's largest industry—the catching, freezing, and canning of fish—an industry that had flourished for five centuries.

Canada and the European Union have since been in conflict over what Canada claims is predatory overfishing by EU boats just outside Canadian territorial waters. These tensions heightened in March 1995 when the Spanish fishing trawler Estai was fired at and forced into St. John's harbour by a Canadian fisheries-protection vessel for fishing turbot just outside Canada's 200-nautical-mile "economic zone." The EU (on behalf of Spain) accused Canada of piracy. Canada accused Spain of overfishing and depleting the value of Canada's turbot fishery.

Some developing countries are taking action to conserve their fish stocks but the majority are encouraging rapid expansion of their own fishing fleets with the all-too-predictable results that their domestic waters will soon be seriously overfished.

Worldwide action saved most species of whales. It remains to be seen how many types of fish will be caught to extinction and how many will recover as individual nations slowly learn the lesson of economic theory. Common-property resources need central management if they are not to be overexploited to an extent that risks extinction.

In July 1997, B.C. fishermen blockaded a U.S. ferry in Prince Rupert in protest over U.S. fishermen catching "Canadian" salmon.

The positive price in some of these cases can be explained by another feature of these goods. What happens in the Canadian Museum of Civilization on a summer Saturday morning? What happens on Highway 401 outside Toronto at rush hour? The answer is *crowds*. When congestion occurs on roads and bridges, or in art galleries and museums, it is no longer true that the marginal cost of providing the good to one more user is zero. By increasing the amount of congestion, providing the good to one more per-

APPLYING ECONOMIC CONCEPTS 16-2

Buffalos, Cows, and Elephants

For centuries, North American bison—commonly called buffalos—were a common-property resource for the Plains Indians, whose populations were small enough that they could kill all they needed without endangering the ability of the herds to reproduce themselves. In a little over a decade following the end of the American Civil War in 1865, white hunters decimated the herds. Buffalo Bill Cody may have been a folk hero, but he, and those like him, were the buffalo's executioners.

The buffalo was replaced by cattle, which did not follow the buffalo into extinction. The difference was that cattle were the private property of the rancher. Rustlers and other predators attacked the herds, but the self-interest of ranchers made it worthwhile for them to protect their cattle.

Many people, watching the decimation of wildlife in Africa and Asia, have argued that property rights should be used to turn these animals from the modern equivalent of the buffalo into the modern equivalent of cattle. Wildlife is a common-property resource. When it becomes endangered, laws are passed to prevent predatory hunting. But no one has any profit motive in enforcing these laws. Government officials are employed to do this job, but they are often few in number and poorly paid. Some become corrupted by the large sums poachers are willing to pay to avoid enforcement. Others find the policing job impossible, given the inadequate resources that their governments devote to enforcement.

Some African governments have dealt with the problem by giving ownership of the wild animals to local villages and allowing them to use animals as a commercial asset. The animals are the subjects of camera safaris whose organizers pay the locals for the privilege. They are also prey for hunters who pay large sums for licences to kill a selected number of animals. Local tribesmen control poachers and keep the licenced kill rate below the reproduction rate because they have a profit motive in protecting what has become their very valuable property.

These schemes have many opponents as well as many supporters. Some opponents object to any permissible "sports hunting" and other commercial use of wild animals. They argue for more effective public enforcement of anti-poaching laws. Supporters counter that leaving the animals as common property is bound to result in their extinction. Farming them, they argue, is better than presiding over their extinction.

son imposes costs on those already using the good. If I enter an already-busy highway, I slow down all the existing traffic. If you visit an already-crowded museum, you make it that much less pleasant for everybody else. In these cases, a good that is non-rivalrous when uncongested becomes rivalrous when congested. At this point it appears much (in economic terms) like an ordinary good.

Governments who provide such goods often charge a price to help ration the good when rivalry becomes significant. An excellent example of this is the new toll highways that, with the aid of powerful cameras and computers, charge motorists a different amount per kilometre driven depending on how crowded the highway is. As the traffic slows down due to congestion, the price per kilometre increases to reflect the higher marginal cost. This higher price is indicated on electronic highway signs posted regularly along the highway. Drivers can then choose either to remain on the highway and pay the higher price or exit the highway and take another route to their destination.

See the website for the World Wildlife Fund to learn about one organization's efforts to protect endangered species: www.wwfcanada.org.

Public Goods

Finally, there are some goods that are neither excludable nor rivalrous. These are called **public goods** or sometimes *collective consumption goods*. The classic case of a public good is national defence. Increasing the population of Canada does not reduce

public goods   Goods or services that can simultaneously provide benefits to a large group of people. Also called *collective consumption goods*.

the extent to which each individual is defended by a given size and quality of armed forces. Also, it would not be possible to provide national defence to some people and not to others.

Information is also often a public good. Suppose a certain food additive causes cancer. The cost of discovering this fact needs to be borne only once. The information is then of value to everyone who might have used the additive, and the cost of making the information available to one more consumer is essentially zero. Furthermore, once the information of the newly discovered carcinogen is available, it is impossible to prevent people from using that information. Other public goods include street-lighting, weather forecasts (a type of information), and police services.

All of these examples raise what is called the *free-rider problem,* which follows from the fact that it is difficult to prevent people from using public goods once they are produced. This in turn implies that the private market will generally not produce efficient amounts of the public good because once the good is produced, it is impractical (or impossible) to make people pay for its use. Indeed, free markets may fail to produce public goods at all. The obvious remedy in these cases is for the government to provide the good, financed from its tax revenues.

Practise with Study Guide Chapter 16, Exercise 2.

Because of the free-rider problem, private markets will not provide public goods.

How much of a public good should the government provide? It should provide the public good up to the point where the *sum* of everyone's individual marginal benefit from the good is just equal to the marginal cost of providing the good. We add everyone's individual marginal benefit to get the total marginal benefit because a public good—unlike an ordinary private good—can be used simultaneously by everyone. It therefore generates value to more than one person at a time. Figure 16-2 shows the optimal provision of a public good in the simple case of only two individuals.

Consider a simple example. Suppose that Andrew, Brenda, Carol, and Dick are all thinking of renting a video. For each of them individually, a video rental is a private good. But for the four of them together, it is a public good because the cost will be the same no matter how many of them decide to watch. Suppose that each honestly expresses his or her value of watching the tape. Say it is worth $1.00 to Andrew, $2.00 each to Brenda and Carol, and 50 cents to Dick. If the rental charge for the tape is $5.50 or less, it is worth renting because the total value to all four consumers will be at least equal to the cost.

Efficient provision of public goods requires that consumers pay the marginal cost of their consumption—zero. Private markets will never provide goods at a price of zero and thus will always underprovide public goods. Public goods are therefore left to be provided by government.

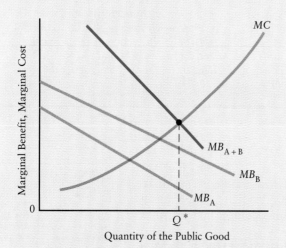

FIGURE 16-2   The Optimal Provision of a Public Good

Determining the optimal provision of a public good requires adding together the marginal benefits for each individual. The figure shows the demand curves (marginal benefit) for a public good by two individuals, Andrew and Brenda. By adding MB_A and MB_B *vertically* (that is, for any given quantity of the public good), we derive society's marginal benefit curve, MB_{A+B}. The marginal cost of providing the public good is shown by MC. The allocatively efficient level of the public good is Q^*, where the marginal cost to society is just equal to the marginal benefit to society.

Asymmetric Information

The role of information in the economy has received increasing attention from economists in recent years. Information is, of course, a valuable commodity, and markets for information and expertise are well developed, as every college student is aware. Markets for expertise are conceptually identical to markets for any other valuable service. They can pose special problems, however. One of these we have already discussed: Information is often a public good and thus will tend to be underproduced by a free market.

Even where information is not a public good, markets for expertise are prone to market failure. The reason for this is that one party to a transaction can often take advantage of special knowledge in ways that change the nature of the transaction itself. Situations where one party to a transaction has special knowledge are called situations of **asymmetric information.** The two important sources of market failure that arise from situations of asymmetric information are *moral hazard* and *adverse selection*.

asymmetric information
A situation in which one party to a transaction has more or better information about the transaction than the other party.

Moral Hazard

In general, **moral hazard** exists when one party to a transaction has both the *incentive* and the *ability* to shift costs onto the other party. Moral hazard problems often arise from insurance contracts. The classic example is the homeowner who does not bother to shovel snow from his sidewalk because he knows that his insurance will cover the cost if the mail carrier should fall and break a leg. The costs of the homeowner's lax behaviour will be borne largely by others, including the mail carrier and the insurance company.

moral hazard
A situation in which an individual or a firm takes advantage of special knowledge while engaging in socially uneconomic behaviour.

Individuals and firms who are insured against loss will often take less care to prevent that loss than they would in the absence of insurance. They do so because they do not bear all of the marginal cost imposed by the risk, whereas they do bear all of the marginal cost of taking action to reduce the risk.

With moral hazard, the market failure arises because the action by the insured individual or firm raises total costs for society. In the first example above, the decision not to shovel the sidewalk reduces costs for the individual but, in the event of an accident, increases by much more the costs to other individuals and firms.

Insurance is not the only context in which moral hazard problems arise. Another example is professional services. Suppose that you ask a dentist whether your teeth are healthy or a lawyer whether you need legal assistance. The dentist and the lawyer both face moral hazard in that they both have a financial interest in giving you answers that will encourage you to buy their services, and it is difficult for you to find out if their advice is good. In both cases, one party to the transaction has special knowledge that he or she could use to change the nature of the transaction in his or her favour. Codes of professional ethics and licensing and certification practices, both governmental and private, are reactions to concerns about this kind of moral hazard.

Adverse Selection

Adverse selection refers to the tendency for people who are more at risk than the average to purchase insurance and for those who are less at risk than the average to reject insurance. A person who is suffering from a heart condition may seek to increase his life insurance coverage by purchasing as much additional coverage as is available without a medical examination. People who buy insurance almost always know more about themselves as individual insurance risks than do their insurance companies. The company can try to limit the variation in risk by requiring physical examinations (for life or health insurance) and by setting up broad categories based on variables, such as age and occupation, over

adverse selection
Self-selection, within a single risk category, of persons of above-average risk.

which actuarial risk is known to vary. The rate charged is then different across categories and is based on the average risk in each category, but there will always be much variability of risk *within* any one category.

People who know that they are well above the average risk for their category are offered a bargain and will be led to take out more car, health, life, or fire insurance than they otherwise would. Their insurance premiums will also not cover the full expected cost of the risk that they are insuring against. Once again, their private cost is less than social cost. On the other side, someone who knows that she is at low risk and pays a higher price than the amount warranted by her risk is motivated to take out less insurance than she otherwise would. In this case, her private cost is more than the social cost.

In both cases, resources are allocated inefficiently because the marginal private benefit of the action (taking out insurance) is not equal to the marginal social cost.

More generally, whenever either party to a transaction lacks information that the other party has, or is deceived by claims made by the other party, market results will tend to be changed, and such changes may lead to inefficiency. Economically (but not legally), it is but a small step from such unequal knowledge to outright fraud. The arsonist who buys fire insurance before setting a building on fire and the business person with fire insurance who decides that a fire is preferable to bankruptcy are extreme examples of moral hazard.

Asymmetric information is involved in many other situations of market failure. The *principal-agent problem,* which we discussed in the appendix to Chapter 7, is one example. In its classic form, the firm's managers act as agents for the shareholders, who are the legal principals of the firm. The managers are much better informed than the principals are about what they do and what they can do. Indeed, the managers are hired for their special expertise. Given that it is expensive for the shareholders (principals) to monitor what the managers (agents) do, the managers have latitude to pursue goals other than maximizing the firm's profits. The private costs and benefits of their actions will thus be different from the social costs and benefits, with the usual consequences for the allocative efficiency of the market system.

A second example of market failure due to asymmetric information is the apparent overdiscounting of the prices of used cars because of the buyer's risk of acquiring a "lemon." See the discussion of this problem in *Applying Economic Concepts 16-3.*

Missing Markets

In the 1950s two American economists, Kenneth Arrow and Gerard Debreu, who were subsequently awarded Nobel Prizes in economics, studied necessary conditions for optimality in resource allocation. One of the conditions is that there must exist a separate market in which each good and service can be traded to the point where the social marginal benefit equals the social marginal cost. Missing markets are the final item in our list of causes of market failure.

Not only do markets not exist for such prominent things as public goods and common-property resources; they are also absent in a number of less obvious but equally important cases.

One important set of missing markets involves risk. You can insure your house against its burning down. This is because your knowledge of the probability of this occurrence is not much better than your insurance company's, and because the probability of your house burning down is normally independent of the probability of other houses burning down.

If you are a farmer, you cannot usually insure your crop against bad weather. This is because the probabilities of yours and your neighbour's crop suffering from bad weather are interrelated. If the insurance company has to pay you, chances are that it will also have to pay your neighbour and everyone else in the region—perhaps even through-

APPLYING ECONOMIC CONCEPTS 16-3

Used-Car Prices: The "Lemons" Problem

It is common for people to regard the large loss of value of a new car in the first year of its life as a sign that consumers are overly style-conscious and will always pay a big premium for the latest in anything. Professor George Akerlof of the University of California at Berkeley suggests a different explanation based on the proposition that the flow of services expected from a one-year-old car that is *purchased on the used-car market* will be lower than those expected from an *average* one-year-old car on the road. Consider his theory.

Any particular model year of automobiles will include a certain proportion of "lemons"—cars that have one or more serious defects. Purchasers of new cars of a certain year and model take a chance on their car turning out to be a lemon. Those who are unlucky and get a lemon are more likely to resell their car than those who are lucky and get a quality car. Hence, in the used-car market, there will be a disproportionately large number of lemons for sale. For example, there may be only one percent of all 1999 Toyota Corollas that have a particular defect and are thus lemons. But, in the market for used 1999 Toyota Corollas, 20 percent of them may be lemons.

Buyers of used cars are therefore right to be on the lookout for low-quality cars, while salespeople are quick to invent reasons for the high quality of the cars they are selling ("It was owned by a little old lady who drove it only on Sundays."). Because it is difficult to identify a lemon or a badly treated used car before buying it, the purchaser is prepared to buy a used car only at a price that is low enough to offset the increased probability that it is of poor quality.

This is a rational consumer response to uncertainty and may explain why one-year-old cars typically sell for a discount that is much larger than can be explained by the physical depreciation that occurs in one year in the *average* car of that model. The large discount reflects the lower services that the purchaser can expect from a used car because of the higher probability that it will be a lemon.

The market failure in this situation arises because of the asymmetric information between the buyers and the sellers. If there were perfect information, prices would better reflect the value of the used car. Good used cars would command higher prices than used cars known to be lemons. Buyers and sellers would then conduct more transactions, for two reasons. First, sellers of good used cars would be more likely to sell them since they know they will get a good price. In contrast, when information is poor, owners of good used cars are less inclined to sell their cars because the price of used cars reflects the average quality, which of course is diminished by the presence of the lemons. Second, when information is good consumers know precisely what it is they are buying. Consumers that wish to spend more on a good used car can do so; other consumers that want the bargain price on a car known to be a lemon can also be satisfied. A larger number of successful transactions between buyers and sellers means more surplus on both side of the market—that is, a more efficient outcome.

Owners have an incentive to keep good-quality used cars because it is difficult to convince buyers that a used car is not a "lemon." As a result, lemons represent a larger proportion of used-car sales than of the total car population.

out the country. An insurance company survives by pooling independent risks. It cannot survive if the same events affect all its clients in the same way. This is why income insurance for farmers is provided by the government (see Chapter 5) rather than by private insurance companies.

If you are in business, you cannot insure against bankruptcy. Here the problem is adverse selection. You know much better than does your would-be insurance company the chances that your business will fail. If insurance were offered against such failure, it would mainly be taken out by people whose businesses had recently developed a high chance of failure.

Another set of missing markets concerns future events. You can buy certain well-established and unchanging products, such as corn or oil, on future markets. But you cannot do so for most manufactured products, such as cars and TV sets, because no one knows the precise specifications of future models. Future markets for these products are missing, so there is no way that the costs and benefits of planned future expenditure on these products can be equated by economic transactions made today.

Summary

Our discussion about market failures has covered a lot of ground. Before we move on to explore some details of government intervention, it is worthwhile to briefly summarize what we have learned. The following five situations result in market failures and, in principle at least, provide a rationale for some government intervention.

1. Firms with market power will charge a price greater than marginal cost. The level of output in these cases is less than the allocatively efficient level.

2. When there are externalities, social and private marginal costs are not equal. If there is a negative externality, output will be greater than the allocatively efficient level. If there is a positive externality, output will be less than the allocatively efficient level.

3. Common-property resources will be overused by private firms and consumers. Public goods will be underprovided by private markets.

4. Situations in which there is asymmetric information—both moral hazard and adverse selection—can lead to allocative inefficiency.

5. Allocative efficiency requires that a separate market exist for each good or service. Missing markets results in allocative inefficiency.

These situations of market failure justify a role for government in a market economy. Let's now explore some reasons for government intervention that are *not* based on market failures.

▌ Other Government Objectives

Suppose that the market did generate the allocatively efficient outcome. That is, suppose that all markets were perfectly competitive and that there were no problems of market power, externalities, public goods, asymmetric information or missing markets. In such an extreme world, does the achievement of allocative efficiency mean that the government would have no reason for intervening in free markets? The answer, in general, is no.

Even if there are no market failures, the government may choose to intervene in markets to achieve broader social goals.

It should not be surprising that even when the free-market system generates an allocatively efficient outcome, it may not always achieve broader social goals. Some of these goals (for example, the desire for an "equitable" income distribution) are basically economic. Some, especially notions that people in a given society should have shared values, such as patriotism or a belief in basic human rights, are clearly not economic. In either set of cases, however, markets are not very effective, precisely because the "goods"

Practise with Study Guide Chapter 16, Exercise 3.

in question are not of the kind that can be exchanged in decentralized transactions. (Indeed, if we stretch the definition a bit, these are public goods, and we have seen that markets tend to underproduce such goods.)

Income Distribution

As we saw in Chapter 13, an important characteristic of a market economy is the *distribution of income* that it determines. People whose services are in heavy demand relative to supply, such as good television anchors and outstanding hockey players, earn large incomes, whereas people whose services are not in heavy demand relative to supply, such as doctorates in classics and high-school graduates without work experience, earn much less.

The distribution of income produced by the market can be looked at in the long run or in the short run. In the long run, in an efficiently operating free-market economy, similar efforts of work or investment by similar people will tend to be similarly rewarded everywhere in the economy. Of course, dissimilar people, or people in dissimilar jobs, will be dissimilarly rewarded.

In the short run, however, similar people making similar efforts may be dissimilarly rewarded. People in declining industries, areas, and occupations suffer the "punishment" of low earnings through no fault of their own. Those in expanding sectors earn the "reward" of high earnings through no extra effort or talent of their own. But these differentials are likely to be temporary, eliminated by the mobility of workers across industries, occupations, or regions.

These rewards and punishments serve the important function of motivating people to adapt. The advantage of such a system is that individuals can make their own decisions about how to alter their behaviour when market conditions change; the disadvantage is that temporary rewards and punishments are dealt out as a result of changes in market conditions that are beyond the control of the affected individuals.

Moreover, even equilibrium differences in income may seem unfair. A free-market system rewards certain groups and penalizes others. Because the workings of the market may be stern, even cruel, society often chooses to intervene. Should heads of households be forced to bear the full burden of their misfortune if, through no fault of their own, they lose their jobs? Even if they lose their jobs through their own fault, should they and their families have to bear the whole burden, which may include starvation? Should the ill and the aged be thrown on the mercy of their families? What if they have no families? Both private charities and a great many government policies are concerned with modifying the distribution of income that results from such things as where one starts, how able one is, how lucky one is, and how one fares in the labour market.

We might all agree that it is desirable to have a more equal distribution of income than the one generated by the free market. We would probably also agree that the pursuit of allocative efficiency is a good thing. It is important to understand, however, that the goal of a more equitable distribution of income invariably conflicts with the goal of allocative efficiency. To understand why this is so, see *Extensions in Theory 16-1* which discusses Arthur Okun's famous analogy of the "leaky bucket."

Preferences for Public Provision

Police protection and justice could in principle be provided by private-market mechanisms. Security guards, private detectives, and bodyguards all provide policelike protection. Privately hired arbitrators, "hired guns," and vigilantes of the Old West represent private

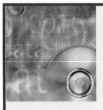

EXTENSIONS IN THEORY 16-1

Arthur Okun's "Leaky Bucket"

Economists recognize that government actions can affect both the allocation of resources and the distribution of income. Resource allocation is easier to talk about simply because economists have developed precise definitions of *efficient* and *inefficient* allocations. Distribution is more difficult because we cannot talk about *better* or *worse* distributions of income without introducing value judgements.

To the extent that society chooses to redistribute income, it is generally the case that allocative efficiency will be reduced. Arthur Okun (1928–1980)—a noted economist at Yale University—developed the image of a "leaky bucket" to illustrate this problem. Suppose we have a well-supplied reservoir of water and we wish to get some water to a household that is not able to come to the reservoir. The only vessel available for transporting the water is a leaky bucket; it works, in that water is deliverable to the intended location, but it works at a cost, in that some of the water is lost on the trip. Thus, to get a litre of water to its destination, more than a litre of water has to be removed from the reservoir. It may be possible to design better or worse buckets, but all of them will leak somewhat.

The analogy to an economy is this: The act of redistribution (carrying the water) reduces the total value of goods and services available to the economy (by the amount of water that leaks on the trip). Getting a dollar to the poor reduces the resources available to everyone else by more than a dollar. Thus, pursuing social goals—like the redistribution of income—conflicts with the goal of allocative efficiency.

Why is the bucket always leaky? Because there is no way to redistribute income without changing the incentives that private households and firms face. For example, a tax-and-transfer system that takes from the rich and gives to the poor will reduce the incentives of both the rich and the poor to produce income. Thus, the redistribution of income will lead to less total income being generated. As another example, a policy of subsidizing goods that are deemed to be important, such as food, shelter, or oil, will cause the market prices of those goods to be lower than marginal costs, a result implying that resources used to produce those goods could be used to produce goods of higher value elsewhere in the economy.

Measuring the efficiency costs of redistribution is an important area of economic research. One result from this research is that some methods of redistribution are more efficient than others. For example, most economists agree that programs that directly redistribute income are more efficient (per dollar of resources made available to a given income group) than programs that subsidize the prices of specific goods. One reason for this is that price subsidies apply even when high-income households purchase the goods in question. These high-income households therefore benefit from the subsidy—an unintended (and perhaps undesirable) consequence of the program.

Redistribution virtually always entails some efficiency cost. However, this inefficiency does *not* imply that such programs should not be undertaken. (That buckets leak surely does not imply that they should not be used to transport water, given that we want to transport water and that the buckets we have are the best available tools.) Whatever the social policy regarding redistribution of income, economics has an important role to play in measuring the efficiency costs and distributional consequences of different programs of redistribution. Put another way, it has useful things to say about the design and deployment of buckets.

---

ways of obtaining "justice." Yet the members of society may believe that a public police force is *preferable* to a private one and that public justice is preferable to justice for hire. The question of the boundary between public and private provision of any number of goods and services became an important topic of debate during the late 1980s and early 1990s, and the debate shows no sign of waning. In Canada, the United States and Western Europe, the issue is framed as *privatization*. In the formerly socialist countries of Eastern Europe, the disposition of much of the productive capacity of entire countries is currently under dispute. In all of these cases, part of the debate is about the magnitude of the efficiency gains that could be realized by private organization, and part is about less tangible issues, such as changes in the nature and distribution of goods and services that may take place when production is shifted from one sector to the other.

Protecting Individuals from Others

People can use and even abuse other people for economic gain in ways that the members of society find offensive. Child labour laws and minimum standards of working conditions are responses to such actions. Yet direct abuse is not the only example of this kind of market failure. In an unhindered free market, the adults in a household would usually decide how much education to buy for their children. Selfish parents might buy no education, while egalitarian parents might buy the same education for all of their children, regardless of their abilities. The rest of society may want to interfere in these choices, both to protect the child of the selfish parent and to ensure that some of the scarce educational resources are distributed according to the ability and the willingness to use them rather than according to a family's wealth. All households are forced to provide a minimum of education for their children, and a number of inducements are offered—through public universities, scholarships, and other means—for talented children to consume more education than they or their parents might choose if they had to pay the entire cost themselves.

Paternalism

Members of society, acting through government, often seek to protect adult (and presumably responsible) individuals, not from others, but from themselves. Laws prohibiting the use of addictive drugs and laws prescribing the installation and use of seat belts are intended primarily to protect individuals from their own ignorance or shortsightedness. This kind of interference in the free choices of individuals is called **paternalism**. Whether such actions reflect the wishes of the majority in the society or whether they reflect the actions of overbearing governments, there is no doubt that the market will not provide this kind of protection. Buyers do not buy what they do not want, and sellers have no motive to provide it.

paternalism
Intervention in the free choices of individuals by others (including governments) to protect them against their own ignorance or folly.

Social Responsibility

In a free-market system, if you can pay another person to do things for you, you may do so. If you persuade someone else to clean your house in return for $35, presumably both parties to the transaction are better off (otherwise neither of you would have voluntarily conducted the transaction). Normally, society does not interfere with people's ability to negotiate mutually advantageous contracts.

Most people do not feel this way, however, about activities that are regarded as social responsibilities. For example, when military service is compulsory, contracts similar to the one between you and a housekeeper could also be negotiated. Some persons faced with the obligation to do military service could no doubt pay enough to persuade others to do their military service for them. Indeed, during the U.S. Civil War, it was common practice for a man to avoid the draft by hiring a substitute to serve in his place. Yet such contracts are usually prohibited by law. They are prohibited because there are values to be considered other than those that can be expressed in a market. In times when it is necessary, military service is usually held to be a duty that is independent of an individual's tastes, wealth, influence, or social position. It is felt that everyone *ought* to do this service, and exchanges between willing traders are prohibited.

Military service is not the only example of a social obligation. Citizens cannot buy their way out of jury duty or legally sell their voting rights to others, even though in many cases they could find willing trading partners.

See Chapter 16 of www.pearsoned.ca/lipsey for an excellent discussion of the government's evolving role in society: John Richards, "The Welfare State as a Valuable Work in Progress," *World Economic Affairs*.

Polices for Economic Growth

Over the long haul economic growth is the most powerful determinant of living standards. Whatever their policies concerning efficiency and equity, people who live in economies with rapid rates of growth find their living standards rising (on average) faster than those of people who live in countries with low rates of growth. Over a few decades these growth-induced changes tend to have much larger effects on living standards than any policy-induced changes in the efficiency of resource allocation or the distribution of income.

For the last half of the twentieth century most economists viewed growth mainly as a macroeconomic phenomenon related to total saving and total investment. Reflecting this view, most textbooks do not even mention growth in the chapters on microeconomic policy.

More recently there has been a shift back to the perspective of earlier economists, who saw technological change as the engine of growth, with the individual entrepreneurs and firms as the agents of innovation. This is a microeconomic perspective, which is meant to add to, not replace, the macroeconomic emphasis on total saving and total investment.

Although most basic textbooks have not yet caught up with the change to a microeconomic perspective on growth, governments have. Today few microeconomic policies escape being exposed to the question "Even if this policy achieves its main goal, will it have unfavourable effects on growth?" Answering yes is not a sufficient reason to abandon a specific policy. But it is a sufficient reason to think again. Is it possible to redesign the policy so that it can still achieve its main objective, while removing its undesirable side-effects on growth?

A General Principle

We have discussed how the free market may fail to achieve social goals that members of society deem to be desirable. This discussion suggests the following general principle:

Even if free markets generated allocatively efficient outcomes, they would be unlikely to generate outcomes consistent with most people's social goals. Furthermore, there is generally a tradeoff between achieving these social goals and achieving allocative efficiency.

Government Intervention

Private collective action can sometimes remedy the failures of private individual action. For example, volunteer fire departments can fight fires or insurance companies can guard against adverse selection by more careful classification of clients. However, by far the most common remedy for market failure is government intervention.

Since markets sometimes *do* fail, there is a potential scope for governments to intervene in beneficial ways. Whether government intervention is warranted in any particular case depends both on the magnitude of the market failure that the intervention is designed to correct and on the costs of the government action itself.

The benefits of some types of government intervention—such as a publicly provided justice system—are both difficult to quantify and potentially very large. Further, government intervention often imposes difficulties of its own. For many types of government activity, however, *cost-benefit analysis* can be helpful in considering the general question of when governments ought to intervene and to what extent.

The idea behind **cost-benefit analysis** is simple: Add up the (opportunity) costs of a given policy, then add up the benefits, and implement the policy only if the benefits outweigh the costs. In practice, however, cost-benefit analysis is usually quite difficult for three reasons. First, it may be difficult to ascertain what will happen when an action is undertaken. Second, many government actions involve costs and benefits that will occur only in the distant future; thus, they will be more complicated to assess. Third, some benefits and costs—such as the benefits of prohibiting actions that would harm members of an endangered animal species—are very difficult to quantify. Indeed, many people would argue that they cannot be and should not be quantified, as they involve values that are not commensurate with money. The practice then is to use cost-benefit analysis to measure the things that can be measured and to be sure that the things that cannot be measured are not ignored when collective decisions are made. By narrowing the range of things that must be determined by informal judgement, cost-benefit analysis can still play a useful role.

In this chapter, we have been working toward a cost-benefit analysis of government intervention. We have made a general case against government intervention, stressing that free markets are great economizers on information and coordination costs. We have also made a general case for government intervention, emphasizing that free markets fail to produce allocative efficiency when there are monopolies, public goods, externalities, information asymmetries or missing markets, and may also fail to achieve broader social goals. We now turn to the more specific questions of what governments do when they intervene, what the costs of government intervention are, and under which circumstances government interventions may fail to improve on imperfect private markets.

> **cost-benefit analysis**
> An approach for evaluating the desirability of a given policy, based on comparing total (opportunity) costs with total benefits.

The Tools of Government Intervention

The legal power of governments to intervene in the workings of the economy is limited only by the Charter of Rights (as interpreted by the courts), the willingness of legislatures to pass laws, and the willingness of the government to enforce them. There are numerous ways in which one or another level of government can prevent, alter, complement, or replace the workings of the unrestricted market economy.

Public Provision.   National defence, the criminal justice system, public schools, the highway system, and national parks are all examples of goods or services that are directly provided by governments in Canada. Public provision is the most obvious remedy for market failure to provide public goods, but it is also often used in the interest of redistribution (e.g., hospitals) and other social goals (e.g., public schools). We shall consider public spending in detail in Chapter 18.

See the Government of Canada's web page to see just how many various government departments and crown corporations exist: www.gc.ca.

Redistribution Programs.   Taxes and spending are often used to provide a distribution of income that is different from that generated by the free market. Government transfer programs affect the distribution of income in this way. We examine the distributive effects of the Canadian tax system in Chapter 18.

Regulation.   Government regulations are public rules that apply to private behaviour. In Chapter 12, we saw that governments regulate private markets to limit monopoly power. In Chapter 17, we will focus on regulations designed to deal with environmental quality. Among other things, government regulations prohibit minors from consuming alcohol, require that children attend school, penalize racial discrimination in housing and labour markets, and require that new automobiles have seatbelts.

Government regulation is used to deal with all of the sources of market failure that we have discussed in this chapter; it applies at some level to virtually all spheres of modern economic life.

Structuring Incentives.   Almost all government actions, including the kinds we have discussed here, change the incentives that consumers and firms face. If the government provides a park, people will have a weakened incentive to own large plots of land of their own. Fixing minimum or maximum prices (as we saw in the discussion of rent control and agriculture in Chapter 5) affects privately chosen levels of output. If the government taxes income, people may have a reduced incentive to work.

The government can adjust the tax system to provide subsidies to some kinds of behaviour and penalties to others. In the United States, for example, deductible mortgage interest makes owned housing relatively more attractive than other assets that a person might purchase. In Canada, tax exemptions for contributions to Registered Retirement Saving Plans (RRSPs) may lead individuals to increase their total saving. Such tax treatment sends the household different signals from those sent by the free market. Scholarships to students to become nurses or teachers may offset barriers to mobility into those occupations.

The Costs of Government Intervention

Consider the following argument: The market system produces an outcome that is deemed to be undesirable; government has the legal means to improve the situation; therefore, the public interest will be served by government intervention.

At first glance the argument is appealing. But it is deficient because it neglects three important considerations. First, government intervention is itself costly since it uses scarce resources; for this reason alone, not every market failure is worth correcting because the intervention itself may use up more resources than are being wasted in the (inefficient) free-market outcome. Second, government intervention is generally imperfect. Just as markets sometimes succeed and sometimes fail, so government interventions sometimes succeed and sometimes fail. Third, deciding what governments are to do and how they are to do it is also costly and intrinsically imperfect.

Large potential benefits do not necessarily justify government intervention, nor do large potential costs necessarily make it unwise. What matters is the balance between benefits and costs.

There are several different costs of government intervention. Economists divide these costs into two categories—*direct resource costs* and *indirect costs*.

Direct Resource Costs

Government intervention uses real resources that could be used elsewhere. Civil servants must be paid. Paper, photocopying, and other trappings of bureaucracy; the steel in the navy's ships; the fuel for the army's tanks; and the pilot of the Prime Minister's jet all have valuable alternative uses. The same is true of the accountants who administer the Canada Pension Plan, the economists who are employed by the Bureau of Competition Policy, and the educators who retrain displaced workers.

Similarly, when government inspectors visit plants to monitor compliance with federally imposed standards of health, industrial safety, or environmental protection, they are imposing costs on the public in the form of their salaries and expenses. When regulatory bodies develop rules, hold hearings, write opinions, or have their staff prepare research reports, they are incurring costs. The costs of the judges, clerks, and court reporters who hear, transcribe, and review the evidence are also imposed by government regulation. All these activities use valuable resources that could have provided very different goods and services.

All forms of government intervention use real resources and hence impose direct costs.

This type of cost is fairly easy to identify, as it almost always involves well-documented expenditures. Other costs of intervention are less apparent but no less real.

Indirect Costs

Most government interventions in the economy impose some costs on firms and households. The nature and the size of the extra costs borne by firms and households vary with the type of intervention. A few examples will illustrate what is involved.

Changes in Costs of Production.   Government safety and emission standards for automobiles have raised the costs of both producing and operating cars. These costs are much greater than the direct budgetary costs of administering the regulations. Taxes used to finance the provision of public goods must be paid by producers and consumers and often increase the cost of producing or selling goods and services.

Costs of Compliance.   Government regulation and supervision generate a flood of reporting and related activities that are often referred to collectively as *red tape*. The number of hours of business time devoted to understanding, reporting, and contesting regulatory provisions is enormous. Regulations dealing with occupational safety and environmental control have all increased the size of nonproduction payrolls. The legal costs alone of a major corporation sometimes can run into tens or hundreds of millions of dollars per year. While all this provides lots of employment for lawyers and economic experts, it is costly because there are other tasks these professionals could do that would add more to the production of consumer goods and services.

Farmers in Canada often request government assistance to offset the effects of low crop prices or bad weather. This is one example of "rent seeking."

Households also bear compliance costs directly. A recent study found that the time and money cost of filling out individual income-tax returns was about eight percent of the total revenue that is collected. In addition to costs of compliance, there are costs borne as firms and households try to avoid regulation. There will be a substantial incentive to find loopholes in regulations. Resources that could be used elsewhere will be devoted to the search for such loopholes and then, in turn, by the regulators to counteracting such evasion.

Rent Seeking.   A different kind of problem arises from the mere existence of government and its potential to use its tools in ways that affect the distribution of economic resources. This phenomenon has been dubbed **rent seeking** by economists because private firms, households, and business groups will use their political influence to seek *economic rents* from the government. These valuable rents can come in the form of favourable regulations, direct subsidies, and profitable contracts. Democratic governments are especially vulnerable to manipulation of this kind because they respond to well-articulated interests of all sorts.

rent seeking
Behaviour whereby private firms and individuals try to use the powers of the government to enhance their own economic well-being.

Rent seeking is endemic to mixed economies. Because of the many things that governments are called on to do, they have the power to act in ways that transfer resources among private entities. Because they are democratic, they are responsive to public pressures of various kinds. If a government's behaviour can be influenced, whether by voting, campaign contributions, lobbying, or bribes, real resources will be used in trying to do so.

In the aggregate, the indirect costs of government intervention are substantial. But they are difficult to measure and are usually dispersed across a large number of firms and households.

Government Failure

Our conceptual cost-benefit analysis of government intervention is almost complete. First, we identify each market failure. Then we make our best estimate of the expected benefits of a government intervention designed to correct that failure. Then we calculate the expected costs of the government intervention, as outlined in the preceding section. If the expected benefits exceed the expected costs, the intervention is warranted. Unfortunately, things are never this simple. For one thing, as we have already noted, many of the benefits of government intervention are extremely difficult to quantify. But even in the cases where the benefits and costs of intervention can be easily measured, governments, like private markets, are imperfect. Often they will fail, in the same sense that markets do, to achieve their potential.

The reason for government failure is not that public-sector employees are less able, honest, or virtuous than people who work in the private sector. Rather, the causes of government failure are inherent in government institutions, just as the causes of market failure stem from the nature of markets. Importantly, some government failure is an inescapable cost of democratic decision making.

Decision Makers' Objectives

By far the most important cause of government failure arises from the nature of the government's own objectives. Until recently, economists did not concern themselves greatly with the motivation of government. The theory of economic policy implicitly assumed that governments had no objectives of their own. As a result economists only needed to identify places where the market functioned well on its own, and places where government intervention could improve the market's functioning. Governments would then stay out of the former markets and intervene as necessary in the latter.

This model of government behaviour never fitted reality, and economists were gradually forced to think more deeply about the motivation of governments. Today economists no longer assume that governments are faceless robots doing whatever economic analysis shows to be in the social interest. Instead they are modelled just as are producers and consumers—as units with their own objectives, which they seek to maximize.

Governments undoubtedly do care about the social good to some extent, but public officials have their careers, their families, and their prejudices as well. As a result, public officials' own needs are seldom wholly absent from their consideration of the actions they will take. Similarly, their definition of the public interest is likely to be influenced heavily by their personal views of what policies are best. The resulting problems are similar to the principal-agent issues that we discussed in Chapter 7. In the present case the principals are the public; they want governments to do certain things. However, their agents—elected and appointed—are motivated by considerations that sometimes pull against what the public wishes.

Modelling governments as maximizers of their own welfare, and then incorporating them into theoretical models of the working of the economy, was a major breakthrough. One of the pioneers of this development was the American economist James Buchanan, who was awarded the 1986 Nobel Prize in economics for his work in this field. The theory that he helped to develop is called *public choice theory*. The key breakthrough was to view the government as just another economic agent engaging in its own maximizing behaviour.

Public Choice Theory

Full-blown public choice theory deals with three maximizing groups. Elected officials seek to maximize their votes. Civil servants seek to maximize their salaries (and their positions in the hierarchy). Voters seek to maximize their own utility. To this end, voters look to the government to provide them with goods and services and income transfers that raise their personal utility. No one cares about the general interest!

On the one hand, this surely is not a completely accurate characterization of motives. Elected statesmen have acted in what they perceive to be the public interest, hoping to be vindicated by history even if they know they risk losing the next election. Some civil servants have exposed inside corruption even though it cost them their jobs. And some high-income individuals vote for the political party that advocates the most, not the least, income redistribution.

On the other hand, the characterization is close to the mark in many cases. Most of us have read of politicians whose only principle is "What will get me the most votes?" And many voters ask only "What is in it for me?" This is why the theory can take us a long way in understanding what we see, even though real behaviour is more complex.

Here is one example that we discussed in Chapter 5. Why, in spite of strong advice from economists, have governments persisted in assisting agriculture for decades, until many governments now have major farm crises on their hands? Public choice theory looks at the gainers and the losers among the voters.

The gainers from agricultural supports are farmers. They are a politically powerful group, and are aware of what they will lose if farm supports are reduced. They would show their disapproval of such action by voting against any government that even suggests it. The losers are the entire group of consumers or taxpayers. Although they are more numerous than farmers, and although their total loss is large, each individual suffers only a small loss. Citizens have more important things to worry about, and so do not vote against the government just because it supports farmers. As long as the average voters are unconcerned about, and often unaware of, the losses they suffer, the vote-maximizing government will ignore the interests of the many and support the interests of the few. The vote-maximizing government will consider changing the agricultural policy only when the cost of agricultural support becomes so large that ordinary taxpayers begin to be concerned by the cost. What is required for a policy change, according to this theory, is that those who lose become sufficiently aware of their losses for this awareness to affect their voting behaviour.

Another example that we will see in Chapter 35 is the use of tariffs. When a tariff is imposed on an imported good, it increases the domestic price of the good. Tariffs therefore provide protection to the domestic firms producing competing products. This protection typically raises prices, profits, and wages in those firms. The costs of such tariffs are borne by a much larger number of consumers, each of whom is hurt a relatively small amount by the higher price. This concentration of benefits and the dispersion of costs explains to a large extent why tariffs, once in place, are so politically difficult to remove.

The ability of elected officials and civil servants to ignore the public interest is strengthened by a phenomenon called **rational ignorance**. Many policy issues are extremely complex. For example, even the experts are divided when assessing the pros and cons of Canada's maintaining a flexible exchange rate rather than pegging the value

rational ignorance
When agents have no incentive to become informed about some government policy because the costs of becoming informed exceed the benefits of any well-informed action the agent might take.

of the Canadian dollar in terms of the U.S. dollar. Much time and effort is required for a layperson even to attempt to understand the issue. Similar comments apply to the evidence for and against capital punishment or lowering the age of criminal liability. Yet one person's vote has little influence on which party gets elected or on what they will really do about the issue in question once elected. So the costs are large, the benefits small. Thus a majority of rational, self-interested voters will choose to remain innocent of the complexities involved in most policy issues.

Who will be the informed minority? The answer is those who stand to gain or lose a lot from the policy, those with a strong sense of moral obligation, and those policy junkies who just like this sort of thing.

Inefficient Public Choices

At the core of most people's idea of democracy is that each citizen's vote should have the same weight. One of the insights of the theory of social choice is that resource allocation, based on the principle of one vote per person, will generally be inefficient because it fails to take into account the *intensity of preferences*. Consider three farmers, Albert, Bob, and Charlie, who are contemplating building access roads. Suppose that the road to Albert's farm is worth $7000 to him and that the road to Bob's farm is worth $7000 to him. Charlie's farm is on the main road, which already exists. Suppose that under the current tax rules, each road would cost each farmer $2000. It is plainly efficient to build both roads because each generates net benefits of $1000 ($7000 gross benefits to Albert and Bob minus $6000 total cost). But each road would be defeated 2-1 in a simple majority vote. (Bob and Charlie would vote against Albert's road; Albert and Charlie would vote against Bob's road.)

Now suppose that we allow Albert and Bob to make a deal: "I will vote for your road if you will vote for mine." Although such deals are often decried by political commentators, the deal enhances efficiency: Both roads now get 2–1 majorities, and both roads get built. However, such deals can just as easily reduce efficiency. If the gross value of each road were $5000 instead of $7000, and Albert and Bob again make their deal, each road will still command a 2–1 majority, but building the roads will now be inefficient. (The gross value of each road is now only $5000, but the cost is still $6000.) Albert and Bob will be using democracy to appropriate resources from Charlie while reducing economic efficiency.

The possibility of inefficient public choices stems in large part from the problems inherent to a democratic system. *Extensions in Theory 16-2* discusses Kenneth Arrow's famous result in the theory of social choice. Arrow's somewhat unsettling theorem is that there is very often a tradeoff between democracy and efficiency.

Governments as Monopolists

Governments face the same problems of cost minimization that private firms do but often operate in an environment where they are monopoly producers without stockholders. Large governments (provinces, big cities, the federal government) face all of the organizational problems faced by large corporations. They tend to use relatively rigid rules and hence to respond slowly to change. Building codes are an example of this type of problem. Most local governments have detailed requirements regarding the materials that must go into a new house, factory, or office. When technology changes, the codes often lag behind. For example, plastic pipe, which is cheaper and easier to use than copper pipe, was prohibited by building codes for decades after its use became efficient. Similarly, much antipollution regulation specifies the type of control equipment that must be em-

EXTENSIONS IN THEORY 16-2

The Problem with Democracy

Nobel laureate Kenneth Arrow from Stanford University has shown that it is generally impossible to construct a set of rules for making social choices that is at once comprehensive, democratic, efficient, and consistent. This striking idea—called Arrow's Impossibility Theorem—has led to decades of work on the part of economists, philosophers, and political scientists, who have tried to find conditions under which democracy can be expected to yield efficient allocations of resources. The news is generally not good. Unless individual preferences or their distribution in the population meet fairly unlikely criteria, either democracy or efficiency must be sacrificed in the design of social-choice mechanisms.

The Arrow theorem can be illustrated by a simple case, depicted in the following table.

	Voter		
Density of Trees	A	B	C
Sparse (1)	3	1	2
Medium (2)	1	2	3
Thick (3)	2	3	1

Imagine that we have a society that consists of three voters who are choosing how many trees to plant in the local park. The three possibilities are as follows: (1) Plant very few trees in one corner. This would make the park suitable for playing Frisbee and soccer but not for walks in the woods. (2) Plant trees in moderate density throughout the park. In this case, the park would be nice for jogging but not usable for most sports. (3) Plant trees densely everywhere. This would make the park a pleasant place to get away from it all (for whatever reasons) but not a good place to jog. Voter A loves jogging, hates Frisbee, and likes walking in the woods. His ranking of the alternatives is 3–1–2. Voter B likes the wide open spaces. His ranking is 1–2–3. Voter C likes to play Frisbee, likes solitude even more, and has little taste for a park that provides neither. Her ranking is 2–3–1.

Now, suppose that the electorate gets to choose between alternatives that are presented two at a time. What does majority rule do? Unfortunately, there is no unique democratic outcome; the result of such voting depends on which two alternatives are presented. In a choice of 1 versus 2, 1 wins, getting votes from B and C. When the choice is between 2 and 3, 2 wins, getting votes from A and B. When 3 is pitted against 1, 3 wins with the support of A and C. Thus, the social-choice mechanism of majority rule is *inconsistent*. It tells us that 1 is preferred to 2, 2 is preferred to 3, and 3 is preferred to 1. There is no way to make a choice without arbitrarily—that is, undemocratically—choosing which set of alternatives to offer the electorate. This is the essence of Arrow's famous argument that, in general, democracy and efficiency cannot both be achieved in issues of social choice.

ployed. Changes in technology may make a regulation inefficient, but the regulation may stay in place for some time.

In the private sector, market forces often push the corporation into revising its view of the problem at hand, whereas there is ordinarily no market mechanism to force governments to use relatively efficient regulations. Put another way, much government failure arises precisely because governments do not have competitors and are not constrained by the "bottom line."

How Much Should Government Intervene?

Do governments intervene too little, or too much, in response to market failure? This question reflects one aspect of the continuing debate over the role of government in the economy. The theoretical principles for determining the optimal amount of government intervention are individually accepted by most economists. What they add up to, however, is more controversial. Moreover, the issue is often framed ideologically. Those on the "right wing" tend to compare heavy-handed government with a hypothetical and perfectly operating competitive market. In contrast, those on the "left wing" tend to compare hypothetical and ideal government intervention with a laissez-faire economy rife with market failures.

Evaluating the costs and the benefits of government intervention requires a comparison of the private economic system as it is working (not as it might work ideally) with the pattern of government intervention as it actually performs (not as it might perform ideally).

Over the last two decades in most of the advanced industrial countries the mix of free-market determination and government ownership and regulation has been shifting towards more market determination. No one believes that government intervention can, or should, be reduced to zero. Do we still have a long way to go in reversing the tide of big intrusive government that flowed through most of the twentieth century? Or perhaps we have gone too far and have given some things to the market that governments could do better? These will be some of the great social debates of the early decades of the twenty-first century.

The cases that we have made for and against government intervention are both valid, depending on time, place, and the values that are brought to bear. At this point, we turn to the issue of what government actually does, something that will perhaps illuminate the question of what it ought to do. In Chapter 12, we discussed government action that is designed to affect monopoly and competition. In the next two chapters, we will discuss in some detail three other important types of intervention in the Canadian economy today: environmental regulation, taxation, and public spending.

SUMMARY

Basic Functions of Government   LO 1

- The government's monopoly of violence gives it the ability to enforce laws and protect its citizens. But restrictions on the government's power are required to ensure that the individual's rights are not violated.

The Case for Free Markets

- The case for free markets can be made in two different ways. The "formal defence" is based on the concept of allocative efficiency. This was the basis for the appeal of competitive markets as discussed in Chapter 12.
- The "informal defence" of free markets is not specifically based on the idea of allocative efficiency, and thus applies to market structures other than just perfect competition. The informal defence of free markets is based on three central arguments:

1. Free markets provide automatic coordination of the actions of decentralized decision makers.

2. The pursuit of profits which is central to free markets provides a stimulus to innovation and economic growth.

3. Free markets permit a decentralization of economic power.

Market Failures

- Market failure refers to situations in which the free market does not achieve allocative efficiency. Five main sources of market failure are

    1. monopoly

    2. externalities

    3. public goods

    4. information asymmetries

    5. missing markets

- Pollution is an example of an externality. A producer who pollutes the air or water does not pay the social cost of the pollution and is therefore not motivated to avoid the costs. Private producers will therefore produce too much pollution relative to what is allocatively efficient.
- National defence is an example of a public good. Markets fail to produce public goods because the benefits of such goods are available to people whether they pay for them or not.
- Information asymmetries cause market failure when one party to a transaction is able to use personal expertise to manipulate the transaction in his or her own favour. Moral hazard and adverse selection are consequences of information asymmetries.

Other Government Objectives

- Changing the distribution of income is one of the roles for government intervention that members of a society may desire. Others include values that are placed on public provision for its own sake, on protection of individuals from themselves or from others, on recognition of social responsibilities, and on the promotion of economic growth.

Government Intervention

- Major tools of microeconomic policy include (a) public provision, (b) redistribution, (c) regulation, and (d) structuring incentives. (The first two are the subject of Chapter 18.) Regulation can take various forms. Incentives can be structured in a number of ways, including the use of fines, subsidies, taxes, and effluent charges (which are discussed in Chapter 17).
- The costs and benefits of government intervention must be considered in deciding whether, when, and how much intervention is appropriate. Among the costs are the direct costs that are incurred by the government, the costs that are imposed on the parties who are regulated, directly and indirectly, and the costs that are imposed on third parties. These costs are seldom negligible and are often large.
- The possibility of government failure must be balanced against the potential benefits of removing market failure. It is neither possible nor efficient to correct all market failure; neither is it always efficient to do nothing.

KEY CONCEPTS

Market failure
Externalities
Private and social cost
Coase theorem
Excludable and non-excludable goods

Rivalrous and non-rivalrous goods
Common-property resource
Public goods
Information asymmetries
Missing markets

Moral hazard and adverse selection
Cost-benefit analysis
Rent seeking
Government failure
Public choice theory

STUDY EXERCISES

1. For each of the situations in the table below, indicate whether there is a positive or a negative externality. Indicate in each case whether social marginal cost (MC_S) is greater than or less than private marginal cost (MC_P).

	Positive or Negative Externality?	MC_S greater than or less than MC_P?
You smoke a cigarette and blow the smoke into others' faces.		
You cut your lawn early on a Sunday morning.		
A firm conducts R&D and generates useful "basic" knowledge that is freely available.		
A firm produces aluminum, but also produces toxic waste as a byproduct.		

2. Consider the following diagram showing the perfectly competitive market for newsprint. The demand curve shows the marginal benefit to society of consuming an extra unit of newsprint. The supply curve shows the firms' marginal costs of producing an extra unit of newsprint.

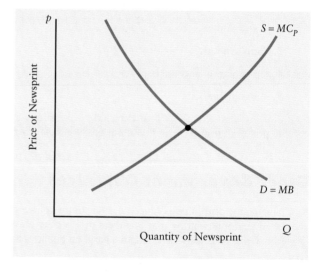

a. Describe the equilibrium in this competitive market.
b. Now suppose that, as a byproduct to producing newsprint, some nasty chemicals are also produced that get dumped in public streams and rivers. Suppose that for each unit of newsprint produced, one unit of nasty chemicals is also produced, imposing an external cost of $100. Show the social marginal cost curve in the diagram.
c. What is the allocatively efficient level of newsprint?

3. For each of the listed goods indicate whether they are rivalrous or non-rivalrous, and also indicate whether the use of them is excludable or non-excludable.

	Rivalrous?	Excludable?
CD player		
Clothing		
Library		
Lighthouse		
Medical services		
Published product safety information		
Pacific salmon		

Number of people	Value of park per person	Total
10	$1000	$10 000
30	500	15 000
30	200	6 000
20	50	1 000
10	0	0
100		$32 000

a. Which of the goods in the table are public goods? Explain.

b. Which are common-property resources? Explain.

4. Art galleries, museums, roads, and bridges are usually provided by the government.

a. Explain why uncrowded goods of this sort should have a price of zero if allocative efficiency is to be achieved.

b. Would allocative efficiency be achieved if private firms provided these goods? Explain.

c. What happens when access to these goods becomes congested? Does efficiency still require a zero price? Explain.

5. Consider a small town deciding whether to build a public park. The town council conducts a survey of its 100 residents and asks them how much they would each value the park. The survey results are as follows:

a. Suppose it costs $35 000 to build the park. Should the town do it?

b. Suppose the park costs only $20 000 to build. Should the town build the park? If so, how should the town pay for building the park?

c. Suppose the town builds the park but charges people $50 for an annual pass. Does this present a problem for efficiency? Explain.

6. In the text we discussed how rent seeking is one of the costs of government intervention. Consider a group of pig farmers who are lobbying the federal government for some form of financial assistance (as they did in 1998 when the world price of pork declined steeply).

a. Explain why economists call such lobbying "rent seeking."

b. Suppose the farmers spend $500 000 in their lobbying efforts but it has no effect on government policy. What is the cost to society of the rent seeking? Explain.

c. Suppose the $500 000 of lobbying *does* lead to a change in government policy. Now what is the social cost of the rent seeking?

DISCUSSION QUESTIONS

1. In each case, identify any divergence between social and private costs.

a. Cigarette smoking
b. Getting a university education
c. Private ownership of guns
d. Drilling for offshore oil

2. Consider the possible beneficial and adverse effects of each of the following forms of government intervention.

a. Charging motorists a tax for driving in the downtown areas of large cities and using the revenues to provide peripheral parking and shuttle buses

b. Prohibiting juries from awarding large malpractice judgements against doctors

c. Mandating no-fault automobile insurance, in which the automobile owner's insurance company is responsible for damage to his or her vehicle no matter who causes the accident

3. The president of Goodyear Tire and Rubber Company complained that government regulation had imposed $30 million per year in "unproductive costs" on his company, as listed here. How would one determine whether these costs were "productive" or "unproductive"?

a. Environmental regulation, $17 million
b. Occupational safety and health, $7 million
c. Motor vehicle safety, $3 million
d. Personnel and administration, $3 million

4. Your local government almost certainly provides a police department, a fire department, and a public library. What are the market imperfections, if any, that each of these seeks to correct? Which of these are closest to being public goods? Which are furthest?

5. Suppose that for $100, a laboratory can accurately assess a person's probability of developing a fairly rare disease that is costly to treat. What would be the likely effects of such a test on health-insurance markets?

6. What market failures do public support of higher education seek to remedy? How would you go about evaluating whether the benefits of this support outweigh the costs?

CHAPTER 17

Environmental Policy

LEARNING OBJECTIVES

1 Explain how an externality can be internalized, and how this can lead to allocative efficiency.

2 Understand why direct pollution controls are inefficient.

3 Explain how market-based policies such as emissions taxes and tradable pollution permits can improve economic efficiency.

4 Have a general understanding of some popular arguments against market-based environmental policies.

In almost everything we do, we are subject to some form of government regulation. The system of criminal law regulates our interactions with people and property. Local zoning ordinances regulate the ways in which the land that we own may be used. Insurance commissions must approve both the insurance contracts that we sign and the rates that we are charged. Regulatory commissions set rates for electricity, natural gas, local telephone service, and a host of other goods and services. Seat belts, brake lights, turn signals, air bags, internal door panels, bumpers, and catalytic converters are subjects of regulation—all in a single industry. The list goes on and on. A good case can be made that various governments in Canada have more effect on the economy through regulation than through taxing and spending.

The focus in this chapter is on a specific type of government regulation, one that has become increasingly important in the eyes of the public in recent years. In particular, we examine the negative externalities of pollution and the various government policies designed to address them. As we will see, policies intended to reduce the amount of environmental degradation do not always do so in an efficient manner. One of the central themes in this chapter is that the information available to the regulatory agencies, especially regarding firms' technologies for reducing pollution, is generally incomplete. This lack of good information leads to the result that *market-based* environmental regulations may be much more successful than methods based on the government's *direct control*.

For information about the new Canadian Environmental Protection Act, see Environment Canada's website: www.ec.gc.ca.

The Economics of Pollution Control

Pollution is a negative externality. As a consequence of producing or consuming goods and services, "bads" are produced as well. Steel plants produce smoke in addition to steel. Farms produce chemical runoff as well as food. Logging leads to soil erosion which contaminates fish-breeding grounds. Households produce human waste and garbage as they consume goods and services. Individuals who smoke impose costs on nearby persons. In all of these cases, the technology of production and consumption automatically generates pollution. Indeed, there are few human endeavors that do not have negative pollution externalities.

The Economic Rationale for Regulating Pollution

When firms use resources that they do not regard as scarce, they fail to consider the cost of those resources. This is a characteristic of most examples of pollution. The valuable resource that polluting firms do not regard as scarce is a clean environment. When a paper mill produces newsprint for the world's newspapers, more people are affected than just its suppliers, employees, and customers. Its water-discharged effluent hurts the fishing boats that ply nearby waters, and its smog makes many resort areas less attractive, thereby reducing the tourist revenues that local motel operators and boat renters can expect. The profit-maximizing paper mill neglects these external effects of its actions because its profits are not directly affected by them.

As shown in Figure 17-1, allocative efficiency requires that the price (the value that consumers place on the marginal unit of output) be just equal to the marginal social cost (the value of the resources that society gives up to produce the marginal unit of output). When there are negative externalities, *social* marginal cost exceeds *private* marginal cost (the cost borne by the producer) because the act of production generates costs for society that are not faced by the producer.

By producing where price equals private marginal cost and thereby ignoring the externality, the firms are maximizing profits but producing too much output. The price that consumers pay just covers the private marginal cost but does not pay for the external damage. The *social benefit* of the last unit of output (the market price) is less than the social cost (private marginal cost plus the social cost imposed by the externality). Reducing output by one unit would increase allocative efficiency and thus make society as a whole better off.

Making polluting firms bear the entire social cost of their production is called **internalizing the externality**.

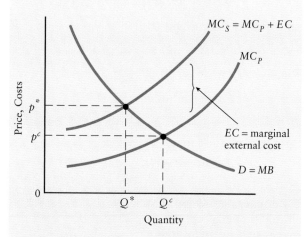

FIGURE 17-1   A Pollution Externality in a Competitive Market

A negative externality implies that a competitive free market will produce more output than the allocatively efficient level. If the externality can be internalized, allocative efficiency can be achieved. A competitive free market will produce where the demand and supply curves intersect—that is, at Q^c and p^c. If each unit of output of this good also generates an external cost of EC, then social marginal cost is greater than private marginal cost by this amount. The allocatively efficient level of output is where marginal benefit equals *social* marginal cost—that is, at Q^*. The competitive free market therefore produces too much output.

If firms in this industry are now required to pay a tax of $\$EC$ per unit of output, then the private marginal cost curve, MC_P, shifts up to MC_S. The externality will thus be *internalized* because firms will now be forced to pay the full social cost of their production. The new competitive equilibrium will be p^*, Q^*, and allocative efficiency will be achieved.

internalizing the externality   A process that results in a producer or consumer taking account of a previously external effect.

This leads them to produce a lower level of output, as shown in Figure 17-1. Indeed, at the optimal output, where the externality is completely internalized, consumer prices would just cover all of the *social* marginal cost of production. We would have the familiar condition for allocative efficiency that marginal benefits to consumers are just equal to the marginal cost of producing these benefits. The difference here is that some of the social marginal cost takes the form of the externality.

Note that in order to successfully internalize the externality, it is necessary to be able to accurately measure the size of the externality. Looking at Figure 17-1, we must be able to measure the magnitude of the marginal external cost, *EC*. In practice, however, external costs are quite difficult to measure. This measurement is especially difficult in the case of air pollution, where the damage is often spread over hundreds of thousands of square kilometres and can affect millions of people. Another difficulty arises because the cost that is imposed by pollution—in addition to the water that it contaminates or the animals that it kills—depends on the mechanisms that are used to undo the damage that it causes. Pollution-control mechanisms are themselves costly, and their costs must also be counted as part of the social cost of pollution. Nevertheless, the basic analysis of Figure 17-1 applies to these more difficult cases.

The socially optimal level of output is at the quantity where all marginal costs, private plus external, equal the marginal benefit to society.

The Optimal Amount of Pollution Abatement

Notice from Figure 17-1 that the allocatively efficient outcome still has some pollution being generated. This is because the production of each unit of output in Figure 17-1 generates some pollution. And this is generally the case. It is simply impossible to produce goods and services without generating *some* environmental damage. The economic problem is then to determine how much environmental damage to allow—this is determined where the costs to society of further pollution reduction equal the benefits to society of further pollution reduction.

Zero environmental damage is generally not economically efficient.

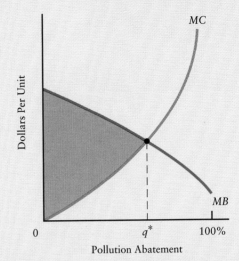

FIGURE 17-2   The Optimal Amount of Pollution Abatement

The optimal amount of pollution abatement occurs where the marginal cost of reducing pollution is just equal to the marginal benefits from doing so. *MB* represents the marginal benefit that is achieved by pollution abatement in some activity. *MC* represents the marginal cost of abating pollution; it rises sharply as more and more pollution is prevented. The optimal level of pollution abatement is *q**, where *MB* = *MC*. *Notice that not all pollution is avoided.* For each unit up to *q**, the marginal benefit derived from pollution abatement exceeds the marginal cost. The total net benefit from the optimal amount of pollution abatement is given by the shaded area—the sum of the difference between marginal benefit and marginal cost at each level of abatement. Any further efforts to prevent pollution beyond *q** would add more to costs than to benefits.

The economics of determining how much pollution to prohibit, and therefore how much to allow, is summarized in Figure 17-2, which depicts the benefits and costs of pollution abatement (reduction). The analysis might be thought of as applying, for example, to water pollution in a specific watershed. It is drawn from the perspective of a public authority whose mandate is to maximize social welfare.

Note that the figure is drawn in terms of the amount of pollution that is prevented (or abated) rather than in terms of the total amount of pollution produced. We do this because pollution abatement (rather than pollution itself) is a "good" of economic value, and we are more familiar with applying the concepts of supply and demand for goods with positive values. If no pollution is abated, the watershed will be subjected to the amount of pollution that would occur in an unregulated market. The greater the amount of pollution abated, the smaller the amount of pollution that remains.

Pollution is an externality. Firms do not take the social costs of their pollution into account when they make their private profit-maximizing decisions.

The marginal cost of abating pollution is likely to be small at low levels but to rise steeply after some point. This is the upward-sloping line shown in Figure 17-2. There are two reasons for believing that this shape is generally accurate. First is the familiar logic behind increasing marginal costs. For each firm that pollutes, because there will be some antipollution measures that can be taken fairly easily, the first portion of pollution prevention will be cheap relative to later portions. In addition, it is likely that pollution prevention of any degree will be easier for some firms than for others. New facilities are likely to run cleaner than old ones, for example. Pollution abatement in a factory that was designed in the era of environmental concern may be much easier than obtaining similar abatement in an older factory. After some point, however, the easy fixes are exhausted, and the marginal cost of preventing pollution further rises steeply.

The downward-sloping curve in Figure 17-2 is the "demand" for pollution abatement, and reflects the marginal benefit of pollution reduction. The curve slopes downward for much the same reason that the typical demand curve slopes downward. Starting at any nonlethal level of pollution, people will derive some benefit from reducing the level of pollution, but the marginal benefit from a given amount of abatement will be lower, the lower the level of pollution (or the higher the level of abatement). Put another way, in a very dirty environment, a little cleanliness will be much prized, but in a very clean environment, a little more cleanliness will be of only small additional value.

The optimal amount of pollution abatement occurs where the marginal benefit is equal to the marginal cost—where "supply" and "demand" in Figure 17-2 intersect. In trying to reach this optimum, the pollution-control authority faces three serious problems.

First, although Figure 17-2 looks like a supply-demand diagram, we have already seen that the private sector will not by itself create a market in pollution control. Hence, the government must intervene in private-sector markets if the optimal level of control shown in Figure 17-2 is to be attained.

The second problem is that the optimal level of pollution abatement is not easily known because the marginal benefit and the marginal cost curves shown in Figure 17-2 are not usually observable. In practice, the government can only estimate these curves, and accurate estimates are often difficult to obtain, especially when the technology of pollution abatement is changing rapidly and the health consequences of various pollutants are not known.

The third problem is that the available techniques for regulating pollution are themselves imperfect. Even when the optimal level of pollution abatement is known, there are both technical and legal impediments to achieving that level through regulation.

Pollution-Control Policies

In what follows we examine three different types of policies designed to bring about the optimal amount of pollution abatement (or the optimal amount of pollution). These are *direct controls*, *emissions taxes*, and *tradable emissions permits*.

Direct Controls

Direct control is the form of environmental regulation that is used most often. Automobile emissions standards are direct controls that are familiar to most of us. The standards must be met by all new cars that are sold in Canada. They require that emissions per kilometre of a number of noxious chemicals and other pollutants be less than certain specified amounts. The standards are the same no matter where the car is driven. The marginal benefit of reducing carbon monoxide emissions in rural Saskatchewan, where there is relatively little air pollution, is certainly much less than the marginal benefit in Montreal, where there is already a good deal of carbon monoxide in the air. Yet the standard is the same in both places.

Direct controls also often require that specific *techniques* be used to reduce pollution. For example, coal-fired electric plants were sometimes required to use devices called "scrubbers" to reduce sulfur dioxide emissions, even in cases where other techniques could have achieved the same level of pollution abatement at lower cost.

Another form of direct control is the simple prohibition of certain polluting behaviours. For example, many cities and towns prohibit the private burning of leaves and other trash because of the air pollution problem that the burning would cause. A number of communities have banned the use of wood stoves. Similarly, the government gradually reduced the amount of lead allowed in leaded gasoline and then eliminated leaded gasoline altogether.

Problems with Direct Controls.   Suppose that pollution of a given waterway is to be reduced by a certain amount. Regulators will typically apportion the required reduction among all of the polluters according to some roughly equitable criterion. The regulators might require that every polluter reduce its pollution by the same percentage. Alternatively, every polluter might be required to install a certain type of control device or to ensure that each litre of water that is dumped into the watershed meets certain quality criteria. Although any of these rules might seem reasonable, each of them will be inefficient.

Pollution is being abated efficiently when the marginal cost of abatement is the same for all firms.

When firms are required to abide by direct pollution controls, however, the marginal cost of pollution abatement is usually *not* equated across firms. To see this, consider two firms that face different costs of pollution abatement, as shown in Figure 17-3. Suppose that, for any level of pollution abatement, Firm A's marginal costs of abatement are lower than those for Firm B. A situation like this is quite likely because pollution comes from many different industries, and it may be easier for firms in one industry to cut back on the amount of pollution that they produce than it is for firms in another industry.

In this situation, consider a system of direct pollution controls that requires Firm A and Firm B to each reduce pollution by a given amount, say Q_R. As shown in Figure 17-3, Firm A's marginal cost at Q_R is less than Firm B's marginal cost. The total cost of abating this much pollution could be reduced by having the low-marginal-cost firm (Firm A) abate more pollution and having the high-marginal-cost firm (Firm B) abate less. As long as the two firms' marginal costs of abatement are not equal, it is possible to further reduce total costs. Only when marginal costs are equal across the two firms is the given level of pollution abatement being achieved at the lowest possible cost.

Direct pollution controls are inefficient because they do not minimize the cost of a given amount of pollution abatement.

Direct controls are also expensive to monitor and to enforce. The regulatory agency has to check, factory by factory, farm by farm, how many pollutants of what kinds are being emitted. It then also needs a mechanism for penalizing offenders. Accurate monitoring of all potential sources of pollution requires a level of resources that is much greater than has ever been made available to the relevant regulatory agencies. Moreover, the existing system of fines and penalties, in the view of many critics, is not nearly harsh

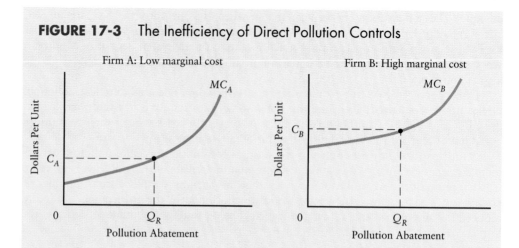

FIGURE 17-3   The Inefficiency of Direct Pollution Controls

Requiring equal amounts of pollution abatement from different polluters is inefficient when the different polluters have different technologies of pollution abatement. Firm A is able to reduce its emissions according to the marginal cost curve MC_A. Firm B, which operates at the same scale but in a different kind of factory, has a higher marginal cost of abatement, MC_B. Suppose that a regulatory authority requires that the two firms reduce pollution by the same amount, Q_R. Firm A will have a marginal cost of pollution abatement of C_A, whereas Firm B's marginal cost will be C_B, which is larger than C_A.

To see that this outcome is inefficient, consider what happens if Firm A reduces its pollution (increases its pollution abatement) by one unit while Firm B increases its pollution by one unit. Total pollution remains the same, but total costs fall. Firm A incurs added costs of C_A, and Firm B saves a greater amount, C_B. Because the total amount of pollution is unchanged, the total social cost of pollution and pollution abatement is lower.

enough to have much effect. A potential polluter, required to limit emissions of a pollutant to so many kilograms or litres per day, will take into account the cost of meeting the standard, the probability of being caught, and the severity of the penalty before deciding how to behave. If the chances of being caught and the penalties for being caught are small, the direct controls may have little effect.

Monitoring and enforcement of direct pollution controls are costly, and this costliness reduces the effectiveness of the controls.

Emissions Taxes

An alternative method of pollution control is to levy a tax on emissions at the source. The great advantage of such a procedure is that it internalizes the pollution externality so that decentralized decisions can lead to allocatively efficient outcomes. Again, suppose that Firm A can reduce emissions cheaply, while it is more expensive for Firm B to reduce emissions. If all firms are required to pay a tax of t for each unit of pollution they produce, then t is equal to each firm's marginal benefit of pollution reduction. The goal of profit maximization will then lead firms to reduce emissions to the point where the marginal cost of further reduction is just equal to t. Thus, Firm A will reduce emissions much more than Firm B and both will then have the same marginal cost of further abatement, which is required for allocative efficiency. Such a situation is illustrated in Figure 17-4.

FIGURE 17-4   The Efficiency of Emissions Taxes

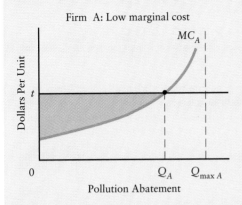

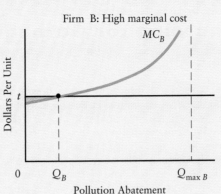

Emission taxes can lead to efficient pollution abatement. As in Figure 17-3, Firm A faces a lower marginal cost of pollution abatement than does Firm B. Suppose that the regulatory authority imposes a tax of t dollars per unit of pollution. Since each firm must then pay t dollars for each unit of pollution it produces, t can be viewed as the firm's marginal benefit of pollution abatement—for each unit of pollution it *does not produce* it avoids paying taxes equal to t.

Firm A will choose to reduce its pollution by Q_A. Up to this point, the tax saved by reducing pollution exceeds the marginal cost of reducing pollution. If Firm A chooses not to reduce pollution at all, it would pay $t \times Q_{maxA}$ in pollution taxes, where Q_{maxA} is the firm's total pollution if it takes no action to prevent pollution. By abating its pollution by Q_A, Firm A saves an amount that is given by the shaded area in the panel on the left.

Firm B chooses to abate only a small amount of pollution, Q_B. Any further abatement would require that the firm incur costs along MC_B, which would be greater than the benefits of taxes saved.

Note that if the regulatory agency is able to obtain a good estimate of the marginal damage done by pollution, it could set the tax rate just equal to that amount. In such a case, polluters would be forced by the tax to internalize the full pollution externality and allocative efficiency would be achieved. In terms of Figure 17-1, the firms' private marginal cost curve would shift up by the full amount of the tax (set to equal the marginal external cost, EC) and thus the allocatively efficient level of output would be produced.

A second great advantage of using emissions taxes is that regulators are not required to specify anything about *how* polluters should abate pollution. Rather, polluters themselves can be left to find the most efficient abatement techniques. The profit motive will lead them to do so because they will want to avoid paying the tax.

Emissions taxes can perfectly internalize pollution externalities so that profit-maximizing firms will produce the allocatively efficient amount of pollution abatement.

Applying Economic Concepts 17-1 discusses a simple type of pollution tax that is becoming quite common in many U.S. cities—charging for household garbage by the bag.

Problems with Emissions Taxes.   Emissions taxes can work only if it is possible to measure emissions accurately. For some kinds of pollution-creating activities, this does not pose much of a problem, but for many other types of pollution, good

APPLYING ECONOMIC CONCEPTS 17-1

Charging for Garbage by the Bag

One of the most common forms of pollution is household garbage. The economic theory of pollution externalities discussed in the text suggests that a tax on household trash should reduce the volume of pollution. In a number of communities in the United States, per-bag charges on household garbage have led to reductions in the amount of trash generated. The waste that is not going into the costly bags is going into compost heaps and into recycling. Communities vary in the way that charges are assessed and in the degree of support that they provide for alternative uses of waste. Typically, the municipal garbage trucks will pick up trash only if the trash bag (or other type of garbage) carries a special sticker. The stickers are sold by the municipal authorities; the fewer a household uses, the less money it spends on having its trash picked up. Fees of $1 to $2 per bag are not uncommon. In one U.S. community (High Bridge, New Jersey), a fee of $1.25 per bag has led to a 25 percent reduction in the volume of garbage.

The externality in this case is the use of landfills. Especially in the more populated areas of the United States, landfills for solid waste are becoming scarce and, consequently, expensive. By charging residents something for use of the landfill, alternative means of dealing with waste are encouraged, and a solid waste facility of given size can last longer.

Even in this case, the problem of finding the optimal charge per bag of garbage poses serious technical difficulties. There are also enforcement problems: Rather than pay the charge, some households will illegally dump their trash, adding to environmental damage. However, the pollution itself is very easy to measure, and it is plain that the optimum charge is greater than zero.

Household garbage is costly to dispose of in landfills. Charging by the bag for garbage internalizes the disposal cost.

measuring devices that can be installed at reasonable cost do not exist. Obviously, in these cases, emissions taxes cannot work, and direct controls are the only feasible approach.

When there is good reason to prohibit a pollutant completely, direct controls are obviously better than taxes. Municipal bans on the burning of leaves fall in this category, as do the occasional emergency bans on some kinds of pollution that are invoked during an air pollution crisis in cities such as Los Angeles and Vancouver.

Another problem with emissions taxes involves setting the tax rate. Ideally, the regulatory agency would obtain an estimate of the marginal social damage caused per unit of each pollutant and set the tax equal to this amount. This ideal tax rate would perfectly internalize the pollution externality. However, the information that is needed to determine the marginal external cost (*EC*) shown in Figure 17-1 is often difficult to obtain. If society is currently far away from the optimum, it may be very difficult to estimate what the marginal external cost will be at the optimum. If the regulatory agency sets the tax rate too high, too many resources will be devoted to pollution control. If the tax is set too low, there will be too little pollution abatement and thus too much pollution.

A potentially serious problem with emissions taxes is that information necessary to determine the optimal tax rate is often unavailable.

Tradable Emissions Permits

One advantage of direct controls is that the regulators can set the standards to limit the total quantity of pollution in a given geographical area. They can do this without knowing the details of either the marginal benefits or the marginal costs in Figure 17-2. The advantage of emissions taxes is that they allow for decentralized decision making, providing firms with an incentive to internalize the negative externality of pollution. **Tradable emissions permits** can combine both of these advantages and thus have the potential for being superior to either direct controls or emissions taxes.

In Figure 17-3, we noted that direct pollution controls are generally inefficient because the marginal cost curves for pollution abatement vary across firms. Tradable permits can achieve efficiency despite differences in firms' marginal cost curves. To see this, we must first figure out how much pollution to allow. This involves reformulating the regulator's problem. Start with the same conditions as those in Figure 17-3, and permit each firm to pollute exactly the same amount as would be allowed by the direct controls. Now suppose that the firms are each allocated Q_R tradable pollution permits—each one being simply a "right to pollute" by one unit. These permits are tradable in that firms are allowed to buy and sell them among themselves, at whatever price the market determines. Trades among firms will lead to discovery of the lowest-cost means of achieving the permitted level of pollution.

To see how the outcome is changed in the presence of tradable emissions permits, note that at the initial allowed amounts of pollution (Q_R), the marginal cost of pollution abatement for Firm A is lower than that for Firm B. Since Firm B must pay C_B to reduce pollution by one unit, it would be willing to pay any amount *less than* C_B to purchase one more pollution permit (and thus avoid reducing that last unit of pollution at cost C_B). Firm A would be willing to sell one pollution permit for any amount *greater than* C_A. By doing so, it earns an amount greater than C_A in return for reducing one more unit of pollution and paying the cost C_A. If Firm A and Firm B made such a trade, Firm A would be selling one of its pollution permits to Firm B. Society would benefit from this transaction because pollution would end up being abated at a lower cost than previously. If such a trade were made, the total amount of pollution would be unchanged, the total cost of abating pollution would fall (by $C_B - C_A$), and both firms would be at least as well off as before. We would thus have a clear efficiency improvement.

Once firms engage in trading pollution permits, an equilibrium market price will quickly be established. Facing this market price for permits, firms will end up equating their marginal abatement costs. To see this, note that the market price for a pollution permit will be each firm's marginal benefit of abatement since reducing pollution by one unit means the firm needs to purchase one less pollution permit. Profit-maximizing firms will therefore choose the level of abatement (and thus the number of permits) that equate this marginal benefit with their marginal abatement costs. Therefore, as in the case of emissions taxes shown in Figure 17-4, the introduction of tradable pollution permits will equate firms' marginal abatement costs and thus minimize the total cost of any given amount of pollution abatement.

With tradable pollution permits, profit-maximizing firms will abate pollution until their marginal abatement costs equal the price of the pollution permit. This will minimize the total cost of any given amount of pollution abatement.

Note, however, that the use of tradable pollution permits requires less information on the part of the regulators than does the use of emissions taxes. With tradable pollution permits, regulators do not need to calculate the optimal pollution tax. Given the permitted quantity of pollution, the market in permits will calculate the equivalent to the tax through the voluntary trades of firms.

tradable emissions permits   Government-granted rights to emit specific amounts of specified pollutants that private firms may buy and sell among themselves.

See Chapter 17 of www.pearsoned.ca/lipsey for an excellent discussion of why tradable emissions permits may be good for developing countries: Georges Tanguay, "Will Kyoto Lead to World Trade in Pollution Permits?" *World Economic Affairs.*

Practise with Study Guide Chapter 17, Exercise 3.

Problems with Tradable Emissions Permits.   Tradable permits pose some problems of implementation. Some of these involve technical difficulties in measuring pollution and in designing mechanisms to ensure that firms and households comply with regulations (some of these problems also exist for direct controls and emissions taxes). Furthermore, the potential efficiency gains arising from tradable permits cannot be realized if regulatory agencies are prone to change the rules under which trades may take place. Such changes have been a problem in the past, but they are a problem that can be corrected.

One problem with tradable permits is more political than economic, but it is certainly important in explaining why such policies are so rare. Opponents of tradable permits often argue that by providing permits, rather than simply outlawing pollution above some amount, the government is condoning crimes against society. Direct controls, according to this argument, have much greater normative force because they say that violating the standards is simply wrong. Emissions taxes and markets for pollution make violating the standards just one more element of cost for the firm to consider as it pursues its private goals.

Most economists find arguments of this kind unpersuasive. An absolute ban on pollution is impossible because any production of goods and services generates at least some pollution. In choosing how much pollution to allow, society must trade pollution abatement against other valuable things. Economic analysis has a good deal to say about how a society might minimize the cost of *any* degree of pollution abatement. By taking the moral attitude that pollution is wrong and pollution permits should not be allowed, the result is that *less* pollution gets abated for any given amount of society's scarce resources that are allocated toward this goal.

The creation of markets for pollution emissions may become one of the most promising strategies for efficiently overcoming the market failure that leads to environmental pollution.

Most experimentation with tradable pollution permits has so far been conducted in the United States. *Applying Economic Concepts 17-2* discusses how the U.S. Clean Air Act of 1990 created a national market in tradable permits for sulfur dioxide, the major cause of acid rain.

The Politics of Pollution Control

To see a copy of the Kyoto Protocol, go to the website for the United Nations Framework Convention on Climate Change: www.unfccc.de.

Tradable emissions permits increased in prominence after the December 1997 conference on global warming held in Kyoto, Japan. At this conference, representatives for 166 countries met to discuss the need for reducing the emissions of greenhouse gases—gases that many scientists believe are capable of trapping enough heat to significantly raise the earth's surface temperature. Thirty-eight countries eventually signed the "Kyoto Protocol," whereby the signing countries agreed to reduce their emissions of greenhouse gases. Central to the Protocol was the agreement in principle to use tradable emissions permits. Though many environmental groups applauded the agreement to reduce the emissions of greenhouse gases, there was widespread scepticism about the use of tradable emissions permits.

What is the basis for this scepticism? We consider, in turn, the views of producers, the public, and environmentalists.

APPLYING ECONOMIC CONCEPTS 17-2

A Market for SO$_2$ Emissions in the United States

Coal-burning electric power plants are the major cause of acid rain. They emit sulfur dioxide (SO$_2$) through their tall smokestacks, and the SO$_2$, which stays in the air for between two and five days, becomes acidic when it combines with moisture. Such emissions from the Ohio Valley and the Midwest, combined with prevailing winds from the southwest, provide a serious pollution problem for New England and parts of eastern Canada. Acid rain (or snow) harms the ability of lakes to sustain aquatic life and damages agricultural crops, forests, and even the surfaces of cars and buildings.

Much of the enthusiasm for tradable emissions permits, in the United States and elsewhere, comes from the success that the United States has had in reducing SO$_2$ emissions from electric utilities. The U.S. Clean Air Act of 1990 established targets for SO$_2$ emissions and implemented those targets by issuing (for free) a fixed number of "permits to pollute." Beginning in 1993, additional permits were auctioned to the highest bidder every year. Starting in 1995, the Environmental Protection Agency (EPA) implemented emissions trading, whereby emissions permits could be bought and sold at market-determined prices. The total number of emissions permits is controlled so that by the year 2000, emissions will be less than half the 1980 level. After 2000, the allowed emissions will be sharply reduced again.

Once firms receive their permits, either from the initial issuance or from the annual auction, they may use them or sell them as they please. But individual utilities are limited in their SO$_2$ emissions by the quantity of the permits that they own. For this system to be effective, monitoring of each firm's emissions is necessary; thus as part of the program all utilities subject to the new law are required to install continuous monitoring equipment. Each ton of emissions for which the polluter does not have a permit is subject to a $2000 fine. In addition, each such violation must be matched with an equivalent amount of underpollution (emissions less than the permitted amount) in the future.

Before the Clean Air Act was passed, utilities warned that annual compliance costs would be very large and that the emissions permits would be very expensive—ranging from $170 to $1000 per ton of emissions. By the end of the 1997, however, the market price was about $90 per ton. As technology for operating power plants with reduced SO$_2$ emissions improves, and thus the cost of emissions abatement falls, the price of the permits will also fall.

In addition to the utilities' participation in the market for emissions permits, several environmental groups have purchased permits, only to retire them from the market. By doing so, such groups can "put their money where their mouth is"—that is, they can express their preference for having a cleaner environment by purchasing the permits themselves and, by so doing, directly reduce the amount of SO$_2$ that can legally be produced.

Producers

Some firms object to the costs that they are asked to pay in terms of emissions taxes or the purchase prices of emissions permits. However, there is no reason why payments to government under any market-based scheme need to be an unjustified "tax grab." Emissions taxes need not be in excess of the costs imposed on society by the industry's activities. If government uses the introduction of a market-based scheme to raise general revenue—and thus levies emissions taxes in excess of the costs generated by the pollution—firms can oppose the extra tax burden without opposing the market-based scheme itself.

The introduction of market-based measures may signal the end of a free ride that producers have been taking at society's expense. If the firms in an industry were bearing none of the cost of their pollution, any efficient antipollution scheme will impose a burden on them—but only to the extent of forcing them to bear the costs of their own ac-

See Chapter 17 of www.pearsoned.ca/lipsey for an argument that stringent environmental standards may improve productivity: Georges Tanguay, "Environmental Standards and Industrial Competitiveness," *World Economic Affairs.*

tivities. The difference between direct controls and the market-based solution, however, is that the former will cost the average firm in the industry more than the market solution. (This difference just reflects the fact that direct controls are generally less efficient than emissions taxes or tradable emissions permits.)

Under market-based schemes (rather than direct controls), many firms feel a sense of unfairness because their competitors continue polluting while they must clean up. Their complaints ignore the fact that those firms that continue to pollute have paid for the right to do so, either by paying effluent taxes or by buying pollution rights, and that the complaining firm could do the same if it wished (it does not do so because cleaning up is cheaper for it than paying to pollute, as the competitors are doing).

These points make clear a key issue in assessing market-based solutions: Such solutions must not be judged relative to a "no action" policy. Given a government's decision to reduce pollution, the market solution must be compared with other alternatives that reduce pollution by the same amount. When such a comparison is made, much of the opposition from producers fades away.

Some firms argue that environmental protection reduces overall welfare because output and employment will fall if firms are required to pay emissions taxes or the price of pollution permits. This argument is misleading. It is surely true, as is clear in Figure 17-1, that firms required to pay for the external cost of the pollution they create will experience an increase in marginal cost—this is precisely how the externality gets internalized. It is also true that the level of output and employment in such firms will fall. But there is no tradeoff here between the environment and overall welfare. The environment is part of overall welfare. When we say that one unit of pollution generates an external cost of $100, we are measuring the cost imposed on the environment (or, equivalently, the amount of resources required to clean up that bit of environmental damage).

If steel-producing firms are required to pay the external cost of their pollution, the reduction in output and employment in those firms will indeed cause some pain. Profits will be lower, and some workers will be laid off. But this reduction in the amount of total resources devoted to the steel industry is part of the solution to the pollution externality. A negative externality in the steel industry means that too much steel is being produced. Thus it will improve overall welfare—not reduce it—to reduce the amount of resources in the steel industry. The resources that are no longer used in the steel industry are now free to be used in other industries, producing goods and services that society values more at the margin than an extra unit of steel.

The General Public

Some members of the general public have a moral opposition to selling anyone the right to pollute. Since it involves human survival, dealing in the right to pollute seems evil to many people. As we said earlier, however, it is not possible simply to ban pollution outright since all production invariably generates some pollution. The relevant question then becomes: How best can society reduce pollution by a given amount? Economic analysis suggests that tradable pollution permits are an efficient way of reducing pollution, and are much more efficient than direct pollution controls.

Opposition to the outcome where those who have the highest costs of cleaning up continue to pollute while those with the lowest costs do the cleaning up. Morality may dictate to many observers that the biggest polluters should do the cleaning up. Economists cannot show this reaction to be wrong; they can only point out the cost in terms of unnecessary resource use and less overall pollution abatement that follow from adopting such a position.

Environmentalists

Many environmentalists are sceptical about the efficiency and desirability of markets. Some do not understand economists' reasoning as to why markets can be, and often are, efficient mechanisms for allocating scarce resources. Others understand the economists' case but reject it, although few complete their argument by trying to demonstrate that direct government controls will be more effective.

Many environmentalists do not like the use of self-interest incentives to solve what they regard as "social" rather than "economic" issues. Economists who point to the voluminous evidence of the importance of self-interest incentives are often accused of ignoring higher motives such as social responsibility, self-sacrifice, and compassion. Although such motives are absent from the simple theories that try to explain the everyday behaviour of buyers and sellers, economists since Adam Smith have been aware that these higher motives often do exert strong influences on human behaviour.

Many environmentalists do not recognize that markets can be an efficient tool for protecting the environment.

Such higher motives are very powerful at some times and in some situations, but they do not govern many people's behaviour in the course of day-to-day living. If we want to understand how people behave in the aftermath of a flood, or an earthquake, or a war, we need motives in addition to self-interest; if we want to understand how people behave day after day in their buying and selling, we need little other than a theory of the self-interested responses to market incentives. Since control of the environment requires influencing the mass of small decisions, as well as a few large ones, the appeal to self-interest is the only currently known way to induce the required behaviour through voluntary actions.

Some environmentalists have the view that resources such as clean air and pure water are above mere monetary calculation and should thus be treated in special ways. The economist can point out that the use of this view to justify departing from market-based solutions ensures that measured material living standards will be lowered. If that is the understood and accepted price of regarding resources as special entities, then so be it!

Summary

This chapter has examined the main economic issues, and some of the political issues, associated with pollution control. The fact that pollution is a byproduct of some other production process means that pollution is a negative externality. Producers think about their own private costs but ignore the pollution costs that their production imposes on the rest of society. The efficient solution to this problem involves *internalizing the externality*—that is, making sure that the producers of the pollution are made to bear its full external cost. In the chapter we reviewed two ways of internalizing pollution externalities: emissions taxes and tradable pollution permits.

If properly designed, such market-based environmental policies can reverse the effects of the pollution externality. In terms of Figure 17-1, these policies have the effect of shifting the private marginal cost curve up by the full amount of the marginal external cost, thus equating private marginal cost with social marginal cost. When this occurs, firms will reduce the output of the goods that produce pollution as a byproduct, and the amount of pollution produced will also decline.

There is considerable opposition among environmentalists and the general public to market-based environmental policies. Tradable pollution permits, especially, appear to generate much scepticism among non-economists. Much of this scepticism has the same source as scepticism toward others policies that advocate the use of markets: *the lack of understanding of how markets work to allocate resources efficiently*. In response, economists can only continue to explain how markets work, illustrate what happens when markets are not permitted to operate, and present the costs and benefits of various environmental policies. Eventually, the message will get through.

SUMMARY

The Economics of Pollution Control   (LO)①②③

- Almost all economic activity is subject to at least some government regulation. Government regulation, of some form or another, is used to deal with every type of market failure—public goods, externalities, natural monopoly problems, and information asymmetries.
- Most pollution problems can be analysed as negative externalities. Polluting firms and households going about their daily business do harm to the environment and fail to take account of the costs that they impose on others.
- In a market that produces pollution as a byproduct, the external cost of the pollution implies that too much of the good is produced compared with what is allocatively efficient.
- The allocatively efficient level of pollution in any activity is generally not zero; it is the level where the marginal cost of further pollution reduction is just equal to the marginal damage done by a unit of pollution. If a firm or a household faces incentives that cause it to internalize fully the costs that pollution imposes, it will choose the allocatively efficient level of pollution.
- Pollution can be regulated either directly or indirectly. Direct controls are used most often. Direct controls are often inefficient because they require that all polluters meet the same standard regardless of the benefits and costs of doing so.
- Market-based environmental controls, such as taxes on emissions, are more efficient; ideally, they cause firms to internalize perfectly the pollution externality. Tradable emissions permits could have the same effect as taxes without requiring regulators to know as much about the technology of pollution abatement.

The Politics of Pollution Control   (LO)④

- There is considerable opposition by the public to the use of market-based environmental policies—especially the use of tradable pollution permits.
- Many firms oppose having to pay for pollution permits. But the market-determined price of pollution permits will equal the marginal external cost of pollution, and thus firms will only pay the external cost that their production imposes on society.
- Some environmentalists and other members of the public oppose on moral grounds that firms should pay for the "right to pollute." These criticisms ignore the fact that pollution is an important economic problem, and a strong case can be made for wanting to minimize the total cost of any given level of pollution abatement.

K E Y   C O N C E P T S

Negative pollution externalities
Marginal external cost

Costs and benefits of pollution abatement
The efficient level of pollution

Direct pollution controls
Emissions taxes
Tradable emissions permits

S T U D Y   E X E R C I S E S

1. Consider the market for lumber, which we assume here to be perfectly competitive.

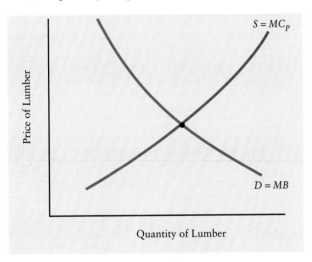

a. Suppose that for each unit of lumber produced, the firm also generates $10 of damage to the environment. Draw the social marginal cost curve in the diagram.
b. What is the allocatively efficient level of lumber output? Explain.
c. Describe and show the new market outcome if lumber producers are required to pay a tax of $10 per unit of lumber produced. Explain.
d. In part c, does the equilibrium price of lumber rise by the full $10 of the tax? Explain.

2. The following diagram shows society's marginal benefit and marginal cost for abating a particular type of pollution—say sulfur dioxide emissions.

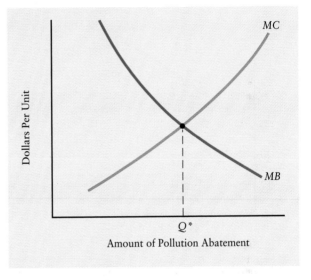

a. Explain why the marginal cost curve is upward sloping.
b. Explain why the marginal benefit curve is downward sloping.
c. At Q^*, are all sulfur dioxide emissions eliminated? Explain.
d. Is there an "optimal" level of sulfur dioxide emissions? Explain.

3. Suppose there are only two firms—Softies Inc. and Cuddlies Inc.—producing disposable diapers. Both firms are releasing dioxins into the same river. To reduce the pollution, the regulatory agency must choose between using direct controls and emissions taxes. The following diagrams show each firm's marginal cost of pollution abatement.

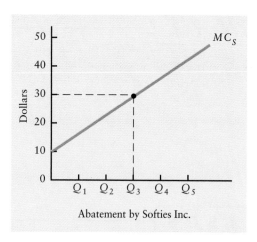

Abatement by Softies Inc.

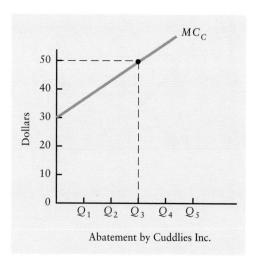

Abatement by Cuddlies Inc.

a. Suppose the regulatory agency requires that the two firms each abate Q_3 units of pollution. What is each firm's marginal abatement cost at Q_3?

b. Could the total cost of this amount of pollution abatement be reduced? Explain how.

c. Now suppose that the regulatory agency instead imposes an emissions tax of $40 per unit of emissions. Explain why this tax can be thought of as each firm's "marginal benefit of abatement".

d. In part c, how much pollution will each firm choose to abate?

e. Is it possible to reduce the total cost of the amount of abatement being done in part d?

4. Suppose that the government issues a fixed quantity of tradable pollution permits, each one permitting the emission of 1 ton of sulfur dioxide. In thinking about the market for pollution permits, think of the demand for permits as reflecting the marginal benefit to firms from being able to avoid costly pollution abatement.

a. If there is a competitive market for pollution permits, explain why the equilibrium price of the permit will equal the marginal abatement cost.

b. Explain why if polluting firms experience a technological improvement that reduces their marginal abatement costs, the equilibrium price of permits will fall.

c. What would happen if firms suffered a deterioration in their abatement technology?

d. One advantage of tradable pollution permits is that they allow the public to express their preferences for pollution reduction through the market. What happens if Greenpeace decides to buy a large number of pollution permits (and "retires" them)?

DISCUSSION QUESTIONS

1. "Pollution is wrong. When a corporation pollutes, it commits assault on the citizens of the country, and it should be punished." Comment on this statement in light of the discussion in this chapter.

2. Consider the following (alleged) facts about pollution control and indicate what influence they might have on policy determination.

a. The cost of meeting government pollution requirements is about $300 per person per year.

b. More than one-third of the world's known oil supplies lie under the ocean floor, and there is no known method of recovery that guarantees that large amounts of oil will not spill into the ocean.

c. Sulfur-removal requirements and strip-mining regulations have led to the tripling of the cost of a ton of coal used in generating electricity.

d. Every million dollars that is spent on pollution control creates 47 new jobs in the economy.

3. Suppose you were given the job of drafting a law to regulate water pollution over the entire length of some river.

a. How would you determine how much total pollution to permit?

b. What control mechanism would you use to regulate emissions into the river? Why?

c. Would you impose the same rules on cities as on farms?

d. Would your answer to parts **a**, **b**, or **c** depend on the quality of information that would be available to you? How and why?

4. The federal government has imposed many regulations aimed at reducing the pollution that is generated by driving. The more familiar regulations are direct—catalytic converters, fuel efficiency, and the like. Given the discussion in the chapter, why do you think the government opted for such direct controls? Can you think of any indirect controls currently in use to reduce automobile pollution?

CHAPTER 18

Taxation and Public Expenditure

LO LEARNING OBJECTIVES

1. Explain progressive, proportional, and regressive taxes.

2. Have a general knowledge of the main taxes used in Canada.

3. Explain how a tax generates both a direct and an excess burden.

4. Understand why high income taxes may act as a disincentive to work.

5. Understand why funds are transferred between various levels of government in Canada.

6. Describe a general outline of Canada's major social programs.

7. Be aware of some common pitfalls in evaluating government's role in the economy.

In Chapter 16, we saw some of the reasons why the scope of government is so extensive. Taxation is needed to raise money for public spending, and it can also play a policy role in its own right. Taxes can affect the distribution of income—some people get taxed more than others. Moreover, by taxing some activities heavily and others lightly or not at all, the tax system can influence the allocation of resources. In some cases, tax policy is carefully designed with such effects in mind; in other cases, the effects are unintentional by-products of policies pursued for other purposes.

In this chapter, we examine the various sources of government tax revenues and the various types of government expenditures. We ask how taxation and public expenditure affect the allocation of resources and the distribution of income, and to what extent they are effective tools of public policy. We examine the basis on which to evaluate a tax system, emphasizing the distinction between equity and efficiency. The types of public expenditures in Canada are examined along with the important concept of fiscal federalism. Finally, we describe the five pillars of Canadian social policy as well as some of the current pressures for reform of Canada's social programs.

Taxation in Canada

There is a bewildering array of taxes in Canada today. These are levied at the federal, provincial, and local levels. Some are highly visible, such as income taxes and the Goods and Services Tax (GST). Others are all but invisible to most people because they do not show up on income-tax forms or on receipts for purchases. For example, there are special taxes

For information on how Canada's tax system compares to those of other countries, see the website for the Canadian Tax Foundation: www.counsel.ca.

TABLE 18-1 Tax Revenues of Canadian Governments, 1997-98

	Billions of Dollars	Percent of GDP
Income taxes	$159.2	17.9
Consumption taxes (GST, provincial sales taxes, and excise taxes)	73.1	8.2
Property and related taxes	27.3	3.1
Other taxes	14.8	1.7
Health and social insurance premiums	27.1	3.0
Total tax revenues	$301.5	33.9
Non-tax revenues (sales of goods and services, investment income)	44.7	5.0
Total government revenues	$346.2	38.9

Canadian governments (at all levels) collect over $300 billion in various taxes, about one-third of the value of GDP. These data show total tax revenues for all levels of government combined. They *do not* include the mandatory contributions to the Canada and Quebec Pension Plans (which would increase the total by about $25 billion). Notice also that Canadian governments have considerable revenue, about $45 billion in 1998, from non-tax sources.

(*Source:* These data are available on Statistics Canada's website: www.statcan.ca)

levied on the sales of alcohol, cigarettes, and gasoline, but these taxes are levied directly on the producers (rather than the retailers) of these goods. People and firms are taxed on what they earn, on what they spend, and on what they own. Not only are taxes numerous, but taken together they raise a tremendous amount of revenue. Table 18-1 shows, for the federal, provincial, and local governments combined, the amount of revenue raised by the different types of taxes in 1998.

Canada lies roughly in the middle of other developed countries in terms of tax revenues as a share of GDP. Among the major industrialized countries, Denmark, Sweden, and the Netherlands collect roughly 50 percent of GDP in taxes. The lowest-tax industrialized country is Turkey, which collects about 25 percent of GDP in taxes. Canada is in the middle of the pack, collecting taxes equal to approximately 34 percent of GDP.

Some Definitions

Before discussing some details about the Canadian tax system, we examine two general concepts—*tax expenditures* and the *progressivity* of taxes.

Tax Expenditures

Sometimes taxes are used in ways that are similar to spending programs. For example, one way to deal with polluted rivers is to spend public funds to clean them up. An alternative, as we saw in Chapter 17, is to use taxes to penalize polluters or to give tax concessions to firms that install pollution-abating devices. Tax concessions that seek to induce market responses are called **tax expenditures**—tax revenue forgone to achieve purposes that the government believes are desirable.

The difference between a tax expenditure and an ordinary budgetary expenditure is that a tax expenditure represents *a reduction in tax revenue* whereas an ordinary expenditure represents *an increase in spending*. Because tax expenditures represent forgone earnings for the government, they are less visible than actual budgetary expenditures. They therefore usually receive little scrutiny from Parliament or the public. But this does not mean that they are small or unimportant. On the contrary, tax expenditures are very significant in the current Canadian economy. Personal income-tax expenditures alone, including such things as RRSP deductions, tuition fee credits, and child-care expense deductions, amount to over $75 billion annually.

Progressivity

When the government taxes one group in society more heavily than it taxes another, it influences the distribution of income. The effect of taxes on the distribution of income can be summarized in terms of *progressivity*. A **progressive tax** takes a larger percentage of income from high-income people than it does from low-income people. A **proportional tax** takes amounts of money from people in direct proportion to their income—

tax expenditures
Tax provisions, such as exemptions and deductions from taxable income, that are designed to induce market responses considered to be desirable.

progressive tax
A tax that takes a larger percentage of income the higher the level of income.

proportional tax
A tax that takes a constant percentage of income at all levels of income and is thus neither progressive nor regressive.

for example, every individual pays 10 percent of their income in taxes. A **regressive tax** takes a larger percentage of income from low-income people than it does from high-income people.

Note that the progressivity or regressivity of a tax is expressed in terms of *shares* of income rather than absolute dollar amounts. Thus a tax that collects $1000 from each individual clearly collects the same dollar amount from everybody, though it collects a higher share of income from low-income people than from higher-income people. A tax of this type—often called a **poll tax** or a *lump-sum tax*—is therefore a regressive tax.

Since a progressive tax takes a larger share of income from high-income people than it does from low-income people, progressive taxes reduce the inequality of income. A regressive tax increases the inequality of income.

For many families, day-care expenditures are tax deductible. The tax revenue forgone through such deductions are called "tax expenditures."

A progressive tax involves an important distinction between the average tax rate and the marginal tax rate. The **average tax rate** is the percentage of income that the individual pays in taxes. The **marginal tax rate** is the percentage *of the next dollar* earned that the individual pays in taxes. Progressivity in the tax system requires an *average* tax rate that rises with income. As you may recall from Chapter 7, where we examined the relationship between average and marginal, a rising average product can be accomplished only by having the marginal product above the average product. This is also true for tax rates: the average tax rate can rise only if the marginal tax rate is above the average tax rate. Figure 18-1 shows the difference between progressive, proportional, and regressive income taxes.

The Canadian Tax System

Taxes are collected by the federal government, by each of the provinces, and by thousands of cities, townships, and villages. Here is a brief guide to the most important of the various taxes.

Personal Income Taxes

Personal income taxes are paid directly to the government by individuals. The amount of tax any individual pays is the result of a fairly complicated series of calculations. All types of income are included in what is called total income, although certain types of income qualify for total or partial exemption. Then a number of allowable deductions are subtracted from total income to determine taxable income. Once taxable income is calculated, the amount of tax payable is then calculated by applying different tax rates to different levels of income. There are three federal personal income tax rates, each applying within what is called a tax bracket. In 1999, the three **tax brackets** were $0–$29 590; $29 590–$59 180; and greater than $59 180. The federal tax rates in these brackets were 17 percent, 26 percent, and 29 percent, respectively.

To see how this system of differential tax rates and tax brackets operates, consider Christine, who has a taxable income of $70 000. To the federal government, she pays at a rate of 17 percent on the first $29 590 ($5030), at a rate of 26 percent on the next $29 590 ($7693), and at a rate of 29 percent on all income *above* $59 180 (0.29 × $10 820 = $3138). Christine's total federal income tax payable is thus $15 861.

Recalling the definition of average and marginal tax rates, Christine's *average* tax rate is $15 861/$70 000, or 22.6 percent. Her *marginal* tax rate—the rate on an additional dollar of income—is 29 percent.

regressive tax A tax that takes a lower percentage of income the higher the level of income.

poll tax A tax that takes the same absolute amount from each person, independent of the level of their income. Also called a *lump-sum tax*.

average tax rate The ratio of total taxes paid to total income earned.

marginal tax rate The fraction of an additional dollar of income that is paid in taxes.

tax bracket A range of income for which there is a constant marginal tax rate.

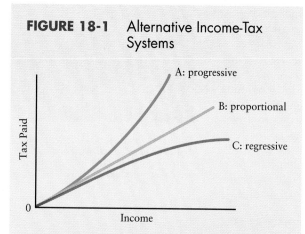

FIGURE 18-1   Alternative Income-Tax Systems

The relationship between income and taxes paid determines whether an income tax is progressive, proportional, or regressive. The average tax rate at any level of income, say $X, can be measured by computing the slope of a straight line from the origin to a point on the curve at income equal to $X. The slope of the curve at that point shows the marginal tax rate.

Along Curve A, the average tax rate rises as income rises. It shows a progressive income tax. The marginal tax rate also rises as income rises. Along Curve B, the average and marginal tax rate are equal to each other and are constant as income rises. This is a proportional tax system. Along Curve C, the average tax rate falls as income rises. This is a regressive tax system. The marginal tax rate is also falling as income rises.

The three federal personal income-tax rates do not represent the complete taxation of personal income in Canada, for two reasons. First, both the federal and many provincial governments have added more progressivity to the personal income tax by levying surcharges that kick in at various higher levels of income.

Second, the provincial governments also tax personal income. Quebec runs its own income-tax system, whereas the other nine provinces simply use the federal tax base (and federally distributed tax forms) and essentially "top up" federal taxes. Except for Quebec, taxpayers pay a single amount to Revenue Canada, which then distributes the total between the federal government and each province according to the amount collected from residents of that province.

The provincial taxation of income implies that Canada's highest marginal income-tax rate is not the federal rate, 29 percent. As of 1999, the highest marginal tax rates vary from a low of about 40 percent in Alberta to over 50 percent in Quebec and Newfoundland.

Corporate Taxes

The federal corporate income tax is, for practical purposes, a flat-rate (proportional) tax on profits as defined by the taxing authorities—which includes the return on capital as well as economic profits. In 1999, the rate was 28 percent.

Some corporate profits get distributed as dividends to shareholders. These dividends represent the shareholder's share of after-tax profits, and would ordinarily be taxed along with their other income. To avoid double taxation on this income, however, individual shareholders get a personal income-tax credit for the amount of corporate tax already paid by the firm. In this way, the corporate and personal income-tax systems are said to be *integrated*.

Excise and Sales Taxes

An excise tax is levied on a particular commodity. In many countries, commodities such as tobacco, alcohol, and gasoline are singled out for high rates of excise taxation. Because these commodities usually account for a much greater proportion of the expenditure of lower-income than higher-income groups, the excise taxes on them are regressive.

A sales tax applies to the sale of all or most goods and services. All provinces except Alberta impose a retail sales tax. Such a tax is mildly regressive, because poorer families tend to spend a larger proportion of their incomes than richer families.

Both excise and sales taxes are often referred to as "indirect" taxes to contrast them with income taxes, which are levied directly on the income of individuals or firms.

Since 1991, Canada has had a country-wide tax which applies at the same rate (7 percent) to the sale of all goods and services (with a few exceptions, such as basic groceries).

The Goods and Services Tax (GST) was introduced—despite enormous political contro-versy—for a number of reasons. First, it followed the modern trend in taxing expenditure rather than income. One problem with taxing income is that interest earnings from accu-mulated savings get counted as income and thus get taxed. Income taxes therefore dis-courage saving by lowering the after-tax rate of return to saving. In contrast, the GST only applies to the value of expenditure. Since the GST does not tax income (and therefore does not tax interest income) it does not discourage saving.

Practise with Study Guide Chapter 18, Exercise 4.

Second, the GST does not distort the relative prices of goods and services because it is applied at the same rate to all goods and services. Third, it followed the trend in almost all other developed nations (except the United States), which levy similar taxes; they are called *value added taxes* (VAT) in Europe.

In practice, the GST works by taxing a firm on the gross value of its output and then allowing a tax credit equal to the taxes paid on the inputs that were produced by other firms. Thus the GST taxes each firm's contribution to the value of final output—its value added. The result is the same as if each good and service bore a 7 percent tax when it was sold to its final user. Figure 18-2 shows how the GST is calculated at each stage from the mining of iron ore to the final retail sale of a washing machine.

Like sales and excise taxes, the GST is applied to ex-penditure rather than income. The GST taken alone would therefore be mildly regressive, because the pro-portion of income saved, and hence not taxed, rises with income. This regressivity is reduced by exempting food and, more importantly, by giving low- and mid-dle-income people a refundable tax credit, which for the poor exceeds the value of GST that they would pay even if they spent all of their incomes on taxable commodities.

Property Taxes

The property tax is the most important Canadian tax that is based on wealth and is an important source of revenue for municipalities. It is different from any other important tax because it is not related directly to a current transaction. In contrast, income taxes are levied on the current payment to a factor of production (in-come) and sales taxes are levied on the value of a cur-rently purchased good or service.

Taxing the value of existing property creates two problems. First, someone has to assess what the prop-erty is worth. Because the assessment is only an esti-mate, it is always subject to challenge. Second, sometimes owners of valuable property have low *in-comes* (though considerable wealth) and thus have dif-ficulty paying the tax.

The progressivity of the property tax has been studied extensively. It is obvious that the rich typically live in more expensive houses than the poor, and thus pay more in property taxes. But this does not mean

FIGURE 18-2   The Operation of the GST

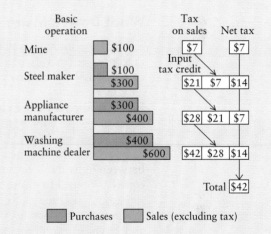

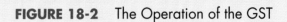

A tax on value added is the same as a tax on the value of final goods with a credit allowed for the tax paid for purchased inputs. The example is for the stages involved as iron ore is mined and then sold to a steel maker, the steel then sold to an appliance manufacturer, and the washing machine sold to a retailer and then to a con-sumer. The example makes the simplifying assumption that no produced inputs are used in the mining operation (so that the value of the iron ore is all value added); at all further stages, however, the use of produced inputs makes the firm's value added less than the value of final out-put at that stage. The steel maker's value added is $200, and its tax is thus $14; $21 on the total value of its out-put less the $7 credit on the taxes already paid by the mine on the value of the iron ore. Total taxes paid equal $42, which is 7 percent of the $600 value of the final product; each firm pays 7 percent of its share in creating that $600 value.

that the rich pay more property taxes *as a fraction of their income* than the poor. Thus it is not readily apparent that property taxes are progressive. Indeed, most studies have shown that the proportion of income spent on housing tends to decrease with income—that is, the property tax is regressive.

For information about the Canadian tax system, see the website for the Canada Customs and Revenue Agency: www.ccra-adrc.gc.ca.

▌Evaluating the Tax System

What makes one tax system better or worse than another? Economists deal with this question by considering two aspects of taxation—equity and efficiency. We deal with equity first.

Taxation and Equity

Debate about income distribution and tax policy usually involves the important but hard-to-define concept of *equity*.

What Do We Mean By Equity?

Equity (or fairness) is a normative concept; what one group thinks is fair may seem outrageous to another. Two principles can be helpful in assessing equity in taxation: equity according to *ability to pay,* and equity according to *benefits received.*

The Ability-to-Pay Principle.   Most people view an equitable tax system as being based on people's ability to pay taxes. In considering equity that is based on ability to pay, two concepts need to be distinguished.

Vertical equity concerns equity *across* income groups; it focuses on comparisons between individuals or families with different levels of income. The concept of vertical equity is central to discussions of the progressivity of taxation. Proponents of progressive taxation argue as follows. First, taxes should be based on ability to pay. Second, the greater one's income, the greater the percentage of income that is available for goods and services beyond the bare necessities. It follows, therefore, that the greater one's income, the greater the proportion of income that is available to pay taxes. Thus, an ability-to-pay standard of vertical equity requires progressive taxation.

Horizontal equity concerns equity *within* a given income group; it is concerned with establishing just who should be considered equal to whom in terms of ability to pay taxes. Two households with the same income may have different numbers of children to support. One of the households may have greater dental expenses, leaving less for life's necessities and for taxes. One of the households may incur expenses that are necessary for earning income (e.g., requirements to buy uniforms or to pay union dues). There is no objective way to decide how much these and similar factors affect the ability to pay taxes. In practice, the income-tax law makes some allowance for factors that create differences in ability to pay by permitting taxpayers to exempt some of their income from tax. However, the corrections are rough at best.

The Benefit Principle.   According to the benefit principle, taxes should be paid in proportion to the benefits that taxpayers derive from public expenditure. From this perspective, the ideal taxes are *user charges,* such as those that would be charged if private firms provided the government services.

The benefit principle is the basis for the gasoline tax, since gasoline usage is closely related to the services obtained from using public roads. There is also a special airline ticket excise tax that is used for airport operations and airport security. Although there are other examples, especially at the local level, the benefit principle has historically played only a minor role in the design of the Canadian tax system. But its use is growing in Canada and elsewhere as governments seek new ways to finance many of their expenditures. For example, a decade ago Statistics Canada supplied data for free to anybody who wanted it. Now, Statistics Canada charges on a "cost recovery basis" for any data other than the most general data which they make available on their website.

The benefit principle can be easily applied to some government-provided goods and services. But it is difficult to see how the benefit principle could be applied to many of the most important categories of government spending. Who gets how much benefit from national defence or from interest on the public debt? It is even more difficult to imagine applying the benefit principle to government programs that redistribute income.

How Progressive Is the Canadian Tax System?

Although most public controversy over tax equity stresses the progressivity or regressivity of particular taxes, what matters in the end is the overall progressivity of the *entire tax system*. For a modern government to raise sufficient funds, many taxes must be used. We have already discussed personal and corporate income taxes, excise and provincial sales taxes, the Canada-wide GST, and municipal property taxes. Not all of them are equally progressive in design and each one has its own loopholes and anomalies. So, how high-, middle-, and low-income people are taxed relative to each other depends on how the entire tax system impacts on each group.

Assessing how the entire tax system affects the distribution of income is complicated by two factors. First, the progressivity of the system depends on the mix of the different taxes. Federal taxes tend to be somewhat progressive; the progressivity of the income-tax system and the use of a low-income tax credit more than offset the regressivity of the federal GST. Provincial and municipal governments rely heavily on property and sales taxes and thus have tax systems that are probably slightly regressive.

Second, income from different sources is taxed at different rates. For example, in the federal personal income tax, income from royalties on oil wells is taxed less than income from royalties on books, and profits from sales of assets (capital gains) are taxed less than wages and salaries. To evaluate progressivity, therefore, one needs to know the way in which different *levels* of income are related with different *sources* of income.

Many economists have concluded that the Canadian tax system is roughly proportional for middle-income classes and mildly progressive for low- and high-income persons. Thus the overall tax system is essentially redistributing income from high-income people to low-income people, and doing little redistribution among the middle-income people.

Taxation and Efficiency

The tax system influences the allocation of resources by altering such things as the relative prices of various goods and factors and the relative profitability of various industries.

Although it is theoretically possible to design a neutral tax system—one that leaves all relative prices unchanged—the conditions are too complex to be met in practice. As a result, any actual tax system, including Canada's, does alter the allocation of resources. The taxes change the relationship between prices and marginal costs and shift consumption and production toward goods and services that are taxed relatively lightly and away from those that are taxed more heavily. Usually, this alteration of free-market outcomes causes allocative inefficiency. In a world without taxes (and without other market imperfections), prices would equal marginal costs, and society's resources could be allocated efficiently.

Of course, in a world without taxes, there would be other problems—it would be impossible to pay for any government programs or public goods desired by society. In practise, then, the relevant objective for tax policy is to design a tax system that minimizes inefficiency, *holding constant the amount of revenue to be raised*. In designing such a tax system, a natural place to start would be with taxes that both raise revenue and enhance efficiency. An example of such a tax is the emissions tax that we discussed in Chapter 17. When taxes are imposed on negative externalities, marginal social benefit is moved closer to marginal social cost, *and* government revenue is raised. Unfortunately, such taxes cannot raise nearly enough revenue to finance all of government expenditure.

The Two Burdens of Taxation

In the absence of externalities, a tax normally does two things. It takes money from the taxpayers, and it changes their behaviour. Taxpayers are typically made worse off by both aspects of the tax. Economists call the revenue collected the **direct burden** of the tax. The additional cost that results from the induced changes in behaviour is called the **excess burden.**

direct burden
Amount of money for a tax that is collected from taxpayers.

excess burden   The amount that taxpayers would be willing to pay, over and above the direct burden of taxes, to abolish the taxes.

The direct burden of a tax is the amount paid by taxpayers. The excess burden of a tax is the amount of money that the taxpayers would have to be given, over and above the taxes paid, in order to be just as well off as they would be without the tax. The excess burden reflects the allocative inefficiency of the tax.

Figure 18-3 shows an example that illustrates this important distinction. Suppose that your provincial government imposes a $2 excise tax on the purchase of compact discs. Suppose further that you are a serious music lover and that this tax does not change your quantity demanded of CDs—that is, your demand for them is perfectly inelastic and hence you continue to buy your usual five CDs per month. In this case, you pay $10 in excise taxes per month, and you therefore have to reduce your consumption of other goods by $10 per month.

In this special case, the burden on you is not reflected by the change in your consumption of CDs (because there is no change), but rather by the change in your overall purchasing power. That is, if you were to be given an additional $10 a month in income, you would be exactly as well off as you were before the tax was imposed. Thus, the total burden on you is equal to the direct burden, $10 a month; there is no excess burden of this tax. The absence of any excess burden from this tax is just another way of saying that there is no allocative inefficiency; the cost of raising $10 a month for the province is just the $10 a month that you pay in taxes. In this case, the tax is *purely* a redistribution of resources from you to the government.

Now suppose that a friend of yours is also a music lover but is not quite so dedicated. The tax leads her to cut back on her consumption of CDs from two per month to none. In this case, your friend pays no taxes and therefore experiences no reduction in her overall purchasing power. The direct burden of the tax is therefore zero. However, your friend *is* worse off as a result of this tax—she has given up the satisfaction that she would have derived from two new CDs per month. She would have to be given some amount of money greater than zero (exactly her consumer surplus from buying two untaxed CDs per month) in order to make her as well off as she was before the tax was imposed. In this case, the direct burden is zero (because no tax is paid) but there *is* an excess burden. The excess burden is equal to her loss in consumer surplus from the two CDs per month that she no longer enjoys.

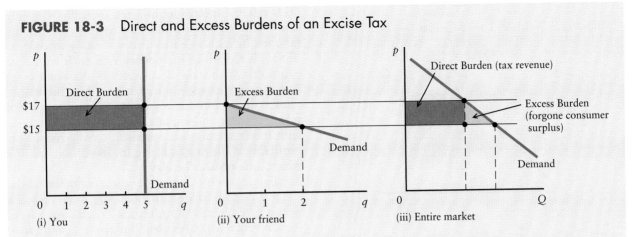

FIGURE 18-3 Direct and Excess Burdens of an Excise Tax

The allocative inefficiency of a tax is measured by its excess burden. The excess burden is greater the more elastic is demand. Part (i) shows your demand for CDs. It is perfectly inelastic at five CDs per month. When the government imposes an excise tax of $2 per CD, the price rises from $15 to $17. Your quantity demanded is unchanged, and so you pay $10 per month in taxes ($2 tax per CD × 5 CDs). The direct burden of the tax is $10; but because your behaviour is unchanged, there is no excess burden.

Part (ii) shows your friend's demand. Her quantity demanded falls from two CDs per month to zero as a result of the tax. Since she pays no tax on CDs, she bears no direct burden of the tax. But because she has lost consumer surplus, she bears an excess burden from the tax.

Part (iii) shows the entire market demand. There is both a direct burden, the dark shaded area, and an excess burden, the light shaded area. The more elastic is the demand curve, the larger is the excess burden of the tax.

When a tax is imposed, some people behave like the music buff and do not change their consumption of the taxed good at all, others cease consuming the taxed good altogether, and most simply reduce their consumption. There will be an excess burden for those in the latter two groups. Thus, the revenue collected will understate the total cost to taxpayers of generating that revenue. Since our exercise in judging the efficiency of a tax system is to hold constant the total revenue raised, and thus to hold constant the direct burden generated by the tax system, *an efficient tax system will be one that minimizes the amount of excess burden.*

As the example above shows, the excess burden is minimized when taxes are imposed on goods with the lowest price elasticities of demand; the extreme case is illustrated by the music fan who has perfectly inelastic demand for CDs. A good with perfectly inelastic demand (one that has a vertical demand curve) can be taxed with no excess burden at all. Unfortunately, because many of life's necessities (such as food) have very price-inelastic demand curves, a tax system that taxed only goods that had inelastic demand curves would prove to be very regressive. This example illustrates an important general point:

Efficiency and equity are often competing goals in the design of tax systems. Improving efficiency often reduces equity; improving equity often reduces efficiency.

Practise with Study Guide Chapter 18, Exercise 2.

Disincentive Effects of Taxation

We have just shown how a tax can change consumers' behaviour. By raising the price of a good or service, the tax can lead consumers to purchase less of that good. What is true for consumers' demand for goods is also true for their demand for leisure. And their demand for leisure is simply the opposite of their supply of work effort. Thus,

FIGURE 18-4   A Laffer Curve

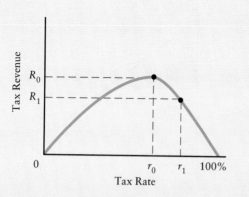

Increases in tax rates beyond some level will decrease rather than increase tax revenues. The curve relates the government's tax revenue to the tax rate. As drawn, revenue reaches a maximum level of R_0 at the tax rate r_0. If the tax rate were r_1, then *reducing* it to r_0 would increase the government's tax revenue from R_1 to R_0.

taxes can be expected to influence individuals' supply of work effort. In particular, an increase in the income-tax rate, by reducing after-tax earnings, may lead individuals to reduce their work effort. (It would be helpful to review the discussion of this point from *Applying Economic Concepts 6-1*.) This possibility leads to the paradoxical result that reducing income-tax rates may lead individuals to work and earn more, with the result that tax revenue actually *rises*. This possibility is illustrated in Figure 18-4, which shows what economists call a *Laffer Curve*.

The reasoning behind the general shape of the Laffer curve is as follows. At a zero tax rate, no revenue would be collected. As rates are raised above zero, some revenue will be gained. But as rates continue to rise, revenue will eventually fall because the very high tax rates will lead people to work less and less. At a tax rate of 100 percent, they will not bother to work at all (because all of their income would go to the government) and so tax revenue will be zero. It follows that there must be *some* tax rate, greater than zero and less than 100 percent, at which tax revenue reaches a maximum.

Figure 18-4 is drawn under the assumption that there is a steady increase in tax revenue as tax rates rise to r_0, and a steady decrease in tax revenues as tax rates continue to rise toward 100 percent. This particular shape—with a single peak in tax revenues—is not necessary. But the precise shape is beside the point. The key point is that there is *some* tax rate like r_0 that maximizes total tax revenue. And as long as this is true, then tax rates both above and below r_0 will raise less tax revenue than is raised at r_0.

Just where this maximum occurs—whether at average tax rates closer to 40 or to 70 percent—is currently unknown for either corporate or personal income taxes. Also, there will be a separate Laffer curve for each type of tax. The curve does, however, provide an important warning: Governments cannot increase their tax revenues to any desired level simply by increasing their tax rates. Sooner or later, further increases in the rates will reduce work incentives so much that total tax revenues will fall.

Public Expenditure in Canada

In recent years, spending by the consolidated public sector—which includes federal, provincial, and municipal governments—has equaled about 40 percent of Canadian GDP. Table 18-2 gives the distribution of consolidated government spending across a number of major *functions* for 1998. As can be seen, health care, education, and social services are very large items; collectively, they make up almost half of the total spending of $357 billion. Interest on the public debt is the largest single item, making up about one-quarter of total spending. The remaining quarter covers everything else, from police protection and sanitation to general administration of government, environmental protection, and foreign aid.

There are three broad categories of government expenditure. First, the government spends to provide goods and services to the public, as when the government pays for physicians' services, highway repair, primary and secondary education, and so on. Included in this category of expenditures are the salaries that the government pays to its employees. The second category of government expenditures is **transfer payments**. These are payments to individuals, firms, or other levels of government that are *not* made in exchange for a good or a service. For example, when the federal government pays employment insurance benefits to an unemployed individual, the government is not getting any good or service in return. Similarly, when the federal government transfers money to the provincial governments, it is not getting any good or service in return. The third category is actually expenditure on a particular type of service, but it is common to treat it separately—this is the interest the government pays on its outstanding stock of debt. Table 18-2, however, does not show a breakdown of expenditures between transfer payments and the provision of goods and services; instead, it shows the breakdown according to the broad area of spending.

transfer payment
A payment to a private person or institution that does not arise out of current productive activity.

Table 18-2 also does not show which of the three levels of government—federal, provincial, and municipal—actually do the spending. For example, of the $40.2 billion spent on education in 1998, the vast majority—over $36 billion—was spent by provincial and municipal governments. In contrast, expenditures on foreign affairs and foreign aid are made exclusively by the federal government. Expenditures on social services are about equally divided between the federal and provincial governments with only a small role played by the municipalities.

Fiscal Federalism

Canada is a federal state with governing powers divided between the central authority and the ten provinces and three territories. Municipalities provide a third level of government, whose powers are determined by the provincial legislatures. Understanding the fiscal interaction of the various levels of government is central to understanding the nature of government expenditure in Canada. In this section, we examine the concept of *fiscal federalism;* in the next section we examine how fiscal federalism affects the operation of Canada's social programs.

The Logic of Fiscal Federalism

The essence of fiscal federalism is the recognition that Canada is a country with many different fiscal authorities (federal, provincial, and municipal governments) that need a certain amount of coordination to be responsive to the needs and desires of the citizens—who are free to move from one area to another. We discuss four motivations for fiscal federalism.

TABLE 18-2 Expenditures by Canadian Governments, 1997–98

Category of Spending	Billions of Dollars	Percent of GDP
General government services	12.9	1.4
Protection of persons and property	28.5	3.2
Transportation and communication	19.4	2.2
Health	50.9	5.7
Social services	84.6	9.5
Education	40.2	4.5
Resource conservation, environment, and industrial development	23.5	2.6
Recreation and culture	9.0	1.0
Housing	4.9	0.5
Labour, employment, and immigration	2.0	0.2
Foreign affairs and international aid	4.0	0.4
Debt charges	72.9	8.2
Other expenditures	3.7	0.4
	356.5	39.8

Expenditures on health, social services, and education together make up almost half of total government expenditure. These data show the various categories of spending by all levels of government combined.

(*Source:* These data are available on the Statistics Canada website: www.statcan.ca.)

Differences in Tax Bases. The ten Canadian provinces vary considerably in terms of their average levels of prosperity. Newfoundland and Quebec have for many years lagged the national average in terms of per capita real incomes, whereas Alberta and Ontario have for many years exceeded the national average. In order to provide public goods such as highways and judicial systems, the provincial governments must levy various types of provincial taxes. Provinces that are more prosperous, and thus have larger tax bases, are able to provide a given amount of public goods while having relatively low tax rates. In contrast, less affluent provinces with smaller tax bases will be able to provide the same amount of public goods only by having higher tax rates.

Why don't we just let the more affluent provinces have lower tax rates than the less affluent provinces? The answer is that one of the guiding principles in Canada's system of fiscal federalism is that individuals, no matter where they live, should have approximately the same access to public goods and should face approximately the same tax rates to finance those public goods.

intergovernmental transfer A transfer of funds from one government to another.

Since revenue sources do not always match revenue needs at each level, **intergovernmental transfers** are required. This is the underlying motivation behind Canada's system of *equalization payments*, which transfers resources from the richer provinces to the poorer ones. We examine this shortly.

Geographic Extent of Externalities. Because the government of a province or a municipality is unlikely to be responsive to the needs of citizens outside its jurisdiction, public services that involve *geographic spillovers* may not be provided adequately unless responsibility for them is delegated to a higher level of government. For example, national defence is normally delegated to the central government for this reason. Control of pollution is another obvious case, since contamination of air and water often literally spills over provincial and municipal boundaries. At the other extreme is fire protection. If fire protection is to be effective, it is necessary that there be fire stations serving small geographic areas. Accordingly, responsibility for fire stations lies with municipal governments.

Regional Differences in Preferences. The delegation of some functions to lower levels of government may provide a political process that is more responsive to regional differences in preferences for public versus private goods. Some people may prefer to live in communities with higher-quality schools and police protection, and they may be prepared to pay the high taxes required. Others may prefer lower taxes and lower levels of services. The differences in provincial tax rates that we noted earlier presumably reflect each provincial government's own view of the appropriate level of taxation.

Administrative Efficiency. Administrative efficiency requires that duplication of the services provided at different levels of government be minimized and that related programs be coordinated. On the revenue side, it is desirable that a particular tax be collected by only one level of government. This consideration has led to the negotiation of federal-provincial tax agreements that provide for efficient tax collection and revenue sharing.

Intergovernmental Transfers

The foregoing discussion of fiscal federalism suggests a role for transfers between various levels of government. For example, if income taxes are paid to the federal government but spending on hospitals and highways is undertaken by provincial governments, then federal-provincial transfers must be made. In addition, if some provinces have large tax bases, while others have much smaller tax bases, there is also a role for transferring resources between provinces. Canada has three major programs of intergovernmental transfers.

Canada Health and Social Transfer. A major reform of the system of federal-provincial transfers occurred in 1996 with the creation of the Canada Health and Social Transfer (CHST). The CHST is a block grant made by the federal government to each provincial government to help finance expenditures on health care, social assistance (welfare) and post-secondary education. Though the CHST transfer is described as being directed at these three categories of expenditure, there is no practical way to prevent the provincial governments from spending the money on whatever they deem to be appropriate. Thus, the CHST is received by the provinces with "no strings attached."

The CHST replaced two previous transfer programs. The first, Established Programs Financing (EPF), was directed at health care and post-secondary education. The second, the Canada Assistance Plan (CAP), was a transfer program in which the federal government financed 50 percent of the province's welfare system. Thus, until the creation of the CHST, the federal government was obliged to increase CAP funding to any province that chose to increase the generosity of its welfare program. The CHST therefore gives the federal government more control over its funding of provincially administered programs. Beginning in 2001–02, the CHST payment to each province is made on a per capita basis, equal to $960 for each resident of that province.

Equalization Payments.   With the object of ensuring that citizens in all regions of the country have access to a reasonable level of public services, **equalization payments** are made out of federal government general revenues to provinces with below-average tax capacity. Though this is not explicitly a revenue-sharing program (provinces with above-average tax capacity do not pay in), the richer provinces (typically British Columbia, Alberta, and Ontario) are, in effect, transferring resources via the federal government to the poorer provinces. The equalization payments are calculated by a complicated formula that involves 30 different revenue sources.

Equalization payments are a relatively new phenomenon in Canada, but they have exhibited rapid growth. From their inception with the 1957 Tax-Sharing Act to the time of the 1977 Fiscal Arrangements Act to their formal inclusion in the Constitution Act of 1982, they have expanded considerably. Equalization payments for the 1999–2000 fiscal year were approximately $9.3 billion.

equalization payments   Transfers of tax revenues from the federal government to the low-income provinces to compensate them for their lower per capita tax yields.

Revenue Sharing.   Since the 1940s, most provinces have maintained **tax-rental arrangements,** whereby the federal government collects income taxes and makes a per capita payment to the provinces for that right. In 1999, with the exception of the Quebec personal income tax and the Ontario and Quebec corporate levies, all income taxes in Canada were collected by the federal government.

Outside Quebec, the provincial income tax is calculated as a percentage of the federal tax payable at rates determined by the individual provinces.[1] Federal income-tax rates are set at levels that allow substantial "tax room" to the provinces. That is, by keeping the federal income-tax rates relatively low the provinces can still raise considerable revenue by taxing income without generating extreme supply-side effects such as those discussed in Figure 18-4. A similar arrangement applies to the corporate income tax. The effect of these measures can be thought of in terms of the "value of tax points." Tax points reflect the taxes levied by the provinces, collected by the federal government, and then returned to the provinces as a transfer.

tax-rental arrangements   An agreement by which the federal government makes a per capita payment to the provinces for the right to collect income taxes.

Canadian Social Policy

Canada has a wide variety of social programs, from unemployment insurance and the Canada Pension Plan to the systems of publicly provided health care and heavily subsidized

---

[1]In 1999, Alberta introduced a flat-rate provincial income tax of 11 percent. The tax is still collected by the federal government.

post-secondary education. Canadian governments—both federal and provincial—have been urged to reexamine and redesign these programs with the twin objectives of improving the benefits delivered to the intended beneficiaries and reducing costs wherever possible. It is not surprising that controversies over Canada's social programs have been major news items in recent years. Indeed, these controversies will likely continue well into the future.

Some social programs are universal, in the sense that they pay benefits to anyone meeting only such minimal requirements as age or residence. These are referred to as **demogrants.** Other programs are selective, in the sense that they pay benefits only to people who qualify by meeting specific conditions, such as by having young children or being unemployed. When these conditions are related to the individual's income, the term **income-tested benefits** is used. Some benefits are expenditure programs (including direct transfers to persons), while others are delivered through the tax system in the form of tax expenditures. Some programs are administered by the federal government, some by the provincial governments, and still others by the municipalities.

In this section we examine the five pillars of Canadian social policy: education, health care, income support, employment insurance, and retirement benefits. Each of these pillars, at various points in recent years, have been the focus of attention as financially strapped governments have explored new ways to provide what many perceive as vital social services.

Education

Public education, one of the earliest types of social expenditure in Canada, remains one of the most important. It has been supplemented over the years by numerous other programs aimed at developing human resources.

Basic Education.   Primary and secondary schools teach literacy and numeracy. These basic skills are needed in order to acquire further marketable skills. Canada has one of the world's highest per capita expenditures on basic education, yet Canadian students do relatively poorly on international comparisons that use standardized tests. Studies show that many Canadian adults (some estimates say as many as one-quarter) are functional illiterates—people who cannot comprehend simple written instructions well enough to carry them out. One educational target should be to reduce illiteracy and innumeracy, deficiencies that are lifetime handicaps.

Postsecondary Education.   Postsecondary education is a provincial responsibility in Canada. As discussed earlier in this chapter, however, the federal government makes large payments to the provinces to support postsecondary education as part of the Canada Health and Social Transfer (CHST).

In Canada, all universities are public institutions, and university education is heavily subsidized by government. In 1998, total revenues for universities and colleges was $17.7 billion, with 62 percent coming from various levels of government. Only 16 percent came from student tuition fees. (The remaining 22 percent comes from various other sources—maybe those overpriced shirts that you can't afford to buy from your campus bookstore!)

Two arguments can be advanced for subsidizing higher education; one is an efficiency argument, and the other concerns equity. The efficiency argument is based on the claim that there are positive externalities from higher education—that is, that the country as a whole benefits when a student receives higher education. In many cases these externalities cannot be internalized by the students receiving the education, so, left to their own maximizing decisions, students who had to pay the whole cost of their education would choose less than is socially optimal. The equity argument is that if students were forced to pay anything like the full cost of the services they receive, a university education would become prohibi-

demogrants   Social benefits paid to anyone meeting only minimal requirements such as age or residence; in particular, *not* income-tested.

income-tested benefits   Social benefits paid to recipients who qualify because their income is less than some critical level.

For data on the financial position of Canadian universities, see Statistics Canada's website: www.statcan.ca. Click on "Canadian Statistics" and then "Education."

tively expensive to low- and even middle-income families. Government subsidies help provide education according to ability rather than according to income.

Arguments to reduce the subsidy to higher education, and thus to finance a larger fraction of the costs of running universities from tuition fees, start with the observation that the value of many kinds of education is internalized and recaptured in higher incomes earned by the recipients later in their life. This is particularly true of professional training in such fields as law, medicine, dentistry, management, and computer science. Yet students in these fields typically pay a smaller part of their real education costs than students in the arts, where the argument for externalities is greatest. Also, subsidized education does represent a significant income transfer from taxpayers to students, even though the average taxpayer may have a lower income than the average student can expect to earn in the future.

Health Care

Taking federal and provincial payments into account, Canada's public health-care system is the country's single most expensive social program. In 1998, government expenditure on health care was $50.9 billion, about 15 percent of total government expenditure and 5.8 percent of GDP. Private spending on health care brought total spending up to about 10 percent of GDP. In other words, one out of every ten dollars in income produced in the Canadian economy gets spent on health care.

"Cost containment" in the health-care sector has become a priority for most provincial governments and the debate currently rages over what reforms are practicable and acceptable. Hospital and bed closures, nurse's strikes, and growing queues for non-critical treatments are part of the daily news. Most observers agree that some type of expenditure-controlling reform is urgently needed. Unfortunately, agreement stops here.

Budget cuts in the health-care sector have led to friction between provincial governments and health-care professionals, such as doctors and nurses.

Private Hospitals in a Public System.   In 1999, the Alberta government announced its proposal to allow private, for-profit hospitals to exist within the publicly funded health-care system. According to this proposal, the provincial government would make the same payment to a private hospital for providing a given service as it would make to a public hospital. The Alberta government saw this proposal as one way to reduce waiting lists in the public health-care system without using scarce public funds to build new hospitals or expand existing ones.

The Alberta proposal has met with strong opposition, in part by the federal government. The main concern is that private hospitals may begin "extra billing" their patients. In this case there would develop a "two-tiered" health-care system in which individuals with higher incomes have better access to health care than do individuals with lower incomes. If extra billing becomes a feature of private hospitals, then only those individuals who can afford to pay the extra fees will be able to use the private hospitals. Furthermore, many nurses and doctors that are currently within the financially strapped public health-care system may move to the private hospitals if salaries or working conditions are better there. The overall concern, therefore, is that the introduction of private hospitals into the existing public health-care system, while reducing waiting lists and providing more health-care services overall, may result in a high-quality system for the wealthy and a low-quality system for lower-income people. Many people think that such a two-tiered health-care system would destroy the equity that the public system was initially designed to promote.

Advocates of private hospitals, on the other hand, argue that to a significant extent, Canada already has a two-tiered system. Many Canadians, frustrated by the long waiting lists in the Canadian public health-care system, travel to the United States for medical treatment. Furthermore, these advocates argue that the lack of public funding in the Canadian health-care system has already caused many doctors and nurses to leave Canada and move to the United States (contributing to Canada's "brain drain" which we discussed in Chapter 13). In this view, the introduction of private hospitals to the Canadian system would not significantly increase the degree to which a two-tiered system already exists. Moreover, it would help stem the flow of nurses and doctors out of Canada, thereby *improving* Canada's overall health-care system.

In the late fall of 1999, the Alberta proposals were very new; only time will tell what will happen in Alberta's health-care system. Other provincial governments are watching Alberta closely.

See Chapter 18 of www.pearsoned.ca/lipsey for an excellent discussion of the government's evolving role in society: John Richards, "The Welfare State as a Valuable Work in Progress," *World Economic Affairs*.

Fee for Service.   One major possibility of cost containment that retains the public nature of the health-care system is to move away from the present system of "fee for service." In the system used in most of Canada, the physician and the hospital charge a prescribed fee for each service that is performed. Since under any provincial health scheme, the doctors and hospitals are assured of receiving these fees from the government, there is no reason for the provider of health services to economize on those services. Indeed, much research shows that the rate of elective surgery—operations that are not necessary for survival but may nonetheless be useful—rises with the ratio of physicians to the population. In areas where there are many physicians, the typical physician has time on his or her hands, and the rate of elective surgery goes up. In areas where doctors are in short supply, much less elective surgery is performed.

This illustrates a general point. The case for the free market is strongest when consumers are the best judges of their own needs. The case for market efficiency is greatly weakened when suppliers, such as physicians, can influence the demand for the product they supply. Thus, in the many cases where judgement is needed to decide among several courses of action, all of which have something to recommend them, the evidence is that doctors often create their own demand.

Health Maintenance Organizations.   Health maintenance organizations (HMOs) provide a possible way around this problem. Large hospitals and large groups of doctors work on what is called a *capitation* basis. This means that the HMO is paid an annual fee for each person registered with it. Since payment is on a per capita basis rather than on a services-rendered basis, there is no incentive to prescribe more care than is needed. Furthermore, to the extent that an individual registers with the same HMO for several years, there is little incentive for the HMO to scimp on necessary services, because scimping today (by ignoring a problem, for example) may mean that much more is spent in the future to correct the problem after it has gotten worse. Thus, one big advantage of HMOs is that each HMO has the incentive to keep its clients healthy *and* to keep costs down. The HMO at Sault Ste. Marie, pioneered by the steelworkers' union and their employers, was an early and successful Canadian example of such an organization.

Income-Support Programs

Canada has various programs that provide assistance for people in financial need—these programs constitute what is often called the "social safety net." The overriding objective of this safety net is to reduce poverty. Though nothing like the serious problem it was in Canada's past and still is in many other countries, poverty remains a matter of real concern to Canadian policy makers.

poverty line   The official government estimate of the annual family income that is required to maintain a minimum adequate standard of living.

Statistics Canada defines the **poverty line** or *low-income cutoff* as the level of income below which the typical household spends more than 55 percent of its income on the three necessities of food, shelter, and clothing. According to Statistics Canada's definition, 17.5 percent of the Canadian population lives below the poverty line. There is considerable debate, however, about the methods used to measure poverty. Some studies find a higher poverty rate, others find a lower rate. But all experts agree that many Canadians live in poverty. Canada has several income-support programs designed to address this important problem.

Income-support programs can be divided into three types. The first is designed to provide income assistance to those individuals whose incomes are deemed to be too low to provide an adequate standard of living. The second is designed to assist specifically those individuals who are in financial need because of temporary job loss—employment insurance. The third is designed to provide income assistance specifically to the elderly. In this subsection, we examine the first type. The next two subsections discuss employment insurance and elderly benefits, respectively.

Welfare.   Social assistance for individuals below retirement age, usually called *welfare,* is mainly a provincial responsibility in Canada. The details of the programs vary considerably across the provinces even though they are partly financed by transfers received from the federal government under the Canada Health and Social Transfer (CHST).

Poverty and homelessness exist in Canada, though there is considerable disagreement about how widespread these problems are.

Suggested reforms to welfare take two main forms. First, most economists advocate reforms of the tax-and-transfer system in an effort to reduce what are called *poverty traps.* **Poverty traps** occur whenever the tax-and-transfer system results in individuals having very little incentive to increase their pre-tax income (by accepting a job, for example) because such an increase in their pre-tax income would make them ineligible for some benefits (such as welfare) and might even make them worse off overall. The presence of such poverty traps reflects a tax-and-transfer system that has been modified in many small steps over many years, the result of which is a plethora of programs often working at cross purposes. The elimination of such poverty traps requires that the tax-and-transfer system be examined in its entirety rather than on a piecemeal basis. *Applying Economic Concepts 18-1* discusses one possible reform of the tax-and-transfer system that maintains progressivity of the system while eliminating poverty traps. This is the idea of the negative income tax.

poverty trap   Occurs whenever individuals have little incentive to increase their pre-tax income because the resulting loss of benefits makes them worse off.

The second type of reform is designed to provide positive incentives to self-help by increasing benefits for recipients who accept work or training for work. A related (and quite contentious) proposal is referred to as *workfare*—the idea that welfare recipients should be required to put in some sort of work in order to be eligible for welfare benefits.[2] In 1997, Ontario reformed its welfare program so that single parents with school-aged children are now required to work in order to receive welfare payments.

Child Benefits.   The support system for families with children has been evolving quite rapidly over the years. Prior to the last change in 1993, the system was a combination of universal family allowance payments and tax credits. In 1993, universality was eliminated. A Child Tax Benefit is now paid according to the number of children in the family and varies according to family income, reaching zero at an income of $60 000.

---

[2]For a wide-ranging discussion of the issues involved in workfare, see John Richards and William Watson (eds.), *Helping the Poor: A Qualified Case for Workfare,* C. D. Howe Institute (Social Policy Challenge No. 5), Toronto, 1995.

APPLYING ECONOMIC CONCEPTS 18-1

Poverty Traps and the Negative Income Tax

A tax is negative when the government pays the taxpayer rather than the other way around. The *negative income tax (NIT)* is designed to increase progressivity by making taxes negative at very low incomes. Such a tax would increase progressivity at the very lowest incomes, and thus help to combat poverty. Furthermore, the NIT achieves its progressivity *without* a schedule of rising marginal income-tax rates and thus potentially avoids some of the extreme disincentive effects that are caused by very high marginal tax rates. Finally, by combining taxes and transfers into a single system, the negative income tax also avoids the occurrence of poverty traps.

The underlying principle of the NIT is that a family of a given size should be *guaranteed* a minimum annual income. The tax system must be designed, however, to guarantee this income without eliminating the household's incentive to be self-supporting.

As an example, consider a system in which each household is guaranteed a minimum annual income of $10 000 and the marginal tax rate is 40 percent. Money can be thought of as flowing in two directions; the government gives every household $10 000, and then every household remits 40 percent of any *earned* income back to the government. The *break-even* level of income in this example is $25 000. All households earning less than $25 000 pay negative taxes overall; they receive more money from the government than they remit in taxes. Households earning exactly $25 000 pay no net taxes—their $10 000 from the government exactly equals the taxes they remit to the government on their earned income. All households earning more than $25 000 pay more than $10 000 in taxes and so they are paying *positive* taxes overall.

The figure shows the operation of this scheme by relating earned income on the horizontal axis to after-tax income on the vertical axis. The 45° line shows what after-tax income would be if there were no taxes. The blue line shows after-tax income with a NIT. It starts at the guaranteed annual income of $10 000, rises by 60 cents for every one dollar increase in earned income, and crosses the 45° line at the break-even level of income, $25 000. The vertical distance between the two lines shows the net transfers between the household and the government.

Employment Insurance

Employment insurance (EI) is a federal program designed to provide temporary income support to workers who lose their jobs. Employers and employees remit EI premiums to the government equal to a small percentage of wages and salaries. These premiums then finance the EI payments to unemployed workers who qualify for the benefits. In boom times, when there is little unemployment, the EI premiums exceed the EI benefits; in times of high unemployment, the benefits exceed the premiums. As a result, the EI program is approximately self-financing over the duration of the average business cycle (6 to 7 years).

EI gives incentives to remain in seasonal jobs and in areas with poor employment prospects and to take EI-financed holidays. Saying that the EI system encourages behaviour that increases unemployment and reduces regional mobility does not say that the unemployed themselves are responsible for the "abuses" of the system that lead to these results. The responsibility lies with the people who designed the incentives and those who strive to preserve them. It is they who can alter the system to make it deliver the intended benefits with fewer incentives for undesired behaviour.

A number of changes have been made during the 1990s. Some respond to the criticisms noted above. For example, rules for qualifying to receive benefits have been tightened, and extended coverage and additional assistance provided for individuals attending approved training courses. Other changes worked in the opposite direction, by expanding coverage into areas some critics had argued were better handled outside of the EI program (for example, expanded parental and sickness benefits).

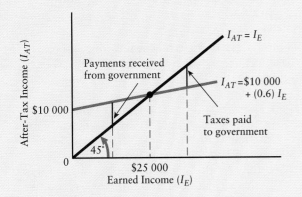

Note that the NIT is a progressive tax, despite the *constant* marginal income-tax rate. To see this, note that a household's *average* tax rate is equal to the total taxes paid divided by total earned income. If I_E is earned income, then

$$\text{Average Tax Rate} = \frac{(0.40) \times I_E - \$10\,000}{I_E}$$

$$= (0.40) - \frac{\$10\,000}{I_E}$$

Thus the average tax rate for the household rises as earned income rises, but the average tax rate is *always less* than the marginal tax rate (40 percent). That the average tax rate rises with earned income means that higher-income households pay a larger fraction of their income in taxes than is paid by lower-income households—that is, the NIT is progressive.

Supporters of the NIT believe that it would be an effective tool for reducing poverty. The NIT provides a minimum level of income as a matter of right, not of charity, and it does so without removing the work incentives for people who are eligible for payments; every dollar earned adds to the after-tax income of the family. Poverty traps are avoided.

One step toward the NIT was taken in 1987 when the personal income-tax system was reformed. In those reforms, many personal exemptions were replaced with tax credits. An exemption reduces an individual's taxable income, whereas a tax credit reduces taxes payable by the amount of the credit. At present, however, the tax credit is not refundable— the credit can be used to reduce taxes payable to zero, but cannot be used to reduce taxes payable to a negative number. Thus, if an individual has taxes payable equal to $5000 and then receives a $6000 tax credit, total taxes payable fall only to zero—any remaining credit ($1000) cannot be claimed back from the government. If the tax credit were fully refundable, however, someone whose taxes on earned income were less than the tax credit would receive the difference from the government. This would be a negative income tax.

Retirement Benefits

There are essentially three components of the system of retirement benefits. These are the Canada Pension Plan (CPP), retirement income support programs such as Old Age Security (OAS) and Guaranteed Income Supplement (GIS), and tax-assisted saving plans.

The Canada Pension Plan (CPP). The CPP provides a basic level of retirement income for all Canadians who have contributed to it over their working lives. (A separate but similar scheme exists in Quebec, the Quebec Pension Plan or QPP.) Unlike some private programs, the pension provided by the CPP is portable—changing jobs does not cause any loss of eligibility. Crucial to understanding the problems faced by the CPP is recognizing that the payments to current retirees are financed by the contributions made by those currently working.

Given the "pay-as-you-go" nature of the Canada Pension Plan, it was inevitable that the CPP would encounter financing problems as the population aged. As the oldest members of the baby boom begin to retire around 2010, the ratio of retirees to contributors will rise rapidly. There will not be enough young workers contributing to the CPP fund to keep the benefits at the generous level received by the current generation of retirees. For young (and even middle-aged) workers today, the CPP is not the good "investment" that it was for people who retired in the past 20 years.

This inevitable financing crisis has led to a great deal of concern, expressed both by young workers and by politicians. By the middle of 1998, politicians of all stripes were discussing the problem. The solution is by no means clear. One alternative is to reduce

See Chapter 18 of
www.pearsoned.ca/lipsey to read Paul
Martin's arguments about reforming
the CPP: "Regaining Canada's Fiscal
Levers," *World Economic Affairs.*

See Chapter 18 of www.pearsoned.ca/lipsey for an interesting discussion of reforms in Hungary's pension system: Antal Deutsch, "Pension Reform for Beginners: The Hungarian Case," *World Economic Affairs.*

benefit payments to retirees. This option, for obvious reasons, is opposed by elderly people who view their current benefits as a contractual obligation of the government. A second alternative is to raise workers' contributions to the CPP fund. The problem with this option, however, is that it worsens what is already a poor "investment" in the eyes of the current young workers. In 1998 the Canadian government introduced modest changes to the CPP, involving both slight reductions in benefit rates and slight increases in contribution rates. Many economists think that the 1998 changes will not be enough to save the CPP.

A third option, one that is getting increasing attention, is the movement toward "privatizing" the Canada Pension Plan. This could be accomplished by having working individuals contribute to privately managed accounts rather than to the CPP fund. In this way, the funds set aside by individuals during their working years would be used to directly finance their retirement—a so-called fully funded pension system. This option would largely solve the problem as seen by the current generation of workers, but it would still require someone (presumably the taxpayers) to finance the pensions of the current retirees and those in the near future.

Retirement Income-Support Programs.   The existing public benefits system for the elderly is in many ways analogous to the child benefits system. There are three parts to the system. First, a universal benefit called the Old Age Security (OAS) program, acts much like the family allowance. Under the OAS program, the government sends out monthly benefit cheques to each Canadian over the qualifying age of 65. Since 1989, however, OAS payments to relatively wealthy individuals have been recaptured by means of a tax "clawback."

Second, in calculating the personal nonrefundable tax credit, provisions available to the elderly serve to reduce their taxes payable. These include a credit available to anyone 65 or older and a pension income credit that offsets the taxes due on the first $1000 of pension income.

Third, an income-tested program, called the Guaranteed Income Supplement (GIS), provides benefits targeted to the low-income elderly. (In some provinces this is supplemented by further targeted assistance.) The GIS provides for most of the progressivity that arises in the elderly benefits system.

Tax-Assisted Saving Plans.   The CPP, OAS, and GIS are programs which involve direct spending on the part of the government. But the government has also introduced programs that require no direct government spending but instead rely on *tax expenditures* (i.e., tax reductions). These tax expenditures are designed to provide incentives for individuals to save more for their retirement. There are essentially two types of programs. The first is through Registered Retirement Savings Plans (RRSPs) and the second is through employer-sponsored Registered Pension Plans (RPPs).

RRSPs provide an incentive for individuals to provide for their own retirement, either because they are not covered by a company plan or because they wish to supplement their company plan. Funds contributed are deductible from taxable income but become fully taxable when they are withdrawn. It is thus a tax deferral plan, and as such it is more valuable the higher one's current taxable income and the lower one's expected future income.

Individuals without RRSPs may still receive some tax assistance for saving if their employer has a Registered Pension Plan. In this case, contributions to the company pension plan (which are often mandatory and are withdrawn directly from the regular paycheque) are tax deductible in a manner similar to an RRSP contribution.

Evaluating the Role of Government

Almost everyone agrees that the government has a major role to play in the economy because of the many sources of possible market failure. Yet there is no consensus that the present level of government intervention is the correct one.

Public Versus Private Sector

When the government raises money by taxation and spends it on an activity, it increases the spending of the public sector and decreases that of the private sector. Since the public sector and the private sector spend on different things, the government is changing the allocation of resources. Is this change good or bad? Should there be more schools and fewer houses or more houses and fewer schools?

For all goods that are produced and sold on the market, consumers' demand has a significant influence on the relative prices and quantities produced and thus on the allocation of the nation's resources. But no market provides relative prices for private houses versus public schools; thus, the choice between allowing money to be spent in the private sector and allowing it to be spent for public goods is a matter to be decided by Parliament and other legislative bodies.

John Kenneth Galbraith's 1958 bestseller, *The Affluent Society*, proclaimed that a correct assignment of marginal utilities would show them to be higher for an extra dollar's worth of public parks, clean water, and education than for an extra dollar's worth of television sets, shampoo, or automobiles. In Galbraith's view, the political process often fails to translate preferences for public goods into effective action; thus more resources are devoted to the private sector and fewer to the public sector than would be the case if the political mechanism were as effective as the market.

The alternative view has many supporters, who agree with Nobel Laureate James Buchanan that society has already reached a point where the value of the *marginal* dollar spent by government is less than the value of that dollar left in the hands of households or firms. These people argue that because bureaucrats are spending other people's money, they care very little about a few million or billion dollars here or there. They have only a weak sense of the opportunity cost of public expenditure and, thus, tend to spend beyond the point where marginal benefits equal marginal costs.

See Chapter 18 of
www.pearsoned.ca/lipsey for an interview with John Kenneth Galbraith: "Unconventional Wisdom," *World Economic Affairs*.

Scope of Government Activity

One of the most difficult problems for the student of the Canadian economic system is to maintain the appropriate perspective about the scope of government activity in the market economy. On the one hand, there are tens of thousands of laws, regulations, and policies that affect firms and households. Many people believe that a general reduction in the role of government is both possible and desirable. On the other hand, private decision makers still have an enormous amount of discretion about what they do and how they do it.

One pitfall is to become so impressed (or obsessed) with the many ways in which government activity impinges on the individual that one fails to see that these only make changes—sometimes large, but often small—in market signals in a system that basically leaves individuals free to make their own decisions. It is in the private sector that most individuals choose their occupations, earn their living, spend their incomes, and live their lives. In this sector too, firms are formed, choose products, live, grow, and sometimes die.

A different pitfall is to fail to see that a significant share of the taxes paid by the private sector is used to buy goods and services that add to the welfare of individuals. By and large, the public sector complements the private sector, doing things the private sector would leave undone or would do differently. For example, Canadians pay taxes that are used to finance expenditures on health and education. But certainly Canadians would continue to use hospitals and attend schools even if the various levels of government did not provide these goods, and instead left more money in peoples' pockets. Thus, in many cases, the government is levying taxes to raise money to finance goods that people would have purchased anyway. To recognize that we often benefit directly from public expenditure in no way denies that there is often waste, and sometimes worse, in public expenditure.

Evolution of Policy

Public policies in operation at any time are not the result of a single master plan that specifies precisely where and how the public sector shall seek to complement or interfere with the workings of the market mechanism. Rather, as individual problems arise, governments attempt to meet them by passing appropriate legislation to deal with the problem. These laws stay on the books, and some become obsolete and unenforceable. This pattern is generally true of systems of law.

Many anomalies exist in our economic policies; for example, laws designed to support the incomes of small farmers have created some agricultural millionaires, and commissions created to ensure competition between firms often end up creating and protecting monopolies. Neither individual policies nor whole programs are above criticism.

In a society that elects its policy makers at regular intervals, however, the majority view on the amount of government intervention that is desirable will have some considerable influence on the amount of intervention that actually occurs. Fundamentally, a free-market system is retained because it is valued for its lack of coercion and its ability to do much of the allocating of society's resources better than any known alternative. But we are not mesmerized by it; we feel free to intervene in pursuit of a better world in which to live. We also recognize, however, that sometimes intervention has proved ineffective or even counterproductive.

S U M M A R Y

Taxation in Canada

● Although the main purpose of the tax system is to raise revenue, tax policy is potentially a powerful device for income redistribution because the progressivity of different kinds of taxes varies greatly.

● The most important taxes in Canada are the personal income tax, the corporate income tax, excise and sales taxes (including the nation-wide GST), and property taxes.

● The progressivity of a tax is determined by how the average tax rate (taxes paid divided by income) changes as income changes. If the average tax rate rises as income rises, the tax is progressive. If the average tax rate falls as income rises, the tax is regressive.

Evaluating the Tax System

LO 3 4

- Evaluating the tax system involves evaluating the efficiency and progressivity of the entire system, rather than of individual taxes within the system. For a given amount of revenue to be raised, efficiency and progressivity can be altered by changing the mix of the various taxes used.
- The total Canadian tax structure is roughly proportional, except for very low-income and very high-income groups (where it is mildly progressive).
- Taxes often generate allocative inefficiency. The allocative inefficiency of a tax is measured by the excess burden.

The greater is the elasticity of demand, the greater will be the excess burden of an excise tax.

- There are potentially important supply-side effects of taxation, as represented by a Laffer curve. A rise in the tax rate initially raises total tax revenue; after some point, however, further increases in the tax rate reduce the incentive to produce taxable income, and so total tax revenue falls. Thus, governments cannot always raise tax revenues by raising tax rates.

Public Expenditure in Canada

LO 5 6

- A large part of public expenditure is for the provision of goods and services. Other types of expenditures, including subsidies, transfer payments to individuals, and intergovernmental transfers are also important.
- Fiscal federalism is the idea that the various fiscal authorities should be coordinated in their spending plans and should have a mechanism for transfers between the various levels of government. Understanding the relationship between the federal government and the various provincial governments is of utmost importance in

understanding many of Canada's most important government spending programs.
- The five pillars of Canadian social policy are:

  1. Education
  2. Health care
  3. Income support programs (welfare and child benefits)
  4. Employment insurance
  5. Retirement benefits (CPP, GIS, OAS, and tax-assisted saving plans)

Evaluating the Role of Government

LO 7

- Government taxation and expenditure has a major effect on the allocation of resources. The government determines how much of society's total output is devoted to education, health care, highways, the armed forces, and so on.
- When evaluating the overall role of government in the economy, we should keep three basic issues in mind:

  1. What is the appropriate mix between public goods and private goods?

  2. Much government activity is directed to providing goods and services that add directly to the welfare of the private sector (health and education, for example).
  3. We should continually reevaluate existing programs; some that were needed in the past may no longer be needed; others may have unintended and undesirable side effects.

K E Y   C O N C E P T S

Tax expenditures
Progressive, proportional, and regressive taxes
The benefit principle and the ability-to-pay principle

Vertical and horizontal equity
Direct and excess burdens of a tax
Disincentive effects of taxation
Transfer payments to individuals

Fiscal federalism
Intergovernmental transfers
Canadian social policy

STUDY EXERCISES

1. Consider an income-tax system that has four tax brackets. The following table shows the tax rate which applies to the income in each tax bracket.

Earned Income	Tax Rate in Bracket
up to $20 000	0%
$20 001-$40 000	15%
$40 001-$80 000	30%
$80 001 and higher	35%

   a. Compute the average income-tax rate at income levels $10 000, $20 000, and each increment of $10 000 up to $120 000.
   b. Compute the marginal income-tax rate for each level of income in part **a**.
   c. On a graph with the tax rates on the vertical axis and income on the horizontal axis, plot the average and marginal tax rates for each level of income.
   d. Is this tax system progressive? Explain.

2. The diagram below shows the market for gasoline in two countries, Midas and Neptune. In Midas, demand is perfectly inelastic; in Neptune, demand is relatively elastic. In both countries, supply is identical and upward sloping. The government in each country imposes an excise tax of $t per litre on the producers of gasoline. This tax shifts the supply curve up by $t.

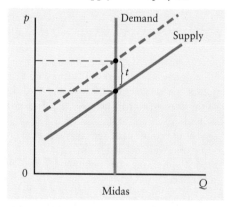

Midas

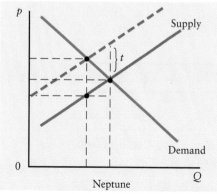

Neptune

   a. In each case, shade the area that is the direct burden of the tax.
   b. In each case, shade the area that is the excess burden of the tax.
   c. In which country does the tax cause the greater allocative inefficiency? Explain.

3. Rank the following taxes according to which has the highest excess burden relative to the direct burden. Start with the highest. Recall that the direct burden of the tax is equal to the revenue that the tax raises.

   a. An excise tax on one brand of breakfast cereal
   b. An excise tax on all breakfast cereals
   c. An excise tax on all food
   d. An excise tax on everything (which is basically what the GST is)

4. Classify each of the following government expenditures as either a transfer payment or a purchase of goods and services. Which ones clearly tend to decrease the inequality of income distribution?

   a. Payments of wages and family living allowances to Canadian peacekeepers overseas
   b. Employment insurance payments to unemployed workers
   c. Payments to provinces for support of highway construction
   d. Pensions of retired Supreme Court justices
   e. Salaries paid to government workers

5. Governments in Canada, at all levels, make considerable transfer payments to individuals and to businesses. This question will show you how significant these transfer payments are. Go to Statistics Canada's website (www.statcan.ca), click on "government" and locate the data on government transfer payments. Then answer the following questions.

   a. For the years 1993–1998, what were the federal transfers for (un)employment insurance benefits? Can you explain why they were falling over those years?
   b. Have total government transfers been growing faster or slower than GDP?
   c. Why did transfers for "family allowance" fall so drastically in 1993? (Hint: Reread the brief section on Child Benefits in the text.)

6. The Negative Income Tax has been proposed as a means of increasing both the efficiency and equity of Canada's tax system (see *Applying Economic Concepts 18-1*). The most basic NIT can be described by two variables, the guaranteed annual income and the marginal tax rate. Suppose the guaranteed annual income is $8000

and the marginal tax rate on *every dollar earned* is 35 percent. With this NIT, after-tax income is given by:

After-tax income = $8000 + (1–0.35) × (Earned Income)

a. On a scale diagram with after-tax income on the vertical axis and earned income on the horizontal axis, draw the NIT relationship between earned income and after-tax income.

b. What is the level of income at which taxes paid on earned income exactly equals the guaranteed annual income?

c. The average tax rate is equal to total *net* taxes paid divided by earned income. Provide an algebraic expression for the average tax rate.

d. On a scale diagram with earned income on the horizontal axis and tax rates on the vertical axis, plot the average and marginal tax rates for the NIT. Is the NIT progressive?

DISCUSSION QUESTIONS

1. In Canada, capitals gains are taxed at three-quarters the rates applicable to other income. Who are the likely beneficiaries of this policy? What are the likely effects on the distribution of income and the allocation of resources? Can you think of both equity and efficiency arguments supporting the special treatment of capital gains?

2. "Taxes on tobacco and alcohol are nearly perfect taxes. They raise lots of revenue and discourage smoking and drinking." In this statement, to what extent are the two effects inconsistent? How is the incidence of an excise tax related to the extent to which it discourages use of the product?

3. Suppose the government spends $1 billion on a new program to provide the poor with housing, better clothing, more food, and better health services.

a. Argue the case for and against assistance of this kind rather than giving the money to the poor to spend as they think best.

b. Should federal transfers to the provinces be conditional grants or grants with no strings attached? Is this issue the same as that raised in **a** or is it a different one?

4. Is the tax deduction allowed for RRSPs progressive or regressive (or neither)?

5. Due to the ageing of the population, the Canada Pension Plan is predicted to become insolvent sometime early in this century. One proposal is to increase the contributions made by workers to the CPP fund. Another proposal is to reduce the benefits paid out to seniors. Who stands to lose and benefit from each proposal? Which proposal is likely to receive more political support?

6. It is common to read articles in the newspapers by people who think Canadians pay too much in taxes. One popular concept is "tax freedom day," the day in the year beyond which you get to keep your income rather than pay it to the government as taxes. For example, if the government collects 33 percent of GDP in taxes, then "tax freedom day" is the 122nd day of the year, May 2.

a. Does everyone in the economy have the same tax freedom day, no matter what their income?

b. How sensible is the concept of "tax freedom day" in a country where the government provides some goods and services to the people that they would otherwise purchase on their own, such as primary education?

PART ELEVEN

International Economics

Does a country always benefit from free trade? If so, why do many people appear to believe the opposite? Can government policy influence a country's pattern of comparative advantage? Is there any connection between the government's budget deficit and the country's current account deficit? How is Canada's exchange rate determined? Should Canada maintain a flexible exchange rate or should it peg the value of its currency to the U.S. dollar? These are the sorts of questions you will be able to answer after reading the final three chapters of this book.*

Chapter 34 explores the gains from trade, and how these gains are based on the important concept of comparative advantage. We discuss the reasons why a country might have a comparative advantage in a particular product, and how some government policies can have the effect of changing a country's pattern of comparative advantage. We will also examine a country's terms of trade, the relative prices at which a country trades with the rest of the world.

In Chapter 35, the focus is on trade policy. We explore the case for free trade as well as the case for protection (we also examine some common but fallacious arguments for protection). We then discuss some methods of protection, such as tariffs, quotas, and nontariff barriers. The chapter then examines current trade policy in Canada, with an emphasis on the North American Free Trade Agreement.

Chapter 36 discusses the exchange rate and the balance of payments. We examine the foreign-exchange market and why the balance of payments accounts are always in balance. The important distinction between fixed exchange rates and flexible exchange rates will be discussed in detail, and we will explore the kinds of events that lead to an appreciation or a depreciation of the Canadian dollar. Finally, we explore three "hot" policy debates, including the cases for and against Canada's adopting a fixed exchange rate.

---

*Chapter 36 does not appear in *Microeconomics*.

CHAPTER 34

The Gains from International Trade

LO LEARNING OBJECTIVES

1 Understand why the gains from trade depend on comparative advantage and not on absolute advantage.

2 Explain the gains from trade due to economies of scale and learning-by-doing.

3 Understand how factor endowments and climate can influence a country's comparative advantage.

4 Explain the law of one price.

5 Explain why countries export some goods and import other goods.

6 Understand what is meant by a country's terms of trade.

Canadian consumers buy cars from Germany, Germans take holidays in Italy, Italians buy spices from Africa, Africans import oil from Kuwait, Kuwaitis buy Japanese cameras, and the Japanese buy Canadian lumber. *International trade* refers to the exchange of goods and services that takes place across international boundaries.

The founders of modern economics were concerned with foreign trade problems. The great eighteenth-century British philosopher and economist David Hume (1711–1776), one of the first to work out the theory of the price system as a control mechanism, developed his concepts mainly in terms of prices in foreign trade. Adam Smith (1723–1790) in his *Wealth of Nations* attacked government restriction of international trade. David Ricardo (1772–1823) developed the basic theory of the gains from trade that is studied in this chapter. The repeal of the Corn Laws—tariffs on the importation of grains into the United Kingdom—and the transformation of that country during the nineteenth century from a country of high tariffs to one of complete free trade were to some extent the result of agitation by economists whose theories of the gains from international trade led them to condemn tariffs.

International trade is becoming increasingly important, not just for Canada but for the world as a whole. As Figure 34-1 shows, the volume of world trade has grown much faster than has world real GDP over the past half-century. Since 1950, the world's real GDP has increased by six times, an average annual growth rate of 3.6 percent. Over the same period, however, the volume of world trade has increased by *seventeen* times, an average annual growth rate of 5.8 percent.

Figure 34-2 shows some data for Canadian trade in 1998. The figure shows the value of Canadian exports and imports in several broad industry groupings. There are three important points to note from the figure. First, international trade is very important for Canada. In 1998, Canada exported and imported over $300 billion in goods—if we added trade in services, the value would rise to over $360 billion. This amounts to over 40 percent of Canada's GDP. Second, exports and imports are roughly the same size, so that the *volume* of trade is much larger than the *balance* of trade—the value of exports equal minus the value of imports. Third, in most of the industry groupings there are significant amounts of both imports and exports. Such *intra-industry trade* will be discussed later in the chapter. Canada does not just export resource products and import manufactured goods; it also imports many resource products and exports many manufactured goods.

In this chapter, we inquire into the gains to living standards that result from such international trade. We find that the source of the gains from trade lies in differing cost conditions among geographical regions. World income is maximized when countries specialize in the products in which they have the lowest opportunity costs of production. These costs are partly determined by natural endowments (geographical and climatic conditions), partly by public policy, and partly by historical accident. We then go on to discuss the terms on which international trade takes place—this refers to the amount that must be exported to obtain a given amount of imports.

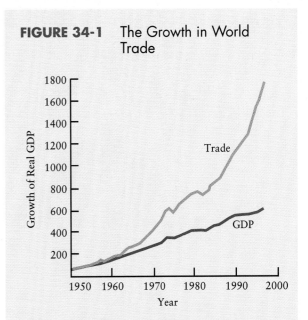

FIGURE 34-1   The Growth in World Trade

The volume of world trade has grown much faster than world GDP over the past fifty years. The figure shows the growth of real GDP and the volume of trade since 1950. Both are expressed as index numbers, set equal to 100 in 1950. Real world GDP has increased six times since 1950; world trade volume has increased seventeen times.

(*Source:* World Trade Organization.)

Sources of the Gains from Trade

An economy that engages in international trade is called an **open economy;** one that does not is called a **closed economy.** A situation in which a country does no foreign trade is called one of *autarky.*

The benefits of trade are easiest to visualize by considering the differences between a world with trade and a world without it. Although politicians often regard foreign trade differently from domestic trade, economists from Adam Smith on have argued that the causes and consequences of international trade are simply an extension of the principles governing domestic trade. What is the advantage of trade among individuals, among groups, among regions, or among countries?

For information on world trade, see the World Trade Organization's website: www.wto.org.

open economy   An economy that engages in international trade.

closed economy   An economy that has no foreign trade.

Interpersonal, Interregional, and International Trade

To begin, consider trade among individuals. Without trade, each person would have to be self-sufficient; each would have to produce all the food, clothing, shelter, medical services, entertainment, and luxuries that he or she consumed. A world of individual self-sufficiency would be a world with extremely low living standards.

Trade among individuals allows people to specialize in activities they can do well and to buy from others the goods and services they cannot easily produce. A good doctor who

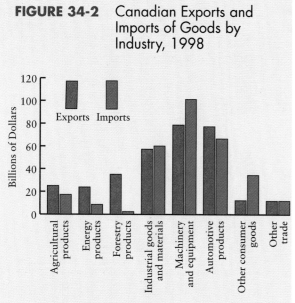

FIGURE 34-2 Canadian Exports and Imports of Goods by Industry, 1998

Canada exports and imports large volumes of goods in most industries. The data show the value of goods exported and imported by industry in 1998 (trade in services is not shown). The total value of goods exported was $322.2 billion; the total value of goods imported was $303.4 billion.

(*Source:* These data are available on Statistics Canada's website: www.statcan.ca.)

is a bad carpenter can provide medical services not only for her own family but also for an excellent carpenter without the training or the ability to practice medicine. Thus, trade and specialization are intimately connected.

Without trade, everyone must be self-sufficient; with trade, people can specialize in what they do well and satisfy other needs by trading.

The same principle applies to regions. Without interregional trade, each region would be forced to be self-sufficient. With trade, each region can specialize in producing products for which it has some natural or acquired advantage. Plains regions can specialize in growing grain, mountain regions in mining and forest products, and regions with abundant power in manufacturing. Cool regions can produce wheat and other crops that thrive in temperate climates, and hot regions can grow such tropical crops as bananas, sugarcane, and coffee. The living standards of the inhabitants of all regions will be higher when each region specializes in products in which it has some natural or acquired advantage and obtains other products by trade than when all regions seek to be self-sufficient.

This same basic principle also applies to nations. A national boundary seldom delimits an area that is naturally self-sufficient. Nations, like regions and individuals, can gain from specialization. More of some goods are produced domestically than residents wish to consume, while residents would like to consume more of other goods than is produced domestically. International trade is necessary to achieve the gains that international specialization makes possible.

With trade, each individual, region, or nation is able to concentrate on producing goods and services that it produces efficiently while trading to obtain goods and services that it does not produce efficiently.

Specialization and trade go hand in hand because there is no motivation to achieve the gains from specialization without being able to trade the goods produced for goods desired. Economists use the term **gains from trade** to embrace the results of both.

gains from trade
The increased output due to the specialization according to comparative advantage that is made possible by trade.

We will examine two sources of the gains from trade. The first is differences among regions of the world in climate and resource endowment that lead to advantages in producing certain goods and disadvantages in producing others. These gains occur even though each country's costs of production are unchanged by the existence of trade. The second source is the reduction in each country's costs of production that results from the greater scale of production that specialization brings.

The Gains from Trade with Constant Costs

In order to focus on differences in countries' conditions of production, suppose that each country's average costs of production are constant. We will use an example below involving only two countries and two products, but the general principles apply as well to the case of many countries and many products.

Absolute Advantage

One region is said to have an **absolute advantage** over another in the production of good X when an equal quantity of resources can produce more X in the first region than in the second. Total production can be increased if each country specializes in producing the product for which it has an absolute advantage.

The gains from specialization make the gains from trade possible. If consumers in both countries are to get the goods they desire in the required proportions, each must export some of the commodity in which it specializes and import commodities in which other countries are specialized.

absolute advantage
The situation that exists when a given amount of resources can produce more of some commodity in one country than in another.

Comparative Advantage

When each product has an absolute advantage over others in a product, the gains from trade are obvious. But what if one country can produce all commodities more efficiently than other countries? This was the question English economist David Ricardo (1722–1823) posed nearly 200 years ago. His answer underlies the theory of *comparative advantage* and is still accepted by economists today as a valid statement of the potential gains from trade.

The gains from specialization and trade depend on the pattern of comparative, not absolute, advantage.

An example will help to make the point. Let us assume that there are two countries, Canada and the European Union. Both countries produce the same two goods, wheat and cloth, but the opportunity costs of producing these two products differ between countries. Recall from Chapter 1 that the opportunity cost is given by the slope of the production-possibility curve, and it tells us how much of one good we have to give up in order to produce one more unit of the other. For the moment we assume that this opportunity cost is constant in each country at all combinations of outputs.

For the purposes of our example we assume that the opportunity cost of producing one kilogram of wheat is 0.60 metres of cloth in Canada, while in the European Union it is 2.0 metres of cloth. These data are summarized in Table 34-1. The second column of this table gives the same information again but expressed as the opportunity cost of one metre of cloth (so the numbers there are reciprocals of the numbers in the first column).

The sacrifice of cloth involved in producing wheat is much lower in Canada than it is in the EU. World wheat production can be increased if Canada rather than the EU produces it. Looking at cloth production, we can see that the loss of wheat involved in producing one unit of cloth is lower in the EU than in Canada. World cloth production can therefore be increased if the EU rather than Canada produces it. The gains from a Canadian shift towards wheat production and an EU shift towards cloth production are shown in Table 34-2.

TABLE 34-1   Opportunity Cost of Wheat and Cloth in Canada and the European Union (EU)

	Wheat (kg)	Cloth (m)
Canada	0.60 m of cloth	1.67 kg of wheat
EU	2.0 m of cloth	0.5 kg of wheat

Comparative advantages reflect opportunity costs that differ between countries. The first column expresses opportunity cost for a kilogram of wheat. The second column expresses the same information for a metre of cloth. Canada has a comparative advantage in wheat production, the EU in cloth.

TABLE 34-2   The Gains from Specialization

	Changes from each country producing one more unit of the product in which it has the lower opportunity cost	
	Wheat (kg)	Cloth (m)
Canada	+1.0	−0.6
EU	−0.5	+1.0
Total	+0.5	+0.4

Whenever opportunity costs differ between countries, specialization can increase the production of both products. These calculations show that there are gains from specialization given the opportunity costs of Table 34-1. To produce one more kilogram of wheat, Canada must sacrifice 0.6 m of cloth. To produce one more metre of cloth, the EU must sacrifice 0.5 kg of wheat. Making both changes increases world production of both wheat and cloth.

FIGURE 34-3   Gains from Trade with Constant Opportunity Costs

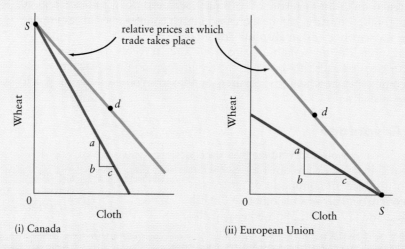

(i) Canada   (ii) European Union

International trade leads to specialization in production and increased consumption possibilities. The purple lines in parts (i) and (ii) represent the production possibility boundaries for Canada and the EU, respectively. In the absence of any international trade these also represent each country's consumption possibilities.

The difference in the slopes of the production possibility boundaries reflects differences in comparative advantage, as shown in Table 34-1. In each part the opportunity cost of increasing production of wheat by the same amount (measured by the distance *ba*) is the amount by which the production of cloth must be reduced (measured by the distance *bc*). The relatively steep production possibility boundary for Canada thus indicates that the opportunity cost of producing wheat in Canada is less than that in the European Union.

If trade is possible at some relative prices between the two countries' opportunity costs of production, each country will specialize in the production of the good in which it has a comparative advantage. In each part of the figure, production occurs at *S* (for specialization); Canada produces only wheat, and the EU produces only cloth.

Consumption possibilities are given by the green line that passes through *S* and has a slope equal to the with-trade relative prices. Consumption possibilities are increased in both countries; consumption may occur at some point such as *d* that involves a combination of wheat and cloth that was not obtainable in the absence of trade.

The gains from trade arise from differing opportunity costs in the two countries.

The slope of the production possibility boundary indicates the opportunity costs, and the existence of different opportunity costs implies comparative advantages that can lead to gains from trade. Figure 34-3 illustrates how two countries can both gain from trade when they have different opportunity costs in production and those opportunity costs are independent of the level of production. An alternative diagrammatic illustration of the gains from trade appears in *Extensions in Theory 34-1* where the production possibility boundary is concave (which means that the opportunity cost for each good is higher when more of that good is being produced).

The conclusions about the gains from trade arising from international differences in opportunity costs are summarized below.

1. Country A has a comparative advantage over Country B in producing a product when the opportunity cost of production in Country A is lower. This implies, however, that it has a comparative *dis*advantage in the other product.

2. Opportunity costs depend on the relative costs of producing two products, not on absolute costs.

3. When opportunity costs are the same in all countries, there is no comparative advantage and there is no possibility of gains from specialization and trade.

4. When opportunity costs differ in any two countries and both countries are producing both products, it is always possible to increase production of both products by a suitable reallocation of resources within each country.

The Gains from Trade with Variable Costs

So far, we have assumed that unit costs are the same whatever the scale of output, and we have seen that there are gains from specialization and trade as long as there are interregional differences in opportunity costs. If costs vary with the level of output, or as experience is acquired via specialization, *additional* gains are possible.

Scale and Imperfect Competition

Real production costs, measured in terms of resources used, generally fall as the scale of output increases. The larger the scale of operations, the more efficiently large-scale machinery can be used and the more a detailed division of tasks among workers is possible. Small countries, such as Switzerland, Belgium, and Israel, whose domestic markets are not large enough to exploit economies of scale would find it prohibitively expensive to become self-sufficient by producing a little bit of everything at very high cost.

Trade allows small countries to specialize and produce a few products at high enough levels of output to reap the available economies of scale.

Wine is a good example of an industry in which there is much intra-industry trade. Canada, for example, imports wine from many countries but also exports Canadian-made wine to the same countries.

Very large countries, such as the United States, have markets large enough to allow the production of most items at home at a scale of output great enough to obtain the available economies of scale. For them, the gains from trade arise mainly from specializing in products in which they have a comparative advantage. Yet, even for such countries, a broadening of their markets permits achieving scale economies in subproduct lines, such as specialty steels or certain lines of clothing.

One of the important lessons learned from patterns of world trade since World War II has concerned imperfect competition and product differentiation. Virtually all of today's manufactured consumer goods are produced in a vast array of differentiated product lines. In some industries, many firms produce this array; in others, only a few firms produce the entire array. In either case, they do not exhaust all available economies of scale. Thus, an increase in the size of the market, even in an economy as large as the United States, may allow the exploitation of some previously unexploited scale economies in individual product lines.

These possibilities were first dramatically illustrated when the European Common Market (now known as the European Union or EU) was set up in the late 1950s. Economists had expected that specialization would occur according to the theory of comparative advantage, with one country specializing in cars, another in refrigerators, another in fashion clothes, another in shoes, and so on. This is not the way it worked out. Instead, much of the vast growth of trade was in *intra-industry* trade—that is, trade of goods or services within the same broad industry. Today, one can buy French, English, Italian, and German fashion goods, cars, shoes, appliances, and a host of other products in London, Paris, Berlin, and Rome. Ships loaded with Swedish furniture bound for London pass ships loaded with English furniture bound for Stockholm, and so on.

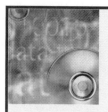

EXTENSIONS IN THEORY 34-1

The Gains From Trade More Generally

Examining the gains from trade is relatively easy in the case where each country's production possibilities boundary is a straight line. What happens in the more realistic case where the production possibilities boundary is concave? As this box shows, the same basic principles of the gains from trade apply to this more complex case.

International trade leads to an expansion of the set of goods that can be consumed in the economy in two ways:

1. by allowing the bundle of goods consumed to differ from the bundle produced; and,

2. by permitting a profitable change in the pattern of production.

Without international trade, the bundle of goods produced is the bundle consumed. With international trade, the consumption and production bundles can be altered independently to reflect the relative values placed on goods by international markets.

Fixed Production

In each part of the figure, the purple curve is the economy's production possibility boundary. In the absence of interna-

tional trade, the economy must consume the same bundle of goods that it produces. Thus, the production possibility boundary is also the consumption possibility boundary. Suppose that the economy produces and consumes at point a, with x_1 of good X and y_1 of good Y, as in part (i) of the figure.

Next suppose that with production point a, good Y can be exchanged for good X internationally. The consumption possibilities are now shown by the line tt drawn through point a. The slope of tt indicates the quantity of Y that exchanges for a unit of X on the international market.

Although production is fixed at point a, consumption can now be anywhere on the line tt. For example, the consumption point could be at b. This could be achieved by exporting y_2y_1 units of Y and importing x_1x_2 units of X. Because point b (and all others on line tt to the right of a) lies outside the production possibility boundary, there are potential gains from trade. Consumers are no longer limited by their own country's production possibilities. Let us suppose that they prefer point b to point a. They have achieved a gain from trade by being allowed to exchange some of their production of good Y for some quantity of good X and thus to consume more of good X than is produced at home.

The same increase in intra-industry trade happened with Canada-U.S. trade over successive rounds of tariff cuts, the most recent being the 1989 Canada-U.S. Free Trade Agreement, and its 1994 expansion into the North American Free Trade Agreement that included Mexico. In several broad industrial groups, including automotive products, machinery, textiles, and forestry products, both imports and exports increased in each country.

What free trade in Europe and North America did was to allow a proliferation of differentiated products, with different countries each specializing in different subproduct lines. Consumers have shown by their expenditures that they value this enormous increase in the range of choice among differentiated products. As Asian countries have expanded into North American and European markets with textiles, cars, and electronic goods, North American and European manufacturers have increasingly specialized their production and now export textiles, cars, and electronic equipment to Asia even while importing similar but differentiated products from Asia.

Learning by Doing

The discussion so far has assumed that costs vary only with the *level* of output. But they may also vary with the *accumulated experience* in producing a product over time.

Variable Production

There is a further opportunity for the expansion of the country's consumption possibilities: With trade, the production bundle may be profitably altered in response to international prices. The country may produce the bundle of goods that is most valuable in world markets. That is represented by the bundle *d* in part (ii). The consumption possibility set is shifted to the line *t't'* by changing production from *a* to *d* and thereby increasing the country's degree of specialization in good *Y*. For every point on the original consumption possibility set *tt*, there are points on the new set *t't'* that allow

more consumption of both goods—for example, compare points *b* and *f*. Notice also that, except at the zero-trade point *d*, the new consumption possibility set lies *everywhere above the production possibility curve*.

The benefits of moving from a no-trade position, such as *a*, to a trading position such as *b* or *f* are the *gains from trade* to the country. When the production of good *Y* is increased and the production of good *X* decreased, the country is able to move to a point such as *f* by producing more of good *Y*, in which the country has a comparative advantage, and trading the additional production for good *X*.

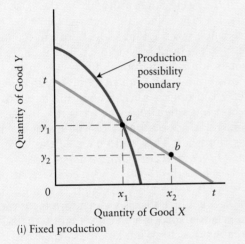

(i) Fixed production

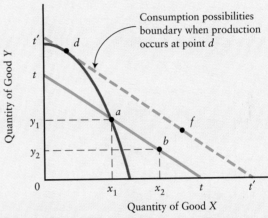

(ii) Variable production

Early economists placed great importance on a concept that is now called **learning by doing**. They believed that as countries gained experience in particular tasks, workers and managers would become more efficient in performing them. As people acquire expertise, costs tend to fall. There is substantial evidence that such learning by doing does occur. It is particularly important in many of today's knowledge-intensive high-tech industries.

The distinction between this phenomenon and the gains from economies of scale is illustrated in Figure 34-4. It is one more example of the difference between a movement along a curve and a shift of the curve.

Recognition of the opportunities for learning by doing leads to an important implication: Policymakers need not accept *current* comparative advantages as given. Through such means as education and tax incentives, they can seek to develop new comparative advantages.[1] Moreover, countries cannot complacently assume that their existing comparative advantages will persist. Misguided education policies, the wrong tax incentives, or policies that discourage risk taking can lead to the rapid erosion of a country's comparative advantage in particular products.

learning by doing
The increase in output per worker that often results as workers learn through repeatedly performing the same tasks. It causes a downward shift in the average cost curve.

---

[1]They can also foolishly use such policies to develop industries in which they do not have and will never achieve comparative advantages.

FIGURE 34-4   Gains from Trade Due to Scale and Learning Effects

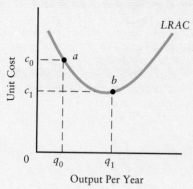

(i) Economies of scale

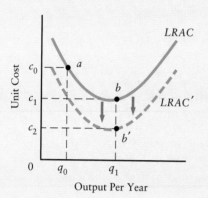

(ii) Learning by doing

Specialization may lead to gains from trade by permitting economies of larger-scale output, by leading to downward shifts of cost curves, or both. Consider a country that wishes to consume the quantity q_0. Suppose that it can produce that quantity at an average cost per unit of c_0. Suppose further that the country has a comparative advantage in producing this product and can export the quantity q_0q_1 if it produces q_1. This may lead to cost savings in two ways.

As shown in part (i), the increased level of production of q_1 compared to q_0 permits it to *move along* its cost curve from a to b, thereby reducing costs per unit to c_1. This is an economy of scale.

As shown in part (ii), as workers and management become more experienced, they may be able to produce at lower costs. This is learning by doing. The downward *shift*, shown by the arrows, lowers the cost of producing every unit of output. At output q_1, costs per unit fall to c_2. The movement from a to b' incorporates both economies of scale and learning by doing.

Sources of Comparative Advantage

We have seen that comparative advantage is the source of the gains from trade. But why do comparative advantages exist? Since a country's comparative advantage depends on its opportunity costs, we could also ask: Why do different countries have different opportunity costs?

Different Factor Endowments

The traditional answer to this question was provided early in the twentieth century by two Swedish economists, Eli Heckscher and Bertil Ohlin. Ohlin was subsequently awarded the Nobel Prize in economics for his work in the theory of international trade. Their explanation for international differences in opportunity costs is now incorporated in the Heckscher-Ohlin model. According to their theory, the international cost differences that form the basis for comparative advantage arise because factor endowments differ across countries. This is often called the *factor endowment theory of comparative advantage.*

To see how this theory works, consider the prices for various types of goods in countries *in the absence of trade.* A country that is well endowed with fertile land but has a small population (like Canada) will find that land is cheap but labour is expensive. It will therefore produce land-intensive agricultural goods cheaply and labour-intensive goods, such as machine tools, only at high cost. The reverse will be true for a second country that is small in size but possesses abundant and efficient labour (like Japan). As a result, the first country will have a comparative advantage in agricultural production and the second in goods that use much labour and little land.

According to the Heckscher-Ohlin theory, countries have comparative advantages in the production of goods that use intensively the factors of production with which they are abundantly endowed.

For example, Canada is abundantly endowed with forests relative to most other countries. According to the Hecksher-Ohlin theory, Canada has a comparative advantage in goods that use forest products intensively, such as newsprint, paper, raw lumber, and wooden furniture. In contrast, relative to most other countries, Canada is sparsely endowed with labour. Thus, Canada has a comparative disadvantage in goods that use labour intensively, such as cotton or many other textile products.

Different Climates

The factor endowment theory has considerable power to explain comparative advantage but it does not provide the whole explanation. One additional influence comes from all those natural factors that can be called *climate* in the broadest sense. If you combine land, labour, and capital in the same way in Nicaragua and in Iceland, you will not get the same output of most agricultural goods. Sunshine, rainfall, and average temperature also matter. If you seek to work with wool or cotton in dry climates, you will get different results than when you work in damp climates. (You can, of course, artificially create any climate you wish in a factory, but it costs money to create what is freely provided elsewhere.)

Canada is extremely well endowed with forests. It is no surprise, therefore, that it has a comparative advantage in a whole range of forestry products.

Climate affects comparative advantage.

Of course, if we consider "warm weather" a factor of production, then we could simply say that countries like Nicaragua are better endowed with that factor than countries like Iceland. In this sense, explanations of comparative advantage based on different climates are really just a special case of explanations based on factor endowments.

Acquired Comparative Advantage

Today it is clear that many comparative advantages are *acquired*. Further, they can change. Thus, comparative advantage should be viewed as being *dynamic* rather than static. New industries are seen to depend more on human capital than on fixed physical capital or natural resources. The skills of a computer designer, a videogame programmer, or a sound mix technician are acquired by education and on-the-job training. Natural endowments of energy and raw materials cannot account for Silicon Valley's leadership in computer technology, for Canada's prominence in communications technology or for Switzerland's prominence in private banking. When countries find their former dominance (based on comparative advantage) in such smokestack industries as cars and steel declining, their firms need not sit idly by. Instead, they can begin to adapt by developing new areas of comparative advantage.

Contrasts

This modern view is in sharp contrast with the traditional assumption that cost structures based largely on a country's natural endowments lead to a given pattern of international comparative advantage. The traditional view suggests that a government interested in maximizing its citizens' material standard of living should encourage specialization of production in goods where it currently has a comparative advantage. If all countries follow this advice, the theory predicts, each will be specialized in a relatively narrow range of distinct products. The British will produce engineering products, Canadians will be producers of resource-based primary products, Americans will be farmers and factory workers, Central Americans will be banana and coffee growers, and so on.

There are surely elements of truth in both extreme views. It would be unwise to neglect resource endowments, climate, culture, social patterns, and institutional arrangements. But it would also be unwise to assume that all of them were innate and immutable.

To some extent, these views are reconciled by the theory of human capital, which is a topic we discussed in *Microeconomics*. Comparative advantages that depend on human capital are consistent with traditional Heckscher-Ohlin theory. The difference is that this type of capital is acquired through conscious decisions relating to such matters as education and technical training.

The Determination of Trade Patterns

Comparative advantage has been the central concept in our discussion about the sources of the gains from trade. If Canada has a comparative advantage in lumber and Italy has a comparative advantage in shoes, then the total output of lumber and shoes could be increased if Canada specialized in the production of lumber and Italy specialized in the production of shoes. With such patterns of specialization, Canada would naturally export lumber to Italy and Italy would export shoes to Canada.

It is one thing to discuss the potential gains from trade if countries specialized in the production of particular goods and exported these to other countries. But do *actual* trade patterns occur along the lines of comparative advantage? In this section of the chapter we use a simple demand-and-supply model to examine why Canada exports some products and imports others. We will see that comparative advantage, whether natural or acquired, does indeed play a central role.

There are some products, such as coffee and mangos, that Canada does not produce (and will probably never produce). Any domestic consumption of these product must therefore be satisfied by imports from other countries. At the other extreme, there are some products, such as nickel or potash, where Canada is one of the world's major suppliers, and demand in the rest of the world must be satisfied partly by exports from Canada. There are also some products, such as houses, that are so expensive to transport that every country produces approximately what it consumes.

Our interest in this section is in the many intermediate cases in which Canada is only one of many producers of an internationally traded product, as with beef, oil, copper, wheat, lumber, and newsprint. Will Canada be an exporter or an importer of such products? And what is the role played by comparative advantage?

For data on Canadian trade by industry and by country, see Statistics Canada's website: www.statcan.ca. Go to "Canadian Statistics" and then "Trade."

The Law of One Price

Whether Canada imports or exports a product for which it is only one of many producers depends to a great extent on the product's price. This brings us to what economists call the *law of one price*.

The law of one price states that when a product which can be cheaply transported is traded throughout the entire world, it will tend to have a single worldwide price.

Many basic products, such as copper wire, steel pipe, iron ore, and computer RAM chips, fall within this category. The world price for each good is the price that equates the quantity demanded worldwide with the quantity supplied worldwide.

The world price of an internationally traded product may be influenced greatly, or only slightly, by the demand and supply coming from any one country. The extent of one country's influence will depend on how important its demands and supplies are in relation to the worldwide totals.

The simplest case for us to study arises when the country, which we will take to be Canada, accounts for only a small part of the total worldwide demand and supply. In this case, Canada does not itself produce enough to influence the world price significantly. Similarly, Canadian purchases are too small a proportion of worldwide demand to affect the world price in any significant way. Producers and consumers in Canada thus face a world price that they cannot influence by their own actions.

Notice that in this case, the price that rules in the Canadian market must be the world price (adjusted for the exchange rate between the Canadian dollar and the foreign currency). The law of one price says that this must be so. What would happen if the Canadian domestic price diverged from the world price? If the Canadian price were below the world price, no supplier would sell in the Canadian market because more money could be made by selling abroad. The absence of supply to the Canadian market would thus drive up the Canadian price. Conversely, if the Canadian domestic price were above the worldwide price, no buyers would buy from a Canadian seller because money could be saved by buying abroad. The absence of demand on the Canadian market would thus drive down the Canadian price.

The Pattern of Foreign Trade

Let us now see what determines the pattern of international trade in such circumstances.

An Exported Product

To determine the pattern of Canadian trade, we first show the Canadian domestic demand and supply curves for some product, say, lumber. This is done in Figure 34-5. The intersection of these two curves tells us what the price and quantity would be *if there were no foreign trade*. Now compare this no-trade price with the world price of that product.[2] If the world price is higher, the actual price in Canada will exceed the no-trade price. In this situation there will be an excess of Canadian supply over Canadian demand. Domestic producers want to sell q_2 units of lumber but domestic consumers want to buy only q_1 units. If Canada were a closed economy, such excess supply would drive the price down to p_d. But in an open economy with a world price of p_w, this excess supply gets exported to Canada's trading partners.

Countries export products whose world price exceeds the price that would exist domestically if there were no foreign trade.

What is the role of comparative advantage in this analysis? We have said that Canada will export lumber if the world price exceeds Canada's no-trade price. Note that in a competitive market the price of the product reflects the product's marginal cost, which in turn reflects the opportunity cost of producing the product. That Canada's no-trade price for lumber is lower than the world price reflects the fact that the opportunity cost of producing lumber in Canada is less than the opportunity cost of producing it in the rest of the world. Thus, by exporting goods which have a low no-trade price, Canada is exporting the goods in which it has a comparative advantage.

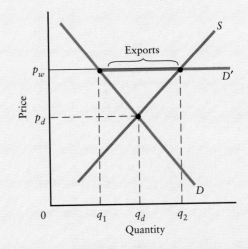

FIGURE 34-5   An Exported Good

Exports occur whenever there is excess supply domestically at the world price. The domestic demand and supply curves are D and S, respectively. The domestic price in the absence of foreign trade is p_d, with q_d produced and consumed domestically. The world price of p_w is higher than p_d. At p_w, q_1 is demanded while q_2 is supplied domestically. The excess of domestic supply over the domestic demand is exported.

The Export Development Corporation is a crown corporation devoted to improving Canada's export prospects. For information about Canada's exports, check out its website: www. edc–see.ca.

---

[2]If the world price is stated in terms of some foreign currency (as it often is), then the price must be converted into Canadian dollars using the current exchange rate between the foreign currency and Canadian dollars.

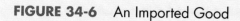

FIGURE 34-6   An Imported Good

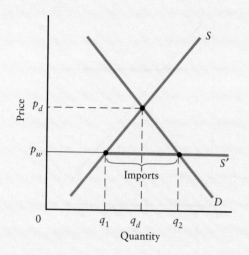

Imports occur whenever there is excess demand domestically at the world price. The domestic demand and supply curves are D and S, respectively. The domestic price in the absence of foreign trade is p_d, with q_d produced and consumed domestically. The world price of p_w is less than p_d. At the world price q_2 is demanded, whereas q_1 is supplied domestically. The excess of domestic demand over domestic supply is satisfied through imports.

Countries export the goods for which they are low-cost producers. That is, they export goods in which they have a comparative advantage.

An Imported Product

Now consider some other product—for example, computer RAM chips. Once again, look first at the domestic demand and supply curves, shown this time in Figure 34-6. The intersection of these curves determines the no-trade price that would rule if there were no foreign trade. The world price of RAM chips is below the Canadian no-trade price so that, at the price ruling in Canada, domestic demand is larger and domestic supply is smaller than if the no-trade price had ruled. The excess of domestic demand over domestic supply is met by imports.

Countries import products whose world price is less than the price that would exist domestically if there were no foreign trade.

Again, this analysis can be restated in terms of comparative advantage. The high Canadian no-trade price of RAM chips reflects the fact that RAM chips are more costly to produce in Canada than elsewhere in the world. This high cost means that Canada has a comparative disadvantage in RAM chips. So Canada imports goods for which it has a comparative disadvantage.

Countries import the goods for which they are high-cost producers. That is, they import goods for which they have a comparative disadvantage.

Is Comparative Advantage Obsolete?

In the debate preceding the signing of both the Canada-U.S. Free Trade Agreement and the North American Free Trade Agreement (NAFTA), some opponents argued that the agreements relied on an outdated view of the gains from trade based on comparative advantage. The theory of comparative advantage was said to be obsolete.

In spite of such assertions, comparative advantage remains an important economic concept. At any one time—because comparative advantage is reflected in international relative prices, and these relative prices determine what goods a country will import and what it will export—the operation of the price system will result in trade that follows the current pattern of comparative advantage. For example, if Canadian costs of producing steel are particularly low relative to other Canadian costs, Canada's price of steel will be low by international standards, and steel will be a Canadian export (which it is). If Canada's costs of producing textiles are particularly high relative to other Canadian costs, Canada's price of textiles will be high by international standards, and Canada will import textiles (which it does). Thus, there is no reason to change the view that Ricardo long ago expounded: *Current comparative advantage is a major determinant of trade under free-market conditions.*

What has changed, however, is economists' views about the *determinants* of comparative advantage. It now seems that current comparative advantage may be more open to change by private entrepreneurial activities and by government policy than used to be thought. Thus, what is obsolete is the belief that a country's current pattern of comparative advantage, and hence its current pattern of imports and exports, must be accepted as given and unchangeable.

The theory that comparative advantage determines trade flows is not obsolete, but the theory that comparative advantage is completely determined by forces beyond the reach of public policy has been discredited.

It is one thing to observe that it is *possible* for governments to influence a country's pattern of comparative advantage. It is quite another to conclude that it is *advisable* for them to try. The case in support of a specific government intervention requires that (1) there is scope for governments to improve on the results achieved by the free market, (2) the costs of the intervention be less than the value of the improvement to be achieved, and (3) governments will actually be able to carry out the required interventionist policies (without, for example, being sidetracked by considerations of electoral advantage).

The Terms of Trade

We have seen that world production can be increased when countries specialize in the production of the products in which they have a comparative advantage and then trade with one another. We now ask: How will these gains from specialization and trade be shared among countries? The division of the gain depends on what is called the **terms of trade**, which relate to the quantity of imported goods that can be obtained per unit of goods exported. They are measured by the ratio of the price of exports to the price of imports.

terms of trade   The ratio of the average price of a country's exports to the average price of its imports, both averages usually being measured by index numbers.

A rise in the price of imported goods, with the price of exports unchanged, indicates a *fall in the terms of trade*; it will now take more exports to buy the same quantity of imports. Similarly, a rise in the price of exported goods, with the price of imports unchanged, indicates a *rise in the terms of trade*; it will now take fewer exports to buy the same quantity of imports. Thus, the ratio of these prices measures the amount of imports that can be obtained per unit of goods exported.

Because actual international trade involves many countries and many products, a country's terms of trade are computed as an index number:

$$\text{Terms of Trade} = \frac{\text{Index of Export Prices}}{\text{Index of Import Prices}} \times 100$$

A rise in the index is referred to as a *favourable* change in a country's terms of trade (sometimes called a terms of trade *improvement*). A favourable change means that fewer goods have to be exported per unit of goods imported than was previously the case. For example, if the export price index rises from 100 to 120 while the import price index rises from 100 to 110, the terms-of-trade index rises from 100 to 109. At the new terms of trade, a unit of imports will require approximately 9 percent fewer exports than at the old terms of trade.

A decrease in the index of the terms of trade, called an *unfavourable* change (or a terms of trade *deterioration*), means that the country can import less in return for any given amount of exports, or, equivalently, it must export more to pay for any given

FIGURE 34-7   Canada's Terms of Trade, 1970–1998

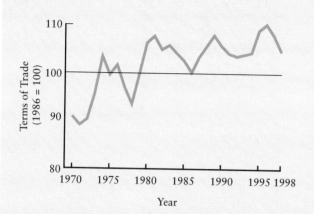

Canada's terms of trade have been quite variable over the past 30 years, but they have also displayed a long-term improvement. The data shown are Canada's terms of trade—the ratio of an index of Canadian export prices to an index of Canadian import prices. As the relative prices of lumber, oil, wheat, electronic equipment, textiles, fruit, and other products change, the terms of trade naturally change. Especially notable are the sharp increases in 1973 and 1980, caused by the OPEC oil shocks. The decline in the late 1990s is due to the reduction in world commodity prices following the Asian crisis in 1997-1998.

(Source: Economic Reference Tables, Department of Finance, and Bank of Canada.)

amount of imports. For example, the sharp rise in oil prices in the 1970s led to large unfavourable shifts in the terms of trade of oil-importing countries. When oil prices fell sharply in the mid 1980s, the terms of trade of oil-importing countries changed favourably. The converse was true for oil-exporting countries.

Canada's terms of trade since 1970 are shown in Figure 34-7. As is clear, the terms of trade are quite variable, reflecting frequent changes in the relative prices of different products. Also clear from the figure is that Canada's terms of trade have displayed a long-term improvement over the past 30 years.

Note the deterioration in Canada's terms of trade in the late 1990s. Deep recessions in several Southeast Asian countries contributed to a dramatic fall in world commodity prices between the middle of 1997 and the end of 1998. Many of these commodities—copper, gold, oil, newsprint, lumber, pork—are important Canadian exports. Thus, a decline in their price implies a deterioration in Canada's terms of trade.

S U M M A R Y

Sources of the Gains from Trade

- One country (or region or individual) has an absolute advantage over another country (or region or individual) in the production of a specific product when, with the same input of resources in each country, it can produce more of the product than can the other.
- Comparative advantage is the relative advantage one country enjoys over another in the production of various products. It occurs whenever countries have different

opportunity costs of producing particular goods. World production of all products can be increased if each country transfers resources into the production of the products in which it has a comparative advantage.

- The most important proposition in the theory of the gains from trade is that trade allows all countries to obtain the goods in which they do not have a comparative advantage at a lower opportunity cost than they would face if they were to produce all products for themselves; specialization and trade therefore allow all countries to have more of all products than they could have if they tried to be self-sufficient.

- As well as gaining the advantages of specialization arising from comparative advantage, a nation that engages in trade and specialization may realize the benefits of economies of large-scale production and of learning by doing.

- Classical theory regarded comparative advantage as largely determined by natural resource endowments that are difficult to change. Economists now believe that some comparative advantages can be acquired and consequently can be changed. A country may, in this view, influence its role in world production and trade. Successful intervention leads to a country's acquiring a comparative advantage; unsuccessful intervention fails to develop such an advantage.

The Determination of Trade Patterns

- The law of one price says that internationally traded goods that are inexpensive to transport must sell at the same price in all countries. Economists call this the world price.

- Countries will export a good when the world price exceeds the price that would exist in the country if there were no trade. The low no-trade price reflects a low opportunity cost and thus a comparative advantage in that good. Thus, countries export goods for which they have a comparative advantage.

- Countries will import a good when the world price is less than the price that would exist in the country if there were no trade. The high no-trade price reflects a high opportunity cost and thus a comparative disadvantage in that good. Thus, countries import goods for which they have a comparative disadvantage.

The Terms of Trade

- The terms of trade refer to the ratio of the prices of goods exported to the prices of those imported. This determines the quantity of imports that can be obtained per unit of exports. The terms of trade determine how the gains from trade are shared.

- A favourable change in the terms of trade—a rise in export prices relative to import prices—means that a country can acquire more imports per unit of exports, and vice versa.

K E Y   C O N C E P T S

Interpersonal, interregional, and international specialization

Absolute advantage and comparative advantage

Opportunity cost and comparative advantage

The gains from trade: specialization, scale economies, and learning by doing

The sources of comparative advantage

Factor endowments

Acquired comparative advantage

The law of one price

The terms of trade

STUDY EXERCISES

1. The following diagram shows the production possibilities boundary for Arcticland, a country that produces two goods, ice and fish. Labour is the only factor of production.

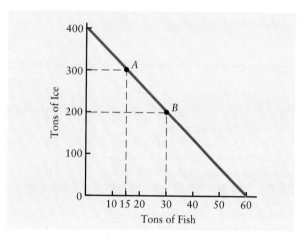

a. Beginning at any point on Arcticland's production possibilities boundary, what is the opportunity cost of producing 10 more tons of fish?
b. Beginning at any point on Arcticland's production possibilities boundary, what is the opportunity cost of producing 100 more tons of ice?

2. The following table shows the production of wheat and corn in Brazil and Mexico. Assume that both countries have one million acres of arable land.

	Brazil	Mexico
Wheat	90 bushels per acre	50 bushels per acre
Corn	30 bushels per acre	20 bushels per acre

a. Which country has the absolute advantage in wheat? In corn? Explain.
b. Which country has the comparative advantage in wheat? In corn? Explain.
c. Explain why one country can have an absolute advantage in both goods but cannot have a comparative advantage in both goods.
d. On a scale diagram with wheat on the horizontal axis and corn on the vertical axis, draw each country's production possibilities boundary.
e. What is shown by the slope of each country's production possibilities boundary? Be as precise as possible.

3. The following diagrams show the production possibilities boundaries for Canada and France, both of which produce two goods, wine and lumber.

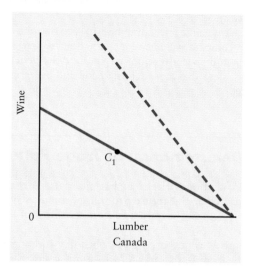

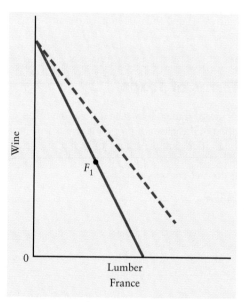

a. Which country has the comparative advantage in lumber? Explain.
b. Which country has the comparative advantage in wine? Explain.
c. Suppose that Canada and France are initially not trading with each other and are producing at points C_1 and F_1, respectively. Suppose when trade is introduced, the free-trade relative prices are shown by the dashed line. Which combination of goods will each country now produce?
d. In this case, what will be the pattern of trade for each country?

4. The diagrams below show the Canadian markets for newsprint and machinery, which we assume to be competitive.

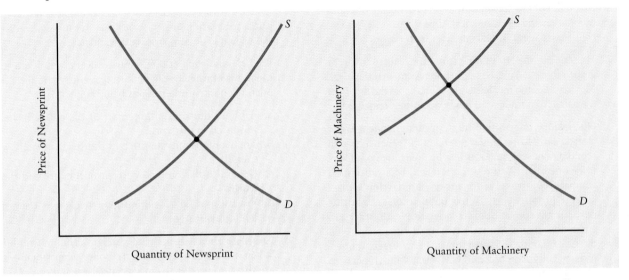

Quantity of Newsprint

Quantity of Machinery

a. Suppose there is no international trade. What would be the equilibrium price and quantity in the Canadian newsprint and machinery markets?

b. Now suppose that Canada is open to trade with the rest of the world. If the world price of newsprint is *higher* than the price of newsprint from part **a**, what will happen to the levels of domestic production and consumption? Explain.

c. If the world price of machinery is lower than the price of machinery from part **a**, what happens to the levels of domestic consumption and production? Explain.

5. The table below shows indexes for the prices of imports and exports over several years for a hypothetical country.

Year	Import Prices	Export Prices	Terms of Trade
1996	90	110	—
1997	95	87	—
1998	98	83	—
1999	100	100	—
2000	102	105	—
2001	100	112	—
2002	103	118	—

a. Compute the terms of trade in each year for this country and fill in the table.

b. In which years does the terms of trade improve?

c. In which years does the terms of trade deteriorate?

d. Explain why a terms of trade "improvement" is good for the country.

6. For each of the following events, explain the likely effect on Canada's terms of trade. Your existing knowledge of Canada's imports and exports should be adequate to answer this question.

a. A hurricane damages much of Brazil's coffee crop.

b. OPEC countries succeed in significantly restricting the world supply of oil.

c. Several new large copper mines come into production in Chile.

d. A major recession in Southeast Asia reduces the world demand for pork.

DISCUSSION QUESTIONS

1. Adam Smith saw a close connection between the wealth of a nation and its willingness "freely to engage" in foreign trade. What is the connection?

2. One critic of the North American Free Trade Agreement argued that "it can't be in our interest to sign this deal; Mexico gains too much from it." What does the theory of the gains from trade have to say about that criticism?

3. One product innovation that appears imminent is the electric car. However, development costs are high and economies of scale and learning by doing are both likely to be operative. As a result, there will be a substantial competitive advantage for those who develop a marketable product early. What implications might this have for government policies toward North American automobile manufacturers' activities in this area? Should the Canadian or U.S. governments encourage joint efforts by Chrysler, Ford, and GM, even if this appears to lessen competition between them?

4. Studies of Canadian trade patterns have shown that industries with high wages are among the largest and fastest-growing export sectors. One example is the computer software industry. Does this finding contradict the principle of comparative advantage?

5. Predict what each of the following events would do to the terms of trade of the importing country and the exporting country, other things being equal.

   a. A blight destroys a large part of the coffee beans produced in the world.
   b. The Koreans cut the price of the steel they sell to Canada.
   c. General inflation of 4 percent occurs around the world.
   d. Violation of OPEC output quotas leads to a sharp fall in the price of oil.

6. Are there always benefits to specialization and trade? When are the benefits greatest? Under what situations are there *no* benefits from specialization and trade?

CHAPTER 35

Trade Policy

 LEARNING OBJECTIVES

1 Understand the various situations in which a country may rationally choose to protect some industries.

2 Recognize the most common fallacious arguments in favour of protection.

3 Explain the effects of placing a tariff or a quantity restriction on an imported good.

4 Recognize that trade-remedy laws are sometimes just thinly disguised protection.

5 Explain the difference between trade creation and trade diversion.

6 Know the main features of the North American Free Trade Agreement.

Conducting business in a foreign country is not always easy. Differences in language, in local laws and customs, and in currency often complicate transactions. Our concern in this chapter, however, is not with these complications but with government policy toward international trade, which is called **trade policy.** At one extreme is a policy of free trade—that is, an absence of any form of government interference with the free flow of international trade. Any departure from free trade designed to protect domestic industries from foreign competition is called **protectionism.**

We begin by briefly restating the case for free trade and then go on to study various valid and invalid arguments that are commonly advanced for some degree of protection. We then explore some of the methods that are commonly used to restrict trade, such as tariffs and quotas. Finally, we examine the many modern institutions designed to foster freer trade on either a global or a regional basis. Of central importance to Canada is the North American Free Trade Agreement (NAFTA).

trade policy
A government's policy involving restrictions placed on international trade.

protectionism Any government policy that interferes with free trade in order to give some protection to domestic industries against foreign competition.

Free Trade or Protection?

Today, most governments accept the proposition that a relatively free flow of international trade is desirable for the health of their individual economies. But heated debates still occur over trade policy. Should a country permit the completely free flow of international trade, or should it sometimes seek to protect its local producers from foreign competition? If some protection is desired, should it be achieved by tariffs or by nontariff barriers? **Tariffs** are taxes designed to raise the price of foreign goods. **Nontariff barriers (NTBs)** are devices other than tariffs that are designed to reduce the flow of imports;

tariff A tax applied on imports of goods or services.
nontariff barriers (NTBs) Restrictions other than tariffs designed to reduce the flow of imported goods or services.

examples are quotas and customs procedures that are deliberately more cumbersome than necessary.

The Case for Free Trade

The case for free trade was presented in Chapter 34. Comparative advantages arise whenever countries have different opportunity costs. Free trade encourages all countries to specialize in producing products in which they have a comparative advantage. This in turn maximizes world production and hence maximizes average world living standards (as measured by the world's per capita GDP).

Free trade does not necessarily make *everyone* better off than they would be in its absence. For example, reducing an existing tariff often results in individual groups receiving a smaller share of a larger world output so that they lose even though the average person gains. If we ask whether it is *possible* for free trade to improve everyone's living standards, the answer is "yes." But, if we ask whether free trade always does so, the answer is "not necessarily."

Given that all countries can be better off by specializing in those goods in which they have a comparative advantage, it is puzzling that most countries of the world continue in some way to restrict the flow of trade. Why do tariffs and other barriers to trade continue to exist two centuries after Adam Smith and David Ricardo stated the case for free trade? Is there a valid case for some protection?

The Case for Protection

Two kinds of arguments for protection are commonly offered. The first concerns national objectives *other than* maximizing total income; the second concerns the desire to increase one country's national income, possibly at the expense of the national incomes of other countries.

Objectives Other than Maximizing National Income

It is possible to believe that a country's national income is maximized with free trade and yet rationally oppose free trade because of a concern with other policy objectives.

Noneconomic Advantages of Diversification.   Comparative advantage might dictate that a small country should specialize in producing a narrow range of products. However, there may be social advantages in a more diverse economy. Citizens would be given a wider range of occupations, and the social and psychological advantages of diversification may more than compensate for the reduction in per capita output.

Countries whose economies are based on the production of only a few goods face risks from fluctuations in world prices. For this reason, protection to promote diversification may be viewed as desirable.

Risks of Specialization.   For a very small country, specializing in the production of only a few products—though dictated by comparative advantage—might involve risks that the country does not wish to take. One such risk is that technological advances may render its basic product obsolete. Another risk, especially for countries specialized in producing a small range of agricultural products, is that swings in world prices lead to large swings in national income. Everyone understands these risks, but there is debate about what governments can do about it. The pro-tariff argument is that the government can encourage a more diversified economy by protecting industries that otherwise could not compete. Opponents argue that governments, being naturally influenced by political motives, are poor judges of which industries can be protected in order to produce diversification at a reasonable cost.

Protection of Specific Groups.

Although free trade—and specialization according to comparative advantage—will maximize per capita GDP over the whole economy, some specific groups may have higher incomes under protection than under free trade. Of particular interest in Canada and the United States has been the effect that greater international trade has on the incomes of unskilled workers.

Consider the ratio of skilled workers to unskilled workers. There are plenty of both types throughout the world. Compared to much of the rest of the world, however, Canada has more skilled and fewer unskilled people. When trade is expanded because of a reduction in tariffs, Canada will tend to export goods made by its abundant skilled workers and import goods made by unskilled workers. (This is the basic prediction of the *factor endowment theory* of comparative advantage that we discussed in Chapter 34.) Because Canada is now exporting more goods made by skilled labour, the domestic demand for such labour rises. Because Canada is now importing more goods made by unskilled labour, the domestic demand for such labour falls. This specialization according to comparative advantage raises average Canadian living standards, but it will also tend to raise the wages of skilled Canadian workers relative to the wages of unskilled Canadian workers.

If increasing trade has these effects, then reducing trade by raising trade barriers can have the opposite effects. Raising trade barriers may raise the incomes of unskilled Canadian workers, giving them a larger share of a smaller total GDP. The conclusion is that trade restrictions can improve the earnings of one group whenever the restrictions increase the demand for that group's services. This is done, however, at the expense of a reduction in *overall* national income and hence the country's average living standards.

This analysis is important because it reveals both the grain of truth and the dangers that lie behind the resistance to reductions in trade restrictions on the part of some labour groups and some organizations whose main concern is with the poor.

Social and distributional concerns may lead to the rational adoption of protectionist policies. But the cost of such protection is a reduction in the country's average living standards.

Economists cannot say that it is irrational for a society to sacrifice some income to achieve other goals. But economists can do three things when presented with such arguments for adopting protectionist measures. First, they can ask if the proposed measures really do achieve the ends suggested. Second, they can calculate the cost of the measures in terms of lowered living standards. Third, they can see if there are alternative means of achieving the stated goals at lower cost in terms of lost national income.

Maximizing One Country's National Income

Next we consider several arguments for the use of tariffs when the objective is to maximize a country's national income.

To Alter the Terms of Trade.

Tariffs can be used to change the terms of trade in favour of a country that makes up a large fraction of the world demand for some product that it imports. By restricting its demand for that product through a tariff, it can force down the price that foreign exporters receive for that product. The price paid by domestic consumers will probably rise but as long as the increase is less than the tariff, foreign suppliers will receive less per unit. For example, a 20 percent U.S. tariff on the import of

Canadian softwood lumber might raise the price paid by U.S. consumers by 12 percent and lower the price received by Canadian suppliers by 8 percent (the difference between the two prices being received by the U.S. treasury). This reduction in the price received by the foreign suppliers of a U.S. import is a terms-of-trade improvement for the United States (and a terms-of-trade deterioration for Canada).

To Protect Against "Unfair" Actions by Foreign Firms and Governments.

Tariffs are used to prevent foreign industries from harming domestic industries by employing predatory practices. Two common practices are subsidies paid by foreign governments to their exporters and price discrimination by foreign firms, which is called *dumping* when it is done across international borders. These practices are typically countered by levying tariffs called *countervailing duties* and *antidumping duties*. The circumstances under which dumping and foreign subsidization provide a valid argument for such tariffs are considered in detail later in this chapter.

To Protect Infant Industries.

infant industry argument The argument that new domestic industries with potential for economies of scale or learning by doing need to be protected from competition from established, low-cost foreign producers so that they can grow large enough to achieve costs as low as those of foreign producers.

The oldest valid argument for protection as a means of raising living standards concerns economies of scale. It is usually called the **infant industry argument.** An infant industry is nothing more than a new, small industry. If such an industry has large economies of scale, costs will be high when the industry is small but will fall as the industry grows. In such industries, the country first in the field has a tremendous advantage. A developing country may find that in the early stages of development, its industries are unable to compete with established foreign rivals. A trade restriction may protect these industries from foreign competition while they grow up. When they are large enough, they will be able to produce as cheaply as foreign rivals and thus be able to compete without protection.

Most of the now industrialized countries developed their industries initially under quite heavy tariff protection. (In Canada's case, the National Policy of 1876 established a high tariff wall behind which many Canadian industries developed and thrived for many years.) Once the industrial sector was well developed, these countries moved to reduce their levels of protection, thus moving a long way toward freer trade.

To Encourage Learning by Doing.

Learning by doing, which we discussed in Chapter 34, suggests that the pattern of comparative advantage can be changed. If a country learns enough by producing products for which it currently has a comparative *dis*advantage, it may gain in the long run by specializing in those products, developing a comparative advantage as the learning process lowers their costs.

Learning by doing is an example of what in Chapter 34 we called *dynamic* comparative advantage. The success over the past three decades of such newly industrializing countries (NICs) as Hong Kong, South Korea, Singapore, Taiwan, Indonesia, and Thailand seemed to many observers to be based on acquired skills and government policies that created favourable business conditions. These successes gave rise to the theory that comparative advantages can change and that they can be developed by suitable government policies, which can, however, take many forms other than restricting trade.

Some countries have succeeded in developing strong comparative advantages in targeted industries, but others have failed. One reason such policies sometimes fail is that protecting local industries from foreign competition may make the industries unadaptive and complacent. Another reason is the difficulty of identifying the industries that will be able to succeed in the long run. All too often, the protected infant grows up to be a weakling requiring permanent protection for its continued existence, or else the rate of learning is slower than for similar industries in countries that do not provide protection from the chill winds of international competition. In these instances, the anticipated comparative advantage never materializes. The NICs mentioned above avoided these problems by insisting that the protected industries serve the export market. If they could not succeed within a few years in the tough world of international competition, they lost their domestic support.

To Earn Pure Profits.   Another argument for tariffs or other trade restrictions is to help create an advantage in producing or marketing some new product that is expected to generate pure profits. To the extent that all lines of production earn normal profits, there is no reason to produce goods other than ones for which a country has a comparative advantage. Some goods, however, are produced in industries containing a few large firms where economies of scale provide a natural barrier to entry. Firms in these industries can earn high profits even over long periods of time. If protection of the domestic market can increase the chance that one of the protected domestic firms will become established and thus earn high profits, the protection may pay off. This is the general idea behind the concept of *strategic trade policy.*

Opponents of strategic trade policy argue that it is nothing more than a modern version of age-old and faulty justifications for tariff protection. Once all countries try to be strategic, they will all waste vast sums trying to break into industries in which there is no room for most of them. Domestic consumers would benefit most, they say, if their governments let other countries engage in this game. Consumers could then buy the cheap, subsidized foreign products and export traditional nonsubsidized products in return. The opponents of strategic trade policy also argue that democratic governments that enter the game of picking and backing winners are likely to make more bad choices than good ones. One bad choice, with all of its massive development costs written off, would require that many good choices also be made in order to make the equivalent in profits that would allow taxpayers to break even overall.

An ongoing dispute between Canada and Brazil illustrates how strategic trade policy is often difficult to distinguish from pure protection. The world's two major producers of regional jets are Bombardier, based in Montreal, and Embraer SA, based in Brazil. For several years, each company has accused their competitor's government of using illegal subsidies to help their domestic company sell jets in world markets. Brazil's Pro-Ex program provides Embraer's customers with low-interest loans with which to purchase Embraer's jets. The Canadian government's Technology Partnerships program is a $300 million annual fund that subsidizes research and development activities in high-tech aerospace and defence companies. As the leading Canadian aerospace company, Bombardier benefits significantly from this program.

See Chapter 35 of www.pearsoned.ca/lipsey for an interview with Bombardier's Laurent Beaudoin on the need for subsidies in the aerospace industry: "Trade and Subsidies in the Air," *World Economic Affairs.*

In 1999, the World Trade Organization (WTO) ruled that both the Brazilian and Canadian governments were using illegal subsidy programs to support their aerospace firms. Both countries, however, naturally view their respective programs as necessary responses to the other country's subsidization. Many economists believe that an agreement to eliminate both programs would leave a "level playing field" while saving Brazilian and Canadian taxpayers a considerable amount of money. By the end of 1999, the two countries had not reached an agreement involving reductions in their subsidy programs.

The Importance of Competition

For a list and discussion of many ongoing trade disputes, see the WTO's website: www.wto.org.

In today's world, a country's products must stand up to international competition if they are to survive. Over time, this requirement demands that they hold their own in competition for successful innovations. Over even so short a period as a few years, firms that do not develop new products and new production methods fall seriously behind their competitors in many industries. Protection, by reducing competition from foreign firms, reduces the incentive for industries to fight to succeed internationally. If any one country adopts high tariffs unilaterally, its domestic industries will become less competitive. Secure in its home market because of the tariff wall, its protected industries are likely to become less and less competitive in the international market. As the gap between domestic and foreign industries widens, any tariff wall will provide less and less protection. Eventually, the domestic industries will succumb to the foreign competition. Meanwhile, domestic living standards will fall relative to foreign ones as an increasing productivity gap opens between domestic protected industries and foreign, internationally oriented ones.

Although restrictive trade policies have sometimes been pursued following a rational assessment of the approximate cost, such policies are often pursued for political objectives or on fallacious economic grounds, with little appreciation of the actual costs involved.

Fallacious Arguments for Protection

We have seen that there are generally gains from trade, although trade does not necessarily make everyone in a country better off. We have also seen that there are some situations in which there are valid arguments for restricting trade. For every valid argument, however, there are many fallacious arguments—many of these are based, directly or indirectly, on the misconception that in every transaction there is a winner and a loser. Here we review a few such arguments that are frequently advanced in political debates concerning international trade.

Keep the Money at Home

This argument says that if I buy a foreign good, I have the good and the foreigner has the money, whereas if I buy the same good locally, I have the good and our country has the money, too. This argument is based on a common misconception. It assumes that domestic money actually goes abroad physically when imports are purchased and that trade flows only in one direction. But when Canadian importers purchase Japanese goods, they do not send dollars abroad. They (or their financial agents) buy Japanese yen and use them to pay the Japanese manufacturers. They purchase the yen on the foreign-exchange market by giving up dollars to someone who wishes to use them for expenditure in Canada. Even if the money did go abroad physically—that is, if a Japanese firm accepted a shipload of Canadian $100 bills—it would be because that firm (or someone to whom it could sell the dollars) wanted them to spend in the only country where they are legal tender—Canada.

Canadian currency, or any other national currency, ultimately does no one any good except as purchasing power. It would be miraculous if Canadian money could be exported in return for real goods. After all, the Bank of Canada has the power to create as much new Canadian money as it wishes (at almost zero direct cost). It is only because Canadian money can buy Canadian products and Canadian assets that others want it.

Protect Against Low-Wage Foreign Labour

This argument says that the products of low-wage countries will drive Canadian products from the market, and the high Canadian standard of living will be dragged down to that of its poorer trading partners. Arguments of this sort have swayed many voters over the years.

As a prelude to considering this argument, think what the argument would imply if taken out of the international context and put into a local one, where the same principles govern the gains from trade. Is it really impossible for a rich person to gain by trading with a poor person? Would the local millionaire be better off if she did all her own typing, gardening, and cooking? No one believes that a rich person gains nothing by trading with those who are less rich.

Why, then, must a rich group of people lose when they trade with a poor group? "Well," some may say, "the poor group will price its goods too cheaply." Does anyone believe that consumers lose from buying in discount houses or supermarkets just because the prices are lower there than at the old-fashioned corner store? Consumers gain when they can buy the same goods at a lower price. If Mexican or Malaysian firms pay low wages and sell their goods cheaply, workers in those countries may suffer, but Canadians will gain by obtaining imports at a low cost in terms of the goods that must be exported in return. The cheaper our imports are, the better off we are in terms of the goods and services available for domestic consumption.

As we said earlier in this chapter, *some* Canadians may be better off if Canada places high tariffs on the import of Mexican goods. In particular, if the Mexican goods compete with goods made by unskilled Canadian workers, then those unskilled workers will be better off if a Canadian tariff protects their firms and thus their jobs. But Canadian income overall—that is, average per capita real income—will be higher when there is free trade.

Exports Are Good; Imports Are Bad

Exports create domestic income; imports create income for foreigners. Thus, other things being equal, exports tend to increase our total GDP, and imports tend to reduce it. Surely, then, it is desirable to encourage exports by subsidizing them and to discourage imports by taxing them. This is an appealing argument, but it is incorrect.

Exports raise GDP by adding to the value of domestic output, but they do not add to the value of domestic consumption. The standard of living in a country depends on the goods and services available for consumption, not on what is produced.

If exports really were "good" and imports really were "bad," then a fully employed economy that managed to increase exports without a corresponding increase in imports ought to be better off. Such a change, however, would result in a reduction in current standards of living because when more goods are sent abroad but no more are brought in from abroad, the total goods available for domestic consumption must fall.

The living standards of a country depend on the goods and services consumed in that country. The importance of exports is that they provide the resources required to purchase imports, either now or in the future.

Create Domestic Jobs

It is sometimes said that an economy with substantial unemployment, such as Canada during much of the 1990s, provides an exception to the case for freer trade. Suppose that tariffs or import quotas cut the imports of Japanese cars, Korean textiles, German kitchen equipment, and Polish vodka. Surely, the argument maintains, this will create more employment in Canadian industries producing similar products. This may be true but it will also *reduce* employment in other industries.

The Japanese, Koreans, Germans, and Poles can buy from Canada only if they earn Canadian dollars by selling their domestically produced goods and services to Canada (or by borrowing dollars from Canada).[1] The decline in their sales of cars, textiles,

See Chapter 35 of www.pearsoned.ca/lipsey for an interview with MIT's Paul Krugman, who explains why countries do not "compete" against each other: Paul Krugman, "Fresh Thoughts from a Saltwater Economist," *World Economic Affairs.*

---

[1] They can also get dollars by selling to other countries and then using their currencies to buy Canadian dollars. But this intermediate step only complicates the transaction; it does not change its fundamental nature. Other countries must have earned the dollars by selling goods to Canada or borrowing from Canada.

kitchen equipment, and vodka will decrease their purchases of Canadian lumber, cars, software, banking services, and holidays. Jobs will be lost in Canadian export industries and gained in industries that formerly faced competition from imports. The major long-term effect is that the same total employment will merely be redistributed among industries. In the process, living standards will be reduced because employment expands in inefficient import-competing industries and contracts in efficient exporting industries.

A country that imposes tariffs in an attempt to create domestic jobs risks starting a "trade war" with its trading partners. Such a trade war can easily leave every country worse off, as world output (and thus income) falls significantly. An income-reducing trade war followed the onset of the Great Depression in 1929 as many countries increased tariffs to protect their domestic industries in an attempt to stimulate domestic production and employment. Most economists agree that this trade war made the Great Depression worse than it otherwise would have been.

There are several fallacious arguments for protection that are often heard in political debate. These arguments suffer from a misunderstanding of the sources of gains from trade or from the misbelief that protection can increase total employment.

Methods of Protection

We now go on to explore the various tools that governments use to provide protection to domestic industries.

Two main types of protectionist policy are illustrated in Figure 35-1. Both cause the price of the imported good to rise and its quantity demanded to fall. They differ, however, in how they achieve these results. The caption to the figure analyses these two types of policy.

Policies that Directly Raise Prices

The first type of protectionist policy directly raises the price of the imported product. A tariff, also often called an *import duty*, is the most common policy of this type. Other such policies are any rules or regulations that fulfill three conditions: They are costly to comply with; they do not apply to competing, domestically produced products; and they are more than is required to meet any legitimate purpose other than restricting trade.

As shown in part (i) of Figure 35-1, tariffs affect both foreign and domestic producers, as well as domestic consumers. The initial effect is to raise the domestic price of the imported product above its world price by the amount of the tariff. Imports fall. As a result, foreign producers sell less and must transfer resources to other lines of production. The price received on domestically produced units rises, as does the quantity produced domestically. On both counts, domestic producers earn more. However, the cost of producing the extra production at home exceeds the price at which it could be purchased on the world market. Thus, the benefit to domestic producers comes at the expense of domestic consumers. Indeed, domestic consumers lose on two counts: First, they consume less of the product because its price rises, and second, they pay a higher price for the amount that they do consume. This extra spending ends up in two places: The extra that is paid on all units produced at home goes to domestic producers, and the extra that is paid on units still imported goes to the government as tariff revenue.

FIGURE 35-1   Tariffs and Quotas to Protect Domestic Producers

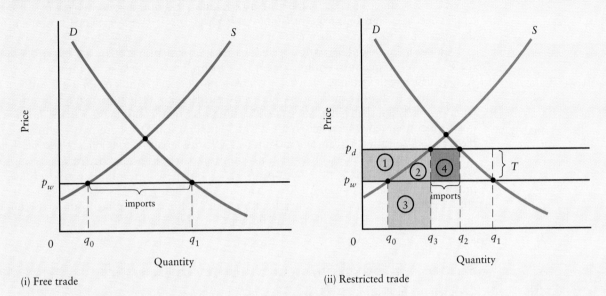

(i) Free trade   (ii) Restricted trade

The same reduction in imports and increase in domestic production can be achieved by using either a tariff or a quantity restriction. In both parts of the figure, D and S are the domestic demand and supply curves, respectively, and p_w is the world price of some product that is both produced at home and imported.

Part (i) of the figure shows the situation under free trade. Domestic consumption is q_1, domestic production is q_0, and imports are $q_0 q_1$.

Part (ii) shows what happens when protectionist policies restrict imports to the amount $q_3 q_2$. When this is done by levying a tariff of T per unit, the price in the domestic market rises by the full amount of the tariff to p_d. Consumers reduce consumption from q_1 to q_2 and pay an extra amount, shown by the shaded areas 1, 2, and 4, for the q_2 that they now purchase. Domestic production rises from q_0 to q_3. Because domestic producers receive the domestic price, their receipts rise by the three light-shaded areas, labelled 1, 2, and 3. Area 3 is revenue that was previously earned by foreign producers under free trade, while areas 1 and 2 are now paid by domestic consumers because of the higher prices they now face. Foreign suppliers of the imported good continue to receive the world price, so the government receives as tariff revenue the extra amount paid by consumers for the $q_3 q_2$ units that are still imported (shown by the dark shaded area, 4).

When the same result is accomplished by a quantity restriction, the government—through either a quota or a voluntary export restriction (VER)—reduces imports to $q_3 q_2$. This drives the domestic market price up to p_d and has the same effect on domestic producers and consumers as the tariff. Since the government has merely restricted the quantity of imports, both foreign and domestic suppliers get the higher price in the domestic market. Thus, foreign suppliers now receive the extra amount paid by domestic consumers (represented by the shaded area labelled 4) for the units that are still imported.

Policies that Directly Reduce Quantities

The second type of protectionist policy directly restricts the quantity of an imported product. A common example is the **import quota,** by which the importing country sets a maximum of the quantity of some product that may be imported each year. Another measure is the **voluntary export restriction (VER),** an agreement by an exporting country to limit the amount of a product that it sells to the importing country.

Figure 35-1 shows that a quantity restriction and a tariff have similar effects on domestic consumers and producers—they both raise domestic prices, increase domestic

import quota   A limit set by the government on the quantity of a foreign commodity that may be shipped into that country in a given time period.

voluntary export restriction (VER)   An agreement by an exporting country to limit the amount of a good exported to another country.

production, and reduce domestic consumption. But a quantity restriction is actually *worse* than a tariff for the importing country because the effect of the quantity restriction is to raise the price received by the foreign suppliers of the good. In contrast, a tariff leaves the foreign suppliers' price unchanged and instead generates tariff revenue for the government of the importing country.

Canada, the United States, and the European Union have used VERs extensively, and the EU makes frequent use of import quotas. Japan has been pressured into negotiating several VERs with Canada, the United States, and the EU in order to limit sales of some of the Japanese goods that have had the most success in international competition. For example, in 1983, the United States and Canada negotiated VERs whereby the Japanese government agreed to restrict total sales of Japanese cars to these two countries for three years. When the agreements ran out in 1986, the Japanese continued to restrict their automobile sales by unilateral voluntary action. Japan's readiness to restrict its exports to North America reflects the high profits that Japanese automobile producers were making under the system of VERs, as explained in Figure 35-1. In recent years, such VERs have become less important because Japan's major automobile producers, Honda and Toyota, both have established manufacturing plants in Canada.

Trade-Remedy Laws and Nontariff Barriers

As tariffs were lowered over the years since 1947, countries that wished to protect domestic industries began using, and often abusing, a series of trade restrictions that came to be known as nontariff barriers (NTBs). The original purpose of some of these barriers was to remedy certain legitimate problems that arise in international trade and, for this reason, they are often called *trade-remedy laws*. All too often, however, such laws are misused to become potent means of simple protection.

Dumping

dumping The practice of selling a commodity at a lower price in the export market than in the domestic market for reasons unrelated to differences in costs of servicing the two markets.

Selling a product in a foreign country at a lower price than in the domestic market is known as **dumping**. Dumping is a form of price discrimination studied in the theory of monopoly. Most governments have antidumping duties designed to protect their own industries against what is viewed as unfair foreign pricing practices.

Dumping, if it lasts indefinitely, can be a gift to the receiving country. Its consumers get goods from abroad at less than their full cost of production.

Dumping is more often a temporary measure, designed to get rid of unwanted surpluses, or a predatory attempt to drive competitors out of business. In either case, domestic producers complain about unfair foreign competition. In both cases, it is accepted international practice to levy antidumping duties on foreign imports. These duties are designed to eliminate the discriminatory elements in their prices.

Unfortunately, antidumping laws have been evolving over the past three decades in ways that allow antidumping duties to become barriers to trade and competition rather than to provide redress for unfair trading practices.

Several features of the antidumping system that is now in place in many countries make it highly protectionist. First, any price discrimination between national markets is classified as dumping and is subject to penalties. Thus prices in the producer's domestic market become, in effect, minimum prices below which no sales can be made in foreign markets, whatever the nature of demand in the domestic and foreign markets. Second, following a change in the U.S. law in the early 1970s, many countries' laws now calculate the "margin of dumping" as the difference between the price that is charged in that country's market and the foreign producer's average cost. Thus when there is a global slump in some industry so that the profit-maximizing price for all producers is below average cost, foreign producers can be convicted of dumping. This gives domestic producers enormous protection whenever the market price falls temporarily below average cost. Third, law in the United States (but not in all other countries) places the onus of proof on the accused. Facing a charge of dumping, a foreign producer must prove within the short time allowed for such a defence that the charge is unfounded. Fourth, U.S. antidumping duties are imposed with no time limit, so they often persist long after foreign firms have altered the prices that gave rise to them.

Governments have often been persuaded that low-price competition from foreign firms is "unfair" competition, and have levied antidumping duties on the imported goods. A recent example in Canada was an alleged case of dumping by Gerber, a U.S.-based producer of jarred baby food. In 1997, Heinz, the only Canadian producer, claimed that Gerber was pricing its products in Canada below costs, causing Heinz to lose sales. Heinz pushed for antidumping duties to be imposed on Gerber imports, and in April of 1998 the Canadian government agreed and imposed a 69 percent duty on Gerber imports. This duty was high enough to cause Gerber to reconsider the value of selling in the Canadian market. Later in the same year, however, consumer groups and the federal Competition Bureau argued that the very high duties on Gerber's products effectively left Heinz as a monopolist in the Canadian market. They urged a reluctant Canadian government to repeal the duty so that consumers could benefit from the competition between Gerber and Heinz.

Countervailing Duties

Countervailing duties, which are commonly used by the U.S. government but much less so elsewhere, provide another case in which a trade-remedy law can sometimes become a covert method of protection. The countervailing duty is designed to act, not as a tariff barrier, but rather as a means of creating a "level playing field" on which fair international competition can take place. Privately owned domestic firms rightly complain that they cannot compete against the seemingly bottomless purses of foreign governments. Subsidized foreign exports can be sold indefinitely at prices that would produce losses in the absence of the subsidy. The original object of countervailing duties was to counteract the effect on price of the presence of such foreign subsidies.

If a domestic firm suspects the existence of such a subsidy and registers a complaint, its government is required to make an investigation. For a countervailing duty to be levied, the investigation must determine, first, that the foreign subsidy to the specific industry in question does exist and, second, that it is large enough to cause significant injury to competing domestic firms.

There is no doubt that countervailing duties have sometimes been used to counteract the effects of unfair competition that are caused by foreign subsidies. Many governments complain, however, that countervailing duties are often used as thinly disguised protection. At the early stages of the development of countervailing duties, only subsidies whose prime effect was to distort trade were possible objects of countervailing duties. Even then, however, the existence of equivalent domestic subsidies was not taken into account when decisions were made to put countervailing duties on subsidized imports. Thus the United States levies some countervailing duties against foreign goods even though the foreign subsidy is less than the domestic subsidy. This does not create a level playing field.

Over time, the type of subsidy that is subject to countervailing duties has evolved until almost any government program that affects industry now risks becoming the object of a countervailing duty. Because all governments, including most U.S. state governments,

Canada's supply-management programs such as those in the dairy industry have been a perpetual source of friction in international trade negotiations.

have programs that provide direct or indirect assistance to industry, the potential for the use of countervailing duties as thinly disguised trade barriers is enormous.

Current Trade Policy

In the remainder of the chapter, we discuss trade policy in practice. We start with the many international agreements that govern current trade policies and then look in a little more detail at the NAFTA.

Before 1947, any country was free to impose tariffs on its imports. However, when one country increased its tariffs, the action often triggered retaliatory actions by its trading partners. The 1930s saw a high-water mark of world protectionism as each country sought to raise its employment and output by raising its tariffs. The end result was lowered efficiency, less trade, but no more employment or income. Since the end of World War II, much effort has been devoted to reducing tariff barriers, both on a multilateral and on a regional basis.

The GATT and the WTO

One of the most notable achievements of the post-World War II era was the creation of the General Agreement on Tariffs and Trade (GATT). The GATT has since been replaced by the World Trade Organization (WTO). The principle of the GATT was that each member country agreed not to make unilateral tariff increases. This prevented the outbreak of "tariff wars" in which countries raised tariffs to protect particular domestic industries and to retaliate against other countries' tariff increases.

The Uruguay Round—the final round of trade agreements under GATT—was completed in 1994 after years of negotiations. It reduced world tariffs by about 40 percent. But a significant failure of these talks was not getting a major liberalization of trade in agricultural goods. Such an agreement was resisted by the EU and Canada. The EU has a scheme called the Common Agricultural Policy (CAP) that provides general support for most of its agricultural products, many of which are exported. The EU's position as a subsidized net exporter causes major harm to agricultural producers in developing countries whose governments are too poor to compete with the EU in a subsidy war.

Canada, which has free trade in many agricultural commodities, was concerned to maintain its supply management over a number of industries including poultry, eggs, and dairy products. These schemes are administered by the provinces who restrict domestic production and thus push domestic prices well above world levels. The federal government made them possible by imposing quotas on imports of these products at the national level.

Canada, the EU, and a number of other countries that lavishly protect some or all of their domestic agricultural producers were finally forced to agree to a plan to end all import quotas on agricultural products. In a process called "tariffication," these quotas have been replaced by "tariff equivalents"—tariffs that restrict trade by the same amount as the quotas did. Canadian tariff equivalents are as high as several hundred percent in some products, showing just how restrictive the Canadian policy is. The hope among countries that are pushing for freer trade in agricultural commodities is that pressure will build to reduce these very high tariffs over the next few decades.

Despite the failure to achieve free trade in agricultural products, the Uruguay Round is generally viewed as a success. Perhaps its most significant achievement was the creation of the World Trade Organization (WTO) to replace the GATT. An important part of the WTO is its formal dispute-settlement mechanism. This mechanism allows countries to take cases of alleged trade violations—such as illegal subsidies or tariffs—to the WTO for a formal ruling, and also obliges member countries to follow the ruling. The WTO's dispute-settlement mechanism is thus a significant step toward a "rules based" global trading system.

The WTO, however, does have its opponents. In December 1999, trade ministers from the WTO member countries met in Seattle to set the agenda for a proposed new round of trade talks. (Not surprisingly, there were difficulties establishing the agenda—not least were the familiar problems in dealing with subsidies to agriculture.) The Seattle meetings were delayed and interrupted by massive protests from environmental and labour groups, among others, who argued that the WTO's process of negotiating trade agreements pays insufficient attention to environmental and labour standards, especially in the developing countries. Many WTO officials and trade ministers, including those from the developing countries, recognized the importance of environmental and labour issues but questioned the wisdom of formally including these concerns in trade agreements. Reaching agreement on trade issues among the 134 member countries of the WTO is difficult enough—it would be almost impossible if the issues were bundled with the even more contentious environmental and labour issues. The result would be an overall agreement that achieved very little in terms of either trade liberalization, environmental protection, or establishing labour standards. Instead, many trade officials argued that the existing International Labour Organization should be strengthened and a separate international organization like the WTO should be created to promote environmental issues. These organizations could then push ahead to achieve in their respective domains the same success that the GATT achieved over fifty years of negotiations.

For further progress to be made on trade liberalization, environmental and labour issues will probably have to be addressed. Either domestic political pressures will push individual member countries to insist that these issues be included within the WTO negotiations, or other organizations like the WTO will be developed and/or strengthened to address the concerns. Whatever approach is followed, it appears that these will surely continue to be hot policy issues into the 21st century.

Despite the obstacles, many economists and policy makers now see multilateral free trade in goods and services as an attainable goal. After notable success in liberalizing trade in goods and services, attention in recent years has swung toward accomplishing the same thing for foreign direct investment (FDI). *Applying Economic Concepts 35-1* discusses the attempt to negotiate a Multilateral Agreement on Investment (MAI), and the political difficulties that were encountered along the way.

For more information on the WTO, see its website at www.wto.org.

Regional Trade Agreements

Regional agreements seek to liberalize trade over a much smaller group of countries than the WTO membership. Three standard forms of regional trade-liberalizing agreements are *free trade areas, customs unions,* and *common markets.*

A **free trade area (FTA)** is the least comprehensive of the three. It allows for tariff-free trade among the member countries, but it leaves each member free to levy its own trade policy with respect to other countries. As a result, members must maintain customs points at their common borders to make sure that imports into the free trade area do not all enter through the member that is levying the lowest tariff on each item. They must also agree on *rules of origin* to establish when a good is made in a member country and hence is able to pass tariff-free across their borders and when it is imported from outside the FTA and hence is subject to tariffs when it crosses borders within the FTA.

free trade area (FTA) An agreement among two or more countries to abolish tariffs on all or most of the trade among themselves while each remains free to set its own tariffs against other countries.

APPLYING ECONOMIC CONCEPTS 35-1
The Multilateral Agreement on Investment

The view that free flows of foreign direct investment (FDI) are necessary to the efficient functioning of the world economy led governments of many developed countries to seek international rules on the treatment of foreign investment. In the absence of such rules, firms and investors face a great deal of uncertainty about how their foreign-located assets will be treated by the government in the host country, especially in regard to expropriation and discriminatory taxation. This kind of uncertainty leads firms to invest less than they otherwise would, thereby reducing the benefits that would otherwise accrue to both host and source countries.

Under the auspices of the Organization for Economic Cooperation and Development (OECD), Canada joined other countries in negotiations toward a Multilateral Agreement on Investment, popularly known as the MAI. The underlying principle of the MAI is that signatory governments would commit themselves to treat foreign-owned firms no differently from domestically owned firms. The proposed MAI also includes a mechanism for the settlement of disputes caused by alleged violations of the agreement.

By early in 1998, the MAI negotiations had stalled for two main reasons. First, many countries (including Canada and France) pushed strongly for some industries to be exempt from the agreement. These countries wanted the ability to discriminate against foreign firms in politically sensitive "cultural" industries, such as publishing and broadcasting. Many other countries argued that such exemptions defeat the purpose of the agreement and were reluctant to grant them. Further, exemptions greatly increase the complexity of the agreement, in part because it

becomes necessary to provide a precise industrial classification for every unit of foreign investment.

The second and probably more important difficulty encountered by the MAI was that many interest groups around the world began expressing their concerns about the MAI's impact on environmental standards and social programs. Environmental lobby groups argued that the MAI would weaken any country's ability to set environmental standards different from those of its trading partners. Grassroots citizens' movements expressed their concerns about a country's ability to continue providing generous social programs. Though these criticisms received considerable attention in the popular press, a careful examination of the proposed MAI suggests that many of the criticisms are baseless.

The text of the proposed MAI clearly specifies that a country party to the agreement is not restricted in its design and implementation of policies, provided the policies treat foreign and domestic firms equally. If Canada, for example, wished to toughen its environmental standards by requiring firms to install better scrubbers in smokestacks, this policy would not contravene the MAI as long as the new policy applied equally to foreign-owned and domestically owned firms.

By the summer of 1998, the member countries of the OECD decided to delay further negotiations of the MAI. But failure in this set of negotiations will not make the issue go away. With over $300 billion of FDI flowing *annually* between many countries of the world, foreign investment has become too important to be ignored. A widespread set of rules for FDI is surely in our future.

customs union
A group of countries who agree to have free trade among themselves and a common set of barriers against imports from the rest of the world.

common market
A customs union with the added provision that factors of production can move freely among the members.

A **customs union** is a free trade area in which the member countries agree to establish a common trade policy with the rest of the world. Because they have a common trade policy, the members need neither customs controls on goods moving among themselves nor rules of origin. Once a good has entered any member country it has met the common rules and regulations and paid the common tariff and so it may henceforth be treated the same as a good that is produced within the union. An example of a customs union is Mercosur, an agreement linking Argentina, Brazil, Paraguay, and Uruguay.

A **common market** is a customs union that also has free movement of labour and capital among its members. The European Union is by far the most successful example of a common market. Indeed, the EU is now moving toward a full *economic union* in which all economic policies in the member countries are harmonized. The adoption of the euro as the common currency of 11 EU countries in 1999 was a significant step in this direction.

Trade Creation and Trade Diversion

A major effect of regional trade liberalization is to reallocate resources. Economists divide these effects into two categories, *trade creation* and *trade diversion*. These concepts were first developed by Jacob Viner, a Canadian-born economist who taught at the University of Chicago and Princeton University and was a leading economic theorist in the first half of the 20th century.

Trade creation occurs when producers in one member country find that they can export to another member country as a result of the elimination of the tariffs. For example, when the North American Free Trade Agreement (NAFTA) eliminated most cross-border tariffs between Mexico, Canada, and the United States, some U.S. firms found that they could undersell their Canadian competitors in some product lines, and some Canadian firms found that they could undersell their U.S. competitors in other product lines. As a result, specialization occurred, and new international trade developed. This trade, which is based on (natural or acquired) comparative advantage, is illustrated in Table 35-1.

Trade creation represents efficient specialization according to comparative advantage.

Trade diversion occurs when exporters in one member country replace foreign exporters as suppliers to another member country. For example, trade diversion occurs when U.S. firms find that they can undersell competitors from the rest of the world in the Canadian market, not because they are the cheapest source of supply, but because their tariff-free prices under NAFTA are lower than the tariff-burdened prices of imports from other countries. This effect is a gain to U.S. firms and Canadian consumers of the product but a loss to Canada overall, which now has to export more goods for any given amount of imports than before the trade diversion occurred. Table 35-1 also illustrates trade diversion.

From the global perspective, trade diversion represents an inefficient use of resources.

The History of Free Trade Areas

The first important free trade area in the modern era was the European Free Trade Association (EFTA). It was formed in 1960 by a group of European countries that were unwilling to join the European Common Market (the forerunner of the European Union) because of its all-embracing character. Not wanting to be left out of the gains from trade, they formed an association whose sole purpose was tariff removal. First, they removed all tariffs on trade among themselves. Then each country signed a free-trade-area agreement with the EU. This made the EU-EFTA market the largest tariff-free market in the world (over 300 million people). In recent years almost all of the EFTA countries have entered the EU.

In 1989, a sweeping agreement between Canada and the United States instituted free trade on almost

trade creation
A consequence of reduced trade barriers among a set of countries whereby trade within the group is increased and trade with the rest of the world remains roughly constant.

trade diversion
A consequence of reduced trade barriers among a set of countries whereby trade within the group replaces trade that used to take place with countries outside the group.

TABLE 35-1   Trade Creation and Trade Diversion

Producing Country	Canadian Delivered Price Without Tariffs (dollars)	Canadian Delivered Price with a 10 Percent Tariff (dollars)
Trade creation		
Canada	40.00	40.00
United States	37.00	40.70
Trade diversion		
Taiwan	20.00	22.00
United States	21.50	23.65

Regional tariff reductions can cause trade creation and trade diversion. The table gives two cases. In the first case, a U.S. good, which could be sold for $37.00 in Canada, has its price increased to $40.70 by a 10 percent Canadian tariff. The Canadian industry, which can sell the good for $40.00 with or without a tariff on imports, is protected against the more efficient U.S. producer. When the tariff is removed by the NAFTA, the U.S. good wins the market by selling at $37.00. Trade is created between Canada and the United States by eliminating the inefficient Canadian production.

In the second case, Taiwan can undersell the U.S. in the Canadian market for another product when neither is subject to a tariff (column 1) and when both are subject to a 10 percent tariff (column 2). But after the NAFTA, the U.S. good enters Canada tariff-free and sells for $21.50, whereas the Taiwanese good, which is still subject to the Canadian tariff, continues to sell for $22.00. The U.S. good wins the market, and Canadian trade is diverted from Taiwan to the U.S. even though Taiwan is the lower-cost supplier (excluding the tariff).

all goods and most nongovernment services and covered what is the world's largest flow of international trade between any two countries. In 1994, this agreement was extended into the North American Free Trade Agreement (NAFTA) by renegotiating the Canada-U.S. agreement to include Mexico. Provision is made within the NAFTA for the accession of other countries with the hope that it may eventually evolve into an agreement linking all countries of the western hemisphere.

The possible expansion of NAFTA is being examined. Indeed, the first accession was to have been Chile. But the negotiations for its entry into NAFTA were held up by domestic political considerations in the United States. The first few years of the 21st century may well see a significant push for expansion of NAFTA.

Australia and New Zealand have also entered into an association that removes restrictions on trade in goods and services between their two countries. The countries of Latin America have been experimenting with free trade areas for many decades. Most earlier attempts failed but, in the past few years, more durable FTAs seem to have been formed, the most successful of which is Mercosur, which includes Argentina, Brazil, Uruguay, and Paraguay. Whether these will remain stand-alone agreements or evolve into a broader continental agreement remains to be seen.

In early 1998, the negotiations for the Free Trade Area of the Americas (FTAA) were formally launched in Santiago, Chile. These negotiations will take many years and will involve discussions of rules of origin, environmental concerns, the treatment of foreign direct investment, agricultural policy, and how best to integrate the many regional agreements into a single comprehensive agreement. Only time will reveal the eventual outcome of these negotiations.

The North American Free Trade Agreement

The NAFTA is an extension of the 1989 Canada-U.S. Free Trade Agreement (FTA) with some important improvements based on the experience of the earlier agreement. It is a free trade area and not a customs union; each country retains its own external trade policy, and rules of origin are needed to determine when a good is made within the NAFTA and thus allowed to move freely among the members.

National Treatment

The fundamental principle that guides the NAFTA is the principle of *national treatment*. The principle of national treatment means that countries are free to establish any laws they wish and that these can differ as much as desired among member countries, with the sole proviso that these laws must not discriminate on the basis of nationality. Canada can have tough environmental laws or standards for particular goods, but it must enforce these equally on Canadian, Mexican, and U.S. firms and on domestically produced and imported goods. The idea of national treatment is to allow a maximum of policy independence while preventing national policies from being used as barriers to trade and investment.

Other Major Provisions

There are several other major provisions in NAFTA. First, all tariffs on trade between the United States and Canada were eliminated by 1999. Canada-Mexico and Mexico-U.S. tariffs are to be phased out over a 15-year period that started in 1994. Also, a number of nontariff barriers are eliminated or circumscribed.

Second, the agreement guarantees national treatment to foreign investment once it enters a country while permitting each country to screen a substantial amount of inbound foreign investment before it enters.

Third, all existing measures that restrict trade and investment that are not explicitly removed by the agreement are "grandfathered," a term referring to the continuation of a practice that predates the agreement and would have been prohibited by the terms of the agreement were it not specifically exempted. This is probably the single most important departure from free trade under the NAFTA. Under it, a large collection of restrictive measures in each of the three countries are given indefinite life. An alternative would have been to "sunset" all of these provisions by negotiating dates at which each would be eliminated. From the point of view of long-term trade liberalization, even a 50-year extension would have been preferable to an indefinite exemption.

Fourth, a few goods remain subject to serious nontariff trade restrictions. In Canada, the main examples are supply-managed agricultural products, beer, textiles, and the cultural industries. Restrictions for the Canadian supply-managed agricultural products may be short-lived because of their tariffication under the Uruguay round of GATT. Textile restriction in both the United States and Canada comes under the Multifiber Agreement, which is being phased out over a 15-year period under the Uruguay round. In the United States, textiles, shipping between U.S. ports, and banking were shielded from free trade in good and services.

APPLYING ECONOMIC CONCEPTS 35-2

Canadian Wine: A Free-Trade Success Story

Before the Canada-U.S. FTA was signed in 1989, great fears were expressed over the fate of the Canadian wine industry, located mainly in Ontario and British Columbia. It was heavily tariff protected and, with a few notable exceptions, concentrated mainly on cheap, low-quality products. Contrary to most people's expectations, rather than being decimated, the industry now produces a wide variety of high-quality products, some of which have won international competitions in Europe.

Why did this surprising result occur? The high Canadian tariff was levied on a per unit rather than on an *ad valorem* basis. For example, the tariff was expressed as so many dollars per litre rather than as a specific percentage of the price. Charging a tariff by the litre gave most protection to the low quality wines with low value per litre. The higher the per-litre value of the wine, the lower the percentage tariff protection. For example, a $5-per-litre tariff would have the following effects. A low-quality imported wine valued at $5 per litre would have its price raised to $10, a 100 percent increase in price, whereas a higher quality imported wine valued at $25 per litre would have its price increased to $30, only a 20 percent increase in price.

Responding to these incentives, the Canadian industry concentrated on low-quality wines. The market

for these wines was protected by the nearly prohibitive tariffs on competing low-quality imports, and also by the high prices charged for high-quality imports. In addition, protection was provided by many hidden charges that the various provincial governments' liquor monopolies levied in order to protect local producers.

When the tariff was removed, the incentives were to move up-market, producing much more value per acre of land. Fortunately, much of the Canadian wine-growing land in the Okanagan Valley in BC and the Niagara Peninsula in Ontario is well-suited for growing the grapes required for good wines. Within a very few years, and with some government transitional assistance, Canadian wines were competing effectively with imported products in the medium-quality range. BC and Ontario wines do not yet reach the quality of major French wines in the $40-$70 (per bottle) range but they compete very effectively in quality with wines in the $10-$25 range, and sometimes even higher up the quality scale.

The success of the wine industry is a fine example of how tariffs can distort incentives and push an industry into a structure that makes it dependent on the tariff. Looking at the pre-FTA industry, very few people suspected that it would be able to survive, let alone produce a world-class product.

APPLYING ECONOMIC CONCEPTS 35-3

Headline Trade Disputes Between Canada and the United States

The flow of goods and services across the Canada-U.S. border is the largest flow of trade between any two countries. In 1998, approximately $500 billion worth of goods and services crossed this border. Although more than 95 percent of this trade passes between the two countries without dispute or hindrance, some items have been beset by persistent disputes. Here is a brief discussion of three of the most contentious areas in U.S.-Canadian trade.

Softwood Lumber

Canada exports large amounts of softwood lumber to the United States. And U.S. producers have persistently claimed that Canadian provincial government policies provide a concealed subsidy that should be evened out with a countervailing duty. The main bone of contention is *stumpage*, which is the royalty that governments charge the logging companies for cutting timber on government-owned land. In the United States, stumpage fees are set by open auction. In Canada, the fees are set in private negotiations between logging companies and the government. U.S. critics argue that the much lower Canadian stumpage fees that emerge from this negotiation process are a subsidy from the government to the lumber industry. Canadians argue that the higher U.S.

stumpage fees reflect the higher services that U.S. governments provide for their lumber companies by way of infrastructure that Canadian lumber companies must provide for themselves.

Just before the Canada-U.S. FTA was finalized, the Canadian government imposed an export tax on lumber going to the United States, to forestall the imposition of a U.S. countervailing duty. When this tax expired, Canada did not renew it and the United States imposed a countervailing duty. Two dispute-settlement panels found in Canada's favour, but largely on the grounds of narrow technicalities. The United States then changed its laws to remove what they saw as the loopholes that the Canadians had used. In 1996, the Canada-U.S. Softwood Lumber Agreement was signed. This agreement restricts the volume of duty-free exports of Canadian softwood lumber to the United States until 2001, with the Canadian government imposing export taxes on any exports that exceed the limit.

Supply-Managed Agricultural Industries

Several of the Canadian provinces use supply-management systems to support farm incomes. Such systems typically involve issuing quotas to farmers to restrict output. The result

For information about NAFTA, go to the website for the NAFTA Secretariat: www.nafta-sec-alena.org.

Fifth, trade in most nongovernmental services is liberalized by giving service firms the right of establishment in all member countries and the privilege of national treatment. There is also a limited opening of the markets in financial services to entry from firms based in the NAFTA countries.

Finally, a significant minority of government procurement is opened to cross-border bids.

Dispute Settlement

From Canada's point of view, by far the biggest setback in the negotiations for the Canada-U.S. FTA was the failure to obtain agreement on a common regime for countervailing and antidumping duties. In view of that failure, no significant attempt was made to deal with this issue in the NAFTA negotiations. The U.S. Congress has been unwilling to abandon the unilateral use of these powerful weapons.

In the absence of such a multilateral regime, a dispute-settlement mechanism was put in place. Under it, the domestic determinations that are required for the levying of antidumping and countervailing duties are subject to review by a panel of Canadians, Americans, and Mexicans. This international review replaces appeal through the domestic courts. Panels are empowered to uphold the domestic determinations or refer the decision to the domestic authority—which in effect is a binding order for a new in-of such quotas is to substantially raise the prices paid by Canadian consumers. For years, the Canadian government had supported these policies by imposing import quotas on the managed products, without which their prices would be driven down to world levels. The Canadian government successfully negotiated exemptions for these quotas under the Canada-U.S. FTA. In the Uruguay round of GATT negotiations, despite spirited resistance, the Canadian government was forced to agree to "tariffication" of these quotas. The United States then took the position that although the quotas had been exempt under the FTA, their tariff equivalents were not. After all, the U.S. argued, all tariffs without exception are to be removed by 1999 under the FTA. At the time of writing, the debate continues without an obvious resolution.

Cultural Industries

Canada has always sought to support its magazines, book sellers, film distributors, and other cultural industries from U.S. competition. Although there was never any pressure to prevent governments on both sides of the border from subsidizing the performing arts, such as music and drama, protection of the cultural industries more widely defined was a serious bone of contention during the FTA negotiations. In the end, Canada got exemption for all of its broadly defined cultural industries.

In the mid 1990s, the Canadian government became concerned over the presence of Canadian editions of U.S. split-run magazines. These magazines, such as *Time* and *Sports Illustrated*, contain mostly U.S. content but also include a few pages of Canadian editorial content. Because the fixed costs of the magazine are covered by the U.S. sales of the magazine, the Canadian advertising rates can be lower than those of Canadian-based magazines. The Canadian government and Canadian magazine publishers argued that the presence of such split-run magazines would make it more difficult for Canadian magazines to sell advertising space, thus putting them in an untenable financial position. Failure of Canadian magazines would then damage an important part of Canadian culture. In 1995, the Canadian government imposed an 80 percent tax on advertising expenditures in the Canadian editions of U.S. split-run magazines.

The U.S. government and U.S. magazine publishers argued that the Canadian government's attempts to protect Canadian culture by protecting their magazines were nothing more than simple trade protection. On this basis, they saw no difference between aid to Canadian magazines and aid to textiles firms or the aerospace industry. The United States brought their complaint to the World Trade Organization and, in 1997, the WTO ruled against Canada—that is, it ruled that Canada's tax on split-run advertising contravened international trade agreements.

The Canadian government then attempted to write new legislation that would be consistent with WTO rules but would still have the effect of preventing the U.S. split-run magazines. This prompted the United States to threaten the imposition of duties on a whole range of Canadian exports if the Canadian government did not drop its attempts to prevent the split-runs. Finally, in 1999, the Canadian and U.S. governments reached an agreement to provide limited access to the Canadian market for the U.S.-based split-run magazines.

---

vestigation. The referral can be repeated until the panel is satisfied that the domestic laws have been correctly and fairly applied.

This is pathbreaking: For the first time in its history, the United States has agreed to submit the administration of its domestic laws to *binding* scrutiny by an international panel that often contains a majority of foreigners.

Results

The Canada-U.S. FTA aroused a great debate in Canada. Indeed, the Canadian federal election of 1988 was fought almost entirely on the issue of free trade. Supporters looked for major increases in the security of existing trade from U.S. protectionist attacks and for a growth of new trade. Detractors predicted a flight of firms to the U.S., the loss of Canadian competitiveness, and even the loss of Canada's political independence.

By and large, however, both the Canada-U.S. FTA and NAFTA agreements have worked out just about as expected by their supporters. Industry has clearly restructured in the direction of greater export orientation in all three countries, and trade creation has occurred. All three countries are importing more from and exporting more to each other. This trend is particularly true between Canada and the United States. As the theory of trade predicts, specialization has occurred in many areas, resulting in more U.S. imports of some product lines from Canada and more U.S. exports of other goods to Canada. In 1988, before the Canada-U.S. FTA took effect, Canada exported $85 billion in goods and services to the United States, and imported $74 billion from the United States. By 1998, the value of Canada-U.S. trade had almost quadrupled—Canadian exports to the United States had increased to $271 billion and imports from the United States had increased to $234 billion.

It is hard to say how much trade diversion there has been and will be in the future. The greatest potential for trade diversion is with Mexico, which competes in the U.S. and Canadian markets with a large number of products produced in other low-wage countries. South-East Asian exporters to the United States and Canada have been worried that Mexico would capture some of their markets by virtue of having tariff-free access denied to their goods. Most estimates predict, however, that trade creation will dominate over trade diversion.

Most transitional difficulties were initially felt in each country's import-competing industries, just as theory predicts. An agreement such as the NAFTA brings its advantages by encouraging a movement of resources out of protected but inefficient import-competing industries, which decline, and into efficient export industries, which expand because they have better access to the markets of other member countries. Southern Ontario and parts of Quebec had major problems as some traditional exports fell and resources had to be moved to sectors where trade was expanding. Eight years after the agreement, however, southern Ontario was booming again and its most profitable sectors were those that exported to the United States.

There were also some pleasant surprises resulting from free trade. Two Canadian industries that many economists expected to suffer from the FTA and NAFTA were wine-making and textiles. Yet both of these industries have prospered as Canadian firms have improved quality, productivity, and benefited from increased access to the huge U.S. market. *Applying Economic Concepts 35-2* discusses the success of the Canadian wine industry after the tariffs on wine were eliminated.

Finally, the dispute-settlement mechanism seems to have worked well. A large number of disputes have arisen and have been referred to panels. Panel members have usually reacted as professionals rather than as nationals. Most cases have been decided on their merits; allegations that decisions were reached on national rather than professional grounds have been rare.

With over $500 billion annually in two-way trade between Canada and the United States, however, it is inevitable that some disputes arise. *Applying Economic Concepts 35-3* discusses three of the most contentious trade disputes that still disturb the generally tranquil state of Canada-U.S. trade.

See Chapter 35 of www.pearsoned.ca/lipsey for an interesting discussion of the results of FTA and NAFTA: Richard Lipsey, "Free Trade—Real Results Versus Unreal Expectations," *World Economic Affairs*.

See Chapter 35 of www.pearsoned.ca/lipsey for an interview with former Prime Minister Brian Mulroney on the political aspects of FTA and NAFTA: "Standing Firm on Free Trade," *World Economic Affairs*.

See the website for the Department of Foreign Affairs and International Trade for information on the dispute-settlement mechanism: www.dfait-maeic.gc.ca.

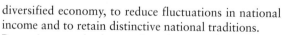

SUMMARY

Free Trade or Protection?

- The case for free trade is that world output of all products can be higher under free trade than when protectionism restricts regional specialization.
- Protection for an individual country can be urged as a means to ends other than maximizing that country's living standards. Examples of such ends are to produce a diversified economy, to reduce fluctuations in national income and to retain distinctive national traditions.
- Protection can also be urged on the grounds that it may lead to higher living standards for the protectionist country than would a policy of free trade. Such a result might come about by using a monopoly position to influence

the terms of trade or by developing a dynamic comparative advantage by allowing inexperienced or uneconomically small industries to become efficient enough to compete with foreign industries.

- Some fallacious protectionist arguments are that (a) mutually advantageous trade is impossible because one trader's gain must always be the other's loss; (b) buying abroad sends our money abroad, while buying at home keeps our money at home; (c) our high-paid workers must be protected against the competition from low-paid foreign workers; and (d) imports are to be discouraged because they lower national income and cause unemployment.

Methods of Protection

(LO)(3)(4)

- Trade can be restricted by policies that either directly raise prices, such as tariffs, or operate in the first instance on quantities, such as import quotas and voluntary export restrictions.
- As tariff barriers have been reduced over the years, they have been replaced in part by nontariff barriers. The two most important are antidumping and countervailing duties which, although providing legitimate restraints on unfair trading practices, are also used as serious nontariff barriers to trade.

Current Trade Policy

(LO)(5)(6)

- The General Agreement on Tariffs and Trade (GATT), under which countries agree to reduce trade barriers through multilateral negotiations and not to raise them unilaterally, has greatly reduced world tariffs since its inception in 1947.
- The World Trade Organization (WTO) was created in 1995 as the successor to GATT. It has 134 member countries and contains a formal dispute-settlement mechanism.
- Regional trade-liberalizing agreements such as free trade areas and common markets bring efficiency gains through trade creation and efficiency losses through trade diversion.

- The North American Free Trade Agreement (NAFTA) is the world's largest and most successful free trade area, and the European Union is the world's largest and most successful common market.
- NAFTA is based on the principle of "national treatment". This allows Canada, the United States, and Mexico to implement whatever social, economic, or environmental policies it chooses providing that such policies treat foreign and domestic firms (and their products) equally.

KEY CONCEPTS

Free trade and protectionism
Tariffs and import quotas
Voluntary export restrictions (VERs)
Countervailing and antidumping duties

The General Agreement on Tariffs and Trade (GATT)
The World Trade Organization (WTO)
Common markets, customs unions, and free trade areas

Trade creation and trade diversion
Nontariff barriers
The North American Free Trade Agreement (NAFTA)

STUDY EXERCISES

1. Canada produces steel domestically and also imports it from abroad. Assume that the world market for steel is competitive and that Canada is a small producer, unable to affect the world price. Since Canada imports steel, we know that in the absence of trade, the Canadian equilibrium price would exceed the world price.

   a. Draw a diagram showing the Canadian market for steel, with imports at the world price.
   b. Explain why the imposition of a tariff on imported steel will increase the price of *both* domestic and imported steel.
   c. Show the effects of such a tariff in the diagram.
   d. Who benefits and who is harmed by such a tariff?

2. The diagram below shows the Canadian market for leather shoes, which we assume to be competitive. The world price is p_w. If the Canadian government imposes a tariff of t dollars per unit, the domestic price then rises to $p_w + t$.

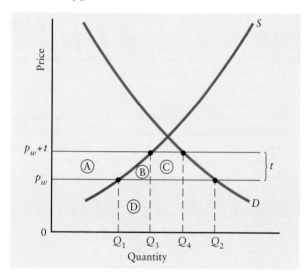

   a. What quantity of leather shoes is imported before the tariff is imposed? After the tariff?
   b. What is the effect of the tariff on the Canadian production of shoes? Which areas in the diagram show the increase in domestic producers' revenue?
   c. With the tariff in place, Canadian shoe producers are earning higher revenues. Which areas in the diagram show how much of this increased revenue is attributed to the higher price paid by Canadian consumers?
   d. The Canadian government earns tariff revenue on the imported shoes. Which area in the diagram shows this tariff revenue?

3. Use the diagram from Question 2 to analyse the effects of imposing an import quota instead of a tariff to protect domestic shoe producers. Draw the diagram as in Question 2 and answer the following questions.

   a. Explain why an import quota of Q_3Q_4 raises the domestic price to $p_w + t$.
   b. With import quotas, the Canadian government earns no tariff revenue. Who gets this money now?
   c. Is the import quota better or worse than the tariff for Canada as a whole? Explain.

4. Under pressure from the Canadian and U.S. governments in the early 1980s, Japanese automobile producers agreed to restrict their exports to the North American market. After the formal agreement ended, the Japanese producers decided unilaterally to continue restricting their exports. Carefully review Figure 35-1 and then answer the following questions.

   a. Explain why such Voluntary Export Restrictions (VERs) are "voluntary."
   b. Explain why an agreement to export only 100 000 cars to North America is better for the Japanese producers than a North American tariff that results in the same volume of Japanese exports.
   c. Who is paying for these benefits to the Japanese producers?

5. Go to Statistics Canada's website: www.statcan.ca. Find the data on "the economy" and then on "international trade," and answer the following questions.

   a. For the most recent year shown, what was the value of Canada's exports to the United States? To the European Union?
   b. For the same year, what was the value of Canada's imports from the United States? From the European Union?
   c. Compute what economists call the "volume of trade" (the sum of exports and imports) between Canada and the United States. How has the volume of trade grown over the past five years? Has trade grown faster than national income?

6. The table below shows the prices *in Canada* of cotton towels produced in the United States, Canada, and Malaysia. All cotton towels are identical.

Producing Country	Canadian Price (in $) without tariff	Canadian Price (in $) with 20% tariff
Canada	4.75	4.75
United States	4.50	5.40
Malaysia	4.00	4.80

a. Suppose Canada imposes a 20 percent tariff on imported towels from any country. Assuming that Canadians purchase only the lowest-price towels, from which country will Canada buy its towels?

b. Now suppose that Canada eliminates tariffs on towels from all countries. Which towels will Canada now buy?

c. Canada and the United States now negotiate a free-trade agreement that eliminates all tariffs between the two countries, but Canada maintains the 20 percent tariff on other countries. Which towels now get imported into Canada?

d. Which of the situations described above is called trade creation and which is called trade diversion?

DISCUSSION QUESTIONS

1. Some Canadians opposed Canada's entry into NAFTA on the grounds that Canadian firms could not compete with the goods produced by cheap Mexican labour. Comment on the following points in relation to the above worries:

   a. "Mexicans are the most expensive cheap labour I have ever encountered"—statement by the owner of a Canadian firm who is moving back from Mexico to Canada.

   b. The theory of the gains from trade says that a high-productivity, high-wage country can gain from trading with a low-wage, low-productivity country.

   c. Technological change is rapidly reducing labour costs as a proportion of total costs in many products; in many industries that use high-tech production methods this proportion is already well below 20 percent.

2. Should Canada and the United States trade with countries with poor human rights records? If trade with China is severely restricted because of its lack of respect for human rights, who will be the gainers and who the losers? Argue the cases that this policy will help, and that it will hinder, human rights progress in China.

3. Import quotas and voluntary export restrictions are often used instead of tariffs. What real difference, if any, is there between quotas, voluntary export restrictions (VERs), and tariffs? Explain why lobbyists for some import-competing industries (cheese, milk, shoes) support import quotas while lobbyists for others (pizza manufacturers, soft drink manufacturers, retail stores) oppose them. Would you expect labour unions to support or oppose quotas?

4. Over the past several years, many foreign automobile producers have built production and assembly facilities in Canada and in the United States. What are some advantages and disadvantages associated with shifting production from, for example, Japan to Canada? Will these cars still be considered "imports"? What is beginning to happen to the definitions of "foreign made" and "domestic made"?

5. Consider a mythical country called Forestland, which exports a large amount of lumber to a nearby country called Houseland. The lumber industry in Houseland has convinced its federal government that it is being harmed by the low prices being charged by the lumber producers in Forestland. You are an advisor to the government in Forestland. Explain who gains and who loses from each of the following policies.

   a. Houseland imposes a tariff on lumber imports from Forestland

   b. Forestland imposes a tax on each unit of lumber exported to Houseland

   c. Forestland agrees to restrict its exports of lumber to Houseland

   d. Which policy is likely to garner the most political support in Houseland? In Forestland?

6. In March 1999, the Canadian government imposed antidumping duties of up to 43 percent on hot-rolled steel imports from France, Russia, Slovakia, and Romania. The allegation was that these countries were dumping steel into the Canadian market.

   a. Who benefits from such alleged dumping? Who is harmed?

   b. Who benefits from the imposition of the antidumping duties? Who is harmed?

   c. Is Canada as a whole made better off by the imposition of the duties? Explain.

MATHEMATICAL NOTES

1. Because one cannot divide by zero, the ratio $\Delta Y/\Delta X$ cannot be evaluated when $\Delta X = 0$. However, as ΔX *approaches* zero, the ratio $\Delta Y/\Delta X$ increases without limit:

$$\lim_{\Delta X \to 0} \frac{\Delta Y}{\Delta X} = \infty$$

Therefore, we say that the slope of a vertical line (when $\Delta X = 0$ for any ΔY) is equal to infinity.

2. Many variables affect the quantity demanded. Using functional notation, the argument of the next several pages of the text can be anticipated. Let Q^D represent the quantity of a commodity demanded and

$$T, \overline{Y}, N, \hat{Y}, p, p_j$$

represent, respectively, tastes, average household income, population, income distribution, the commodity's own price, and the price of the jth other commodity.

The demand function is

$$Q^D = D(T, \overline{Y}, N, \hat{Y}, p, p_j), \qquad j = 1, 2, \ldots, n$$

The demand schedule or curve is given by

$$Q^D = d(p) \,\Big|\, T, \overline{Y}, N, \hat{Y}, p_j$$

where the notation means that the variables to the right of the vertical line are held constant.

This function is correctly described as the demand function with respect to price, all other variables being held constant. This function, often written concisely as $q^d = d(p)$, shifts in response to changes in other variables. Consider average income: if, as is usually hypothesized, $\partial Q^D/\partial \overline{Y} > 0$, then increases in average income shift $q^d = d(p)$ rightward and decreases in average income shift $q^d = d(p)$ leftward. Changes in other variables likewise shift this function in the direction implied by the relationship of that variable to the quantity demanded.

3. Quantity demanded is a simple and straightforward but frequently misunderstood concept in everyday use, but it has a clear mathematical meaning. It refers to the dependent variable in the demand function from note 2:

$$Q^D = D(T, \overline{Y}, N, \hat{Y}, p, p_j)$$

It takes on a specific value whenever a specific value is assigned to each of the independent variables. The value of Q^D changes whenever the value of any independent variable is changed. Q^D could change, for example, as a result of a change in any one price, in average income, in the distribution of income, in tastes, or in population. It could also change as a result of the net effect of changes in all of the independent variables occurring at once.

Some textbooks reserve the term *change in quantity demanded* for a movement along a demand curve, that is, a change in Q^D as a result *only* of a change in p. They then use other words for a change in Q^D caused by a change in the other variables in the demand function. This usage is potentially confusing because it gives the single variable Q^D more than one name.

Our usage, which corresponds to that in more advanced treatments, avoids this confusion. We call Q^D *quantity demanded* and refer to any change in Q^D as a *change in quantity demanded*. In this usage it is correct to say that a movement along a demand curve is a change in quantity demanded, but it is incorrect to say that a change in quantity demanded can occur *only because of* a movement along a demand curve (because Q^D can change for other reasons, for example, a *ceteris paribus* change in average household income).

4. Similar to the way we treated quantity demanded in note 2, let Q^S represent the quantity of a commodity supplied and

$$C, X, p, w_i$$

represent, respectively, producers' goals, technology, the product's price, and the price of the ith input.

The supply function is

$$Q^S = S(C, X, p, w_i), \qquad i = 1, 2, \ldots, m$$

The supply schedule or curve is given by

$$Q^S = s(p) \,\Big|\, C, X, w_i$$

M-1

This is the supply function with respect to price, all other variables being held constant. This function, often written concisely as $q^s = s(p)$, shifts in response to changes in other variables.

5. Equilibrium occurs where $Q^D = Q^S$. For *specified values of all other variables*, this requires that

$$d(p) = s(p) \qquad [5.1]$$

Equation 5.1 defines an equilibrium value of p; hence, although p is an *independent* or *exogenous* variable in each of the supply and demand functions, it is an *endogenous* variable in the economic model that imposes the equilibrium condition expressed in Equation 5.1. Price is endogenous because it is assumed to adjust to bring about equality between quantity demanded and quantity supplied. Equilibrium quantity, also an endogenous variable, is determined by substituting the equilibrium price into either $d(p)$ or $s(p)$.

Graphically, Equation 5.1 is satisfied only at the point where the demand and supply curves intersect. Thus, supply and demand curves are said to determine the equilibrium values of the endogenous variables, price and quantity. A shift in any of the independent variables held constant in the d and s functions will shift the demand or supply curves and lead to different equilibrium values for price and quantity.

6. The definition in the text uses finite changes and is called *arc elasticity*. The parallel definition using derivatives is

$$\eta = \frac{dq}{dp} \cdot \frac{p}{q}$$

and is called *point elasticity*. Further discussion appears in the Appendix to Chapter 4.

7. The propositions in the text are proved as follows. Letting TE stand for total expenditure, we can write

$$TE = p \cdot q$$

It follows that the change in total expenditure is

$$dTE = q \cdot dp + p \cdot dq \qquad [7.1]$$

Multiplying and dividing both terms on the right-hand side of Equation 7.1 by $p \cdot q$ yields

$$dTE = \left[\frac{dp}{p} + \frac{dq}{q} \right] \cdot (p \cdot q)$$

Because dp and dq are opposite in sign as we move along the demand curve, dTE will have the same sign as the term in brackets on the right-hand side that dominates—that is, on which percentage change is largest.

A second way of arranging Equation 7.1 is to divide both sides by dp to get

$$\frac{dTE}{dp} = q + p \cdot \frac{dq}{dp} \qquad [7.2]$$

From the definition of point elasticity in note 6, however,

$$q \cdot \eta = p \cdot \frac{dq}{dp} \qquad [7.3]$$

which we can substitute into Equation 7.1 to obtain

$$\frac{dTE}{dp} = q + q \cdot \eta = q \cdot (1 + \eta) \qquad [7.4]$$

Because η is a negative number, the sign of the right-hand side of Equation 7.4 is negative if the absolute value of η exceeds unity (elastic demand) and positive if it is less than unity (inelastic demand).

Total expenditure is maximized when dTE/dp is equal to zero. As can be seen from Equation 7.4, this occurs when elasticity is equal to -1.

8. The axis reversal arose in the following way. Alfred Marshall (1842–1924) theorized in terms of "demand price" and "supply price," these being the prices that would lead to a given quantity being demanded or supplied. Thus,

$$p^d = d(q) \qquad [8.1]$$
$$p^s = s(q) \qquad [8.2]$$

and the condition of equilibrium is

$$d(q) = s(q)$$

When graphing the behavioural relationships expressed in Equations 8.1 and 8.2, Marshall naturally put the independent variable, q, on the horizontal axis.

Leon Walras (1834–1910), whose formulation of the working of a competitive market has become the accepted one, focused on quantity demanded and quantity supplied *at a given price*. Thus,

$$q^d = d(p)$$

$$q^s = s(p)$$

and the condition of equilibrium is

$$d(p) = s(p)$$

Walras did not use graphical representation. Had he done so, he would surely have placed p (his independent variable) on the horizontal axis.

Marshall, among his other influences on later generations of economists, was the great popularizer of graphical analysis in economics. Today, we use his graphs, even for Walras's analysis. The axis reversal is thus one of those historical accidents that seem odd to people who did not live through the "perfectly natural" sequence of steps that produced it.

9. The distinction made between an incremental change and a marginal change is the distinction for the function $Y = Y(X)$ between $\Delta Y/\Delta X$ and the derivative dY/dX. The latter is the limit of the former as ΔX approaches zero. We shall meet this distinction repeatedly—in this chapter in reference to marginal and incremental *utility* and in later chapters with respect to such concepts as marginal and incremental *product, cost,* and *revenue.* Where Y is a function of more than one variable—for example, $Y = f(X,Z)$—the marginal relationship between Y and X is the partial derivative $\partial Y/\partial X$ rather than the total derivative, dY/dX.

10. The hypothesis of diminishing marginal utility requires that we can measure utility of consumption by a function

$$U = U(X_1, X_2, \ldots, X_n)$$

where $X_1, \ldots, X_n$ are quantities of the n goods consumed by a household. It really embodies two utility hypotheses: first,

$$\partial U/\partial X_i > 0$$

which says that the consumer can get more utility by increasing consumption of the commodity; second,

$$\partial^2 U/\partial X_i^2 < 0$$

which says that the utility of *additional* consumption of some good declines as the amount of that good consumed increases.

11. Because the slope of the indifference curve is negative, it is the absolute value of the slope that de-

clines as one moves downward to the right along the curve. The algebraic value, of course, increases. The phrase *diminishing marginal rate of substitution* thus refers to the absolute, not the algebraic, value of the slope.

12. The relationship between the slope of the budget line and relative prices can be seen as follows. In the two-good example, a change in expenditure (ΔE) is given by the equation

$$\Delta E = p_C \cdot \Delta C + p_F \cdot \Delta F \qquad [12.1]$$

Expenditure is constant for all combinations of F and C that lie on the same budget line. Thus, along such a line we have $\Delta E = 0$. This implies

$$p_C \cdot \Delta C + p_F \cdot \Delta F = 0 \qquad [12.2]$$

and thus

$$-\Delta C/\Delta F = p_F/p_C \qquad [12.3]$$

The ratio $-\Delta C/\Delta F$ is the slope of the budget line. It is negative because, with a fixed budget, one must consume less C in order to consume more F. In other words, Equation 12.3 says that the negative of the slope of the budget line is the ratio of the absolute prices (i.e., the relative price). Although prices do not show directly in Figure 6A-3, they are implicit in the budget line: Its slope depends solely on the relative price, while its position, given a fixed money income, depends on the absolute prices of the two goods.

13. *Marginal product,* as defined in the text, is really *incremental* product. More advanced treatments distinguish between this notion and marginal product as the limit of the ratio as ΔL approaches zero. Marginal product thus measures the rate at which total product is changing as one factor is varied and is the partial derivative of the total product with respect to the variable factor. In symbols,

$$MP = \frac{\partial TP}{\partial L}$$

14. We have referred specifically both to diminishing *marginal* product and to diminishing *average* product. In most cases, eventually diminishing marginal product implies eventually diminishing average product. This is, however, not necessary, as the accompanying figure shows.

In this case, marginal product diminishes after v units of the variable factor are employed. Because marginal product falls toward, but never quite reaches, a value of m, average product rises continually toward, but never quite reaches, the same value.

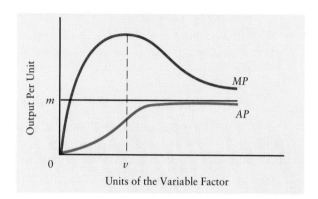

Units of the Variable Factor

15. Let q be the quantity of output and L the quantity of the variable factor. In the short run,

$$TP = q = f(L) \qquad [15.1]$$

We now define

$$AP = \frac{q}{L} = \frac{f(L)}{L} \qquad [15.2]$$

$$MP = \frac{dq}{dL} \qquad [15.3]$$

We are concerned with the relationship between these two. Where average product is rising, at a maximum, or falling is determined by its derivative with respect to L:

$$\frac{d(q/L)}{dL} = \frac{L \cdot (dq/dL) - q}{L^2} \qquad [15.4]$$

This may be rewritten

$$\frac{1}{L} \cdot \left[\frac{dq}{dL} - \frac{q}{L} \right] = \frac{1}{L} \cdot (MP - AP) \qquad [15.5]$$

Clearly, when MP is greater than AP, the expression in Equation 15.5 is positive and thus AP is rising. When MP is less than AP, AP is falling. When they are equal, AP is neither rising nor falling.

16. The text defines *incremental cost*. Strictly, marginal cost is the rate of change of total cost with respect to output, q. Thus,

$$MC = \frac{dTC}{dq}$$

From the definitions, $TC = TFC + TVC$. Fixed costs are not a function of output. Thus, we may write $TC = Z + f(q)$, where $f(q)$ is total variable costs and Z is a constant. From this we see that $MC = df(q)/dq$. MC is thus independent of the size of the fixed costs.

17. This point is easily seen if a little algebra is used:

$$AVC = \frac{TVC}{q}$$

but note that $TVC = L \cdot w$ and $q = AP \cdot L$, where L is the quantity of the variable factor used and w is its cost per unit. Therefore,

$$AVC = \frac{L \cdot w}{AP \cdot L} = \frac{w}{AP}$$

Because w is a constant, it follows that AVC and AP vary inversely with each other, and when AP is at its maximum value, AVC must be at its minimum value.

18. A little elementary calculus will prove the point:

$$MC = \frac{dTC}{dq} = \frac{dTVC}{dq} = \frac{d(L \cdot w)}{dq}$$

If w does not vary with output,

$$MC = \frac{dL}{dq} \cdot w$$

However, referring to note 15 (Equation 15.3), we see that

$$\frac{dL}{dq} = \frac{1}{MP}$$

Thus,

$$MC = \frac{w}{MP}$$

Because w is fixed, MC varies negatively with MP. When MP is at a maximum, MC is at a minimum.

19. Strictly speaking, the marginal rate of substitution refers to the slope of the tangent to the isoquant at a particular point, whereas the calculations in Table 8A-1 refer to the average rate of substitution between two distinct points on the isoquant. Assume a production function

$$Q = Q(K,L) \qquad [19.1]$$

Isoquants are given by the function

$$K = I(L,\overline{Q}) \qquad [19.2]$$

derived from Equation 19.1 by expressing K as an explicit function of L and Q. A single isoquant relates to a particular level of output, Q. Define Q_K and Q_L as an alternative, more compact notation for $\partial Q/\partial K$ and $\partial Q/\partial L$, the marginal products of capital and labour. Also, let Q_{KK} and Q_{LL} stand for $\partial^2 Q/\partial K^2$ and $\partial^2 Q/\partial L^2$, respectively. To obtain the slope of the isoquant, totally differentiate Equation 19.1 to obtain

$$dQ = Q_K \cdot dK + Q_L \cdot dL$$

Then, because we are moving along a single isoquant, set $dQ = 0$ to obtain

$$\frac{dK}{dL} = -\frac{Q_L}{Q_K} = MRS$$

Diminishing marginal productivity implies $Q_{LL} < 0$ and $Q_{KK} < 0$, and hence, as we move down the isoquant of Figure 8A-1, Q_K is rising and Q_L is falling, so the absolute value of MRS is diminishing. This is called the *hypothesis of a diminishing marginal rate of substitution.*

20. Formally, the problem is to maximize

$$Q = Q(K,L)$$

subject to the constraint

$$p_K \cdot K + p_L \cdot L = C$$

To do this, form the Lagrangean,

$$\mathcal{L} = Q(K, L) - \lambda(p_K \cdot K + p_L \cdot L - C)$$

The first-order conditions for this maximization problem are

$$Q_K = \lambda \cdot p_K \qquad [20.1]$$

$$Q_L = \lambda \cdot p_L \qquad [20.2]$$

$$p_K \cdot K + p_L \cdot L = C \qquad [20.3]$$

Dividing Equation 20.1 by Equation 20.2 yields

$$\frac{Q_K}{Q_L} = \frac{p_K}{p_L}$$

That is, the ratio of the marginal products, which is -1 times the MRS, is equal to the ratio of the factor prices, which is -1 times the slope of the isocost line.

21. Marginal revenue is mathematically the derivative of total revenue with respect to output, dTR/dq. Incremental revenue is $\Delta TR/\Delta q$. However, the term *marginal revenue* is used loosely to refer to both concepts.

22. For notes 22 through 24, it is helpful first to define some terms. Let

$$\pi_n = TR_n - TC_n$$

where π_n is the profit when n units are sold.

If the firm is maximizing its profits by producing n units, it is necessary that the profits at output q_n be at least as large as the profits at output zero. If the firm is maximizing its profits at output n, then

$$\pi_n \geq \pi_0 \qquad [22.1]$$

The condition says that profits from producing must be greater than profits from not producing. Condition 22.1 can be rewritten as

$$TR_n - TVC_n - TFC_n \geq TR_0 - TVC_0 - TFC_0 \qquad [22.2]$$

However, note that by definition

$$TR_0 = 0 \qquad [22.3]$$

$$TVC_0 = 0 \qquad [22.4]$$

$$TFC_n = TFC_0 = Z \qquad [22.5]$$

where Z is a constant. By substituting Equations 22.3, 22.4, and 22.5 into Condition 22.2, we get

$$TR_n - TVC_n \geq 0$$

from which we obtain

$$TR_n \geq TVC_n$$

This proves Rule 1.

On a per-unit basis, it becomes

$$\frac{TR_n}{q_n} \geq \frac{TVC_n}{q_n} \qquad [22.6]$$

where q_n is the number of units produced.

Because $TR_n = q_n \cdot p_n$, where p_n is the price when n units are sold, Condition 22.6 may be rewritten as

$$p_n \geq AVC_n$$

23. Using elementary calculus, we may prove Rule 2.

$$\pi_n = TR_n - TC_n$$

each of which is a function of output q. To maximize π, it is necessary that

$$\frac{d\pi}{dq} = 0 \qquad [23.1]$$

and that

$$\frac{d^2\pi}{dq^2} < 0 \qquad [23.2]$$

From the definitions,

$$\frac{d\pi}{dq} = \frac{dTR}{dq} - \frac{dTC}{dq} = MR - MC \quad [23.3]$$

From Equations 23.1 and 23.3, a necessary condition for attaining maximum π is $MR - MC = 0$, or $MR = MC$, as is required by Rule 2.

24. To prove that for a negatively sloped demand curve, marginal revenue is less than price, let $p = p(q)$. Then

$$TR = p \cdot q = p(q) \cdot q$$

$$MR = \frac{dTR}{dq} = q \cdot \frac{dp}{dq} + p$$

For a negatively sloped demand curve, dp/dq is negative, and thus MR is less than price for positive values of q.

25. The equation for a downward-sloping straight-line demand curve with price on the vertical axis is

$$p = a - b \cdot q$$

where $-b$ is the slope of the demand curve. Total revenue is price times quantity:

$$TR = p \cdot q = a \cdot q - b \cdot q^2$$

Marginal revenue is

$$MR = \frac{dTR}{dq} = a - 2 \cdot b \cdot q$$

Thus, the MR curve and the demand curve are both straight lines, and the (absolute value of the) slope of the MR curve ($2b$) is twice that of the demand curve (b).

26. The marginal revenue produced by the factor involves two elements: first, the additional output that an extra unit of the factor makes possible and, second, the change in price of the product that the extra output causes. Let Q be output, R revenue, and L the number of units of labour hired. The contribution to revenue of additional labour is $\partial R/\partial L$. This, in turn, depends on the contribution of the extra labour to output $\partial Q/\partial L$ (the marginal product of the factor) and $\partial R/\partial Q$ (the firm's marginal revenue from the extra output). Thus,

$$\frac{\partial R}{\partial L} = \frac{\partial Q}{\partial L} \cdot \frac{\partial R}{\partial Q}$$

We define the left-hand side as marginal revenue product, MRP. Thus,

$$MRP = MP \cdot MR$$

27. The proposition that the marginal labour cost is above the average labour cost when the average is rising is essentially the same proposition proved in note 15. Nevertheless, let us do it again, using elementary calculus.

The quantity of labour supplied depends on the wage rate: $L^s = f(w)$. Total labour cost along the supply curve is $w \cdot L^s$. The average cost of labour is $(w \cdot L^s) / L^s = w$. The marginal cost of labour is

$$\frac{d(w \cdot L^s)}{dL^s} = w + L^s \cdot \frac{dw}{dL^s}$$

Rewrite this as

$$MC = AC + L \cdot \frac{dw}{dL^s}$$

As long as the supply curve slopes upward, $dw/dL^s > 0$; therefore, $MC > AC$.

28. In general, for any growth rate per unit of time, g, and starting value, P_0, the price level at time t will be $P_0(1 + g)^t$. This is the formula for *compound* growth at rate g per unit of time. For small values of g, $(1 + g)^t$ will be very close to $(1 + tg)$. But as g gets larger, so does the difference. For example, if prices are growing at 2 percent per month, the annual growth will be $(1.02)^{12} = 1.268$, yielding a growth rate of 26.8 percent per year. This is considerably more than 24 percent, which is just the monthly rate times 12. Generally, annual rates of growth are calculated by compounding rates of growth that are measured over shorter or longer periods than one year.

29. In the text, we define *MPC* as an incremental ratio. For mathematical treatment, it is sometimes convenient to define all marginal concepts as derivatives: $MPC = dC/dY_D$, $MPS = dS/dY_D$, and so on.

30. The basic relationship is

$$Y_D = C + S$$

Dividing through by Y_D yields

$$\frac{Y_D}{Y_D} = \frac{C}{Y_D} + \frac{S}{Y_D}$$

and thus

$$1 = APC + APS$$

Next, take the first difference of the basic relationship to get

$$\Delta Y_D = \Delta C + \Delta S$$

Dividing through by ΔY_D gives

$$\frac{\Delta Y_D}{\Delta Y_D} = \frac{\Delta C}{\Delta Y_D} + \frac{\Delta S}{\Delta Y_D}$$

and thus

$$1 = MPC + MPS$$

31. The total expenditure over all rounds is the sum of an infinite series. If we let A stand for autonomous expenditure and z for the marginal propensity to spend, the change in autonomous expenditure is ΔA in the first round, $z \cdot \Delta A$ in the second, $z^2 \cdot \Delta A$ in the third, and so on. This can be written as

$$\Delta A \cdot (1 + z + z^2 + \ldots + z^n)$$

If z is less than 1, the series in parentheses converges to $1/(1 - z)$ as n approaches infinity. The total change in expenditure is thus $\Delta A/(1 - z)$. In the example in the box, $z = 0.80$; therefore, the change in total expenditure is five times ΔA.

32. This is easily proved. The banking system wants sufficient deposits (D) to establish the target ratio (v) of deposits to reserves (R). This gives $R/D = v$. Any change in D of size ΔD has to be accompanied by a change in R of ΔR of sufficient size to restore v. Thus, $\Delta R/\Delta D = v$, so $\Delta D = \Delta R/v$ and $\Delta D/\Delta R = 1/v$. This can be shown also in terms of the deposits created by the sequence in Table 26-7.

Let v be the reserve ratio and $e = 1 - v$ be the excess reserves per dollar of new deposits. If X dollars are initially deposited in the system, the successive rounds of new deposits will be X, eX, e^2X, e^3X, ... The series

$$X + eX + e^2X + e^3X + \ldots$$
$$= X \cdot [1 + e + e^2 + e^3 + \ldots]$$

has a limit of $X \cdot \dfrac{1}{1 - e}$

$$= X \cdot \frac{1}{1 - (1 - v)} = \frac{X}{v}$$

This is the total new deposits created by an injection of \$X of new reserves into the banking system. For example, when $v = 0.20$, an injection of \$100 into the system will lead to an overall increase in deposits of \$500.

33. Suppose that the public wishes to hold a fraction, c, of deposits in cash, C. Now suppose that X dollars are injected into the system. Ultimately, this money will be held either as reserves by the banking system or as cash by the public. Thus, we have

$$\Delta C + \Delta R = X$$

From the banking system's reserve behaviour, we have $\Delta R = v \cdot \Delta D$, and from the public's cash behaviour, we have $\Delta C = c \cdot \Delta D$. Substituting into the above equation, we get the result that

$$\Delta D = \frac{X}{v + c}$$

From this we can also relate the change in reserves and the change in cash holdings to the initial injection:

$$\Delta R = \frac{v}{v + c} \cdot X$$

$$\Delta C = \frac{c}{v + c} \cdot X$$

For example, when $v = 0.20$ and $c = 0.05$, an injection of \$100 will lead to an increase in reserves of \$80, an increase in cash in the hands of the public of \$20, and an increase in deposits of \$400.

34. Let $L(Y,r)$ give the real demand for money measured in purchasing power units. Let M be the

supply of money measured in nominal units and P the price level, so that M/P is the real supply of money. Now the equilibrium condition requiring equality between the demand for money and the supply of money can be expressed in real terms as

$$L(Y, r) = \frac{M}{P} \qquad [36.1]$$

or in nominal terms by multiplying through by P,

$$P \cdot L(Y, r) = M \qquad [36.2]$$

In Equation 36.1, a rise in P disturbs equilibrium by lowering M/P, and in Equation 36.2, it disturbs equilibrium by raising $P \cdot L(Y, r)$.

35. This is based on what is called the "rule of 72". Any sum growing at the rate of X percent per year will double in approximately $72/X$ years. For two sums growing at the rates of X percent and Y percent per year, the *difference* between the two sums will double in approximately $72/(X - Y)$ years.

36. The time taken to break even is a function of the *difference* in growth rates, not their *levels*. Thus, if 4 percent and 5 percent or 5 percent and 6 percent had been used in the example, it still would have taken the same number of years. To see this quickly, recognize that we are interested in the ratio of two growth paths:

$$\frac{e^{r_1 t}}{e^{r_2 t}} = e^{(r_1 - r_2)t}$$

37. A simple example of a production function is $GDP = z(LK)^{1/2}$. This equation says that to find the amount of GDP produced, multiply the amount of labour by the amount of capital, take the square root, and multiply the result by the constant z. This production function has positive but diminishing marginal returns to either factor. This can be seen by evaluating the first and second partial derivatives and showing the first derivatives to be positive and the second derivatives to be negative.

For example,

$$\frac{\partial GDP}{\partial K} = \frac{z \cdot L^{1/2}}{2 \cdot K^{1/2}} > 0$$

and

$$\frac{\partial^2 GDP}{\partial K^2} = -\frac{z \cdot L^{1/2}}{2 \cdot K^{3/2}} < 0$$

38. The production function $GDP = z(LK)^{1/2}$ displays contant returns to scale. To see this, multiply both L and K by the same constant, θ, and see that this multiplies the whole value of GDP by θ:

$$z(\theta L \cdot \theta K)^{1/2} = z(\theta^2 \cdot LK)^{1/2} = \theta z(LK)^{1/2} = \theta \cdot GDP$$

Time Line of Great Economists

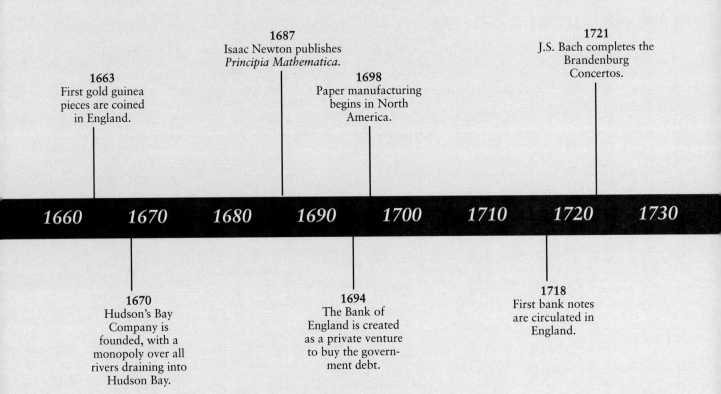

1663
First gold guinea pieces are coined in England.

1687
Isaac Newton publishes *Principia Mathematica*.

1698
Paper manufacturing begins in North America.

1721
J.S. Bach completes the Brandenburg Concertos.

1660   1670   1680   1690   1700   1710   1720   1730

1670
Hudson's Bay Company is founded, with a monopoly over all rivers draining into Hudson Bay.

1694
The Bank of England is created as a private venture to buy the government debt.

1718
First bank notes are circulated in England.

ADAM SMITH (1723–1790)

Adam Smith was born in 1723 in the small Scottish town of Kirkcaldy. He is perhaps the single most influential figure in the development of modern economics, and even those who have never studied economics know of his most famous work, *The Wealth of Nations*, and of the terms *laissez faire* and the *invisible hand,* both attributable to Smith. He was able to describe the workings of the capitalist market economy, the division of labor in production, the role of money, free trade, and the nature of economic growth. Even today, the breadth of his scholarship is considered astounding.

Smith was raised by his mother, as his father had died before his birth. His intellectual promise was discovered early, and at age 14 Smith was sent to study at Glasgow and then at Oxford. He then returned to an appointment as professor of moral philosophy at University of Glasgow, where he became one of the leading philosophers of his day. He lectured on natural theology, ethics, jurisprudence, and political economy to students who traveled from as far away as Russia to hear his lectures.

In 1759, Smith published *The Theory of Moral Sentiments*, in which he attempted to identify the origins of moral judgment. In this early work, Smith writes of the motivation of self-interest and of the morality that keeps it in check. After its publication, Smith left his post at the University of Glasgow to embark on a European tour as the tutor to a young aristocrat, the Duke of Buccleuch, with whom he traveled for two years. In exchange for this assignment Smith was provided with a salary for the remainder of his life. He returned to the small town of his birth and spent the next 10 years alone, writing his most famous work.

An Inquiry into the Nature and Causes of the Wealth of Nations was published in 1776. His contributions in this book (generally known as *The Wealth of Nations)* were revolutionary, and the text became the foundation of much of modern economics. It continues to be reprinted today. Smith rejected the notion that a country's supply of gold and silver was the measure of its wealth—rather, it was the real incomes of the people that determined national wealth. Growth in the real incomes of the country's citizens—that is, economic growth—would result from specialization in production, the division of labor, and the use of money to facilitate trade. Smith provided a framework for analyzing the questions of income growth, value, and distribution.

Smith's work marked the beginning of what is called the Classical period in economic thought, which continued for the next 75 years. This school of thought was centered on the principles of natural liberty (laissez faire) and the importance of economic growth as a means of bettering the conditions of human existence.

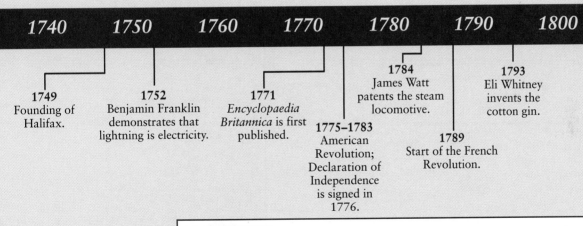

| 1740 | 1750 | 1760 | 1770 | 1780 | 1790 | 1800 |

1749
Founding of Halifax.

1752
Benjamin Franklin demonstrates that lightning is electricity.

1771
Encyclopaedia Britannica is first published.

1775–1783
American Revolution; Declaration of Independence is signed in 1776.

1784
James Watt patents the steam locomotive.

1789
Start of the French Revolution.

1793
Eli Whitney invents the cotton gin.

THOMAS MALTHUS (1766–1834)

Thomas Malthus was born into a reasonably well-to-do English family. He was educated at Cambridge and from 1805 until his death he held the first British professorship of political economy in the East India Company's college at Haileybury. In 1798 he published *An Essay on the Principle of Population as It Affects the Future Improvement of Society*, which was revised many times in subsequent years until finally he published *A Summary View of the Principle of Population* in 1830.

It is these essays on population for which Malthus is best known. His first proposition was that population, when unchecked, would increase in a geometric progression such that the population would double every 25 years. His second proposition was that the means of subsistence (i.e. the food supply) cannot possibly increase faster than in arithmetic progression (increasing by a given number of units every year). The result would be population growth eventually outstripping food production, and thus abject poverty and suffering for the majority of people in every society.

Malthus's population theory had tremendous intellectual influence at the time and became an integral part of the Classical theory of income distribution. However, it is no longer taken as a good description of current or past trends.

DAVID RICARDO (1772–1823)

David Ricardo was born in London to parents who had immigrated from the Netherlands. Ricardo's father was very successful in money markets, and Ricardo himself had earned enough money on the stock exchange that he was very wealthy before he was 30. He had little formal education, but after reading Adam Smith's *The Wealth of Nations* in 1799, he chose to divide his time between studying and writing about political economy and increasing his own personal wealth.

Ricardo's place in the history of economics was assured by his achievement in constructing an abstract model of how capitalism worked. He built an analytic "system" using deductive reasoning that characterizes economic theorizing to the present day. The three critical principles in Ricardo's system were (1) the theory of rent, (2) Thomas Malthus's population principle, and (3) the wages-fund doctrine. Ricardo published *The Principles of Political Economy and Taxation* in 1817, which dominated Classical economics for the following half-century.

Ricardo also contributed the concept of comparative advantage to the study of international trade. Ricardo's theories regarding the gains from trade had some influence on the repeal of the British Corn Laws in 1846—tariffs on the importation of grains into Great Britain—and the subsequent transformation of that country during the nineteenth century from a country of high tarrifs to one of completely free trade.

1814
British forces burn Washington, D.C., in the War of 1812.

1831
The first horse-drawn buses appear in New York.

1837
Victoria becomes Queen of England (until 1901). Rebellions in Upper and Lower Canada.

1800   *1810*   *1820*   *1830*

1805
Admiral Horatio Nelson's victory (and death) at Trafalgar.

1815
Napoleon defeated at Waterloo and exiled to St. Helena; Corn Laws passed in Britain.

1822
First textile mills are built in Lowell, Massachusetts.

JOHN STUART MILL (1806–1873)

John Stuart Mill, born in London, was the son of James Mill, a prominent British historian, economist, and philosopher. By age 12 he was acquainted with the major economics works of the day, and at 13 he was correcting the proofs of his father's book, *Elements of Political Economy*. J. S. Mill spent most of his life working at the East India Company—his extraordinarily prolific writing career was conducted entirely as an aside. In 1848 he published his *Principles of Political Economy*, which updated the principles found in Adam Smith's *The Wealth of Nations* and which remained the basic textbook for students of economics until the end of the nineteenth century. In *Principles*, Mill made an important contribution to the economics discipline by distinguishing between the economics of production and of distribution. He pointed out that economic laws had nothing to do with the distribution of wealth, which was a societal matter, but had everything to do with production.

Previous to Mill's *Principles* was his *System of Logic* (1843), which was the century's most influential text on logic and the theory of knowledge. His essays on ethics, contemporary culture, and freedom of speech, such as *Utilitarianism* and *On Liberty*, are still widely studied today.

KARL MARX (1818–1883)

Karl Marx was born in Trier, Germany (then part of Prussia), and studied law, history, and philosophy at the universities of Bonn, Berlin, and Jena. Marx traveled between Prussia, Paris, and Brussels, working at various jobs until finally settling in London in 1849, where he lived the remainder of his life. Most of his time was spent in the mainly unpaid pursuits of writing and studying economics in the library of the British Museum. Marx's contributions to economics are intricately bound to his views of history and society. *The Communist Manifesto* was published with Friedrich Engels in 1848, his *Critique of Political Economy* in 1859, and in 1867 the first volume of *Das Kapital*. (The remaining volumes, edited by Engels, were published after Marx's death.)

For Marx, capitalism was a stage in an evolutionary process from a primitive agricultural economy toward an inevitable elimination of private property and the class structure. Marx's "labor theory of value," whereby the quantity of labor used in the manufacture of a product determined its value, held the central place in his economic thought. He believed that the worker provided "surplus value" to the capitalist. The capitalist would then use the profit arising from this surplus value to reinvest in plant and machinery. Through time, more would be spent for plant and machinery than for wages, which would lead to lower profits (since profits arose only from the surplus value from labor) and a resulting squeeze in the real income of workers. Marx believed that in the capitalists' effort to maintain profits in this unstable system, there would emerge a "reserve army of the unemployed." The resulting class conflict would become increasingly acute until revolution by the workers would overthrow capitalism.

1859
Charles Darwin publishes *On the Origin of Species.*

1846
Britain repeals the Corn Laws.

1867
British North America Act establishes the Dominion of Canada. Alfred Nobel invents dynamite.

1840

1850

1860

1870

1844
Electric telegraph opens between Washington and Baltimore.

1861–1865
The U.S. Civil War; Abraham Lincoln is assassinated in 1865.

1869
Opening of the Suez Canal.

1840
Act of Union unites Upper and Lower Canada.

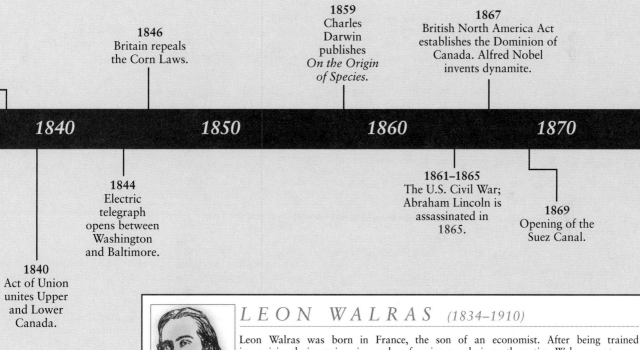

LEON WALRAS (1834–1910)

Leon Walras was born in France, the son of an economist. After being trained inauspiciously in engineering and performing poorly in mathematics, Walras spent some time pursuing other endeavors, such as novel writing and working for the railway. Eventually he promised his father he would study economics, and by 1870 he was given a professorship in economics in the Faculty of Law at the University of Lausanne in Switzerland. Once there, Walras began the feverish activity that eventually led to his important contributions to economic theory.

In the 1870s, Walras was one of three economists to put forward the marginal utility theory of value (simultaneously with William Stanley Jevons of England and Carl Menger of Austria). Further, he constructed a mathematical model of general equilibrium using a system of simultaneous equations that he used to argue that equilibrium prices and quantities are uniquely determined. Central to general equilibrium analysis is the notion that the prices and quantities of all commodities are determined simultaneously because the whole system is interdependent. Walras's most important work was *Elements of Pure Economics*, published in 1874. In addition to all of Walras's other accomplishments in economics (and despite his early poor performance in mathematics!), we today regard him as the founder of mathematical economics.

Leon Walras and Alfred Marshall are regarded by many economists to be the two most important economic theorists who ever lived. Much of the framework of economic theory studied today is either Walrasian or Marshallian in character.

CARL MENGER (1840–1921)

Carl Menger was born in Galicia (then part of Austria), and he came from a family of Austrian civil servants and army officers. After studying law in Prague and Vienna, he turned to economics and in 1871 published *Grundsatze der Volkswirtschaftslehre* (translated as *Principles of Economics*), for which he became famous. He held a professorship at the University of Vienna until 1903. Menger was the founder of a school of thought known as the "Austrian School," which effectively displaced the German historical method on the continent and which survives today as an alternative to mainstream Neoclassical economics.

Menger was one of three economists in the 1870s who independently put forward a theory of value based on marginal utility. Prior to what economists now call the "marginal revolution," value was thought to be derived solely from the inputs of labor and capital. Menger developed the marginal utility theory of value, in which the value of any good is determined by individuals' subjective evaluations of that good. According to Menger, a good has some value if it has the ability to satisfy some human want or desire, and *utility* is the capacity of the good to do so. Menger went on to develop the idea that the individual will maximize total utility at the point where the last unit of each good consumed provides equal utility—that is, where marginal utilities are equal.

Menger's emphasis on the marginal utility theory of value led him to focus on consumption rather than production as the determinant of price. Menger focused only on the demand for goods and largely ignored the supply. It would remain for Alfred Marshall and Leon Walras to combine demand and supply for a more complete picture of price determination.

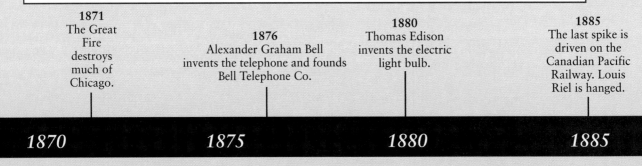

1871
The Great Fire destroys much of Chicago.

1876
Alexander Graham Bell invents the telephone and founds Bell Telephone Co.

1880
Thomas Edison invents the electric light bulb.

1885
The last spike is driven on the Canadian Pacific Railway. Louis Riel is hanged.

1870 *1875* *1880* *1885*

ALFRED MARSHALL (1842–1924)

Alfred Marshall was born in Clapham, England, the son of a bank cashier, and was descended from a long line of clerics. Marshall's father, despite intense effort, was unable to steer the young Marshall into the church. Instead, Marshall followed his passion for mathematics at Cambridge and chose economics as a field of study after reading J. S. Mill's *Principles of Political Economy*. His career was then spent mainly at Cambridge, where he taught economics to John Maynard Keynes, Arthur Pigou, Joan Robinson, and countless other British theorists in the "Cambridge tradition." His *Principles of Economics,* published in 1890, replaced Mill's *Principles* as the dominant economics textbook of English-speaking universities.

Marshall institutionalized modern marginal analysis, the basic concepts of supply and demand, and perhaps most importantly the notion of economic equilibrium resulting from the interaction of supply and demand. He also pioneered partial equilibrium analysis—examining the forces of supply and demand in a particular market provided that all other influences can be excluded, *ceteris paribus.*

Although many of the ideas had been put forward by previous writers, Marshall was able to synthesize the previous analyses of utility and cost and present a thorough and complete statement of the laws of demand and supply. Marshall refined and developed microeconomic theory to such a degree that much of what he wrote would be familiar to students of this textbook today.

It is also interesting to note that although Alfred Marshall and Leon Walras were simultaneously expanding the frontiers of economic theory, there was almost no communication between the two men. Though Marshall chose partial equilibrium analysis as the appropriate method for dealing with selected markets in a complex world, he did acknowledge the correctness of Walras's general equilibrium system. Walras, on the other hand, was adamant (and sometimes rude) in his opposition to the methods that Marshall was putting forward. History has shown that both the partial and the general equilibrium approaches to economic analysis are required for understanding the functioning of the economy.

THORSTEIN VEBLEN (1857–1929)

Thorstein Veblen was born on a farm in Wisconsin to Norwegian parents. He received his Ph.D. in philosophy from Yale University, after which he returned to his father's farm because he was unable to secure an academic position. For seven years he remained there, reading voraciously on economics and other social sciences. Eventually, he took academic positions at the University of Chicago, Stanford University, the University of Missouri, and the New School for Social Research (in New York). Veblen was the founder of "institutional economics," the only uniquely North American school of economic thought.

In 1899, Veblen published *The Theory of the Leisure Class,* in which he sought to apply Charles Darwin's evolutionism to the study of modern economic life. He examined problems in the social institutions of the day, and savagely criticized Classical and Neoclassical economic analysis. Although Veblen failed to shift the path of mainstream economic analysis, he did contribute the idea of the importance of long-run institutional studies as a useful complement to short-run price theory analysis. He also reminded the profession that economics is a *social* science, and not merely a branch of mathematics.

Veblen remains most famous today for his idea of "conspicuous consumption." He observed that some commodities were consumed not for their intrinsic qualities but because they carried snob appeal. He suggested that the more expensive such a commodity became, the greater might be its ability to confer status on its purchaser.

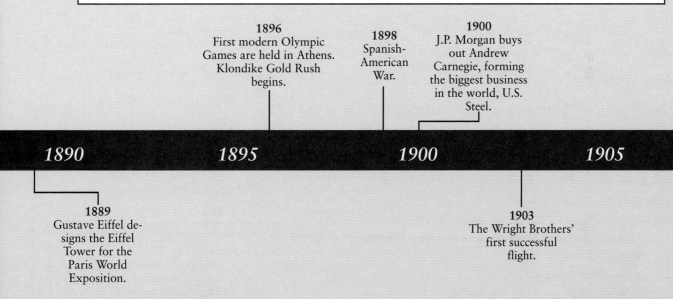

1896
First modern Olympic Games are held in Athens. Klondike Gold Rush begins.

1898
Spanish-American War.

1900
J.P. Morgan buys out Andrew Carnegie, forming the biggest business in the world, U.S. Steel.

1890   1895   1900   1905

1889
Gustave Eiffel designs the Eiffel Tower for the Paris World Exposition.

1903
The Wright Brothers' first successful flight.

VILFREDO PARETO (1848–1923)

Vilfredo Pareto was an Italian, born in Paris, and was trained to be an engineer. Though he actually practiced as an engineer, he would later succeed Leon Walras to the Chair of Economics in the Faculty of Law at the University of Lausanne.

Pareto built upon the system of general equilibrium that Walras had developed. In his *Cours d'économie politique* (1897) and his *Manuel d'économie politique* (1906) Pareto set forth the foundations of modern welfare economics. He showed that theories of consumer behavior and exchange could be constructed on assumptions of ordinal utility, rather than cardinal utility, eliminating the need to compare one person's utility with another's. Using the indifference curve analysis developed by F. Y. Edgeworth, Pareto was able to demonstrate that total welfare could be increased by an exchange if one person could be made better off without anyone else becoming worse off. Pareto applied this analysis to consumption and exchange, as well as to production. Pareto's contributions in this area are remembered in economists' references to *Pareto optimality* and *Pareto efficiency.*

JOSEPH SCHUMPETER *(1883–1950)*

Joseph Schumpeter was born in Triesch, Moravia (now in the Czech Republic). He was a university professor and later a Minister of Finance in Austria. In 1932, he emigrated to the United States to avoid the rise to power of Adolf Hitler. He spent his remaining years at Harvard University.

Schumpeter, a pioneering theorist of innovation, emphasized the role of the entrepreneur in economic development. The existence of the entrepreneur meant continuous innovation and waves of adaptation to changing technology. He is best known for his theory of "creative destruction," where the prospect of monopoly profits provides owners the incentive to finance inventions and innovations. One monopoly can replace another with superior technology or a superior product, thereby circumventing the entry barriers of a monopolized industry. He criticized mainstream economists for emphasizing the static (allocative) efficiency of perfect competition—a market structure that would, if it could ever be achieved, retard technological change and economic growth.

Schumpeter's best known works are *The Theory of Economic Development* (1911), *Business Cycles* (1939), and *Capitalism, Socialism and Democracy* (1943).

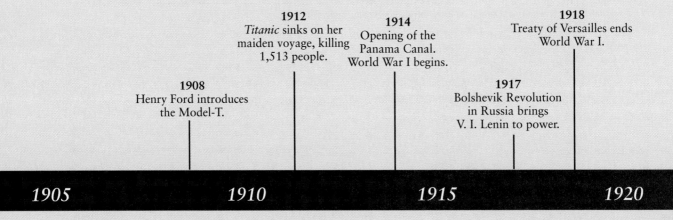

1912
Titanic sinks on her
maiden voyage, killing
1,513 people.

1914
Opening of the
Panama Canal.
World War I begins.

1918
Treaty of Versailles ends
World War I.

1908
Henry Ford introduces
the Model-T.

1917
Bolshevik Revolution
in Russia brings
V. I. Lenin to power.

1905   **1910**   **1915**   **1920**

JOHN MAYNARD KEYNES *(1883–1946)*

John Maynard Keynes was born in Cambridge, England. His parents were both intellectuals, and his father, John Neville Keynes, was a famous logician and writer on economic methodology. The young Keynes was educated at Eton and then at Kings College, Cambridge, where he was a student of Alfred Marshall and Arthur Pigou. His career included appointments to the Treasury in Britain during both World Wars I and II, a leading role in the establishment of the International Monetary Fund (through discussions at Bretton Woods, New Hampshire, in 1944), and editorship of the *Economic Journal* from 1911 to 1945, all in addition to his academic position at Kings College.

Keynes published extensively during his life but his most influential work, *The General Theory of Employment, Interest, and Money,* appeared in 1936. This book was published in the midst of the Great Depression when the output of goods and services had fallen drastically, unemployment was intolerably high, and it had become clear to many that the market would not self-adjust to achieve potential output within an acceptable period of time. Fluctuations in economic activity were familiar at this point, but the failure of the economy to recover rapidly from this depression was unprecedented. Neoclassical economists held that during a downturn both wages and the interest rate would fall low enough to induce investment and employment and cause an expansion. They believed that the persistent unemployment during the 1930s was caused by inflexible wages and they recommended that workers be convinced to accept wage cuts.

Keynes believed that this policy, though perhaps correct for a single industry, was not correct for the entire economy. Widespread wage cuts would reduce the consumption portion of aggregate demand, which would offset any increase in employment. Keynes argued that unemployment could be cured only by manipulating aggregate demand, whereby increased demand (through government expenditure) would increase the price level, reduce real wages, and thereby stimulate employment.

Keynes's views found acceptance after the publication of his *General Theory* and had a profound effect on government policy around the world, particularly in the 1940s, 1950s, and 1960s. As we know from this textbook, Keynes's name is attached to much of macroeconomics, from much of the basic theory to the Keynesian short-run aggregate supply curve and the Keynesian consumption function. His contributions to economics go well beyond what can be mentioned in a few paragraphs—for, in effect, he laid the foundations for modern macroeconomics.

EDWARD CHAMBERLIN *(1899–1967)*

Edward Chamberlin was born in La Conner, Washington, and received his Ph.D. from Harvard University in 1927. He became a full professor at Harvard in 1937 and stayed there until his retirement in 1966. He published *The Theory of Monopolistic Competition* in 1933.

Before Chamberlin's book (which appeared more or less simultaneously with Joan Robinson's *The Economics of Imperfect Competition*), the models of perfect competition and monopoly had been fairly well worked out. Though economists were aware of a middle ground between these two market structures and some analysis of duopoly (two sellers) had been presented, it was Chamberlin and Robinson who closely examined this problem of imperfect markets.

Chamberlin's main contribution was explaining the importance of product differentiation for firms in market structures between perfect competition and monopoly. Chamberlin saw that though there may be a large number of firms in the market (the competitive element), each firm created for itself a unique product or advantage that gave it some control over price (the monopoly element). Specifically, he identified items such as copyrights, trademarks, brand names, and location as monopoly elements behind a product. Though Alfred Marshall regarded price as the only variable in question, Chamberlin saw both price and the product itself as variables under control of the firm in monopolistically competitive markets.

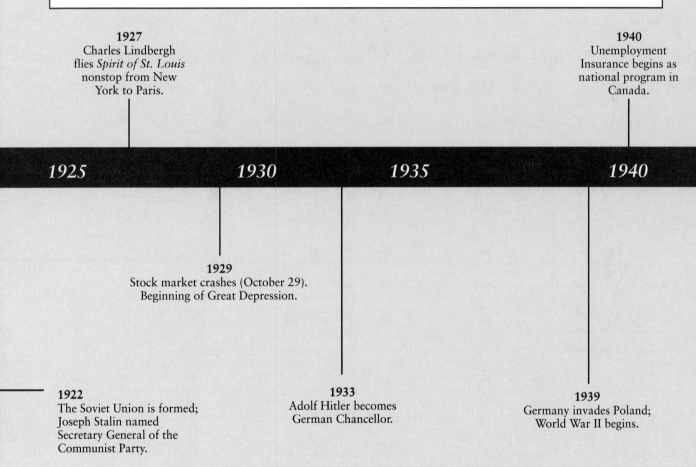

1927
Charles Lindbergh flies *Spirit of St. Louis* nonstop from New York to Paris.

1940
Unemployment Insurance begins as national program in Canada.

1925   **1930**   **1935**   **1940**

1929
Stock market crashes (October 29).
Beginning of Great Depression.

1922
The Soviet Union is formed; Joseph Stalin named Secretary General of the Communist Party.

1933
Adolf Hitler becomes German Chancellor.

1939
Germany invades Poland; World War II begins.

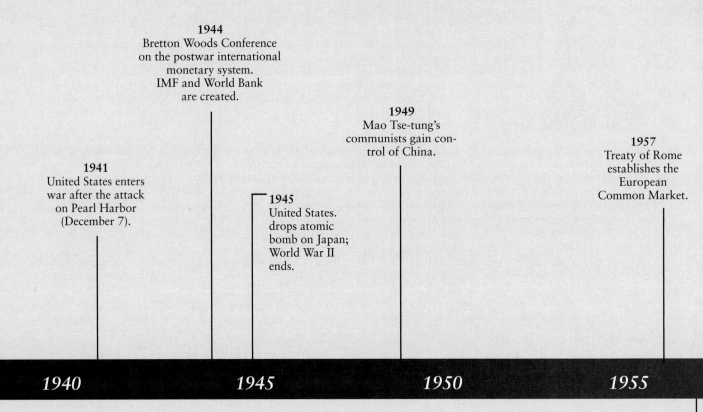

1944
Bretton Woods Conference
on the postwar international
monetary system.
IMF and World Bank
are created.

1949
Mao Tse-tung's
communists gain con-
trol of China.

1957
Treaty of Rome
establishes the
European
Common Market.

1941
United States enters
war after the attack
on Pearl Harbor
(December 7).

1945
United States.
drops atomic
bomb on Japan;
World War II
ends.

| 1940 | 1945 | 1950 | 1955 |

FRIEDRICH AUGUST VON HAYEK *(1899–1992)*

1959
Fidel Castro
overthrows
Fulgencio Batista
in Cuba.

Friedrich von Hayek was born in Vienna and studied at the University of Vienna, where he was trained in the Austrian tradition of economics (a school of thought originating with Carl Menger). He held academic positions at the London School of Economics and the University of Chicago. He returned to Europe in 1962 to the University of Freiburg in what was then West Germany and the University of Salzburg in Austria. He was awarded the Nobel Prize in Economics in 1974.

Hayek contributed new ideas and theories in many different areas of economics, but he is perhaps best known for his general conception of economics as a "coordination problem." His observation of market economies suggested that the relative prices determined in free markets provided the signals that allowed the actions of all decision makers to mesh—even though there was no formal planning taking place to coordinate these actions. He emphasized this "spontaneous order" at work in the economy as the subject matter for economics. The role of knowledge and information in the market process became central to Hayek, an idea that has grown in importance to the economics profession over the years.

Hayek's theory of business cycles provided an example of the breakdown of this coordination. A monetary disturbance (e.g., an increase in the money supply) would distort the signals (relative prices) by artificially raising the return to certain types of economic activity. When the disturbance disappeared, the boom caused by these distorted signals would be followed by a slump. Although Hayek's business-cycle theory was eclipsed by the Keynesian revolution, his emphasis on economics as a coordination problem has had a major influence on contemporary economic thought.

Hayek was also prominent in advocating the virtues of free markets as contributing to human freedom in the broad sense as well as to economic efficiency in the narrow sense. His *The Road to Serfdom* (1944) sounded an alarm about the political and economic implications of the then-growing belief in the virtues of central planning. His *Constitution of Liberty* (1960) is a much deeper philosophical analysis of the forces, economic and otherwise, that contribute to the liberty of the individual.

INDEX

The page on which a key term is defined is printed in boldface.